1994

NATIVE AMERICAN RESOURCES SERIES

Advisory Board

R. David Edmunds, Indiana University/Arlene B. Hirschfelder, Teaneck, NJ/Karl Kroeber, Columbia University/James H. May, California State University, Chico, CA/LaVonne Ruoff, University of Illinois, Chicago/Emory Sekaquaptewa, University of Arizona/Virginia Driving Hawk Sneve, Rapid City, SD/Clifford E. Trafzer, University of California, Riverside

Jack W. Marken, *General Editor,* South Dakota State University

1. *Handbook of the American Frontier: Four Centuries of Indian-White Relationships,* by J. Norman Heard
   Volume I: *Southeastern Woodlands.* 1987
   Volume II: *Northeastern Woodlands.* 1990
   Volume III: *The Great Plains.* 1993
2. *Oliver La Farge and the American Indian,* by Robert A. Hecht. 1991.
3. *Native American Resurgence and Renewal: a reader and a bibliography,* by Robert N. Wells, Jr. 1994.

NATIVE AMERICAN RESURGENCE AND RENEWAL

a reader and bibliography

by
ROBERT N. WELLS, JR.

Native American Resources Series, No. 3

The Scarecrow Press, Inc.
Metuchen, N.J., & London
1994

British Library Cataloguing-in-Publication data available

Library of Congress Cataloging-in-Publication Data

Native American resurgence and renewal : a reader and
bibliography /
Robert N. Wells.
   p. cm. -- (Native American resources series ; no. 3)
   Includes bibliographical references and index.
   ISBN 0-8108-2784-0 (alk. paper)
   1. Indians of North America--Government relations--1934-
2. Indians of North America--Social conditions. 3. Indians of
North America--Ethnic identity. I. Wells, Robert N. II. Series.
E93.N286 1994
970.004'97—dc20   93-39199

To Ted

His determination and will to live
has been an inspiration to all of us.

iii

COPYRIGHT ACKNOWLEDGMENTS

iv

CONTENTS

page

vii

EDITOR'S FOREWORD

This collection of essays by American scholars focusing on the complex issues of Native American life in the decades of the seventies and eighties chronicles a renascence in almost all facets of American Indian society. Professor Robert Wells, who has worked closely with the St. Regis Mohawks for over two decades and regularly teaches courses to Native Americans on campus and on the nearby reservation, has brought together a collection of essays that will be useful to the general public as well as to those who teach college or university courses in applied anthropology, race and culture, minority politics, or politics of poverty and dependence.

The main objectives of the collection, as Professor Wells notes, are to document Native revitalization in the United States and to describe the direction it has taken and to compile a body of literature which broadly describes major aspects of Native American life today, particularly on the reservations. Some of the articles directly or indirectly support the idea of extending federal support in the areas of education, medical and social services and legal protection to Native Americans living off reservation.

The book is enhanced by the inclusion of a Glossary of Terms section which contains definitions of important words and thumb-nail histories of events. And there is a useful bibliography at the end of the collection.

Jack W. Marken
South Dakota State University

PREFACE

The road to self-determination for Native Americans has been a long and difficult one. For over one hundred and fifty years, Indian communities were surrounded by a federal bureaucracy which controlled virtually every aspect of tribal life. The long-term impact on Native Americans has been poverty, economic and social dependency, tribal disintegration, linguistic and cultural loss, and political factionalism.

The resurgence of Native American communities has taken many avenues. At all levels, Native Americans are taking over the education of their children. Through cooperation and legal initiatives, Indian tribes are gaining control of their tribal resources: land, water, minerals, energy sources and wildlife. With the immense reductions of federal financial support to Native American communities during the Reagan Administration, Indian tribes were forced to seek out other sources of income. While many communities suffered dearly, others embarked upon economic enterprises such as fish farming, tourism, gaming, mail order sales of cigarettes, and solid waste disposal. Some of these initiatives have been controversial within the Indian world, but gaming alone has brought six billion dollars of new revenue into over 100 tribal communities.

A principal objective of this anthology is to document this Native revitalization and describe the direction it has taken. There has been a strong movement to preserve and regain native language and cultural traditions, and develop tribal histories from the tribal viewpoint. This cultural revitalization has become very important as over two-thirds of all Native Americans live off reservation in cities, towns and rural areas. Beginning with the Indian fish-ins in the state of Washington and the Red Power movement in the 1960's, Native Americans have become proactive about their treaty rights and the need for the federal government to protect the Indian land and resource base. When the courts have failed them they have appealed directly to Congress for support and redress.

A second objective of this project is to compile a body of literature which broadly describes major aspects of Indian life today. For guidance, I drew upon an excellent anthology edited by Stuart Levine and Nancy Lurie, *The American Indian Today*, Everett/Edwards Inc., 1968. The unique relationship which Native Americans have with federal and state governments is central to any study of Indian-white relations. Native American health, education, economic viability and resource base are key to any movement toward self-determination. These topics, along with chapters on Native American women, urban Native Americans, and a comparison of Canada-United States policies regarding Native peoples, complete the survey.

I would like to thank the authors and publishers who kindly consented to allow me to include their articles in this study. I am indebted to Akwesasne (St. Regis) Mohawk people who have been leaders in Native American educational reform. Our close association over a quarter of a century has enhanced my understanding of Native Americans and their unique place in American culture. My student research assistants Molly Crowe, Kevin Todd and Bridget Kobor provided invaluable assistance in assembling this work. Sheila Murphy, Bethany Taylor and Bonnie Enslow were ever available to provide editorial assistance, manuscript typing and assembling bibliographies. The index was prepared by Carolyn G. Weaver of Weaver Indexing Service, Bellevue, WA. Laurie Olmstead prepared the entire manuscript for the publisher and her assistance was invaluable.

I would like to acknowledge my gratitude to St. Lawrence University for its generous financial support and encouragement. To my students, the Mohawks and the student volunteers in Operation K and Upward Bound, a special thanks. Their interest and enthusiasm have provided me with the incentive to pursue my interest in Native Americans and edit this anthology.

Robert N. Wells, Jr.
Munsil Professor of Government
St. Lawrence University
1993

Chapter I

Introduction

Resilience and Revitalization: Native Americans Enter the 21st Century

Robert N. Wells, Jr.

The past two decades have witnessed a revitalization of Native American communities and strenuous efforts to achieve Indian self-determination. In the areas of education, tribal government, economic development, health and resource management, Indian tribes and communities have made substantial progress in their goals of local control and tribal control and management of their internal affairs. These advances have been made at a time when Indian nations have been plagued by significant economic difficulties and social problems. High levels of infant mortality, suicide, substance abuse, unemployment, extreme poverty and poor health are common features of Indian life. By every social indicator, Native Americans are our most disadvantaged minority group. They are also our fastest growing population, with a 38 percent increase in ten years (see Table 1).

For more than a century, Native Americans have had little say about the direction of their affairs. Until very recently, every facet of Indian life was controlled by the federal government through the Bureau of Indian Affairs. The Native American relationship with the federal government, and later state government after termination, was one of extreme dependency. The governments controlled the purse strings and the management of all Indian resources. Although former President Nixon announced a new era of "Indian Self-Determination" in 1970, the withdrawal of government control

1

of Indian policy was halting and lacked the financial resources to fully support a new era of tribal self-determination.

Table 1: U.S. Population Estimates, 1980 and 1990

Race/Ethnicity	1980		1990		Percentage Growth
	Number	Percent	Number	Percent	
Total U.S. Population	227,757,000	100.0%	248,709,873	100.0%	9.2%
White	195,571,000	85.9%	199,686,070	80.3%	2.1%
African American	26,903,000	11.8%	29,986,060	12.1%	11.5%
Asian American	3,834,000	1.7%	7,273,662	2.9%	89.7%
Hispanic Origin*	14,608,673	6.4%	22,354,059	9.0%	53.0%
American Indian	**1,420,400**	**0.6%**	**1,959,234**	**0.9%**	**37.9%**

*persons of Hispanic origin may be of any race.
Note: The 1990 figures have not been statistically adjusted to account for persons who identified themselves as "other race."
Source: U.S. Bureau of the Census, Preliminary Population Estimates, unpublished data, 1991.

Figure 1: States with the Largest American Indian Populations, 1990

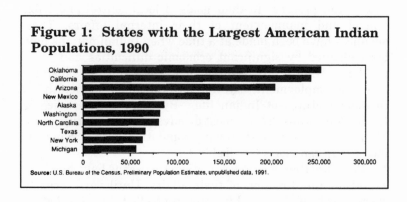

Source: U.S. Bureau of the Census. Preliminary Population Estimates, unpublished data, 1991.

The most impressive strides have been in the field of Native American Education. Almost overnight, twenty-six Indian controlled tribal colleges have sprung up. Before the 1969 Senate Subcommittee Report on Indian Education, there were fewer than five predominately Native American post-secondary institutions. Title V of the Indian Education Act has opened the door for Native Americans to be involved in the teaching of their children and integrating native language, history and culture into the school curriculum.

Although the Native American high school dropout rate exceeds the national average by seven percent, it is gradually decreasing and over 103,000 Native Americans attend two- and four-year post-secondary institutions, an increase of 36 percent over 1976.[1] Of all the states with large numbers of Native Americans, Minnesota has done the most to improve the level of Native American education from pre-school through post-secondary, and the Minnesota compact between the states and Indian communities serves as a viable model to follow.

Ever since Chief Justice Marshall's opinion in "Cherokee Nation v. Georgia," 1831, there has been controversy as to what constitutes Indian tribal sovereignty. Substantial inroads were made into tribal sovereignty by the 1885 Major Crimes Act, the Indian Allotment Act, 1883, and a series of court cases beginning with "United States v. Kagama," 1886. Indian policies following World War II to terminate and relocate Indian tribes further eroded tribal sovereignty. The enactment of the Indian Self-Determination Act (PL93-638) provided the mechanism and authority for Indian tribes to take over a broad area of tribal responsibility and contract for services. Unfortunately, it has never been funded to the level to accomplish these goals. Also, beginning with the Oliphant decision[2] the courts and state governments began to intrude upon the criminal and civil jurisdiction of Indian tribes.

With their assault upon tribal sovereignty, Indian nations turned to the U.S. Congress to stem the impact of court decisions and state actions which infringed upon internal tribal functions. Legislation protecting Indian child welfare, Indian gambling, tribal enterprise, trust lands from exploitation and sacred Indian burial sites was passed by Congress. Forty-five tribes formed the Coalition of Energy Resource Tribes to protect the Indian resource base and negotiate agreements which would guarantee tribal communities a fair market value for the land, mineral, energy and water resources. NARF, the Native American Rights Fund was established with the support of foundation money to provide legal defense to Native Americans and tribal communities in support of their individual and communal tribal rights.

When one reviews Native American health figures, it appears that the statistics are from an underdeveloped country in Asia or Africa. The infant mortality rate among Native Americans is 27.5 percent per thousand births, almost double the U.S. rate.[3] Death from alcoholism among all Native Americans is 27 percent, over five times the average U.S. rate. Indian suicides ran at 15 per thousand in 1988, four percentage points higher than the United States as a whole. However, suicides among Native American males 18-44 years of age exceeds the national average by almost 100 percent.

Common diseases among Native Americans are diabetes, influenza, tuberculosis and heart disease (stroke). Indians have a shorter life span than other Americans, 71 years compared to the national average of 75.[4] Beyond alcohol abuse, drugs have become a major source of physical and mental problems for younger Native Americans. Tribal communities have attempted to undertake a proactive response to physical and mental health problems by contracting for health care with local agencies and setting up substance abuse programs, well child clinics and promoting the use of traditional medicine practices.

Native resources, particularly land, have always been central to the relationship of the dominant white society with Native Americans. In over 400 treaties, American Indians ceded to the United States and its political subdivisions over one billion acres. In return for these land and resource cessions, Indian tribes were to receive treaty protection, reserved land and annuities held by the U.S. government.

Although it was not intended, the 285 Indian reservations on which almost one-third of Native Americans live contain valuable resources in the form of coal, uranium, gas, oil, timber and grazing land. Historically, the leasing of these resources was the responsibility of the Bureau of Indian Affairs. Royalties from the leases were to be given to the tribe. BIA leasing policy and protection of the Indian resource base constitutes one of the great historical misjustices of the federal government's trust responsibility. To void these unprofitable and exploitive leases, Indian tribes have gone into court to cancel the leases and formed a resource coalition known as CERT (Coalition of Energy Resource Tribes).

Native Americans are fighting a continuous battle to protect their resources, particularly water in the west, and the hunting, fishing, trapping and gathering rights guaranteed by treaties. The famous "Bolt decision"[5] on the division of Columbia River Salmon between Indian tribes and commercial fishermen generated strong anti-Indian feelings in the northwest and led to a spate of tribal and treaty termination bills in Congress. Since their resource base constitutes a principal source of Indian revenue, tribes have aggressively attempted to market these resources directly without BIA involvement. Tribal enterprise and resource exploitation has created resentment among traditional Native Americans who reject attempts to utilize valuable tribal resources, and in some instances, sacred lands, for commercial exploitation.

The use of tribal tax exemption from state sales and income taxes has generated a large over-the-counter sales market for Indian gasoline, cigarettes and alcoholic beverages. Today there are over one-hundred tribal gaming enterprise operations on Indian reservations grossing approximately six billion dollars per year. These initiatives, too, have generated strong state and local reaction to Indian sales of those products to non-Indians on reservations and gambling casinos in states where gambling is prohibited.

Opponents contend that exemption from direct federal and state taxes on Indian land were never meant to apply to non-Indian purchases. Several court cases have resulted with the Kansas Supreme Court ruling against the Indian tribe and the New York State Court of Appeals upholding the exemption in June, 1993.

Almost two-thirds of all 1.9 million Native Americans live off reservation in cities, towns and rural areas. This exodus from the reservation began after World War II and was accelerated by federal government policies of "termination" and "relocation." This fact, perhaps, presents the single greatest challenge to Native Americans in the years ahead. Historically, the reservation has been the center of Indian life and culture for over 150 years. "Indianness" and cultural identity of Native Americans is intimately bound up with language, culture, lifestyle, family and community (tribe).

Few of these support systems exist in the off reservation setting to the degree they do on reservation. Moreover, off reservation Native Americans do not necessarily receive the legal, educational and medical services and entitlements that their tribal counterparts do. Despite the attempts of urban Indians to organize in support of their entitlements as "enrolled Indians" or legally recognized Native Americans (1/4 Indian blood quantum) both the lack of federal funding and reluctance to extend federal services to off reservation Indians have greatly hampered the extension of services and federal protection to a majority of Native Americans.

A related issue, terminated Indian nations and non-federally recognized tribes, denies hundreds of thousands of Native Americans from receiving federal protection and services. In the 1960's over two-hundred tribes and barrios (small California Indian bands) were terminated from federal protection and services. Many of these tribes became the responsibility of the states. Numerous other tribes, many in the Eastern part of the United States and home to 500,000 Native Americans, lost federal recognition or never gained it as state authority in the thirteen original colonies was dominant. The Lumbee in North Carolina are a good example of this non-recognition of a tribal grouping numbering close to 50,000 people.

The B.I.A. has been very reluctant to grant federal status to non-recognized tribes or return former recognized tribes, which were terminated to federally recognized status. The Menominee Restoration Act is an exception to this principle. Currently, the federal government recognizes 309 Indian tribes or nations, while Native leaders claim there are 500 Indian tribal groups in existence.

California, a state where Indian tribes and barrios were terminated in the 1960's, has taken an active role in support of the educational, economic and social needs of resident Native Americans. There are also large number of urban Indians in Los Angeles and other California cities. However, as a rule, those tribes which were terminated or never recognized by the federal government do not receive the level of support or legal protection which federally recognized tribes do.

Since most Native Americans who reside off reservation as a result of impoverished conditions on the reserves (41 percent unemployment rate)[6] and federal government policy, it is the responsibility of the government to address this matter forthrightly. Education, employment opportunity, medical services, social services and legal protection should be extended to Native Americans who reside off reservation who are either enrolled tribal members or legally recognized Native Indian people (1/4 blood quantum). The rationale is that these are Indian people who are entitled to such services and federal protection by virtue of their treaties, federal laws and court decisions.

Ralph W. Johnson's article, "Fragile Gains: Two Centuries of Canadian and United States Policy Toward Indians," traces the development of Indian policy in both Canada and the United States since the end of British rule in North America. Native peoples in Canada constitute a larger segment of the total population, almost ten percent compared to one percent in the United States, yet have even less political power and legal protection. For the student of U.S. Indian policy, this article is an excellent opportunity to review the development of Indian-white relations in this century and compare it with Canada's policy regarding Native peoples. Much of the current resurgence in Canada is related to Indian civil rights efforts in the United States in the 1960's and 70's. One major difference is the circumstances regarding Native peoples in both countries. In Canada about 60 percent of all the land is still aboriginal title, whereas there is no aboriginal title existing in the United States. Therefore, Canada has a long process of land claim negotiations with Indian bands in resolving territorial issues.

The purpose of this volume is to document the Native American's quest for self-determination. The keys are education, economic opportunity, tribal integrity and cultural preservation in the face of a continuing assimilationist pull of the larger white society. Whereas the courts have historically supported Indian treaty rights and federal responsibilities to Native Americans, the political tide has turned with the advent of the Renquest Supreme Court. Tribes have now turned to

Congress to deflect unfavorable court rulings and state encroachment into "Indian country."

The sobering economic and social statistics which profile Native Americans will not soon vanish. The abject poverty of most reservations and the cycle of dependency will not be reversed over night. However, for the first time Indian people are being placed in charge of the management of their own affairs, and now will have a firmer grasp on the direction of their communities. There are more college graduates, including professionals, and economic opportunities in a broad range of areas have been explored.

Perhaps most important, a new generation of Indian leadership, on and off the reservation, has emerged: better educated, assertive, entrepreneurial and schooled in dealing with the larger white society. It is increasingly determined to find Indian solutions to Indian problems. The emergence of twenty-six Indian controlled colleges provides the nucleus of an indigenous higher education system run by Native Americans. Whether the cloak of dependency will be lifted in the near future is dependent upon federal recognition of Indian self-determination and the ability of Native American communities to come forward with creative solutions to problems which have plagued Indian people for a century and a half. Without doubt, that renaissance is underway in "Indian country" and it has taken many forms.

NOTES

1. Eileen M. O'Brien, "American Indians in Higher Education," *Research Briefs*, Washington, D.C.: American Council on Education 3(3), (1992), 4.

2. "Oliphant v. Squamish Indian Tribe," 1978.

3. "Reviving Native Economies." Dollars and Sense," 1(9), (October 1991), 18-20.

4. "Native Americans: In Search of an Identity." *Scholastic Update* 21, (May 26, 1989), 5.

5. U.S. Supreme Court in Washington v. Washington State Commercial Passenger Fishing Vessel Association, 1979.

6. "Native Americans: In Search of an Identity." *Scholastic Update* 21, (May 26, 1989), 5.

Chapter II

Federal Indian Policy

In commenting on Federal Indian Policy one Native American leader said that Indian policy is as changing as the phases of the moon. From the earliest days of the republic there has always been a concern about the "Indian problem." In the 19th century federal policies of civilization, removal, forced assimilation, land cession and military subjugation characterized governmental approaches to the Indian question. When the Indian population declined to approximately 350,000 after the Civil War, the full impact of federal policies was evident.

What earlier policies didn't accomplish later federal initiatives further impoverished and subordinated Indian people: the Dawes Act, Major Crimes Act, Federal Boarding Schools, and repressive laws outlawing Indian religion. The 1926 Merium Report on the Conditions of American Indians painted a depressing picture of the conditions under which most Indian people were living: poor health, inadequate housing and sanitation, unemployment, and economic poverty. The New Deal and the reform policies of BIA Commissioner John Collier attempted to reverse previous assimilationist and paternalistic policies of the federal government. This reform period was short lived, and immediately subsequent to the Second World War the government embarked upon a program of terminating federal trust responsibility for Indian tribes. This disastrous policy was closely followed by a policy of relocation which offered tribal members economic and job incentives to move off reservation to the cities. Both of these policies, as well as severe federal funding limits for tribal services, forced many Indian people to leave the reservation. The outcome of this human migration is the phenomenon of the urban Native American, currently over 50% of the entire American Indian population.

In 1970, the Nixon administration enunciated a policy of "self determination" and the reversal of termination and assimilation. The centerpiece of this policy was the 1975 Indian Self-Determination and Education Assistance Act (PL 93-638). Unfortunately, insufficient funding has hobbled full implementation of this legislation. During the Reagan Administration federal financial support of Indian programs was cut by one billion dollars. One critic called this tribal termination by "accountants."

To replace this reduction of federal subsidies the Reagan and Bush Administration have encouraged tribal capitalism and extensive leasing and exploitation of tribal resources. One outgrowth of this policy is the explosion of gambling on Indian reservations. To protect tribal natural resources and insure adequate leasing royalties for their use, forty-three Indian Tribes have formed a consortium (CERT) to protect tribal interests.

9

The Bureau of Indian Affairs has encouraged tribal self-determination through a policy of subcontracting of services. However, tribal self-determination will continue to be hampered until sufficient funds are appropriated to provide services to an exploding Native population. Over four hundred treaties ceding one-billion acres were signed by the U.S. government and Indian nations. These agreements serve as the basis of the federal government's responsibility to Native Americans. Any federal policy of recognition of tribal sovereignty and self-determination, devoid of adequate financial support, is no program at all and back door return to the termination policies of the 1950's. It may be the appropriate time for the federal government to withdraw from the Indian business and let Native Americans manage their communities, however, abdicating the trust responsibility to federally recognized tribes is another matter and not subject to unilateral action.

—RNW

Federal Indian Policy: A Framework for Evaluation

Thomas R. McGuire

Unlike many agencies of the United States government, the Bureau of Indian Affairs has not developed a coherent set of standards for evaluating the impacts of specific actions on reservation-based Native Americans. Nor, many would claim, have the judicial, executive, and legislative branches of government offered clear policy directives to the implementing agency. It is argued here, however, that three dominant policy objectives can be abstracted from the corpus of federal laws, regulations, and court decisions. These objectives are: tribal sovereignty, economic self-sufficiency, and cultural self-determination. After defining these objectives, I suggest operational measures which may serve as guides for evaluating specific programs. I then illustrate the framework with a review of residential leasing programs on reservations, and examine the effects of exogenous factors on the implementation of these three objectives of federal Indian policy.

Key words: social impact assessment, Native Americans, policy

Many observers of contemporary federal Indian policy would argue that there is no such policy and hence no clear and consistent set of objectives for the human and natural resources of Native American reservations.[1] There is much in the nature of the way policy is made to support this view.

Few significant presidential statements about Indians have been issued since the Nixon administration. The plenary powers of the Congress over Indian affairs, and the discretion given to the Secretary of the Interior as trustee for tribal resources, can and do lead to capricious policy formation. Inconsistencies may be introduced into the policy process by the semi-autonomous regionalism of legislative districts, area offices of the Bureau of Indian Affairs, and by circuits of the federal, district and appeals courts. Moreover, much of the action on Indian affairs is generated outside the designated agency for such business. On many reservations in the west, the U.S. Bureau of Reclamation has a more salient presence than does the BIA. Even in matters of direct concern to the BIA, actions are guided only loosely by congressional mandates and the Code of Federal Regulations.

In addition, there are many field solicitors' opinions, internal office memoranda, and the daily decisions of the Secretary's delegated spokesmen—the directors of area offices and the heads of reservation-level field agencies. The role of the federal court system itself may even foster inconsistency, as relatively narrow canons of construction for Indian decisions give way to calls for a socially responsive judiciary. There is also the weight of prior action taken toward past objectives, which still constrains policy. Finally, and of most significance, there is the constant tension between the diverse desires of Indians themselves and the government's reading of, and response to these desires. Even when desires are correctly perceived, responses have frequently been grudging at best.

I will argue, nevertheless, that there is indeed a relatively clear and definable set of federal objectives toward Native Americans on reservations. In brief, these objectives are to enhance tribal sovereignty, promote economic self-sufficiency, and foster cultural self-determination.

First, I attempt to justify the selection of these overriding objectives by a review of federal actions—those repudiated as well as those still valid. Next, I will define these objectives and suggest in a preliminary fashion ways that the objectives might be measured. In a subsequent section, I examine how these objectives may be applied to an evaluation of reservation leasing policies. The primary purpose of that discussion is to suggest how the independently defined objectives "behave" when confronted with proposals for action. This mode of analysis is expanded in the final section by looking at how the self-contained objectives of Indian policy interact with exogenous policy goals, those of the federal government toward its non-Indian constituents.

Throughout the endeavor, the distinction between policy goal and implementation, between ends and means is retained. The intent of the exercise is both descriptive and normative. I hope to lend some order to the complexity of federal actions toward Native Americans—to abstract a set of enduring objectives that accurately describes the intent of diverse actions, although implementation may certainly contravene goals, as demonstrated by the drastically reduced levels of funding for Indian programs in the Reagan administration.[2] Morris is perhaps justified in speaking of the recent administration's "policy" as one of "termination by accountants,"[3] but for purposes of program evaluation, it seems essential to distinguish relatively durable objectives from the actions of specific administrations. I suggest the following: if modern federal Indian policy objectives are as I say they are here, then specific programs for Indian reservations ought to address these objectives and ought to be evaluated against these objectives.[4]

Nixon's Legacy

In his reasoned attack on the termination policies of the 1950s and 1960s, Richard Nixon laid the groundwork for contemporary Indian policy. His presidential address of July 1970 argued that the severance of the federal trust relationship and the privatization of reservation resources failed to achieve the goal of economic advancement, jeopardized or destroyed tribal sovereignty and implicitly weakened cultural self-determination. Nixon acknowledged that

> . . . the practical results have been clearly harmful in the few instances in which termination actually has been tried. The removal of Federal trusteeship responsibility has produced considerable disorientation among the affected Indians and has left them unable to relate to a myriad of Federal, State and local

assistance efforts. Their economic and social condition has often been worse after termination than it was before.[5]

Nixon prefaced his address with an explicit call for a new approach:

The time has come to break decisively with the past and to create the conditions for a new era in which the Indian future is determined by Indian acts and Indian decisions.[6]

This philosophy underlies the Indian Self-Determination and Education Assistance Act of 1975 (Public Law 638), now the governing statement on federal policy for Native Americans. The Act redefined and, most agree, bolstered the sovereignty of tribes. PL 638 was followed shortly by the American Indian Religious Freedom Act of 1978 (PL 95-341), which, though narrowly addressing the religious rights of individual Indians, was promulgated in the spirit of cultural self-determination. A number of acts and judicial rulings in the last several decades have sought to promote the economic self-sufficiency and economic well-being of Indians.

Statements of these three overarching objectives in federal Indian policy can be derived from contemporary statutes and decisions but, as described below, none of these objectives is wholly new. What does appear to be unique about the modern policy after Nixon's 1970 address is that these objectives should be pursued concurrently.[7] Even a cursory reading of the history of Indian policy suggests that one or another of these objectives has dominated, even destroyed, others. Little balance among the goals has been achieved or even sought. The desirability of such a balance is Nixon's legacy; its actual achievement subsequently has proven to be a great deal more difficult.

The Objectives of Federal Indian Policy

TRIBAL SOVEREIGNTY. In *American Indians, Time, and the Law*, Charles Wilkinson[8] traces the modern definition of tribal sovereignty to the decisions of Chief Justice John Marshall in the 1830s and to the seminal legal scholarship of Felix Cohen in the 1940s. Assigned by the Department of the Interior to catalogue and evaluate Indian law, Cohen was led to the conclusion that sovereignty was "perhaps the most basic principle of all Indian law."[9] To Cohen, this was not the absolutist political power of the 18th century European theorists, but a more limited "legal sovereignty," a more "narrow sense of the power of a people to make governmental arrangements to protect and limit personal liberty by social control."[10] For Native Americans, this degree of sovereignty stemmed from the fundamental rulings of Justice Marshall. As defined by Wilkinson, the concept of sovereignty Marshall developed in his famous rulings on "Worcester v. Georgia" and "Cherokee Nation v. Georgia" implied a "largely autonomous tribal government subject to an overriding federal authority but essentially free of state control."[11]

Felix Cohen's contribution, in his *Handbook of Federal Indian Law*,[12] was to establish firmly the modern salience of this definition. Drawing on Cohen's careful arguments, there appear to be several core elements of the concept of tribal sovereignty.

First, Indian tribes have been given substantial authority to define their own citizenry, an inherent right of any sovereign society, albeit one historically exercised as a means of controlling access to resources. It was usually accompanied by some mechanism for territorial defense—to keep "others" from utilizing "our" resources. There were typically a variety of criteria invoked to determine group membership, usually including both ascriptive markers and performance standards. Thus, for example, membership might be determined by an individual's descent as well as a judgment of how successfully that person measures up to some set of rules for appropriate behavior. Quite recently, in the wake of the Indian Reorganization Act of 1934, membership criteria have largely become ascriptive ones which, I argue below, have significant if ironic implications for preserving cultural self-determination. Here, however, the importance of this tribal prerogative lies in determining access to the resources and services of the reservation. Tribal members have rights to them; all others gain such rights only at the sufferance of the tribe.

A second major element of tribal sovereignty is closely related to the first. Tribal officials can exercise governmental, not just proprietary, control over the reservation's land and natural resources. In addition to determining who gets access to these resources, governments may in theory determine how such resources are utilized—or left unused. Tribal authorities can regulate and tax the use of resources[13] and can determine as well that some resources remain intact for future generations, without fear that those resources will be appropriated in the interim.[14] This last principle of "tribal non use" was established unequivocally in a 1982 decision involving the Jicarilla Apache's mineral deposits, a ruling that directly spoke to sovereignty: "sovereign power, even when unexercised, is an enduring presence that governs all contracts subject to the sovereign's jurisdiction, and will remain intact unless surrendered in unmistakable terms."[15]

On many reservations, however, tribal authorities must contend with the legacy of the General Allotment Act of 1887, an effort to privatize tribal resources. Although the process was stopped in the 1920s, heirs to the original allottees still retain a voice in how the land can be used. In theory, such individual rights do not preclude the enforcement of tribal land-use ordinances on allotted land, but in practice many tribal governments have been reluctant to interfere with the decisions of allottees.

The existence of this incongruous land-holding pattern in no way weakens another core element of sovereignty—the judicial control over civil actions of tribal members. Tribal courts are empowered to hear such issues, based on their own rules of procedure and their own culturally specific rules of judgment.[16]

Many observers, both Indian and non-Indian, argue that this is a very restricted manifestation of tribal sovereignty, for there is much that remains outside the tribal court's jurisdiction. The 1978 "Oliphant" decision is the case in point. The Supreme Court denied tribal court jurisdiction over criminal activities of non-Indians within reservations, reminding the tribes that they are only "quasi-sovereign."[17]

"Oliphant" was indeed an assault on full sovereignty, but the impact of the decision has been mitigated by the common practice of cross-deputization. Trained Indian police have been given full authority to act on behalf of county and state law enforcement agencies and can monitor the activities of non-Indians within the reservation. Moreover, tribes retain the significant rights to deny entry of private non-Indian citizens to the reservation, and to expel unwanted trespassers. Thus, while courts have no jurisdiction over criminal activities, the tribes are in a position to prevent and police such actions.

Finally, tribal authorities, acting in their proper capacities, enjoy "sovereign immunity." Under most circumstances, tribal governments cannot be sued—a protection identical to that of municipal, state, and federal governments. Some have argued that such immunity, while serving the cause of sovereignty, severely dampens the potential for economic development. Investors, the argument runs, will be unwilling to commit financial resources to on-reservation projects when they may not sue for redress if the tribe fails to keep its promises.[18] There are alternatives to litigation, however, which have proven successful in overcoming this obstacle. Leases frequently contain arbitration clauses. Tribes may choose to waive their immunity, and offer assets other than tribal real estate as collateral in business transactions.[19]

On balance, modern legislative and judicial actions have quite consistently fostered tribal sovereignty, a sovereignty that was defined more than a century ago by Justice Marshall. To be sure, this is the "quasi-sovereignty" that Marshall distilled in his notion of "domestic dependent nations," a sovereignty limited importantly by congressional and administrative review of tribal decisions. Nonetheless, the governmental powers retained by the tribes are significant.

Are there operational proxies for these contemporary elements of tribal sovereignty? Consider the general aim of these core elements. First, one crucial decision arena of a sovereign entity—that of determining citizenship—is largely routinized. Second, the "tribal sovereignty" line of reasoning has the effect of minimizing the amount of time tribes must devote to shoring up their rights against outside intervention. Finally, the tribes' governmental, as opposed to proprietary, control over natural and human resources within the boundaries of Indian country has the effect of allowing—indeed requiring—active, substantive decisions of an administrative, legislative and judicial nature over actions and people. There are, of course, administrative costs associated with these activities.

Perhaps the simplest measures to approximate these aims are time and money. Sovereignty could be measured by the ratio of administrative time devoted to internal issues over the total time expended on all administrative efforts. Tribal sovereignty would be enhanced as this ratio approaches one. Absolute measures of administrative costs expended on internally and externally directed activities would capture the related factor of bureaucratic scope. Tribal sovereignty would thus be enhanced as the organization expands to manage additional activities. But there are some upper limits to the promotion of sovereignty. Such limits might be reached when the available finances for administrative activities are reallocated from internally focused to externally oriented functions.[20]

The Kansas Kickapoo, studied by Stull, Schultz, and Cadue,[21] provide suggestive evidence for such a limit. Since the early 1970s, the tribe has consistently pursued strategies to "hunt the federal buffalo,"[22] to tap all available sources of federal financing. During the Reagan era of severe budgetary restrictions on Indian assistance, the tribal budget (excluding education funds, outside the control of the tribe) fell from a high of $1,500,000 in 1981 to $921,000 in 1984. In absolute terms, however, line item expenditures for tribal government and administration rose significantly during this period. Funds for economic development showed an inverse and extenuated trend, from $661,000 in 1981 to $120,000 in 1984. By 1984, governing costs represented 48% of the entire budget; funds for economic development accounted for only 13% of tribal expenditures.[23] Hunting the federal buffalo, an externally oriented activity in the terms utilized here, had become an onerous and unrewarding activity.

As one might have predicted, this economic crisis precipitated a political one. In 1983, recall petitioners accused five council members of "illegally passing tribal resolutions, improperly disposing of government property, and misappropriating tribal funds."[24] The council rejected the recall petition, the dissidents formed a shadow council and seized the tribal offices, the existing council sought a restraining order in Federal Court, and the BIA "refused to intercede, because of a directive that Indian tribes should settle their own internal disputes."[25] Efforts to resolve the conflict, however, did little to foster tribal sovereignty, nor to promote economic stability:

> Soon both Kickapoos and local non-Indians were calling for an investigation. Pressure from the U.S. Attorney General's office and the congressional delegation led to a freeze on some new program funds and audits of existing programs.[26]

Another disputed election occurred the following year. The result, as Stull, Schultz, and Cadue observe simply, "was a tribe without a functioning government."[27]

The Kickapoo case makes a clear point. While tribal sovereignty and economic self-sufficiency may be distinguished analytically, they are closely embedded in each other. The interconnections are strongest for reservations, like Kickapoo, where the mainstay of the economy is the public sector—transfer funds from the federal government. But sovereignty and self-sufficiency intertwine, too, in those cases where energy- and resource-rich tribes seek private development. I will return to such connections in an extended discussion of reservation leasing; for the present purpose, however, it is useful to disentangle economic self-sufficiency from sovereignty.

ECONOMIC SELF-SUFFICIENCY. Over the last several decades, scores of programs have been authorized by the U.S. Congress to address the economic and social well-being of Native Americans. Despite this variety of means, the overriding objective of federal policy has seldom been clearly articulated. This objective, however defined, has never been isolated from other policy objectives of the federal government. Particularly in the arena of natural resources, federal goals for Indians have been confounded by the demands of competing non-Indian users as well as by overall requirements for national productivity. Nonetheless, some progress towards defining economic self-sufficiency may be made by examining four relatively explicit statements of federal intent.

The final report of the Senate's American Indian Policy Review Commission, issued in 1977, invoked a long-standing federal trust responsibility in the following definition of goals:

> The purpose behind the trust doctrine is and always has been to ensure the survival and welfare of Indian tribes and people. This includes the obligation to provide those services required to protect and enhance Indian lands, resources, and self-government, and also includes those economic and social programs which are necessary to raise the standard of living and social well-being of the Indian people to a level comparable to the non-Indian society.[28]

One legislative vehicle for promoting the survival and well-being of Native Americans was the Indian Financing Act of 1974. The Act endeavored to stimulate economic activity within the existing constraints on property ownership. Reservation lands, held in trust by the federal government, generally cannot be offered as collateral to potential investors. While necessary to preserve remaining lands in Indian ownership, the restriction serves to dampen outside economic aid. The Financing Act authorized the Secretary of the Interior to make federal loans to tribes or individual Indians for economic development, as well as guarantee the loans of private investors.[29]

The Act was meant to underscore the intent of the government that economic development should not be pursued at the expense of Indian ownership of resources. In practice, however, the legislation did little to achieve substantial progress in raising standards of living. It has never been adequately funded.[30]

The federal judiciary has also addressed the question of an appropriate standard of living for Indians, but the answers are similarly vague. In its 1963 "Arizona v. California" decision, the U.S. Supreme Court articulated the concern for social well-being and awarded water to the tribes along the Colorado River in the expectation that living conditions would improve. The award, however, was not based on any calculations of projected returns for specific uses of water. Rather, the quantities were determined by the amount of irrigable acres on the reservations, with the additional provisions that such water need not be put to agricultural use, nor that the award would be revoked for "tribal non use." Thus the decision, vague as it was in specifying a targeted standard of living, nevertheless sought to guarantee the economic viability of future generations of reservation residents as well as present ones.

In a brief passage contained in the 1979 decision on Indian rights to salmon runs in the Pacific Northwest, the "moderate living standard" was invoked again, but without much refinement. Indians were to be allowed 50% of the fish, at a maximum:

> As in "Arizona v. California" and its predecessor cases, the central principle here must be that Indian treaty rights to a natural resource that was once thoroughly and exclusively exploited by the Indians secures so much as, but not more than, is necessary to provide the Indians with a livelihood—that is to say, a moderate living.[31]

Yet the "Passenger Fishing Vessel" argument seemingly introduced the "use it or lose it" concept that "Arizona v. California" adamantly rejected. If the tribe's population should decrease or "if it should find other sources of support that lead it to abandon its fisheries," the allocation of fish could be decreased. In sum, though, the decision clearly acknowledged that Indians do have rights to sufficient resources, fish or otherwise, to provide a "moderate living."

Specific policies, programs, and legal rulings over the last several decades have sought—in intent if not in implementation—to maximize the possibilities for achieving adequate standards of economic and social well-being on reservations. Rulings on taxation quite consistently have favored Indians by exempting monies earned on the reservation from state personal income taxes, by precluding the enforcement of most other state taxing powers, and by allowing tribes to tax non-members engaged in economic pursuits within the reservation.

This collection of taxing powers and exemptions has two economic goals. First, it seeks to give some financial incentives to individuals and tribes for the development of on-reservation resources and employment opportunities. Second, it empowers tribes to generate revenue for the provision of social services to their members—ultimately with the expectation that federal and state transfer payments for such services can be reduced.

The federal government, however, retains fairly strict obligations over the management of natural and monetary resources of reservations. This trust responsibility is fundamental, but ambiguous. Legislative and judicial rulings hold the trustee to high fiduciary standards in managing "money accounts, parcels of land, or mineral deposits for tribes or individual Indians."[32] The recent decision in "Mitchell II" exemplifies this standard: the Department of the Interior was faulted for mismanaging the valuable timber lands of Washington's Quinault Reservation.[33] The standard bends, however, in cases where "a single federal agency must administer a multipurpose project providing benefits both to Indians and to numerous parties other than Indians."[34] I will examine this exogenous factor—articulated in the famous decision over Pyramid Lake in Nevada—in a subsequent section.

Finally, many specific social and economic programs have sought to foster economic self-sufficiency. Employment preference policies have been upheld, job training programs have been instituted, Indian-run lending institutions have been certified, aid to dependent Indian children and the elderly has been offered, and housing assistance programs have been extended widely to the tribes. The benefits deriving from these programs are contingent on the levels of funding and the efficiency of administration, but the purpose is quite unequivocal: to enhance the economic well-being of individuals and tribes.

Three operational measures can be used to capture the objective of economic self-sufficiency. First, this goal would be enhanced as mean family income on the reservation approaches the regional income mean. Second, on the assumption that economic development programs should benefit all reservation residents, economic self-sufficiency would be enhanced as a Gini coefficient approaches zero (indicating a homogeneous distribution), or, more realistically, as that coefficient approaches the prevailing value nation-wide. Finally, a measure of the ratio of available tribal revenues against total requirements for funding social services and infrastructure development would reveal the extent to which tribes must rely on transfer payments from other sources. Economic self-sufficiency would be fostered to the extent that reservations are able to generate their own revenues to underwrite these services and construction needs, and thus not have to rely on external—and frequently unreliable or inadequate—sources.

CULTURAL SELF-DETERMINATION. Federal Indian policy has been informed by anthropological notions of culture but more often than not they are archaic ones. A close connection between values and institutionalized behavior has been presumed in support of efforts to manipulate the fates of Native Americans. During the reservation era of the 1800s, for example, many reformers believed that the preservation of a land base and other core elements of traditional economic behavior would enhance the ability of Indian tribes to retain their "culture." An identical presumption fostered the allotment policy of the 1880s. By radically altering the basis for land holding, from community property to individual ownership, "tribalism" and "communism" would be rapidly replaced by private initiative and assimilation into the mainstream of American society.

In both cases, the results frequently ran counter to expectations. Restricted to reservations that were often inadequate to support traditional economies, Indians had to lose themselves in the surrounding white towns, working for wages. And during the allotment era paper title to land often did little to alter the institutions of communal labor and the exchange of goods and services. The core values justifying such behaviors did not disappear.

John Collier's philosophy, built into the Indian Reorganization Act (IRA), contained a similar conception of the workings of Indian society. Collier assumed that by strengthening or recreating tribal political institutions, he could preserve and enhance the culture of Native Americans.[35] There was some justification for this view, but more often than not, the tribal governments had to be created *de novo*, modeled along the lines of state and municipal governments, sanctioned by constitutions that read very much like the United States Constitution. These developments frequently destroyed those vestiges of traditional authority that had survived previous assaults. Simultaneously, though, the efforts to fabricate new governing institutions introduced necessary elements of behavioral variability. New leaders emerged to deal with a substantially changed environment, one of complex federal programs and new arenas of decision-making, an environment that demanded frequent visits to legislators and administrators in Washington.

One of the powers accorded to these newly constituted IRA governments was that of defining the criteria for tribal enrollment. The implication of this right has not been adequately addressed in discussions of Indian policy. Initially, it was a legal necessity attendant to the IRA. As anthropologist James Clifton observes of the Southern Ute,

> . . . one of the purposes of this Act was to provide a stable legal basis for the continuity of the tribe as a legal entity, hence the provision of perpetual succession in the tribe's Corporate Charter. Following from this provision, it was also necessary to write into this charter provisions for admitting members to the corporation. In this way the existing reservation community was made over into a fixed-membership group.[36]

The "fixed-membership group" is one in which membership rests on ascriptive criteria, not achievement- or performance-oriented standards. Like the Southern Ute, most Indian tribes adopted some measure of blood quantum as the key to defining tribal membership. The significance of the concept of fixity is that it allows for cultural heterogeneity. Clifton explores the implications:

> What is important is to consider that, notwithstanding their differences, these diversely constituted persons partly orient themselves in terms of membership in the tribe, and at least at a minimal level, the tribe as a corporate unit services each individual member, regardless of whether he is a semi-nomadic rodeo cowboy, a resident sheepherder, or a listless alcoholic. The fact is that, when and where the individual desires or can be made to expend his energies in the interest of furthering the achievement of tribal goals, the tribe employs him. Thus the tribe harnesses and manages a highly diverse reservoir of values, skills, and ambitions for both its own and the individual's benefit. In this way it would not be inappropriate to consider the new tribal unit as culturally adaptive.[37]

As Clifton further observes, there can be some limits placed on this degree of cultural variability. The fixed-membership principle may apply only to the most encompassing level of social organization—the legally constituted tribe. Below this, performance-oriented membership criteria may be invoked. Thus,

> ... like any large social system the Southern Ute tribe is differentiated, and ... the valuation of the fixity of membership on the tribal level does not necessarily drift downward evenly to influence all of the lesser contained groupings equally. Some of the Southern Ute social units such as cattle-raising co-ops and nativistic groups are clearly based on flexible-membership principles; that is, they are associative groupings

where there is an emphasis upon performance norms and adherence to a specific ideology.[38]

The concept allows at once for stability and variation, for continuity and change.[39]

There was some irony to this reliance on blood quantum as the defining element of tribal membership. The measurement had served, during the allotment period, as a direct and unquestioned proxy for competency. That is, Indians with less than one-half Native American blood were assumed by the Indian agents to be competent to handle their own property and affairs, and were thus given title in fee simple to their lands.[40] This was an extreme application of archaic notions of culture—not only were values presumed to be tightly linked to economic institutions, but to race as well.

The fixed-membership principle adopted by the IRA tribes nevertheless laid the structural basis for a decidedly more enlightened concept of culture, as Clifton suggests, since the principle allows for behavioral variability and a range of values to be maintained within a reservation population. This variation is adaptive. It provides a necessary basis for responding to shifts in the social, institutional, and political environment. At the same time, the principle allows at least some degree of stability. Some social networks, economic groups, and institutions within reservation society are built not simply on descent, but also on ascriptive criteria, on an allegiance to core cultural values.[41]

For decades, however, the implications of the IRA would not be formalized into a distinct federal policy toward Indian "culture." The termination era of the 1950s and 1960s was, once again, a direct attempt to destroy Native American cultures by dissolving tribal organizations. While much land was lost from Indian control and existing political organizations became ineffective, values proved to be more resilient. The Supreme Court, hearing a series of cases on termination, confirmed this resilience and, significantly, laid the groundwork for a policy of cultural self-determination. Discussing two of these, Wilkinson[42] summarizes the Court's actions: 150,166

Taken together, "Menominee Tribe" and "John" held that tribalism is ultimately a matter of self-definition. Federal recognition may be withdrawn. The tribal unit may change when a catastrophic event occurs, as with the Choctaws [removal of most of the tribe from its aboriginal territory], and a tribe may redefine itself ethnologically. But tribalism continues until the members themselves extinguish it. Tribalism depends on a tribe's own will.

These two cases, decided in 1968 and 1978 respectively, bracket a series of federal policy initiatives to bolster cultural self-determination. The Indian Civil Rights Act of 1968 had the effect of validating the diversity of behaviors and values implicit in the concept of the fixed-membership group. Individual Indians were accorded important constitutional rights vis-à-vis tribal governments, including the guarantee that tribal officials cannot "make or enforce any law prohibiting the free exercise of religion, or abridging the freedom of speech, or of the press, or the right of the people peaceably to assemble and to petition for a redress of grievances."[43]

Similar protections for individual religious beliefs were solidified in the American Indian Religious Freedom Act of 1978:

. . . it shall be the policy of the United States to protect and preserve for American Indians their inherent right of freedom to believe, express, and exercise the traditional religions of the American Indian . . . .[44]

While these two acts addressed the cultural self-determination of Indians as individuals, the overriding policy statement of the 1970s—the operative legislation now governing Indian affairs—firmly supported self-determination at the tribal level. This, of course, is the Indian Self-Determination and Education Assistance Act of 1975, reviewed above. While much of the act addresses tribal rights to make decisions over the disposition of natural resources and thus to enhance tribal sovereignty, the statement on educational choice reflects a somewhat different intent. There was an implicit recognition that the longterm viability of Native American societies rests with adequate human resources—with present and future generations trained to make their own choices. This concern was reiterated more forcefully in the Indian Child Welfare Act of 1978. Objecting to the historic practice of placing Indian children in non-Indian settings, Congress stated that "there is no resource more vital to the continued existence and integrity of Indian tribes than their children and that the United States has a direct interest, as trustee, in protecting Indian children. . . ."[45]

Taken together, these court decisions and acts of Congress reflect a rather sophisticated understanding of cultural self-determination. The core elements of the federal policy objective can be summarized as follows: a recognition that the tribes themselves, not the federal government or outside experts, have the right and duty to define their own basis of cultural identification; that individuals within tribal entities are guaranteed the right to choose what social and religious values they will uphold; and that future generations of Indians will have this right, likewise, to choose their own values and beliefs. As a policy objective, this set of elements simultaneously addresses group strength and internal flexibility.

A potential source for operationalization would seem to be the role and network analyses contained in *Measuring Culture: A Paradigm for the Analysis of Social Organization*[46] by Jonathan Gross and Steve Rayner. The work itself is an effort to objectify the grid/group theory of Mary Douglas.[47] While the lines of congruence between that theory and the present discussion need not be fully explored here, the overlap should be clear from Michael Thompson's succinct characterization:[48]

> Douglas holds that just two dimensions are enough to describe the important variations of social context: one, the extent to which a person's social life depends on his membership of [sic] social groups (group), and two, the extent to which his social life is restricted by rules which

preordain his social relationships (grid). Further, she holds that simple qualitative distinctions between strong and weak group and between strong and weak grid are sufficient to describe the correlation between social context and cosmology (by cosmology is meant the theories about the nature of the universe that sustain moral judgment).

Several of the quantitative measures developed by Gross and Rayner to assess group and grid dimensions may be adapted to the concern here with strength and flexibility. For proxies of group strength, their variables of *scope* and *impermeability* may be utilized. For flexibility (equivalent to low grid scores), the Gross/Rayner concepts of *specialization* and *entitlement* are of relevance.

Scope is explained as follows:

> If a given social unit is a subnetwork of some larger system, or if its membership overlaps with the membership of other networks, then a person's commitment might extend beyond the given unit. The *scope score* measures a person's diversity of interactive involvement in the activities of a given unit, relative to his interactive involvement outside the unit.[49]

Thus a scope score approaching one (i.e., the ratio of the number of activities performed with members of the social unit over the total number of activities performed, both inside and outside the social unit) would indicate that an individual (or a group, the averaged scores of all members) interacts primarily with members of the same social unit. While it is clear that extensive interaction takes place between Indians and non-Indians, I would suspect that there are critical levels of interaction within the social unit—the reservation community—that must be maintained for the perpetuation of group norms.

Impermeability is a second useful indication of group strength, one which seeks to measure "the likelihood that a non-member who satisfies the categorical requirements for membership and wants to join will actually attain membership."[50] For the purpose at hand, the Gross-Rayner measurement must be modified. Fixed-membership groups, based solely on ascriptive criteria, would have a high permeability index: individuals satisfying the categorical requirements of blood quantum would be rather automatically enrolled. A more appropriate discrimination would be the extent to which reservation residents (Indian *and* non-Indian) are given a franchise in tribal elections. On some reservations with programs of residential leasing this is a contested issue, as non-Indians press for representation and Indians attempt to thwart such permeability. The impermeability score would be defined as high if, to paraphrase Gross and Rayner,[51] few non-Indian reservation residents who want to join/vote are actually allowed to in a given timespan.

The extent of flexibility within the fixed-membership group can be measured by two grid variables. First, an entitlement score measures the "proportion of ascribed roles to all roles."[52] Second, the variable of specialization quantifies the proportion of possible roles in a social unit that are actually assumed by an individual in a given timespan. I would suggest that a social group is more adaptive the less specialization there is, and more conducive to retaining members if there are roles to be filled through achieved means. Both of these grid measures, it should be noted, also have intergenerational implications. A narrowly defined set of roles, either (or both) highly specialized or predominantly ascribed, is likely to promote rigidity at the expense of adaptability.[53]

Much additional work is needed to operationalize these variables. My purpose here is simply to review what appear to be some promising efforts to measure rather intractable elements of society and culture. If such efforts are not extended, more readily quantified indicators, strictly economic ones, are likely to dominate the assessment of programs and policies.

SUMMARY. I have endeavored to isolate and define the guiding objectives of federal Indian policy. I have done so by examining major statements of congressional and administrative policy, significant decisions of the courts, and specific programs designed to further one or another of the objectives of tribal sovereignty, economic self-sufficiency, and cultural self-determination. It has been argued that these three objectives have roughly equivalent weights as a result of Nixon's influence. Historically, this has not always been the case. Indeed, through some eras in the development of Indian-white relations, the very signs attached to these objectives have differed. During the allotment period, for example, programs and policies sought specifically to destroy any semblance of tribal sovereignty and to assimilate individual Indians into the mainstream of American society and culture. Although the difficulties caused by fractionated ownership of allotments now impinge on many efforts at economic development, the policy objectives of the allotment era have been effectively repudiated. Cultural self-determination, tribal sovereignty, and economic self-sufficiency are now concurrent goals of federal policy toward Indians.

Interaction of Objectives and Means

In practice, three objectives cannot be maximized simultaneously. Moreover, the federal government is mandated to serve multiple constituencies. Thus, complications to the framework developed above quickly arise. Here the issue of trade-offs among objectives is examined in the context of a lease proposal on the San Xavier Reservation, Tohono O'Odham Nation. Subsequently, I review the effects of exogenous influences on these objectives of federal Indian policy.

LONG-TERM LEASING. Since the mid-1950s, long-term leasing of reservation lands and resources has been a favored means employed by the Bureau of Indian Affairs to promote economic development and generate revenues for tribes and individual Indians. Legislation permits land leases of up to 99 years, on the assumption that extended terms will facilitate the procurement of financing. Two observers of this program note that long-term leasing

. . . can be the cornerstone of a reservation economic development program. Leasing can now be a strategy whereby land—a major economic factor of production on most reservations—is conveyed for a term to non-Indians as an inducement to invest capital and to bring industries, jobs, or services to the reservation.[54]

But Chambers and Price immediately urge caution, for leasing, a means to foster economic development, may simultaneously affect tribal sovereignty and cultural self-determination:

The issues that come before the Secretary [of the Interior] in the context of approval of long-term business leases are of enormous significance in terms of the law-making power of the tribe and its cultural and political future. Some leases may bring large numbers of non-Indians onto the reservation or may entice states to attempt to exercise regulatory and taxing powers over reservations. More than the landscape may be changed: an influx of non-Indians or state authority may interfere with tribal control over the reservation and continuation of tribal culture.[55]

Despite the gravity of the issues, the Department of the Interior has developed very few specific guidelines for the approval or rejection of leases. The Code of Federal Regulations simply requires the Secretary to assure that Indians receive fair financial returns for their land that activities on the leased lands do not detrimentally affect the surrounding communities and their natural environment. More importantly, neither the Department nor Congress has formulated an overriding policy for balancing tribal sovereignty, cultural self-determination, and economic self-sufficiency in the consideration of leases.

A brief examination of a recent proposal for leasing on the San Xavier Reservation in Arizona can suggest how these three federal objectives may interact. The proposal was rather extraordinary, calling for a 90-year lease of 18,000 acres of largely unutilized reservation land on the outskirts of Tucson. The intent of the developer was to build an entire "planned community" of 100,000 inhabitants. The tribe's council ultimately rejected the proposal in 1986, fearing, in part, that the planned development would indeed have serious repercussions on tribal sovereignty and cultural self-determination.[56]

Some of these repercussions may be briefly sketched. Tribal sovereignty, it can be argued, is at a low point when there is little or no economic activity to require administrative decision-making. As land use increases, the governing capacities of tribal officials will be exercised, and sovereignty will be enhanced. After some point, however, the issues raised by the presence of significant numbers of non-Indians on substantial reservation acreage will overwhelm tribal officials and debilitate their capability to respond to internal, Indian issues. For example, as the income generated by non-Indian activities on the reservation increases, states and municipalities are likely to intensify their efforts to assert taxing powers, and tribal officials would have to devote time and money to ward off such efforts. And, of course, it is possible that resident non-Indians would push for representation in tribal affairs.

Economic self-sufficiency, the second objective, is unlikely to be fostered to any great extent by small-scale, short-term lease activities. Without the security of long terms, outside investors would not be willing to develop substantial improvements, nor to pay significant ground rentals. Thus the revenues accruing to individuals and tribes would be nominal. As the length of lease increases sufficiently to attract investment, substantial rents, taxes, and other revenues may be paid to the tribe. This income will not increase linearly with increasing size and length, however. By standard real estate practice, per-acre ground rents will be smaller the larger the size of the total leased parcel. Moreover, at some point the employment-generating capabilities of a large-scale development will become superfluous to Indian economic self-sufficiency. Such a point would be reached, for example, when all Indians desiring employment have been satisfied. Beyond this point, the multiplier effects of the development may continue to benefit the regional economy, but have little positive impact on the reservation itself.

Finally, cultural self-determination may be expected to show a tendency similar to the other two objectives. With little or no on-reservation economic activity, many Indians will be drawn into the off-reservation labor force and be prone to the assimilative forces of the surrounding society. Within some range of economic development on the reservation, cultural self-determination will be enhanced by enabling individuals to remain within Indian social networks and affording them a choice of activities, without assimilative pressures. Again, however, at some point cultural self-determination may be jeopardized. As leases become longer and larger, land-use decisions become irreversible, and future generations are locked in to the choices made by the present one. At the extreme, too, pressures to assimilate may come not only from the society surrounding the reservation, but additionally from a dominant non-Indian society within the bounds of the reservation itself.

A schematic representation of the three objectives of federal Indian policy may be drawn to indicate the positioning of alternative leasing options. The representation is meant to be suggestive only, since the optimum will vary according to local conditions, specific provisions of a given lease, and variable weights accorded to the three objectives (Figure 1).

It became increasingly clear through the process of evaluating the proposed lease on the San Xavier Reservation, for example, that the lease fell well outside of any acceptable intersection of sovereignty, self-sufficiency, and self-determination.

I suggested above that these three objectives of federal Indian policy should be equally salient. In practice, the question of reservation land-leasing reveals a somewhat different pattern. The Bureau of Indian Affairs and its higher authority, the Secretary of the Interior, are inclined to give tribal sovereignty more weight than the other objectives. Once the Department of the Interior was assured that its minimal responsibilities under the Code of Federal Regulations were being addressed in the environmental impact assessment of the proposed lease on San Xavier, it chose to leave the decision to the governing bodies of the tribe and to the individual land-holders of allotments on the reservation. It was clear from the start that these decision-makers faced a binary decision on an unalterable proposal. To the developer, the large size and long duration of the lease were essential to his design for an entire planned city, so he was unwilling to entertain more modest ones counterproposals, ones which may have reflected local optima.

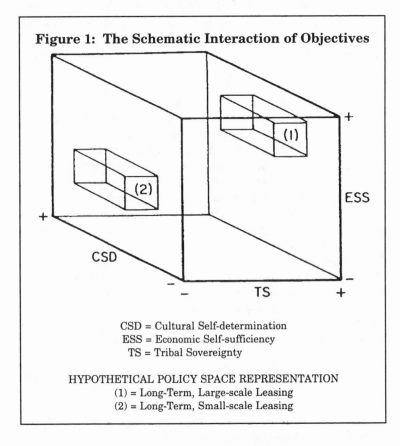

Figure 1: The Schematic Interaction of Objectives

CSD = Cultural Self-determination
ESS = Economic Self-sufficiency
TS = Tribal Sovereignty

HYPOTHETICAL POLICY SPACE REPRESENTATION
(1) = Long-Term, Large-scale Leasing
(2) = Long-Term, Small-scale Leasing

During much of the study and evaluation process, the tribal council appeared reluctant to take a position. In essence, it passed its sovereign authority onto the landholders, the heirs to the original allottees on San Xavier. These individuals struggled privately to make a decision on whether to encumber their own parcels in the development. By addressing this question they had to weigh, at least implicitly, the three objectives against one another.

Unfortunately for the task at hand, there is no way to reconstruct these individual decision processes. Extraordinary conflict developed on the reservation over the proposal, out of which emerged an organized and vocal opposition and an anonymous set of lease proponents who, in the face of the opposition, remained steadfastly quiet about their reasons for signing the lease. Not a single voice in favor of the lease was heard at the public hearings on the draft environmental impact statement. At these hearings, the opponents, however, expressed a rather clear theme—that the proposed lease would have some undeniable economic benefits but would unacceptably and irresponsibly constrain the land-use options of future generations. Although the issue was not fully articulated, opponents to the lease drew quite close connections between this option value of land and the cultural viability of the tribe itself. The potential threats to cultural self-determination overrode most of the other issues raised by the proposed city on the reservation.

Exogenous Influences on Federal Indian Policy

The Secretary of the Interior is required to give at least a cursory review to off-reservation environmental and social impacts of leasing. The provision appears to impose only a light exogenous constraint on action. Environmental impacts frequently can be mitigated; socio-economic impacts may quite easily be designated as neutral or beneficial, contributing some stimuli to the regional economy. A more significant area of conflict arises when the federal government must allocate scarce natural resources among competing users, Indian and non-Indian. Land, water, fish, and congressional appropriations are pre-eminent examples of such scarce resources.

Wilkinson relies on a close analysis of significant judicial decisions to argue that reservations today remain relatively insulated from deleterious outside influence. The exceptions prove the rule. In "Rosebud Sioux Tribe v. Kneip," for example, the Court upheld the "justifiable expectations" of long-term non-Indian residents within the exterior boundaries of the reservation. But the facts, Wilkinson argues, were peculiar:

In "Rosebud Sioux," the Court bowed to practicality. The decision can be explained in part as an exceptionally difficult case for tribal powers: it is anomalous in the extreme to uphold tribal self-government over a vast region of non-Indian land overwhelmingly populated by non-Indians.[57]

Similarly, two 1983 cases acknowledged specialized situations to support rulings against additional Indian water claims. In the first, "Nevada v. United States," the Pyramid Lake Paiutes were not awarded their claims to a fishable lake because the case had already been adjudicated in the 1940s. Justice Brennen, as Wilkinson observes,

noted that a result of the res judicata holding was that "thousands of small farmers in northwestern Nevada can rely on specific promises made to their forebears two and three generations ago. . . ."[58]

An identical ruling of finality was delivered in the second round of "Arizona v. California": the initial 1963 delineation of irrigable acreage on the Colorado River Reservation held fast.[59]

These cases involved the expectations of historic, non-Indian claimants to resources. Wilkinson[60] observes, nonetheless, that the Supreme Court has shown an "extreme reluctance to allow settled expectations, even over lengthy periods of time, to deny tribal prerogatives." One important vehicle for supporting this position is the well-established canon of construction that instructs the courts to rule in favor of Indian claims when those claims derive from ambiguities in the original treaties and settlements.[61]

Yet this canon is not without bounds. Of particular relevance are the string of cases invoking the McCarran Amendment, a 1952 statute that waived the sovereign immunity of the United States as trustee for Indian water rights in general stream adjudications. Such cases are given over to state courts to decide. It should be noted that Senator McCarran represented Nevada and regularly initiated legislation to retrieve land and water from the Pyramid Lake Paiutes.[62] To Wilkinson, the cases governed by the McCarran Amendment "demonstrate the kinds of limits that are inherent in the canons of construction favoring Indians."[63]

The nature of these inherent limits, and likewise the workings of the principle of settled expectations, are not easily specified. Clearly, though, the judicial actions reviewed by Wilkinson warn of powerful exogenous influences on the goals of federal Indian policy.

The Pyramid Lake decision is rightly viewed as critical, for it addressed not only the legal implications of *res judicata*, but the fundamental meaning of the trust relationship as well. On this issue, Wilkinson differs significantly from the interpretation of another leading commentator on Indian law, Reid Chambers. Writing in the early 1970s, Chambers argued that the Department of the Interior, as trustee for Indian land and resources, frequently violated its responsibility by serving diverse clients. In Chambers' view, the trust relationship is unique:

> In analyzing the conflict of interest between government agencies and the Indians, it is imperative to perceive that the federal government as trustee is charged with the protection of what are essentially *private property rights*. As trustee for private rights, the government does not act in its usual political capacity, but is charged with the same general obligations as are imposed on private trustees.[64]

The conflict arises because the Department of the Interior, in its larger mission, is manager and conservator of "*public* property and resources."[65] Its bias as an agency is thus against the private property rights of Indian tribes.

In the 1983 decision on Pyramid Lake, the Supreme Court disagreed with this fundamental contention. Wilkinson reluctantly acknowledges the appropriateness of this ruling:

. . . when government officials are directed simultaneously to advance both Indian interests and those of competing parties, then the rigid standards applicable to private trusts do not apply in full force.[66]

The frequent invocation of settled expectations, the ambiguities over canons of construction, and, finally, this reliance on balance in interpreting trust issues, all impose constraints on the pursuit of federal objectives toward Native Americans. The success or failure of many Indian policies and programs ultimately lies not in the courts, however, but in the legislature.[67] To the extent that the congressional appropriations process is a zero-sum game (and there are those who disagree, such as Wildavsky),[68] Indians must compete directly with other interests to ensure adequate funding for federally supported programs. While several observers have applauded the increase in lobbying skills among tribes,[69] the necessary presence of Indian leaders in Washington cannot help but to reduce their usefulness on their home reservations—reduce the time and effort they can devote to local issues.

Conclusions

Federal Indian policy, defined as the simultaneous enhancement of tribal sovereignty, economic self-sufficiency, and cultural self-determination, appears relatively benign. Yet there is ample evidence to suggest that many reservations and their inhabitants are not much better off—politically, economically, and culturally—than when Richard Nixon delivered his address on Indian affairs. Does the framework constructed here make any sense out of this paradox?

"Termination by accountants," the mildly hyperbolic phrase employed by Morris to characterize the Reagan administration's efforts, affords a clue. In the absence of sustained and healthy reservation-based economies, the public sector comes to the fore. Transfer payments and bureaucratic employment may contribute a veneer of self-sufficiency to reservation economies and, by forestalling difficult choices about jobs and the often irretrievable commitment of natural resources, may appear to promote cultural self-determination. But, as the brief review of the Kansas Kickapoo case revealed, reliance on the public sector may endanger the fledgling sovereignty of tribes. Most significantly, though, recourse to the public sector inevitably implicates the exogenous pressures on Indian livelihood—the competing demands of non-Indians on the federal budget.

Reagan's response was to corral the federal buffalo and to encourage the kind of resource development exemplified—in the extreme, to be sure—by the attempt to build a city of 100,000 people on the San Xavier Reservation. Unlike many mineral developments, that project would indeed have produced a substantial multiplier effect on the reservation and the regional economy. It would have enhanced tribal sovereignty to a point—and then most likely would have destroyed that sovereignty. It would have promoted cultural self-determination, perhaps, but only briefly.

What has been missing, recently, in the implementation of Indian policy is an intelligent middle course. In the discussion of the choices facing San Xavier, I alluded to the possibility of local optima, of projects that service all three objectives. But there is abundant space in the cube formed by the dimensions of sovereignty, self-sufficiency and self-determination. Too often, in recent years, policy implementors, evaluators, and entrepreneurs have worked at one or another corner of that box.

NOTES

1. Vine Deloria and Clifford M. Lytle, *American Indians, American Justice*, (Austin: University of Texas Press, 1983); Vine Deloria and Clifford M. Lytle, *The Nations Within: The Past and Future of American Indian Sovereignty*, (New York: Pantheon Books, 1984).

2. Joseph G. Jorgensen, "Sovereignty and the Structure of Dependency at Northern Ute," *American Indian Culture and Research Journal* 10, (1986), 75-94; C. Patrick Morris, "Termination by Accountants: The Reagan Indian Policy," *Policy Studies Journal* 16, (1988), 731-750; Donald R. Stull, Jerry A. Schultz, and Ken Cadue, "Rights Without Resources:

The Rise and Fall of the Kansas Kickapoo," *American Indian Culture and Research Journal* 10, (1986), 41-59.

3. Morris, "Termination by Accountants," (1988), 731-750.

4. The intent here is to define, in a preliminary fashion, a set of federal policy objectives for Indians similar to those of the U.S. Bureau of Reclamation for water development projects. That agency is mandated to address four objectives in its planning efforts: social well-being, regional economic development, environmental quality, and national economic benefits. See Stephen J. Fitzsimmons, Lorrie I. Stuart, and Peter C. Wolff, *Social Assessment Manual: A Guide to the Preparation of the Social Well-Being Account for Planning Water Resource Projects*, (Boulder, CO: Westview Press, 1977). Observations on how the Bureau of Reclamation has implemented that evaluative framework in recent years give impetus to the tentative measurement exercises carried out in this paper. Reclamation planners have found it all too easy to ignore or accord low weight to sociocultural factors, which are difficult to quantify. In fact, "social well-being" has been reduced from a co-equal planning objective to an "account" or display of "other social effects." See William B. Lord, "Objectives and Constraints in Federal Water Resources Planning," *Water Resources Bulletin*, 17, (1981), 1060-1065. The preliminary measurements reviewed in this commentary are intended simply to open a discussion of how to reinstate sociocultural factors into the planning and policy analysis process.

5. Monroe E. Price, *Law and the American Indian: Readings, Notes and Cases*, (Indianapolis: Bobbs-Merrill Co., 1973), 599.

6. Ibid., 597.

7. The issue of the weights to be placed on objectives in a multi-criterion (trade-off) decision-making problem is critical. In the context of Indian program and policy analysis, the problem is complicated by the fact that there are several appropriate decision-makers, minimally those administering and program or policy and those affected by the action. Each body may have justifiably different preferences. Moreover, specific programs are not generally designed to address the full range of objectives. As a general guideline, I would

suggest an analogy to "Pareto optimality" in welfare economics. See Frank H. Stephen, *The Economics of the Law*, (Ames: Iowa State University Press, 1988), 41-45. No specific program designed to enhance a single objective would be acceptable if it resulted in a "loss" on other dimensions. For an alternative—and promising—approach to multicriterion decision-making problems on reservations, see Ronald L. Trosper, "Multicriterion Decision-Making in a Tribal Context," *Policy Studies Journal*, 16, (1988), 826-842.

8. Charles F. Wilkinson, *American Indians, Time, and the Law*, (New Haven: Yale University Press, 1987).

9. Ibid., 57.

10. Ibid., 54-55.

11. Ibid., 24.

12. Felix S. Cohen, *Handbook of Federal Indian Law*, (Washington, D.C.: U.S. Government Printing Office, 1942).

13. Wilkinson, *American Indians, Time, and the Law*, (1987), 62, 73, 177.

14. Ibid., 39.

15. Ibid.

16. Deloria and Lytle, *American Indians, American Justice*, (1983).

17. Wilkinson, *American Indians, Time, and the Law*, (1987), 61.

18. Price, *Law and the American Indian*, (1973), 635.

19. Antoinette G. Houle, "Non-Lease Agreements Available for Indian Mineral Development," *Natural Resources Journal* 24, (1984), 195-201; Price, *Law and the American Indian*, (1973), 636.

20. Alternative measures of tribal sovereignty could be constructed. There is substantial variation across reservations in the extent to which tribes have chosen to implement governmental "police powers"—a definable set of regulatory functions such as zoning controls, law enforcement, game and fish regulations, taxation and business licensing, and judicial responsibility for the civil actions of non-Indians on the reservation. A simple enumeration of such powers exercised by tribes may approximate the objective of sovereignty, with one caveat. The likelihood that these governmental powers are put to the service of *Indians* can be expected to vary with the ratio of

Indians to non-Indians living on the reservation.

21. Stull, Schultz, and Cadue, "Rights Without Resources," (1986), 41-59.

22. Ibid., 45.

23. Ibid., 51.

24. Ibid., 52.

25. Ibid.

26. Ibid.

27. Ibid., 53.

28. American Indian Policy Review Commission, *Final Report*, (Washington, D.C.: U.S. Government Printing Office, 1977); Stephen L. Pevar, *The Rights of Indians and Tribes*, (New York: Bantam Books, 1983).

29. Ibid., 258.

30. Ibid.

31. "Washington v. Washington State Commercial Passenger Fishing Vessel Association 1979,' in Wilkinson, *American Indians, Time, and the Law*, (1987), 212.

32. Wilkinson, *American Indians, Time, and the Law*, (1987), 85.

33. Antoinette G. Houle, "Federal Government Held Accountable for Damages on Theory of Breach of Trust," *Natural Resources Journal* 24, (1984), 783-799.

34. Wilkinson, *American Indians, Time, and the Law*, (1987), 85.

35. Francis Paul Prucha, *The Great Father: The United States Government and the American Indians* vol. II, (Lincoln: University of Nebraska Press, 1984), 917-1012; Kenneth R. Philp, *John Collier's Crusade for Indian Reform, 1920-1954*, (Tucson: University of Arizona Press, 1977).

36. James A. Clifton, *The Southern Ute Tribe as a Fixed Membership Group*, in Deward E. Walker (ed.), *The Emergent Native Americans: A Reader in Culture Contact*, (Boston: Little, Brown and Co., 1972), 491.

37. Ibid., 500.

38. Ibid., 488.

39. Thomas R. McGuire, *Mixed-Bloods, Apaches, and Cattle Barons: Documents for a History of the Livestock Economy on the White Mountain Reservation, Arizona*, (Tucson: University of Arizona, Arizona State Museum, 1980); Thomas R. McGuire, *Politics and Ethnicity on the Rio Yagni:*

Potam Revisited, (Tucson: University of Arizona Press, 1986).

40. Prucha, *The Great Father*, (1984), 659-686.

41. Jorgensen provides an interesting example to counter the claim that the ability of tribes to establish their own criteria for membership is a sovereign right. See Joseph G. Jorgensen, "Sovereignty and the Structure of Dependency at Northern Ute," *American Indian Culture and Research Journal*, 10, (1986), 88-89. On the Uintah and Ouray Ute Indian Reservation, with a long history of tension between mixed- and full-bloods, the tribal court, acting on an apparent reading of congressional intent in earlier legislation separating the Northern Ute from the Affiliated Ute Citizens, overturned the membership criteria established by the tribe and supported by the BIA. While there are sufficient idiosyncracies in the case so as not to overturn the general principle, the example illustrates the complex intertwining of sovereignty, economy, and culture. The membership dispute exploded in the context of a severely depressed economy in the 1980s. At stake was the $400 monthly per capita payment.

42. Wilkinson, *American Indians, Time, and the Law*, (1987), 77.

43. American Indian Resources Institute (AIRI), *Indian Tribes as Sovereign Governments*, (Oakland, CA: American Indian Lawyer Training Program, Inc., 1987), 92.

44. Ibid., 98.

45. Ibid., 96.

46. Jonathan L. Gross and Steve Rayner, *Measuring Culture: A Paradigm for the Analysis of Social Organization*, (New York: Columbia University Press, 1985).

47. Mary Douglas, *Cultural Bias*, (London: Royal Anthropological Institute of Great Britain and Ireland, 1978).

48. Michael Thompson, "A Three Dimensional Model," in Mary Douglas (ed.), *Essays in the Sociology of Perception* (London: Routledge and Kegan Paul, 1982), 32.

49. Gross and Rayner, *Measuring Culture*, (1985), 78.

50. Ibid.

51. Ibid., 78-79.

52. Ibid., 81.

53. The data requirements for this set of measures are onerous. It is quite likely in practice that the single measures

of "entitlement" and "scope" will be found to capture most of the variation in the two variables, easing at least some of the measurement difficulties. It should be noted, however, that the "scope" argument is predicated on assimilationist notions, and would thus not accurately reflect phenomena such as "retribalization" and the "new ethnicity." See John W. Bennett (ed.), *The New Ethnicity: Perspectives from Ethnology*, (St. Paul, MN: American Ethnological Society, 1975; George L. Hicks and David I. Kertzer, "Making the Middle Way: Problems of Monhegan Identity," *Southwestern Journal of Anthropology* 28:1-24, 1972; Thomas R. McGuire, *Politics and Ethnicity on the Rio Yaqui: Potam Revisited*, (Tucson: University of Arizona Press, 1986, 1-19). Discussions of the "new ethnicity," however, are most appropriate to populations without fixed-membership principles, i.e., Native Americans not yet recognized as legal entities or populations of urban Indians who have left the reservations. For the specific case under review here—reservation-based, fixed-membership groups—the scope measure ought to more accurately reflect and differentiate group strength. It might be expected, for example, that "scope" would differ substantially among reservations situated within urban areas (e.g., the Agua Caliente Reservation, on checkerboarded land within Palm Springs, CA), those adjacent to, but distinct from, urban zones (the Salt River Pima-Maricopa Indian Community, bordering Scottsdale, AZ), and those relatively remote from urban centers of employment and interaction (e.g., the main area of the Tohono O'Odham [Papago] reservation).

54. Reid P. Chambers and Monroe E. Price, "Regulating Sovereignty: Secretarial Discretion and the Leasing of Indian Lands," *Stanford Law Review* 27, (1974), 1063. Jorgensen, however, warns that the multiplier effects of such investments are frequently less than anticipated. This is especially evident in the case of oil and mineral leasing, where royalties are often low and static, where production levels respond to demand, not to yearly revenue requirements of the tribes, and where the income received through leases may be diverted immediately to necessary social services, not economic development. See Joseph G. Jorgensen, "Sovereignty and the Structure of Dependency at Northern

Ute," *American Indian Culture and Research Journal* 10:75-94, 1986.

55. Reid P. Chambers and Monroe E. Price, "Regulating Sovereignty: Secretarial Discretion and the Leasing of Indian Lands," *Stanford Law Review* 27, (1974), 1063-1064.

56. Thomas R. McGuire, "Operations on the Concept of Sovereignty: A Case Study of Indian Decision Making," *Urban Anthropologist* 17, (1988), 75-86; Thomas R. McGuire and Marshall A. Worden, *Draft Socio-Cultural Impact Assessment of the San Xavier/Tucson Planned Community, Papago Indian Reservation, Pima County, Arizona*, (Tucson: University of Arizona, Bureau of Applied Research in Anthropology, 1984).

57. Wilkinson, *American Indians, Time, and the Law*, (1987), 43.

58. Ibid., 42-43.

59. Ibid., 43.

60. Ibid., 44.

61. Norris Hundley, "The 'Winters' Decision and Indian Water Rights: A Mystery Reexamined," *Western Historical Quarterly* 13 (1982), 17-42.

62. Martha C. Knack and Omer C. Stewart, *As Long as the River Shall Run: An Ethnohistory of Pyramid Lake Indian Reservation*, (Berkeley: University of California Press, 1984).

63. Wilkinson, *American Indians, Time, and the Law*, (1987), 50.

64. Reid P. Chambers, "Discharge of Federal Trust Responsibility to Enforce Claims of Indian Tribes: Case Studies of Bureaucratic Conflicts of Interest." In [hearings on] Federal Protection of Indian Resources, Senate Subcommittee on Administrative Practice and Procedure of the Committee on the Judiciary (ed.), (Washington, D.C.: Government Printing Office, 1971), 235-249.

65. Ibid., 237.

66. Wilkinson, *American Indians, Time, and the Law*, (1987), 84.

67. Daniel McCool, *Command of the Waters: Iron Triangles, Federal Water Development and Indian Water*, (Berkeley: University of California Press, 1987).

68. Charles F. Wildarsky, *The Politics of the Budgetary Process, 3rd ed.*, (Boston: Little, Brown and Co., 1979).

69. Robert Bee, *The Politics of American Indian Policy*, (Cambridge, MA: Schenkman Publishing Co., 1982); George P. Castile, "Mau Mau in the Mechanism: The Adaptations of Urban Hunters," *Human Organization* 35, (1976), 394-397.

Chapter III

Social and Economic Consequences of Federal Indian Policy: A Case Study of the Alaska Natives

Gary C. Anders

Introduction

Responding to the potent lobbying efforts of major energy companies, Congress resolved the land disputes of Alaska Natives by passing the Alaska Native Claims Settlement Act (ANCSA) in 1971. Among other things, this law mandated that corporations be formed and that everyone of at least one-quarter Alaska Native blood (Indian, Eskimo, or Aleut) born before December 18, 1971 be enrolled as a shareholder. Subsequent distributions of both land and money went to these corporations in place of tribal entities.

This article discusses ANCSA (Public Law 92-203) and its impact on the Native people of Alaska. First, the article briefly examines the historical events that lead to the passage of ANCSA. Next it outlines some important aspects of the settlement terms. Then it compares ANCSA with other federal policies toward the American Indian. Finally, the article evaluates the effects of ANCSA on the development potential of Alaska Natives.

Historically in the United States, pressures to open new lands for an expanding immigrant population, combined with opportunities to exploit valuable natural resources, resulted in a fluctuating national policy toward the American Indian. The historical consistency of the federal government's assimilationist attitudes with regard to Native Americans can be seen through a comparison of two major federal Indian policies, namely, the Dawes Allotment Act, 1887, and the termination of Indian tribes' trust status during the 1950s. Although ANCSA bears certain similarities to allotment, it combines elements of other policies. A principal focus of this article is to

47

examine the similarities between ANCSA and termination. This orientation will allow a closer study of a contemporary policy periodically undergoing congressional revision.

Owing to the nature of the study, this article will not provide econometric analyses to support the inferences that it draws. Rather, research issues will be raised regarding the impact of federal policy on Native Americans and Alaska Natives. In a study of this breadth, it is not possible to reduce the analysis to a set of testable hypotheses or even to a number of fully documented propositions. Moreover, the data necessary to conduct such empirical investigations either do not exist or are considered proprietary.

Historical Background

The ANCSA is usually traced back to the Russian/American Treaty of Cession (1867).[1] From that time and for over a century, the destiny of Alaska Natives was defined by dominant elements of white America (i.e., government bureaucrats, missionaries, and the military). While perhaps well intentioned, their policies have tended to be culturally ethnocentric and morally indurate with frequent devastating side effects.[2] For example, in the 1950s the U.S. Army Corp of Engineers examined the feasibility of constructing a dam at a narrow portion of the Yukon River near the Koyukon village of Rampart. Costs were estimated at $1.3 billion, and the dam would flood approximately 10,000 miles of land in order to create a reservoir bigger than Lake Erie. The project was to produce 5 million kilowatts of electricity per year. It was to be the largest dam in the world at that time. Little consideration was given to the fact that the lake would flood seven Athabascan villages and cause several thousands of Natives to suffer the loss of their homes and traditional subsistence economy. In another instance, the Atomic Energy Commission, in a demonstration of the peaceful use of nuclear power, proposed "Project Chariot," which would create a deep water harbor by means of an atomic blast.[3] The designated site of this undertaking was Cape Thompson, the home of several hundred Inupiat Eskimos.

Attempts by Alaska Natives to protect and prevent the loss of their land have taken place since the late nineteenth century.[4] But it was not until after oil was discovered on the

North Slope in 1968 that a statewide movement was organized to fight for Native land claims. When one looks at the history of the ANCSA, it is apparent that a concerted effort was needed to bring regionally and culturally different Native groups together to form a statewide organization called the Alaska Federation of Natives (AFN).[5] During the intense lobbying that preceded ANCSA's passage, the AFN was the unifying entity that helped resolve differences between various groups of Alaska Natives.

The younger, more educated Natives who formed the core of AFN leadership sought a settlement that would allow them to keep a portion of their aboriginal lands and quickly learned to organize politically to gain power.[6] Although the usual procedure for resolving Native land disputes was to litigate these cases before the U.S. Indian Claims Commission, the decision to seek a Congressional settlement was based on several important considerations.[7] For obvious reasons, many white Alaskans did not favor a settlement and hoped that the Natives would get lost in the federal system. Native leaders, however, knew that the issues that pertained to their people could only be addressed in Congress. Therefore, they concentrated their energies and political skills into developing an effective lobbying effort strengthened by the assistance of major oil companies. Oil companies such as British Petroleum knew a settlement was needed to secure a right-of-way for the construction of the Trans-Alaska Oil Pipeline. It has been pointed out by J. Hanrahan and P. Gruenstein that the lobbying by multinational oil companies was the major impetus for congressional intervention.[8]

Almost from the beginning, the AFN leadership seemed to insist on corporations as a settlement vehicle. Reasons given for the selection of corporations deal mainly with the Natives' desire to reduce the bureaucratic control of the Bureau of Indian Affairs (BIA). There was a general distrust of the BIA based on the history of its involvement in Native affairs. More important were the heterogeneous interests of the various Native groups. To quote a representative of the Arctic Slope Native Association during land claims negotiations, "Since this is a settlement extinguishing property rights, it is our deep conviction that the settlement's land and money should be distributed on the basis of the quantum of land within each native region. This to us is the most fair allocation for it directly relates that which is received to that which is taken in exchange."[9] Accepting this principle, at least in part, one of the earliest bills submitted to Congress called for the division of Alaska into seven Native regions according to a common heritage and provided for the formation of a statewide corporate structure that would be "for the purpose of promoting economic opportunity for the benefit of the Natives and their descendants."[10]

The final version of ANCSA, the result of numerous compromises, modified the bill in such a way that it lost much of its original intent.[11] The original version had emphasized a single statewide corporation with social responsibilities going well beyond business functions. Congress handled the state's objections to this proposal by calling for the creation of two types of regional corporations, one strictly for profit making and a second nonprofit social service agency. Although these two types of corporations were established for each region, in the belief that they would be equals, the for-profit corporations quickly became dominant. And, while ANCSA was ratified by the 600 delegates at the AFN annual meeting, in truth the majority of Alaska Natives had little appreciation for the settlement's highly complex terms.[12]

Given their limited understanding of ANCSA and major differences between Western and traditional Native views of land ownership, it is possible to argue that ANCSA was not a legitimate expression of Alaska Native self-determination. The numerous discontinuities arising from ANCSA, especially with regard to the effects of external forces on the organic texture of Alaska Native communities, indicate that the probable intent of ANCSA was not to preserve Alaska Native land ownership. As F. Ferguson, a former AFN president, surmised, "I believe the Natives who were shooting for this [ANCSA] won a fair settlement, but the people who devised the bill knew that this was very complicated and that failure was likely."[13]

In retrospect, it appears that corporations may not have been the most suitable choice of a development institution for Alaska Natives because of their low educational levels and general unfamiliarity with capitalism on anything larger than a village scale. But the means for cultural survival seemed to depend on adopting some element of the larger society that would allow Native people to maintain their basic identity.[14] As B. Garber remarks: "With little faith in federally supervised property, Native leaders opted for parity with non-Natives in land tenure and saw in ANCSA an alternative through stock ownership in landed corporations. With thousands of years of experience in holding communal property and relatively little experience living with private property, it's no wonder that conflicts arise between the new land tenure under ANCSA and the older notions of communal property."[15] Most Alaska Native leaders understood that previous federal policies had broken up Indian land holdings, factionalized tribal memberships, and in some instances terminated the relationship between tribal groups and the federal government. Given this, they believed that corporations would provide a more effective buffer from the capriciousness of the federal government.

ANCSA Settlement Terms
Although there are complex facets of ANCSA providing for allotments to individuals, its main thrust is a combination cash and land award that went to state chartered Native-owned corporations.[16] In return for extinguishing aboriginal claims, ANCSA provided a cash settlement of $962.5 million and approximately 44 million acres of land. ANCSA designated 12 Native regions in the state, each region reflecting common culture and language whenever possible (see fig. 1). Native lands in each of these regions were to be managed by a regional corporation, and by complementary village corporations established in local communities with at least 25 Native residents. The 12 regional corporations, and a thirteenth later established for nonresident Alaska Natives, were incorporated as for-profit enterprises as stipulated by the act. (See table 1 for information on Alaska Native corporations.)

Of 211 Native villages qualified for ANCSA benefits, most chose to form for-profit corporations. Only seven villages chose not to participate in the settlement and, instead, selected ex-reserve lands that were transferred to a traditional village council.[17] These villages received land taken from public domain and a relatively small cash award. Regional corporations were entitled to receive 16 million acres under a complicated formula based on the number of shareholders within the region as well as on historical use and occupancy. Participating village corporations had 3 years to select from three to seven townships (69,120-161,280 acres). National parks or land already in private ownership could not be selected.

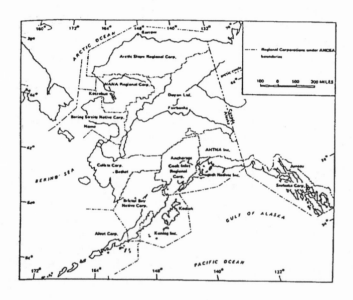

Fig. 1—The Alaska Native Regional Corporations

Alaska Natives of at least one-fourth Indian, Eskimo, or Aleut descent were awarded 100 shares of stock in both a regional and village corporation. In the event that a Native could not identify a home village, he or she was given at-large shareholder status in the regional corporation. Instead of village corporation stock, they received a per capita share of the monies paid by the regional corporation to its villages from the settlement fund. Settlement benefits in the form of stock were made available to approximately 80,000 Natives born before December 18, 1971.

TABLE 1

Alaska Native Regional Corporations: Enrollment, Number of Villages, Ethnicity, Land Award, and Employment Sources

Regional Corporation	Number of Shareholders	Number of Villages	Ethnic Group	Land Base*	Employment Sources
Ahtna	1,057	8	Ahtna	1.7	Wage labor
Aleut	3,124	13	Aleut	1.3	Wage labor Fishing
Arctic Slope	3,710	8	Inupiat	5.1	Subsistence Wage labor
Bering Straits	6,271	17	Inupiat, Yup'ik	2.1	Subsistence Wage labor Fishing
Bristol Bay	5,315	30	Yup'ik, Aleut, Athabascan	2.9	Fishing Subsistence Wage labor
Calista	13,193	56	Yup'ik, Athabascan	6.2	Subsistence Fishing Wage labor
Chugach	1,881	5	Alutiq, Eyak	.9	Fishing Wage labor
Cook Inlet	6,052	7	Athabascan mixed urban migrants	2.2	Wage labor Subsistence
Doyon	8,905	34	Athabascan	12.0	Subsistence Fishing Wage labor
Koniag	3,267	16	Koniag	1.0	Fishing Wage labor
NANA	4,761	11	Inupiat	2.2	Subsistence Wage labor Fishing
Sealaska	15,388	12	Tlingit, Haida	.2	Fishing Wage labor Subsistence

SOURCE.—U.S. Department of Interior, Bureau of Land Management, Information Bulletin no. AK 87-167 (Anchorage, Alaska: Bureau of Land Management, 1987).

* In millions of acres, including subsurface village estates, and excluding former reserves.

Of the $962.5 million, the state of Alaska paid $500 million from the 12.5% royalty it receives from Prudhoe Bay oil. The federal government appropriated the remaining $462.5 million over a 10-year period. Monies paid into the Alaska Native Fund by both parties were allocated to the regional corporations on the basis of their shareholder enrollments. During the first 5 years of the settlement (1971-76), 10% of the cash was distributed to individuals, and 45% went to the village corporations. Thereafter, all payments were kept by the regional corporations.

Lands selected by Natives were divided between village and regional corporations. Although intraregional distributions were determined by village enrollment, the overall land allocation between regional corporations followed a much more complex formula. Because village corporation lands include only the surface rights, the regional corporations control the subsurface rights to all Native-owned lands within their respective boundaries. ANCSA regional corporations have certain controlling powers over village corporations within their region; imposition of this supernumerary power over the villages has generated conflicts over the use of village lands that have, in a few instances, been resolved by mergers. ANCSA allows mergers between villages and regional corporations; however, section 7-B requires that there be no fewer than seven regional corporations.

Section 7-I of ANCSA calls for a 30%-70% distribution of net revenues between a regional corporation generating income on timber sales or subsurface mineral developments and all of the regional corporations. According to the negotiated terms of a costly legal dispute between ANCSA corporations, a regional corporation is to receive 30% of its net revenues and a per capita share of the remaining 70%, divided with all other regional corporations. This requirement has reduced the revenues of financially profitable corporations—making certain investments uneconomic, given the risks associated with full liability but limited returns.

In addition to the competition between regional corporations and villages, there is substantial competition between regional corporations for profits and for qualified Native employees. Although some regions have reduced these internal conflicts through mergers with village entities, rivalry between villages and their regional corporations has led to lawsuits that have practically bankrupted the corporations involved. Such events substantiate the frequently heard claim that the principal ANCSA beneficiaries have been the state's attorneys.

Some ANCSA provisions were modified through the 1980 Alaska National Interest Lands Conservation Act (ANILCA), Public Law 96-487. These changes include an extension of the tax exemption for underdeveloped lands and an amendment that gives the Native corporations the "first right of refusal" when shareholders are able to sell stock. Still another provision allows Native corporations to enact by-laws that prohibit voting rights from being transferred to non-Natives. ANILCA called for a congressional review of ANCSA, which was undertaken in 1985. This review process also led to the recent enactment of amending legislation.

ANCSA and Other Indian Policies

Several scholars have emphasized parallels between ANCSA and allotment policy. M. Price argues that the federal government attempts to periodically recreate Natives "to reflect their own image of the perfect society."[18] L. Fuller argues that "the Alaska Native Claims Settlement Act of 1971 may well parallel the predicament of the Indians following enactment of the General Allotment Act [Dawes Act] of 1887. Both pieces of legislation arose during a period of economic fluctuation and uncertainty, and were promulgated at a point in history when Indian-White contact was at a precarious stage with regard to social adaptation. In addition, integrating the Natives into the dominant white culture was the expressed goal of each settlement."[19] S. Langdon further extends this comparison by considering the effects of Alaska's limited entry fishery program on Native fishing rights.[20]

Signed into law on February 8, 1887, the General Allotment Act contained five basic provisions: (1) Indian reservations would be divided, with each tribal member receiving a grant of land consisting of 160 acres for family heads (single Indians over the age of 18 and juveniles received lesser grants of 80 and 40 acres, respectively); (2) allotees would receive fee simple title to their holdings, but the lands were to be held in trust by the government for a period of 25 years, during which time the land could not be sold; (3) Indians would be given 4 years to make their selections, after which time their selections would be made by representatives of the federal government; (4) U.S. citizenship would be conferred on any Indian who maintained his allotment and adopted a "civilized" way of life; (5) unallotted tracts of land were declared surplus and sold by the government.[21]

In a study of allotment policy, D. Otis argues that the most powerful motivating force behind the implementation of the Dawes Act was "the pressure from land hungry white settlers." This assertion seems to be corroborated by the historical evidence.[22] Therefore, comparisons between ANCSA and the Dawes Act suggest that a mix of white economic interests was the principal force for their enactment, but there were other similarities as well. Like the Dawes Act, the Alaska Native Claims Settlement Act imposed time restrictions on the sale or dispossession of the award. Congress mandated a 20-year protection period so that shares of stock in ANCSA Native corporations could not be sold until December 18, 1991. Congress further stipulated additional provisions that prevent taxation of undeveloped Alaska Native lands.

Although the assimilationist purpose of these two policies appears similar, the settlement mechanics differ significantly. Alaska Natives were organized into regional and village corporations, whereas with allotment, Indians received their lands purely on an individual basis. While corporations were to become the vehicle for integrating geographically isolated Alaska Natives into the dominant capitalist political economy, allotment was intended to spread agrarian values among nomadic Indian tribes.

An important thing to keep in mind when considering the allotment program and the ANCSA as assimilationist devices is that allotment was followed by New Deal efforts to reconstruct reservations through the Indian Reorganization Act (IRA).[23]

While offering some useful insights, comparisons between ANCSA and allotment fail to consider the progression of federal policy toward Natives. After much consideration I have come to realize that the policy of termination adopted during the Eisenhower administration provides a much better analogy. Under the guise of removing economically successful tribes from the BIA's protective yoke, Congress terminated the trust relationship with several tribes with disastrous consequences. The Menominee tribe is a case study of termination that closely resembles ANCSA.

In 1953, these Wisconsin Indians were among the most prosperous tribes in the United States. In addition to owning prime timber land, they were estimated to have financial assets of over 90 million dollars. Under the Menominee Termination Act of 1954, the tribe took over responsibility for the tribal paper mill and the social service programs previously provided by the BIA. A tribal corporation, Menominee Enterprises, Inc., was created to run the mill, and each tribal member (approximately 3,000 persons) was issued a bond paying 4% interest and 100 shares of stock. Tribal enrollment was stopped in 1961 so that a Menominee born after that date could only get shares through inheritance.

Though supposedly inalienable until the year 2000, shares were soon passing into white hands. Speculators also accepted shares against loans that Indians took out without means for repayment. Within a relatively short time, the high cost of providing tribal services, along with poor management, and the loss of the tribe's tax exempt status eventually forced the company to liquidate its assets in order to pay mounting debts. The enterprise finally collapsed with the remaining resources being absorbed by creditors.[24]

Although the Menominee succeeded in eventually getting their termination repealed and their reservation restored, other tribes were not so fortunate. The Klamath reservation in Oregon, for example, was dissolved and each tribal member received a per capita share in land or money (approximately $43,000 in 1961). According to W. Trulove and D. Bunting, most of the payments were quickly spent on consumer goods, and little was invested in businesses or education. They found that by 1965, over 40% of the recipients had no cash or savings.[25]

When compared to previous federal policies resulting in white absorption of Native land and natural resources, ANCSA appears to have a similar capacity only raised to a higher power.[26] ANCSA imposes the institution of private property rights, pressures for assimilation and an individualistic economic orientation. A settlement based on limited participation has been established with limited opportunities for success. Given the primacy of this model, it is necessary to consider its impact on the Alaska Natives' future prospects.

ANCSA's Impact on Alaska Native Potential for Self-Determination and Development

ANCSA was the outgrowth of a congressional desire to resolve a land dispute so that the Trans-Alaska oil pipeline could be built. In settling the conflict, Congress sought to assimilate and integrate Alaska Natives by organizing them into profit-making corporations. How does one evaluate such a public policy except by considering what would have occurred in its absence or the lost potential of a different approach? In other words, are Alaska Natives better off because of ANCSA? Has it made a perceptible difference? The overall evaluation is mixed.

On the one hand, the act has empowered Alaska Natives, helping them to become an economic and political force; Alaska Natives, through AFN and various Native associations created to defend their lands and ways of life, have achieved a strong voice in state politics. But, on the other hand, after almost 20 years, it is increasingly apparent that ANCSA has not benefited most Alaska Natives in practical economic terms by improving their ability to make a living or to get a job.

ANCSA has done little to reduce Native dependence on welfare and subsidies. As R. Arnold, a long-time ANCSA observer, puts it, "Despite the cash payments received by Eskimo, Indian and Aleut shareholders or the value of shares they own in their corporations, and the prosperity and political influence that some possess, the lives of most Natives appear to be little changed by the most extraordinary aboriginal land claims settlement in American history."[27] Alaska Native family income remains far below white Alaskan levels. At least one Native in four lives below the poverty level even with welfare payments. According to data presented in table 2, over 60% of Alaska Natives over the age of 16 were unemployed. Of those with jobs, almost 39% earned less than $7,000 per year. It has been estimated that in 1979 18% of Native households received 46% of all the income earned by Alaska Natives, and that 5% received 20% of that total.[28] It is likely that the distribution of income will become even more inequitable, especially between rural and urban Alaska Natives.

Forty-six percent of the Alaskan population is concentrated in Anchorage, and only about 19% live in over 200 widely scattered villages and small towns that are predominantly Native. Yet, over one half of the Alaska Native population lives in rural communities with populations under 1,000.[29] The economic and social opportunities of urban and rural Alaska Natives differ substantially. Most rural Natives maintain to a nominal degree traditional culture and language. Subsistence hunting and fishing still provide a significant portion of the village food supply. The vast majority of rural communities in Alaska are not connected with a road system, and often the only form of transportation is a boat or snowmobile. The local economy is heavily dependent on state expenditures and transfer payments. Yet, these cash injections are largely insufficient to cover expensive imported goods. In traveling around rural Alaska, one has the sense of entering a world that has been largely bypassed by the mainstream development. Although rural Alaska Natives have been afforded basic services such as electricity, running water, and health care, most of these service systems are expensive to operate and maintain and are vulnerable to breakdowns that require white technicians to repair them.[30]

In the past, Alaska Natives survived by subsistence hunting and fishing, which were materially poor and unpredictable. Famines were common, and mass starvation periodic. After the arrival of Westerners, Natives continued subsistence hunting and fishing, but over time, expensive modern technology replaced traditional techniques. Today the rural subsistence economy is heavily dependent on cash. An active hunter, for example, spends about $4,000 every few years for a snowmobile, plus gas and oil. These shifts have increased monetary dependence for the subsistence component maintained in village economies.

In addition, cash needs have been reinforced by the rapid growth of state spending in rural Alaska during the oil

TABLE 2

Population and Employment of Alaska Natives, 1985

	Total	Male	Female
Resident Alaska Native population	84,816	44,434	40,382
Total Native population under 16 years old	32,945	16,913	16,032
Total Native population over 16 years old	51,871	27,521	24,350
Native population by age cohort:			
16-24 years	14,973	8,190	6,783
25-34 years	18,006	9,568	8,438
35-44 years	7,516	4,118	3,398
45-64 years	7,799	3,948	3,851
65 years and older	3,577	1,697	1,880
Persons not in labor force, 16 years and older	14,381	5,956	8,425
Persons classified as students, 16 years and older	6,643	3,559	3,084
Potential labor force (a)	37,490	21,565	15,925
Total employed (b)	14,188	8,810	5,378
Total not employed (c)	23,302	12,755	10,547
Percentage unemployed (c/a)	62.1	59.1	66.2
Persons unemployed and actively seeking work (d)	14,255	7,959	6,296
Prospective labor force (d/a)	38.0	36.9	39.5
Total employed earning more than $7,000 per year ($e$)	8,681	5,678	3,003
Total employed earning less than $7,000 per year ($f$)	5,507	3,132	2,375
Percent of f/b	38.8	35.5	44.2

SOURCE.—U.S. Department of the Interior, Bureau of Indian Affairs, Juneau Office, *Report on Service Population and Labor Force* (Juneau, Alaska: Bureau of Indian Affairs, August 13, 1986).

boom of the 1970s and early 1980s. Responding to the high incidence of rural poverty, a variety of transfer programs provided rural Alaska Natives with subsidized incomes, state and federal capital projects (e.g., schools, clinics, housing, and electrification) exacerbated a growing dependence on entitlement programs and wage incomes.[31] Except in villages with commercial fishing alternatives, almost eight out of every 10 jobs are dependent on state spending.[32]

Prior to ANCSA, Native tribal identity had long been under assault. Imposition of Western institutions (i.e., religion, schools, legal systems, etc.) effected a substantial disintegration of the traditional cultural patterns and language. Although ways of life, culture, and economic orientation are different among regions, Alaska Natives have been traditionally sparsely distributed relative to the total land area. As late as the 1940s a considerable population of Natives did not live in permanent settlements but moved to follow the seasons of game harvesting. The factors that brought about a more sedentary social pattern can be traced to missionaries and schools as well as to developments that occurred during the Second World War. Accordingly, Natives moved from a kinship-based society to one differentiated according to education, position, religion, wealth, and geographical location. Over time, this stratification has been strengthened by out-migration, inter-marriage with whites, and other factors that allow urban Natives better access to education, economic opportunities, and social prestige.

Social stratification or the hierarchical ordering of people from a common background can be traced to the externally imposed division of Native society and the reactions of individual Natives to opportunities for personal gain or the threat of dispossession. The erosion in Alaska Native cohesiveness and the attendant effects of social disintegration are exacerbated by value conflicts between traditional common property ways and the new emphasis on private property and accumulation. Traditional Native economies integrated welfare considerations into household relations, with the Native leadership dividing responsibility for their people. The ANCSA corporations have encouraged a new rank and file of bureaucratic Natives to take up the nonprofit responsibilities of shareholders. These innovations often do not reflect traditional features of Native culture. Anomie and suicide have resulted because the village economy is incapable of generating enough jobs, especially for young adult males already suffering from a loss of esteem and self-worth.[33] A high incidence of Native mental health disorders and medical pathologies are correlated with associated social dislocations.

The Alaska Native Claims Settlement Act has largely benefited white professionals (mainly lawyers but also accountants, business consultants, and others) as well as a small number of Natives who moved into privileged positions in regional corporations or nonprofit social service agencies created to serve Alaska Natives. Because of ANCSA's complexity and the numerous legal and financial responsibilities it imposes on the corporations, Native leaders lost considerable control over the institutions that they had fought to establish. Reflecting their dependence on white technocrats, ANCSA corporations demonstrate in many instances that they have internalized the values of white society. While a relatively small number of Natives employed in high-paying jobs enjoy the opportunities that ANCSA created, most Alaska Natives face much more limited prospects. By and large, they have received minuscule benefits from ANCSA and have been only marginally affected by the corporations' activities. In the villages, the primary occupation is still subsistence, with supplementary cash coming from seasonal jobs or from transfer payments. While some concerned Native leaders have tried to expand rural employment opportunities, their corporate fiduciary responsibilities impose severe trade-offs between profit and the pursuit of social objectives.

At the outset, Congress had naive expectations regarding the economic benefits obtainable from the corporations, believing that it was possible to move Alaska Natives off welfare by using the corporations as a development vehicle. For various reasons, however, ANCSA corporations did not become institutions that could accommodate the shareholders' needs for both money and services.[34] The dividends of most ANCSA corporations have never been enough to support even a minimum income. Moreover, the typically poor financial performance of ANCSA corporations has further weakened their already narrow base of shareholder support. Early on, for example, several regional corporations encountered serious financial problems or bankruptcy, and more than one-half of the 200 ANCSA village corporations do not prepare government-required status reports.[35]

Because many shareholders are dissatisfied with their corporations, a major sellout of ANCSA corporate stock in 1991 is likely even though the law has been changed to prevent such transfers. The possibility of Native corporate takeovers, although reduced by recent legislation permitting Native corporations to sell their losses as tax write-offs, is very real. Thomas Berger, who recently completed a 2-year study of ANCSA for the Inuit Circumpolar Conference, finds that many Alaska Natives fear that "through corporate failure, corporate takeovers, and taxation, they could lose their land."[36]

Given this situation it seems reasonable to ask what can be done to improve the participation of Alaska Natives in the state's economic development. This is, of course, a very complex problem as G. Rogers points out: "In addition to such adverse factors as lack of education and skills, racial discrimination, etc., the present geographical distribution of the Native population is heaviest in areas which are away from the centers of recent economic development and anticipated future growth."[37] Since the regional profit-making corporations are powerful institutions in terms of the assets and resources they control, it is important to understand the extent to which they assume the responsibility for formulating regional development strategies.

Earlier research indicates that except for perhaps NANA and the North Slope regional corporations, there is little evidence that adaptive innovations have occurred or will occur soon, which will allow the pursuit of broader objectives.[38] Without a development strategy either on the state or regional level it appears that most villages have been left to find their own way without the resources, markets, or technical expertise to promote the development of viable local economies.

Conclusion

In the late 1960s, Alaska Native leaders realized that wealth and power would emerge from land claims producing a substantial land base. Through their determined efforts, and with the help of big oil companies, the Alaska Native leadership successfully lobbied for and won title to over 44 million acres of land. But while the Natives were capable of effective political innovation, it seems that it was not possible for them to anticipate the full consequences brought about by their decision to adopt corporations. Congress, as holders of the trust responsibility for Native affairs, should have anticipated the problems with ANCSA based on what had occurred as a result of other federal Indian policies.

A comparison with the policies of allotment and those of termination indicates more than a continuation of federal efforts to promote the assimilation of Natives. This research strongly suggests the possibility of a hidden agenda—one that may result in the cultural and economic conquest of Alaska Natives. The corporate institutions imposed by ANCSA may have been intended to establish a developmental infrastructure mainly for non-Native beneficiaries. Such a realization prompted the Alaska Federation of Natives to seek a series of amendments dealing with the 1991 potential sale of stock by Native shareholders.[39]

If Natives sell off their shares of ANCSA stock, it could lead to corporate takeovers and a further reduction of Native control over their valuable timber and mineral resources. While this would be a powerful incentive for outside corporations, in reality the entities most likely to instigate takeovers would be the small handful of successful ANCSA regional corporations. They alone have the access and means for acquiring the stock. Because they have the right of first refusal, there is the strong possibility that regional corporations could execute a buy-out, leaving a smaller set of closely held corporations. Given that there are fewer than 16,000 shares in the largest regional corporation, this scenario is not difficult to envision.

Although it is too early to draw conclusions regarding the struggle of Alaska Natives to maintain control of their corporations and land, it is possible to make some reasonable extrapolations based on insights drawn from comparisons with other federal Indian policies. If ANCSA is consistent with the historical experiences of Native Americans, the likely result will be the further immiserization of the more traditional Alaska Natives. A takeover of the corporations even by other Native corporations will not prevent the development of land and wilderness areas important to subsistence hunting and fishing.

Given these prospects and the severe recession in the state's oil based economy, which dramatically reduced the funding available for rural programs, some village leaders have begun to push for the reconveyance of Native lands to federally recognized tribal entities (IRA councils). Currently there is mounting pressure over the competition between native supporters of the "sovereignty movement" and the ANCSA corporate establishment. In a recent decision, the State Supreme Court has taken the position that the concept of Indian territory cannot be legally applied to Native villages. This, however, has not reduced the growing number of villages implementing various forms of Indian sovereignty, including law enforcement, courts, game regulation, and tribal government.[40]

Certainly the sovereignty movement constitutes a serious challenge to ANCSA, but the dominant patterns of political and economic power favor the existing arrangement while militating against any further effort to alter the corporate framework to allow for greater rural participation. Thus it leaves the majority of Alaska Natives shareholders in an estranged corporation that they do not understand, let alone control.

The history of the federal government's policies toward the Native populations covers a wide spectrum ranging from allotment to reorganization of tribes, termination, and finally self-determination. Yet, in the face of these far-flung efforts, it is apparent that government policy makers still have not found a way to increase Native participation in a state's economic development and protect the traditional cultural and economic basis of tribes without having these policies compromised by competing vested interests, greed, and apathy.

NOTES

1. The Alaska Native leadership and their attorneys argued that when Alaska was sold to the United States the 1867 treaty contained a clause in article 3 that stated that "the uncivilized tribes will be subject to such laws and regulations as the United States may, from time to time, adopt toward aboriginal tribes of that country." Because

Native Americans did not become citizens of the United States until 1924, the treaty specifically excluded Natives. Moreover, it left the title of ownership of their lands unclear. In 1884 Congress, through the Organic Act, attempted to provide Alaska with a basis for civil government. A clause in section 8 further emphasized the Native ownership issue: "Indians or other persons in said district shall not be disturbed in the possession of any lands actually in their use or occupation or now claimed by them, but the terms under which such persons may acquire title to such lands is reserved for future legislation by Congress." When Alaska became a state in 1959, the issue of Native land claims was still unsettled. According to section 4 of the Statehood Act, "as a compact with the United States said State and its people do agree and declare that they forever disclaim all right and title to any lands or other property not granted or confirmed to the State or its political subdivisions by or under the authority of this Act, the right or title to which is held by the United States, and to any lands or other property (including fishing rights) the right or title to which may be held by any Indians, Eskimos, or Aleuts (hereinafter called Natives) or is held by the United States in trust for said Natives; that all such lands or other property, belonging to the United States or which may belong to said Natives, shall remain under the absolute jurisdiction and control of the United States until disposed of under its authority." For more discussion, see Monica E. Thomas, "The Alaska Native Claims Settlement: The Next Decades" (paper presented at the annual meeting of the Western Regional Science Association, Monterey, California, February 22-25, 1984).

    2. Such side effects result despite the good intentions of missionaries such as Sheldon Jackson, who endeavored to "fit them [Natives] for the social and industrial life of the white population of the United States, and to promote their not-too-distant assimilation" (Margaret Lantis, "The Current Nativistic Movement in Alaska," in *Circumpolar Problems: Habitat, Economy, and Social Structures in the Arctic* (London and Exeter: Wheaton, 1973), 21:99-118.

    3. Robert D. Arnold et al., *Alaska Native Land Claims*, 2d ed. (Anchorage: Alaska Native Foundation, 1978).

    4. In 1912, e.g., a group of Indian leaders, called the

Tanana Chiefs, attempted to persuade the territorial governor to create reservations for their people.

5. Under the Statehood Act, Alaska received 104 million acres of land from the public domain. Consequently, when the state began to select its lands, it ran into opposition from Natives. In the 1960s, the Alaska Native claims movement began to gather new leaders who formed a statewide organization, the Alaska Federation of Natives (AFN), in 1966. These younger, more acculturated leaders felt it necessary to try to do something to prevent the loss of their land. The traditional leadership had little or no experience dealing with these types of problems. As Willie Hensley, one of the young Native leaders, once explained, "If we had waited on the elders, nothing would have happened. The elders were too kind, too tribal, to take this approach. They preferred not to place people in positions of saying no." In reality, the choice was either to do nothing or to attempt some action that would prevent state land selection. The alternative of letting the system work its will obviously was not in the interests of the Natives (class lecture, Native Studies Program, University of Alaska, Fairbanks, February 20, 1981).

6. Gerald McBeath and Thomas A. Morehouse, *The Dynamics of Alaska Native Self-Government* (Lanham, Md.: University Press of America, 1980), 12.

7. The Indian Court of Claims (1946) was a mechanism created to provide compensation to Indians for lands taken but not necessarily to help them acquire land. The form of compensation was generally a cash payment that went to the tribal government, usually for a per capita distribution. A previous 7.5 million dollar settlement for lands taken from the Tlingit and Haida Indians in Southeast Alaska took 35 years to work its way through the court.

8. According to these writers, "The oil companies saw that the Native land claims stood in the way of a pipeline permit, but they soon realized that many of the Native leaders also favored development of oil and minerals on land they might receive under a claims act. Accepting the reality that the pipeline would not be built until the claims issue was settled, the oil companies joined with the Natives to lobby for a just land settlement" (John Hanrahan and Paul Gruenstein, *Lost Frontier*, (New York: Norton, 1972), 95.

9. Statement of Charles Edwardsen, Jr., Executive Director, Arctic Slope Native Association, "Alaska Native Land Claims, Hearings before the Committee on Interior and Insular Affairs, United States Senate," *Congressional Record*, 92d Cong., 1st sess., February 18, 1971.

10. Section 10, S. 3580, 90th Cong., 2d sess.

11. For a discussion of the various bills and the compromise negotiations, see Mary C. Berry, *The Alaska Pipeline, the Politics of Oil, and Native Land Claims*, (Bloomington: Indiana University Press, 1975), 165-214.

12. A fairly accurate characterization of the Alaska Native socioeconomic situation prior to ANCSA passage is provided by McBeath and Morehouse: "Most natives at the time of statehood were unprepared for the demands of life in a modern economy. Many did not speak English fluently; few had adjusted to the demands of time and the achievement orientation of the dominant cultural group in America. Traditional attitudes and values were different from those of the dominant culture and did not bend easily under the disruptive pressures of a changing environment," 12.

13. Mary Lenz, "Native Claims Settlement Act—Was It Meant to Fail?" *Tuandra Drums* 9, no. 26 (1981): 19.

14. A somewhat similar attempt to preserve tribal integrity through adoption of white institutions occurred much earlier among the Five Civilized Tribes. For discussion, see Charles E. Royce, "The Cherokee Nation of Indians," *Fifth Annual Report of the Bureau of American Ethnology, 1883-84* (Washington, D.C.: Government Printing Office, 1887).

15. Bart Garber, "1991 Roundtable Discussion Paper," (paper presented to the Alaska Native Review Commission, Anchorage, Alaska, November 14, 1984).

16. In section 14(H), Congress set aside 2 million acres for individual allotments of 160 acres or less that would be registered in a 4-year period after passage but canceled opportunities for Alaska Natives to receive individual allotments under the General Allotment Program. Lands remaining after the application deadline were conveyed to regional corporations on the basis of their shareholder enrollments. Section 14(C) required village corporations to convey to individual Natives title to surface estates for lands used as primary places for residence, business, or subsistence.

17. Villages that voted to retain their ex-reserve lands and status include Venetie Elim, Gamble, Savoonga, Tetlin, Klukwan, and Arctic Village.

18. Monroe E. Price, "A Moment in History: The Alaska Native Claims Settlement Act," *UCLA-Alaska Law Review* 8 (1979): 89-99.

19. Lauren L. Fuller, "Alaska Native Claims Settlement Act: An Analysis of the Protective Clauses of the Act through a Comparison of the Dawes Act of 1887," *American Indian Law Review* 4, no. 2 (1976): 269-78.

20. Steve J. Langdon, "Alaska Native Land Claims and Limited Entry: The Dawes Act Revisited" (paper presented at the annual meeting of the American Anthropological Association, Washington, D.C., December 4-7, 1982).

21. D. S. Otis, *The Dawes Act and the Allotment of Indian Lands* (Norman: University of Oklahoma Press, 1973), 3-12.

22. Angie Debo, *And Still the Waters Run* (New York: Gordian, 1966).

23. The IRA (Wheeler-Howard Act) was an effort to reconstitute tribal governments and reestablish their land base. A 1928 study conducted by the Brookings Institution called attention to the impoverishment of American Indians and the crusading efforts of John Collier, then Commissioner of Indian Affairs; and Solicitor General Felix Cohen championed its passage in 1934. It was hoped that the IRA would reverse the disastrous effects of allotment and further provide mechanisms to encourage tribal self-government. Natives of Alaska were later included in a 1936 amendment that led to the formation of numerous federally recognized tribal governments. While noble in its efforts and impressive in its accomplishments, IRA policy has been the subject of frequent criticism by Native American leaders. For more discussion, see Kenneth R. Philip, ed., *Indian Self-Rule* (Salt Lake City, Utah: Howe Brothers, 1986).

24. Nancy O. Lurie, "Menominee Termination: From Reservation to Colony," *Human Organization* 31, no. 3 (1972): 257-70.

25. W. T. Trulove and David Bunting, "The Economics of Paternalism: Federal Policy and the Klamath Indians" (Department of Economics, University of Oregon, Eugene,

Oregon, 1971, photocopy).

26. Gary C. Anders, "A Critical Analysis of the Alaska Native Claims and Native Corporate Development," *Journal of Ethnic Studies* 13, no. 1 (1985): 1-12.

27. Robert D. Arnold, "71 Settlement in Retrospect," *Alaska Native News* (November 1982).

28. Institute for Social and Economic Research, "A Summary of Changes in the Status of Alaska Natives" (Anchorage: Eductional Services Corporation, January 15, 1984).

29. Ibid., 14.

30. Harold Sparck, "The Other Village" (Nunam Kitlustsisti [a Yupik Eskimo nonprofit organization], Bethel, Alaska, 1980, photocopy).

31. A partial listing is available in Alaska State Legislature, House of Representatives, Research Agency Report, "Assistance for Alaska Natives and Rural Alaskans," April 9, 1982.

32. David Marshall, "Jobs Planning: Aniak, 1987," report prepared for the city of Aniak, Alaska, July 13, 1987.

33. The suicide rate for Natives is more than twice that for non-Natives, and the accidental death rate is over 3.5 times the national average (Institute for Social and Economic Research, 6).

34. Gary C. Anders and Kathleen K. Anders, "Incompatible Goals in Unconventional Organization: The Politics of Alaska Native Corporations," *Organization Studies* 7, no. 3 (1986): 213-33.

35. For more discussion concerning the financial problems of regional corporations, see *Alaska Business* (September 1983), 27. Regarding status reports, see U.S. General Accounting Office, "Information on Alaska Native Corporations," GAO/RCED 83-173 draft report, June 9, 1983.

36. Thomas R. Berger, *Village Journey, the Report of the Alaska Native Review Commission* (New York: Hill and Wang, 1985), 6.

37. George W. Rogers, "Party Politics or Protest Politics? Current Political Trends in Alaska," *Polar Record* 14, no. 91 (1969): 445-58.

38. Gary C. Anders and Steve J. Langdon, "Alaska Native Regional Strategies," *Human Organization* (in press).

39. These amendments include: extending land bank provisions to prevent taxation; allowing corporations to grant voting rights to Natives receiving stock through inheritance; issuance of special classes of stock to elders and Natives born after 1971; and allowing the corporations to purchase stock from shareholders before 1991. These would also entail changes in by-laws among corporations to prevent non-Natives from securing voting rights.

40. Two forms of Native self-government (traditional village councils and IRA councils) are recognized by the federal government. Of the 211 villages recognized under ANCSA, 70 have organized IRAs and 90 are governed by traditional councils. Recently there had been a renewal of interest in the formation of IRAs and some villages have transferred their lands to these newly created governments. Because these two governmental forms compete for resources and control within existing municipal governments and village corporations, there is increasing conflict in Alaska Native communities where leadership does not overlap. The concept of limited sovereignty applied to Indian tribal governments over its reservation jurisdiction is known as "Indian country." Some Alaska Native villages are attempting to extend this concept to lands conveyed to IRAs and traditional councils in the hope that these powers will help them avoid taxes and prevent corporate take-overs. The question of whether or not Alaska Native lands can be considered to be Indian country is a controversial political and legal issue that has not yet been decided. For more discussion, see David H. Getches and Charles F. Wilkinson, *Federal Indian Law*, 2nd ed. (St. Paul, Minn.: West Publishing, 1986), 773-820; and Robert E. Price, "Legal Status of the Alaska Natives," report to the Alaska Statehood Commission (Juneau, Alaska, July 30, 1982).

Chapter IV

Tribal Sovereignty

Beginning with the Supreme Court's "Oliphant" decision ("Oliphant v. Suquamish Tribe," 1978) the federal courts have chipped away at Indian tribal sovereignty. The "Oliphant" decision denied tribal courts criminal jurisdiction over non-Natives for crimes committed on Indian reservations. Before the "Oliphant" decision, federal law recognized that Indians retained all powers of sovereign nations except where it had been surrendered by treaty or abrogated by Congressional statute.

Historically the federal courts have been the protectors of Indian sovereignty. Beginning with the decision of the Marshall Court in "Cherokee Nation v. Georgia" (1831) the federal judiciary has guarded tribal sovereignty, particularly against the encroachment of states. A major blow to tribal sovereignty was the policy of termination in the 1950's and Public Law 280 which allowed states to acquire criminal and civil jurisdiction over Indian tribes within their state. The 1968 Indian Civil Rights Act halted state takeover of law enforcement on Indian reservations and provided a means for tribes to re-acquire federal and tribal jurisdiction.

The largest problem facing Indian nations is the presence of non-Indians on Indian land and ownership of land and businesses within a federal reserve by non-Indians. What civil jurisdiction does the tribe have over such individuals and their enterprises? Recent federal court decisions have had the effect of limiting tribal sovereignty in the areas of zoning, health and welfare, police powers and gaming. What has crept into the courts' legal reasoning is a new rule of "implicit divestiture" which would provide federal judges wide discretionary authority to limit tribal sovereignty by determining that a specific tribal power was inconsistent with its status as an Indian nation. Moreover the courts have added another limitation on tribal sovereignty by introducing tests of "national interest" and "overriding sovereignty" of the United States when measuring the limits of tribal sovereignty.

Tribal sovereignty is the most fundamental characteristic of Indian nations. It was secured by treaty and recognition by the courts and Congress of the distinct legal nature of Indian tribes. A key attribute of sovereignty is legal jurisdiction within Indian country. Recent court decisions, beginning with "Oliphant," have had the effect of severely encroaching on both the civil and criminal jurisdiction of Indian tribes. Moreover, states have entered the picture by attempting to impose their jurisdiction in the areas of taxation, gaming laws and general police powers. Congress has the power to stem this incursion into tribal sovereignty and should send a clear signal to the federal

72

courts and the states that a policy of tribal self-determination requires respect for tribal sovereignty and federal law will protect this status.

—RNW

Indian Nations Under Legal Assault: New Restrictions on Native American Sovereignty: Are They Constitutional? Are They Moral?

Curtis Berkey

During the last ten years, the sovereign authority of American Indian governments has come under legal attack. On many reservations, non-Indians comprise a large part of the population, and Indian governments naturally assert authority over them as part of the inherent and historic power of territorial self-government.

Non-Indians are increasingly resorting to the federal courts to challenge those actions as beyond the scope of Indian self-government under federal law.

With the Supreme Court leading the way, the federal courts have produced an array of contradictory rules and principles which have been interpreted by some to undermine the jurisdictional authority of Indian governments. The doctrine of Indian sovereignty, which once provided modest protection for self-government, is now so eviscerated that the powers of those governments are said to exist completely at the whim of the federal government. Cherished rights of self-government are being trammeled as federal supremacy over Indian governments becomes more firmly entrenched in the law.

The transmutation of the Indian sovereignty doctrine can be traced to the Supreme Court's "Oliphant v. Suquamish Indian Tribe" decision in 1978 that stripped the Suquamish Tribe of its power to exercise criminal jurisdiction over non-Indians who violate tribal laws.

The case grew out of two incidents that occurred during the tribe's annual Chief Seattle Days celebration on the Port Madison Reservation in Washington State. Mark David Oliphant, a non-Indian resident of the reservation, was charged with assaulting a tribal police officer. In a separate incident, Daniel Belgarde was arrested after a high-speed chase on reservation highways that ended when he collided with a tribal police vehicle. In a 6-2 decision, the Court denied the tribe's criminal jurisdiction over Oliphant and Belgarde.

Rewriting law and history, Justice Rehnquist reasoned that the Indian nations' exercise of criminal jurisdiction over non-Indians is inconsistent with their inferior legal status under United States law. The Court announced an unprecedented restriction on the powers of the Indian governments.

"Upon incorporation into the territory of the United States, the Indian tribes thereby come under the territorial sovereignty of the United States and their exercise of separate power is constrained so as not to conflict with the interests of this overriding sovereignty," the Court wrote.

The Court's decision in "Oliphant" seriously undermined the legal protection Indian nations had enjoyed for their right of self-government under federal law. It fundamentally changed the conception of Indian nations as sovereign governments within the United States legal system.

Before "Oliphant," federal law recognized that Indian nations retained all powers of sovereign nations, except where elements had been given up in treaties or where Congress abrogated their powers by federal statute. In its decision, the Supreme Court supplanted the clarity of this doctrine with the concept that Indian nations have been divested by operation of law of all powers "inconsistent with their status."

Federal courts have since imposed new and far-reaching limitations on Indian self-government. Judicial abrogation of Indian sovereignty has replaced congressional abrogation as the principal danger, although it is doubtful that the Supreme Court intended such a harsh result.

Many feared a new era of judicial activism in curtailing the powers of Indian governments, particularly as regards non-Indians. Measured solely by results in particular cases, the impact of "Oliphant" may not have been the total disaster that was predicted. In fact, the Indian parties have won about as many sovereignty cases as they have lost.

The effect of "Oliphant," however, cannot be accurately measured simply by tallying up wins and losses. The decision may have paved the way for an unprecedented erosion of

Indian rights to self-government. The so-called implicit divestiture rule could be interpreted as giving federal judges broad discretion to abolish sovereign powers by simply finding that a particular power is inconsistent with the status of Indian nations.

The new rule is exceedingly difficult to apply fairly because of the elasticity of the concept that the status of Indian nations, as subjugated under the sovereignty of the United States, necessarily restricts Indian powers of self-government. Despite these problems, the Supreme Court has not sufficiently clarified the meaning and scope of the "Oliphant" doctrine.

Although it is unlikely that the Supreme Court intended to cripple Indian sovereignty, its decisions since have further empowered the lower federal courts to impose severe restrictions on Indian self-government. The Court can be faulted for its indifference to the doctrinal confusion its opinions have created, and for its striking lack of concern for the adverse effect this confusion may have on treasured Indian rights to self-government.

Although the Court often pays lip service to venerable doctrines of Indian sovereignty, its uncertainty about the manner in which Indian sovereignty questions are to be decided has created a vacuum that the lower federal courts by necessity must fill. Thus, Indian sovereignty is endangered by the proclivity of some lower federal courts to treat selected Supreme Court dicta as rules for decision, despite the absence of clear evidence that the Court intended its statements to establish new doctrine.

To be sure, the Court has sent very confusing signals to the lower federal courts. Shortly after "Oliphant," the Court issued a warning about the potential impact of the implicit divestiture rule in "United States v. Wheeler." The Court suggested that virtually all powers touching, "the relations between an Indian tribe and nonmembers of the tribe" had already been lost through the mysterious process of implicit divestiture.

Ironically, this statement came in a case which has been regarded as a victory for the sovereignty of Indian nations. The Court upheld the sovereign authority of Indian nations to try and punish its own members for violations of tribal law.

After "Wheeler," the Court issued a string of inconsistent statements about the scope of Indian sovereignty. "Wheeler's" broad statement about the reach of the implicit divestiture rule was contradicted two years later in "Washington v. Confederated Tribes of the Colville Indian Reservation." In that case, the Court upheld the power of Indian nations to tax the business activities of non-Indians on Indian land, noting that the federal government has "consistently recognized that Indian tribes possess a broad measure of civil jurisdiction over the activities of non-Indians on Indian reservation lands in which the tribes have a significant interest."

"Colville" raised additional questions about the meaning of implicit divestiture because of internal inconsistencies in the opinion. On the one hand, the Court appeared to repudiate the implicit divestiture rule, while affirming its own holding that divestiture can occur "where the exercise of tribal sovereignty would be inconsistent with the overriding interests of the National Government. . . ." The contradiction is neither acknowledged nor resolved by any reasonably clear explanation of the appropriate governing principle.

Apart from the confusion about what the law is, "Oliphant" and "Colville" left unanswered a number of important questions about the application of the implicit divestiture rule. If, for example, the governing principle is that tribes are constrained from exercising any power inconsistent with the national interest of the United States, how is that interest to be defined? How does a court decide what the national interest is, and what sources can it properly examine?

Can it rely on policy statements of executive agencies that do not have the force of law? Are certain national interests more important than others, and how should they be weighted in importance? These difficult questions, which no court has sought to address, suggest that the implicit divestiture rule may be incapable of precise and evenhanded application, if it is to be regarded as a test at all.

The U.S. Supreme Court's indifference to doctrinal inconsistency was again illustrated in "Montana v. United States," a 1981 ruling. In that decision, the Court ruled that the Crow Tribe had no authority to regulate hunting and fishing by non-members on lands within the reservation but no longer owned by the Tribe.

Ignoring completely "Colville's" general principle that tribes retain civil jurisdiction over non-Indians, the Court resurrected "Wheeler's" broad declaration that divestiture has occurred in areas "involving the relations between an Indian tribe and nonmembers of the tribe." The Court also said that Indian nations have been divested of all powers beyond what is necessary to protect tribal self-government or to control internal relations."

Thus, the Court purported to find support for the "general proposition that the inherent sovereign powers of an Indian tribe do not extend to the activities of nonmembers of the tribe."

The fact that this formulation is so impractical to apply suggests that the Court may not have intended to lay down a stringent test for deciding Indian sovereignty questions. The distinction between internal and external relations is exceedingly difficult to draw precisely in today's world, where non-Indians comprise major parts of many reservation communities and where the conduct of non-Indians often has a direct effect on the internal workings of tribal governments, particularly on their ability to govern the reservation.

"Montana" did not establish new tests for Indian sovereignty questions, a fact found in the Court's explanation of those areas where a tribe may have retained civil authority over non-Indians. The Court devised, without sound legal or historical authority, two categories that it said may be exceptions to the general principle that tribal powers do not apply to the activities of nonmembers.

First, tribes may have the power to tax or otherwise regulate the activities of nonmembers who enter into "consensual relationships," such as commercial dealings, with Indian tribes. Second, tribes may have authority over nonmembers when their conduct "threatens or has some direct effect on the political integrity, the economic security, or the health or welfare of the tribe."

The Court left no clues as to whether these statements are intended to be rules that supplant the "necessary to self-government and to control internal relations" principles set forth earlier in the same opinion. In any event, if treated as rules by lower federal courts, they impose a discriminatory burden on Indian tribes to justify exercises of power over non-Indians. For no other government is the validity of sovereign powers tied to the effect the conduct sought to be regulated has on that government.

"Montana" failed to resolve the contradictions and inconsistencies in the Supreme Court's Indian sovereignty jurisprudence. Instead, it added to the growing number of bewildering statements and principles in this area. In particular, the Court did not say whether divestiture of tribal powers was to be determined according to a perceived conflict with the paramount national interest mentioned in earlier rulings, or according to one or another of "Montana's" so-called rules.

One year later in "Merrion v. Jicarilla Apache Tribe," the Court raised additional doubts about whether "Montana" should be read as establishing rules for decisions in Indian sovereignty cases. In deciding that Indian tribes had inherent authority to impose a severance tax on non-Indian producers of oil and gas on reservation lands, the Court did not even cite "Montana," much less apply any "rules" from that decision.

Nor did the Court analyze whether this power had been divested by reason of some overriding interest of the United States, as "Colville" seemed to invite the Court to do. The Court acknowledged that tribal powers can be limited in that way, but it summarily dismissed that issue as "not presented here." Instead, the Court relied on the principle that tribes retain inherent powers over their territories, and on the assumption of all three branches of the federal government that the taxing power over non-Indians is retained by tribes.

Because of the failure of the Supreme Court to provide clear guidance, the lower federal courts have exercised very broad discretion in deciding these issues. Despite the absence of compelling evidence that the Court intended its statements on Indian sovereignty to be ironclad rules, the lower federal courts have tended to seize on specific language in this case or that, elevate it to the status of a rule of law and mechanically apply it to the facts in the case being decided. As a result, the Court's confused pronouncements have perhaps unwittingly contributed to the development of a new set of rules on Indian sovereignty questions.

Treating selected Supreme Court statements as rules, the lower federal courts transformed the analytical framework of Indian sovereignty issues. The traditional presumption that Indian nations retain all those powers not expressly given up in treaties or taken away by Congress has been eliminated. In its place some courts have applied a new presumption that Indian tribes do not have governmental authority unless they can prove it is necessary to control "internal relations," or to protect the political integrity, economic security or welfare of the tribe and its government.

The Supreme Court's jurisprudence also permits, if it does not absolutely require, judges to balance the interest of Indian tribes in maintaining strong governments against the "national interest" or "overriding sovereignty" of the United States, with very little guidance from the Court as to the meaning of those terms.

This trend can be seen in the increasing frequency with which lower federal courts seized on "Montana's" explanation of the implicit divestiture phenomena as the dispositive test for determining the scope of Indian sovereignty over non-Indians.

This means the courts will assume that Indian nations have been divested of authority over non-Indians unless the exercise of sovereign power falls within two exceptions: where a consensual relationship exists between the tribe and the non-Indian, and where the non-Indian conduct threatens the welfare of the tribe in a concrete way.

Until recently, tribal litigants generally fared better under that analysis than under the "overriding national interest" test of "Colville" and "Oliphant." For example, the Court of Appeals for the Ninth Circuit upheld the authority of the Quinault Indian Nation to enforce its building, health and safety regulations against a non-Indian operating a store on non-Indian land within the reservation.

In that case, "Cardin v. De La Cruz," the court ruled that the exercise of such authority was permissible because it fit within both of the "Montana" exceptions to Indian authority over non-Indians.

Similarly, the Court of Appeals for the Tenth Circuit upheld the authority of the Shoshone and Arapahoe Indian Tribes to enforce a zoning ordinance on lands owned by non-Indians within the reservation. In that case, "Knight v. Shoshone and Arapahoe Indian Tribes," the court found that the "interest of the Tribes in preserving and protecting their homeland from exploitation justifies the zoning code."

Although the results are laudable, these decisions, by purporting to identify and apply a new Supreme Court test for the exercise of tribal powers, further entrench the supposed rules or tests. By doing so, they enhance the power of the federal courts to place limits on tribal authority. As a practical matter, moreover, these legal victories may be illusory, because the law still permits Congress to eradicate the powers of Indian governments without legal limitation.

None of these decisions sought to balance the interests of the Indian government against the "national interest" or "overriding sovereignty" of the United States, as the Supreme Court has permitted. Indian sovereignty will have little real legal protection as long as the law permits courts to engage in such balancing or requires Indian governments to prove that the exercise of a particular power is necessary for their survival.

The danger to Indian sovereignty posed by "Montana" is illustrated by "Swift Transportation, Inc. v. John." In that case, a non-Indian sued in federal court to enjoin the Navajo Nation District Court from exercising jurisdiction over a lawsuit brought by members of the Navajo Nation against non-Indians for injuries arising out of an automobile accident within the Navajo Reservation.

The federal court granted the injunction, ruling that the Navajo Nation had been divested of its jurisdiction over the case by virtue of its "dependent status." The court refused to find that the Nation's authority came within either of the "Montana" categories for validly exercising power over non-Indians, and it concluded that the primary effect of the accident fell on the Indian individuals, and the Navajo Nation, therefore, could not claim any adverse effect on itself.

This strained, narrow interpretation of "Montana" completely ignores the adverse political and economic impact on the Nation if it is disabled from compelling non-Indians to compensate Nation members for civil wrongs. This ruling graphically shows the broad discretion federal judges have under the new rules.

The Supreme Court's assortment of declarations and principles in sovereignty cases has permitted the lower courts to choose arbitrarily the rules they intend to apply. The district court in Arizona has ruled that the Navajo Nation courts do not have jurisdiction to hear suits by Navajos against a non-Indian corporation for injuries resulting from a uranium waste spill.

For support, the court cited the "Montana" proposition that Indian governments generally do not have authority over the activities of nonmembers, but it neglected to determine whether this case fell within either of the two categories in which the exercise of Indian governmental authority over non-Indians may be valid.

Another danger of "Montana" is exposed by a case brought by UNC Resources against members of the Navajo Nation. In that case, the federal district court in New Mexico agreed with the Arizona court that the Nation had no civil jurisdiction over suits by Nation members against UNC Resources for injuries from the uranium spill. Here, the court applied virtually all the permutations of "Montana," concluding that the Navajo Nation's power to impose civil penalties on non-Indian corporations is not necessary to protect tribal self-government "because the tribal government has always been able to function without it."

This is the "Montana" rationale carried to its logical extreme: the validity of an exercise of Indian governmental power may come to depend on whether that power has been exercised historically and, if so, how effective such power has been in regulating conduct. This novel concept ignores the fundamental fact that Indian governmental powers are exercised in response to changing conditions on the reservations.

Several decisions in Indian sovereignty cases in the past few years have relied at least in part on a finding that the exercise of tribal power is inconsistent with the national interest of the United States. In both UNC Resources cases, the courts held that the exercise of tribal jurisdiction would conflict with the overriding sovereignty of the United States. In the New Mexico case, the court reasoned that a civil judgment in the Navajo court against UNC Resources would be an "unwarranted intrusion" on the property interests of the corporation, which presumably also conflicted with the interest of the United States in protecting UNC Resources's property.

The Arizona district court went even further, holding that the assertion of Navajo jurisdiction "also conflicts with the superior federal interest in regulating the production of nuclear power."

The range of "superior federal interests" which could conceivably void Indian governmental authority appears to be very broad indeed. What is particularly disturbing about these cases is their conclusion that the exercise of Navajo jurisdiction per se conflicted with the interests of the United States. There was no finding that the Navajo courts are incapable of administering justice fairly and equitably.

Despite erratic lower court decisions, the Supreme Court appears to be unwilling to rectify the deficiencies of its Indian sovereignty opinions. The Court's recent decision concerning tribal power to zone non-Indian land within reservation boundaries shows that the members of the Court continue to be sharply divided about the governing principles in these cases.

In "Brendale v. Confederated Tribes and Bands of the Yakima Indian Nation," the Court recently ruled that the Yakima Nation retains sovereign authority to zone non-Indian land within that part of the reservation that has a relatively small percentage of non-Indian land and that has almost no residential or commercial development.

In that case, the Yakima Nation sought to enforce its zoning ordinance against Philip Brendale, a nonmember who planned to develop several summer cabin sites on his land in the forested, or "closed," portion of the reservation. The Nation further sought to enforce its zoning ordinance against Stanley Wilkinson, a non-Indian who proposed to subdivide his property into lots for single family homes. Both proposed developments violated the zoning ordinance.

Based largely on differences in the character of the communities where the properties were located, the Court upheld the Nation's power to zone the Brendale property in the closed part of the reservation, but denied the power to zone the Wilkinson property in the so-called open portion of the reservation, where the majority of the land is owned or farmed by non-Indians, and where a large number of non-Indians live and work.

Thus, the Court is willing to sanction tribal authority to zone non-Indian land only in reservation areas containing a relatively small percentage of non-Indian land and where there is almost no residential or commercial development. In reaching this conclusion, three different views were expressed about the scope of Indian powers over non-Indians, none of which commanded a majority of the Court's members.

Only Justices Stevens and O'Connor agreed with both of these rulings. In Justice Stevens's opinion, the power to zone is derived exclusively from the Yakima Nation's inherent power to exclude nonmembers from the reservation. He reasoned that this power necessarily includes the lesser power to "define the essential character of that area" through zoning regulation. He concludes that because most of the land located in the open area is owned by non-Indians and the Nation no longer has the power to exclude nonmembers, the power to define the character of the area has been lost as well.

If applied beyond the zoning context, Justice Stevens's theory would add a new element to the implicit divestiture concept first announced in 1978 in "Oliphant v. Suquamish Indian Tribe." It raises the specter that tribal powers could be implicitly lost due to changes in the composition and character of the reservation community, changes caused primarily by larcenous congressional enactments and anachronistic federal policies.

There is no indication, however, that this new theory, if indeed it can be called that, is intended to replace the long standing rule that tribal powers derive from the status of Indian nations as inherently sovereign bodies. Among the other Justices, only Justice O'Connor joined Justice Stevens's opinion.

Justice White, in an opinion joined by Justices Scalia and Kennedy and Chief Justice Rehnquist, took the position that the Yakima Nation lacked inherent authority to zone non-Indian land anywhere on the reservation. Justice White concluded that the "governing principle is that the tribe has no authority itself, by way of tribal ordinance or actions in tribal courts, to regulate the use of free land."

Justice White would hold that Indian tribes have been implicitly divested of all powers over non-Indians, by virtue of their "dependent" status under federal law. In so doing, the plurality of four justices would, for all practical purposes, discard the principle recognized in "Montana" that tribes have inherent authority to regulate the conduct of non-Indians when it "threatens or has some direct effect on the political integrity, the economic security, or the health or welfare of the tribe."

Justice Blackmun, joined by Justices Brennan and Marshall, would have upheld the Yakima Nation's inherent authority to regulate non-Indian land anywhere on the reservation. Blackmun acknowledged the inconsistencies of the Court's prior statements on the applicable principle, especially the contradictions between the "Montana" and "Colville" approaches. For Blackmun, tribes have power to zone non-Indian land because such authority is central to the "economic security, or the health or welfare of the tribe."

The lack of consensus in "Yakima" about the proper approach to Indian sovereignty questions raises doubts about the decision's precedential value. The result in the case, that tribes have authority only in areas with a small percentage of non-Indian land, cannot be mechanically applied with precision to other circumstances.

The assault on Indian sovereignty may now come from two sources. Congress is still said to have plenary power to terminate Indian governments at will. And now, as a result of confusing Supreme Court decisions, the federal courts could exercise a plenary power of their own.

The increased power of the courts may be a greater threat to Indian sovereignty in the long run than the plenary power of Congress. At least when Congress intends to act, there is an opportunity through political advocacy to prevent the erosion of Indian self-government. But there is no effective check on the power of the courts. Moreover, when courts take away Indian governmental powers, their action has an appearance of legitimacy that is scarcely deserved.

What can Indian governments, lawyers and Indian people do to achieve better legal protection for Indian sovereignty? Most important, the notion that Congress has plenary power over Indian governments must be challenged at every opportunity. Acquiescence in the idea of federal supremacy over Indian nations historically has helped create a legal climate in which concepts of inherent limitations on Indian sovereignty seem acceptable to the Supreme Court.

Perhaps the Supreme Court would not have created the implicit divestiture doctrine if lawyers and tribes had consistently and aggressively challenged the idea that Indian governments are subjugated under the sovereignty of the United States. Reform of the law of Indian sovereignty must necessarily be based on a consensus about appropriate limitations on the power of the United States to abolish Indian governmental authority.

As a practical matter, lawyers and Indian rights advocates may need to change their approach to understanding and applying Supreme Court opinions on Indian sovereignty. Perhaps it is time to discard the old analysis which seeks uncritically to distill every court decision into a test or rule that can be routinely applied in other circumstances.

Ultimately, a coherent and sensible legal theory must be developed which recognizes the historic status of Indian tribes as independent sovereign nations and their legitimate aspirations for greater powers of self-government.

There should be a critical reexamination of the assumption that the federal government has supreme and practically unlimited powers over Indian nations. And a way should be found to reestablish the concept of consent as the governing principle for the legal and political relationship between the United States and Indian nations. This restructuring would lay a strong foundation for the restoration of much of the autonomy Indian nations have lost at the hands of the United States.

Chapter V

Native American Education

Despite advances in Native American education, continued developments are needed before the efforts can be considered a success. More students are graduating from high school and going to college than ever before, but many are not as successful. The high school dropout rate among Native American students is seven percent above the national average. Dropout is also a major problem among Native American college students, where 50 percent of freshmen leave school. In order to improve the quality of education that Native American students receive, it is vital that they remain in school. This will only occur if educators take steps to encourage and support these students throughout their educational experience.

Support services, such as Head Start, Title V, and Upward Bound, must continue to address the cultural and educational needs of Native American students. Because almost two-thirds of all Native Americans do not live on the reservation, these services are often their sole link to their cultural heritage. These services also provide the generally educationally disadvantaged Native American population a source of academic support.

For the most part, Native American students attend integrated public schools. In these schools, the Native American community and tribal leadership have little control over the administration of the schools. Native Americans are underrepresented on school boards, which leads to a lack of attention to the needs of Native American students.

American school systems must develop a curriculum designed to encourage success among the Native American student population. In 70 percent of schools serving Native Americans, the native language is not offered. Just under half of schools attended by Native American students do not offer classes in Indian culture or history. Native American students need to learn about their culture, history and language to develop a strong sense of cultural identity and a positive self-image which will lead them to greater personal confidence and academic success.

Teachers of Native American students play an important role in their academic success. The number of Native American teachers at schools with large Indian populations must be increased. Non-native teachers can be made more effective through training programs on the culture and learning styles of Native American students and on the issues of racism that often hinder the students' success.

Because over half of living Native Americans have not completed high school, adult educational opportunities are important to the Indian community.

86

With opportunity to get a high school diploma, a G.E.D., a college degree or vocational training, more Native American adults can become literate, gain valuable vocational skills and further their education, leading to greater employability.

The social, cultural and economic obstacles that often prevent Native American students from excelling in academics can be overcome through education, support and self-determination.

—RNW

Transforming Native American Education: The Long Road from Acculturation to Cultural Self-Determination[*]

Robert N. Wells, Jr.

It has been twenty-four years since the U.S. Senate Special Subcommittee on Indian Education issued its report and findings on Indian Education (Indian Education: A National Tragedy—A National Challenge). In the interim, there have been significant changes in the education of Native Americans. More Native Americans are completing high school, going to college, graduating and moving into positions of responsibility in Indian education and other areas of tribal leadership. There are now twenty-six Indian, tribally controlled, two- and four-year colleges (see Figure 1).

However, despite these positive developments, the educational needs of Native Americans are still far from being met. Even today, 35.5 percent of Indian students drop out of high school, seven percent above the national average.[1] Over 92 percent of Native American students attend state public schools and tribal communities exercise little or no control of those schools.[2] In 48 percent of all schools which Indian students attend, there are no Native American teachers and in 70 percent of those schools, the native language is not offered in the curriculum.[3] Just under 50 percent of schools serving

---

[*] *This article was originally presented as a keynote address at the First Annual Conference on the Native American Indian Education Conference at St. Bonaventure University, July 18-21, 1993 in Olean, NY.*

Native American students do not offer any courses in Indian culture and history. About 25 percent of graduating Native American students go on to college, but only about 29 percent

Figure 1: Tribally Controlled Community Colleges

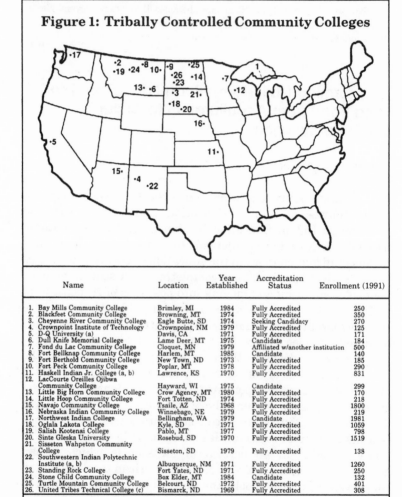

	Name	Location	Year Established	Accreditation Status	Enrollment (1991)
1.	Bay Mills Community College	Brimley, MI	1984	Fully Accredited	250
2.	Blackfeet Community College	Browning, MT	1974	Fully Accredited	350
3.	Cheyenne River Community College	Eagle Butte, SD	1974	Seeking Candidacy	270
4.	Crownpoint Institute of Technology	Crownpoint, NM	1979	Fully Accredited	125
5.	D-Q University (a)	Davis, CA	1971	Fully Accredited	171
6.	Dull Knife Memorial College	Lame Deer, MT	1975	Candidate	184
7.	Fond du Lac Community College	Cloquet, MN	1979	Affiliated w/another institution	500
8.	Fort Bellknap Community College	Harlem, MT	1985	Candidate	140
9.	Fort Berthold Community College	New Town, ND	1973	Fully Accredited	185
10.	Fort Peck Community College	Poplar, MT	1978	Fully Accredited	290
11.	Haskell Indian Jr. College (a, b)	Lawrence, KS	1970	Fully Accredited	831
12.	LacCourte Oreilles Ojibwa Community College	Hayward, WI	1975	Candidate	299
13.	Little Big Horn Community College	Crow Agency, MT	1980	Fully Accredited	170
14.	Little Hoop Community College	Fort Totten, ND	1974	Fully Accredited	218
15.	Navajo Community College	Tsaile, AZ	1968	Fully Accredited	1800
16.	Nebraska Indian Community College	Winnebago, NE	1979	Fully Accredited	219
17.	Northwest Indian College	Bellingham, WA	1979	Candidate	1981
18.	Oglala Lakota College	Kyle, SD	1971	Fully Accredited	1059
19.	Salish Kootenai College	Pablo, MT	1977	Fully Accredited	798
20.	Sinte Gleska University	Rosebud, SD	1970	Fully Accredited	1519
21.	Sisseton Wahpeton Community College	Sisseton, SD	1979	Fully Accredited	138
22.	Southwestern Indian Polytechnic Institute (a, b)	Albuquerque, NM	1971	Fully Accredited	1260
23.	Standing Rock College	Fort Yates, ND	1971	Fully Accredited	250
24.	Stone Child Community College	Box Elder, MT	1984	Candidate	132
25.	Turtle Mountain Community College	Belcourt, ND	1972	Fully Accredited	401
26.	United Tribes Technical College (c)	Bismarck, ND	1969	Fully Accredited	308

(a) Not located on a reservation
(b) Established and operated by the Bureau of Indian Affairs
(c) Not located on a reservation, does not receive funds under the Tribally Controlled Community College Assistance Act

Note: In addition, two Canadian institutions are members of the American Indian Higher Education Consortium: Saskatchewan Indian Federated College is Saskatchewan, Canada, and Red Crow Community College in Cardston, Alberta.

Source: American Indian Higher Education Consortium, unpublished tabulations, 1992.

complete the baccalaureate compared with the national average of 53 percent.[4]

As we approach the twenty-first century, the goals of Native American education would appear to be quite precise:

• Reduce school dropout.

• Increase substantially the number of Native American teachers.

• Increase local and tribal control over Indian education.

• Greatly expand Native American curricular elements.

• Target the one-third of Native students who are at risk and provide support services for them.

• Address the educational needs of Native Americans living off reservation or in urban areas (over 60 percent of all Native students).

• Reward success. Set high standards for Indian students by developing educational programs which reward achievement.

For the 380,000 Native Americans attending elementary and secondary schools, the above mentioned objectives constitute the core of programmatic needs which will reverse a cycle of dropout, failure and low performance levels. Because of where they live, in the city or remote rural areas, most Native Americans attend below average schools which lack the support services and enrichment programs to address their educational needs. Since 75 percent of these students attend schools in ten states, the schools and curriculum of these state public schools should be a high priority for improvement. The Minnesota comprehensive educational program for Native Americans stands out as a model to follow when reforming state educational practices for Native American students. From pre-school through post-secondary education, the state of Minnesota has developed in conjunction with Native American leaders a comprehensive educational and social program which addresses the needs of Indian students at all levels. With so many Native American students attending state public schools, there needs to be educational programs similar to those in Minnesota established in the schools where Indian students attend.

The Native American population is the fastest growing population in the United States. There are now 1.9 million Native Americans, and the Indian growth rate from 1980-1990 was 38 percent, compared to the national average of 9 percent.[5] In many school districts, particularly in the ten states which have 75 percent of the Native American population, Native Americans constitute the majority of students. Yet, with regard to Indian staffing and school board membership, they are in a distinct minority. In my survey of tribal leaders, only 55 percent of respondents indicated that Indian people were represented on school boards, and in only 34 percent of the schools where they were represented were they a majority. These facts, along with the absence of courses in Native language, history and culture, constitute a major hurdle to Native American communities' efforts to achieve self-determination in education for their children.

In my study on Native Americans in higher education, I discovered that 75 percent of Indian students attended a group of 79 institutions enrolling four percent or more Native Americans.[6] Only 16 of those institutions had Native American teacher education programs. There is an obvious need for more institutions, particularly those with teacher training programs, to recruit and save Native Americans. Although Native American college enrollment is up 11 percent over the past decade, less than half attend four-year colleges, and 47 percent of all Indian college students attend part time. Financial considerations are paramount as only 50 percent of Native Americans receive financial aid.[7]

Indeed, there is a critical need to open college doors to Native American students. Over one third of all post-secondary institutions had no Indian students. Over 88 percent of Native Americans attending college attend public institutions. If the higher education objectives of the Native American community are to be met, substantially more *four-year* and *private* institutions need to reach out to Native American students.

For the immediate future, colleges and universities will need to focus on the development of academic and personal support programs for Native American students. The highest level dropout for Indian students in college is the freshman year (50 percent).[8] However, in the years ahead, Native American education needs to move beyond remediation and concentrate on developing curricular programs which are centered around attaining high achievement among Native American students. Head Start and other pre-school programs are not too early to identify well-qualified Indian students. Since many Native American students, including the brightest, are "at risk," special attention should be given to gifted students to ensure their educational success. Too often, highly qualified Native Americans are tracked by guidance counselors into either vocational or general, non post-secondary programs. It is for these reasons that there needs to be present, in substantially greater numbers, Native American teachers, counselors and administrators in schools where Native Americans attend.

Head Start, Title V (Indian Education Act) and Johnson-O'Malley are the three federal programs which provide educational support to Indian students. As the Native American school population increases at an accelerating rate (38 percent), funding for these programs needs to keep pace. Since most school curricula do not provide offerings in native language, culture and history, these support programs are often the sole mechanism to introduce native content into the curricula. Moreover, they provide opportunities for Indian employment in the school and guidance services to Native American students. Their advisory committees also serve as a vital link between the native and school communities.

Beginning in the 1950's, Indian people began moving off reservation into the cities and towns. This exodus was created by poverty on the reservation and a series of federal programs initialed by the Bureau of Indian Affairs to depopulate reservations in order to lessen the financial responsibility of the federal government to Indians. It almost succeeded! However, the fallout from this pernicious policy was the creation of the urban and off reservation Indian. Today, a majority of Native Americans, almost two-thirds, live off reservation and attend schools when Native Americans are a distant minority.

Little research has been done regarding the educational achievement of the off reservation Native American. Some are served by Head Start, Title V, Upward Bound and other state and federal programs which serve minority and educationally disadvantaged students. But, for the most part, these students are lumped in with others and receive little recognition concerning their cultural heritage or special educational needs. Many have never had contact with their tribal community and receive no benefits based on tribal membership. Indian Clubs, Native Friendship Centers and Title V programs which cover entire urban areas attempt to fill the educational gap.

Since many of these students attend the poorest and least educationally advanced schools in urban and rural areas, they are at a substantial educational disadvantage. Lacking both tribal and school support systems which their reservation counterparts have, off reservation Indian students constitute the most "at risk" group of Native Americans in American schools. The educational challenge of this decade is to devise a strategy which will salvage these students, educationally and culturally. It has been suggested that in urban areas with large numbers of Native American students that magnet schools for Indian students be established.

Since most Native American students attend integrated schools and are taught predominantly by non-Indian teachers, the learning environment for Native American students requires important changes. I have already spoken for the need to offer the native language in the school system. This is essential for two reasons: the language is dying on the reservation and without the language, critical elements of the native culture and value system will be lost. Speaking and learning in their own language will enhance Indian culture identity and self concept.

Other changes in integrated schools where Native Americans attend would be strong affirmative action programs to hire Indian personnel. Classes should be taught in Native American language, culture and tribal history by Indian elders when certified teachers are not available, which is almost always the case. Perhaps, most important of all, a thorough orientation and sensitization of non-native personnel about Indian culture, values and learning styles. An important element of this orientation for non-native staff would be workshops focusing on racism and Indian stereotyping. As a minimum, school districts with significant numbers of Native Americans should have ongoing in-service educational programs for school personnel working with Indian children. Tribal personnel and specialists on Native American education and cultural values should be part of these programs.

In a national survey of Native American tribal leaders, literacy education, vocational education, and securing tribal educators were the three highest rated tribal educational needs.[9] Over half of living Native Americans have not completed high school and this group generally lacks vocational skills. Along with improving the educational environment for Native American youth, a major challenge in the decade ahead is developing programs for adult learners who dropped out of the system. For these reasons, tribal leaders placed literacy education (G.E.D., high school diploma) and vocational education at the top of their educational priorities.

Programs like the New York State Regents' provision for achieving high school equivalency by attending and graduating from a two-year community college with an associates degree (including vocational programs) are a stimulus to adult Native Americans to return to school. Mater Dei College of Ogdensburg, New York, has had significant success in attracting adult Mohawks who have dropped out to return to school and earn a degree and their high school equivalency. Fifty percent of Indian tribes are within fifty miles of a two- or four-year college and respondents to the survey indicated that 63 percent of the tribes had college level courses on or near the reservation.[10] With the growth of the twenty-six Indian controlled tribal colleges and the proximity of college level extension courses to reservations, the educational base is available to respond to this priority need in Indian education, literacy and vocational education for Native American adults.

Without a doubt, education is the key to Native American self-determination. "Without knowledgeable tribal members, Indian tribes will continue to be dependent upon others for expertise and advice in the several areas of tribal responsibility. It should be the policy of the federal government to enhance Indian control over educational programs designed to serve Indian people, promoting local tribal control and by strongly encouraging state educational leadership to develop programs which improve the educational advantage of Indians and preserve their cultural identity."[11] Two obvious objectives remain to be reached: the improvement of the quality of Indian education and Indian control over the education of their children. Since the majority of Native Americans (90 percent) attend state public schools, it is the responsibility of the federal government to see that Native Americans are fully served by state education programs. The compact which characterizes the educational relationship between Native Americans and the State of Minnesota is a concrete step in this direction. Newfound wealth from gambling sources, mineral land and water leases, land claim settlements, etc., should serve as the base for tribal support of educational institutions at a time when state and federal funding for education is diminishing.

Even when one accounts for the cultural bias, Native American students score 36 points below the national average on the verbal section of SAT's and 39 points below on the mathematical part.[12] There has been little improvement in stemming the high school dropout rate over the past five years.[13] Tribal leaders point to lack of funding, poor facilities, lack of family support and involvement, dysfunctional family environment, alcohol and substance abuse and the low quality of education as obstacles to the educational achievement of their children.[14] Despite these handicaps, immense strides have been made by Native Americans in regaining the control and direction of the education of Indian students. However, the appalling poverty, social problems, pervasive unemployment and lack of political influence in state capitals hamper further advances. Further advances in the improvement of Indian education over the next decade are intimately tied in with addressing the aforementioned problems and seeking solutions.

NOTES

1. Eileen M. O'Brien, "American Indians in Higher Education," *Research Briefs*, Washington, D.C.: American Council on Education, 3(3), 1992, 1.

2. Robert N. Wells, "Indian Education from the Tribal Perspective: A Survey of American Indian Tribal Leaders," unpublished paper, January, 1991, 10.

3. Ibid., 2.

4. Eileen M. O'Brien, "American Indians in Higher Education," *Research Briefs*, Washington, D.C.: American Council on Education, 3(3), 1992, 6.

5. Ibid., 1.

6. Robert N. Wells, "The Native American Experience in Higher Education: Turning Around the Cycle of Failure." Presentation at Minorities in Higher Education Conference

sponsored by Hofstra University, March 10, 1989, 6.

7. Eileen M. O'Brien, "American Indians in Higher Education," *Research Briefs*, Washington, D.C.: American Council on Education, 3(3), 1992, 6.

8. Robert N. Wells, "Indian Education from the Tribal Perspective: A Survey of American Indian Tribal Leaders," unpublished paper, January, 1991, 2.

9. Ibid., 3.

10. Ibid., 6.

11. Ibid., 8.

12. Eileen M. O'Brien, "American Indians in Higher Education," *Research Briefs*, Washington, D.C.: American Council on Education, 3(3), 1992, 4.

13. Robert N. Wells, "Indian Education from the Tribal Perspective: A Survey of American Indian Tribal Leaders," unpublished paper, January, 1991, 7.

14. Ibid., 6.

Chapter VI

Native American Health

Since the arrival of Europeans in North America centuries ago, Native American populations have suffered greatly from poor health. Currently, Native American rates of infant mortality, alcoholism, mental illness, teen pregnancy, drug abuse, diabetes, and HIV infection are much higher than the rates for the general population.

Most Native American health problems are related to poverty and social disadvantage. The American health care system is based on ability to pay, so it is natural that any social group which is predominantly poor will be disadvantaged medically. Native American health problems are closely related to social, economic, and political conditions under which Indian people must live. Therefore, the solutions to these problems must be socially and politically conceived.

During the last twelve years, Federal funding for Native American health services has become less and less adequate, as overall aid to Native Americans has decreased. The most disadvantaged of American minorities, Native Americans thus find themselves without adequate disease prevention and health care. An effective Native American health program depends upon the creation of social and political conditions which allow Indians to enjoy greater educational and economic opportunities. Native Americans will not cease to be medically disadvantaged until they cease to be socially, economically, and politically disadvantaged.

Low socio-economic status for Native Americans has manifested itself in a poor diet, which has led to obesity, diabetes, and other health problems. Lack of opportunity has caused many Indians, young and old, male and female, to resort to alcohol, drugs, and sexual promiscuity as escape mechanisms. As a result, Native Americans suffer from a high level of alcoholism, drug addiction, and unplanned pregnancy. In addition, certain of these high risk activities have caused the rate of sexually transmitted diseases, including AIDS, to increase among Native Americans.

Indian infants and elderly are hit particularly hard by the inadequacy of Native American health care and the external factors which increase the likelihood of disease for Indians. High alcoholism rates have resulted in a large number of infants suffering from Fetal Alcohol Syndrome.

Any attempt to improve the health care situation of Native Americans must support traditional culture, recognizing the age-old Indian emphasis on harmony and balance with nature, and must make every effort not to conflict with tribal values.

—RNW

96

The Changing Dimension of Native American Health: A Critical Understanding of Contemporary Native American Health Issues

Gregory R. Campbell

THE UNNATURAL HISTORY OF DISEASE

The health problems Native Americans are confronting today did not arise out of an historical vacuum. Diseases and ill health have a history. Health levels are linked to the social, political, and economic forces present at any historical moment. Thus, in order to understand some of the present day factors determining Native American health levels, it is imperative to examine the historical context from which these health patterns emerged.

The medical history of Native Americans since European contact can be characterized as an "unnatural history of disease"—unnatural because the epidemiology of Native American people changed under the hegemony of European contact.[1] Native Americans, from the sixteenth through the mid-twentieth century, experienced a new set of afflictions which decimated their populations.[2] Epidemics such as smallpox, rubella, influenza, malaria, yellow fever, and cholera ravaged Native American societies, creating societal disorganization. It is not surprising that these epidemic episodes coincided with European expansion and development of the frontier.[3]

By the time most Native Americans were forced onto reservations, they had experienced centuries of cultural change, including a decline in health status. Reservation life brought further alterations to Native American societies. Under full governmental control, the Bureau of Indian Affairs launched its assimilation program, which was designed to move Native American people out of "savagery" and into "civilization." Native Americans were subjected to rapid changes in settlement pattern, social organization, diet, and ideology. These rapid changes gave rise to new health problems rarely experienced by prereservation Native Americans. Reservation Indian populations experienced an increase in tuberculosis, trachoma, otitis media, venereal disease, and alcoholism.[4]

As part of its assimilation program the Bureau of Indian Affairs took charge of medical care for Native American people. Bureau medical personnel set about treating reservation diseases that had been created by the social and economic conditions engendered by the bureau's policies. The role of reservation medicine therefore was never separate from the political policy of assimilation. Hospitals, for example, were not constructed to isolate infectious Indian people or to provide a sanitary location to perform medical services, but were constructed to "civilize" sick Indian people away from tribal influences.[5] Needless to say, ill health continued into the mid-twentieth century.

Following the Second World War, governmental policies shifted toward terminating the government's trust responsibility with Native Americans. The policy shift coincided with rapid social changes. As social and economic services were phased out on reservations, many Indian people entered into the cash economy, migrated off the reservation to more urban locations, and began to consume more manufactured products. In addition, the responsibility of health care was shifted from the Bureau of Indian Affairs to the United States Public Health Service. The transfer represented not only the administrative restructuring of responsibility, but also the emergence of a new medical ideology. Assimilation through medicine was no longer the explicit goal; it was replaced by a medical ecological paradigm. The poor health of American Indians was attributed no longer to "savage ignorance," but to a lack of sufficient medical knowledge.

Parallel to these rapid alterations in Native American lifestyle and political relationship with the federal government, significant health changes were taking place. As the Indian Health Service brought trachoma and tuberculosis under control, new chronic diseases emerged to take their place. Native Americans began to suffer from substance abuse, diabetes mellitus, carcinoma, heart disease, accidents, violence, and abuse.[6] To solve these health problems, the federal government passed the Indian Self-Determination and Education and Assistance Act of 1975 and the Indian Health Care Improvement Act of 1976.

The Indian Health Care Improvement Act declared as a national goal that Native Americans should be afforded the highest possible health status and should be provided the resources necessary to effect that policy.[7] Despite this policy objective, the health status of Native American people remains below the national average.[8] What health improvements have been accomplished over the last three decades are being erased by current United States governmental policy. The fiscal year budget request for 1990 proposes the total elimination of funding for housing, sanitation, and outpatient health facilities, and significant reductions in funding for Indian child welfare, rights protection, and housing improvements.[9] Health services and care, like other services provided by the federal government, are slowly being dissolved under the guise of self-determination through private sector investment. The government's argument is that the private sector will continue social programs. Such a policy amounts to termination by de-funding. As Ortiz has stated,

> although termination has been disavowed as an active federal policy, . . . there is a kind of de-facto termination. It is occurring by de-funding—by just not funding programs, but ignoring the law of the land and just cutting the funding out from programs. Without funds, there is de-facto termination.[10]

This is the "unnatural history of disease" for Native American people. It is a history in which health levels were, and still are, intimately linked to the social, economic, and political conditions under which Indian people must live. Native American health levels and health care are determined outside of the health sector.[11]

The papers presented in this volume represent some of the most salient health problems facing contemporary Native Americans. The diversity of subject matter in the articles reflects the complexity of various health issues confronting Native Americans. They are health problems that have a history and will certainly affect the future. Perhaps the most perplexing and ambiguous issue that these papers address is the solution to these health problems. Intervention and prevention have always been elusive, but all the authors conclude, either explicitly or implicitly, that the health dilemmas of the American Indian will ultimately be solved by social means, rather than exclusively in the medical arena.

ACQUIRED IMMUNE DEFICIENCY SYNDROME: AN EMERGING EPIDEMIC

Since contact with Europeans, Native Americans have had to contend with the importation of fatal diseases. Today, a new contagion is beginning to impact Indian people. This deadly new communicable disease is caused by a human immuno-deficiency virus and is called "Acquired Immune Deficiency Syndrome" (AIDS). Just as with other imported communicable diseases, Native Americans are particularly vulnerable. Acquired Immune Deficiency Syndrome is the most pressing health problem facing the Native American community. Yet, it is the most underrated and ignored health dilemma. Since 1981, considerable effort has been expended to examine the public health ramifications of the disease. Thus far, over 60,000 cases of AIDS have been reported in the United States, with a fatality rate of over 50 percent within two years of diagnosis. Recent projections indicate that by 1991 over 300,000 AIDS cases will have been diagnosed; a disproportionate number of these cases will be among minorities.[12]

Native Americans (including Native Alaskans) represent approximately 1.6 percent of the total United States population, but currently account for less than .07 percent of the reported AIDS cases. The Native American population is composed of a broad biogenetic, sociocultural, and economic spectrum. Currently, few Indian people have attained a degree of economic security, and over 50 percent of the population can be described as chronically poor. Furthermore, the Native American population is younger and more poorly educated, and earns less than the larger population.[13] These sociodemographic variables contribute to a significant decline in the health status of Native Americans, subjecting them to higher forces of morbidity and mortality. Like other minorities and the poor, Native Americans are at a significant risk for contracting HIV and developing AIDS. Qualitative and medical observations suggest that American Indians possess a number of high-risk social behavior patterns which could result in a dramatic rise in AIDS cases among American Indians.[14]

Recent studies have demonstrated that sexually transmitted disease (STD) rates among American Indians are significantly higher than among non-Indians. According to Center for Disease Control statistics for 1985, Indian syphilis and gonorrhea rates are approximately 20 times higher than for non-Indians.[15] In Arizona, for example, Indian people had syphilis rates of 79.1 per 100,000, compared to a nationwide rate of 7.1 per 100,000 for non-Indians.[16] It has been well established that high STD rates correlate with promiscuity, multiple sex partners, bisexuality, homosexuality, and other high-risk behaviors associated with HIV infection. Sexually transmitted diseases may be a marker for infection with the HIV virus.[17]

Emerging evidence suggests there is a link between STD contact investigations on reservations and migration patterns from natal communities to urban centers and back again. This cyclical migration pattern is poorly documented, but it is common knowledge that American Indians who reside, either permanently or temporarily, in metropolitan locations frequently return to their home communities for various reasons.[18] Moreover, American Indians residing in an urban setting have a wider range of sexual contacts with non-Indians. In many cases, these contacts are with members of other minority groups or sub-populations which are at high risk for being carriers of the HIV virus.[19] American Indian migrants provide a direct transmission route from higher risk population areas (i.e., urban centers) to lower risk communities (i.e., reservations or natal communities, which are largely rural).[20]

Concomitantly, there is little data regarding the extent of bisexual or homosexual behavior among contemporary American Indians. Native American homosexuality and bisexuality remain largely "closeted" phenomena and, hence, a hidden reservoir for potential HIV infection. Such information is critical to our understanding of AIDS, especially if we are to adequately assess the level of knowledge and provide sound intervention strategies in Indian country.

The above risk factors are further compounded by substance abuse. Approximately one-third of all Indian people die before the age of 45 from diseases directly related to alcohol.[21] Acute alcohol abuse leads some American Indian people to engage in sexually promiscuous behavior that would normally be avoided. For many years, alcoholism has been an Indian Health Service priority, but the IHS has

> . . . focused exclusively on the alcohol problem without monitoring and analyzing possible changes in patterns of abuse, especially among young Indian people . . . [E]vidence from residents and providers in California Indian alcoholism treatment programs as well as among tribal leaders appears to indicate that growing numbers of Indian youth are shooting drugs, especially amphetamines.[22]

Although the extent of drug use is not well documented, recent survey data in the San Francisco Bay area suggest that 50 percent of young American Indian alcoholics are using drugs intravenously.[23] The failure of health administrators to track the changes in substance abuse patterns (Finley, this volume), coupled with withdrawal of funding for urban Indian health clinics (Brod and LaDue, this volume), places Native American people at risk.

Because of the time lag in the development of AIDS after HIV infection has taken place and the lack of an effective treatment of the underlying disease process, those exposed to the virus must be presumed to be chronically infectious. Therefore, the most effective means of altering the course of the epidemic lies in education and in modifying high risk behaviors among uninfected Native Americans.

The number of Indian people developing AIDS has been increasing every year since 1985. The Center for Disease Control reports that at least 55 American Indians have the disease. Of that number, 21.8 percent have been reported in

California. Current estimates indicate that for every reported AIDS case, there are 40 to 100 people infected with the HIV virus.[24]

Although the majority of the American Indian cases were from urban areas, AIDS is not exclusively an urban affliction. Already six people have died on the Navajo Reservation.[25] With only 1,500,000 Native Americans in the United States, any further spread of the disease could drive many tribal groups once again to the brink of extinction.

It is a political, economic, and health reality that a general correlation is emerging between ethnicity, poverty, and the impact of AIDS. Recent epidemiological data suggest that minorities will represent a significant number of AIDS cases by 1991. It is also an unfortunate truth that those most at risk for contracting AIDS are the most poorly informed. The youth, poverty, poor education, and cultural behaviors of Native Americans often militate against utilization of available services. Because of the unique political relationship American Indians have with the federal government, many are denied access to private health services and health education.

Since clinical treatment has had little impact in stopping the spread of AIDS in the general population, it is recognized that prevention through community education is the most viable intervention strategy. This is especially important in American Indian populations, where basic demographic and attitudinal data are nearly nonexistent. Claymore's work provides a timely and important starting point for critically evaluating the need for and the barriers to developing an AIDS health education and intervention program.

Claymore's paper points out the urgency with which the Indian Health Service and various tribal communities must involve themselves in AIDS prevention. The author correctly points out that prevention efforts should be based on health education policies developed from factual, culturally specific, and relevant educational materials in order to enhance the level of knowledge about AIDS among American Indians.

Claymore's argument is well taken, but current Native American health policies view Native Americans as a homogeneous ethnic group, despite the fact that there are over 483 distinct Native American cultures recognized by the United States federal government and over 100 non-federally recognized groups. Each of these societies has unique cultural traditions. To be successful, AIDS risk reduction education must be culturally specific. This requires accounting for the cultural values and dynamics that have an important impact on high-risk behaviors. Any attempt to reach and educate Native Americans must present health information in a culturally sensitive and relevant manner, addressing American Indian high-risk behavior patterns. The next logical question that must be posed is whether the Indian Health Service is willing to model education programs based not only on cultural constructs, but also on the demographic realities of twentieth-century Native American life.

SUBSTANCE ABUSE AND TYPE II DIABETES MELLITUS: DISEASES OF SOCIAL CHANGE

The prevalence of alcohol and drug abuse among Native Americans is alarming. As of 1985, the age-adjusted alcoholism mortality rate for Native Americans was 4.2 percent higher than the United States all races rate.[26] Currently, seven of the ten leading causes of death among Indian people are directly attributed to alcohol abuse.[27] The problem is so acute that it led the United States Congress and the Indian Health Service to target alcoholism and substance abuse as "the most severe health and social problem facing Indian Tribes."[28]

A growing trend in Indian country is the abuse of alcohol and drugs among the youth. Finley's article attests to the importance of substance abuse prevention among today's Native American youth. In a comparison of Indian and non-Indian students between the sixth and twelfth grades, Finley discovered that both Native American males and females drank more often and more regularly than their non-Indian counterparts. By her criteria, 29 percent of Native American girls and 100 percent of Native American boys were heavy drinkers by the ninth grade. Further, in a previous survey, Finley found a 37 percent prevalence rate of marijuana, a 42 percent prevalence of inhalants, and an 11 percent rate of using hallucinogens, stimulants, and sedatives.[29] The Native American youth who abused alcohol and drugs cited boredom, peer pressure, poor economic hope, family instability, and lack of Native American spiritual values as primary contributing factors in their decision to drink and use drugs. The consequences of substance abuse are dropping out of school, sexual promiscuity, illegitimate pregnancies, possible physical and sexual abuse, delinquency, and high morbidity and mortality, including suicide.[30]

Health professionals and organizations that serve Native Americans must develop an intervention model for substance abuse. The intervention strategy should not only treat the symptoms of abuse but should also, as Finley suggests, reify Native American values and identity. Although such an intervention strategy could go far in treatment and prevention, it is obvious that major social, economic, and political changes will have to take place if the problem of substance abuse is to be overcome.

Type II diabetes mellitus is a new disease among Native American people. Previous to 1940, few cases of diabetes were recorded for Native Americans. Since then, Type II diabetes mellitus (commonly called adult onset diabetes) has become a major epidemic. Diabetes mellitus is currently the seventh leading cause of death among Native Americans, exceeding by 2.8 times the United States all races age-adjusted mortality rate.[31] Diabetes is also a major cause of debilitation. Each year, thousands of Indian people undergo amputations and experience blindness, vascular complications, and kidney dialysis because of this chronic disease.

Justice's study of the prevalence of diabetes on the Warm Springs Reservation in Oregon traces the appearance of the disease since 1965. Justice outlines the changes in diet, food availability, activity output, and medical intervention which contributed to a cycle of obesity, high blood sugar levels, and, eventually, the onset of diabetes. By 1978, diabetes mellitus at Warm Springs was a growing and recognized health problem.

Although currently the explanation for the diabetes epidemic among Native Americans implicates a genetic predisposition for the disease, the appearance of Type II diabetes is directly related to rapid social change.[32] It is a political and economic scenario that has taken place among other Native American people and other indigenous people worldwide.[33] In reality, diabetes ". . . is a debilitating byproduct of the U.S. government's forced changes in Indian lifestyle, diet, and psychology."[34] Like alcoholism, drug abuse, suicide, and many other afflictions that plague Native American people, diabetes is a disease of colonialism in which social and economic circumstances, to a great extent, determine the onset and prevalence of the disease.

NATIVE AMERICAN DISABLED, INFANTS, AND ELDERLY: AN UNDERSERVED POPULATION AT RISK

Many of the identified health problems among Native Americans are preventable but continue to exist within a cycle of social disadvantage. In general, Native American people suffer from higher rates of fetal alcohol syndrome, bacterial meningitis, otitis media, diabetes, accidents, mental disorders, and substance abuse than the national averages. All of these afflictions lead to major disabilities among Indian people.

Recognizing the needs of Native Americans for prevention and rehabilitation, Congress passed Public Law 99-506, the Rehabilitation Act Amendments of 1986. The act specified governmental responsibility in serving Native American disabled and handicapped. Despite the legislation, involvement by federal and state health agencies was often fragmented and lacked any empirical data on the problems, barriers, and limitations confronting disabled Native Americans. Hodge's work begins to fill this void. Collaborating with the Native American Research and Training Center at the University of Arizona and three tribally operated vocational and rehabilitation centers located on the Navajo, Rocky Boy, and Fort Hall reservations, Hodge conducted a needs assessment of Native Americans with disabilities. The study revealed the social and economic burden that disabilities place on Native American communities. Hodge discovered that the

. . . adult disabled Indian was relatively young (average age 33 years) and unemployed, resided in a state of poverty, and required a multitude of services incorporating medical care, rehabilitation, training, and financial assistance. Chronic health problems were evident; such problems as high blood pressure, arthritis, coughs, heart problems, and diabetes were noted. Multiple disabilities and health problems were also reported.[35]

The tragedy is that most of the diseases that contributed to the disabilities are associated with poverty and social disadvantage. Moreover, treatment of these disabilities is retarded by lack of services, lack of viable prevention strategy, and cultural insensitivity on the part of many health service providers. Until the maldistribution of health services is corrected and culturally sensitive preventive measures become policy and practice, disabled Native Americans, as Hodge's analysis demonstrates, will continue to be confronted with institutional and medical barriers that limit their potential as viable members of their tribal community.

Demographically, Native Americans continue to constitute one of the fastest growing segments of the United States population. Between 1970 and 1980, the Native American population increased by 70 percent. If this rate of growth continues, the Native American population will increase by 150 percent over the next two decades.[36] The current Native American profile indicates a young, growing population. This age structure has important implications for health and health delivery services.

Population dynamics play a prominent role in defining the various dimensions of health and health-related behavior. These relationships include the effects of changing age and sex composition of a population on patterns of disease and on health programs.[37] Two age cohorts that are facing health problems at opposite ends of the epidemiologic continuum are Native American infants and elderly. The elderly experience health problems that are largely chronic, while the infants continue to suffer from infectious diseases, especially during the postneonatal period. Although Native American infants and elderly suffer from different types of diseases, they share the common bonds of higher rates of morbidity and mortality than the general United States population. Their health dilemma attests to the political and economic nature of the problem.

In 1980, 10.7 percent of the Native American population was under the age of five, and most of these children were one year of age or younger.[38] While medical technology has resulted in an 84 percent decrease in the national Native American infant mortality rate since 1954-1956, significant differences between native Americans and other populations remain when comparisons are made on a regional basis.[39] This is especially true when the infant mortality rate is broken down into neonatal and postneonatal rates.

Campbell's article examines the differential infant mortality rates which existed between American Indians and non-Indians in the state of Montana between 1979 and 1987. According to a 1986 United States congressional study, the 1980 to 1982 neonatal and postneonatal infant mortality rates for the Billings Indian Health Service Area (which includes Native Americans residing in Montana and Wyoming) were higher than the United States all races rates.[40] Campbell contends that the differences between the Montana American Indian and non-Indian rates is the result of poverty and social disadvantage, rather than biology. Thus, the solution to the infant mortality crisis should not solely be sought in the medical arena, but in political and economic change.

Over the past two decades, health professionals have come to realize that minority elders represent an underserved population.[41] This is especially true for Native American elderly.[42] As a segment of the total United States population, Native American elderly are statistically an insignificant minority subpopulation.[43] Even within the Native American population, the elderly, age 60 years and older, represent only 7.6 percent of the total population.[44] Because of their relatively small numbers, Native American elderly have experienced limited access to health service resources and are not a primary target population for the distribution of these resources.

The maldistribution of health resources magnifies the already poor health conditions of Native American elderly. In general, Native American elderly suffer from poverty, a poor diet, and inordinately high rates of disease associated with poverty and a low standard of living. Health conditions are worse for Native American elders on reservations or in rural areas, and they have greater unmet service needs. These Native American elders ".. . are poorer, have greater financial concerns, support more people on less income, have fewer social contacts and somewhat lower life satisfaction, and are in poorer health than urban Indians."[45] Regardless of their residence, many Native American elderly are unaware of available health resources, however limited those resources may be.[46] The result is a population that is invisible and grossly underserved in the health arena.

Recent evidence indicates that the full range of services is usually unavailable to tribal elders and that those services that are available are largely directed toward secondary health care needs. The resultant services are underserving American Indian elders. In addition, health care is often perceived as culturally insensitive.[47] That is, most services rendered provide the minimal instrumental assistance necessary to maintain physical, but not psychosocial, well-being.

Awareness and accessibility of services for eligible American Indian elderly do not guarantee service utilization. Most Native American elderly, especially those who are members of recognized tribal entities, face a myriad of complex rules and governmental regulations before services can be rendered. This fact, combined with other obstacles such as lack of transportation, language barriers, and other difficulties, severely limit full utilization of health care services.[48]

American Indian elderly suffer from a service system modeled by policymakers from a different cultural context, who are frequently unaware of the specific legal history each Indian community maintains with the federal, state, and county governments. At the heart of the issue is the degree of empowerment Native American communities have in formulating health policies for their elderly.[49]

Although a significant literature about Native American elders is emerging, there remains a fundamental gap in our knowledge about health and well-being among the American Indian elderly. The article by Weibel-Orlando entitled "Elders and Elderlies: Well-Being in Indian Old Age" begins to fill an important gap in our knowledge of the specific factors associated with well-being among Native American elderly. Weibel-Orlando discovered that successful aging was associated with ethnically inflected community statuses and roles that involved active participation in community and family. In other words, well-being was defined in large part by sociocultural criteria.

Weibel-Orlando's analysis points out the importance of cultural values in the delivery of health services.[50] Existing social and health services should construct a system utilizing ethnic community membership and participation as a positive resource toward well-being.[51] Such knowledge is essential to learning the delivery needs and problems of Native American elderly.

URBAN HEALTH CARE, UTILIZATION, AND SURVIVAL: A POLITICAL DILEMMA FOR THE 1990s

During the 1950s, the federal government encouraged Native Americans to relocate to selected urban centers. This relocation policy was carried out under the dubious theory that American Indians would find secure employment and eventually assimilate into the "mainstream" of urban American life. Although many Native Americans returned to their home communities, many stayed in the cities. According to the 1980 census, 54 percent of the total United States Native American population resides in metropolitan areas.[52]

The urbanization of the Native American population has brought a number of serious threats to Native American health and well-being. Although the federal government encouraged Native Americans to urbanize, most recently there has been a general retreat on the part of the Indian Health Service from extending comprehensive health care to urban Native Americans. Faced with service population increases, mismanagement, escalating health care costs, shortages of qualified personnel, and federal budget restraints, the Indian Health Service has been forced to curtail or discontinue many health programs, including urban health programs.

Historically, support for Native American urban-based health care clinics has been tenuous at best. Since 1972, the Indian Health Service has funded urban health services through its community development branch. Appropriations were derived from Public Law 94-437, the Indian Health Improvement Act. The Indian Health Service funds only 51 percent of the total urban Indian health care program. The remaining economic resources are sought through other federal funds, private donations, and charges for services rendered.

Since 1980, Indian Health Service funding has increased, but funds reaching urban areas are decreasing. As of 1984, there were 37 health clinics or programs in urban areas in 20 states.[53] As a result of decreased funding, however, Native American urban health clinics have been reduced to 28 (circa 1987) and have experienced a significant decline in client caseload. These reductions, coupled with the conflicts that have arisen about the eligibility of clients, the servicing of non-Indians, and the desire of reservation governments to have greater control over urban programs, have led the Indian Health Service to call for the elimination of urban health programs. The withdrawal of support for health services for urban Native American people contradicts three decades of United States federal policy encouraging Native American people to leave their natal communities and relocate to metropolitan areas.[54]

Given the current nationwide assault on health services for Native Americans residing in urban areas, the papers by Brod and LaDue, Taylor, and Joe and Miller are a timely addition to this volume. Utilizing a micro-level analysis of the Billings Indian Health Service Area, Brod and LaDue examine the political mobilization of the urban Indian community is Missoula, Montana and the western region of the Billings Indian Health Service Area in response to the proposed elimination of their programs. The study by Brod and LaDue, while regional in scope, demonstrates two critical realities of urban Native American life: first, that political mobilization is necessary if urban Native Americans are to receive any degree of equity with regard to health and community services; second, that there is a lacuna of research on urban health needs and utilization.

Taylor's work (this volume) addresses the issue of urban health care utilization. By regression analysis, Taylor explored the determinants of medical care utilization among urban Native Americans in Oklahoma City. The results of his research indicate that the primary reason for patient visits to the Oklahoma City Indian Health Clinic was for acute and chronic health problems. More importantly, the clinic served the two most underprivileged segments of the urban native American population—impoverished young women and the elderly.

Complementing the work of Brod and LaDue and Taylor, the article by Joe and Miller focuses on the economic, organizational, and political problems faced by the Tucson Indian Clinic and its clients. The authors paint a picture similar to that of the Brod and LaDue study. The Tucson clinic continues to maintain a precarious existence while providing vital health care services to Native American people who are often impoverished and experiencing a high degree of cultural discontinuity. Culture is an important key in forging a positive health outcome. This is especially true for many Native American people who maintain a different perspective of health, disease, and illness from that of the general population.

WORLD VIEW AND HEALTH

The final paper in this volume, by Swentzell and Naranjo, reminds us that healing and well-being transcend the Western European biophysical model of ill health. Many Native American societies still maintain a viable ethnomedical system which defines health, disease, and healing within their own cultural traditions and values. For the Tewa Pueblos, as the authors point out, health is "a state of balance"—an interconnectedness and interdependency which engenders a wholeness of the individual's body, spirit, and self, with society, the natural and physical environment, and the cosmos. Thus the entire Pueblo world, including health, is based on a broad, natural rhythm which is dualistic and largely symmetrical.[55] This symmetrical dualism is reflected in Tewa architecture, social organization, life cycle, and religious symbolism. It is not surprising, therefore, that health and healing powers emanate from all aspects of society.

In opposition, ill health must be defined as imbalance, not only in a biophysical sense, but in relation to society and the surrounding world. Diseases and ill health are symbolically classified into this dualistic model of the world. "[F]or a Tewa is never just ill;" according to Ortiz, "he has either a 'hot' illness or a 'cold' one, and it must be treated with appropriate herbs."[56] In the Tewa case study, presented by Swentzell and Naranjo, health is not merely the absence of illness; it is a social construct which is tied to the structure of society. If intervention and prevention strategies are to be successful, the health care policy must not conflict with but must support the prevailing cultural paradigm of health, disease, and healing.

THE SOCIAL CONSTRUCT OF HEALTH

Just as health is connected to society, so, too, are the origins of ill health. If we are ultimately to understand the nature of ill health among Native American people, we must examine health levels within the particular historical and social context in which they have arisen. By doing so, we can begin to comprehend the "contending forces in and out of the health arena that impinge on health and healing."[57] It is a credit to the authors of this volume that they have critically addressed these particular Native American health problems within their wider social context. As the commentary by Red Horse, Johnson, and Weiner indicates, the next essential task will be to build solutions within the same social arena.

ACKNOWLEDGMENTS

As an author and general editor, I owe a debt of gratitude to a number of people and institutions. I would like to thank the authors of this volume, particularly Dr. John Red Horse, Dr. Jennie Joe and Dr. Joan Weibel-Orlando, for their constructive suggestions during the initial planning of this volume. I also would like to thank Dr. Duane Champagne, Mr. Hanay Geiogamah, the publication staff of the *American Indian Culture and Research Journal*, and the anonymous reviewers for their critical comments, editorial and production assistance. Their commentary and support made this a better volume. Initially, support for this project was received from the Institute of American Cultures and the American Indian Studies Center, University of California, Los Angeles. I am in their debt. Finally, I would like to express my appreciation to the Department of Anthropology at the University of Montana. Their support and encouragement greatly contributed toward the completion of this volume.

NOTES

1. Meredeth Turshen, *The Political Ecology of Disease in Tanzania* (New Brunswick: Rutgers University Press, 1984), 9-19.

2. Gregory R. Campbell, "Plains Indian Historical Demography and Health," *Plains Anthropologist*, Memoir 23 (Lincoln, NE: Agustums Printing Service Incorporated, 1989); Shereburne F. Cook, *Essays in Population History* (Berkeley: University of California Press, 1971); Henry F. Dobyns, "Estimating Aboriginal American Population: An Appraisal of Techniques with a New Hemispheric Estimate," *Current Anthropology* 7(4), (1966), 495-516; Henry Dobyns, *Their Number Become Thinned*, (Knoxville, TN: University of Tennessee Press, 1983); Russell Thornton, *American Indian Holocaust and Survival: A Population History Since 1492*, (Norman: University of Oklahoma Press, 1987).

3. Gregory R. Campbell, *Plains Indian Historical Demography and Health; The Political Economy of Ill-Health: Changing Northern Cheyenne Health Patterns and Economic Underdevelopment*, Ph.D. diss., (Ann Arbor: University of Michigan, 1987); Diane T. Putney, *Fighting the Scourge: American Indian Morbidity and Federal Policy*, Ph.D. diss., (Ann Arbor: University of Michigan, 1980); Paul T. Stuart, *Nation Within a Nation*, (New York: Greenwood Press, 1987).

4. Campbell, *Plains Indian Historical Demography and Health; Political Economy*, (1987); Putney, *Fighting the Scourge*, (1980); Stuart, *Nation Within a Nation*, (1987).

5. Gregory R. Campbell, "Medicine as Civilization: American Indian Health Care Under the Bureau of Indian Affairs" (Manuscript, 1989).

6. U.S. Department of Health and Human Services, *Indian Health Service Chart Series Book, April 1988*, (Washington, D.C.: U.S. Government Printing Office, 1988).

7. Office of Technology Assessment, *Indian Health Care*, (Washington, D.C.: U.S. Government Printing Office, 1986), 45.

8. U.S. Department of Health and Human Services, *Indian Health Service Chart Series Book*, April (1988); Office of Technology Assessment, *Indian Health Care*, (1986).

9. Letter, Representative Pat Williams to Mrs. Betty A. Peace, 2 June 1989.

10. Alfonso Ortiz, "Half a Century of Indian Administration: An Overview." In Jennie R. Joe (ed.), *American Indian Policy and Cultural Values: Conflict and Accommodation*, (Los Angeles: American Indian Studies Center, 1986).

11. Hans Baer, Merrill Singer, and John H. Johnsen, "Toward a Critical Medical Anthropology," *Social Science and Medicine* 23(2), (1986), 95.

12. J. W. Curran, H. W. Jaffe, et al., "Epidemiology of HIV Infection and AIDS in the United States," *Science* 239, (1988), 610-616.

13. M. B. Tucker, W. M. Herron, et al., *Ethnic Groups in Los Angeles: Quality of Life Indicators*, (Los Angeles: UCLA Ethnic Studies Center, 1986).

14. R. Rowell and T. Tafoya, *Acquired Immune Deficiency Syndrome: The Basics*, (Oakland, CA: National Native American AIDS Prevention Center, 1986).

15. Ron Rowell, "Native Americans: Historic Problems Hamper AIDS Prevention and Care," *NAN Multi-Cultural Notes of AIDS Education and Service* 1(11), (1988), 1.

16. Ibid.

17. Patrick Johannes and Rice C. Leach, "The Indian Health Service AIDS Prevention Program," *The IHS Primary Care Provider* 13(6), (1988), 53-57.

18. Ibid., 54.

19. Recent data indicate that minority populations, especially blacks and Latinos, are disproportionately

represented among the reported AIDS cases. Blacks and Latinos comprise 12 percent and 6 percent of the United States population, respectively, yet now account for 25 percent and 14 percent of all reported AIDS cases. Current evidence indicates that these populations are at significantly higher risk of HIV infection because of increased exposure through high-risk behaviors and lack of sufficient educational services. Behavioral evidence indicates that AIDS could impact Native American people in a similar manner. See S. R. Friedman, J. L. Sotheran, et al., "The AIDS Epidemic among Blacks and Hispanics," *The Milbank Quarterly* 65, (1987), 455-499; and Ron Rowell, "Native Americans: Historic Problems Hamper AIDS Prevention and Care," *NAN Multi-Cultural Notes of AIDS Education and Service*, 1(11), (1988).

20. Rowell, "Native Americans," (1988), 1.

21. Ibid., 2.

22. Ibid.

23. Ibid.

24. Johannes and Leach, "The Indian Health Service AIDS Prevention Program," (1988), 53-57.

25. Ibid., 55.

26. U.S. Department of Health and Human Services, *Indian Health Service Chart Series Book, April 1988*, (1988), 46.

27. Ibid., 35.

28. U.S. Congress, "Indian Alcohol and Substance Abuse Prevention and Treatment Act of 1986," *Congressional Record* H11259, (Washington, D.C.: U.S. Government Printing Office, 1986).

29. Britt Finley, *Patterns of Alcohol and Drug Related Behavior Among Missoula County Youth: Indian and Non-Indian*, (Missoula, MT: Missoula City-County Health Department, 1988), 35.

30. Office of Technology Assessment, *Indian Health Care*, (1986), 92, 95.

31. Ibid., 97.

32. Dennis W. Weidman, "Type II Diabetes Mellitus, Technological Development, and the Oklahoma Cherokee," in Hans A. Baer (ed.), *Encounters With Biomedicine*, (New York: Gordon and Breach Science Publishers, 1987), 43-71.

33. Ibid., 47-49.

34. Chuck Cook, Mike Masterson, and M. H. Trahant, "Diabetes Epidemic Linked to Sundering of Lifestyle," *The Arizona Republic*, 7, (October 1987), 19.

35. Felicia Hodge, "Disabled American Indians: A Special Population Requiring Special Considerations," *American Indian Culture and Research Journal*, 13 (3, 4), (1989).

36. Thornton, *American Indian Holocaust and Survival*, (1987), 182.

37. Abdel R. Omran, "Population Epidemiology," *American Journal of Public Health* 64 (7), (1974), 676.

38. U.S. Department of Health and Human Services, *Indian Health Service Chart Series Book, April 1988*, (1988), 15.

39. Ibid., 22.

40. Office of Technology Assessment, *Indian Health Care*, (1986), 129.

41. Laculine J. Jackson, *Minorities and Aging*, (Belmont, CA: Wadsworth Publishers, 1980); Ron C. Manuel (ed.), *Minority Aging: Sociological and Social Psychological Issues*, (Westport, CT: Greenwood Press, 1982); R. L. McNeely and John N. Colen (eds.), *Aging in Minority Groups*, (Beverly Hills, CA: Sage Publications, 1983); National Council on Aging, *Indian Elderly and Entitlement Programs: An Assessing Demonstration Project*, (Albuquerque, NM: NICOA, 1981); National Council on Aging, *Access, A Demonstration Project: Entitlement Programs for Indian Elders 1*, (Albuquerque, NM: NICOA, 1983); E. Percil Stanford and Shirley A. Lockery, eds., *Trends and Status of Minority Aging*, (San Diego, CA: Campanile Press, 1982).

42. National Council on Aging, *Indian Elderly and Entitlement Programs*, (1981); National Council on Aging, *Access, A Demonstration Project*, (1983).

43. Marilyn R. Block, "Exiled Americans: The Plight of Indian Aged in the United States." In Donald E. Gelfand and Alfred J. Kutzik (eds.), *Ethnicity and Aging*, (New York: Springer Publishers, 1979), 184.

44. U.S. Department of Health and Human Services, *Indian Health Service Chart Series Book, April 1988*, (1988), 15.

45. Robert John, "Social Policy and Planning for Aging

American Indians: Provision of Services by Formal and Informal Support Networks." In Jennie R. Joe (ed.), *American Indian Policy and Cultural Values: Conflict and Accommodation*, (Los Angeles: American Indian Studies Center, 1986), 126.

46. Ibid., 111.

47. E. Daniel Edwards, Margie E. Edwards and Geri M. Daines, "American Indian/Alaska Native Elderly: A Current and Vital Concern," *Journal of Gerontological Social Work* 2, (1980), 213-224.

48. Frank C. Dukepoo, *The Elderly American Indian*, (San Diego, CA: Campanile Press, 1975).

49. The problem of empowerment faces all elderly in the United States. For a discussion of this issue, see M. A. Mendelson, *Tender Loving Greed: How the Incredibily Lucrative Nursing Home Industry is Exploiting America's Old People*, (New York: Knopf Publishers, 1974); and B. Vladeck, *Unloving Care*, (New York: Basic Books, 1980).

50. Wynne H. DuBray, "American Indian Values: Critical Factor in Casework," *Social Casework* 66, (1985), 30-37; Jimm G. Good Tracks, "Native American Non-Interference," *Social Work* 18, (1973), 30-34; Ronald G. Lewis and Man Keung Ho, "Social Work with Native Americans," *Social Work* 20, (1975), 379-382; C. T. Goodluck and D. Short, "Working with American-Indian Parents—A Cultural Approach," *Social Casework* 61, (1980), 472-475; Taylor J. Satala, "Multi-Cultural Skill Development in the Aging Network: An Indian Perspective," in Jacob V. Gordon (ed.), *Multi-Cultural Dimensions in the Aging Network: Cross-Cultural Perspectives in Gerontology*, (Lawrence, KS: National Caucus on Black Aged, 1981).

51. Block, "Exiled Americans", (1979); Robert M. Moroney, *Families, Social Services, and Social Policy: The Issue of Shared Responsibility*, (Washington, D.C.: U.S. Government Printing Office, 1980); Steve H. Murdock and Donald F. Schwartz, "Family Structure and Use of Agency Services: An Examination of Patterns Among Elderly Native Americans," *Gerontologist* 18, (1978), 475-481; C. Jean Rogers and Teresa E. Gallion, "Characteristics of Elderly Pueblo Indians in New Mexico," *Gerontologist* 18, (1978), 482-487.

52. U.S. Department of Commerce, Bureau of the

Census, *American Indians, Eskimos and Aleuts on Identified Reservations and in the Historic Areas of Oklahoma (Excluding Urbanized Areas)*, (Washington, D.C.: U.S. Government Printing Office, 1986).

53. U.S. Department of Health and Human Services, *Indian Health Service Chart Series Book, April 1988*, (1988), 36.

54. Thornton, *American Indian Holocaust and Survival*, (1987), 235-239.

55. Alfonso Ortiz, *The Tewa World: Space, Time, Being, and Becoming in a Pueblo Society*, (Chicago: University of Chicago Press, 1969).

56. Ibid., 118.

57. Baer, Singer, and Johnsen, "Toward a Critical Medical Anthropology," (1986), 95.

Chapter VII

American Indian Mental Health Policy

Teresa D. LaFromboise

The American Indian population is culturally heterogeneous, geographically dispersed, and remarkably young. There are 200 tribal languages still spoken today. The diversity found in some 511 federally recognized native entities and an additional 365 state-recognized American Indian tribes defies distinct categorizations.[1] The 1980 census indicated that the American Indian population numbered approximately 1.5 million, nearly double the 1970 count.[2] It also verified that American Indians have become increasingly urbanized, both for subsistence and for gainful employment. In 1980, 24% of the American Indians in this country lived on reservations. The 20.4 year median age of American Indians and 17.9 year median age of Alaska Natives is significantly younger than the median age of the U.S. population in general (30.3 years).

American Indians are generally unaffected by national economic cycles; unemployment is consistently extremely high among Indians and Alaska Natives. It hovers at about 30% on most reservations and ranges from a high of over 70% on some plains reservations to a low of 20% in the case of more prosperous tribes.[3]

Poverty and prolonged unemployment have combined with substandard housing, malnutrition, inadequate health care, shortened life expectancy, and high suicide rates to affect and limit opportunities for educational attainment. American Indians and Alaska Natives 25 years and older have an average of 9.6 years of formal education. This is below the national mean of 10.9 years and is the lowest of any major ethnic group in the United States.[4] Nearly one third of all American Indian adults are classified as illiterate, and only one in five men has a high school education.[5] Dropout

120

rates between the eighth and ninth grades in some urban areas range from 48% to 85%[6] and approach 50% in Bureau of Indian Affairs boarding schools and day schools on reservations.[7] Only 16% of the American Indian students who enter universities complete an undergraduate degree, compared to 34% of their White counterparts.[8] This can undoubtedly be attributed to the stressful pressures American Indian students have experienced in the dominant White culture of higher education institutions.[9]

Although it is apparent that American Indians have shown impressive reservoirs of strength and coping mechanisms in the face of these environmental realities,[10] they experience high rates of mental health disorders associated with social stress. For example, overall rates of alcohol and drug abuse are high, but prevalence varies tremendously from tribe to tribe and by age within tribes.[11] A congressional hearing on Indian juvenile alcoholism and drug abuse reported that 52% of urban Indian adolescents and 80% of reservation Indian adolescents engaged in moderate to heavy alcohol or drug use as compared to 23% of their urban, non-Indian counterparts.[12] The hearing revealed that in some American Indian communities, children as young as four years of age can be found drinking and using inhalants.

Delinquency and arrest rates of American Indians are among the highest of any ethnic minority group in this nation.[13] American Indians in urban areas are taken into police custody for violations committed under the influence of drugs or alcohol four times as often as Blacks and ten times as often as Whites.[14] Youth are likewise arrested more often than the norm for offenses committed while under the influence of alcohol.

American Indians have been characterized as "aliens in their own land" for the past 100 years. Cultural epidemiologists claim that forced acculturation to urban living increases individuals' vulnerability for developing psychological problems.[15] Barter and Barter[16] noted the heightened stress involved when Indians adapt to the dominant culture and at the same time are forced by their choice of residency into relinquishing their sovereign rights to health, education, and welfare on reservation land.

Psychological disturbance is often primarily a reaction to life conditions, and mental illness can be a tragic manifestation of unsatisfactory adjustment to a social-psychological environment that provides few satisfactory options for human action.[17] There is a severe imbalance in favor of studies that focus on pathological disorders of American Indians to the neglect of investigations of milder transient problems and of research on familial or sociocultural antecedents of psychopathology. The most glaring gap, however, is the failure to examine the effective strategies currently employed by American Indians for coping with numerous stressors.

Only three community-wide American Indian epidemiological studies of psychopathology exist. The prevalence rates of psychological dysfunction range from a low of 1% per 2,000 to a high of 37% per 1,000; depression and adjustment reactions are the most prevalent problems.[18] Manson, Shore, and Bloom[19] recently reported that the prevalence of depression within select Indian communities may be four to six times higher than that in the studies noted above. Media attention to American Indian suicide recently stimulated national concern over a problem emphasized by service providers and researchers for quite some time.[20] The suicide rate among Indian adults is over twice as high and that of school-aged children three times greater than that of the American White majority.[21] Harras[22] reported that the annual suicide rate in some tribes has increased by about 200% in the past two decades to a rate of 18 per 100,000.

Given the magnitude of these social and psychological problems, what mental health services are currently available to American Indians?

Available Psychological Service Providers

In 1976 there was only one psychologist of any ethnic background for every 43,000 American Indian people.[23] A recent survey of psychological personnel reported that 180 American Indians held master's or doctoral degrees in psychology,[24] boosting the personnel rate to one American Indian psychologist for every 8,333 Indian people. This rate compares most unfavorably to the current availability rate of one psychologist for every 2,213 people in the general population.[25] Of those 180 self-identified American Indian psychologists, 102 reported involvement in research activities and 36 in educational activities in addition to their involvement in mental health service delivery. These figures suggest that American Indian underrepresentation in fields of applied psychology continues to be a serious concern.

Because there are so few American Indian psychologists as role models and so few psychologists serve American Indians on Indian reservations, few Indian students seriously consider university training in psychology. For example, there are currently only five American Indian American Psychological Association (APA) minority Fellows despite extensive, continuous efforts to recruit applicants. Moreover, tribal efforts at career development have placed priority on training in the medical and legal professions since the early 1970s. Finally, the Indian Health Scholarship Program only recently began to consider counseling psychology in addition to clinical psychology applications from American Indian students for clinical scholarships.

There is only one American Indian employed by the National Institute of Mental Health[26] and one by the APA.[27] Few American Indian psychologists are involved in mental health legislative decision making beyond the provision of testimonial support.[28] The Society of Indian Psychologists[29] and the National Indian Counselors Association, the two professional organizations that have emerged to articulate the need for more Indian psychologists in Indian communities, also try to counteract the high turnover rate of mental health service providers in the Indian Health Service and provide support for mental health workers who must often cope with undesirable working conditions. Members have found it advantageous to have a professional forum to articulate American Indian philosophical underpinnings within psychology as well as share strategies for the coordination of coexisting conventional and traditional Indian psychological service delivery. Members of both of these organizations frequently express difficulty in delivering psychological services to Indian clients, even to those who may come from their own tribe. Too often, educators assume that because a person is of American Indian descent, that person knows how to organize, support, and develop indigenous community resources.

Utilization of Psychological Services

The U.S. government initiated mental health programs for American Indians and Alaska Natives in 1965. By 1977, 40 reservation mental health programs were supported by the federal Indian Health Service. In that same year, there were 60,000 visits by American Indian and Alaska Native clients to outpatient facilities.[30] Forty percent of all clients who utilize the Indian Health Service mental health programs were treated for depression, anxiety, and adjustment reactions.[31] An unpublished summary of a random sample of patient caseloads in three urban health clinics indicated that 30% of the presenting complaints were attributable to mental health problems.[32] However, 55% of the American Indian clients seen in Seattle mental health centers were highly unlikely to return after their initial contact as compared to a 30% dropout rate among other groups.[33] The disparity between American Indians in need and those who use psychological services has been attributed to difference in values and expectations among practitioners and clients, but it is also due to neglect by representatives of the U.S. government and the profession of psychology itself in promoting adequate mental health services or health maintenance activities.[34]

A number of surveys suggest that American Indians in need of help are less aware of the kinds of psychological services available to them than are most Americans.[35] Even those aware of available services underutilize them because of perceptions that the existing services are unresponsive to their needs.[36] Dukepoo[37] identified fear, mistrust, and insensitivity as major barriers to mental health service utilization in the Southwest. Manson and Trimble[38] further suggested that underutilization is the result of negative attitudes toward non-Indian psychologists who are presumably insensitive to the cultural complexities of Indian problems. In some cases, tribal judges and school administrators have considered bussing Indian children in need of psychological assessment as far as 2,044 miles to assure that American Indian psychometricians could conduct the evaluation.[39] Alternatives proposed for these situations often represent attempts to link traditional community-based practices with relevant modern approaches to mental health. Realistically, however, there are many obstacles to the implementation of more effective delivery systems.

Delivery of Services

The Indian Health Service

The largest single provider of mental health services to American Indians is the Indian Health Service (IHS). The IHS annually provides inpatient and outpatient care to more than .75 million urban and rural American Indians and their family members through direct care or contract services. The Mental Health Program administrative center in Albuquerque, New Mexico administers social service and mental health programs in eight regional areas through 100 units composed of hospitals, clinics, and satellite centers.[40] Unfortunately, the IHS fails to distinguish between initial visits and repeat visits in its record keeping, which obfuscates any estimates of American Indian mental health service utilization rates.[41]

Funds appropriated for mental health services within the IHS budget for the fiscal year 1985 amounted to $10,518,000, and funds for alcoholism services amounted to $24,149,800. Together, these categories accounted for only 7.3% of the total IHS budget allocations for direct and contract care. If the Indian Health Care Improvement Act were authorized, then previously authorized awarded funds could be allocated to decrease the backlog of mental health care services, expand services to include prevention services, and provide more rehabilitative interventions for substance abuse and other problems. The presently allocated budget covers, at best, crisis intervention and emergency care.[42] For this reason, the IHS is now drafting a national plan for more culturally responsive mental health services to Indians.[43]

More services are delivered by paraprofessionals and social workers in the IHS system than by psychologists, psychiatrists, or psychiatric nurses. The stark absence of psychologists in many IHS service centers is of less concern to tribal leaders than the need for 1,500 physical health professionals (e.g., physicians, registered nurses, dentists, optometrists, audiologists, and pharmacists). The standard rationale for mental health prevention efforts—that from 60% to 70% of medical office visits among the U.S. general population are for problems primarily psychological rather than physical in nature[44]—falls on deaf ears. Also, reports of a wide range of problems for which Indian people seek services, including alcohol misuse, anxiety, depression, cultural conflict, and suicide attempts, often are overlooked.[45]

Bureau of Indian Affairs

In addition to the IHS, the Department of the Interior's Bureau of Indian Affairs (BIA) maintains 123 offices across 12 geographic areas, serving 281 tribes with a total population of approximately 649,000 people. Its community service division coordinates educational and social service branches where psychological services are also available. The educational branch is charged with consultant, advisory, and administrative responsibility for programs with American Indian youth and adults. These programs are supported by tribal and state contracts and conducted in federal boarding schools and other BIA educational and vocational guidance centers. The social service branch provides child welfare and family services, including help with problems from family disintegration and emotional instability. Unfortunately, diagnostic observations are seldom a matter of formal record keeping in the BIA, and there is little or no postreferral monitoring.

Urban Indian Health Care Programs

In the early 1970s, American Indian communities began to assume more direct control of the management and provision of health services. In 1972 the IHS began funding urban programs through its community development branch under the general authority of the Snyder Act.[46] By 1984, 37 urban health programs in 20 states were implemented on a contractual basis with the Indian Health Service. Recently, some of these programs have expanded to include as high as

20% of the fiscal expenditure for a wide range of programs designed to help urban Indians alleviate individual and family problems.[47] More innovative programs include the Seattle Indian Health Board's seminar series on traditional medicine, tribal beliefs and mental health, culture conflict, and self-awareness for service providers[48] and the San Francisco Urban Indian Health Board's weekend drop-in mental health clinic primarily for homeless clients. It is difficult to determine whether the most innovative programs are found on or off Indian reservations because urban Indian mental health programs receive more attention than reservation programs among those interested in contract care services.

State and Local Mental Health Services

The extent to which Indians use private or public mental health services is unknown. Relatively few Indians seek private care given the availability of services provided by other institutions, but cases do exist where American Indians travel substantial distances to seek services from therapists known to be effective by the Indian community. Many urban and reservation Indians are served by city, county, or state mental health facilities. The points of entry into these facilities are diverse—state hospitals, Veterans Administration hospitals, day treatment centers, other programs such as the Job Training Partnership Act Program, and families.[49] Referral activities to acquaint potential clients with the mental health services in the surrounding area are conducted by Indian centers and Indian social service programs. Unfortunately, record keeping in these service delivery agencies is also uncoordinated, complicating an assessment of client satisfaction with services or utilization patterns.

University Counseling Centers

An increasing number of American Indian university students are seeking psychological services during their academic training, especially if American Indian psychologists are available. University environments typically reinforce formal methods of seeking help. The utilization rate of American Indian students for initial visits at the University of California-Berkeley clinic was 75%.[50] Haskell Indian Junior College reported a direct referral rate of 50% and an indirect referral rate of 79% primarily for alcohol-related problems, personal counseling, and campus violations.[51] American Indian women in private university settings reported using formal psychological services when difficulties arose in their academic programs more frequently than their counterparts in state universities.[52] University students in their home environment indicate they would seek help from family members before seeking psychological services. Increased utilization of psychological services in academic settings by American Indians attests to the supportive functions of counseling in competitive educational arenas. This service use also provides an excellent opportunity to demonstrate the benefits of psychological interventions because the clientele will likely return to their communities upon completion of a degree.

Tribally Based Mental Health Care Programs

American Indian tribes residing on reservations were empowered with freedom to design a wide range of services, including mental health care, through the Indian Self-Determination and Education Assistance Act of 1975.[53] To date, 61 different tribal health programs have been established under contract to the Indian Health Service, but fewer than half of these programs have a mental health component.

The use of traditional healers who both help and heal remains a priority over all other forms of clinical treatment in several tribally based communities. In recent years there appears to have been a renaissance and revitalization of traditional healing practices.[54] A research and intervention project on the Rosebud Reservation in South Dakota was designed by Sioux medicine men in collaboration with Western psychologists and was entitled "Identity Through Traditional Lakota Methods." The psychological interventions employed were deemed successful by community members because they reinforced traditional ways of life.[55] Attneave[56] reported a successful two-way referral system between Indian

Health Service staff and traditional healers in an Eskimo village. The first director of the IHS mental health program also reported recurring evidence of successful collaboration with Navajo healers and the establishment of a school for traditional healers.[57]

Not all attempts at collaboration with traditional healers are considered successful. In fact, Dinges, Trimble, Manson, and Pasquale[58] asserted that most attempts by psychologists to establish working relationships with healers failed due to confusion regarding credibility, fee for service, professional efficacy, technical explanations, and patient expectations. Traditional community and kinship networks of support may be the most effective delivery agencies.

American Indian communities both on and off reservations have traditionally practiced informal caregiving through the extended family. Even though diverse Indian families have transformed over time because of geographic movements and intertribal marriages, relational values have remained intact, and extended family networks provide extensive psychological support.[59] Carolyn Attneave[60] saw the need to make more explicit the ongoing reciprocal support of Indian extended families with urban Indians through "network therapy." This support was necessary because their residence within the dominant culture constrained cultural activities that normally sustained network exchanges. In network therapy the focus of help giving is to mobilize the family, relatives, and friends into a socially interdependent force that can be attentive and responsive to emotional distress within the family in order to counteract the depersonalizing atmosphere of urban life. Red Horse[61] applied the cultural network model in Minneapolis with Indian adolescents in a family-as-treatment model entitled the Wido-Ako-Dade-Win Program. Political organizations also represent an important source of support. Over 200 Indian political organizations exist in the United States and Canada that provide psychological and social support, as well as support for advocacy within various levels of the government to bring about changes in everything from the treatment of American Indians in history books to increased funds for the economic development of American Indian resources. The "elders' movement" is a social network that actively seeks older people to provide religious and personal counseling.[62] The actions of these networks and political organizations reflect general American Indian value systems and beliefs, as well as particular notions concerning health.

Assumptions American Indians Hold About Psychology

American Indian communities are distinguished by many ties among tribal members and strong group cohesion, particularly in times of crisis. Indian people have concerns about psychological concepts like "mental health," "personality," and "self" because of the absence of naturalistic or holistic concepts in the design and implementation of therapeutic processes. Mental health translates in the Lakota (Sioux) language as *ta-un* (being in a state of well-being). Ta-un requires certain categories of action and introspection prior to engagement in social relations or group collective actions.[63] Among the Hopi, a person in a state of well-being is peaceful and exudes strength through self-control and adherence to the universal American Indian values of wisdom, intelligence, poise, tranquility, cooperation, unselfishness, responsibility, kindness, and protectiveness toward all life forms.[64]

Further guidance in understanding American Indian assumptions about psychology emerges from an analysis of the work of traditional healers who have challenged Western psychologists for centuries not to separate cultural ideals and practice.[65] Primeaux[66] stated that traditional medicine potentially embraces a broad spectrum of forces that are interwoven in all aspects of being. Carl Gorman stated that a traditional healer is actually a doctor, counselor, priest, and historian.[67] Additionally, a healer is viewed as a safekeeper of ancient legends, which are maintained through the power of the spoken word. The healer uses the wisdom of spiritual legends for insight into human behavior and to explain emotional and behavioral problems.[68]

Many American Indians believe that mental illness is a justifiable outcome of human weakness or the result of avoiding the discipline necessary for the maintenance of cultural values and community respect. The Coyote stories, for example, contain a theme of danger associated with excessively individualistic behavior (e.g., greed, envy, trickery). Individualization of responsibility is emphasized as a means of achieving community solidarity rather than a mechanism for personal achievement. Thus, the focus on maintaining cultural values is one way of controlling individuals' preoccupation with themselves and their personal symptoms.

American Indian psychologists generally describe only a few culturally specific categories of disease causation[69] and tend to attach diagnostic labels to clients less frequently than non-Indian psychologists.[70] When problems arise in Indian communities, they become not only problems of the individual but also problems of the community. The family, kin, and friends coalesce into a network to observe the individual, find reasons for the individual's behavior, and draw the person out of isolation and back into the social life of the group. The strong social and symbolic bonds among the extended family network maintain a disturbed individual within the community with minimal coercion.

In some cases the tribe has ritually adopted the individual suffering from mental disorders into a new clan group.[71] Disturbed individuals in certain tribes are encouraged to attend peyote meetings that involve confession of a ritualized rather than personal nature and collective discussions.[72] The cure may involve confession, atonement, restoration into the good graces of family and tribe, and intercession with the spirit world. Treatment usually involves a greater number of individuals than simply the client and healer; often the client's significant others and community members are included.

The informal resources and reciprocal exchanges of goods and services in American Indian communities diminish the impact of troubled individuals on group functioning. This system allows typically autonomous individuals sanctioned opportunities to unite in the social control of disruptive behavior. Thus, the collective treatment of psychologically troubled individuals in tribal groups not only serves to heal the individual but also to reaffirm the norms of the entire group.[73] The goal of therapy is not to strengthen the client's ego but to encourage the client to transcend the ego by experiencing the self as embedded in and expressive of community.[74] Inner motivations and unique experiences involving repression, self-esteem, ambivalence, or insight are ignored, and symptoms are transformed into elements of social categories rather than personal states. New solutions to problems or new ways to see old problems become possible through interconnectedness with the community.

American Indians who engage in individual therapy often express concern about how conventional Western psychology superimposes biases onto American Indian problems and shapes the behavior of the client in a direction that conflicts with Indian cultural life-style orientations and preferences. The incompatibility between conventional counseling approaches and indigenous approaches has been discussed by numerous writers.[75] Many American Indians recognize the need for professional assistance only when informal community-based networks are unavailable.

Assumptions Psychology Holds About American Indians

Psychologists have sought to describe, measure, and understand tribal social phenomena; discover cultural patterns; and explain the practices of diverse American Indian groups of numerous decades. Unfortunately, little has been done regarding their psychological problems other than to document them.[76] Most psychological interventions have been culturally myopic and have not accepted assumptions or procedures that could be helpful to Indian clients. Treatment reports rarely account for the functional aspects of American Indian problems, nor do they recognize the efficacy of coping interventions that have been used for centuries.

A primary difference between Western and American Indian psychology involves a difference of values. Beginning with the work of Freud, psychologists have tried to conduct therapy within a "value-free" framework. Even though the accepted view is that many of the central targets of therapy (e.g., matters of work, marriage, and adjustment) are value laden, most psychologists choose to adopt a quasi-medical, value-free position in order to avoid the diverse social and religious values of Western society.[77] In contrast, however, many well-intentioned psychologists believe that they could best help American Indians by helping them adjust to Western value systems or create a more personal value system of their own. As noted earlier, the American Indian approach to psychology assigns importance to healers and therapists as value keepers of the tribe. Much of the work of American Indian therapy centers around the process of deciphering traditional American Indian values that come into conflict with the values espoused by the dominant culture.[78]

The current U.S. mental health care system operates primarily on a scarcity paradigm regarding mental health resources, with university-trained specialists being considered the only valid healers.[79] This paradigm still holds even though professionals have argued persuasively that communities can play a vital role in promoting mental health.[80] Unfortunately, the same psychologists trained during the progressive social era of the 1960s now appear aligned with fiscal conservatives who emphasize the cost ineffectiveness of helping grass-roots institutions involved in therapeutic efforts.[81] As psychology becomes increasingly more guild oriented, its members attend to pronouncements of the zero-sum gain and restrict mental health delivery to those individuals and agencies who are properly licensed and accredited (i.e., those that are reimbursable by insurance or are supported by grants or by established social agencies).

The Euro-American tradition, on which contemporary psychology[82] is based, espouses an Aristotelian worldview that promotes dualisms, weakens community, and diminishes a sense of rootedness in time and place. The Anglo-American emphasis on personal agency has fostered material prosperity, freedom, and autonomy for the privileged classes. However, the consequences include alienation and narcissistic self-absorption.[83]

Psychology also maintains a distinction between scientific and alternative therapeutic styles.[84] Psychologists believe that working class clients rely on superstitious or physical explanations of personality problems rather than insight-oriented therapies. Para-professionals, traditional healers, and community mental health representatives who run essential programs in American Indian communities are not considered to be bona fide professionals and are often subjected to excessive scrutiny. The profession assesses techniques used by Western, licensed therapists with PhDs as scientific, whereas practices of paraprofessional and indigenous healers are considered to be "largely magical."[85]

Even the process of prevention is different between Western psychologists and American Indians.[86] Western psychologists often select high-risk clients and offer them prepackaged programs to teach them how to adjust to circumstances.[87] Thus, prevention efforts maintain a self-serving, aloof flavor unlike the transforming intention of American Indian prevention ceremonies. Further evidence of the individualistic orientation of psychology involves a reluctance to combine therapies despite the fact that consumers make pragmatic decisions to do so, often blending theoretically conflicting psychological interventions.[88] American Indian clients experience little, if any, conflict about integrating both traditional and "modern" conventional psychological approaches.[89] These distinctions must be considered in light of American Indian approaches that emanate from a holistic, community-involved perspective that implies a spiritual dimension as well.[90]

Even recently trained psychologists are quick to develop a "clinical mentality" that emphasizes action and a sense of responsibility to individual clients and professional colleagues over a service orientation to the larger community.[91] Therapy as currently practiced by American Indians is often seen by Anglo professionals as having comparative insignificance within an overall system of health care delivery. These professionals view the perceptions of the community as unimportant and focus on the therapeutic process between the client and the therapist. This therapeutic enterprise is very individualistic. It emphasizes immediate experiencing, intrapsychic processes, and individual motivation rather than community-oriented social causes of illnesses and issues of cohesiveness. Psychologists help clients develop the ego or defenses to mediate between the influences of significant others and the larger society.[92] Psychologists also tend to use the strategies common in most theoretical orientations to provide clients with new, corrective experiences and offer them direct feedback in order to somehow change their psychological and emotional lives.[93]

Currently, psychologists are trained within a university model that emphasizes lecture-dominated and cognitive-centered pedagogy. Training has conceptually changed little despite the recommendations of the Vail and Dulles conferences.[94] Trimble[95] has described this model as leaving students dramatically lacking in the necessary skills for work in unique cultural settings. A typical program in counseling and clinical psychology, for example, involves technical training in everything from principles of psychopathology to research methods, but it rarely includes training in community consultation and social change intervention or alternatives to individual intervention.[96] Courses on culturally distinct clients are relegated "to the periphery of the curriculum where they have been subject to the vagaries of faculty politics, budgetary constraints, and student activism or apathy."[97] Sandwiched in the program are clinical practicums, supervised instruction and internships, and some sort of resident practicum, which is often devoid of professional character development in areas such as empowerment, transformation, and synergy paradigms. Following the completion of course work and successful defense of a dissertation or thesis, the trainee is granted a degree (usually the doctorate). The trainee subsequently may seek a state license to practice his or her chosen profession. Such a situation, whether intentional or not, tends to inhibit the student from pursuing cross-cultural interests and subtly influences the student's socialization more solidly into the mainstream profession of psychology.

If non-Indian professionals are to be trained in American Indian cultural styles of healing, it is necessary to understand the process by which Indians become competent as healers. The process begins with the search to find a master teacher or healer willing to accept the student as an apprentice. The decision of who is trained by whom is solely decided by the two people involved. The apprenticeship process can begin as early as adolescence, and the apprenticeship can last for the full duration of training. The healer decides what tasks an apprentice is ready to perform.[98] The interaction of student and healer combines elements of course work, supervision, therapy, and scholarship.

Although apprentices receive formal education, the main structure of their education is determined by needs apparent in the apprenticeship. Classes, laboratories, and other university trappings are regarded as adjuncts, not the essence of education.

Recommendations for Policy and Action

Recruitment, Education, and Training

1. Academic institutions should make every effort to acquaint American Indians with the benefits of pursuing careers in psychology and increase and expedite the recruitment of American Indian students to psychological training programs.

2. Psychological training programs should revise their curriculum to include the impact of cultural environment and contextual effects on American Indian behavior.[99]

Course work should begin with a non-Western point of departure, relying on the history of past practice to remind students to analyze indigenous methods and learn from them prior to developing psychological interventions. The sociopolitical history that American Indians have undergone and the present impact of that history should be reviewed. Topics on social influence variables,[100] appropriate problems for presentation in therapy,[101] styles of therapeutic communication,[102] and the personal attributes of a psychologist[103] should be included.

3. The training of psychologists should include community-based practicum internships in order that psychologists develop a sensitivity to the effects of their own worldviews on American Indian clients.

Students must learn how American Indian communities are organized, supported, and developed, in order to use networking skills with them.[104] Mohatt[105] suggests a tribally based community internship year consisting of intense exposure to American Indian religious and transcendental values and experiences. Interns would study interactions among the therapist, the client, and the client's culture[106] and learn to use individuals and families as brokers, interpreters, and supporters for clients. American Indians would witness the potential of psychology to improve American Indian mental health as they interact with interns endeavoring to integrate cultural healing beliefs and psychotherapy practices.

4. Mental health service providers should build on clients' strengths while helping clients maintain their membership in social networks and remain in natural communities in the least restrictive environment.[107] The empowerment of American Indians relies on diagnostic methods that evaluate the functioning of an individual's natural support system, examines the established linkages between the natural support systems and the professional caregiving systems, and maintains respect for privacy and general collaboration. In a community-empowerment model, the community functions as the locus for services, mechanism for the development of professional and lay helping networks, foundation for the development of community-relevant mental health programming, and means of client involvement.[108]

Rappaport and Rappaport[109] recommended a two-stage process that focuses on different aspects of the disturbance process. Psychologists would treat symptoms, and traditional support systems would function to manage secondary anxiety or existential value-laden issues. The coordination of psychologists with resources in the Indian community (e.g., community volunteers, indigenous helpers, extended family resources, and other nonprofessional sources) in help-giving activities enhances organizational effectiveness. By working with already established channels of communication and power structures, psychologists could more easily increase their social influence.[110] Katz[111] recommended community empowerment through the expansion of community healing resources. He advocated a process of transformation that involves linking individuals and organizations so that disparate groups might create agreement on how to manage central issues. In order to operate within a transformational system or an empowerment system, the psychologist needs to emphasize developmental processes rather than treatment processes.

Political-Organizational Involvement

5. American Indian tribal governments must assume a more active stance in regulating the quality of psychological service provision.

McShane and Bloom[112] have recently encouraged American Indian tribes to assume a more active role in the provision of mental health services through regulatory authority of the Indian Self-Determination and Education Assistance Act of 1975. They exhorted tribes to require tribal licensure in addition to state licensure for psychologists who practice within reservations or within American Indian programs in urban areas. This procedure has already been employed, with researchers conducting investigations on reservations in the form of "scientific ordinances."[113]

Tribal licensure would allow Indian communities the control necessary to set their own priorities for development and their own criteria for competence in service provision. Presumably, tribal governments would try their best to recruit American Indian and non-Indian psychologists who meet the highest available standards, who are eligible for licensure in the surrounding vicinity, and who can move freely in bicultural, professional circles surrounding the reservation. It has been suggested that requirements for tribal licensure include prior course work or supervised experience in American Indian studies and in cross-cultural psychology. It is hoped that this approach to demonstrate firm guidance and concern by tribal governments would attract more psychological professionals to work in American Indian communities.

6. Those interested in improving the status of American Indians within psychology should become actively involved in all levels of professional and governmental organizations. Increased American Indian involvement in policy-making arenas will sensitize professionals to their needs and allow opportunities for American Indians to use their skills and knowledge in advocating for appropriate actions to redress their mental health needs. Professionals can add relevance to social policy matters by fostering coalitions between grass roots representatives and professional associations.

The formulation of mental health policy should begin with affected people articulating to officials what social policies and programs are necessary.[114] By mobilizing efforts and funding resources for improvement in these critical areas, psychologists can practice their ethical responsibility to use their clinical skills and academic knowledge to work for change in eliminating social and racial inequality.

NOTES

1. S. M. Manson and J. E. Trimble, "American Indian and Alaska Native Communities: Past Efforts, Future Inquiries." In L. R. Snauden, ed. *Reaching the Underserved: Mental Health Needs of Neglected Populations*, (Beverley Hills, CA: Sage, 1982), 143-163.

2. U.S. Department of Commerce, Bureau of the Census, *1980 Census of Population: Characteristics of the Population*, (Washington, D.C.: U.S. Department of Commerce, Bureau of the Census, May 1983).

3. U.S. Senate Select Committee on Indian Affairs, *Indian Juvenile Alcoholism and Eligibility for B.I.A. Schools* (Senate Hearing 99-286), (Washington, D.C.: U.S. Government Printing Office, 1985).

4. R. L. Brod and J. M. McQuiston, "American Indian Adult Education and Literacy: The First National Survey," *Journal of American Indian Education* 1, (1983), 1-16.

5. J. A. Price, "North American Indian Families." In C. Mendel and R. Habenstein, eds. *Ethnic Families in America*, (New York: Elsevier, 1981), 245-268.

6. D. Jacobsen, Alaskan Native High School Dropouts. A Report Prepared for Project ANNA. (ERIC Document Reproduction Service No. ED 088651, 1973).

7. T. R. Hopkins and R. L. Reedy, "Schooling and the American Indian High School Student," *BIA Education Research Bulletin* 6, (1978), 5-12; U.S. Senate Committee on Labor and Public Welfare, *Indian Education: A National Tragedy — A National Challenge*. Special Subcommittee on Indian Education Report No. 91-501. (Washington, D.C.: U.S. Government Printing Office, 1969).

8. A. W. Astin, *Minorities in American Higher Education*, (San Francisco: Jossey-Bass, 1982).

9. J. L. Edgewater, "Stress and the Navajo University Students," *Journal of American Indian Education* 20, (1981), 25-31.

10. Special Populations Subpanel on Mental Health of American Indians and Alaska Natives, *A Good Day to Live for One Million Indians*, (Washington, D.C.: U.S. Government Printing Office, 1978).

11. P. Mail and P. R. McDonald, *Tulapai to Tokay, A Bibliography of Alcohol Use and Abuse Among Native Americans of North America*, (New Haven, CT: HRAF, 1980); E. R. Oetting, B. A. Edwards, G. S. Goldstein and V. G. Mason, "Drug Use Among Adolescents of Five Southwestern Native American Tribes," *The International Journal of Addictions* 15 (1980), 439-445.

12. U.S. Senate Select Committee on Indian Affairs, *Indian Juvenile Alcoholism and Eligibility for B.I.A. Schools*, (1985).

13. U.S. Department of Justice, Federal Bureau of Investigations, *Crime in the United States 1972: Uniform Crime Reports*, (Washington, D.C.: U.S. Government Printing Office, 1976).

14. Jepsen, G. F., J. H. Strauss and V. W. Harris, "Crime, Delinquency and the American Indian," *Human Organization* 36, (1977), 252-257.

15. L. S. Kemnitzer, "Adjustment and Value Conflict in Urbanizing Dakota Indians Measured by Q-Sort Technique," *American Anthropologist* 29, (1974), 441-449; G. D. Spindler and L. S. Spindler, "Identity, Militancy and Cultural Congruence: The Menomonee and Kainai," *Annals of the American Academy* 436, (1978) 73-85.

16. E. R. Barter and J. T. Barter, "Urban Indians and Mental Health Problems," *Psychiatric Annals* 4, (1974), 37-43.

17. P. H. DeLeon, "Psychology and the Carter Administration," *American Psychologist* 32, (1977) 750-751.

18. C. Roy, A. Chaudhuri and O. Irvine, "The Prevalence of Mental Disorders Among Saskachewan Indians," *Journal of Cross-Cultural Psychology* 1, (1970), 383-392; B. M. Sampath, "Prevalence of Psychiatric Disorders in a Southern Baffin Island Eskimo Settlement," *Canadian Psychiatric Association Journal* 19, (1974), 363-367; J. H. Shore, J. D. Kinzie, D. Thompson and E. M. Pattison, "Psychiatric

Epidemiology of an Indian Village," *Psychiatry* 36 (1973), 70-81.

19. S. Manson, J. Shore and J. Bloom, "The Depressive Experience in American Indian Communities: A Challenge for Psychiatric Theory and Diagnosis." In A. Kleinman and B. Good (eds.), *Culture and Depression* (Berkeley: University of California Press, 1985), 331-368.

20. "Suicides of Young Indians Called Epidemic," *New York Times*, (1985, October 6), 4.

21. U.S. Congress, Office of Technology Assessment, *Indian Health Care*, (OTA-H-290) (Washington, D.C.: U.S. Government Printing Office, 1986).

22. A. Harras, *Issues in Adolescent Indian Health: Suicide* (Division of Medical Systems Research and Development Monograph Series) (Washington, D.C.: U.S. Department of Health and Human Services, 1987).

23. W. Welch, "Wanted: An American Indian Psychologist," *Behavior Today*, (1976, April), 2, 3.

24. J. Stapp, A. M. Tucker and G. R. VandenBos, "Census of Psychological Personnel: 1983," *American Psychologist* 40, (1985), 1317-1351.

25. This figure was arrived at by dividing the 1980 U.S. population of 226 million people by Stapp, Tucker, and VandenBos's (1985) estimate of 102,101 available psychological personnel.

26. Raglin, personal communication, July 15, 1986.

27. J. Jones, personal communication, April 4, 1986.

28. P. Zell, personal communication, May 2, 1986.

29. T. LaFromboise, "Special Commentary from the Society of Indian Psychologists," *American Indian Alaska Native Mental Health Research* 1, (1987), 51-53.

30. M. Beiser and C. Attneave, "Mental Health Services for American Indians: Neither Feast Nor Famine," *White Cloud Journal* 1, (1978), 3-10.

31. E. R. Rhodes, M. Marshall, C. L. Attneave, M. Echohawk, J. Bjork and M. Beiser, "Mental Health Problems of American Indians Seen in Outpatient Facilities of the Indian Health Service," *Public Health Reports* 96 (1980), 329-335.

32. American Indian Health Care Association, *Six Studies Concerning the Assessment of Mental Health Needs in*

the Minneapolis-St. Paul Area: A Summary, (Unpublished manuscript, American Indian Health Care Association, Minneapolis, MN, 1978).

33. S. Sue, "Community Mental Health Services to Minority Groups: Some Optimism, Some Pessimism," *American Psychologist* 32, (1977), 616-624.

34. D. Liberman and R. Knegge, "Health Care Provider-Consumer Communication in the Miccosukee Indian Community," *White Cloud Journal* 1, (1979), 5-13.

35. N. Dinges, J. Trimble, S. Manson and F. Pasquale, "The Social Ecology of Counseling and Psychotherapy with American Indians and Alaska Natives." In A. Marsella and P. Pedersen (Eds.), *Cross-cultural Counseling and Psychotherapy*, (New York: Pergamon Press, 1981), 243-276; J. G. Red Horse, R. L. Lewis, M. Feit and J. Decker, "Family Behavior of Urban American Indians," *Social Casework* 59, (1978), 67-72; J. E. Trimble, S. M. Manson, N. G. Dinges and B. Medicine, "American Indian Concepts of Mental Health: Reflections and Directions." In P. Pedersen, N. Sartorius and A. Marsella (Eds.), *Mental Health Services: The Cross Cultural Context* (Beverly Hills, CA: Sage, 1984), 199-220.

36. Barter and Barter, "Urban Indians and Mental Health Problems," (1974), 37-43.

37. P. C. Dukepoo, *The Elder American Indian*, (San Diego, CA: Campanile, 1980).

38. S. M. Manson and J. E. Trimble, *American Indian and Alaska Native Communities: Past Efforts, Future Inquiries*, (1982), 143-163.

39. R. LaFromboise, personal communication, July 10, 1980.

40. J. L. Schultz, *White Medicine Indian Lives...As Long as the Grass Shall Grow...*, (Fort Collins: Colorado St. University, 1976).

41. W. B. Hunter, personal communication, July 23, 1986.

42. U.S. Committee on Interior and Insular Affairs, Reauthorizing and Amending the Indian Health Care Improvement Act, (House of Representatives Report No. 99-94), (Washington, D.C.: U.S. Government Printing Office, 1985).

43. S. Nelson, personal communication, September 8,

1987.

44. H. Dörken and Associates, *The Professional Psychologist Today: New Developments in Law, Health Insurance, and Health Practices*, (San Francisco, CA: Jossey-Bass, 1976).

45. Rhodes, Marshall, Attneave, Echhawk, Bjork and Beiser, "Mental Health Problems of American Indians Seen in Outpatient Facilities of the Indian Health Service," (1980), 329-335.

46. Snyder Act, 25 U.S.C. 13 (1921).

47. U.S. Congress, Office of Technology Assessment, *Survey of Urban Indian Health Programs*, (Internal Document) (Washington, D.C.: U.S. Government Printing Office, 1985).

48. J. S. Putnam, *Indian and Alaska Native Mental Health Seminars: Summarized Proceedings*, (Seattle, WA: Seattle Indian Health Board, 1982).

49. Manson and Trimble, "American Indian and Alaska Native Communities," (1982), 143-163.

50. A. Uemura, personal communication, July 10, 1986.

51. B. Smith, personal communication, July 8, 1986.

52. T. LaFromboise, *Bicultural Competence for American Indian Self-Determination*. Paper presented at the Thirteenth Annual McDaniel Conference, Stanford, CA, (June 1986).

53. Indian Self-Determination and Education Assistance Act, Pub. L. No. 93-638 (1975).

54. C. L. Attneave, "Medicine Men and Psychiatrists in the Indian Health Service," *Psychiatric Annals* 4, (1974), 37-43; G. V. Mohatt, *Cross-Cultural Perspectives on Prevention and Training: The Healer and Prevention*, paper presented at the Meeting of the American Psychological Association, Los Angeles, CA (August 1985).

55. G. V. Mohatt and A. W. Blue, "Primary Prevention as it Relates to Traditionality and Empirical Measures of Social Deviance." In S. M. Manson (ed.), *New Directions in Prevention Among American Indian and Alaska Native Communities* (Portland, OR; National Center for American Indian and Alaska Native Mental Health Research, 1982), 91-116.

56. Attneave, "Medicine Men and Psychiatrists in the

Indian Health Service," (1974), 37-43.

57. R. L. Bergman, "The Medicine Men of the Future — Reuniting the Learned Professions." In A. B. Tulipan, C. L. Attneave and E. Kingston (Eds.) *Beyond Clinic Walls*, (University, AL: University of Alabama Press, 1974), 131-143.

58. Dinges, Trimble, Manson, and Pasquale, "The Social Ecology of Counseling and Psychotherapy with American Indians and Alaska Natives," (1981), 243-276.

59. Red Horse, Lewis, Feit and Decker, "Family Behavior of Urban American Indians," (1978), 67-72.

60. C. L. Attneave, "Therapy in Tribal Settings and Urban Network Intervention," *Family Process* 8, (1969), 192-210.

61. Y. Redhorse, "A Cultural Network Model: Perspectives for Adolescent Services and Paraprofessional Training." In S. M. Manson (Ed.), *New Directions in Prevention Among American Indian and Alaska Native Communities*, (Portland, OR: National Center for American Indian and Alaska Native Mental Health Research, 1982), 173-185.

62. Price, "North American Indian Families," (1981), 245-268.

63. B. Medicine, "New Roads to Coping — Siouan Sobriety." In S. Manson (Ed.), *New Directions in Prevention Among American Indian and Alaska Native Communities*, (Portland, OR: National Center for American Indian and Alaska Native Mental Health Research), 91-116

64. J. E. Trimble, "Value Differentials and Their Importance in Counseling American Indians." In P. Pedersen, J. Draguns, W. Loner, and J. Trimble (Eds.), *Counseling Across Cultures*, (Honolulu: University Press of Hawaii, 1981), 203-226.

65. P. F. Dell, "The Hopi Family Therapist and The Aristotelian Parents," *Journal of Marital and Family Therapy*, 6, (1980), 123-130.

66. M. H. Primeaux, "American Indian Health Care Practices: A Cross Cultural Perspective," *Nursing Clinics of North America* 12, (1977), 55-65.

67. H. Greenberg and G. Greenberg, *Carl Gorman's World*, (Albuquerque: University of New Mexico Press, 1984).

68. W. K. Powers, *Yuwipi, Vision and Experience in*

Oglala Ritual, (Lincoln: University of Nebraska Press, 1982).

69. Trimble, Manson, Dinges and Medicine, "American Indian Concepts of Mental Health," (1984), 199-220.

70. A. V. Horowtiz, *The Social Control of Mental Illness*, (New York: Academic Press, 1982); D. R. Kelso and C. L. Attneave, *Bibliography of North American Indian Mental Health*, (Westport, CT: Greenwood Press, 1981).

71. J. R. Fox, "Witchcraft and Clanship in Cochiti Therapy." In A. Kiev (Ed.), *Magic, Faith, and Healing: Studies in Primitive Psychiatry Today*, (New York: Free Press, 1964).

72. For specific examples, see A. Wallace, "Dreams and Wishes of the Soul: A Type of Psychoanalytic Theory Among Seventeenth Century Iroquois," *American Anthropologist* 60, (1958), 234-248.

73. B. Kaplan and D. Johnson, "The Social Meaning of Navajo Psychology." In A. Kiev (Ed.), *Magic, Faith, and Healing*, (New York: Free Press, 1964), 203-229.

74. R. Katz and E. Rolde, "Community Alternatives to Psychotherapy," *Psychotherapy Theory, Research, and Practice* 18, (1981), 365-374.

75. L. Jilek-Aall, "The Western Psychiatrist and his Non-Western Clientele," *Canadian Psychiatric Association Journal* 21, (1976), 252-257; J. E. Trimble, "American Indian Mental Health and the Role of Training for Prevention." In S. M. Manson (Ed.), *New Directions in Prevention Among American Indian and Alaska Native Communities*, (Portland: Oregon Health Sciences University, 1982), 147-168; J. E. Trimble and T. LaFromboise, "American Indians and the Counseling Process: Culture, Adaptation, and Style." In P. Pedersen (Ed.), *Handbook of Cross-Cultural Mental Health Services*, (Beverly Hills, CA: Sage, 1985), 127-134.

76. T. LaFromboise and B. Plake, "Toward Meeting the Educational Research Needs of American Indians," *Harvard Educational Review* 53, (1983), 45-51; J. E. Trimble, "The Sojourner in the American Indian Community: Methodological Issues and Concerns," *Journal of Social Issues* 33, (1977), 159-174.

77. H. Rappaport and M. Rappaport, "The Integration of Scientific and Traditional Healing," *American Psychologist* 36, (1981), 774-781.

78. J. E. Trimble, "Value Differentials and their Importance in Counseling American Indians," (1981), 203-226.

79. R. Katz, "Healing and Transformation: Perspectives on Development, Education and Community." In M. White and S. Pollack (Eds.), *The Cultural Transition: Human Experience and Social Transformation in the Third World and Japan*, (London: Routledge and Kegan Paul, 1986), 41-64.

80. C. Jung, *Two Essays on Analytical Psychology* (Princeton, N.J.: Princeton University Press, 1972); J. Rappaport, "In Praise of Paradox: A Social Policy of Empowerment over Prevention," *American Journal of Community Psychology* 9, (1981), 1-25; S. Sarason, *The Psychological Sense of Community: Prospects for a Community Psychology*, (San Francisco, CA: Jossey-Bass, 1977).

81. Rappaport, "In Praise of Paradox," (1981), 1-25.

82. J. T. Spence, "Achievement American Style: The Rewards and Costs of Individualism," *American Psychologist* 40, (1985), 1285-1295.

83. R. N. Bellah, R. Madsen, W. Sullivan, A. Swidler and S. M. Tipton, *Habits of the Heart*, (Berkeley, CA: University of California Press, 1985).

84. E. F. Torrey, "What Western Psychotherapists Can Learn from Witch Doctors," *American Journal of Orthopsychiatry* 42, (1972), 69-76.

85. A. E. Hippler, "Thawing Out Some Magic," *Mental Hygiene* 59, (1975), 24.

86. M. Robbins, "Project Nak-nu-we-sha: A Preventive Intervention in Child Abuse and Neglect Among a Pacific Northwest Indian Community." In S. M. Manson (Ed.), *New Directions In Prevention Among American Indians and Alaska Native Communities*, (Portland: Oregon Health Sciences University, 1982), 233-248; J. H. Shore and W. M. Nichols, "Indian Children and Tribal Group Homes: New Interpretations of the Whippler Man," *American Journal of Psychiatry* 132, (1975), 454-456.

87. J. Rappaport, "In Praise of Paradox: A Social Policy of Empowerment Over Prevention," *American Journal of Community Psychology* 9, (1981), 1-25.

88. Katz and Rolde, "Community Alternatives to Psychotherapy," (1981), 365-374.

89. G. G. Meyer, "On Helping the Casualties of Rapid Change," *Psychiatric Annals* 4, (1974), 44-48.

90. Katz, "Healing and Transformation," (1986), 41-64; Mohatt, "Cross-Cultural Perspectives on Prevention and Training," (August 1985).

91. M. S. Goldstein and D. J. Donaldson, "Exporting Professionalism: A Case Study of Medical Education," *Journal of Health and Social Behavior* 20, (1979), 322-337.

92. J. D. Frank, *Persuasion and Healing: A Comparative Study of Psychotherapy*, (Baltimore, MD: Johns Hopkins University Press, 1973).

93. W. Schofield, *Psychotherapy: The Purchase of Friendship*, (Englewood Cliffs, NJ: Prentice-Hall, 1964), 994.

94. T. J. Boll, "Graduate Education in Psychology: Time for Change?" *American Psychologist* 40, (1985), 1029-1030; Dulles Conference Task Force, *Expanding The Roles of Culturally Diverse Peoples in the Profession of Psychology*, (Report Submitted to the Board of Directors of the American Psychological Association, Washington, D.C.: American Psychological Association, 1978); M. Korman, "National Conference on Levels and Patterns of Professional Training in Psychology," *American Psychologist* 29, (1974), 441-449.

95. J. E. Trimble, "American Indian Mental Health and the Role of Training for Prevention," (1982), 150.

96. D. Atkinson, "Selections and Training for Human Rights Counseling," *Counselor Education Supervision* 21, (1981), 101-108.

97. J. T. Gibbs, "Can We Continue to be Color-Blind and Class-Bound?" *The Counseling Psychologist* 13, (1985), 426.

98. Bergman, "The Medicine Men of the Future," (1974), 131-143.

99. J. Trimble, T. LaFromboise, D. Mackey, and G. France, "American Indians, Psychology and Curriculum Development: A Proposal Reform with Reservations." In J. Chunn, P. Dunston, and F. Ross-Sheriff (Eds.), *Mental Health and People of Color*, (Washington, D.C.: Howard University Press, 1982), 43-64.

100. T. LaFromboise and D. Dixon, "American Indian Perceptions of Trustworthiness in a Counseling Interview,"

Journal of Counseling Psychology 28, (1981), 135-139.

101. A. W. Blue, "A Study of Native Elders and Student Needs," *B.I.A. Education Research Bulletin* 5, (1977), 15-24; Dauphnais, LaFromboise and Rowe, "Perceived Problems and Sources of Help for American Indian Students," (1980), 37-46.

102. P. Dauphnais, T. LaFromboise and W. Rowe, "Effects of Race and Communication Style on Indian Perceptions of Counselor Effectiveness," *Counselor Education and Supervision* 20, (1981), 72-80.

103. M. G. Haviland, R. K. Hosswill, J. T. O'Connell and V. V. Dynneson, "Native American College Students' Preference for Counselor Race and Sex and the Likelihood of their Use of a Counseling Center," *Journal of Counseling Psychology* 30, (1983), 267-270.

104. L. M. Brammer, "Nonformal Support in Cross-Cultural Counseling and Therapy." In P. Pedersen (Ed.), *Handbook of Cross-Cultural Counseling and Therapy*, (Westport, CT: Greenwood Press, 1985), 87-92.

105. See, T. LaFromboise and J. Trimble, "Counseling intervention and American Indian tradition: An integrative approach," *The Counseling Psychologist*, (in press).

106. P. Lenrow, "Dilemmas of Professional Helping: Continuities and Discontinuities with Folk Helping Relationships." In L. Wispe (Ed.), *Altruism, Sympathy, and Helping*, (New York: Academic Press, 1978), 263-290.

107. President's Commission on Mental Health, *Task Panel Report to the President* (Vols. 1-4) (Washington, D.C.: U.S. Government Printing Office, 1978).

108. D. E. Biegel and A. J. Naparstek (Eds.), *Community Support Systems and Mental Health*, (New York: Springer, 1982).

109. Rappaport and Rappaport, "The Integration of Scientific and Traditional Healing," (1981), 774-781.

110. Kiesler, C. A. "Mental Health Policy as a Field of Inquiry for Psychology," *American Psychologist* 35, (1980), 1066-1080.

111. R. Katz, "Employment and Synergy: Expanding the Community's Healing Resources," *Prevention in Human Services* 3, (1983-1984), 201-225.

112. D. McShane and J. Bloom, *Transcultural Training and Service Delivery: Training and Certifying of Mental*

Health Professionals. Unpublished manuscript, Oregon Health Sciences University, Portland, OR.

113. B. Efrat and M. Mitchell, "The Indian and the Social Scientist: Contemporary Contractual Arrangements on the Pacific Northwest Coast," *Human Organization* 33, (1974), 405-407.

114. R. F. Elmore, "Backward Mapping: Implementation Research and Policy Decisions," *Political Science Quarterly* 80, (1979), 601-612.

Chapter VIII

Resource Rights

For thousands of years before the arrival of Europeans on the North American continent, Native Americans enjoyed lives of comfort without harming the natural environment. To natives, growth which sacrifices any portion of the natural world has always been considered illogical and illegitimate. Non-native North American culture, however, is based upon a very different land ethic and economic system. European settlers immediately envisioned endless expansion, exploitation, and economic growth. "Manifest Destiny" was the United States' battle cry for the nineteenth century.

As non-native Americans expanded westward, native populations found themselves pushed with the frontier, until no frontier existed. At that point, the Federal Government of the United States concentrated on native lands which it considered to be unnecessary for the non-native economy's endless growth process. Ironically, many of these native reservation lands have since been found to contain considerable natural resource wealth.

Predictably, the Federal Government has allowed, even encouraged, large private corporations to contract with these native populations for the extraction of oil, uranium, low-sulfur coal, and other extremely valuable resources. Sixty percent of America's uranium reserves, for instance, are found under Native Americans' reserved lands. The supposed needs of the ever-expanding American economy seem to dictate that further expropriation of Indian lands must take place. The process of expansion which began with the first American settlers has continued to this day, and the natural environment has been the victim.

Valuable grazing lands, water rights, fishing waters, oil, uranium, and coal reserves are currently being depleted within native territories by the large companies which seldom take the needs of native populations into consideration. Natives are paid rates far below market value for the rights to their resources, and they are often left to deal with terrible environmental degradation once the companies leave. High rates of cancer plague Indian nations whose lands have been mined for uranium, for instance. Native American communities remain impoverished, lose their resources, suffer health risks, and see the lands they love ravaged in the process. The "Four Corners" Indian territory of Utah, Arizona, Colorado, and New Mexico, and the Black Hills Indian region of the Dakotas, which together constitute about ten percent of the United States' land area, are currently treated as "national sacrifice areas," where toxins are dumped, resources are irresponsibly extracted, waters are polluted and depleted, and environments are made uninhabitable for mankind.

150

Thus, Native American peoples find themselves in a no-win situation. If their lands contain no highly valuable resources, they reman impoverished, with little leverage or opportunity to improve their economic situations. Likewise, if their lands contain resources valuable to the non-native economy, their lands are likely to be degraded, without an appreciable improvement in native American economic prospects.

—RNW

Native American Control of Tribal Natural Resource Development in the Context of the Federal Trust and Tribal Self-Determination

Mark Allen

I. INTRODUCTION

When the United States and the Indian Tribes entered into treaties last century, in exchange for the tribes' land the government promised protection and assistance.[1] The fulfillment of this promise is the historic trust owed by the federal government to the tribes.[2] Today, the trust still plays a role, and the official federal policy supports tribal self-determination.[3] One manifestation of this policy is the recent set of amendments to environmental protection statutes[4] that grant the tribes a role in reservation regulation.[5] This manifestation of the federal policy supporting tribal self-determination is particularly fitting because a number of tribes are leasing their land for the development of natural resources,[6] and these amendments offer some ways to control such development, control that for several reasons often seems beyond the tribes' capacities. The control of such development is crucial to the tribes' quest for economic self-determination.

This Comment first examines the historic trust and the history of federal-tribal relations, including the present era of the official federal policy encouraging tribal self-determination. The Comment then explores recent amendments to environmental protection statutes that permit the tribes a new role, tribal natural resource development under the auspices of the federal government and the problems therein, and the role of the United States

Environmental Protection Agency in facilitating tribal self-regulation. The Comment then considers President Reagan's Indian policies and the general position of reservation economies. This Comment ultimately suggests ways of improving the tribes' self-determination posture through increasing tribal control over reservation resource development.

II. THE HISTORIC TRUST AND THE HISTORY OF FEDERAL GOVERNMENT-INDIAN RELATIONS

The European colonial powers that explored this continent, and later the United States government, entered into many treaties with various Indian tribes.[7] Under mounting pressure from the government, the tribes surrendered their lands.[8] The Indians understood that, in exchange for their land, they were to receive services relating to education, health, welfare, and economic development.[9] This exchange included a guarantee by the United States government to give the Indians certain lands for the sole use and benefit of the Indian people forever.[10] This guarantee is commonly known as the historic trust that the federal government holds for the tribes.[11]

The trust has three basic characteristics.[12] First, the trust covers a wide range of areas, from protection and enhancement of Indian trust resources[13] and tribal self-government to social and economic programs designed to raise the Indians' standard of living.[14] Second, the trust extends to individuals as well as to tribes in general.[15] Third, the responsibility to honor the trust applies to all federal agencies, not only to those charged specifically with administering tribal affairs.[16]

The federal government, as trustee, can be liable for breach of the trust.[17] The government's liability, however, is limited.[18] Although the federal government exercises a general fiduciary relationship with the tribes that governs federal-tribal relations, liability only attaches in cases where the trust responsibility breached is one where the federal government clearly plays a specific dominant role.[19] In "United States v. Mitchell," for example, the Supreme Court found the federal government liable to the Quinault Tribe for damages for mismanaging the harvesting of the tribe's timber, a specific fiduciary duty.[20]

The federal government continues to invoke the trust today.[21] President Reagan spoke of the trust in his 1983 Statement on Indian Policy: "[W]e shall continue to fulfill the federal trust responsibility for the physical and financial resources we hold in trust for the tribes and their members. The fulfillment of this unique responsibility will be accomplished in accordance with the highest standards."[22]

Despite the presence of the trust, federal-tribal relations have not been consistent. The history of federal-tribal relations has evolved through several stages, each distinguishable by the government's attitude and action toward the tribes. These stages alternate between federal government respect for tribal self-determination and federal attempts to assimilate the tribes into mainstream American society.[23]

In 1831, Chief Justice Marshall wrote for the Supreme Court in "Cherokee Nation v. Georgia" that the Cherokee tribe was in effect a state, a distinct political society separate from others, and was therefore able to manage its own affairs and govern itself.[24] In "Cherokee Nation," Marshall recognized that the Cherokee had indeed "been uniformly treated as a state from the [time of the] settlement of our country."[25] Despite this recognition, however, the Court denied the Cherokee claim to status as an independent nation.[26] The Court stated that the tribes were not foreign nations but rather were "domestic dependent nations."[27]

One year after the "Cherokee Nation" decision, the Court in "Worcester v. Georgia" stated that the laws of the state of Georgia had no effect in Cherokee territory.[28] Significantly, the Court ignored the wishes of the State of Georgia and recognized the Cherokee tribeal sovereignty to the state's exclusion.[29] Justice Marshall stated:

> The Cherokee Nation, then, is a distinct community, occupying its own territory, with boundaries accurately described, in which the laws of Georgia can have no force, and which the citizens of Georgia have no right to enter, but with the assent of the Cherokees themselves or in

conformity with treaties, and with the acts of Congress.[30]

"Worcester" and "Cherokee Nation" set the framework of federal Indian law that remains to this day. Within this framework, Indian policy is the prerogative of the federal government and the tribes are sovereign entities "with inherent powers of self-government."[31]

The tribal right of self-government, however, did not serve to protect the tribes from white encroachment. Even though the case law remained essentially undisturbed for more than a century after Marshall's opinions, the federal government has since that time inconsistently supported tribal self-government.[32] Congress and the Executive branch have alternated between policies supportive of tribal self-government and those facilitating the alienation of Indian lands and the termination of tribes' official recognition and status.[33]

In the late 19th and early 20th centuries, the goal of the United States government was to assimilate Indians into mainstream American society.[34] Central to this policy was separating the Indians from their tribal-held land.[35] The government gave individual Indians land, interests known as allotments,[36] in exchange for the allottee's interest in the tribal estate.[37] Humanitarian reformers supported this method of terminating tribal existence because they were convinced that the Indian could and should participate fully in the American system.[38] Between 1887 and 1934, the Indians sold two-thirds of their land allotted under this method.[39] The federal government's role in this mass disenfranchisement was to increase the ease with which the Indians could sell or lease their land.[40]

Congress enacted the Indian Reorganization Act (IRA)[41] in 1934 as a result of a new attitude[42] toward the tribes. Specifically, the new attitude resulted from an emerging historical and anthropological respect for the tribes, in contrast to the previous desire to see Native Americans wholly assimilated into mainstream America.[43] Congress specifically intended the IRA to encourage Indian tribes to revitalize their self-government.[44] The IRA provided a congressional sanction of tribal self-government under which the tribes could adopt a constitution and enter into negotiations with local, state, and federal governments.[45] Many of these constitutions, however, were standard boilerplate documents "prepared by the Bureau of Indian Affairs (BIA)[46] and based on federal constitutional and common law notions rather than on tribal custom."[47] The good intentions of Congress notwithstanding, then, this procedure was a form of assimilation, because tribal custom was not the basis of the written constitutions.[48] In addition, the federal government did not realize that only a minority of tribal members, consisting of those members who had already assimilated, supported the newly sanctioned tribal councils.[49]

Assimilation and termination have recurred in a number of forms, some of them benign.[50] Examples include the education by missionaries and the present-day leasing of land to energy companies in exchange for royalties and jobs.[51] Given that traditional tribal existence in most cases was no longer possible, self-determination under the white man's tutelage was the best available course of action to preserve the tribes as cultural entities. The IRA signalled the beginning of the modern era of federal-tribal relations, characterized by support of Indian self-government and self-determination.[52]

Unfortunately for the development of tribal self-government and self-determination, congressional and executive branch opponents of the IRA policies, citing the expense and dubious nature of the programs, had by the mid-1940s, shifted the emphasis of federal Indian policy back to assimilation.[53] In the early 1950s, termination of many tribes' official status accomplished this pre-IRA directive of assimilation.[54] Congress also enacted Public Law 280 (PL 280),[55] which gave many of the states criminal[56] and civil[57] jurisdiction over Indian lands. Previously, the federal government had exercised such jurisdiction exclusive of the states.[58]

Later in the decade, however, the Supreme Court ruled more favorably for the interests of Indian self-determination. In the 1959 case of "Williams v. Lee,"[59] the Court emphasized that the basic policy of "Worcester v. Georgia"[60] was still in effect, that policy being that the tribes were to be respected as sovereign, distinct communities occupying their own territory under federal, not state, jurisdiction.[61] The Court did state, however, that the "Worcester" principles would be modified "in cases where essential tribal relations were not involved and the rights of Indians would not be jeopardized."[62] The federal policies in effect at this time reflected the changes since "Worcester," not the continuation of the "Worcester" principles. Assimilation, termination, and PL 280 clearly jeopardized essential tribal relations and the rights of Indians.[63] For example, taking away a tribe's official recognition is the opposite of recognizing a tribe as a distinct political society that is able to manage its own affairs.

This contradiction between the stated continuation of the recognition of tribal self-determination and the reality of federal policy lessened in the 1960s with the advent of the self-determination era, which continues to the present time.[64] The federal government began to actively "promote the practical exercise of inherent sovereign powers possessed by Indian tribes."[65] This policy change reflected the increased public concern for minorities' civil rights[66] and the reform-oriented presidential administrations of that decade.[67]

The tribes themselves were very much in favor of increasing their role in self-governance. Early in the modern self-determination era, in June of 1961, representatives from sixty-seven tribes adopted the "Declaration of Indian Purpose," calling for a change in the federal administration of Indian affairs.[68] "The Indians, as responsible individual citizens, as responsible tribal representatives, and as responsible tribal councils, want to participate, want to contribute to their own personal tribal improvements and want to cooperate with their Government on best how to solve the many problems . . . ."[69]

A statutory landmark during the modern self-determination era of Native American-federal government relations was the 1968 Indian Civil Rights Act (ICRA).[70] According to the Supreme Court, which interpreted the congressional purpose of ICRA in "Martinez v. Santa Clara Pueblo,"[71] the Act contained two competing purposes.[72] In addition to granting individual tribal members rights against tribal governments similar to some of the rights granted in the first ten and fourteenth amendments to the United States Constitution, Congress intended ICRA to promote the well-established federal policy of furthering Indian self-government.[73] In "Martinez," the Court held that the latter purpose prevailed over the former.[74] Thus the Court held that ICRA promoted tribal self-determination.

A more recent statute affecting the self-determination of the tribes is the Indian Self-Determination and Education Assistance Act (IS-DEAA).[75] In 1975, Congress enacted ISDEAA after reviewing the federal government's historical relationship with, and resulting responsibilities to, the American Indian people. This Act recognized that

> (1) the prolonged Federal domination of Indian service programs has served to retard rather than enhance the progress of Indian people and their communities by depriving Indians of the full opportunity to develop leadership skills crucial to the realization of self-government, and has denied to the Indian people an effective voice in the planning and implementation of programs for the benefit of Indians which are responsive to the true needs of Indian communities; and
> (2) the Indian people will never surrender their desire to control their relationships both among themselves and with non-Indian governments, organizations, and persons.[76]

ISDEAA represented Congress' recognition of the tribes' desires to control their own destinies.[77] Various groups such as national task forces, commissions, and congressional committees had investigated reservation living conditions and had brought the need for new legislation to the attention of Congress.[78] These investigations uncovered many problems, such as poor health care and poor education.[79] Presidents Johnson and Nixon both recognized the need to address these problems.[80]

ISDEAA is only one manifestation among many of the federal government's policy supporting Indian self-determination and self-government. Other manifestations include court holdings,[81] statutes,[82] and policy statements.[83] This language affirming tribal self-determination had been used in Supreme Court decisions in the 1830s[84] as well as in

1980s policy statements of the Reagan Administration.[85] Thus, the federal government has made very clear its policy of promoting tribal self-determination. Unfortunately, the federal government has inconsistently promoted this tribal right, and the future of tribal self-determination remains uncertain.

In the 1970s and 1980s, the Supreme Court has handed down inconsistent holdings affecting the jurisdictional rights and the self-determination prospects of Indians.[86] Most of the cases address the encroachment of state jurisdiction into Indian affairs.[87] The Court has clouded Marshall's mandate[88] despite its reaffirmation in "Williams."[89] As a result, there is no longer a clear federal prerogative of jurisdiction over Indian lands to the exclusion of the states.[90]

The doctrine of pre-emption has replaced exclusive federal jurisdiction over Indian lands.[91] State law applies unless pre-empted by federal law:[92] "[T]he trend has been away from the idea of inherent Indian sovereignty as a bar to state jurisdiction and toward reliance on federal pre-emption."[93] In upholding the pre-emption doctrine, the Court ignores the tradition of interpretation of treaties and statutes in favor of the right of tribal self-government.[94]

Although the behavior of the federal government in meeting its trust duties to the tribes has been questionable, the states are less suitable to exercise jurisdiction over the tribes.[95] As one commentator has observed, "[f]rom the earliest days of this Republic, local interests have placed the greatest pressures on Congress to limit the land bases and powers of tribal governments."[96] To allow state encroachment upon the tribes, endangering Indian sovereignty, could represent a violation of the federal government's trust responsibility.

In 1978, the Supreme Court struck down tribal jurisdiction over crimes committed by non-Indians on reservations.[97] The Court, in "Oliphant v. Suquamish Indian Tribe,"[98] held that tribal courts do not have inherent criminal jurisdiction to try and to punish non-Indians, and that only Congress could authorize such tribal criminal jurisdiction.[99] The "Oliphant" holding was based, inter alia, on a century-old notion that tribes need protection from illegal and harmful intrusion into their territory, which they could not themselves provide.[100] Because this reasoning denies the tribes a crucial aspect of sovereignty, "Oliphant" is one of the least popular Court decisions among the tribes.[101] As the dissent pointed out, because the power to preserve order on a reservation is inherent in a tribe's original sovereignty and is not affirmatively withdrawn by treaty or statute, the tribes should continue to enjoy this aspect of their sovereignty.[102]

In contrast to "Oliphant," the Court's recent decisions have not all served to limit tribal self-determination. In "Merrion v. Jicarilla Apache Tribe"[103] and "Kerr-McGee Corp. v. Navajo Tribe,"[104] the Court upheld the tribal right to tax non-Indians' natural resource development activities on the reservation.[105] The Court considered the power to tax an essential attribute of Indian sovereignty[106] because taxation is a necessary device for carrying out self-government and territorial management, that is, raising revenues for essential government services.[107] The Court has thus recognized a tribe's right as a sovereign entity to control economic activity within its territory.[108]

These cases provide positive developments for the tribes in that the tribes receive a better return from the development of their natural resources, effected by the collection of taxes, an important governmental function. There is another side to the "Merrion" decision, however, that serves to limit the tribes' sovereignty.[109] The "Merrion" Court recognized that tribal authority to tax non-members is "subject to constraints not imposed upon other government entities."[110] The Secretary of the Interior must approve taxes placed on non-members and the federal government has the power to take away a tribe's right to tax.[111] These constraints ensure that the tribes do not tax "in an unfair or unprincipled manner" and that tribal taxation is exercised in a manner "consistent with national policies."[112]

The federal government's Indian policy has evolved over time, resulting in today's official respect for tribal self-determination, although federal policies in practice at least partly contradict the official line. The judiciary has shaped the self-determination policy of the executive and legislative branches. Nevertheless, the Supreme Court, with its recent emphasis on the preemption doctrine may be limiting the tribe's sovereignty by allowing the states greater opportunity for jurisdiction over tribal affairs.

III. TRIBAL NATURAL RESOURCE DEVELOPMENT

A crucial application of federal Indian policy and practice affecting tribal self-determination is in the area of natural resources found on or under tribal lands. Natural resource development presents a significant application of federal policy and practice both because of the United States' need for natural resources and because the resources represent a number of tribes' economic wealth, potential or realized. Not suprisingly, there are many conflicting interests in the consideration of tribal natural resources and their development. The country's need to develop sources of energy, the energy companies that extract and refine the minerals, protection of the tribes' physical and cultural environments, the tribes' economic needs, and the federal trust responsibility for the tribes' physical and financial resources[113] combine to create a complicated situation. Conflicts of interest abound. Most relevant to tribal self-determination is the inherent conflict within the federal government between the need to develop energy supplies and the traditional trust responsibility to protect the tribes' physical and financial resources. Given the unequal economic forces that affect this conflict, development dominates.

The tribes do possess a great deal of natural mineral wealth. About sixty percent of known United States uranium reserves lie under Indian lands, as does one-third of the country's low-sulphur coal.[114] The Indians receive an average of 3.4 percent of the market value of their uranium and about two percent for their coal from the energy companies that extract the minerals through tribal leases.[115] These 1984 figures run up to eighty-five percent less than the royalty rates paid to non-Indians for the same minerals.[116]

As of 1986, twenty-one Indian tribes in this country had entered into about 4,600 lease agreements with mining and energy companies for exploration and/or development of natural resources.[117] The statutory authority permitting the leasing of Indian lands specifically includes the development and utilization of natural resources.[118] Statutory law empowers the Secretary of the Interior to approve tribal mineral agreements.[119] In approving or disapproving a mineral agreement, the Secretary must take into account such concerns as the potential economic return to the tribe and potential environmental, social, and cultural effects of the agreement on the tribe.[120] The Secretary, however, apart from the requirements of the National Environmental Policy Act (NEPA),[121] is not required to prepare any study of these effects on the tribe.[122]

Although the Secretary's mandatory duties are limited, the Secretary does have a statutory responsibility to respect the trust obligation in order to ensure that tribal and individual rights are not violated.[123] The Federal Circuit Court of Appeals in "Pawnee v. United States" recently imposed this fiduciary duty on the Secretary of the Interior.[124] As a result, the Secretary is responsible for ensuring that the tribes are treated fairly with respect to the making and administration of leases and the collection and payment of royalties on the tribes' lands leased for mineral extraction purposes.[125]

The Materials Management Service (MMS) branch of the Department of the Interior oversees the lease and payment process, collecting the royalties from minerals and energy companies holding tribal leases.[126] The Bureau of Indian Affairs (BIA)[127] then distributes the royalties to the tribes and to individual Native Americans holding land allotments.[128] A major problem with the MMS and the lease system in general is underpayment and undercollection of royalties.[129] Five to ten percent of the royalties due to the tribes from leases for the tribes' natural resources go uncollected.[130] A congressional subcommittee found that more than twenty percent of royalties due from energy companies is not paid under the present system, which is, in effect, an honor system.[131] A study showed that for oil royalties in the years 1978-1983, tribes in Oklahoma lost $3.7 million, tribes in Utah lost $6.5 million, and tribes in Wyoming lost $12 million in royalties.[132] A recent Department of Interior Inspector General Report acknowledged the problem of underpayment and undercollection.[133]

Congressional commentators have suggested that the Department of the Interior let another agency, probably the

IRS, handle royalty collection.[134] The Department has not fulfilled the federal government's obligations to the tribes under the trust.[135] One problem is that the BIA, also under the Department, is at odds with the MMS.[136] The BIA is supposed to assert itself against the Department to ensure adequate collection for and distribution to the tribes.[137] Considering the amount of royalties not collected, it is clear that this system is not working.[138] In response to this failure, a Senate Committee recently approved financing for an investigation of the BIA, hoping to recover "billions of dollars in mineral royalties to which Indians are entitled."[139]

The MMS contends that it has instituted mechanisms to improve the collection of royalties.[140] MMS has for several years audited a portion of the leases, resulting in the collection of millions of dollars in additional royalties.[141] In addition, MMS has instituted a "comprehensive enforcement and penalty strategy to assure prompt and accurate reporting and payment,"[142] consisting of interest charges,[143] erroneous, late, and non-reporting assessments,[144] and civil penalties.[145] For example, since 1980 MMS has collected $3.2 million for the tribes through interest charges.[146]

Although the MMS claims that it has reduced underpayment to two to three percent, the tribes and states are not satisfied.[147] The tribes and states, along with allies in Congress, complain that the Department of the Interior continues to allow the energy industry to set its own values for the gas and oil produced.[148] Critics of the Department are calling for the establishment of netback pricing, whereby the values of the natural resources are set according to the open market price of the end products.[149] The combined effect of more effective royalty collection and netback pricing would allow tribes to earn a greater return from the development of their natural resources. For example, the greater return would benefit the Navajo, who depend on natural resource development for revenue and have been hurt by the decrease in oil and gas prices.[150]

Despite the royalties owed and paid to the tribes, many tribal members do not share in the benefits from resource development,[151] and all tribal members endure the side effects of development such as pollution.[152] In the Southwest, the energy produced in local power plants from locally mined coal is delivered to cities hundreds of miles away, while half the Navajo and Hopi homes are without electricity.[153] Much of the coal is extracted by strip mining.[154] Reclamation[155] attempts in the arid west have not been successful, according to the National Academy of Sciences, and true reclamation "will take centuries."[156] Devastation of the land, overuse of scarce water resources for coal slurries, and air pollution emitted from power plants are the side effects of the mineral extraction that provides the benefits of royalties and jobs.[157]

In addition to recurrent problems such as air pollution, several incidents of major environmental degradation connected with the mineral exploitation process have occurred on and near reservations,[158] and some are arguably the result of company carelessness.[159] The Kerr-McGee Corporation, operating a uranium[160] mine through a lease by the BIA and endorsed by the Navajo tribal council, allowed improper ventilation in its mine shafts which, by 1959, had exposed miners to levels of radiation ninety to one hundred times the permissible safety limits.[161] By 1980, thirty-eight of the approximately one hundred fifty Navajo miners had died of radiation-induced lung cancer and ninety-five others were ill with cancer or other serious respiratory ailments.[162] When the company left the area in 1970, they left behind about seventy acres of mounds of radioactive uranium tailings.[163] Some of these mounds lay only sixty feet from a river that was the only significant surface water in the area.[164] The tailings contaminated drinking water and radiation-related birth defects dramatically increased.[165] Despite the Kerr-McGee experience, many similar uranium mines operate today on or near Navajo land.[166]

A more recent example of environmental degradation caused by corporate carelessness was the 1979 United Nuclear Corporation radioactive spill, the largest radioactive spill in United States history.[167] A uranium tailings impoundment dam burst, releasing millions of gallons of contaminated liquid and 1100 tons of hazardous solid waste.[168] The radioactive and chemically dangerous materials flowed through an arroyo into a river flowing through Navajo grazing lands, eventually leaving a trail of contamination nearly one hundred miles long.[169] The company knew about cracks in the dam structure at least two months before the break,[170] and yet made no repairs.[171]

As a result of the spill, the sole water source of 1700 Navajos was contaminated, as was their livestock.[172] United Nuclear, however, contested the findings of contamination.[173] The company refused to supply needed food and water to the people,[174] and made no redress until an out-of-court settlement a year later.[175] The Governor of New Mexico, faced with this crisis, did not declare the site a disaster area.[176] Navajo leaders complained that congressional hearings three months after the spill represented the first expression of serious national concern, whereas a smaller incident at Three Mile Island commanded a Presidential Commission.[177]

The Navajo reservation has been plagued by many of the preceding problems associated with natural resource development, such as radioactive spills[178] and air pollution.[179] Despite these problems, Navajo leaders have embarked on a pro-development course. For example, Peter MacDonald, tribal chairman, advocates resource exploitation at the best price the tribe can get from an energy company.[180] Tribes such as the Navajo are turning to resource development to make up for federal budget cuts, which along with a depressed energy market have hit the tribes hard in recent years.[181] As a result, tribal leaders are "hoping for prosperity through large-scale private-sector development."[182]

The experience of a Montana tribe with a less pro-development attitude exposes some of the problems of resource development. The Northern Cheyenne initially leased one-half of their land to coal companies.[183] Although they had originally been attracted by the prospect of jobs and money, the tribe realized at some point that strip mining and gasification plants presented a permanent trade of their land for money.[184] In addition, the tribe felt that their right to fair dealing had been violated by both the energy company and the BIA.[185] The tribe proceeded to direct the BIA to cancel its leases. The Secretary of the Interior suspended all the leases the following year.[186]

Among other charges, the tribe claimed that the Department of the Interior had failed to include the required environmental protection clauses in the leases and had not completed environmental impact statements.[187] The tribe also charged that the BIA had violated its trust responsibility to the tribe by not informing them of the negative aspects of mining and energy development and by recommending that the tribe accept an unconscionably low price for the coal.[188]

Resource development is clearly fraught with dangers such as not receiving a fair return on the extracted minerals and suffering from the pollution resulting from the extraction and refining process. The federal government has a well-recognized trust responsibility to the tribes regarding the tribes' physical and financial resources.[189] By facilitating financially and environmentally irresponsible company activity on tribal land, the government has been less than vigilant in fulfilling its trust responsibilities to the tribes insofar as providing protection.

IV. THE EPA, ENVIRONMENTAL PROTECTION STATUTES, AND TRIBAL SELF-DETERMINATION

One of the major problems associated with mineral extraction is pollution. Reservations currently face many other pollution problems as well.[190] Serious deficiencies exist in water quality, solid waste disposal, hazardous waste management, sewage treatment and disposal, and other areas.[191]

The executive branch of the federal government, through the Environmental Protection Agency (EPA), facilitates tribal jurisdiction over environmental protection, thereby manifesting its promised support of tribal self-determination.[192] Recent amendments to various pollution control statutes and the ensuing regulations grant the tribes the right to act as states for certain purposes under these statues.[193]

The policies and practices of the EPA reflect a federal commitment to tribal self-regulation.[194] The EPA was the first federal agency to issue a policy pursuant to President Reagan's Indian policy.[195] The agency's existing policy also favored tribal self-regulation.[196] A 1980 EPA statement announced the agency policy as "promot[ing] an enhanced role for tribal government in relevant decisionmaking and implementation of Federal environmental programs on Indian reservations."[197] The EPA policy includes working with tribal governments in a government-to-government relationship and recognizing "tribal governments as the primary parties for setting standards, making environmental policy decisions and managing programs for reservations, consistent with agency standards and regulations."[198]

In contrast to the agency's ambitious policy, however, the EPA is beset by constraints such as decreased grants and personnel resources.[199] The EPA is working with level or decreased funding in most programs.[200] In addition, the agency recognizes that "[i]n general, EPA programs have not been effectively applied on Indian reservations."[201]

Interestingly, however, there may be a positive effect of the EPA's limitations. The limited effective application of EPA programs spurs on the need for improved local tribal environmental regulation.[202] In addition to aiding the process of tribal self-government by supplying an opportunity for the tribes to take on a challenging government role, the EPA's policy is expected to result in better environmental protection on reservations.[203]

A recent manifestation of this policy is the 1986 Amendment to the Safe Drinking Water Act (SDWA).[204] The SDWA Amendment allows tribes to act as states in carrying out primary enforcement responsibility for public water systems and for underground injection control programs[205] if the tribes meet the criteria qualifying them to be treated as states.[206] To be eligible for such responsibility, (1) the tribe must be recognized by the Secretary of the Interior;[207] (2) the governing body of the tribe must be such that it carries out "substantial governmental duties and powers over a defined area";[208] (3) the tribe must show that the public water systems and/or injection wells that the tribe intends to regulate are within the area of the tribe's jurisdiction;[209] and (4) the tribe must demonstrate a reasonable capability to administer an effective program in accordance with the terms and purposes of the SDWA.[210]

In the interest of encouraging tribal participation in these programs, tribes can apply for programs one at a time so as not to overtax limited tribal government infrastructure and resources.[211] Several small tribes located in proximity to each other can apply for group primary enforcement authority status.[212] The EPA also recognizes that many tribes may decide, for one reason or another, not to apply for primary enforcement authority.[213] The EPA will continue to regulate these tribes' public water systems and underground injection wells.[214]

The regulations also take into account the limited tribal facilities. For example, tribes do not have to act as states for the purposes of utilizing their own testing laboratories or exercising criminal jurisdiction.[215] In fact, the Supreme Court in "Oliphant v. Suquamish Indian Tribe"[216] held that tribal courts do not have inherent criminal jurisdiction to try and to punish non-Indians, and may not assume such jurisdiction unless specifically authorized to do so by Congress.[217]

The 1987 Amendments to the Clean Water Act[218] provide a similar opportunity for tribes to act as states, subject to similar qualifications.[219] For example, the tribe may bring enforcement actions against persons in violation of the Act.[220] Another important function authorized by the Amendment is that a tribe may administer its own permit program for discharges into navigable waters within its jurisdiction.[221]

Another significant manifestation of the tribal right of self-determination is found in the Clean Air Act.[222] Under this statute, tribes have the right to redesignate reservation air quality standards.[223] Pursuant to this right, the Ninth Circuit Court of Appeals upheld EPA approval of the Northern Cheyenne redesignation of their reservation into the cleanest category so as to prevent deterioration.[224] This decision is a significant victory for the Northern Cheyenne in that the tribe used an environmental statute to protect itself from the environmental effects of coal mining.[225] The tribe thus used the statute to facilitate its self-determination.[226]

Congressional enactment of these statutes and EPA promulgation of the necessary regulations manifest the federal policy of supporting tribal self-government and self-determination.[227] The EPA issued an Indian Policy Statement[228] in 1980 that commentators have heralded as "an excellent model for other Federal Agencies"[229] and thus is important to the encouragement of overall tribal self-government.

Some commentators feel that the EPA is not inclined to impose economically burdensome controls on Indian activities, and is thus not likely to take a strong enforcement position "except where serious environmental problems exist."[230] This position may be consistent with tribal self-determination because the tribes are left with the responsibility for making choices regarding development and environmental protection. A problem with the EPA practice, however, has been the agency's unwillingness to request funds for the Indian programs.[231] After supporting the Indian amendments in Congress, the EPA did not ask for the funds necessary to conduct the surveys and inventories of reservation pollution problems called for in the statutes.[232]

Because the EPA is less likely to respond to "ordinary" environmental problems,[233] the burden falls on the tribe to develop environmental protection programs. Many tribes do have their own programs.[234] These local pollution control efforts are very important, both for improving the environment and for exercising tribal self-government, the stated goal of federal policy.[235]

There are two factors that serve to retard these local efforts, however, in addition to the usual problems of poor facilities and lack of trained personnel. One factor is the necessity of, and sometimes overriding concern with, resource development as a source of tribal income.[236] The other factor is the budget cuts at the hands of the Reagan Administration.[237] These two factors interrelate in that a reduction in federal grant money pushes the tribes toward more resource development in order to compensate for budget cuts.[238] As a result, the tribes with natural resources are likely to both increase pollution due to development and to be less capable of environmental self-regulation.

Protection of the environment is surely one of the most vital and most difficult government functions. Environmental protection requires identifying the problems,[239] supplying financial and personnel resources including scientific expertise, and most basic, a balancing of societal values.[240] The tribes' acquisition of jurisdiction over this challenging matter is indicative of their desire to exercise sovereign authority over their lands.[241] The environmental protection statute amendments that grant this jurisdiction also indicate Congress' belief that at least some tribes are or will be capable of handling such a complex matter. Logically, tribal environmental jurisdiction should be co-extensive with the tribes' ability to exercise practicable jurisdiction over the natural resources whose exploitation contributes to such pollution. Unfortunately, current federal practice will not facilitate tribal control over their natural resources.

V. CURRENT FEDERAL INDIAN POLICY AND PRACTICE

Economic pressure to exploit natural resources has led many developing nations to exploit their resources without fully considering all the impacts.[242] American Indian tribes are similarly pressured, especially given the recent federal budget cuts in Indian allotments.[243] Resource development, whatever the environmental impacts, could help compensate for the cuts as well as provide jobs.[244] Ironically, the budget cuts in education "have stalled development of desperately needed *human* resources."[245] This lack of human resources may effectively prevent the tribes from fully developing their natural resources, the alleged means to tribal self-sufficiency. These budget cuts expose the Reagan Administration's policy supporting tribal self-determination as an empty concept, where basic needs such as housing and health care cannot be met,[246] let alone tribal-controlled resource development. Current federal Indian policy has been described as flowing from the budget rather than the usual method of the budget flowing from the policy.[247]

In his 1983 Statement on Indian Policy, President Reagan stated that the answer to the tribes' economic woes lay in the free market, which would "supply the bulk of the capital investments required to develop tribal energy and other resources."[248] Reagan's vision was aimed at reducing the federal presence on reservations and increasing private sector investment.[249] Unfortunately for the tribes, reducing the federal presence meant sizable cuts in vital programs.[250] One commentator complained that Reaganomics and the new federalism are being mechanically applied to the tribes without taking into account the tribes' needs.[251] Moreover, it may be unrealistic to expect a capitalist economy to bloom in just a few years.[252]

In his 1983 Statement, President Reagan also called for the establishment of a Commission on Indian Reservation

Economies to assess the tribal economic situation and advise the President on Indian matters.[253] In November 1984, the Commission announced its recommendations.[254] The Commission called for a change in the direction of tribal development efforts from social goals to private ownership and the profit motive.[255]

Tribal leaders overwhelmingly rejected these recommendations.[256] The leaders were disturbed by the emphasis on "altering the communal philosophy behind tribal enterprises."[257] This alteration represents a subtle but powerful attempt by the federal government to assimilate the tribes into mainstream society, a position contrary to the stated federal policy supporting tribal self-determination.[258] Many tribal leaders felt that the recommendations, if implemented, would separate the tribes from their natural resources.[259]

Through its budget cuts and its desire to redefine the tribes' group-oriented philosophy, the Reagan Administration is violating the historic trust responsibility of the federal government[260] to the tribes as well as the spirit of the Self-Determination Act.[261] While simply pouring money into reservations is not the answer, true self-determination will require continuing federal-tribal cooperation.[262] For example, the relationship between the EPA and the tribes[263] represents a hopeful partnership. The success of such cooperative efforts will influence federal government decision-making as to whether the tribes will be given the opportunity to develop true self-determination, even if the end result is not aligned with the American individual-oriented and profit-oriented mainstream.

VI. TRIBAL CONTROL OVER NATURAL RESOURCE DEVELOPMENT IS VITAL TO SELF-DETERMINATION

The tribes need to control the development of their natural resources if they are to gain a profound measure of self-determination. A number of tribes own great mineral wealth. For example, about sixty percent of North America's uranium deposits lie within reservation boundaries.[264] Eighty percent of the mining and one hundred percent of the national production, however, was taking place there as of the late 1970s.[265] One possible reason for the one hundred percent is that mining companies can operate more cheaply on reservations, both for leasing[266] and for labor costs.[267] Another possibility is the desirability of company mining operations in an environment where the companies may take fewer precautions, even to the extent of avoiding those precautions required by law.[268] Arguable examples of such corporate exploitation are the Kerr-McGee and United Nuclear incidents.[269]

Whether or not these incidents involved violations of laws and regulations,[270] they nonetheless portray a disregard for the safety of employees and local inhabitants.[271] This disregard represents exploitation of people and the environment in the name of profit. Whether this disregard for human life and property is purposely facilitated by the federal government, as some commentators assert,[272] or is the result of the federal government's failure to regulate properly the energy companies that do business with the tribes,[273] the government is not meeting its trust responsibilities regarding the tribes' physical environment and physical resources.[274]

Another contemporary event, the forced relocation of Hopi and Navajo from a portion of their traditional homeland at Big Mountain, Arizona,[275] exemplifies the failure of the federal government to meet its responsibilities to the tribes. In the case of Big Mountain, one of the government's major partners is the pro-development Hopi Tribal Council.[276] Contrary to the media-purchased[277] image of this relocation as the result of a dispute between the Hopi and Navajo, the conflict was really between the Hopi Council and the traditional Navajo and Hopi at Big Mountain.[278] The two tribes had held the land at Big Mountain jointly since 1882, land which happens to lie above huge deposits of low-sulphur coal.[279] Most Navajo and Hopi opposed the development of these minerals.[280] In spite of this opposition, the pro-development Hopi Council proceeded to convince Congress to divide the land in order to open the land up to mining.[281] Congress obliged in 1974 by enacting Public Law Number 93-531,[282] a law that required thousands of Navajos to leave their homeland.[283] This forced relocation, legal under United States law, violates the traditional Navajo and Hopi right to self-determination under international law.[284] The right to live in one's homeland is one of the most basic rights of peoples everywhere. The federal government, by enforcing the relocation, has ignored its policy supporting tribal self-determination.

A more general criticism of the federal government's treatment of the tribes concerns reservation economic and political conditions. Although some tribes are endowed with large mineral resources, the tribes are not even able to support themselves.[285] The system in which the tribes only share in a minority of the wealth generated by the exploitation of their natural resources may be termed a metropolis-satellite economy,[286] or neocolonialism.[287] In this model, a tribe on a reservation acts as a satellite by providing the natural resources and the labor necessary to extract the resources,[288] but does not own or control the mining industry.[289] The metropolis, or urban center of political and economic power, owns and controls the industry.[290] The metropolis grows at the expense of the satellite,[291] which does not share proportionately in the surpluses from its own area, and has little political and economic power.[292]

In the context of Indian reservations, which play the role of satellite, the mining companies and the federal government facilitate the dominance by the metropolis. The metropolis, most broadly, consists of these companies and the government, as well as other businesses, shareholders, and consumers. All of these persons benefit, directly or indirectly, from the mineral extraction and the energy produced therefrom. They benefit, in fact, to a much larger degree than the reservation inhabitants, who live amidst the stripped land and the pollution.

The federal government, which led the tribes into the prejudicial mining lease agreements with the energy companies,[293] facilitates the companies' role. The companies can mobilize legal and political clout far beyond the tribes' capability.[294] The metropolis-satellite relationship has blossomed since natural resources were discovered on tribal land, although the relationship has historical roots. The framework was set more than 150 years ago when Chief Justice Marshall, although ostensibly supporting tribal self-determination, termed the tribes "domestic dependent nations,"[295] thereby limiting the tribes' autonomy.

Tribal self-determination requires the ending of the colonial relationship facilitated by the energy companies and the government,[296] and the tribes' genuine assumption of control over their resources.[297] Ideally, the tribes themselves should undertake the resource development.[298] The tribes receive royalties and tax revenues from the mining and energy companies under natural resource development leases,[299] resulting in the collection of significant funds.[300] Additionally, the federal government could provide the necessary capital to allow tribes to start resource development companies. The tribes' lack of trained personnel,[301] however, makes this scheme not realistic at present. Reinstatement of the education and training programs cut by President Reagan would help compensate for the personnel shortage. In addition, the tribes could require lessee energy companies to participate in joint ventures that would assure management positions to tribe members, and generally "promote a transfer of technical and managerial skills."[302] In order for the tribes to gain control over the development of their natural resources, both the tribes and the federal government must take bold steps. Unfortunately, the Reagan Administration practices have further removed the tribes from this goal.

Control over resources is a major element of control of the tribal economy, which in turn is a prerequisite for self-determination. In addition to actually conducting exploration and mining, the tribes can assert a measure of control over reservation resource development under environmental regulation.[303] Congress has already amended several statutes to permit tribal participation in environmental regulation.[304] More federal action should follow, including regulations granting greater tribal participation in resource development itself.

Exploitation of natural resources is a course of action available to tribes, but most of the benefits should flow to the people who own the land and suffer the side effects of the development process. For all of the federal government's rhetoric about Indian self-determination,[305] the tribes will not really attain this state until they control their resources. This control becomes all the more critical because natural resources such as coal, oil, and uranium are non-renewable. For example, the Navajo reservation's mineral resources are expected to be depleted by the year 2010.[306] If development continues at the present rate or increases, there is little time left for the tribes to increase their control over, and/or the benefits they receive from, resource development.[307]

Some commentators believe that the tribes will never be granted political and economic justice inside the United States, and therefore must seek international recognition of their plight and must pressure the United States government to grant the tribes greater autonomy.[308] If the tribes were able to act as independent nation-states, they might nationalize the mining operations in their territory, as many former colonies have done.[309] Customary international law recognizes the legitimacy of such expropriation, whereby the expropriating state makes a good-faith effort, over time, to reimburse the individuals and corporations whose property the state expropriates.[310] This law dictates that the expropriating state compensate foreign individuals and corporations in the same manner that the state compensates native citizens.[311]

Domestically, the tribes may wish to reorganize their tribal leadership or restructure the leases, perhaps by challenging the royalty payments as unfairly low. In addition, the tribes may find the long-term nature of leases unacceptable. Presently, the statutory limit is twenty-five years.[312] Leases shorter than this maximum would allow greater tribal flexibility. Tribes could renegotiate leases as conditions change, such as market prices of natural resources, tribal attitudes toward development, and increasing tribal capacity to undertake development on their own.

In the interest of protecting the environment, the tribes should utilize the provisions in the recent statutory amendments permitting them to "act as states" for purposes of setting standards and/or enforcing the provisions.[313] In line with this latter duty, tribes should be granted jurisdiction over energy companies for the purposes of enforcing environmental regulations. This jurisdiction would include the use of a NEPA-type written requirement to study potential societal and environmental effects of any significant resource development. This study would be most effective if required before any disturbances began. A tribe would use this study to design a development plan that would include the roles and requirements for the tribal government and the energy companies.

It makes sense that the tribes should have increased practicable control over the development of their natural resources, because given the tough choices inherent in this development, the tribes will benefit most if the choices are made as freely as possible in the economic circumstances. The tribes with energy-rich reservations have reached a turning point with regard to political and economic choices.[314] Many people feel that the tribes' dependency on the federal government can be fought with economic development.[315] In addition, there is a perception that energy development can be the manifestation of economic development.[316] Energy development alone, however, is not the answer. As one commentator stated:

> [w]hatever decisions individual tribes make about energy development, it is clear that without substantial changes, energy development is not the panacea to end Indian poverty and underdevelopment. And if the problems raised here are not solved, energy development will prove to be the latest and most devastating fiasco of federal Indian policy.[317]

There already exists a distressing model for one possible future of tribal natural resource development, the coal mining areas of Appalachia. The poverty and scoured land of Appalachia provide us with the realization that economic colonialism in America is not limited to Indian reservations.[318] The post-coal mining depression in parts of Appalachia provides the tribes with a vision of their own future if they do not act to control their resources and their land.[319]

VII. CONCLUSION

Congress has honored the historic trust and the modern federal policy supporting tribal self-determination by amending environmental protection statutes to allow tribal participation. There are impediments, however, that serve to make these amendments the exception rather than the rule. The Reagan Administration's budget cuts and the federal government's apparent tacit approval of corporate economic domination over the tribes amount to a violation of the trust. This government and corporate partnership serves to further remove the Indians from their goal of self-determination.

Natural resources development serves as both a prerequisite for and a manifestation of self-determination for some tribes. If the federal government carries out its stewardship over tribal natural resources in a manner conducive to increasing tribal control, the tribes will have the opportunity to control the methods, pace, and location of resource development. Tribal control would allow into the resource extraction process consideration of tribal lifestyles, traditional as well as modern, protection of the environment, and financial needs. Such control would also recognize that the allotment of ultimate control over resource development should not come down to a choice between development and tribal existence. Control over and the benefits of resource development should flow to the people who live on the land and whose lifestyle and environment suffer from the extraction and refinement processes.

NOTES

1. See generally, Fromboise and Fromboise, "Critical Legal and Social Responsibilities Facing Native Americans," in *Indians and Criminal Justice,* v. 25, (L. French ed. 1982).

2. See generally, ibid.

3. See notes 8-22 and accompanying text. The term "self-determination" is described as the realization of self-government, the group act of controlling the relationships both among themselves and with outside governments, organizations, and persons. "1975 Indian Self-Determination and Educational Assistance Act," codified at U.S.C., 25,

(1982), 450(a)(1)-(2).

4. See, e.g., "Safe Drinking Water Act (SDWA)," U.S.C., 42, (1982 and Supp. IV, 1986), 300f - 300j-11; "Clean Water Act (CWA)," U.S.C.A., 33, (West 1986 and Supp. 1988), 1251-1387; "Clean Air Act (CAA)," U.S.C., 42, (1982 and Supp. IV 1986), 7401-7642.

5. See, e.g., "SDWA," U.S.C., 42, 300j-11; "CWA," U.S.C.A., 33, 1377; "CAA," U.S.C., 42, 7474(c).

6. For example, the Navajo and Crow tribes are involved with coal mining. See "Indians Seek Coal Development to Offset Federal Aid Cuts," *Coal Age*, (Jan. 1985), 19 [hereinafter *Coal Age*]. The Navajo have been involved in uranium mining for decades. See notes 161-66 and accompanying text.

7. "Statement by President Reagan: Indian Policy," (Jan. 24, 1983), reprinted in *Department of Interior and Department of Health and Human Services, Moving Toward Self-Sufficiency for Indian People, 2*, (1984), [hereinafter Reagan Indian Policy].

The Supreme Court has also expressed their opinion on the status of treaties between the tribes and the federal government. "[A] treaty was not a grant of rights to the Indians, but a grant of rights from them . . . a reservation of those [rights] not granted." "United States v. Winans," U.S., 198, (1905), 371, 381. The Supreme Court used this definition recently in "United States v. Wheeler," U.S., 435, (1978), 313, 327.

8. Fromboise and Fromboise, supra note 1, 25.

9. Ibid.

10. Ibid.

11. The trust was first described in 1831 by Chief Justice Marshall in "Cherokee Nation v. Georgia," U.S. 30, (1831), (5 Pet.), 1. Marshall described the Cherokee as a "domestic dependent nation" that looked to the federal government for protection, to "rely on its kindness and power [and to] appeal to it for relief to their wants." Ibid., 17. An earlier source, the Northwest Ordinance of 1787, also supplied a basis for the federal trust responsibility to Native Americans. Leventhal, "American Indians—The Trust Responsibility: An Overview," *Hamline Law Review*, 8, (1985), 625, 627. The Ordinance, ratified by the first Congress,

declared: "The utmost good faith shall always be observed towards the Indians; their land and property shall never be taken from them without their consent; and in their property, rights and liberty, they shall never be invaded or disturbed, unless in just and lawful wars authorized by Congress; but laws founded in justice and humanity shall from time to time be made, for preventing wrongs being done to them, and for preserving peace and friendship with them." Ibid., 627-28 (citing Stat. 1, [1789], 50 52). The Supreme Court recently discussed the trust in "United States v. Mitchell," U.S., 463, (1983), 206, 225. The "Mitchell" Court stated that the trust principle "has long dominated the [federal] Government's dealings with Indians." Ibid.

12. Arkansas, Louisiana, New Mexico, Oklahoma, and Texas Advisory Comm., "Indian Tribes: Unique Sovereign Governments," in *The New Wave of Federalism: Block Granting and Civil Rights in the Southwest Region*, (1983), 23, (Report to the United States Commission on Civil Rights) [hereinafter *Advisory Commission*].

13. See P. Reno, *Mother Earth, Father Sky, and Economic Development*, 8-9, (1981), 24-25.

14. *Advisory Comm.*, supra note 12, 23.

15. Ibid. This duty extends to Native Americans living off reservations. See, Leventhal, supra note 11, 655, 662-65.

16. *Advisory Comm.*, supra note 12, 23; see also, Leventhal, supra note 11, 645.

17. Leventhal, supra note 11, 667-69. See also, infra note 20 and accompanying text.

18. Leventhal, supra note 11, 669.

19. Ibid., 668-69.

20. U.S. 463, (1983), 206. The Court concluded that "a fiduciary relationship necessarily arises when the Government assumes such elaborate control over forests and property belonging to Indians." Ibid., 225. See also, "Seminole Nation v. United States," U.S., 316, (1942), 286, 300 (recognizing that the federal government would be liable for damages for trust violations if the government knowingly assisted a corrupt tribal council).

21. The trust exists without formal trust documents. A recent congressional commission summarized the trust as follows: "the Federal duty can be likened to the 'impled trust'

in common law whereby a trust is created by operation of law. Generally, such trusts are recognized by the courts on the basis of an implied intention of the parties to a transaction (resulting trust) or on the basis that recognition of a trust is necessary in order to prevent the unjust enrichment of one party who committed fraud, deception or some other wrongdoing (constructive trust). In such circumstances, the requirements and restrictions imposed on a trustee are recognized even though no formal trust document creates them. The analysis of the United States duty to Indians as that of a trustee to his beneficiary is supported by many judicial decisions where common law trust principles were used to measure the actions of the Federal Government toward Indians. Whether the creation of the responsibility is deemed an express trust or implied trust and whether the nature of the duty is identified as an active trust or a passive trust, the results are the same; the Federal Government is a fiduciary and as such is "judged by the most exacting fiduciary standards." This means that it must act with good faith and utter loyalty to the best interests of the beneficiary. It must keep the beneficiary informed of all significant matters concerning the trust and must not engage in "self-dealing." *American Indian Policy Review Commission, Final Report 125*, quoted in Leventhal, supra note 11, 633.

22. "Reagan Indian Policy," supra note 7, 3. See notes 248-63 and accompanying text for a discussion of President Reagan's Indian policy. The Reagan Administration's goal was to "limit" the focus of the trust to physical and financial resources. See Leventhal, supra note 11, 656. For example, shortly before his January 1983 Statement on Indian Policy, President Reagan pocket vetoed a bill containing language construing the trust responsibility to include education for American Indian students. Ibid., (citing S. Rep. No. 64, 98th Cong., 1st Sess. 5, reprinted in 1983 U.S. Code Cong. and Admin. News 2055, 2059).

23. See notes 24-86 and accompanying text.

24. U.S. (5 Pet.), 30, 1, 16.

25. Ibid., 15. This treatment of the tribe as a state provides the historical basis for the contemporary treatment of the tribes as states for the purposes of environmental protection statutes. See notes 193-241 and accompanying

text. Unfortunately, this recognition of treatment as a state did not protect the Cherokee and other tribes from being driven from their homelands in the southwestern United States to Oklahoma in what the Cherokee, Creek and Choctaw tribes called the "Trail of Tears." See G. Jahoda, *The Trail of Tears*, (1975), foreword.

26. "Cherokee Nation," U.S., 30, 17.

27. Ibid. For a modern-day detrimental effect of the court-imposed limitation on tribal sovereignty, see note 295 and accompanying text.

28. U.S. (6 Pet.), 31, (1832), 515, 561.

29. Ibid., 539-40.

30. Ibid., 561.

31. Canby, "The Status of Indian Tribes in American Law Today," *Washington Law Review* 1, 62 (1987), 1.

32. See generally F. Cohen, *Handbook of Federal Indian Law*, (1982 ed.), 47-206. Cohen divides the past 100 years of federal government-tribal relations into four periods: Allotments and Assimilation (up to 1928); Indian Reorganization (1928-42); Termination (1943-61); and Self-Determination (1961-present).

33. Ibid.

34. See ibid., 130-31.

35. Ibid., 136.

36. Ibid., 129.

37. Ibid., 130.

38. Ibid., 131.

39. Ibid., 138.

40. See ibid., 136-37.

41. "Pub. L. No. 73-383," Stat., 48, (1934), 984. For a thorough background on the IRA, see V. Deloria and C. Lytle, *The Nations Within*, (1984); see also, C. Kelly, *The Navajo Indians and Federal Indian Policy, 1900-1935*, (1968), 163-66.

42. See F. Cohen, supra note 32, 144, 145.

43. Ibid., 144. "Unquestionably, the Act reflected a new policy of the Federal Government and aimed to put a halt to the loss of tribal lands through allotment." "Mescalero Apache Tribe v. Jones," U.S. 411, (1973), 145, 151.

44. "Mescalero," U.S. 411, 151.

45. F. Cohen, supra note 32, 149.

46. The BIA is the federal agency, under the Department of the Interior, charged with conducting relations with the tribes.

47. F. Cohen, supra note 32, 149.

48. Ibid.

49. Howland, "U.S. Law as a Tool of Forced Social Change: A Contextual Examination of the Human Rights Violations By the United States Government Against Native Americans At Big Mountain," *B.C. Third World Law Journal*, 7, (1987), 61, 65. For example, the Hopi Tribal Council was created in a 1936 election in which only 29% of the eligible members voted. The Council collapsed the next decade and the traditional leaders reestablished their roles. The traditional leaders were unwilling to exploit minerals discovered near the reservation. In 1952, a pro-developmen' tribal council was reinstated with the help of a lawyer wh was attorney for both the Hopi and a coal company. T majority of the Hopi boycotted the 1952 election as well a' subsequent tribal council elections. Ibid., 66-67. The Tribal Council played a key role in the forced relocation Mountain. For a discussion of the role of the Hopi Co contemporary resource development, see notes 275 accompanying text.

50. B. Johnson and R. Maestas, *Wasi'chu*, (J¹e Wasi'chu is a Lakota (Sioux) word for "greedy p'ay tribes used the word to describe the white newco with the term refers to "those corporations and ind¡ covet their governmental accomplices, which cont' Ibid., Indian lives, land, and resources for privat vorks of introduction. For a discussion supporting the' and the people who have experienced discrimination stem, see like as key sources for criticisms of the Studies and Matsuda, "Looking to the Bottom: Critica' (1987), 323, Reparations," *Harv. C. R. - C. L. Law Re* 343-49. _e 50, 211.

51. B. Johnson and R. Maestas, sext.

52. See notes 64-85 and accompa 32, 154-56.

53. See generally, F. Cohen, su ngress announced

54. See generally, ibid., 170 al, supra note 11, this termination policy in 1953.

630, (citing H. R. Con. Res. 108, 83d Cong., 1st Sess., (1953)). For an account of the federal termination policy, see generally L. Burt, *Tribalism in Crisis*, (1982).

55. "Act of Aug. 15, 1953, Pub. L. No. 83-280," Stat. 67, (1953), 588, amended by U.S.C., 25, (1982), 1321-1322.

56. U.S.C., 18, (1982), 1162.

57. U.S.C., 28, (1982), 1360.

58. F. Cohen, supra note 32, 174-75. Skibine, "The Courts," *Am. Indian Journal*, (Jan. 1980), 11.

59. U.S., 358, (1959), 217.

60. U.S. (5 Pet.), 30, (1831), 1; see also supra notes 24-31 and accompanying text.

61. Williams, U.S., 358, 219. The Court stated that "[t]here can be no doubt that to allow the exercise of state jurisdiction here would undermine the authority of the tribal courts over Reservation affairs and hence would infringe on the right of Indians to govern themselves." Ibid., 223.

62. Ibid., 219.

63. See supra notes 53-55 and accompanying text. Perhaps the Court intended to author a narrow holding in "Williams," one covering the tribal court's jurisdiction over ᵗe petitioner American Indian. Such limited jurisdiction is ᵗ (the language of "Williams"), because although tribal ᵗt jurisdiction is a vital ingredient in tribal sovereignty, ᵗdeliberate federal policies of assimilation and tribal ᵗation contradict the Court's assurances that Marshall's ᵗe still controlled. Another possible explanation of this ᵗy is that there was inconsistency between the ᵗᵗranches of the federal government—Congress and ᵗs on the one hand, and the Court on the other.

Cohen, supra note 32, 180.

"Publ, For example, in 1968 Congress amended of crim₃0" to require tribal consent to state assumption Civil Rił civil jurisdiction over Indian territory. Indian (1968), 7ᵗ, Pub. L. No. 90-284," 401, 402, Stat., 82, According 9, (codified at U.S.C., 25, (1982), 1322). Law 280" aˢupreme Court, Congress amended "Public extension of ił t of dissatisfaction "with the involuntary they were reᶜrisdiction over Indians who did not feel threatened by accept such jurisdiction, or who felt ᵗhree Affiliated Tribes of the Fort

Berthold Reservation v. Wold Eng'g," U.S., 476, (1986), 877, 892, "Tribes have been critical of 'Public Law 20' because it authorizes the unilateral application of state law to all tribes without their consent and regardless of their needs or circumstances." Ibid., 892-93, (quoting S. Rep. No. 721, 90th Cong., 1st Sess., (1967), 32), (statement of Sen. Ervin).

66. F. Cohen, supra note 32, 180-81.

67. See Danziger, "A New Beginning or the Last Hurrah: American Indian Response to Reform Legislation of the 1970's," *Am. Indian Culture and Res. Journal*, v. 69, no. 4, (1983), 71. Unfortunately, documenting legal rights on paper does not guarantee their availability and protection. For example, "Brown v. Board of Education," U.S., 347, (1954), 483, did not automatically desegregate schools. Years of struggle and much time in the courtroom finally overcame the resistance to the Court's mandate. The same is true for American Indian tribes except that the more legally nebulous right of self-determination is even more difficult to enforce. Significantly, however, these legal rights in themselves provide for only minimal change regarding equality of opportunity and respect for diversity. The Northern Cheyenne used a provision in the Clear Air Act to enforce its right to clearn air. See notes 224-26 and accompanying text.

68. F. Cohen, supra note 32, 183-84.

69. Ibid.

70. "Pub. L. No. 90-284," Stat., 82, (1968), 77, (codified at U.S.C., 25, (1982), 1301-1341). For an analysis of the ICRA, see Zionitz, "In Defense of Tribal Sovereignty: An Analysis of Judicial Error in Construction of the Indian Civil Rights Act," *S.D.L. Rev.*, 20, (1975), 1. de Raismes, "The Indian Civil Rights Act of 1968 and the Pursuit of Responsible Tribal Self-Government," *S.D.L. Review*, 20, (1975), 59.

71. U.S., 436, (1978), 49. For commentary on "Martinez," see note, "Tribal Sovereignty: 'Santa Clara Pueblo v. Martinez': Tribal Sovereignty 146 Years Later," *Am. Indian Law Review*, (1980), 139.

72. U.S., 436, 62.

73. Ibid., 61-62. For example, individual tribal members are granted the right not to be compelled to be a witness against oneself in a criminal case. U.S.C., 25, (1982), 1302(4).

74. U.S., 436, 62-64. See, e.g., U.S.C., 25, 1321-1326,

which repealed "Public Law 280." See supra notes 55-57 and accompanying text. In "Martinez," the Court denied federal court jurisdiction to an individual tribal member plaintiff who claimed that the Pueblo government had violated her ICRA rights. The Court stated that where Congress seeks to promote dual objectives in a single statute, courts must be very hesitant to infer a cause of action that, while serving one legislative purpose, will thwart another. The Court explained that although the availability of a federal remedy might be useful in securing tribal government compliance with the protection of individual rights afforded under ICRA, the federal remedy "plainly would be at odds with the congressional goal of protecting tribal self-government." Ibid., 64. For example, the availability of the federal remedy would undermine the authority of the tribal forum. Ibid.

75. "Indian Self-Determination and Education Act, Public L. No. 93-638," Stat., 88, (1975), 2203, (codified at U.S.C. 25, (1982), 450(a), 450a.

76. Ibid. The stated purpose of this statute was to "promote maximum Indian participation in the government and education of the Indian people." H.R. Rep. No. 1600, 93d Cong., 2d Sess. 1, reprinted in 1974 *U.S. Code Cong. and Admin. News 7775*. The tribes could now contract with the Departments of the Interior and Health, Education, and Welfare (now divided into the Departments of Education and Health and Human Services) for the operation of programs and services provided by the Bureau of Indian Affairs and the Indian Health Services. *1974 U.S. Code Cong. and Admin. News at 7776*. The intent of ISDEAA was to promote more extensive tribal self-determination through the contracting process. R. Bee, *The Politics of American Indian Policy*, (1982), 95. By 1978, however, it was clear that the Bureau of Indian Affairs was not effectively implementing the Act. See ibid., 95-104. Some commentators feel that the Bureau has thwarted attempts to increase tribal self-determination. See, e.g., Nelson and Sheley, "Bureau of Indian Affairs Influence on Indian Self-determination." See, e.g., Nelson and Sheley, "Bureau of Indian Affairs Influence on Indian Self-determination," in *American Indian Policy in the Twentieth Century*, (V. Deloria, ed., 1985), 177-96. The "Indian Self-Determination Amendments of 1987 Bill" stated that the

Indian Self-Determination and Education Assistance Act "has furthered the development of local self-government and education opportunities for Indian tribes, but its goal and progress have been impeded by lack of clarity and direction on the part of Federal agencies regarding implementing the Federal policy of Indian self-determination." H.R. 1223, 100th Cong., 1st Sess. 2(a), *Cong. Rec.* 133, 9018 (1987) (statement of Rep. Richardson). The amendments were intended to address such problems. *Cong. Rec.*, 133, H9019-20, (daily ed. Oct. 27, 1987). The bill also reiterated the federal policy of self-determination for Indian tribes: "the Federal responsibility for the welfare of Indian tribes demands effective self-government by Indian tribal communities." H.R., 1223, 100th Cong., 1st Sess., 2(a), *Cong. Rec.*, 133, 9018. A law similar to ISDEAA, the "Indian Health Care Improvement Act of 1976," allows the tribes to contract for public health programs. "Pub. L. No. 94-437," Stat., 90, (1976), 1400, (codified as amended at U.S.C.A., 42, (West, 1983 and Supp., 1988), 1601-1680.

77. "Pub. L. No. 93-638," Stat., 88, (1975), 2203, (codified at U.S.C., 25, (1982), 450(a) 450a). Not all tribal leaders are satisfied with the extent of the changes brought about by the Act. See Danziger, supra note 67, 69-70.

78. Danziger, supra note 67, 70.

79. Ibid.

80. President's Message to Congress on the Problems of the American Indian: "The Forgotten American," *Pub. Papers*, 113, (Mar. 6, 1968), 335-44; President's Message to Congress on Indian Affairs, *Pub. Papers*, 213, (July 8, 1970), 564-76.

81. See, e.g., "State of Washington, Dept. of Ecology v. EPA," *F.2d*, 752, (9th Cir., 1985), 1465, 1470.

82. See, e.g., U.S.C., 25, (1982), 450(a) 450a.

83. See, e.g., "The Environmental Protection Agency and Tribal Governments," *Am-Indian L. Newsletter*, 18, (1985), 4, 4-5, [hereinafter "EPA Statement"].

84. "Cherokee Nation v. Georgia," U.S., (5 Pet.), 30, (1831), 1; "Worcester v. Georgia," U.S. (6 Pet.), (1832), 515.

85. Reagan Indian Policy, supra note 7, 2-7.

86. See notes 88-112 and accompanying text.

87. See Skibine, supra note 58, 10. For examples of these cases, see "McClanahan v. Arizona State Tax Comm'n,"

U.S., 411, (1973), 164; "Ramah Navajo School Bd. v. Bureau of Revenue," U.S., 458, (1982), 832.

88. See "McClanahan," U.S., 411, (1973), 172; "Rice v. Rehner," U.S., 463, (1983), 713, 718; "Three Affiliated Tribes of the Fort Berthold Reservation v. Wold Eng'g," U.S., 476, (1986), 877, 884.

89. U.S., 358, (1959), 217.

90. See "McClanahan," U.S., 411, 172.

91. Canby, supra note 31, 6-7.

92. "McClanahan," U.S., 411, 172; "Rice," U.S., 463, 718; "Three Tribes," U.S., 476, 884.

93. "McClanahan," U.S., 411, 172.

94. F. Cohen, supra note 32, 273.

95. See Knapp, "Search for Common Ground," *State Gov't News*, (June, 1984), 5. There does appear to be some tribal-state cooperation on the horizon. Ibid., 5-6.

96. Wilkinson, "Basic Doctrines of American Indian Law," in *Indians and Criminal Justice*, (L. French, ed., 1982), 90. The Supreme Court recognized the hostility of the locals toward the tribes in "United States v. Kagama," U.S., 118, (1886), 375, 384, ("Because of the local ill feeling, the people of the States where [the tribes] are found are often their deadliest enemy.").

97. "Oliphant v. Suquamish Indian Tribe," U.S., 435, (1978), 191.

98. Ibid.

99. Ibid., 212.

100. Ibid., 207.

101. Skibine, supra note 58, 13.

102. "Oliphant," U.S., 435, 212, (Marshall, J., dissenting).

103. U.S., 455, (1982), 130.

104. U.S., 471, (1985), 195.

105. "Merrion," U.S., 455, (1982), 130, 137, (citing "Washington v. Confederate Tribes of Colville Indian Reservation," U.S., 447, (1980), 130, 137, "Kerr-McGee," U.S., 471, 198.

106. "Washington," U.S., 447, 152, "Merrion," U.S., 455, 137; "Kerr-McGee," U.S., 471, 198.

107. "Merrion," U.S., 455, 137.

108. Ibid.

109. Williams, "Redefining the Tribe," *Indian Truth*, (April 1985), 8.

110. "Merrion," U.S., 455, 141.

111. Ibid.

112. Ibid.

113. See *Reagan Indian Policy*, supra note 7, 2-7.

114. Churchill, "American Indian Lands: The Native Ethic Amid Resource Development," *Environment*, (July/Aug. 1986, 16).

115. Ibid.

116. Ibid.

117. "Department of the Interior and Related Agencies Appropriations For 1987, Part 12: Royalty Management, Hearings Before the Subcomm. on Interior Appropriations of the House Comm. on Appropriations," 99th Cong., 2d Sess., (1986), 218, [hereinafter "Royalty Hearings"], (letter of William D. Bettenberg, Director, Materials Management Service, to Donald Hodel, Sec. of the Interior, (Sept. 30, 1986)).

118. "Indian Long-Term Leasing Act of 1909," Stat. 35, 783, (codified as amended at U.S.C., 25, (1982), 396); "Mineral Leasing Act of 1938, Pub. L. No. 75-506," Stat., 52, 347, (codified as amended at U.S.C., 25, (1982), 396a-396g; "Indian Mineral Development Act of 1982, Pub. L. No. 97-382," Stat., 96, (1938), (codified at U.SC., 25, (1982), 2101-2108). Congress enacted the Indian Long-Term Leasing Act in order to allow the Department of the Interior to "oversee the leasing of the Indian lands so as to prevent exploitation of and prejudice to the Indians' interest, or injustice to them." "Pawnee v. United States," F.2d, 820, (Fed. Cir. 1987), 187, 189, n. 2, (citing H.R. Rep. No. 1225, 60th Cong., 1st Sess., (1908), 1-2) cert. denied, 108 S. Ct. 3818 (1988). A major purpose of the Mineral Leasing Act was to ensure that Indians received "the greatest return from their property." H.R. Rep. No. 1872, 75th Cong., 3d Sess. 2, (1938), quoted in "Montana v. Blackfeet Tribe of Indians," 471 U.S. 759, 767, n. 5, (1985). Congress enacted the Indian Mineral Development Act in response to business limitations inherent in the Mineral Leasing Act. See H.R. Rep. No. 746, 97th Cong., 2d Sess., 1-5, reprinted in *1982 U.S. Code Cong. and Admin. News*, 3465-67.

119. U.S.C., 25, (1982), 2102. Regulations for the surface exploration, mining, and reclamation of tribal land are listed at C.F.R., 25, (1988), 216.

120. U.S.C., 25, 2103(b).

121. U.S.C., 42, (1982), 4332(2)(C). NEPA requires a written environmental impact statement for major federal actions "significantly affecting the quality of the human environment." Ibid.

122. U.S.C., 25, 2103(b).

123. Ibid., 2103(e).

124. F.2d, 830, (Fed. Cir. 1987), 187, 189, cert. denied, S. Ct., 108, (1988), 3818; see also "United States v. Mitchell," U.S., 463, (1983), 206, 226, (recognizing the federal government's fiduciary obligation in the management and operation of Indian natural resources). The federal government's trust responsibilities were also recognized by Congress in the enactment of the "Federal Oil and Gas Royalty Management Act of 1982, Pub. L. No. 97-451," Stat., 96, 2447, (codified at U.S.C., 30, (1982), 1701-1757). The purposes of the Act include "to fulfill the trust responsibility of the United States for the administration of Indian oil and gas resources." U.S.C., 30, 1701(b)(4).

125. "Pawnee," F.2d, 830, 189; "Mitchell," U.S., 463, 226.

126. See "Royalty Hearings," supra note 117, 1-3, (statement of Rep. Yates, Subcomm. Chairperson). The MMS manages royalty payments from mineral-producing activities on federal and tribal lands. Barnes, "Interior's Struggle to Track Billions in Oil and Gas Royalties," *Government Executive* , (June 1988), 38. The states receive one-half the royalties from federal lands within their borders. The tribes receive 100 percent of the royalties from production on their land. Ibid. The regulations applying to the calculation of the value of the oil and gas extracted are listed at C.F.R., 25, (1988), 206.

127. For an account of the past, present, and possible future of the BIA, see T. Taylor, *The Bureau of Indian Affairs*, (1984).

128. Barnes, supra note 126, 38. For Bureau regulations concerning the leasing of tribal lands for mining, including rents and royalties, see C.F.R., 25, (1988), 211.

129. See "Royalty Hearings," supra note 117, 1-3. The "[f]ederal royalty management and collection system is in disarray. Hundreds of millions of dollars due [from developer company lessess] to the U.S. Treasury, the States, Indian tribes, and individual Indian allottees are going uncollected every year due to the inadequacies in the system." Ibid. For letters from several states and one Indian tribe expressing dissatisfaction with the MMS, see ibid., 136-47. Critics have labeled the MMS royalty collection as "Washington's worst-run program." Barnes, supra note 126, 38.

130. "Royalty Hearings," supra note 117, 3, (statement of Rep. Yates, Subcomm. Chairperson).

131. Hershey, "Washington Watch: Underpayment of Oil Royalties," *N.Y. Times*, (Feb. 23, 1987, D2, col. 1; *United States Dep't of the Interior Inspector General Report, No. 88-63*, (April 1988), 7, [hereinafter *Inspector General*].

132. "Royalty Hearings," supra note 117, 26-30 (Investigative Staff Study: Oil Royalties on Indian Lands, 1978-1983).

133. *Inspector General*, supra note 131, 1. The Report recognized that the MMS has improved its operations. For example, the change to a comprehensive audit system resulted in a 500 percent increase in findings of royalties due the Navajo tribe. Ibid., 6. See also Barnes, supra note 126, 38.

134. See, e.g., "Royalty Hearings," supra note 117, 2, (statement of Rep. Yates, Subcomm. Chairperson).

135. See B. Johnson and R. Maestas, supra note 50, 198, 204-05, 257. On July 4, 1976, when most of the United States was celebrating the Bicentennial, a group of American Indians calling itself the Trail of Self-Determination Caravan delivered to Congress a statement on the Department of the Interior: "[citing other events] and the strip mining monstrosity on the Northern Cheyenne point out the Interior Department's perversion of responsibility to Indian people.... In truth the Interior Department serves oil, mineral, land-trust, transportation, fisheries, shipping, forestry and other energy interests at the expense of Indian lives." Ibid., 198.

136. Ibid., 184.

137. Ibid.

138. See generally, ibid., 1-3.

139. *N.Y. Times*, (Oct. 31, 1987), A8, col. 6.

140. See "Royalty Hearings," supra note 117, 217-18, 227-28, (letter of William D. Bettenberg, Director, MMS, to Donald Hodel, Secretary of the Interior).

141. Ibid., 218.

142. Ibid., 227.

143. Ibid.

144. Ibid., 228.

145. Ibid., 227, 229.

146. Ibid., 227-28.

147. Hershey, supra note 131, D2, col. 1.

148. Ibid.

149. Ibid., D2, col. 2.

150. *New York Times*, (Dec. 11, 1986), B19, col. 1, 4; Knudsen, "Zoning the Reservations for Enterprise"; *New York Times*, (Jan. 25, 1987), 4, col. 1, graph.

151. See Garitty, "The U.S. Colonial Empire Is As Close As the Nearest Reservation: The Pending Energy Wars," in *Trilateralism*, (H. Sklar, ed., 1980), 245; B. Johnson and R. Maestas, supra note 50, 147.

152. See P. Reno, supra note 13, 9.

153. Garitty, supra note 151, 245.

154. For a description of the devastating effects of strip mining, see B. Johnson and R. Maestas, supra note 50, 143-49.

155. C.F.R., 25, (1988), 216.104(a), dictates that all areas affected by surface coal mining "shall be restored in a timely manner . . . to conditions that are capable of supporting the uses which they were capable of supporting before any mining," or in some circumstances, restored to higher or better uses.

156. B. Johnson and R. Maestas, supra note 50, 149, 154.

157. See generally, Garitty, supra note 151, 245.

158. See infra notes 161-77 and accompanying text.

159. See, e.g., "Mill Tailings Dam Break At Church Rock, New Mexico: Hearings Before the Subcommittee on Energy and the Environment of the House Committee on Interior and Insular Affairs," 96th Cong., 1st Sess., (1979), 1-3, [hereinafter "Dam Break Hearings"], (statement of Rep. Udall, Comm. Chairperson).

160. For an account of the Navajo experience with

uranium mining, see P. Reno, supra note 13, 133-42.

161. Churchill, supra note 114, 17.

162. Ibid., 17, 18.

163. Ibid., 17. Uranium tailings are the "waste by-products of uranium ore refinement [which] retain 85% of the original radioactivity of the ore." LaDuke and Churchill, "Native America: The Political Economy of Radioactive Colonialism," *The Insurgent Sociologist*, (Spring 1986, 57) [hereinafter "Radioactive Colonialism"].

164. Churchill, supra note 114, 17.

165. Ibid., 28.

166. Ibid. "[U]ranium mining and milling are the most significant sources of radiation exposure to the public of the entire nuclear fuel cycle, far surpassing nuclear reactors and nuclear waste disposal. . . ." La Duque, "Native America: The Economics of Radioactive Colonialism," *Rev. of Radical Pol. Econ.*, (Fall 1983), 18, (statement of Victor Gillinsky, United States Nuclear Regulatory Commission, 1978).

167. Garitty, supra note 151, 260. The Nuclear Regulatory Commission called the spill, before Chernobyl, "the worst contamination in the history of the nuclear industry." Johnson, "Indian Land, White Greed," *The Nation*, (July 4, 1987), 16. A U.S. Geological Survey report stated that trace elements and radionuclides exceeded Arizona standards in many water samples. Ibid. Radioactive spills have long-term effects. A spill similar to that of United Nuclear Corporation occurred in South Dakota in 1962. Churchill, supra note 114, 30. Indian Health Service groundwater testing eighteen years later revealed radioactive contamination. "Radioactive colonialism," supra note 163, 59. In addition to accidental damage to groundwater, aquifers are susceptible to contamination from regular mining activities and natural leaching from uranium ore. "Dam Break Hearings," supra note 159, 8, (statement of Frank E. Paul, Vice Chairman, Navajo Tribal Council).

168. "Dam Break Hearings," supra note 159, 1 (statement of Rep. Udall). Although the dam was not on reservation land, the spill nonetheless affected such land. Ibid., 8 (statement of Frank E. Paul, Vice Chairman, Navajo Tribal Council).

169. Ibid., 1, (statement of Rep. Udall).

170. Churchill, supra note 114, 28. Before the dam was licensed, a United Nuclear consultant predicted that the soil under the dam "was susceptible to extreme settling which was likely to cause the cracking and subsequent failure of the structure." "Dam Break Hearings," supra note 159, 2, (statement of Rep. Udall). Apparently, none of the state and federal agencies involved required detailed independent assessments of United Nuclear's construction practices. Ibid. The Army Corps of Engineers reviewed the site after the accident, concluding that the dam contained design defects. Ibid., 3. The company contended that the 1977 cracks in the dam were not related to the failure of the dam at the time of the spill. Ibid., 27, (statement of Lawrence A. Hansen, Engineer).

171. Churchill, supra note 114, 28.

172. Ibid. United Nuclear contended that the spill "did not and does not represent a significant hazard to local representatives or to downstream communities." "Dam Break Hearings," supra note 159, 25, (statement of J. David Hann, Vice President, United Nuclear Corp.). There is disagreement within the scientific community as to the health effects of exposure to low level radiation. Ibid., 10, (statement of Dr. Thomas Gesell, Health Physics).

173. "Dam Break Hearings," supra note 159, 20-25, (statement of J. David Hann, Vice President, United Nuclear Corp.). The company claimed that no substantial radiological danger was created by the spill. Ibid., 23-24. The company measurements of the radioactivity of the surface waters were much lower than the measurements conducted by the state of New Mexico. Ibid., 11, (statement of Dr. Thomas Gesell, Ph.D., Health Physics). United Nuclear attributed the variation to differences in analytical techniques. Ibid., 28, (statement of Todd Miller, Manager, Environmental Operations for Mining and Milling Division, United Nuclear Corp.). Measurements taken of groundwater at a thirty to forty foot depth before and after the spill showed a ten-fold increase in alpha radiation and uranium. Ibid., 94, (letter of Paul Robinson, Environmental Analyst, Southwest Research and Information Center, to Andrea Dravo, Staff Consultant, Comm. on Interior and Insular Affairs, (Feb. 22, 1980)).

174. Churchill, supra note 114, 28; contra "Dam Break

Hearings," supra note 159, 25, ("United Nuclear has acted with responsibility and dispatch in cleaning up the spill, . . . aiding local residents . . ."), (statement of J. David Hann, Vice President, United Nuclear Corp.). At the time of the congressional hearings, three months after the spill, United Nuclear had cleaned up less than one percent of the volume of the material spilled. Ibid., 47, (statement of Paul Robinson, Environmental Analyst, Southwest Research and Information Center).

175. The level of citizen outrage in this type of event may be tempered by the uranium industry's position as supplier of local jobs and income. Such a muted reaction has been described as the result of a locality held "economic hostage," "Radioactive colonialism," supra note 163, 58.

176. Garitty, supra note 151, 260. Some commentators allege that the governor did not even admit that an emergency existed, "for fear of hurting the uranium mining industry in his state." Ibid.

177. "Dam Break Hearings," supra note 159, 6, (statement of Frank E. Paul, Vice Chairman, Navajo Tribal Council).

178. See supra notes 160-77 and accompanying text.

179. See supra note 157 and accompanying text.

180. B. Johnson and R. Maestas, supra note 50, 151-52. For a recent account of the controversial Chairman MacDonald, see *The Boston Globe*, (Feb. 13, 1989), 2, col. 2.

181. Forty percent of the adults on the Navajo reservation are unemployed. Forty-nine percent of the households live below the poverty line, versus an overall United States figure of twelve percent. Knudsen, supra note 150, 4, col. 3; *New York Times*, (July 27, 1987), D2, col. 5.

182. *New York Times*, (July 27, 1987), D2, Col. 5.

183. B. Johnson and R. Maestas, supra note 50, 171.

184. See ibid., 171-72.

185. Ibid., 172.

186. Ibid., 172, 173. The neighboring Crow tribe, which had entered similar coal leases, also successfully persuaded the Department of the Interior to cancel the leases. Ibid., 173. The original lease contract provided for a royalty of seventeen and one-half cents a ton, and the tribe was later reported to be negotiating for three dollars a ton. P. Reno, supra note 13,

116.

187. B. Johnson and R. Maestas, supra note 50, 172.

188. Ibid.

189. See *Reagan Indian Policy*, supra note 7, 2.

190. See generally, *Environmental Protection Agency, Survey of American Indian Environmental Protection Needs on Reservation Lands: 1986*, (1986), [hereinafter, *"EPA Survey"*].

191. Ibid., 7-13; "EPA Surveys Indian Tribes for First Look at Environmental Problems on Reservations," *Env't Rep. (BNA)*, 17, (Dec. 19, 1986), 1424; See also "Cook Stresses Enforcement in EPA's Safe Drinking Water Office," *Env't Report (BNA)*, 16, (Jan. 31, 1986), 1822, [hereinafter "EPA Enforcement"]; "Study Finds 1200 Sites Near Indian Lands," *Env't Report, (BNA)*, 16, (Nov. 8, 1985), 1228.

192. "Department of Housing and Urban Development, and Certain Independent Agencies Appropriations for Fiscal Year 1987: Hearings Before the Subcomm. on HUD—Independent Agencies of the Senate Comm. on Appropriations, Part 2," 99th Cong., 2d Sess., (1986), 806, (EPA Indian Policy), [hereinafter "EPA Hearings"]. For a recent account of tribal sovereignty in the context of environmental protection, see Breslin, "Addressing Environmental Problems on Indian Lands: Issues of Tribal Sovereignty Versus State and EPA Regulatory Authority," *Env't Rep, (BNA)*, 19, (Jan. 27, 1989), 1920.

193. See notes 204-26 and accompanying text.

194. "State of Washington, Dept. of Ecology v. EPA," *F.2d*, 752, (9th Cir. 1985), 1465, 1471.

195. *Offices of Federal Activities and External Affairs: EPA Indian Policy Interim Strategy* [hereinafter *"Interim Strategy"*], reprinted in "EPA Hearings," supra note 192, 815. For a presentation of Reagan's policy, see *Reagan Indian Policy*, supra note 7, 2-7.

196. See "EPA Policy for Program Implementation on Indian Lands," (Dec. 19, 1980), quoted in State of Washington, *F.2d*, 752, 1471, [hereinafter "EPA Policy"].

197. Ibid.

198. EPA Statement, supra note 83, 5.

199. *Interim Strategy*, supra note 195, 817.

200. Ibid.

201. Ibid.

202. Ibid.

203. Ibid.

204. "Pub. L. No. 99-339," Stat., 100, (1986), 642. The United States' reliance on groundwater has dramatically increased over the past thirty years and scientists are unsure as to the extent of groundwater pollution. Habicht, "Protecting Groundwater: State and Federal Roles," *Environment*, (July/Aug. 1986), 4. Thus, groundwater contamination is high on the list of national environmental priorities. "EPA Enforcement," supra note 191, 1822. Tribal water systems are particularly poor; as many as one-half do not meet minimal national standards for purity. *Cong. Rec.*, 132, (daily ed. May 21, 1986), S6294, (statement of Sen. Hart). A co-sponsor of the amendment stated that although Indian water systems only represent one and one-half percent of the small systems in the country, their impurity standards exceedance is almost four times greater than all other public water supply systems. Ibid., S6295, (statement of Sen. Burdick). Senator Hart, another co-sponsor of the SDWA Amendment, invoked the trust responsibility as requiring the federal government to remedy the water problem. Ibid., S6294. The sponsors of the amendments "recognized that tribal governments, unlike state governments, do not have a regulatory program base, an underlying financial and budgetary foundation or a supporting tax infrastructure which could be used in cost-sharing on these programs." Ibid., S6295, (statement of Sen. Durenberger). The tribes are exempt from the 25% matching funds requirement. Ibid., (statement of Sen. Burdick). Congress recognized that the tribes were capable and willing to begin assuming responsibility for safe drinking water programs but that they could not "act as states" insofar as contributing funds. See notes 205-12 and accompanying text.

205. U.S.C., 42, (Supp. IV, 1986), 300j-11(a).

206. Fed. Reg., 52, (1987), 28, 119, 28, 121 (to be codified at C.F.R., 40, 142.72, 145.52) (proposed July 27, 1987). The concept of treating the tribes as states has its historical roots in "Cherokee Nation v. Georgia," U.S., 30, (5 Pet.) 1 (1831). See supra notes 24-27 and accompanying text.

207. Fed. Reg., 52, (1987), 28, 113.

208. Ibid., The EPA thus requires that the tribe perform "essential governmental functions traditionally performed by sovereign governments," such as taxation and police power. Ibid.

209. Ibid., 28, 114. In determining whether a tribe is capable of administering a public water system, the EPA will consider several factors, including the tribe's previous managerial experience and existing environmental or health programs administered by the tribe. Ibid.

210. Ibid.

211. Ibid.

212. Ibid.

213. Ibid., 28, 112.

214. Ibid.

215. Ibid., 28, 115.

216. U.S., 435, (1978), 191.

217. Ibid., 212. Two Justices dissented, arguing that the power to preserve order on the reservation is inherent in the original sovereignty that the tribe possessed. Ibid. (Marshall, Brennan, J.J., dissenting). Because this power was not affirmatively withdrawn by treaty or statute, "Indian tribes enjoy as a necessary aspect of their retained sovereignty the right to try and punish all persons who commit offenses against tribal law within the reservation." Ibid. (Marshall, J., dissenting). Native American writers agreed with the dissent. See Oliverio and Skibine, "The Supreme Court Decision That Jolted Tribal Jurisdiction," *Am. Indian J.*, (May 1980), 2. The lack of criminal jurisdiction is unfortunate in that it is an important aspect of sovereignty, and would be useful in the context of enforcing environmental statutes.

218. "Pub. L. No. 100-4," Stat., 101, (1987), 7.

219. U.S.C.A., 33, (West. Supp. 1988), 1377(e).

220. U.S.C.A., 33, (West 1986 and Supp. 1988), 1319.

221. U.S.C., 33, (1982), 1342(b).

222. U.S.C., 42, (1982), 7474(c), implemented by C.F.R., 40, (1987), 52.21(g). The prevention of significant deterioration section of the "Clean Air Act," U.S.C., 42, (1982 and Supp. IV. 1986), 7470-7491, addresses the need to protect clean air from becoming dirty due to the construction of new sources of air pollution. Will, "Indian Lands Environment— Who Should Protect It?," *Nat. Resources J.*, 18, (1978), 465,

484.

223. U.S.C, 42, 7474(c).

224. "Nancy v. EPA," *F.2d*, 645, (9th Cir. 1981), 701, 704.

225. See ibid., 701-18.

226. Congress has also enacted amendments to allow tribes to act as states for purposes of the Federal Insecticide, Fungicide, and Rodenticide Act (FIFRA), U.S.C., 7, (1982), 136(u), and the "Comprehensive Environmental Response, Compensation, and Liability Act," (CERCLA), 126; U.S.C., 42, (Supp. IV 1986), 9626.

227. See supra notes 75-85 and accompanying text.

228. *EPA Survey*, supra note 190, ii-iii.

229. Ibid., iii. Tribal environmental regulation can serve as a model for other areas of self-government.

230. Will, supra note 222, 504.

231. "Department of Housing and Urban Development—Independent Agencies Appropriations for 1988: Hearings Before the Subcomm. on HUD—Independent Agencies of the House Comm. on Appropriations," 100th Cong., 1st Sess., (1987), 675 [hereinafter "1987 Hearings"], (statement of the Council of Energy Resources Tribes).

232. Ibid. For examples of the statutory authority for the surveys, see CERCLA 126, U.S.C., 42, (Supp. IV, 1986), 9626(c); CWA 518(a), U.S.C.A., 33, (West Supp. 1988), 1377(b); SDWA, 302(e), Pub. L. No. 99-339, Stat., 100, (1986), 666. The EPA told the Committee on Appropriations that the Agency was using 1987 funds to undertake the survey of Indian land drinking water. "1987 Hearings," supra note 231, 672, (statement of Rep. Traxler).

233. Will, supra note 222, 504.

234. *EPA Survey*, supra note 190, 5.

235. *Reagan Indian Policy*, supra note 7, 3, (reaffirming the national commitment "to strengthen tribal governments . . . and to pursue the policy of self-government for Indian tribes").

236. See generally *Coal Age*, supra note 6, 19, (tribes such as the Navajo and Crow have become more receptive to coal mining on their reservations).

237. See Winslow, "Reagan's Indian Policy: Speaking With Forked Tongue," *The Nation*, (Feb. 12, 1983), 177. Four

tenths of one percent of President Carter's proposed 1982 budget was dedicated to Federal Indian programs. Ibid. The Reagan Administration singled out these programs for 2.9 percent of their proposed budget cuts. Ibid. Federal funding for programs affecting American Indians was cut by 22 percent from 1982 to 1983. Ibid.

238. See *Coal Age*, supra note 6, 19.

239. See *EPA Survey*, supra note 190, 7-13.

240. See Will, supra note 222, 500.

241. See Ibid., 465.

242. Arthur, "Preface" to *Native Americans and Energy Development*, (Anthropology Resource Center, ed., 1978), 2.

243. Ibid. Government financing for employment and anti-poverty programs decreased from $264 million in 1980 to $117 million in 1984. *New York Times*, (Dec. 11, 1986), B19, cols. 3-4.

244. *Coal Age*, supra note 6, 19. Unemployment on reservations is several times the national average. Hertzberg, "Reaganomics on the Reservation," *New Republic*, (Nov. 22, 1982), 17.

245. Beck, "Reservations on Reaganomics: 'Beggars in Our Own Land," *Newsweek*, (Nov. 29, 1982), 49 (emphasis in original).

246. Winslow, supra note 237, 178 (quoting the House Interior Appropriations Subcommittee). "Reservation Indians are the poorest people in the nation, with the lowest income, the fewest economic opportunities, the highest death rate, and the least education." Hertzberg, supra note 244, 16.

247. Hertzberg, supra note 244, 15.

248. *Reagan Indian Policy*, supra note 7, 6.

249. Williams, supra note 109, 6.

250. See Winslow, supra note 237, 177-78.

251. Hertzberg, supra note 244, 15.

252. The industrial capitalism of Europe and the United States evolved gradually and was facilitated by imperialism and colonialism to ensure a supply of raw materials and cheap labor. Ortiz, "Choices and Directions," in *Economic Development in American Indian Reservations*, (R. Ortiz ed., 1979), 152. Today's newly developing nations, such as American Indian tribes, cannot develop on the same time scale and in the same manner as did the nations that

industrialized in the nineteenth century. Ibid.

253. *Reagan Indian Policy*, supra note 7, 6.

254. Williams, supra note 109, 6.

255. Peterson, "Indians Resist Shift in Economic Goals Urged By U.S. Panel," *New York Times*, (Jan. 13, 1985), A1, col. 6.

256. Ibid.

257. Ibid., A16, col. 1.

258. See generally Williams, supra note 109, 7. Contrast this subtle assimilation with the blatant methods in the late nineteenth and early twentieth century and again in the 1940s and 1950s. See supra notes 34-40, and 53-58 and accompanying text.

259. Peterson, supra note 255, A16, col. 1.

260. See supra notes 7-22 and accompanying text.

261. "Pub. L. No. 93-638," Stat., 88, (1975), 2203, (codified at U.S.C., 25, (1982), 450(a) 450a. Senator Daniel K. Inouye has ordered a study of government injustices toward American Indians. Barnes, supra note 126, 38. Part of this study will focus on MMS royalty collection. Ibid.; see also supra notes 126-33, and accompanying text.

262. See Beck, supra note 245, 49, (comments of David Lester, Executive Director, Council of Energy Resource Tribes).

263. See supra notes 192-203 and accompanying text.

264. Churchill, supra note 114, 16. It is ironic that such mineral wealth lies under some Indian reservations, for the tribes were placed on these lands because such land was considered useless to whites. Ibid.

265. Ibid., 17.

266. See ibid., 16.

267. See ibid., 17.

268. See ibid., 16-17. Taking fewer precautions allows for bigger profits. Ibid.

269. See supra note 159-77 and accompanying text.

270. History has shown that the legality of actions does not guarantee their "rightness." See, e.g., "Plessy v. Ferguson," U.S., 163, (1896), 537, (upholding "separate but equal" facilities for blacks and whites); "Hirabayashi v. United States," U.S., 320, (1943), 81, (upholding curfew applying to only the Japanese-Americans). Criticism of the

use of law to legitimize the illegitimate is a central tenet of the Critical Legal Studies movement. Matsuda, supra note 50, 329. "The Constitution, [the incarcerated Japanese-Americans] found, offered no protection from the guns of military police or from the orders of racist generals. . . ." Ibid., 339.

271. See supra notes 161-66 and accompanying text for a description of such an event involving radioactive poisoning.

272. See, e.g., Churchill, supra note 114, 16-17; "Radioactive Colonialism," supra note 163, 55-56.

273. See Owens, "Can Tribes Control Energy Development?," in *Native American and Energy Development*, 60, (Anthropology Resource Center, ed. 1978). For an example of this failure, see supra notes 183-188.

274. See supra notes 7-22 and accompanying text for a discussion of the trust doctrine. See supra notes 123-25, and accompanying text for a discussion of the federal government's specific fiduciary duty concerning the leasing of tribal lands for mineral extraction.

275. Howland, supra note 49, 61, 63; see also Johnson, supra note 167, 15-18.

276. Howland, supra note 49, 65.

277. The council hired an advertising agency "to secure passage of a bill that would divide" the Joint Use Area. Ibid., 62.

278. Ibid.; see also Johnson, supra note 167, 17. One commentator addressed non-Native Americans regarding the development of tribal natural resources: "Your people will do *anything* to get their hands on our mineral-rich lands. They will legislate, stir up internal conflicts, cause inter-tribal conflicts, dangle huge amounts of monies as compensation for perpetual contracts and promise lifetime economic security. If we object, or sue to protect our lands, these suits will be held in litigation for fifteen to twenty years with "white" interests benefitting in the interim." Sanchez, "Sex, Class, and Race Intersections, Vision of Women of Color," in *Gathering of Spirit: Writing and Art by North American Indian Women*, 163, (B. Brant ed., 1984), 166, quoted in "Matsuda," supra note 50, 327.

279. Howland, supra note 49, 61.

280. Ibid., 61-62.

281. Ibid., 62-63.

282. "Pub. L. No. 93-531," Stat., 88, (1974), 1712, (codified as amended at U.S.C., 25, (1982 and Supp. IV 1986), 640d-640d-28. The 1980 amendment, "Pub. L. No. 96-305," Stat., 94, (1980), 929, somewhat mitigated the effects of the relocation, but did not address the basic problems of the statute. Members of Congress and traditional Native Americans felt that the relocation act, as amended, was "harsh, inhumane, and in need of repeal." Howland, supra note 49, 70-71.

283. Howland, supra note 49, 61. This program will result in the largest removal of an ethnic group in the United States since the Japanese-Americans during WWII. Ibid., 63.

284. Ibid., 80. Native Americans meet the definition of "peoples" as defined by the International Court of Justice. Article 55 of the United Nations Charter mandates the self-determination of peoples. Ibid. The Article states: "With a view to the creation of conditions of stability and well-being which are necessary for peaceful and friendly relations among nations based on respect for the principle of equal rights and self-determination of peoples, the United Nations shall promote . . . universal respect for, and observance of, human rights and fundamental freedoms for all without distinction as to race, sex, language or religion." *U.N. Charter* art. 55, reprinted in Howland, supra note 49, 80. Forced relocation violates the Native Americans' right to self-determination. This right is also recognized in Article One of the International Covenant on Economic, Social, and Cultural Rights, Article One of the International Covenant on Civil and Political Rights, and Article II of the International Convention on the Suppression and Punishment of the Crime of Apartheid. Howland, supra note 49, 80-81. For an account of the United States treatment of the tribes in the context of the recognized international rights of indigenous peoples, see O'Brien, "Federal Indian Policies and the International Protection of Human Rights," in *American Indian Policy in the Twentieth Century*, (V. Deloria, ed., 1985), 35-60.

285. See Churchill, supra note 114, 16.

286. For a discussion on metropolis-satellite economies, see Jorgensen, "Energy, Agriculture, and Social Science in the American West," in *Native Americans and Energy*

Development, 9-12, (Anthropology Resource Center, ed., 1978).

287. See ibid., 12-13. Neocolonialism occurs worldwide. For a description of its effects in the Caribbean, see Seigle, "'We Caribbean Revolutionaries Can Overcome Insularity': Interview with Don Rojas," *The Militant*, (Feb. 5, 1988), 9, col. 2. For a description of the distinction between old colonialism, with its reliance on territorial conquest and manpower, and the new neocolonialism, see R. Davis and M. Zannis, *The Genocide Machine in Canada: Pacification of the North*, quoted in La Duque, supra note 166, 12.

288. Jorgensen, supra note 286, 9.

289. Page, "Reservation Development in the United States: Peripherality in the Core," *Am. Indian Culture and Res. J.*, 9, (1985), 21, 28, (No. 3).

290. Ibid.

291. Jorgensen, supra note 286, 10.

292. Ibid., 9. The Navajo, for example, are not receiving a fair return on their energy resource leases. P. Reno, supra note 13, 116. For example, a 1957 agreement between the tribe and the Utah Mining and Construction Company provided for tribal royalties of 15 cents a ton for "as long as coal is being produced in paying quantities." Ibid., 114. Since 1957, coal prices have risen and inflation has lowered the value of that 15 cents. The loss to the tribe means gain to the company. Ibid., 114-15.

293. P. Reno, supra note 13, 116.

294. Ibid.

295. "Cherokee Nation v. Georgia," U.S. (5 Pet.), 30, (1831), 1, 17. See supra notes 24-27 and accompanying text. A modern commentator has similarly described the tribes as "internal colonies." Jorgensen, supra note 286, 12.

296. B. Johnson and R. Maestas, supra note 50, 211-12.

297. See *Interim Strategy*, supra note 195, 816.

298. Some tribes are undertaking development on their own. Beck, supra note 245, 50; see also P. Reno, supra note 13, 115-16. For example, the Crow tribe announced plans to mine its own coal. Ibid. Federal law recognizes the right of the tribes to develop mineral resources. U.S.C., 25, (1982), 2108; see also *1982 U.S. Code Cong. and Admin. News 3470*.

299. See supra notes 103-08 and accompanying text.

300. See La Duque, supra note 166, 12; "Radioactive Colonialism," supra note 163, 56.

301. See Owens, supra note 273, 50.

302. See Ruffing, "Strategy for Asserting Control Over Mineral Development in American Indian Reservations," in *Economic Development in American Indian Reservations*, 142, CR. Ortiz, ed., 1979). The Navajo tribe in the 1950's attempted to create a partnership with a major corporation for the purpose of developing uranium resources, but the Department of the Interior never approved the plan. *U.S. Commission on Civil Rights, The Navajo Nation: An American Colony*, 133, (1975), [hereinafter *American Colony*].

303. See supra notes 222-25 and accompanying text.

304. See, e.g., SDWA, U.S.C., 42, (Supp. IV 1986), 300j-11j; *CWA*, U.S.C.A., 33, (West Supp. 1988), 1377; *CAA*, U.S.C., 42, (1982), 7474(c).

305. Some tribal leaders feel that President Reagan's motives were "to get the Indians off the government's back by pandering to their desire for independence while ignoring their needs." Winslow, supra note 237, 177.

306. *American Colony*, supra note 302, 24.

307. Ibid.; see also P. Reno, supra note 13, 10.

308. B. Johnson and R. Maestas, supra note 50, 215-16; Owens, supra note 273, 61.

309. See "U.S. Department of State Report on Nationalization, Expropriation, and Other Takings of U.S. and Certain Foreign Property Since 1960," I.L.M., 11, (1972), 84. Argentina, Chile, Mexico, Algeria, Congo, Libya, and the People's Republic of Yemen, among other nations, have nationalized foreign corporations' natural resource extraction operations, providing a variety of forms and degrees of compensation. Ibid., 89-115. A 1962 United Nations General Assembly Resolution declared that "[t]he right of people's [sic] and nations to permanent sovereignty over their natural wealth and resources must be exercised in the interest of their national development and of the well-being of the people in the state concerned." "Permanent Sovereignty Over Natural Resources General Assembly Resolution 1803, (XVII)," (Dec. 14, 1962), reprinted in J. Sweeny, C. Oliver, and N. Leech, *The International Legal System*, 1114-15, (2d. ed., 1981), [hereinafter Sweeny].

310. Sweeny, supra note 309, 1112. This is known as the Calvo doctrine. Ibid. This doctrine was incorporated into the 1962 U.N. General Assembly Resolution. Ibid., 1115. The United States opposes the Calvo doctrine, asserting instead an international minimum standard under which the entity whose property is expropriated is entitled to prompt, adequate, and effective compensation from the expropriating country. Ibid., 1108-12; see also Carasco, "A Nationalization Compensation Framework in the New International Economic Order," in *Third World Attitudes Toward International Law*, 659-89, (F. Snyder and S. Sathirathai, eds., 1987).

311. Sweeny, supra note 309, 1112.

312. U.S.C., 25, (1982), 415(a). The tribes may also want to petition the federal government to end the MMS and BIA intermediary roles and to require the lessee energy and minerals companies to pay royalties directly to the tribes. For a discussion on the problems of the MMS, see supra notes 126-33 and accompanying text.

313. See supra notes 192-229 and accompanying text.

314. La Duque, supra note 166, 12.

315. Ibid.

316. Ibid.

317. Owens, supra note 273, 62. The implications of resource development on culture and vice versa cannot be overestimated. See Vinje, "Cultural Values and Economic Development on Reservations," in *American Indian Policy in the Twentieth Century*, 155-75 (V. Deloria, ed., 1985). Native American cultures include a relationship to the land that differs from that of Western white culture. For traditional Native Americans, the Earth is alive and people are part of the Earth. See P. Allen, *The Sacred Hoop*, 119, (1986). Many Southwestern tribes, for example, share a belief that when they lose their land the world will end. P. Reno, supra note 13, 10. A land deadened by excessive exploitation may have the same effect as the loss of land.

318. See B. Johnson and R. Maestas, supra note 50, 232.

319. Ibid.

Chapter IX

American Indian Lands: The Native Ethic amid Resource Development

Ward Churchill

Within the industrial wasteland of the late twentieth century, the traditional Native American relationship to the environment has become the stuff of pop mythology. A television public-service announcement features an aging Indian, clad in beads and buckskins, picking his way carefully among mounds of rusting junk along a well-polluted river. He concludes his walk through the modern world by shedding a tragic tear induced by the panorama of rampant ecological devastation surrounding him.

The undergirding message is clear enough: The common good requires that we clean up the habitat before it becomes uninhabitable. The use of an archaic Indian image is intended not only to stir the country's sense of survival but to strum the strings of collective guilt as well; having slaughtered the native population as a means to expropriate its land base, the new North Americans now have an obligation to make things right by preserving and protecting that which was stolen.

This tidy mental construction effectively obscures several important realities. Among these are:

• the fundamental—rather than mythological—nature and requirements of the American Indian world view, which allowed ecologically sound occupancy of the hemisphere for many thousands of years before the coming of the European (see pages 228-231). In contrast, the European-derived system has generated environmental crisis on the same land, and over a span of barely 200 years.

205

• the capability, in many cases, of the contemporary Indian to articulate and practice the traditional world view. The Indian still retains both aboriginal and treaty-guaranteed title to much of North America's land and resources. Hence, functioning models of Indian interaction with the natural world should stand today as adaptable examples of ecological alternatives available to all.

• the continued removal from rightful Indian owners of a goodly portion of the resources by which America today maintains its style of living. As in the nineteenth century, both the fact and methods employed in this theft continue to have the direst impact upon Indian people and their environments.

• the displacement of some of the worst aspects of industrially related pollution of the past quarter-century to remote Indian land. This has the effect of hiding (temporarily, at least) rather than resolving many of the inherent issues of advanced industrialization, while imposing a number of its worst consequences upon those who have tended to be the most philosophically and practically resistant to it.

Although the traditional Indian world view survives, contemporary use of the perspective it supports is prevented. The examples here of the results of such prevention are intended not merely to share information or to instill guilt in non-Indians, but to add to the message of Winona LaDuke, an Anishinabe activist:

> They sometimes call us "the First Americans." I've wondered what that means, and the only thing I've come up with is that Indians are always the first to feel the sharp end of the stick: the first to suffer biological and chemical warfare at the hands of the U.S. government, the first to lose their land to big business, the first to lose their legal and human rights in the national interest, the first to be laid off from any jobs they mange to find, the first to be cut from the social services budget every year. . . .

> But we are never the last to suffer what we first experience, and I think that's something everybody

might think about. Non-Indians will be next. . . . And if you don't want to believe me, go ask a farmer about his land these days. Go ask somebody from Love Canal or Three Mile Island about their health. Go ask an Appalachian miner about his job and the benefits of transient, extractive industries.[1]

Carving Up Indian Country

In the moral sense, Indians retain what is generally termed "aboriginal rights" to at least a portion of the lands they have occupied for thousands of generations. It is recognized in law that such rights exist, and that the U.S. government has an obligation to ensure the basis for survival (including land and water) of the indigenous peoples that the government has subsumed.[2] However, doctrines for application of this principle have been left so fuzzy and used so seldom that it may be accurately noted that the concept holds no real force in law.

Much more pragmatically focused are the 371 treaties existing between the federal government and various American Indian nations. In many of these documents, native people reserved sizable and clearly defined territories for their own exclusive use and occupancy, free from internal interference by the United States.[3] For its part the U.S. government concurred with such arrangements, and congressional ratification made them "the supreme Law of the Land" under Article VI (2) of the U.S. Constitution.

Equally clear under both U.S. domestic and international law is the Indian right to sovereign control over reserved territories conveyed by use of treaty instruments. The federal government is not empowered to enter into treaty relations with any entity other than a fully sovereign nation. Hence, the treaty-making process amounted to formal recognition of each Indian people with which a treaty was signed as a nation separate from the United States, as well as the mutual agreement of both parties as to the borders of such nations.

Hence, one would expect to find a number of presently functioning and self-sufficient indigenous North American societies. But the federal government has acted unilaterally and quite illegally—under both its own and international law—to prevent this from happening in two primary ways:

• The U.S. government has steadily usurped Native American national sovereignty by imposition of its own jurisdiction over Indians' reserved land base, supplanting traditional governmental and juridical forms in the name of a self-proclaimed "trust responsibility."
• This expedient has been employed to legally strip away much of the Native Americans' treaty-guaranteed land base and to deny them direct control over residual areas, especially on terms of control over water and resources.

A patent example occurred in 1887 with passage of the General Allotment Act (usually called the Dawes Act), in which the U.S. Congress decided that American Indians should not practice "collective ownership" of their treaty areas (national territories), but that each individual should own a private parcel of 160 acres. This policy, backed by the U.S. Army, was intended to "civilize" the Indians, in effect to deliberately undercut the traditional way of relating to the land. Once each eligible Indian (as defined by the United States) had received his or her individual parcel, the remainder of the reservation land base was declared "surplus" and opened up to non-Indian acquisition. In this manner, Indian landholdings within the 48 contiguous United States was reduced from some 138 million acres in 1887 to 48 million acres in 1934 (see Figure 1).[4]

In 1924 Congress passed the so-called Indian Citizenship Act, in which Native Americans were unilaterally declared to be "dual citizens" (of both their respective indigenous nations and the United States) with all the legal responsibilities to the national interest that such a role involved.[5] This act was followed in 1934 by the Indian Reorganization Act (IRA), under which Congress decided that traditional Indian governmental structures were not legitimate, and "democratized" American Indian government by imposing structures designed to replicate corporate directorates. This is to say that the IRA governments served as boards of directors validating various business leases and other contractual arrangements negotiated by the Department of the Interior between corporations and

Indian peoples. Thereafter, the IRA "tribal council" apparatus was the only form of Indian representation the federal government would acknowledge or deal with.[6]

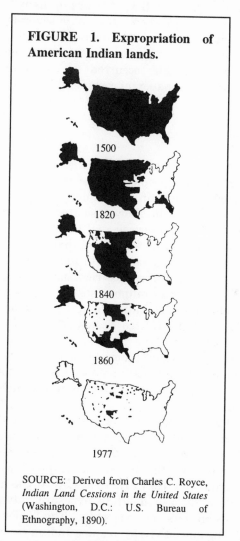

FIGURE 1. Expropriation of American Indian lands.

1500

1820

1840

1860

1977

SOURCE: Derived from Charles C. Royce, *Indian Land Cessions in the United States* (Washington, D.C.: U.S. Bureau of Ethnography, 1890).

By 1953, under the House Concurrent Resolution 108, Congress assigned itself the right to "terminate" Indian nations—that is, to declare them nonexistent—at its discretion.[7]

This was more or less coupled with the passage of Public Law 280 the same year; under this legislation the federal government placed Indian nations at a civil and criminal jurisdictional level below that of states in many cases.[8]

At the present juncture, the fully sovereign status of American Indian nations has been reduced by federal fiat to where it falls roughly between the status of counties and of municipalities. This has occurred despite Indian nations' nominal retention, on paper, of considerable land and resource holdings.

Resource-Rich Lands

The unstated rationales guiding the federal government in its handling of native peoples and territories after the treaty-making period are not difficult to decipher. It is simply not geopolitically efficient to allow a scattering of small, mostly landlocked nations to exercise real sovereignty within one's own borders. Moreover, it was found that, perhaps ironically, the barren residual land base left to Indians in the twentieth century was extremely resource rich: some 60 percent of all known U.S. domestic uranium reserves and one-third of its low-sulfur coal lie under Indian land. In addition, about one-quarter of the oil the United States counts as its own, and perhaps 15 percent of the natural gas, are in reservation areas.[9] Substantial assets of commercial and strategic minerals such as gold, copper, and bauxite are at issue, as are water in the arid West and subsidiary considerations such as grazing land, timber, and the like.[10]

With such holdings, it would seem logical that the 1.5 million Indians would be among North America's wealthiest inhabitants. However, as even the federal government's figures reveal, they receive the lowest per capita income of any population group and they experience by far the highest rates of malnutrition, disease, death by exposure, infant mortality, and other signifiers of poverty.[11] The government has discovered long since that, by keeping Indian resources pooled in reservation areas under trust, it is able to channel the resources at very low rates to preferred corporations, using the tribal council apparatus it established in 1934 as a medium for leasing purposes.[12] Thus, as of 1984, Indians were receiving for uranium extracted from their land an average of 3.4 percent of the market value, 1.6 percent of the value for their oil, 11.3 percent for natural gas, and about 2 percent for coal. These figures run as much as 85 percent under the royalty rates paid to non-Indians for the same items.[13]

This boon to the U.S. economy is enhanced by the government's utilization of its trust position over Indians and Indian land to relax or dispense with environmental protection standards and job safety regulations, further lowering extraction and production costs.[14] Certain of the more odious forms of production and waste disposal associated with advanced industrial technologies may have come to be conveniently located—out of sight and mind of the mainstream public—in Indian areas.

From the government's perspective, the advantages of maintaining discrete Indian territories under direct U.S. trust control vastly outweigh any potential benefit accruing from final absorption of these residual areas. The history of conquest that has always marked the U.S. relationship to Native Americans has correspondingly been transformed into a process of colonization, albeit of an internal variety peculiar to highly evolved settler states. (Australia, New Zealand, Canada, and South Africa are other prime examples of this phenomenon.) The impacts of this system on American Indian environments and the people who inhabit them are best demonstrated by focusing on the two U.S. regions with the greatest concentrations of Indian population.

The Four Corners Region

Although less than 65 percent of North America's uranium deposits are known to lie within reservation areas, 80 percent of the mining and 100 percent of the national production have occurred there since uranium became a profitable commodity between 1950 and 1952.[15] The bulk of this activity has occurred in the Grants Uranium Belt of the Colorado Plateau—the so-called Four Corners region, where the boundaries of Utah, Arizona, Colorado, and New Mexico intersect. The area is also home to the greatest concentration of Indian population remaining in North America: the Navajo, Southern Ute, Ute Mountain, Hopi, Zuni, Laguna, Acoma, and several other Pueblo nations.

In 1952 the U.S. Interior Department's Bureau of Indian Affairs awarded the Kerr-McGee Corporation the first contract (duly endorsed by the Navajo Tribal Council) to mine uranium on Navajo land, employing 100 Navajo miners at two-thirds the off-reservation wage scale.[16] In the same year a federal mine inspector at the Shiprock, New Mexico, facility discovered that the ventilation fans in the mine's primary shaft were not functioning.[17] When the same inspector returned in 1955, the ventilation fans ran out of fuel during his visit. By 1959 radiation levels in the shaft of the Shiprock facility were estimated at 90 to 100 times the permissible limits for worker safety.[18] Nothing was done about the situation before the uranium deposit played out and the Shiprock operation was closed in early 1970. At that point, Kerr-McGee pulled out, leaving the local community to contend with some 70 acres of raw uranium tailings containing approximately 80 percent of the original radioactivity found in uranium ore, piled in huge mounds beginning less than 60 feet from the San Juan River—the only significant surface water in the Shiprock area.[19]

Of the 150-odd Navajo miners who worked underground at the Shiprock facility over the years, 18 had died of radiation-induced lung cancer by 1975.[20] By 1980 an additional 20 were dead of the same disease and another 95 had contracted other serious respiratory ailments and cancers.[21] The incidence of cleft palate and other birth defects linked to increased radiation exposure had risen dramatically, both at Shiprock and at downstream communities that had drinking water contaminated by the uranium tailings.[22] Yet by 1982, 42 similar mining operations and 7 milling operations were installed on or immediately adjacent to Navajo land; 15 new uranium-oriented projects were on the drawing board.[23] The Kerr-McGee facility at Churchrock by itself discharges some 80,000 gallons of water from its primary shaft (dewatering) per day, water that is introduced directly into local and downstream water supplies.[24]

In July 1979 the United Nuclear Corporation uranium mill, also located at Churchrock, was the site of the largest radioactive spill in U.S. history. A mill tailings dam broke under pressure and released more than 100 million gallons of highly contaminated water into the Rio Puerco. Although United Nuclear had known of cracks in the dam structure at least two months before the break, no repairs were made.[25] About 1,700 Navajo people were immediately affected, their single water source contaminated beyond any conceivable limit. Sheep and other livestock were found to be heavily contaminated in the aftermath.[26] United Nuclear refused to supply emergency water and food supplies to the community, and stonewalled for over a year before agreeing to pay even a minimal out-of-court settlement to the victims.[27] The same sort of situation prevails across the Navajo nation lands, from the windswept tailings piles at Dalton Pass in the east to those of Tuba City in the west.[28]

At the neighboring Laguna Pueblo in New Mexico, the situation is perhaps worse. The Anaconda Corporation, which leases 7,000 acres of Laguna land via an arrangement negotiated by the Interior Department, conducted a uranium stripping operation there from 1952 to 1981 when, as in the case of Kerr-McGee's Shiprock mine, the profitably extractable ore played out. In 1973 the Environmental Protection Agency (EPA) informed the Indians that Anaconda's Jackpile Mine had seriously contaminated the Rio Paguate, the pueblo's only surface water.[29] In 1975 it was revealed that the groundwater underlying the whole of the Grants Uranium Belt, into which Laguna's wells are tapped, was also highly contaminated.[30] In 1978 EPA discovered that the tribal council building, community center, and newly constructed Jackpile Housing Project were also very contaminated, and that the corporation had used low-grade uranium ore as the material with which to "improve" the Laguna road network.[31] In addition, it was soon found that disturbed ore pockets had permeated much of the arable land available to the pueblo.[32]

The "radioactive colonization"[33] of the Four Corners is hardly the end of the environmental havoc in the region (see Figure 2). WEST Group, a consortium of 23 energy-production companies based in Salt Lake City, Utah, has established a rapidly proliferating complex of coal-fired generating facilities in the area. The largest of these, the Four Corners Power

Plant, emits a huge and dense plume of smoke that is observable from space. The formerly crystalline air of Monument Valley—sporting a visibility of some 100 miles in 1950—is now clogged with enough pollution to reduce lines of vision to 15 miles or less in many cases. The smoke has also caused a radical increase in the acidity of rainfall throughout the region, with all the consequent damage to wildlife and vegetation that this entails.[34]

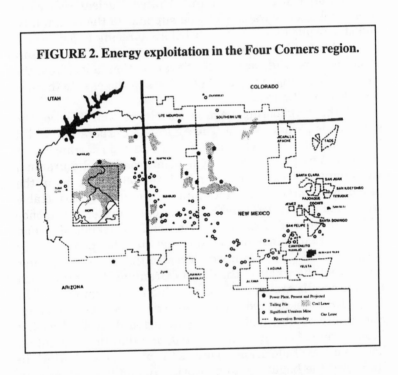

FIGURE 2. Energy exploitation in the Four Corners region.

The coal that fires these generators comes from the same land. One location, Black Mesa in the Navajo-Hopi Joint Use Area of Arizona, contains the largest (at least 20 billion tons) and most accessible (less than six inches below the surface of the ground in some places) deposit of low-sulfur coal in North America. Given that strip-mining of arid terrain such as Black Mesa leaves the land largely unreclaimable, fruition of plans to expand present Peabody Coal mining operations to full development of the deposit will render the area uninhabitable by both Navajos and Hopis.[35] Indeed, under provisions of Public Law 93-531, the U.S. government is presently engaged in the relocation of some 13,000 Indians from the Joint Use Area as an expedient to clearing the way for accelerated coal stripping.[36]

Finally, it has been found that the most cost-effective means of transporting coal from mine pits, both at Black Mesa and elsewhere in the area, to railheads and power plants is by slurry, that is, by literally washing it in a solution of 50 percent water and 50 percent coal through pipelines extending from point to point. Water for this purpose is already being pumped from subterranean aquifers at the rate of millions of gallons per year. Should mining operations be expanded as projected, it is predicted that all groundwater in the area will be depleted by the early twenty-first century, resulting in an "American Sahara."[37]

The National Science Advisory Commission perhaps had all of these factors in mind when, in 1972, it informally recommended to the Nixon administration that serious consideration be given to designating the Four Corners region a "National Sacrifice Area" for purposes of attaining "national energy self-sufficiency" by 1999.[38] While no U.S. president has employed such terminology publicly, it is clear that the advisory commission's prospectus of converting the Colorado Plateau into a gigantic, uninhabited energy park, available for use as a repository for toxic waste disposal and storage, is well under way. For the ecosystem of the area and the native nations in it, the scenario spells a final liquidation.

The Black Hills Region

The Four Corners region is not alone. Also informally designated as a National Sacrifice Area[39] is the Black Hills region, homeland to the various western Sioux (Teton Lakota) nations, and the Arapahoe, Shoshoni, Crow, and Northern Cheyenne Indians. Although the entire region was guaranteed by the 1868 Fort Laramie Treaty as permanent Indian territory, 90 percent of it has now passed from native control (see Figure 3). Nevertheless, the area holds the second greatest concentration of landed Indians in North America. It is also one of the most mineral-rich regions in the United States, with vast quantities of gold, uranium, coal, and zeolites.

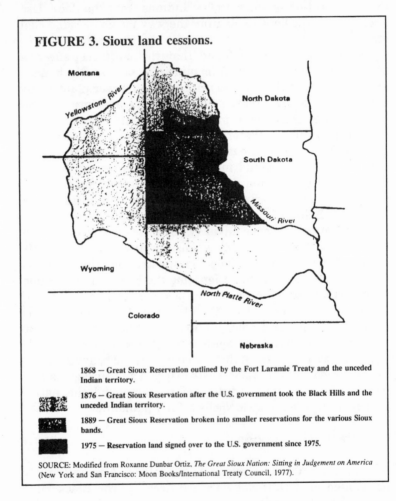

FIGURE 3. Sioux land cessions.

1868 — Great Sioux Reservation outlined by the Fort Laramie Treaty and the unceded Indian territory.

1876 — Great Sioux Reservation after the U.S. government took the Black Hills and the unceded Indian territory.

1889 — Great Sioux Reservation broken into smaller reservations for the various Sioux bands.

1975 — Reservation land signed over to the U.S. government since 1975.

SOURCE: Modified from Roxanne Dunbar Ortiz, *The Great Sioux Nation: Sitting in Judgement on America* (New York and San Francisco: Moon Books/International Treaty Council, 1977).

As of 1979 some 5,160 uranium claims by non-Indian businesses and corporations were held in the Black Hills National Forest alone, while an additional 218,747 acres of private land were under similar mining leases.[40] Although development and consolidation of the uranium industry within the 1868 treaty territory is not as pronounced as that on the Colorado Plateau, the environmental effects are similar. One June 11, 1962, an estimated 200 tons of uranium mill tailings washed into the Cottonwood Creek, a tributary of the Cheyenne River, which is the primary source of surface water for the Pine Ridge (Oglala Lakota) Reservation in South Dakota.[41] The tailings came from a mass of some 3.5 million tons abandoned by a U.S. government milling operation that ran from 1953 to 1966 at Igloo, a former ammunition depot located near the town of Edgemont, immediately west of Pine Ridge.[42]

The same governmental/corporate entities (the Department of Defense and the former Atomic Energy Commission) that in the mid-1950s claimed the uranium works near Edgemont constituted no public health hazard are now announcing that the area is so heavily contaminated it should become a national nuclear waste dump.[43] According to residents, the cancer rate among long-term Edgemont residents is spiraling, as are birth defects at nearby Pine Ridge. Both federal and business spokespersons have stated that putting such a facility in the Black Hills presents "no danger" to the population or the environment.[44] South Dakota Governor William Janklow, who campaigned on a platform against further nuclear development in the state, has apparently reversed his field and begun to advocate the dump siting.

Groundwater has also been heavily affected, as witnessed by a 1980 Indian Health Service report indicating well tests at the reservation village of Slim Buttes showed gross levels of alpha radiation in the water three times the national safety standard. At a newer well at Slim Buttes, tests recorded radiation levels fourteen times the standard.[45] Then Tribal Chairman Stanley Looking Elk requested that $175,000 of a $200,000 federal allocation for reservation water management be committed to securing uncontaminated emergency water supplies for the community. The Bureau of Indian Affairs agreed, but stipulated that such water be provided only for consumption by cattle, the beef being sold in non-Indian markets.[46]

Groundwater could well be the most immediately crucial issue. The plans for the Burdock coal mine, stripping the Fort

Union deposit underlying much of the region, entails the pumping of 675 gallons per minute from the area's quite limited groundwater resources. Dozens of other industrial undertakings relying on the Oglala aquifer are projected for the area (see Figure 4). As was noted in 1980:

> Overall, the plans for industrializing the Black Hills are staggering. They include a gigantic energy park featuring more than a score of 10,000 mega-watt coal-fired plants, a dozen nuclear reactors, huge coal slurry pipelines designed to use millions of gallons of water to move crushed coal thousands of miles, and at least 14 major uranium mines.[47]

Beyond the Myth

The same sort of portrait can be drawn throughout contemporary Native America, from the expropriation of copper-rich Papago land and water rights on the Mexican border earlier in this century (an issue currently escalating as the city of Tucson expands into the Papago Reservation to avail itself of Indian water) to the Alaskan North Slope today where, under provisions of the Alaska Native Claims Settlement Act, indigenous people stand to lose 44 million acres of their ancestral homelands. In California the same thing has already occurred as the government Indian Claims Commissioner resolved the question of indigenous title to most of the state via the expedient of forced compensation to the region's Native Americans at approximately $0.03 per acre.[48]

The environmental consequences of such actions are readily apparent in the Reynolds Aluminum Corporation's flouride contamination of the St. Regis Mohawk Reservation in upstate New York[49] or in the U.S. government's plan to situate a high-level nuclear waste dump at the Hanford site adjoining Washington state's Yakima reservation, as well as in the Four Corners or the Black Hills. In Canada, as the immersion of the James Bay Cree homeland by the James Bay hydroelectric project (generating additional power for the New York megalopolis) demonstrates, things are not very different.[50]

The James Bay situation is actually similar to the project

sponsored by the U.S. Army Corps of Engineers that immersed a portion of the traditional Sioux homeland in the central Dakotas by damming the Missouri River.[51] Likewise, river

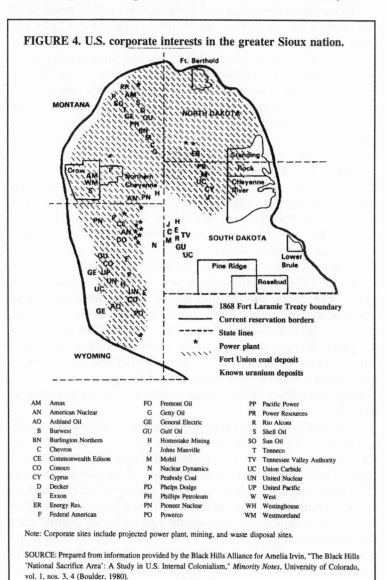

FIGURE 4. U.S. corporate interests in the greater Sioux nation.

1868 Fort Laramie Treaty boundary
Current reservation borders
State lines
★ Power plant
Fort Union coal deposit
Known uranium deposits

AM	Amax	FO	Fremont Oil	PP	Pacific Power
AN	American Nuclear	G	Getty Oil	PR	Power Resources
AO	Ashland Oil	GE	General Electric	R	Rio Alcom
B	Burwest	GU	Gulf Oil	S	Shell Oil
BN	Burlington Northern	H	Homestake Mining	SO	Sun Oil
C	Chevron	J	Johns Manville	T	Tenneco
CE	Commonwealth Edison	M	Mobil	TV	Tennessee Valley Authority
CO	Conoco	N	Nuclear Dynamics	UC	Union Carbide
CY	Cyprus	P	Peabody Coal	UN	United Nuclear
D	Decker	PD	Phelps Dodge	UP	United Pacific
E	Exxon	PH	Phillips Petroleum	W	West
ER	Energy Res.	PN	Pioneer Nuclear	WH	Westinghouse
F	Federal American	PO	Powerco	WM	Westmoreland

Note: Corporate sites include projected power plant, mining, and waste disposal sites.

SOURCE: Prepared from information provided by the Black Hills Alliance for Amelia Irvin, "The Black Hills 'National Sacrifice Area': A Study in U.S. Internal Colonialism," *Minority Notes*, University of Colorado, vol. 1, nos. 3, 4 (Boulder, 1980).

projects by the Tennessee Valley Authority beginning in 1953 have immersed many important sites within the Cherokee nation's traditional southeastern territory.[52]

Even when damming and hydroelectric power projects do not directly drown Indian lands, other effects devastating to traditional economics and environments are readily observable. Dam construction has destroyed numerous salmon runs—upon which area tribal economies depend—in the states of Oregon, Washington, and Idaho.[53] And, in a seemingly paradoxical reversal, the Seminole of the Florida Everglades suffer from the systematic drying out of their environment by the many private and public development projects, a matter that is rapidly destroying their traditional autonomous way of life.[54]

The Four Corners region represents approximately 5 percent of the continental United States. The Black Hills region constitutes another 5 percent. No one knows what effect the sacrifice of 10 percent of the U.S. land base will have on the remainder of the North American ecosystem, but overall it will not be positive. Acid rain and windblown radioactivity have no regard for reservation boundaries. It makes no sense to clean up the drinking water in urban areas while radioactive heavy metals dumped on Indian land leach into aquifers shared by both Indians and mainstream society. There is a certain futility to fighting the proliferation of nuclear weaponry and power plants unless such action is coupled with elimination of the front end of the production process—uranium mining and milling operations. What happens to American Indian lands ultimately happens to the rest of the environment as well.

In many ways, Indian activists seem to have absorbed and acted upon this principle much more readily than have their mainstream counterparts. Evidence of this is to be found in the high degree of direct participation of American Indian Movement (AIM) members in a wide variety of off-reservation actions. Indian delegates to Europe have also put themselves on the line in environmental campaigns called by groups such as the German Green Party.[55] At another level, indigenous nongovernmental organizations to the United Nations—the International Indian Treaty Council, American Indian Law Resource Center, and the World Council of Indigenous

Peoples—have consistently worked to keep broad environmental issues before the international community.

For their part, mainstream activists appear to have been reticent in supporting Indian issues. Even such well-publicized actions as the sustained AIM occupation of Yellow Thunder Camps in the Black Hills (a successful effort to remove a small parcel of the 1868 Fort Laramie Treaty territory from the effects of mining) obtained only meager and short-lived non-Indian participation.[56] The "TREATY" program for autonomy, self-sufficiency, and environmental protection launched by Indians on the Pine Ridge Reservation received even less support.[57] Direct non-Indian involvement in AIM campaigns in the Four Corners area has also been sporadic; it took nearly 10 years to attract significant mainstream involvement in opposition to the planned mining-related forced relocation of thousands of traditional Indians from Black Mesa (scheduled for implementation this year).[58]

Such default seems due to Native Americans' insistence on linking the issue of their own sovereignty to environmental concerns, a matter which many mainstream activists feel is irrelevant at best, retrograde at worst.[59] In this cause, Indians realized that sacrifice of native rights simply forecloses the (re)emergence of ecologically viable social countermodels in North America. Put another way, every inch of land returned to its rightful Indian occupants is an inch withdrawn from the ravages of the present industrial order.

Given that the land in question represents precisely those areas of the continent most imminently threatened, the return of Indian land to Indian owners is rendered doubly important. What is needed, and immediately so, is an increasing awareness of the realities of Indian existence, both historical and contemporary. Only from the basis of such awareness can impending environmental catastrophe throughout Indian country be prevented.

NOTES

1. Winona LaDuke, speech presented at American Indian Women's Symposium, International Women's Week, (Boulder: University of Colorado, 12 March 1984).

2. This concept dovetails nicely, at least in theory, with the provision under Article II of the 1948 United Nations Convention on the Prevention and Punishment of the Crime of Genocide that makes it an aspect of this crime to "bring about conditions leading to the destruction, in whole or in part, of an identified racial, ethnic, religious or national group." The United States finally ratified the convention in 1986.

3. For the full texts of all 371 treaties, see Charles J. Kappler, *Indian Treaties, 1778-1883,* (New York: Interland Publishing Co., 1973).

4. Vine Deloria, Jr., and Clifford M. Lytle, *American Indians, American Justice,* (Austin: University of Texas Press, 1983), 10.

5. Ibid., 11, 217-18.

6. Vine Deloria, Jr., and Clifford M. Lytle, *The Nations Within: The Past and Future of American Indian Sovereignty,* (New York: Pantheon Books, 1984); see also Lawrence C. Kelly, *The Assault on Assimilation: John Collier and the Origins of Indian Policy Reform,* (Albuquerque: University of New Mexico Press, 1983).

7. Deloria and Lytle, note 4 above, 17.

8. Ibid., 18-19; see also Carole E. Goldberg, *Public Law 280: State Jurisdiction over Reservation Indians,* (Los Angeles: University of California American Indian Culture and Research Center, 1975).

9. See Lorraine Turner Ruffing, "The Role of Policy in American Indian Mineral Development," in Roxanne Dunbar Ortiz, ed., *American Indian Energy Resources and Development,* (Albuquerque: University of New Mexico Institute for Native American Development, 1980), 51.

10. Ibid., 41-69; concerning water, see Norris C. Hundley, Jr., "The Dark and Bloody Ground of Indian Water Rights," in Roxanne Dunbar Ortiz and Larry Emerson, eds., *Economic Development in American Indian Reservations,* (Albuquerque: University of New Mexico Institute for Native American Development, 1979), 46-60.

11. See U.S. Department of Health, Education, and Welfare, *A Statistical Portrait of the American Indian,* (Washington, D.C.: U.S. Government Printing Office, 1976). Subsequent updates and addenda reveal no appreciable change

in the situation.

12. See Klara B. Kelly, "Federal Indian Land Policy and Economic Development in the United States," in Ortiz and Emerson, eds., note 10 above, 30-41; see also Lynn A. Robbins, "Structural Changes in Navajo Government Related to Development," in Ortiz and Emerson, eds.,note 10 above, 129-135.

13. See Joseph G. Jorgensen, "The Political Economy of the Native American Energy Business," in Joseph G. Jorgensen, ed., *Native Americans and Energy Development II,* (Boston: Anthropology Resource Center, Seventh Generation Fund, 1984), 10-51; see also Richard Nafzinger, "Transnational Energy Corporations and American Indian Development," in Ortiz, ed., note 9 above, 9-38. Of additional interest is the film *Broken Rainbow,* (Earthworks Productions, Los Angeles, 1985).

14. For a succinct articulation of this principle, see Jorgensen, note 13 above.

15. See Nancy J. Owens, "Can Tribes Control Energy Development?," in Joseph G. Jorgensen, ed., *Native Americans and Energy Development I,* (Boston: Anthropology Resource Center, 1978), 53-54.

16. In addition to the Navajos employed as underground miners by Kerr-McGee during this period, somewhere between 300 and 500 were involved in "independent" Small Business Administration-supported operations (mining shallow—50 feet or less—deposits of rich uranium ore), sold in small lots to an Atomic Energy Commission-buying station located at the Kerr-McGee milling facility. They left behind between 100 and 200 open shafts, all emitting radon gas into the atmosphere. See Harold Tso and Lora Mangum Shields, "Navajo Mining Operations: Early Hazards and Recent Interventions," *New Mexico Journal of Science,* 12:1, (1980), 13.

17. J. B. Sorenson, "Radiation Issues: Government Decision Making and Uranium Expansion in Northern New Mexico," Working Paper no. 14, (San Juan Basin Regional Uranium Study, Albuquerque, 1978), 2.

18. Ibid; Tom Barry, "Bury My Lungs at Red Rock," *The Progressive,* October 1976, 25-27; see also Winona LaDuke, "The History of Uranium Mining," *Black Hills, Paha Sapa Report,* 1:1, (1979), 2; Tso and Shields, note 16 above.

19. Author's measurement. As Tso and Shields note in their article (note 16 above), "This tailings pile is also within one mile of a day care center, the public schools . . . the Shiprock business district and cultivated farmlands."

20. M. J. Samel et al., "Uranium Mining and Lung Cancer Among Navajo Men," *New England Journal of Medicine,* 310, (1984), 1481-84.

21. See Rich Nafziger, "Indian Uranium Profits and Perils," *Red Paper,* (Albuquerque: Americans for Indian Opportunity, 1976); see also Winona LaDuke, "How much Development?," *Akwesasne Notes,* (Mohawk Nation via Rooseveltown, NY), 11:1, (1979), 5.

22. Lora Mangum Shields and Alan B. Goodman, "Outcome of 13,300 Navajo Births from 1964-1981 in the Shiprock Uranium Mining Area," (paper delivered at the American Association of Atomic Scientists Symposium, New York, 25 May 1984).

23. Winona LaDuke, "The Council of Energy Resource Tribes," in Jorgensen, ed., note 13 above, 62.

24. New Mexico Environmental Improvement Agency, Memorandum, (Santa Fe, 21 May 1980).

25. Christopher McCleod, "Kerr-McGee's Last Stand," *Mother Jones,* (December 1980).

26. New Mexico Environmental Improvement Agency, note 24 above. In this document, it was acknowledged that spill-area livestock exhibited "higher than normal" levels of lead 210, polonium 210, thorium 230, and radium 236. Indian Health Service area director William Mohler nonetheless suggested the Indians go ahead and eat their animals, while cautioning that they should "perhaps" avoid consuming "organ tissues," where radioactive toxins were expected to lodge most heavily. McCleod (Ibid.) points out that Churchrock sheepherders were still having difficulty locating commercial markets for their mutton three years after the spill. In other words, the animals were deemed safe by the government for consumption by Navajos, but not by non-Indians in New York and London.

27. Lynn A. Robbins, "Energy Development and the Navajo Nation: An Update," in Jorgensen, ed., note 13 above, 121-23.

28. For Dalton Pass, Ibid., 123-24; for Tuba City, see the

film *The Four Corners: A National Sacrifice Area?*, (Earth Image Films, San Francisco, 1981).

29. Richard Hoppe, "A Stretch of Desert Along Route 66—The Grants Belt—Is Chief Locale for U.S. Uranium," *Engineering and Mining Journal,* 179:11, (1978), 79-93.

30. U.S. Environmental Protection Agency, unpublished report, number deleted (filed with the Southwest Research and Information Center, Albuquerque, June 1973).

31. *Newsletter of the Native American Solidarity Committee,* (Berkeley, CA, Spring 1979), 12-13.

32. Michael Garrity, "The U.S. Colonial Empire is as Close as the Nearest Reservation," in Holly Sklar, ed., *Trilateralism: The Trilateral Commission and Elite Planning for World Management,* (Boston: South End Press, 1980), 242.

33. Winona LaDuke and Ward Churchill, "Native America: The Political Economy of Radioactive Colonization," *Journal of Ethnic Studies,* 13:33, (1985), 107-32.

34. Winona LaDuke and Faye Brown, "Water, Water Everywhere. . . ." *New Age,* (April 1983), 42-50.

35. See Jerry Kammer, *The Second Long Walk: The Navajo-Hopi Land Dispute,* (Albuquerque: University of New Mexico Press, 1980), 1-19.

36. See Ward Churchill, "Genocide in Arizona? The Navajo-Hopi Land Dispute in Perspective," *The Camp Crier,* 3:6,7, (1985); see also Ward Churchill, "Report to the Big Mountain Elders; Implications of U.S. Forced Relocation Policy in the 'Navajo-Hopi Joint Use Area' of Arizona under Provisions of International Law," *Akwesasne Notes,* 17:3,4, (1985).

37. See Jerry Mander, "Kit Carson in a Three-Piece Suit," *The CoEvolution Quarterly,* (Winter 1981), 52-63.

38. The notion of national sacrifice areas must have been in mind when the authors of the February 1979 Los Alamos National Laboratory "Mini-Report" wrote, "Perhaps the solution to the radon emission (radiation) problem is to zone the land into uranium mining and milling districts so as to forbid human habitation."

39. U.S. Department of the Interior, *North Central Power Study,* (Washington, D.C.: U.S. Government Printing Office, 1971).

40. Amelia Irvin, "Energy Development and the Effects of

Mining on the Lakota Nation," *Journal of Ethnic Studies*, 10:1, (1982), 89-102.

41. Henry Wasserman, "The Sioux's Last Fight for the Black Hills," *Rocky Mountain News*, 24 August 1980.

42. See Peter Matthiessen, *Indian Country*, (New York: Viking Press, 1984), 203-18.

43. "Nuclear Waste Facility Proposed near Edgemont," *Rapid City Journal*, 19 November 1982, 3.

44. "Edgemont Waste Facility No Hazard Says Chemical Nuclear Corp.," *Rapid City Journal*, 10 December 1982, 5.

45. Madonna Gilbert (Thunderhawk), "Radioactive Water Contamination on the Red Shirt Table, Pine Ridge Reservation, South Dakota," (Women of All Red Nations, Porcupine, S.D., March 1980).

46. Irvin, note 40 above, 99.

47. Wasserman, note 41 above.

48. See M. Annette Jaimes, "The Pit River Land Claim Dispute in Northern California," *Akwesasne Notes*, 17:6, (1985). In both the Black Hills and Pit River examples, the government has used monetary compensation of $0.05 to $0.50 per acre as a means of securing clear title to hundreds of thousands of acres of aboriginally reserved land.

49. H. Likke, "St. Regis: The Shrouded Nation," *Alternatives*, 31, (January 1983), 36-40.

50. See Mark Davis and Robert Zannis, *The Genocide Machine in Canada*, (Toronto: Black Rose Books, 1973).

51. See Michael L. Lawson, *Damned Indians: The Pick-Sloan Plan and the Missouri River Sioux, 1944-1980*, (Norman: University of Oklahoma Press, 1982).

52. Matthiessen, note 42 above, 105-26.

53. See American Friends Service Committee, *Uncommon Controversy: Fishing Rights of the Muckleshoot, Puyallup and Nisqually Indians*, (Seattle: University of Washington Press, 1970); see also Vine Deloria, Jr., *Indians of the Pacific Northwest*, (Garden City, N.Y.: Doubleday and Co., 1977).

54. Matthiessen, note 42 above, 1-14.

55. For an excellent recounting of the activities of this campaign, see Winona LaDuke, "Journey of Peace: The 1988 Native American Delegation to West Germany," *Akwesasne Notes*, 16:2, (1984), 19-21.

56. See Ward Churchill, "The Extralegal Implications of Yellow Thunder Tiospaye: Misadventure or Watershed Action?" *Policy Perspectives,* 2:2, (1982), 322-44.

57. See TREATY, "TREATY: Toward an Independent Oglala Nation" (TREATY, Porcupine, S.D., 1983).

58. See Ward Churchill, "The Navajos: No Home on the Range," *The Other Side,* 21:1, (1985), 22-27.

59. A very lucid articulation of this position is offered by Bill Tabb, "Marx versus Marxism," in Ward Churchill, ed., *Marxism and Native Americans,* (Boston: South End Press, 1983), 159-74.

The Indian View

The general conception of Native Americans before European contact holds that they wandered perpetually in scattered bands, grubbing out a marginal subsistence from hunting and gathering, without developing serious apprehensions of art, science, mathematics, governance, and so on. Aside from the Indians' utilization of furs and hides for clothing, the manufacture of stone implements, use of fire, and domestication of the dog, there is little in this view to distinguish Indians from the higher orders of mammalian life surrounding them in "the American wilderness."[1]

The conclusions reached by those who idealize "Indianness" are no different at base from the findings of those who denigrate it: Native Americans were able to inhabit the hemisphere for tens of thousands of years without causing appreciable ecological disruption only because they lacked the intellectual capacity to create social forms and technologies that would substantially alter their physical environment. In effect, a sort of sociocultural retardation on the part of Indians is typically held to be responsible for the pristine quality of the Americans at their point of "discovery" by the Europeans.[2]

In contrast to this perspective, it has recently been demonstrated that, far from living hand-to-mouth, "Stone Age" American Indians adhered to an economic structure that not only met their immediate needs but provided considerable surplus of both material goods and leisure time.[3] It has also been established that most traditional Native American economies were based in agriculture rather than in hunting and gathering—a clear implication of a stationary, not nomadic, way of life[4]—until Europeans dislocated the native populations in North America.

It is often argued that indigenous Americans' long-term coexistence with the environment was possible only because of the extremely low population level before European contact. However, serious historians have lately documented that statistics on native population levels in North America were deliberately set low during the nineteenth century to lessen the implications of genocide bound up in U.S. policy.[5] A noted ecological demographer has recently determined that, rather than being dramatically underpopulated at the point of European contact, North America was in fact saturated with people in 1500. The feasible carrying capacity of the continent, however, was outstripped by the European influx by 1840, despite massive reductions of native populations and numerous mammal groups.[6]

Another myth is contained in the suggestion that indigenous governmental forms were less advanced than their European counterparts. The enlightened republicanism, established by the United States during the late 1700s—usually considered a great advance over European norms—was lifted directly from the still functioning model of the Iroquois confederacy (with considerable dilution of Iroquois egalitarianism).[7] In many ways the Iroquois were indicative of the native political status quo across North America. Native Americans made similar achievements in preventive medicine,[8] calendrical mathematics,[9] astronomy, construction,[10] and architecture,[11] all without engendering appreciable environmental disruption. Such a juxtaposition of advanced sociocultural matrices and sustained ecological equilibrium is inexplicable from the vantage point of conventional European-derived assumptions.

Unlike Europeans, Native Americans long ago achieved a profound intellectual apprehension that human progress must be measured as an integral aspect of the natural order, rather than as something apart from and superior to it. Within this structure, elaborated and perfected through oral tradition and codified as "law" in ceremonial and ritual forms, the indigenous peoples of this hemisphere lived comfortably and in harmony with the environment, the health of which they recognized as an absolute requirement for their continuing existence.

In simplest terms, the American Indian world view may be this: Human beings are free (indeed, encouraged) to develop their innate capabilities, but only in ways that do not infringe upon other elements—called "relations," in the fullest dialectical sense of the word—of nature. Any activity going beyond this limitation is considered as "imbalance," a transgression, and is strictly prohibited. For example, engineering was and is permissible, but only insofar as it does not permanently alter the earth itself. Similarly, agriculture was widespread, but only within forms that did not supplant natural vegetation.

Key to the indigenous American world view is the firm acknowledgement that the human population may expand only to the point, determined by natural geographical and environmental circumstances, where it begins to displace other animal species and requires the permanent substitution of corp land for normal vegetation in any area. Indian populations never entered a trajectory of excessive growth, and even today, many Native American societies practice a self-regulation of population size that allows the substance of their traditional world view with its interactive environmental relationship to remain viable.

NOTES

1. References in this regard are legion. In general, we might say that the view was initiated with Christopher Columbus's reports to the Spanish Crown upon his discovery of the New World, were well codified by the time of John Smith and other English colonial journals and reports, and were academically perfected in the works of Mooney, Boas and other seminal anthropologists. By the present day it amounts to academic doctrine.

2. For a particularly virulent exposition of this view, and from a radical progressive source, see the Revolutionary Community Party, U.S.A. "Searching for the Second Harvest: Russell Means' Attack on Revolutionary Marxism," in Ward Churchill, ed., *Marxism and Native Americans* (Boston: South End Press, 1983), 35-58.

3. Marshall Sahlins, *Stone Age Economics* (Chicago: Aldine Publishing Co., 1972), 1-40.

4. See Roxanne Dunbar Ortiz, statements at the so-called Sioux Sovereignty Hearings held in Lincoln, Nebraska (1974), in Roxanne Dunbar Ortiz, ed., *The Great Sioux Nation: Sitting in Judgement on America* (New York and San Francisco: International Indian Treaty Council/Moon Books, 1977).

5. Francis Jennings, *The Invasion of America: Indians, Colonialism and the Cant of Conquest* (New York: W. W. Norton & Co., 1976), 15-31.

6. William Catton, *Overshoot* (Urbana: University of Illinois Press, 1981), 17-23.

7. For an excellent overview of the Iroquois role in the founding of the U.S. government, see Donald A. Grinde, Jr., *The Iroquois and the Founding of the American Nation* (San Francisco: Indian Historian Press, 1977); see also Barbara Graymont, *The Iroquois in the American Revolution* (Syracuse, NY: Syracuse University Press, 1972).

8. See Virgil Vogel, *American Indian Medicine* (Norman: University of Oklahoma Press, 1970); see also Alma R. Hutchins, *Indian Herbology of North America* (Ontario: Merco Publishers, 1969).

9. See Peter Tompkins, *Mysteries of the Mexican Pyramids* (New York: Harper and Row Publishers, 1976).

10. George Cumerman and Emil W. Haury, "Prehistory: Hohokam," in Alphonso Ortiz, ed., *Smithsonian Handbook on the American Indian: The Southwest,* vol. 9 (Washington, D.C.: Smithsonian Institution, 1979), 83.

11. See George S. Esber, Jr., "Indian Housing for Indians," *Kive* 37:3, (1972), 141-47; see also Patricia J. O'Brien, "Urbanism and Middle Mississippian," *Archaeology* 25:3, (1972), 189-97.

Chapter X

Other People's Trash: A Last Ditch Effort to Keep Corporate Garbage Off the Reservation

Paul Schneider and Dan Lamont

When you stand at Horseshoe Butte with two members of the Rosebud Sioux Tribe and look out over the rolling South Dakota prairie, one of the first thoughts to go through your head is that Connecticut is a long way to come from to build a trash dump, no matter how large. Another thought is that this particular piece of the Rosebud Indian Reservation—dotted with a few cattle and a few more trees and dissected by stream-carved draws that snake their way to the distant White River—cannot possibly be the "unproductive tract of land" described by those who plan to build a 6,000-acre mega-regional trash ranch here.

"Hey, you want a cookie?" Oleta Mednansky interrupts, holding out a tin of thick, chewy chocolate-chip and oatmeal cookies. She is of medium height and strong build, with dark eyes, black hair, and rich red-brown skin. With her husband, Rodney, she raises cattle on land within the proposed site. "My son loves to make cookies," she says.

But mostly what you wonder, standing there on Horseshoe Butte on a winter day, is whether these two Lakota women—"Sioux" was never this people's word for themselves—and their white husbands, and their friends both on and off the reservation, are really equipped to stop this dump from happening. The company that intends to build the facility, O&G Industries, Inc., of Torrington, Connecticut, is a $125-million-a-year construction firm. They have already set up a subsidiary, RSW, specifically to develop the dump. There is already an agreement to go ahead with the project signed by the tribal chairman and endorsed by the elected tribal council. And representatives from O&G and the tribal

232

government have already flown to Washington, D.C., to meet with the Bureau of Indian Affairs to try to ease the project through the bureaucracy that administers Native American policy.

"Take a few more than that," Mednansky says, pushing the cookie tin closer. "Around here we always say eat up," adds Marilyn Gangone, who also has the dark eyes, black hair, and red-brown skin of the Lakota. "Because we never know when we're going to get more to eat." Everyone laughs.

The taste of the homemade cookies, the speck of a hawk too far away to identify, and the sheer vastness of the land below all conspire to empty the mind. For a few minutes everyone just stands on Horseshoe Butte and looks. Then Oleta's husband, a tall, thin, cowboy-hatted man with "Rodney Mednansky" stamped in big letters on his belt, takes the cigaret out of his mouth. "See that little house way down there?" he says, squinting and pointing to a place in the middle of the proposed dump site. He blows some smoke. "That's where our son lives."

"Along the way we should stop and see if the Englands are home," Oleta says as everyone climbs back into the vehicles. "We can tell them about the meeting. Maybe we can get them to come." Tonight in St. Francis, South Dakota, is the first-ever meeting of citizens concerned about the proposed dump site. Marilyn and Oleta want as many people there as possible. "This is what we call the Indian telegraph," Gangone says, and everyone laughs again. "We use it when it's too windy for smoke signals," her husband Frank adds.

O&G Industries has other methods. Before the crucial tribal council vote, they flew three council members to company headquarters in Torrington for an all-expenses-paid fact-finding mission. They have a slide show extolling the environmental virtues of the dump and showing lush green examples of what a reclaimed landfill can look like. They have handouts that say in bold letters, "The RSW project is environmentally sound." But most of all, O&G has the tempting promise that in exchange for the Indians' accepting millions of tons of other people's trash—garbage, incinerator ash, coal ash, sewage sludge ash, shredded tires—each year, money and jobs will flow to a reservation sorely in need of both. Unemployment on the reservation runs to 65 percent or more; the tribal government is perennially broke. The landfill will bring lots of money, lots of jobs, the company says. It might even make the tribe's 18,000 members rich.

Nevertheless, the little group of brand-new activists driving the steep road down off of Horseshoe Butte is in relatively good spirits. For one, it's a beautiful day to be out rattling around the high prairie. For another, they all know that O&G came to Rosebud only after having a similar dump proposal stopped by grassroots opposition on the neighboring Pine Ridge Indian Reservation. They've heard, in fact, that all over the country Native Americans are running corporate garbage men off their reservations.

"I don't know why they didn't come and talk to the people around here," Marilyn says from the back seat. She is not the first person of the day to make that observation. "If they did, they would know we don't want this dump. We don't need other people's trash."

Regarding other people's trash, the Rosebud Sioux Tribe is not the first, only, or even most threatened group of Native Americans. Over the past five years Indian lands have become a favorite place to propose waste facilities of all kinds. The Navajo of Dilkon, Arizona, turned down an incinerator. The Kaw Tribe in Oklahoma narrowly defeated a similar proposal, as did the Paiute-Kaibab in Arizona. Last spring, the Mississippi Choctaw voted down a proposal for a hazardous waste dump on their land. The Mohawk of Canada and New York State have been approached at least nine times with waste proposals. Chikaloon Village in Alaska has been approached, as have the Moapa-Paiute. The Campo. The Standing Rock Sioux.

Most tribes eventually rejected the offers, but not all. Outside San Diego W.R. Grace & Co. is still trying to convince the La Posta Indian Reservation to become the final resting place for waste. In Palm Springs, California, the Cabazon Indian Reservation is experimenting with what proponents call a "safe incinerator." And the Rosebud Sioux Tribal Council has signed an agreement with O&G/RSW.

"It's safe to say, and I really am not exaggerating," says Bradley Angel of Greenpeace, "that dozens of companies—large and small, established and fly-by-night—have approached and are approaching literally hundreds of tribes." Angel spends most of his time assisting Native American groups doing battle with waste proposals.

What exactly attracts the trash peddlers to Indian land depends, of course, on who you ask. Companies usually claim coincidence; the search for a safe site just happened to lead to a reservation. "We looked at sites in South Carolina and in Florida, which from a marketing point of view are much better than South Dakota, but we didn't like the geological characteristics of the land," says Maurice Hoben, president of RSW. "We feel that because of the geography and the geology of this particular site in South Dakota, it may well eventually be the safest landfill in North America."

Sometimes companies portray themselves as environmentalists, playing to Native American pride in their own heritage as caretakers of the land. "I have heard Indians say that, because they love Mother Earth so much, they want to participate in environmental problem solving," a spokesperson for Waste-Tech Services, Inc., told a reporter from the *St. Louis Post-Dispatch* last year. Until it was turned away in short order by the Kaw and the Paiute-Kaibab, Waste-Tech, a subsidiary of Amoco, was considered to be at the forefront of the movement to site facilities on Native land.

At the Rosebud reservation, the appeal to Native environmentalism is buttressed by the tribe's need to clean up its own dumps. "'Mother Earth' is being contaminated by open, uncontrolled waste disposal and dumping," reads an O&G/RSW handout. Part of the company's deal with the tribe is that in exchange for hosting what Hoben describes as a "high-tech landfill capable of accepting all the Class I waste from South Dakota and much of the upper Midwest," the tribe can dump their own trash there for free. For a fee, O&G/RSW will even advise the reservation on how to clean up its own existing dumps. If the tribe doesn't clean them up, the company and pro-landfill officials are fond of saying, the tribe will be heavily fined by the federal government.

What O&G/RSW doesn't stress is that EPA regulations allowing for such fines are not yet in place, though they have been proposed, and that EPA has been notoriously lax about enforcement even off the reservation.

"Given [EPA's record] it is almost ludicrous to suggest that Native Americans are in any serious danger of being cited," says Peter Montague, a waste disposal expert at the Environmental Research Foundation. "Quite frankly, it sounds to me like bull."

"The Rosebud tribe will eventually be forced to clean up their own dumps and find some way to dispose of their trash in an acceptable landfill," insists Hoben. "They can pay to ship their waste somewhere else, which they cannot afford, or they can have a site on their own land and earn income from it. The tribe is no different from any other community in America with a solid waste problem."

But Native Americans are different: Their land is not subject to the same set of environmental regulations as the rest of the country. As semi-sovereign nations within the United States, tribes must comply with federal law, but are exempt from state and local regulations, environmental or otherwise. By law, state regulations governing hazardous and solid waste must be at least as strict as federal regulations; in practice, they are often tougher. And most tribes do not have strong environmental or zoning standards of their own that might make up for their state and local exemptions.

"We as a tribe don't have any sort of regulations at all when it comes to the environment," says Ike Schmidt, vice-president of the Rosebud Sioux Tribe and one of the only elected tribal officials to speak out against the proposed dump. "These companies know this, and that's why they're here." Critics also charge that the federal government is even less vigilant about enforcing federal environmental regulations on tribal land than off the reservation.

Not surprisingly perhaps, the suggestion that Native lands have become a vast regulatory loophole causes some at the Bureau of Indian Affairs to bristle.

"Look, let's just say that Greenpeace and all those others don't know what the hell they are talking about," says Carl Shaw from the Washington, D.C., BIA office. Shaw is in charge of maintaining good press relations for the bureau. "We don't rule these tribes. We don't have a policy one way or the other. How would I know why these companies are going to the reservations?"

The head of BIA's environmental office, George Farris, has a few more ideas. After explaining that the bureau requires environmental impact statements on all projects of the sort O&G/RSW wants to construct, he says, "It is my understanding that it is much easier to get a permit from the EPA and the bureau than it is at the state level. It's not that the companies get a free ride here at BIA, but they get a short ride."

The difference, Farris believes, is not that states have stricter standards—though he admits they sometimes do—but that the politics involved in getting a permit at the state level are prohibitive. This is because "not in my backyard" (NIMBY) is the most often voiced through state legislatures, popular referenda, and zoning. Voters in Rosebud's own state of South Dakota, for instance, approved a resolution last fall that prohibits the importation of out-of-state garbage.

O&G/RSW of course denies any connection between the regulatory climate and its selection of the Rosebud reservation. "That's just not the case," Hoben says. "We intend to abide by the law." But later he offers, somewhat curiously, "Whether or not EPA wants to enforce the laws on the reservations is, of course, up to them."

It's worth noting in this regard that an opening sentence of the agreement between the Rosebud Sioux Tribe and O&G/RSW states: "The parties understand, contemplate, and agree that in no event shall any environmental regulations or standards of the State of South Dakota be applicable to this project." The agreement further specifies that should the reservation ever wish to strengthen its own (currently nonexistent) environmental standards, the costs of such improvements will come entirely out of the tribe's pocket.

Ultimately, it is the emptiness of tribal pockets that draws waste management corporations to Indian land. The fact that the Indians are so poor, and yet in possession of relatively sizable amounts of land makes them obvious targets. O&G/RSW has promised an immediate payment of $100,000 to the tribe within a month of the project's receiving BIA/EPA approval, and a dollar per ton of waste dumped on the reservation thereafter. The rate would be even more generous if the company brought in more than three million tons a year. O&G/RSW gives no number of jobs that will be created, promising only that it will hire as many locals as possible.

Such promises don't go as far in wealthier places. Armed with newsletters, phone support networks, videotapes, and a growing band of "have expertise, will travel" advocates, the NIMBY movement has long since driven waste companies from middle-class American neighborhoods. Even formerly compliant Third World countries have gotten finicky of late. In the late 1980s, a barge of solid waste ash from Philadelphia was turned away by five continents, and the waste was presumably dumped at sea. The Marshall Islanders, Africans, and Mexicans—traditional recipients all—are becoming increasingly nervous about noxious exports from the United States.

But the trash keeps coming. Americans produce 320 *billion* pounds of garbage annually; almost three and a half pounds for each person daily. There is also somewhere between 290 million and 3 billion tons a year—even EPA doesn't know for sure—of hazardous industrial and medical waste looking for a cheap home. Meanwhile, many domestic landfills are filling up or are being shut down because pollutants are leaching into groundwater. It all has to go somewhere. But where?

Indian reservations, it would seem—the Third World within. "To me it's a real cynical exploitation of my people," says Carter Camp, a Ponca Indian who did battle with a proposed toxic waste incinerator in Oklahoma. Camp is a former president of the American Indian Movement and was one of the leaders of the uprising at Wounded Knee in 1973. "It is not quite as direct as the old attacks, but if you take the poorest people in the country and offer them these kinds of blandishments—that's what I call a very cynical exploitation."

Others see even more than cynicism. "This is all just another phase in the five-hundred-year-old policy of genocide against the American Indian," says Bill Koenen. He is a Chippewa who lives with his Lakota wife, Iron Cloud, on the Pine Ridge reservation near Rosebud. The two of them, along with another Lakota, JoAnn Tall, organized the opposition to O&G's proposal for a landfill on Pine Ridge. "I see EPA as a clearinghouse for the waste industry," says Koenen. "It is not a coincidence that this is happening on our land."

In his visions of conspiracy Koenen oddly sounds more like Cleve Neiss than either he or Neiss probably would care to admit. Neiss is the Rosebud tribal official who approached O&G and promised they would more easily get a site approved at Rosebud than at Pine Ridge. "Look, we all wish there was another way," Neiss said one morning in the rundown mobile home that serves as his office. The sign outside lists six different responsibilities, including solid waste management. "But we're being forced by EPA and Indian Health Service and everybody else. We can't afford to pay if they fine us, and we can't afford to ship our trash elsewhere." Neiss smiled. "We have no choice."

Whether cynical, diabolical, or coincidental, the trashing of America's reservations probably shouldn't be surprising. After all, waste companies are not entirely disingenuous when they say reservations are the best possible land for waste management. "A lot of times the land the federal government gave the Indians was the armpit of the nation," observes Roccena Lawatch, an Indian affairs specialist at EPA's San Francisco office. "It often actually is as good a site as any for a waste facility."

The unpleasant truth is that our waste is heading for the reservations because that is where we have always put things that we are uncomfortable with having in our own backyards. NIMBY is old news to Native Americans.

There is a small complication with all this white guilt, however, and it is on my mind heading into the tribal offices in Rosebud, South Dakota, some five days after the trip to Horseshoe Butte. In the front hall several elderly men and women sit beneath large bulletin boards covered with announcements, newspaper clippings, and posters. They nod and smile as I head down the narrow hallway that leads to the office of Ralph Moran, the elected chairman of the Rosebud Sioux Tribe. Moran's signature is on the landfill agreement with O&G/RSW. He is a Lakota. So is Cleve Neiss. So are the tribal councilors who voted in favor of the project. This is the complication: They are all Lakota people, and they all want this dump.

"I'd like to be there when people ask all these questions about Mother Earth," Moran says from behind his desk. He is a big man, carefully tucked into the blue jeans and western shirt that are the standard dress of men on the reservation. "If they are all so concerned about Mother Earth why did they continue to have these open dumps on the reservation? Why didn't they make sure those dumps were not harming Mother Earth?

"Over the past years we've been digging holes with no linings in them and filling them with trash. All of these things are seeping down into the aquifer." Moran stops and rubs his hands together uncomfortably. "So if you compare those with the modern-day landfill that we are presenting, with liners and monitoring wells around it to see that it won't seep, there is no comparison whatsoever about who is protecting Mother Earth, this administration or the past ones."

Moran begins or ends all of his comments with a summary of what he sees as the failings of the past tribal administrations, and with an assurance that all dump opponents just want to see his administration fail. He is very much a politician. But to be fair, so are a lot of people on the reservation. Dump opponents sometimes preface their own opinions with a litany of the unrelated past failings of Moran's administration. Or they launch into a not-unconvincing discussion of why the tribal government system has always represented the interests of outsiders rather than those of Native Americans. Or they claim that their very own mothers took money to vote for the current tribal government.

"Look," Moran says a few minutes later. "This is a done deal and you know it. It's gone through the council and that means it's done." He looks out the window at the sky, then back. "Do you understand tribal politics and procedures?" he asks. It sounds like an accusation. "The tribal council was elected by the local communities. There is nothing that states they have to go back to the community for a consensus." Pause. "There is no doubt in my mind that this project will happen." He is beginning to sound slightly irritated. "We don't need a referendum."

Two things are true, and interconnected. The proposed regional landfill at Rosebud is neither a done deal, nor is it necessarily environmentally sound. The citizens' meeting in St. Francis, the one that Oleta Mednansky and Marilyn Gangone were canvassing for that day on Horseshoe Butte, was considered by its organizers to be a success. The Englands turned out, along with another white rancher who operates on land adjoining the proposed dump site. A few reporters came. But mostly, the sixty or so people seated on folding chairs arranged at one end of the school gymnasium were Lakota. The meeting began with two prayers, one in Lakota and one in English.

There were a few moments of awkwardness when Cleve Neiss and Rhett Albers, an engineer from O&G/RSW, tried to convince the crowd to let them show their slides. "All of your questions are easily answered," Neiss pleaded, "if you will only let us speak."

"No, thank you," said Cheryl Crazy Bull, who was moderating the meeting. "Sometime in the future we will watch your presentation, but right now we'd just like to talk about our concerns. We don't even know what questions to ask you. We don't want you to take over our meeting." Crazy Bull is the vice-president of the Sinte Gleska College in St. Francis, and she was very firm. Neiss and Albers talked audibly at the back of the room for a few minutes with some of the men who were clustered around the coffee maker and then left. "I don't know why we were invited if we aren't going to be allowed to speak," Neiss said on the way out. Albers nodded, projector in hand.

Toward the end of the meeting a slight woman with straight black hair got up to speak. "My name is JoAnn Tall," she said quietly. "I came over here this evening from Pine Ridge reservation, where I live, because I wanted to tell you that this same company was there with almost the same proposal." Pine Ridge is more than an hour's drive away. "They told us their dump was the only solution. They told us it was perfectly safe. They told us everything they are telling you, and they almost got it through our council. But so far we have been able to stop them. I wanted to come and tell you that, because you can stop them here if you want to."

The room grew quiet for the first time that evening. Tall did not seem nearly as comfortable talking in front of crowds as the previous speakers. She stood perfectly still, her arms fidgeting a little at her sides. But somehow she cut through as no one before her had, and even the men at the coffee maker listened.

"They will try to divide you," Tall went on. "They will try to use the question of sovereignty to divide Indian against white. They will try to divide full-blood against half-breed. They will tell you you will be fined. They told us that. But we weren't fined." The Pine Ridge reservation, in fact, received federal monies to clean up its own dumps.

"You can stop them, but it will take your time and commitment. There are people outside who are concerned and can help you, but in the end you have to do it." Tall stopped for a moment and thought. "That's all I really have to say."

It was agreed that another citizens' meeting would take place the following week in the town of White River. An ad hoc committee was formed to plan a strategy.

"The most important thing that we need to do is learn more about this whole thing," Ronald Valandra said over dinner the evening after the first strategy meeting. He wore, as usual, a crisp blue shirt from the convenience store he owns is Rosebud. On his left breast pocket was a patch that said "Beanie," which is what everybody calls him. "It's difficult, you know, because Rhett Albers is a professional engineer, and they can say 'Oh, we can answer all your questions, we know everything.' So the first thing for us to do is to read everything we can and call everybody we can. The other thing we want to do is try to keep this nonpolitical; we want to stress that this is just the wrong thing for us, as Indians especially, to be doing to the environment."

By the time the third citizens' meeting was held a few weeks later, attendance had swelled to one hundred and fifty people. By then the organization had a name, "The Good Road Coalition," chosen partly because of the Good Road Cemetery, which is located on the proposed landfill site, and partly because it was a name that would not be tied only to the landfill issue. The Good Road Coalition intends to outlast this particular issue. Oleta Mednansky was elected coalition secretary, and Marilyn and Frank Gangone, to the board of directors. Beanie Valandra and Russell Eagle Bear—a big, friendly man from the tiny community of Norris, South

Dakota, who is helping to lead a revival of traditional Lakota beliefs—were elected co-chairmen.

The coalition leaders began to make good on their goal of educating themselves in the relevant issues. JoAnn Tall visited Rosebud again to help coach everyone on questions they should ask at O&G/RSW's slide shows. And up at the Valandra's house, a big cardboard box was nearly full of literature about modern landfills.

They learned, for instance, that when Neiss said the landfill's plastic liners would probably last forever, they could remind him that EPA says all liners will leak eventually. They were aware of the growing body of studies that prove that even though the type of municipal waste ash that O&G/RSW wants to put in the landfill isn't technically "toxic" or "hazardous," it is loaded with lead, cadmium, and other heavy metals. Metals that will eventually leach into the water supply to the detriment of livestock and humans. They knew of other landfills in the country that weren't supposed to have toxic waste in them but did. They knew that before he worked for O&G/RSW, Rhett Albers worked for a company that illegally dumped several hundred tons of ash in Edgemont, South Dakota, and then proceeded to go bankrupt. And Beanie had even found out that O&G/RSW has never before built a facility like the one proposed.

Soon, instead of preventing the trash-ranch advocates from speaking at their meetings, members of the Good Road Coalition began attending the community meetings/company slide shows set up by the tribal government and asking tough questions.

The meetings were often quite heated. At one, Maurice Hoben told the audience that the dump opponents were all secretly being paid by local white ranchers. Another time, Christine Dunham, an elder, rose and said she would like to return to the company the twenty-dollar bill that she claimed her son had been given to sign a petition in favor of the landfill. "You can keep your money and your trash," she said, to great applause.

"Mostly, what we have learned to do," Valandra says, "is to say 'prove it' every time they promise something. They say it's safe, we say, 'Show us.' They promise jobs, we say,

'How many?' They say it won't cost us much to have our trash collected and taken up there, we say, 'Tell us how much.'"

This tactic has generally served the coalition well. So far, one section of the agreement signed by Moran and Hoben has been declared null and void by the council, and at least four of the eleven council members have publicly softened or reversed their support for the landfill. Half of the tribe's twenty communities have held meetings and voted to instruct their councilmen either to oppose the landfill or to hold a reservation-wide referendum.

At the end of one series of community meetings, the activists held an anti-dump pow-wow, complete with traditional Lakota dress and dances. Native American leaders from all over the U.S. showed up to lend their support for the Good Road Coalition.

Only one community so far, Okreek, has voted in favor of the proposed landfill. But, as tribal vice-president Ike Schmidt and other opponents of the dump are quick to point out, Okreek was the only community meeting that the Good Road Coalition did not attend. They did not attend, Valandra says, because the meeting was not well publicized. In fact, only a dozen people attended.

The policy of not publicizing community meetings is not the only evidence that O&G/RSW and the tribal government do not intend to take the efforts of the Good Road Coalition sitting down. Early this year Chairman Moran sent a memo to all tribal employees informing them that it was mandatory that they attend information meetings with representatives of O&G/RSW. The tribe is by far the largest employer on the reservation, and at the start of each meeting, employees say, Moran asked everyone to remember who it was who signed their paychecks.

For its part, O&G/RSW has changed its brochure a number of times to eliminate the most glaring complaints of its opponents. Rhett Albers has been on the reservation giving slide shows almost as much as he's been home. And last spring, after Albers was told he couldn't circulate a pro-dump petition because he is not a tribal member, paid canvassers collected some 1,700 signatures from tribal members. Almost immediately thirty people swore out affidavits that their names had been forged on the document, and, curiously, at least three signees were found to be deceased. The tribal prosecutor is investigating.

Both sides are still predicting ultimate victory. The tribal government says it will happen whenever the environmental impact statement is complete and everyone sees that this is a great opportunity for the tribe. The Good Road Coalition says the dump will be dead by this fall, at the very latest, when tribal elections take place and the current council and chairman are swept from office.

"It will be political suicide for anyone to run on a platform in favor of the dump," Valandra says.

"Oh, yeah, we're going ahead," says Moran. "We expected opposition. This is the same bunch who have opposed everything—it's nothing."

There is a joke on the Rosebud reservation these days that always gets a big laugh. It can be told a lot of ways, but usually it works the way I first heard it, on that unseasonably warm day driving around the proposed dump site with Marilyn and Frank Gangone and Olera and Rodney Mednansky.

It goes like this:

"You know in the end how we're really going to have to do it to make sure we don't end up with everybody else's trash up here?" Marilyn Gangone asks in a serious voice, but with an ever-present twinkle in her eyes.

"No," I say. "How?"

"Well, we're going to have to get Russell Eagle Bear up here, or somebody else who looks like a real Indian, and dress him up in the old way. And then, when they come to dump that trash, he'll turn his head around real slowly, and he'll have one big old tear right here on his cheek, just like that old commercial on T.V."

She touches her own cheek, and everybody laughs. We all laugh as if it really were funny.

Chapter XI

Western Reservations and the Politics of Water

Lewis Hinchman and Sandra Hinchman

On March 31, 1992, work began near Cortez, Colorado on the final stage of Reach Three of the Towaoc-Highline Canal, designed to bring water from the Dolores River to the Ute Mountain Ute Indian Reservation in the state's southwestern corner. Regional newspapers celebrated the event as a "major economic chapter" in the tribe's history, since it will supply much-needed water to the reservation and permit irrigation on a larger scale than before. The papers mentioned, in passing, that the Dolores project will also serve the Montezuma Valley Irrigation Company, a non-Indian water users' association.[1]

Behind all the fanfare, informed readers may glimpse some of the harsh realities facing Western Native Americans who attempt to secure reliable water supplies for their reservations. Most reclamation/irrigation projects have been built mainly for the benefit of non-Indian settlers, often at the expense of indigenous peoples' water rights. Rarely do Indians have projects built exclusively for them; they usually have to ride along on the coattails of "Anglo" projects like the Dolores. Indeed, water development in the West sometimes has compromised the Indians' ability to earn a living and has undermined their way of life, as reservoirs inundate their best land. In a word, Native Americans have been vulnerable, politically disadvantaged players in the ruthless, high powered game of controlling Western water. The Ute Mountain Utes, in particular, did not even get piped-in drinking water until 1989. This essay will tell the story, in outline, of Native Americans' efforts to secure and develop what is, in the arid West, their most valuable resource. It will present some case studies to illustrate important variations

246

on the theme of water politics and will take stock of the Indians' current prospects for influencing water policy in directions more favorable to them.

I. A Brief History of Western Water Development

West of the 100th meridian, annual rainfall averages less than twenty inches, much of it coming in brief, torrential downpours that quickly run off into usually-dry "washes." Consequently, farmers in the West normally cannot rely on rainfall alone to grow crops. European-descent settlers in the region, after some hard experience, learned a lesson that the Pueblo Indians and before them the ancient Hohokam of Arizona had discovered: to make the land yield consistently, you must irrigate it. Some Native American peoples had practiced irrigation for many centuries, but usually on a small scale, limited both by available technology and often by an aversion to wholesale transformations of their natural environment.[2] Non-Indian settlers, by contrast, could draw upon fast-developing engineering and hydrological know-how, as well as the enormous resources and organizational power of their governments, to control and allocate nearly every acre-foot of water in the West.[3]

At first, "Anglo" irrigators in the West usually relied on private capital and their own labor to build a system of earthen dams and canals. By the 1920s, however, they had pieced together a coalition of local water users' associations (soon to be joined by cities and electric power consumers), Congressional delegations, and executive agencies specializing in water development, all bent on involving the state and federal governments in irrigation. This coalition, in its embryonic form, had helped to pass the Reclamation Act of 1902, which established the Reclamation Service (now the Bureau of Reclamation or "BuRec") and fostered a relatively straightforward scheme for making it work—one that became more Byzantine as time went on. The U.S. government would create a reclamation fund from the proceeds of public land sales, mostly to land-hungry settlers. The Reclamation Service would build dams and aqueducts to store and distribute water to farmers, who would then pay for "their" project over the next ten years out of income derived from crops. No interest was to be charged during the entire pay-back period. In theory, repayments would flow back into the fund, supporting still more projects. Over time, however, Congress postponed or forgave most of these debts, thereby unofficially transforming the Reclamation Act into a direct subsidy of Western irrigated farming.

Paradoxically, the Great Depression strengthened this water development coalition, which previously had enjoyed only mixed success in getting its projects approved. The BuRec began to combine irrigation with electric power production, constructing mammoth dams like Hoover and Grand Coulee that were capable of generating millions of kilowatts of electricity. Projects that would not have made economic sense if they had been built solely for irrigation could now be justified if income from electricity sales were factored into cost-benefit analyses. The "new economics" of dam building appealed especially to politicians from the high, dry upper basin of the Colorado River, whose home states (Colorado, Utah, Wyoming, and New Mexico) so far had derived relatively little benefit from BuRec operations. They proposed, and succeeded in passing in 1956, a bill to create the Colorado River Storage Project, designed to store 48.5 million acre-feet of water, generate over 1.5 million kilowatts of electricity, and subsidize dozens of new irrigation projects. However, as Senator Douglas of Illinois pointed out at the time, the BuRec would have to spend roughly $2,000 per acre to irrigate mainly alfalfa fields and cow pastures that could never be worth even a tenth of the money invested.[4] But "river basin accounting," which offset losses on irrigation projects against income from electricity sales, could make the CRSP appear to be a wise investment. To upper basin Congressmen who did not want to lose "their" water to California, such accounting methods provided useful ammunition against Douglas' objections; in the end, upper basin politicians corralled enough votes for project approval and funding.

Eventually, another government agency, the Army Corps of Engineers, joined the water development coalition, in order to expand its own geographical reach from the Eastern states to the West. At first, the Corps adhered to its original mandate of providing flood control and improving navigation.

But before long it entered the irrigation and power-generation business, too, competing directly with its rival, the BuRec, for projects in the Dakotas, California, and other Western states.[5]

The rationale for water project construction in the West invoked venerable republican and frontier traditions that partly concealed its centralized, bureaucratic core. Initially, the Reclamation Service had a "populist" and Jeffersonian ethos, since it labored to create small (160 acre maximum), prosperous farms for land-hungry yeomen. Then, during the 1930s and 1940s, the BuRec represented to many Americans the New Deal promise of social cooperation, planning, and the harmonious, publicly-guided development of resources. The Reclamation Act, as one commentator remarks, was envisioned as a "social program designed to bring the 'Democracy of the Desert' to the common man."[6] These narratives, together with its undeniable successes in hydropower development, assured the BuRec of widespread support in Congress and public opinion until roughly the 1970s.

Of course, the reclamation program never actually worked in as populist a manner as many had hoped. Especially in California, land speculators and large operators often circumvented restrictions on the size of farms eligible for project water.[7] Moreover, as we shall see, large-scale water development in the West frequently created hardship and even disaster for Native Americans. But Jeffersonian rhetoric, coupled with the increasing political efficacy of the water coalition's policy network in Washington, enabled the BuRec and the Corps to transform the West's landscape and to entice millions of new residents to some of its driest recesses.

Ultimately, however, both of these agencies overreached themselves, especially during the 1950s and 1960s, when it seemed that any project, no matter how expensive and ill-conceived, would receive Congressional funding. The agencies downplayed the environmental and human consequences of their works and eventually stirred up (as in the continuing controversy over proposed dams in the Grand Canyon) widespread antipathy and protest from once-admiring citizens. Last but not least, the water agencies simply began running out of suitable rivers to dam and land to irrigate, at least at a cost that could be made to appear reasonable. The budget deficits of recent years have also forced a scaling-back of the BuRec's and Corps' more ambitious projects. Under relentless pressure to trim expenses, even Congress cannot forever authorize billions of taxpayer dollars for projects that may enable only a few hundred farmers to grow (already surplus) crops. The BuRec and Corps, erstwhile bureaucratic empires locked in a duel for power and appropriations, have had to make do with reduced funding, look for new tasks such as relining aging, leaky aqueducts, and even (at least in theory) worry about the environmental consequences of their projects.[8]

Ironically, the weakening of the water development "iron triangle" may end up disproportionately harming Native Americans. Many Western tribes have been battling for decades not only to have their water rights officially and legally recognized, but also to bring to fruition projects that would allow them to use their water. Meanwhile, large projects like the Dolores have fallen into disfavor, and few tribes have the political influence to initiate all-Indian projects. Thus, it may be the case that the agencies that have done the Native Americans so much harm over the years will now be politically or financially unable to do them much good, just when it is the tribes' "turn" to benefit.

II. Native American Water Rights:
The Courts' Ambiguous Legacy

To understand the Western tribes' conflicts with the water development agencies, one must recall the familiar story of the "winning of the West" by European-stock settlers. Although some Native Americans (for example, the Pueblos, the Hopi, the Tohono O'odham, and the Mandans) long ago had adopted a sedentary, agricultural way of life, the majority of Western tribes, when white explorers arrived, were at least partly nomadic, roaming over large territories to hunt, fish, or gather wild foods as the seasons dictated. During the latter part of the nineteenth century, the U.S. government forced the nomadic tribes into reservations under the pretext that they would be taught to till the soil and thus be able to survive on a much smaller land base. But in the West, the only hope that many tribes had of succeeding in agriculture was to irrigate their reservations.

Such was the Indians' situation when, starting in the waning years of the nineteenth century, white settlers began diverting waters that flowed through, or past, tribal lands and pumping their groundwater at unsustainable rates. Before long, the streams and aquifers upon which Indian agriculture would have to rely began to diminish or even, on occasion, to dry up completely. The tribes, barred by law from hiring their own lawyers, had to petition the Bureau of Indian Affairs (BIA) and its parent, the Interior Department, to defend their interests. The most momentous case to emerge from this turn-of-the-century litigation was "Winters v. U.S." (1908), which pitted Anglo water users on Montana's Milk River against the Gros Ventre and Assiniboine tribes living on the Fort Belknap reservation downstream.

The settlers invoked the laws of the state of Montana, ones that were similar to those in other Western states, to justify their water diversions. They pointed out that state codes in the West had recognized, since the California mining boom of the 1850s, two supreme principles in water law: "prior appropriation" and "beneficial use." According to the prior appropriation doctrine, rights to water receive priority in time according to the earliest date that a stream was diverted. When a senior user's claims are completely fulfilled, the next most senior appropriator may divert enough water to meet his or her quota, and so on until all claims have been satisfied or until there is no more water remaining for junior appropriators (a common circumstance in dry years). "Beneficial use" means that appropriators must actually be using the amount of water that they claim in what the state would consider a beneficial way, such as for irrigation or mining. Let it be noted that many states have been reluctant to recognize fishing as a beneficial use, an interpretation that has wrought havoc with traditional ways of life in many tribes, especially the Pyramid Lake Paiutes in Nevada.[9] The beneficial use doctrine implies that there can be no reserved or unexploited rights to water. To appropriate water, one must actually build some structure to divert or store it. And any water right that goes unused for several years may revert to the public domain and be "up for grabs" once again.

Furthermore, the first user or users may appropriate as much water as they like, as long as they put it to beneficial use. Theoretically, one senior user could appropriate an entire stream. In short, Western state water laws diverge markedly from the "riparian" rights typical of Eastern states. Appropriators in the West, that is, need not own property along a stream to acquire rights to it; they need only divert it to some beneficial purpose, possibly hundreds of miles away, even if in diverting it they dry it up.

In the "Winters" case, the white settlers argued that under Montana law, their diversions of water conformed precisely to the two principles sketched above. They believed that they had appropriated their water first and put it to good use irrigating their fields. And they insisted that the Fort Belknap tribes should be treated no differently from anyone else: since they had not been the first parties to use the water of the Milk River, the tribes deserved to lose out to those who had invested in irrigation.

Lawyers for the tribes invoked several different and even conflicting arguments to buttress their clients' claims.[10] But the argument that impressed the lower courts—and ultimately the Supreme Court of the United States— concerned Congress' intent in creating Indian reservations. The Supreme Court noted that Fort Belknap was only a fragment of the original territory occupied by the Blackfeet, Gros Ventre, and Assiniboine, most of which the tribes had ceded to the United States by treaty in 1888. The court reasoned that the Indians could not have intended to relinquish, in that treaty, the only resource that promised to make their dry reservation arable, and that Congress could not have meant, in the words of Justice McKenna, to take "from them the means of continuing their old habits, [without leaving] them the power to change to new ones." Since the reservation system was supposed to allow many of the tribes to shift from a "nomadic" to a "pastoral" and "civilized" way of life, Congress surely intended that the Indians should have enough water to make the transition.

However, one troubling ambiguity that the "Winters" decision has bequeathed to future courts concerns the exact nature of the transition. Did the Court mean to say that Indian tribes should be granted only enough reserved water rights to help them become farmers or herdsmen, and that other uses were not included? Or did the Court wish to reaffirm the tribes' "command of all . . . beneficial use" of their water to master the "arts of civilization" in whatever ways they saw fit?[11] Generally, a narrow and restrictive reading of the reservations' purpose suits opponents of Indian reserved water rights, since it limits them to an increasingly marginal vocation, agriculture. Meanwhile, advocates of Indian reserved water rights have often read "Winters" as an affirmation of the tribes' right to dwell in permanent "homelands," the occupational structures of which would evolve along with the rest of the outside economy.

The exact source of the reserved rights in "Winters" has been another matter of controversy. Some authorities argue that the aboriginal peoples of North America possessed sovereign rights to the water in their territories "from time immemorial"[12] and must be assumed to have retained them in signing treaties with the U.S. government. In other words, while those treaties restricted their territory, they did not involve a waiver of water rights. The opposing view holds that, when the U.S. government created the reservations, it bestowed water rights upon the Indians. On this reading, the source of the right to water derives from the government's having reserved it to carry out its purposes, as would be true of water in a national park or wildlife refuge. The reason that this debate is important is clear. The first interpretation would normally favor the Native Americans' interests, since it would give them undisputed seniority in any "prior appropriations" adjudication of stream flows. Moreover, it would permit the tribes to challenge the United States government whenever it seemed that government actions failed to respect or protect their "immemorial" rights.[13]

Yet whatever conflicts there may be between these two interpretations of "Winters" rights pale into insignificance when compared to the contradictions that have emerged between the "Winters" and "prior appropriations" doctrines. For these doctrines are irreconcilable on nearly every major point. They pit states against the federal government, rights of use against reserved rights, and rights to specific amounts of water against (relatively) undefined and elastic rights to enough water to fulfill a reservation's purposes.[14] The prior appropriation doctrine is, one might say, individualistic and "Lockean," in the sense that it rewards "industrious and rational" (not to mention well-financed and well-connected) persons who try to develop the land and make it profitable.[15] "Winters" rights, by contrast, are implicitly communitarian, historically conscious, and concerned with the long-term needs of collectivities. They embody a policy stance taken by the United States toward Native American peoples as once-sovereign communities, whose future survival the government has pledged to ensure.

To the extent that "Winters" rights are recognized in state water adjudications, most tribes would have to be given high seniority, since (a) the treaties or executive orders creating their reservations go back well into the nineteenth century, or (b) their water rights date from "time immemorial." The Pueblo tribes of New Mexico form an important exception to the seniority implication of "Winters." This is because they do not actually live on reservations, but in long-established city-states that antedate the arrival of European colonists. Moreover, the Pueblos lived for centuries under other sovereign powers (Spain, then Mexico after 1821) that recognized their water rights, albeit on different principles than those embedded in either the "Winters" case or state "prior appropriation" laws. Finally, they are surrounded by non-Indian (mainly Hispanic) water users who began irrigating their land over 300 years ago, in fact that beclouds the seniority issue.[16]

At least until recently, federal court decisions after "Winters" have tended to confirm and expand the rights of native peoples established in the 1908 case. Indeed, the courts have been one of the few institutions of the U.S. political system in which Indians could expect a modicum of justice.[17] For example, in "Skeem v. the United States" (1923), the Ninth Circuit Court ruled that Indian water rights were not restricted to lands presently under cultivation, but could increase in scope as the tribe brought irrigation water to additional acreage.[18] In "Arizona v. California I" (1963), the Supreme Court developed the implications of the "Skeem" decision more concretely.

In one sense, "Arizona v. California I" appears to limit "Winters" rights. The Court ruled that, in creating Indian reservations along the Colorado River in 1865 and expanding them later by executive order, the United States government reserved water rights *for* the tribes as of the date when the reservations were established. In this case, then, the Court seemed to reject the argument that Indian tribes (or at least those that did not actually sign treaties with the U.S. government) possess water rights from time immemorial.

But on a more important issue the Court clearly affirmed and expanded "Skeem." The justices ruled that the "Special Master" appointed to adjudicate disputes on the Colorado River had been correct in apportioning to several California reservations a relatively large share of water. The Court held further that the quantity of water reserved under "Winters" doctrine rights ought to be determined by calculating all the "practically irrigable acreage" on the reservation and thus assuring that the tribes living there would have enough water in the future, should their population increase or their needs change.[19]

On one level, "Arizona v. California I" would appear to clear up some of the uncertainty and confusion occasioned by the "Winters" ruling, since henceforth state and local water planners would know how to calculate maximum Indian water rights. But matters become murky again when one tries to determine what the term "practically irrigable" means. If engineering skill were the measure of practicability, then almost any land could be made irrigable by investing enough money in terracing, aqueducts, pumps, and drainage tiles. Obviously, however, costs also must be taken into account. And depending upon technology and cost, one can calculate Indian water rights in different ways. The point is that "practically irrigable" acreage does not self-evidently imply a certain quantity of water to irrigate it. For example, the Interior Department has tried to reduce the Navajo tribe's San Juan River water rights from a previously agreed-upon figure of 508,000 acre-feet to 370,000 acre-feet, on the grounds that the Navajo Indian Irrigation Project would need less water if the tribe would install more modern sprinkler-irrigation systems.[20] However, the courts have recently signaled impatience with continued litigation over the meaning of practically irrigable acreage. In a 1963 rehearing ("Arizona v. California II"), the Supreme Court declared that the amount of irrigable acreage specified in the original decree should be considered final precisely in order to buttress "certainty of rights" for all water-users in the region who had made decisions based on the amounts granted twenty years earlier.[21] The court, in other words, seems more concerned to guarantee secure expectations for non-Indian water-users than it does when Native Americans' plans and projects are suddenly thrown into turmoil by the Interior Department and other agencies.

However, another set of decisions, unrelated to "Winters" doctrine rights, has given support to those who want to interpret Indian reserved water rights as narrowly as possible. "Cappaert v. U.S." in 1976 stipulated that, when the United States government reserves water for some specific purpose (in this case, setting aside a small desert pool to protect a rare fish species), its reserved right extends only as far as is necessary to meet the "minimal need" for which the reservation was created.[22] Two years later, in "United States v. New Mexico," the Supreme Court drew a distinction between the primary and secondary purposes for which water rights had been reserved. In this case, the federal government could claim only as much water as it needed to fulfill the specific purpose for which national forests had been established (mainly to preserve timber and assure flows to state users); all other "secondary" uses, such as aesthetics, recreation, and wildlife preservation, would not qualify for federally reserved water. If the U.S. government wanted water for these purposes, it would have to apply for it under state law like anyone else.[23]

If applied to Native Americans' "Winters" rights, these two cases affect both the amount of water the tribes could claim (only enough to fulfill the "minimal need" of turning Indians into farmers) and the specific purposes to which their water could be turned (possibly only agriculture). One observer has surmised that these decisions, along with some more recent ones, indicate that the Supreme Court does not want to allow federally reserved water rights to disrupt the patterns of water use established under state laws. Hence, the Court is trying to contain reserved rights within narrow bounds.[24] Still, it is not clear whether the "Cappaert" and "New Mexico" rulings would imply any reduction at all in

Indians' water rights, since those are determined by the "practicably irrigable acreage" standard outlined in "Arizona v. California I." A lower court ruled in "Colville Confederated Tribes v. Walton" that the language of the "New Mexico" case ("primary purposes") could mean something as broad as providing a homeland for Native American tribes, in which case the tribes should get all the water coming to them under the "practicably irrigable acreage" standard and be entitled to use it for whatever purposes they chose.[25]

The Supreme Court's trend toward greater sympathy for state water rights was confirmed in another set of cases decided in 1976: "United States v. Akin" and "Colorado River Water Conservation District v. United States." Both strengthened the states' ability to limit "Winters" water rights claims, since the Supreme Court ruled that states could now, as part of basin-wide adjudications, resolve all vague or conflicting adjudications of water rights on the streams within their boundaries, including federal reserved water rights previously treated as outside state jurisdiction.[26] Native Americans retained their rights to pursue water rights claims in federal courts. Nevertheless, these rulings suggested that Indian water rights could now be subjected to scrutiny by often-unsympathetic state court judges.

In 1983, reviewing "Arizona v. San Carlos Apache Tribe," the Supreme Court explicitly rejected arguments defending the immunity of "Winters" rights from state court adjudications and concluded that the latter should be the preferred forum for allocating water rights in the West.[27] These jurisdictional cases amounted to a serious setback to Native Americans' campaigns to regain their lost water. They would now have to settle with the states or else go to court again, spending millions to defend water rights that they had believed secure on account of previous agreements or federal decisions. Still, as we shall see, state judges have not been uniformly hostile to Indian claims. While the Wyoming Supreme Court, for example, has rejected many of the claims made by the Wind River Reservation tribes, Arizona courts have reaffirmed the Pima-Maricopa community's claims to substantial reversed water rights.

But the relative ineffectiveness of the "Winters" doctrine in affording protection to the tribes also has deeper causes than these jurisdictional shifts. First, the Interior Department is actually only a "holding company" for its component agencies and services. One of these, the Bureau of Indian Affairs, supposedly looks after the interests of native peoples. But in the meantime, another Interior Department agency, the Bureau of Reclamation, has been building dams and irrigation projects for over 90 years, and these in many cases have either flooded or de-watered tribal lands. Thus, in effect, the Interior Department has been saddled with a permament, built-in conflict of interest in its charge to protect Indian rights and at the same time promote Western water development. The government's legal arm, the Justice Department, therefore has had to respond to conflicting signals from Interior: to clear away legal obstacles to BuRec projects, and—often simultaneously—to assert Indian water rights.

Within Interior, the B.I.A. has had far less political clout than the BuRec (not to mention the relevant Congressional committees), since it lacked the level of external support characteristic of the water development lobby. Thus, the B.I.A. over the years has moved pragmatically and ultra-cautiously in defending Indian water rights. Until 1934, native peoples could not even hire their own attorneys, so they had to acquiesce in whatever strategy the B.I.A. chose to pursue on their behalf. Often, that meant that the B.I.A. would assert "Winters" rights in court, on the one hand, while on the other hand sponsoring Indian irrigation projects that would qualify the tribes for water rights under the Western states' "prior appropriations" doctrine.[28]

That strategy foundered, however, on the second great obstacle to successful assertion of tribes' "Winters" rights. In the West, it is not enough to have the courts confirm water rights on paper; to make use of those rights, the claimant must actually divert water onto fields or use it in some other "beneficial" way. But building water projects costs a great deal of money. Practically speaking, at least for the Indians, only Congressional appropriations could provide sufficient funds to convert "paper" water into real water. To be sure, the B.I.A. over the years has managed to obtain funding for 125 "all-Indian" projects, but only about seven percent of potentially irrigable lands on Western reservations have in fact received irrigation water. Many projects have been left unfinished, while completed sections deteriorate for lack of maintenance.[29] As one observer put it, "without the political power necessary to get budgetary appropriations for Indian reclamation projects, the tribes were incapable of converting the "Winters" rights guaranteed them by the Supreme Court into actual beneficial use of their waters. Meanwhile, the remaining water resources were being rapidly appropriated by non-Indians, with BuRec acquiescence and support, under state law."[30]

Until recently, the states and non-Indian appropriators of water could live with "Winters" and its successor cases, despite the fact that these sowed uncertainty, because they believed that time was on their side. Even if a given tribe should win its case in the courts, citing "Winters" as a precedent, its members could rarely afford to build the dams and aqueducts required to divert and use the water. And in the interim, state delegations in Congress could block any measures that might upset the status quo, such as translating "Winters" principles into federal statutes, appropriating money to build Indian projects, or even allowing unrestricted leasing of "Winters" doctrine water rights by Indian tribes to off-reservation users, such as the West's rapidly growing cities. In effect, non-Indians could continue appropriating and using what were, according to the federal courts, tribal waters without paying compensation for them, merely by following their own states' "prior appropriation" laws. Only recently, when "Winters" rights claims have threatened to stymie federal water projects, has there been real movement toward accommodation of tribal demands for more water.

One obvious, though hardly uncontested, conclusion that might be drawn from these experiences is that Native Americans in the West must find ways not only to defend their water rights in the courts, but to obtain funding for transforming those rights into actual benefits. After all, the tribes on the Fort Belknap reservation that won the "Winters" case in 1908 still have not seen the projects completed that would bring the promised water to their lands.[31] Likewise, the Pyramid Lake Paiutes have won some important victories in the courts during their decades-long struggle to restore the lake's fish life (threatened by irrigation-induced salinity and obstacles to spawning), yet they still have not reversed the lake's decline.[32] The options that Western Indians have for putting teeth into the "Winters" doctrine will be considered below. First, however, we need to review some case studies that may indicate the direction in which Native American water rights claims are moving.

The Indians' battles against Anglo water development interests have dragged on, in some instances, for over eighty years as cases wend their way through the process of appeals and remands, while new lawsuits are triggered by new incursions on tribal rights.[33] We have chosen to focus on several cases that exemplify certain patterns of legal/political maneuvering and may offer insights about the tribes' options in the future. But we wish to stress one theme at the outset. When indigenous peoples began their struggle against the Western water coalition early in this century, everyone assumed that the fight was about irrigation. Who would enjoy the agricultural benefits of the rapidly expanding network of dams, aqueducts, canals, and wells in the West—Anglo settlers or Native Americans? In the meanwhile, however, agriculture has been eclipsed economically by an urban-based economy. Consider the case of Colorado. Twenty eight percent of that state's water is diverted for irrigating alfalfa fields, which provide fodder for cattle; yet this industry only produces $156 million for the state economy. In comparison, the recreation and hunting economies alone (which consume very little water) produce about $4 billion.[34] In Arizona, a state seemingly ideal for irrigated agriculture, farmers cannot even afford to buy water from the enormous Central Arizona Project and are going bankrupt or selling their land.[35] By the same token, the most efficient and profitable farming operations have tended to squeeze out smaller operations everywhere; agribusiness is replacing the family farm. One can no longer assume, as the Court still could in "Winters," that irrigated agriculture would become the economic mainstay of Western reservations. Nor can one any longer assume that most Indians will become farmers on small plots, emulating their Anglo neighbors.

Thus, the case studies we will review suggest a further complication in the resolution of Indian-Anglo disputes. Why should the amount of water the tribes receive depend on practically irrigable acreage, if irrigated agriculture is not their best hope of achieving prosperity? And why should some negotiated settlements virtually compel tribes to irrigate, if farming itself (especially when conducted on a small scale) is a dead-end vocation? It may turn out that the best possible outcome for Native Americans would involve settlements and/or judicial decisions that build some flexibility into the use of water and provide the means for the tribes to branch out into other activities besides agriculture. Certainly, that is the hope of those who interpret "Winters" broadly as guaranteeing dynamic, economically viable homelands to tribes that agreed to live on reservations. It would be a supreme irony if those tribes finally were to obtain long-sought irrigation water, only to discover that most members who used it for farming would end up going broke. What the tribes really need is legal recognition of their right to use water in whatever ways are most likely to sustain their culture and communal institutions.

III. Case Studies

The Navajos and the Colorado River Basin[36]

In 1948, the states that had a claim on water in the upper basin of the Colorado River—that is, the Colorado and its tributaries upstream from Lee's Ferry, Arizona—met to decide how to divide up their 7.5 million acre-feet of water. (The other portion of the Colorado's supposed annual flow had been allotted previously to the lower basin states of California, Nevada, and Arizona downriver from Lee's Ferry.) The Upper Basin Compact ignored the Navajos and other Indian tribes in the region even though (or perhaps because) their "Winters" rights' claim would have been enormous.

Rather than go to court and try to claim their entire "Winters" entitlement, tribal leaders opted to strike deals with officials in Arizona and New Mexico as well as with involved federal agencies, notably the BuRec. The Navajos agreed in 1968 to allow the Salt River Project to build and operate a coal-burning generating station at Page, Arizona on tribal land. The mammoth plant would consume the lion's share of Arizona's upper water basin water right (34,000 out of a possible 50,000 acre-feet). Did the 1968 agreement constitute a waiver of the Navajos' "Winters" rights? Certainly, tribal attorneys then and now would deny it. To them, the issue of how much water the tribe should get under its "Winters" claim has not yet been resolved. At any rate, the tribe was promised significant industrial development: the plant itself, which employs hundreds of Navajo workers, and the Black Mesa coal strip mine, opened up by the Peabody Company to supply fuel to the generating station.

Over in New Mexico, the Navajos encountered a familiar obstacle to their aspiration to use water from the San Juan River (a major Colorado tributary) for irrigation. The federal government, pressured by the state's Congressional delegation, would not appropriate money for any project that would benefit only Navajos. But in 1962, a deal was struck. The tribe would allow water from the San Juan basin to be diverted into the Rio Grande basin, mostly to supply water to the city of Albuquerque. This massive interbasin transfer, known as the San Juan-Chama Project, was to be built by the BuRec. In return, the Navajos would be guaranteed 508,000 acre feet of San Juan River water (considerably less, it should be pointed out, than their potential "Winters" claim of 787,000 acre feet), plus a dam and irrigation project to bring this water to Navajo fields. Moreover, the agreement required them to share shortages in dry years and not to claim their full entitlement under the "prior appropriation" doctrine. Thus, the Navajo Indian Irrigation Project (NIIP) was twinned with the Anglo San Juan-Chama Project, a pattern of symbiosis that has since repeated itself many times in other water development schemes.

Yet the outcome of these supposedly amicable and cooperative agreements has not been satisfactory for the Navajos. Certainly, they did not benefit from the arrangement nearly to the degree that Anglos did. Although the Navajo generating station and its support operations do create jobs and revenue (and also air, groundwater, and soil pollution and pollution-related illnesses) for the reservation, one can ask how much more the tribe might have received if leaders had pressed for full "Winters" rights to Colorado River water. One Navajo economist calculates that the water "donated" to the Page plant would be worth $6.8 million per year.[37]

In New Mexico, the tribe fared even worse: the settlement turned into a nightmare for the eastern part of the reservation. Although the BuRec hastened to complete the San Juan-Chama Project for the state's politically powerful Anglo interests (even though much of the water from the project still has not been used yet by the city of Albuquerque), it dragged its feet on the NIIP. What is more, in 1966, the whole project was "re-evaluated" on the grounds that small-scale irrigated family farms, as foreseen in the NIIP plan, were no longer economically feasible. Further, the Interior Department, as noted above, sliced the Navajos' water share from 508,000 to 370,000 acre feet. Finally, the Navajos' claims became entangled in an effort by the state to adjudicate *all* waters in New Mexico in the face of another Indian lawsuit, this one initiated by the Jicarilla Apaches. Thus, the Navajos have been stuck with a half-completed NIIP, a reduced water allocation, successive Republican administrations determined to reduce domestic expenditures, and a new court case in which they must again defend their water rights in a potentially hostile forum, the state court. The NIIP experience, especially, has hoisted a warning flag to other tribes considering negotiated settlements of their water rights claims. Somehow, native peoples henceforth would have to discover ways to build into their agreements ironclad guarantees that non-Indian parties to the settlement will perform what they promise. They especially would need to craft their agreements in such a way that the U.S. government would incur hefty financial penalties for non-performance.

The Northern Utes and the Central Utah Project[38]

Like the Navajos, the Utes living on the Uintah and Ouray reservations in north-central Utah hoped to negotiate a deal with state and federal officials that would assure them a supply of irrigation water. In 1965, the tribe agreed to defer its right to develop 15,234 acres of unirrigated land until the year 2005. The deferral agreement cleared the way for construction of the sprawling Central Utah Project (CUP), designed to capture Utah's share of Colorado River basin water (28 percent of the basin's 7.5 million acre feet). The CUP would transfer water from tributaries of the Green River in eastern Utah to the Wasatch front cities and to croplands in the western part of the state. In return for deferral, the Northern Utes were supposed to get a water project built that would deliver their share of CUP water. But Congress never even authorized the Indian portion of the project, which in any case has been considerably scaled back due to cost.

During the late 1970s, after a change in tribal leadership, the Utes sued (unsuccessfully) to escape from an agreement that had come to seem more and more unfair to them. In the decade that followed, two new settlement offers were made by the state, both of which failed to win ratification by the tribe and/or by Congress. Eventually, the state and federal governments tendered a new, more attractive offer, which found its way into the CUP reauthorization bill of 1992. The new offer achieves something that previous settlements did not: it would compensate the tribe for damages incurred during all the time that its promised water project remained unbuilt. If ratified by a tribal referendum in 1993, the new settlement will give the Northern Utes 480,000 acre feet of water, $125 million for ranching and farming operations, and $27 million for smaller projects, plus a percentage of the money that will be repaid for the already-built Bonneville unit of the CUP.

The 1992 settlement, if ratified, will result in a better deal for the Utes than they would have received under the terms of earlier offers, though far less than what had been promised them by the deferral agreement. Indeed, the new bargain leaves much to be desired. The tribe still has no ironclad guarantee that its promised water will ever flow into Ute fields. What it will receive, initially, is only a cash payment, not so different from the payments that Indian tribes received in the last century for territory ceded to whites. The tribe will have the right to market its water, but only within the state of Utah. State officials obviously included this provision because they feared losing their share of Colorado River water to lower-basin states if Utahns did not use it. But this stipulation forecloses an attractive option to the tribe: marketing its water to wealthy but parched metropolises such as Los Angeles or San Diego. We will return to the issue of water marketing later, in hopes of evaluating its advantages and disadvantages for Native Americans.

The Pyramid Lake Paiutes and the Newlands Project[39]

In 1859, one of the numerous bands of Northern Paiutes in western Nevada was assigned a reservation encircling Pyramid Lake. Unlike many intermountain lakes, Pyramid was a deep, permanent body of water fed by the Truckee River. By tradition, this band of Paiutes had spent much of its time near the lake (especially in winter) and relied heavily for subsistence on the fishery there. But in 1906, the Reclamation Service finished work on the Newlands irrigation project, intended to divert "excess" water from the Truckee into the nearby Carson River valley, where it would irrigate the fields of newly arrived settlers. The diversion quickly began to affect the tribe. The Paiutes' few fields no longer received enough water from the Truckee to make irrigation succeed. Worse, the lake level began to decline precipitously, resulting in an increased salinity that made it difficult for native fish to survive. Besides making the lake considerably more saline, Derby Dam—Newlands' center-piece—caused a wide, flat, silty delta to appear as the lake level dropped. Eventually, fish could no longer swim up the Truckee to spawn, and by the 1930s, the Pyramid Lake fishery had declined disastrously.

The Paiutes, represented by the United States government, filed a number of lawsuits to try to halt the lake's deterioration. These culminated, temporarily, in the 1944 Orr Water Ditch Decree[40] that granted to the tribe 30,000 acre-feet of water annually for irrigation purposes, but none to restore the lake's fish habitat. Incredibly, when the Paiutes offered to give up their meager irrigation water allotment and simply let it flow into Pyramid Lake to help improve water quality, the Interior Department ruled that fisheries were not a "beneficial use," and thus, should the tribe do as it had suggested, it would lose its entire water right!

During the 1970s, the Paiutes returned to Court hoping to challenge the terms of the Orr Water Ditch Decree. Despite some initial successes in winning judicial recognition of the Pyramid Lake fishery as a beneficial use under state law, the Paiutes lost their suit before the Supreme Court a decade later.[41] The tribunal ruled that old water rights settlements ought not to be reopened even if the tribes had not received adequate representation from the U.S. government (here again plagued by a conflict of interest, since it also represented the BuRec and its operational arm, Truckee-Carson). Technically, suing Truckee-Carson would constitute double jeopardy, because the Irrigation District, as successor to the Newlands Project, had already been a party to the Orr Ditch Decree.

Nevertheless, affected parties (including the states of California and Nevada, the tribe, the Department of the Interior, and local power and water districts, as well as Truckee-Carson officials) still had reason to seek a negotiated settlement, since further litigation always would remain a possibility. After long negotiations, President Bush signed into law in November of 1992 a bill sponsored by Senator Harry Reid (D-Nev.) that resolved at least some of the legal and political issues originating in the 1906 Truckee diversion. The tribe will receive $25 million to restore the lake's fishery, a provision that bodes well for recovery of two food fish traditionally important to the Paiutes. They will also receive $40 million for economic development over five years. More significantly, the settlement recognizes other beneficial uses of Newlands Project water besides irrigation: recreation, municipal supplies for two Nevada counties, and above all, preservation of endangered fish species. Where the extra water to restore Pyramid Lake will come from has not yet been determined. Certainly conservation, probably including metering of supplies in nearby Reno and Sparks, will meet some of the anticipated demand. But the new law also grants the Interior Department broad authority to allocate water supplies as it sees fit. Both the tribe and the Truckee-Carson Irrigation District are forbidden to litigate decisions about water allocation until 1997, so that the Interior Department will have a free hand. By and large, Truckee-Carson officials appear far more disappointed by this provision than the Paiutes do, undoubtedly because they anticipate "losing" water to the river and ultimately the lake. Assuming that the Paiutes actually get the promised water and funds (perhaps an overly optimistic assumption, in light of past experience), the Reid bill probably represents the best settlement they could hope to have reached at this point.

The Dakotas' Pick-Sloan Project[42]

The U.S. government has other ways to exploit Native American water besides diverting it for Anglo irrigation, as tribes in the Dakotas discovered several decades ago. An acrimonious struggle for project "turf" between the BuRec and the Army Corps of Engineers culminated in Congressional authorization of the Pick-Sloan Plan in 1944, named after its sponsors in the two agencies. The Corps ended up building five immense dams on the mainstem of the Missouri River during the 1940s and 50s, ostensibly for flood control in the lower Missouri basin, while the BuRec received funding to construct smaller dams and irrigation works along its tributaries. Some of these dams were begun without the affected Native Americans ever having been informed, let alone consulted. Altogether, the dams inundated 550 square miles of tribal land along the Missouri in North and South Dakota, causing wrenching dislocations and economic havoc among the flooded-out residents. The project's chief chronicler and critic, Michael Lawson, flatly asserts that Pick-Sloan was "without doubt, the single most destructive act ever perpetrated on any tribe by the United States."[43]

Statistical measures of inundated acreage and numbers of families displaced do not capture the true extent of the disaster endured by the Sioux and (on the Fort Berthold Reservation) the three affiliated tribes: Mandan, Arikara, and Hidatsa. The land that they lost was by far the most productive and habitable on their reservations, since it was what Westerners call "bottomland": a relatively sheltered, fertile, and game-rich valley environment that yields good crops and a cornucopia of useful wild plants. When the Pick-Sloan dams forced resident Native Americans to leave the

Missouri bottoms, most had to move to the windy, dry prairies above, where both agriculture and traditional hunting and gathering proved far more difficult.

Of all the Dakota reservations, Fort Berthold probably suffered the most from Pick-Sloan, in this case from Garrison Dam. The affiliated tribes lost a quarter of their total land base and 94 percent of their agricultural land. Four of five families had to leave their former homes and relocate to adjacent Anglo towns or sterile government-built settlements. Unemployment, virtually zero before construction of Garrison Dam, soared to 79 percent,[44] while hopelessness and dislocation fostered social problems like alcoholism. Tribal members, formerly neighbors, were separated by the rising waters of the new reservoir and eventually had to travel for hours to visit one another. There is a special irony in the fate of the affiliated tribes. The reservation system had originally been justified, as we noted previously in reviewing the "Winters" decision, as a means of "civilizing" the Indians, i.e., transforming them into independent tillers of the soil able to survive on a drastically reduced land base. The Mandans, however, had practiced agriculture for many centuries before the Europeans arrived. Indeed, Lewis and Clark, who wintered with them in 1804-05, admired their "civilized" ways even then. But Pick-Sloan, by flooding all their agricultural land, made it virtually impossible for the Mandans to make a living as farmers. As far as Colonel Lewis Pick was concerned, the Indians were once again standing in the way of "civilization" and had to be sacrificed for the good of European-stock Americans.

Other dams in the Pick-Sloan system devastated the Sioux nearly as much as Garrison had the affiliated tribes. The Oahe Dam, for example, cost the Sioux on the Cheyenne River and Standing Rock Reservations over 160,000 acres of their best arable and timber lands. But here again, the tribes' dislocations have to be evaluated in ways that statistics cannot convey. Most tribal members still lived very close to the land and depended on traditional skills and knowledge to survive, since cash was very scarce on the reservations. The Pick-Sloan project, however, drove them pell-mell into a market economy, the rigors of which they could not easily master. In many respects, the Sioux's and the affiliated tribes' destinies mirror that of the Pyramid Lake Paiutes. Just as the latter had to abandon their age-old fishing economy, and the forms of life and religious practices that went with it, when the BuRec ruined the lake's ecosystem by diverting Truckee River water, so the Dakota tribes suffered a similar fate when their water was impounded by the Army Corps of Engineers. The constant feature of these very different events is the failure of government agencies and elected officials to recognize, or care about, the specific and complex ways in which water previously had been used by Native Americans, and to grasp the full impact of dam-building on the traditional ties between water and human life.

Whereas many of the water rights issues we consider here involve quantification of "Winters" claims, the Pick-Sloan Project raised the issue of how much, and what sort of, compensation the affected tribes ought to expect for the loss of their land. The tribes' efforts to gain redress form a sorry chapter in the history of Indian-U.S. government relations. The Fort Berthold tribes suffered especially because the Corps' project superintendent, Lewis Pick, never forgave them for insulting him at a meeting to discuss compensation. In retaliation, Pick saw to it that the affiliated tribes got the least possible indemnity for their losses, and that they were not even permitted to salvage the timber that would be drowned by the rising waters of the Sakakawea Reservoir.

Having witnessed the many reverses and humiliations of their neighbors, the Sioux pressed for better settlements in whatever ways they could, particularly by appealing to Congress to add extra compensation and "rehabilitation" funds beyond what the Corps would pay. The Standing Rock Sioux hired a Washington lawyer of their own who, unlike B.I.A. lawyers, challenged the Corps' procedure of simply condemning and then taking tribal lands. The tribe won a significant victory in 1958, when the Courts affirmed that Indian land, having been established by treaty, could not be taken by the customary eminent domain proceedings, but only by an act of Congress that guaranteed the Native Americans adequate compensation. Still, the Standing Rock Sioux received only a little over $12 million in their settlement, less than half of what they had asked for.

One would imagine that the Pick-Sloan Project at least would have provided irrigation water to Native American farmers now forced to cultivate arid high plains instead of fertile bottomlands. In fact, however, the irrigation segments of Pick-Sloan mostly have never been built, and the few projects now functioning have delivered almost no irrigation water to Native Americans. The tribes have not yet had their "Winters" rights quantified, so at this point no one even knows to what amount they are entitled. Like other Native American farmers (and Anglos too), the Indians of the Dakotas have been hard pressed by the long-term decline of agriculture. It has become ever more difficult to convince Congress to appropriate billions of dollars for irrigated farming that will never pay back even the maintenance and delivery costs, let alone the original investment of tax money. For example, on the Standing Rock Reservation, a Sioux farmer would need to invest $24,000 initially, plus $4000 annually (in 1982 dollars) to irrigate a 160 acre farm. But such a large investment exceeds the value of the property itself, not to mention the limited means of most Sioux.[45] Thus, it appears that the tribes of the Dakotas will never be able to replace their lost bottomlands by irrigated prairie. For most of them, the Pick-Sloan Project will have made farming impossible, without having provided any other reliable alternative for making a living.[46]

The Tohono O'odham Settlement and the Case of the Pima-Maricopas[47]

Despite its legacy of cowboy politics and aversion to water planning, Arizona recently has been the venue for several negotiated settlements between resident native peoples and non-Indian water users. These settlements followed costly, protracted legal battles, launched *de facto* regional hydrological planning, and assured the tribes of some water, though certainly less than they wanted or deserved. As we shall see, the linchpin of all of these settlements has been the promise of water from the Central Arizona Project (CAP). That promise meant that negotiations would not have to follow a zero-sum pattern in which Indian claims could be satisfied only at the expense of current Anglo users. Furthermore, the involvement of Indian tribes in the construction of the CAP has given project proponents a subtle but effective weapon in Congress as they fight for appropriations. They can claim that a vote against CAP will hurt long-suffering Arizona Indians as well as prosperous real estate developers and agribusinesses, thus presenting a moral dilemma to more liberal members of Congress.

The largest tribe to settle was the Tohono O'odham or "Desert People" (formerly Papago), who inhabit a huge reservation in the southern part of the state that is split into eleven districts, one very near Tucson. The Tohono O'odham had long practiced irrigated agriculture, drawing water from wells for their crops. But non-Indians outside reservation boundaries, making use of the same aquifer, began depleting the groundwater supply upon which the tribe depended. The "U.S. v. Cappaert" decision cited earlier affirmed that reserved water rights apply to groundwater as well as surface water. Applying this ruling to their own situation, the Tohono O'odham in 1975 sued the city of Tucson as well as various mines and farms, asking for 160,000 acre-feet of water as compensation for their dwindling aquifer. By 1977, Congressman Morris Udall, representing the Tucson area, became involved in the dispute, hoping to find a resolution acceptable to all parties. Within a year, a committee was established—the Water Resources Coordinating Committee of Eastern Pima County—that included representatives of all affected interests, and that soon became a *de facto* water planning board for the entire region. Several settlements were proposed, but eventually dropped, until, in 1982, Udall steered through Congress the Southern Arizona Water Rights Act. President Reagan vetoed the bill in June of that year, mainly because he did not want the federal government to bear the whole cost of the settlement. Eventually, however, a revised bill that shifted some costs to the local level gained approval.

The Tohono O'odham settlement includes some important features that were conspicuously absent in, for example, the NIIP agreement discussed above. First, in return for relinquishing "Winters" rights, the San Xavier and Schuk Toak districts of the reservation have received a promise of 76,000 acre-feet of water, of which almost 40,000 will flow from the CAP, a project that enjoys wide support from the water development "iron triangle." The rest of the water will come from established groundwater sources and/or from willing sellers outside the reservation. (However, two other districts with "Winters" claims, Sif Oidak and Gila Bend, were not included in this settlement, an omission that has generated conflicts within the tribe.) Second, and perhaps most importantly, funding for water development on the reservation will come from interest generated by a $15 million trust fund, to be created jointly by federal and local contributions. Thus, the Tohono O'Odham will not have to rely on continuing appropriation from Congress, as the Navajos have. If the federal government has not completed the Tucson aqueduct within a decade of the settlement date, it will be required to pay costly penalties to the tribe. Finally, the tribe is authorized to market water off-reservation, though only within the Tucson basin. The settlement bill, interestingly enough, stipulates that its terms should not be considered applicable to any other tribe. This language was inserted by Western Congressmen who feared that the settlement might set a precedent elsewhere.

Unfortunately, the Southern Arizona Water Rights Settlement Act has not proved the unmitigated blessing to the Tohono O'odham that many had hoped it might be. To begin with, the communities in the Tucson basin will not need reservation water until the twenty-first century, which means that the tribe will have no large market for its water unless—as now contemplated—the terms of the settlement are revised. Moreover, the Settlement Act has caused division within the tribe, as many members have questioned the wisdom of their leaders in advocating, for example, the creation of an irrigated farm on land containing prehistoric artifacts and human remains. As McGuire points out, the Indians in this situation were, in effect, being "asked to negotiate [their] cosmology."[48] But the Act locks the Tohono O'odham into agricultural uses for some of its water, and if a farm were not established, the tribe would lose many of the financial incentives built into the Act, such as the federal government's promise to build canals to the reservation.

Nearby, to the east of Phoenix, the Salt River Pima-Maricopa Community seems to have obtained a less ambiguously positive outcome in respect to water rights, though it took eight decades to arrive at that equitable resolution. Dams built under the auspices of the Salt River Project (SRP), which serves the metropolitan area, had deprived the combined tribes of most of their water since 1910. To make matters worse, the SRP failed to deliver them the subsidized water that Anglo farmers in the area enjoyed, with the result that agricultural costs to the Pima and Maricopa farmers—whose ancestors had practiced irrigated agriculture for millennia—averaged $130 per acre, or more than triple the costs incurred by other local farmers.

In the wake of frustrating negotiations and legal maneuvers, a settlement finally was reached in 1988. It stipulated that Pima-Maricopa Community water rights would be quantified at 85,000 acre-feet and that metropolitan users would need to raise enough money to purchase that amount of water annually for the two tribes. This water can subsequently be leased back to other users by the tribes if they so choose. The Pimas and Maricopas were also awarded $50 million in damages for having been deprived of their water unjustly for 80 years. Finally, it was agreed that failure on the part of Anglos to abide by the terms of the settlement would result in lawsuits brought against them by the federal government. What pushed Anglos to the negotiating table in 1988 was the threat of an unpalatable court-imposed resolution, combined with an urge to address any claims that might stand in the way of the Central Arizona Project's completion. Even so, some of the principals fought the settlement, and it was not until November, 1991, when the Arizona Superior Court dismissed their objections, that the settlement was at last secure.

The Utes of Colorado[49]

The political formula that worked in Arizona to help settle Indian water rights claims also seems to have brought results in Colorado. In the southwestern corner of the state, tribal leaders on two Ute reservations—the Southern Ute and the Ute Mountain Ute, referred to in our introduction—have struggled for decades to bring water and economic development to their rugged and dry but beautiful lands. Ute water rights became a major issue in the 1970s after state officials had sought a stream adjudication for three water districts, including the Animas River basin. The 1976 "Colorado River Water Conservation" decision mentioned earlier had established the principle that Indian water rights in Colorado could be determined in state courts (though subject to concurrent jurisdiction in federal courts). It appeared as though Colorado and the Utes would have to embark on a lengthy, expensive round of litigation to resolve the issue of how much water the Utes could reserve.

However, two factors—similar to the ones that emerged in Arizona—helped speed the conflict toward resolution. Southwestern Colorado's then Representative Ben Nighthorse Campbell (now a Senator), the only Native American in Congress, became involved as a broker in the case during the early 1980s, much as Morris Udall had been in regard to the Tohono O'odham. Campbell urged the Utes to reach a negotiated settlement, suggesting certain provisions that would make such an agreement acceptable to all parties, especially an accord that would give the Utes water from two BuRec projects, the Dolores and the Animas-La Plata, if they relinquished their "Winters" claims. As in the Arizona cases, the availability of "new" water made the negotiations less confrontational, creating opportunities for all parties to improve their positions.

In 1986, the Utes gave up their lawsuits in return for roughly 70,000 acre-feet of water annually, once the two BuRec projects reach completion. They are to receive just over $60 million in development money to launch irrigation and coal mining efforts, part of which will be supported through interest from a trust fund. Also, Congress has formally obligated the United States government to build the Animas-La Plata project, although federal support is premised on contributions from local sources of over $100 million.

The Colorado Ute settlement resembles the Arizona pattern in many respects, yet it rests on much shakier ground. While the Dolores project is almost completed and already delivering some water to the Ute Mountain Reservation, Animas-La Plata is a different story. This project was part of BuRec's sprawling Colorado River Basin Project, which (as noted already) has run into difficulties because its underlying economic rationale is so weak. The Animas-La Plata project, expected to cost (as of December, 1992) $641 million, will allow the irrigation of only low value, high altitude crops such as apples, alfalfa, and pasturage. Ecologically irresponsible, it will destroy long stretches of runnable rapids, harm endangered species, and provide water at a very high cost (roughly $190 to $200 per acre-foot for the Southern Utes, about five times more than Arizona farmer pay for CAP water).[50] Moreover, the Anglo portions of Animas-La Plata will be built first; the Ute segments are not scheduled to come on line until the late 1990s, a pattern all too reminiscent of the NIIP twenty-five years earlier. Even Senator Campbell has not defended the project on cost-benefit grounds; he simply points out that it represents the Utes' only real hope for gaining water and developing economically.

In our view, the Colorado Ute settlement involves significant drawbacks for the tribes. While it is true that they will receive at least some water from the Dolores project, they have staked a great deal on the outcome of Animas-La Plata, now stymied in court because of lawsuits filed by environmentalists and river-running enthusiasts, and vulnerable to future budget-cutting. Experience shows that the Indian portions of these monumental projects are usually the most likely to be deferred or de-authorized. But even if the tribes should receive all the water promised them, it will cost a great deal. It might have been cheaper and wiser, from every angle, for the U.S. government to have bought up water rights from existing sellers in the region until it had enough to supply the 70,000 acre-feet promised to the Utes. However much buying up water rights might have cost, it surely would have proven far less expensive and less environmentally damaging than building the Animas-La Plata project. Moreover, any new irrigation projects in southwestern Colorado will add significantly to the salinity of the Colorado River, affecting all users downstream. And since the U.S. is committed by treaty to remove those salts before the river flows into Mexico, the indirect cost of Animas-La Plata will rise still higher. Senator Campbell rightly insists that the Utes deserve water and economic development on their reservations, even if the U.S. government must subsidize it. Nevertheless, there may be ways to achieve those ends other than building uneconomical, ecologically unsound projects like Animas-La Plata, and mortgaging the tribes' future to irrigated agriculture on marginal land.

The Shoshone and Bannock of Idaho[51]

The experience of the Shoshone and Bannock tribes on Idaho's Fort Hall Reservation also suggests the possible benefits of negotiated settlements for all parties. Unlike some other Western states, Idaho can count on multiple, often copious sources of water: rainfall in the north, the Snake River and its tributaries in the south, and the Snake River Aquifer underneath. Consequently, the politics of water in that state has never seemed quite the Hobbesian melee that has been witnessed in, say, the lower-basin Colorado River states. Both state officials and the tribes themselves have enjoyed some room for maneuver and compromise.

In 1990, the two tribes reached an agreement with the state (together with the federal government and certain Idaho water users) to quantify their water rights and to grant them legal recognition in state tribunals. Like other Western states, Idaho, starting in 1984, had sought an adjudication of rights to its greatest water resource, the Snake River. Given the Supreme Court decisions noted earlier, the tribes might not have prevailed if they had chosen to boycott the adjudication process. And even if they did prevail in the courts, litigation would have proven time-consuming and expensive.

Instead, the Shoshone-Bannocks decided to participate in negotiations with state officials. Fractious and difficult, these negotiations lasted almost five years, but in the end, the tribes gained some of the same concessions that their Arizona counterparts, under very different circumstances, had wrested from Anglos. The Fort Hall reservation received a total of 581,000 acre-feet of water, of which 200,000 would be "new," not heretofore used by the two tribes. Rather than irrigating additional acres—and thus locking themselves into the declining agricultural sector, like the Tohono O'odham—the Shoshone-Bannocks acquired the right to use their water to maintain in-stream flows on tribal lands. Since the Fort Hall Reservation abuts the Snake River, that would mean keeping more water in the Snake as well as its tributary, the Blackfoot. The tribes' decision could have a significant payoff, since they are also allowed now to market their water within the Snake River basin. The Bonneville Power Administration has agreed to pay them $1 million per year to maintain in-stream flow levels that should improve conditions for the annual salmon migration, now in decline. In short, the tribes receive income without having to find funds for expensive irrigation projects, while the Power Authority acquires a relatively cheap way to mitigate a public relations and environmental disaster.

Meanwhile, the burden of securing new water supplies will fall on the European-stock water users of southern Idaho, whose rights, according to the Fort Hall agreement, will be junior to those of the Shoshone-Bannocks. To compensate them for "lost" water rights, they will be granted unclaimed rights in other basins, and will be able to purchase extra water from the Native Americans. In effect, Idaho's relatively plentiful supply of water served the same purpose in the Snake River negotiations as CAP water had in Arizona: since additional supplies could be found to satisfy all parties, the negotiation did not have to become a zero-sum game.

The Wind River Cases[52]

Negotiated settlements such as the ones described here have been a fairly recent avenue for resolving Indian-Anglo water disputes. But many other cases have dragged on for years, costing all parties small fortunes in court and yielding no definite result. On occasion, Native Americans have won significant legal victories, although it remains unclear whether they will be able to derive substantial benefits from their success. One such ongoing dispute that merits examination has pitted the Arapaho and Shoshone tribes on Wyoming's Wind River Reservation against the state, the BuRec, and thousands of farmers and ranchers who have been irrigating their lands with water from the Wind River. In many respects, this dispute typifies the patterns of Anglo-Indian conflict already noted. In 1905, the U.S. government, seeking more land for white settlers, coerced the Arapaho and Shoshone tribes into relinquishing their "surplus" lands to non-Indians. The latter, organized as the Midvale irrigation district, prevailed upon the BuRec to build them a water project that diverted Wind River water (theoretically belonging to the Indians) into the Wyoming canal and thence to Midvale fields. In some years, irrigation by Midvale farmers dried up the river completely. Again typically, the tribes received from the B.I.A. a few small irrigation works, which since have fallen into disrepair.

In 1977, Wyoming filed for a stream adjudication of the Big Horn River basin, of which the Wind River is a major tributary. The federal government and the tribe claimed, together, over 800,000 acre-feet of water for the reservation under the "Winters" doctrine. The state, of course, considered that amount excessive, especially since non-Indian irrigation and energy development plans would be hampered by recognition of such a large Indian water right. Initially, the tribes lost a battle over jurisdiction when they were compelled to participate in a state-mandated stream adjudications (in accordance with the "Colorado River Water Conservation District" and "Akin" decisions).

However, the State and U.S. Supreme Courts did uphold at least some of the tribes' claims. For one thing, they granted the reservation a right to 500,717 acre-feet of water from the Wind River—less than the tribe, backed by the U.S. government, had demanded, but still almost half of the river's average annual flow. The tribes also were granted the most senior rights in the basin, dating from 1868, the year the reservation was created. On the other hand, the Courts have not recognized any Arapaho and Shoshone right to market water off the reservation, nor does the state of Wyoming, which administers the tribes' water, acknowledge in-stream flows as a beneficial use. The state Supreme Court's 3-2 majority held that the tribe had been given reserved water exclusively to create an agricultural community, not to develop a homeland, as tribal lawyers had argued. Since the U.S. Supreme Court issued no written opinion in affirming this decision, we cannot know for sure what its reasoning was. Still, one legal scholar who has examined the record of oral arguments believes that the Court is beginning to lean toward a more restrictive reading of "Winters" and that, indeed, several justices have even begun to question the reserved rights doctrine itself as well as the "practically irrigable acreage" quantification standard.[53]

The Wind River case has reaffirmed the old observation that Indian legal victories do not always translate into actual benefits. The state of Wyoming since 1989 has essentially refused to recognize the Indians' legal rights to water. The state engineer summarily declared the river to be "in surplus" for 1990 and awarded non-Indian irrigators all the water they wanted, even though his ruling played havoc with the tribes' plan to create a first-class trout fishery that would attract sportsmen to the reservation. The frustrated Indians sued again to force the state to carry out the terms of the 1989 court decision confirming their "Winters" rights.

In March of 1991, Wyoming state judge Gary Hartman took the unprecedented (in this sort of conflict) step of stripping the state engineer of his administrative powers over Wind River water and vesting them in the tribes' water engineer. In effect, the judge declared that the state engineer could not be trusted to give the tribes the water they had been awarded by the courts. However, the Wyoming Supreme Court overturned his verdict in June of 1992, reaffirming state jurisdiction over water in the Wind River. The Court told the tribes that they could not leave water in the river to maintain in-stream flows, but would have to "appropriate" the water for the "beneficial use" of irrigation. So the tribes have retreated to the *status quo ante*; they enjoy extensive formal water rights, but have few means to develop and perfect them under state law. At least for now (as of December, 1992), the tribes have decided not to appeal the case to the U.S. Supreme Court, since prospects there seem bleak. The Wind River Indians may try to build diversion projects to hold onto their water or pursue a settlement with Midvale and the state.

Even though the Arapaho and Shoshone have gained a great deal from their lawsuits, the results scarcely have been ideal for them. Up to 1989, they had spent approximately $9 million on litigation, an enormous sum for two small, impoverished Indian nations. They still do not have enough money to build irrigation projects, yet their water rights depend, in principle, on their ability to irrigate their land. They have no right to market water off-reservation and, except for their trout fishery scheme, few options for deriving income from it on the reservation. Last but not least, they have incurred the bitter enmity of local Anglo ranchers and farmers, as well as state officials. There has been talk of violence in the small communities around the reservation; residents feel that their expectations of a reliable water supply have been betrayed and their property rendered virtually worthless by tribal claims.

It seems clear that the results of litigation in Wyoming have proven far less satisfactory for all parties concerned than the outcomes of the various negotiated settlements discussed above. The ingredients of other successful settlements—e.g., a Congressional sponsor of Morris Udall's or Harry Reid's stature and judgment; potential new water sources to compensate parties who stand to lose water; federal and local money for tribal development—simply have not been present in Wyoming. By contrast, the example of the Wind River case probably has spurred negotiators in other cases, especially state officials, to seek grounds for compromise. The Utes probably would not have been able to strike a deal in Colorado without the spectre of the Wind River case to galvanize state officials.[54] In this sense, even though that litigation has not yet produced many benefits (except for lawyers), it indirectly abetted the cause of Indian water rights generally and for tribal sovereignty and self-administration of water.

IV. Conclusion: The Future of Native American Water Rights

Although the court cases and negotiations whereby Western tribes are pursuing their "Winters" claims have yielded diverse outcomes, certain patterns seem to be emerging. Clearly, most tribes *are* going to get water, though surely less than their theoretical entitlement. Even in state stream adjudications, Native American claims have been recognized. The era when their water rights could simply be ignored has long passed.

On the other hand, federal and state courts have other agendas besides redressing the grievances of indigenous peoples whose water has been illegally appropriated. The impact of the Reagan and Bush administrations' appointments has been to move the federal courts, especially the Supreme Court, across the board toward a more "states rights"-type interpretation of the Constitution, thereby diluting the sovereignty and immunity from state law that Indians had hoped to assert for their water resources. The upshot is that in the future, Native Americans will have to defend their claims in state courts. One way or another, then, reserved, open-ended "Winters" rights will be quantified and brought into harmony with rights derived from the prior appropriation/beneficial use tradition.

Another observation that can be offered about recent decisions is that the courts—as well as Anglo negotiators—often have placed a high value on security of future expectations. The Supreme Court would not undo the Orr Ditch Decree of 1944 or the original findings in "Arizona v. California I" because doing so would inject doubt and confusion into water rights adjudications throughout the West. In Arizona and elsewhere, the courts' concern to finalize judicial proceedings places limits on their willingness to reopen old water cases, which sometimes works to the detriment of Native American claims. On the other hand, that same interest in finally settling such nettlesome disputes may have helped bring recalcitrant Anglos to the bargaining table in some of the settlements reviewed here. Negotiators have made concessions to Native Americans in order to dispel the uncertainty inherent in a situation in which broad, ill-defined and elastic claims have been levied on a strictly limited, finite resource. Be it noted, however, that negotiated settlements do not necessarily yield the security of expectations that at least Anglo negotiators hoped for.[55]

Native Americans and even (albeit grudgingly) their Anglo counterparts in negotiations have recognized that Indians must be given the means to derive tangible benefits from water that they have been promised in negotiated settlements. Thus, virtually all of their settlements provide either money for irrigation or other activities, or permission to market water off the reservation in-state, or both. And some agreements pledge additional support for on-reservation industrial development using newly acknowledged tribal water resources. They also include features that guarantee full funding of whatever projects have been promised, so that the Congress and executive branch cannot evade their responsibilities to the tribes, as happened to the Navajos and Northern Utes.

Western tribes will get, and in some instances are already benefiting from, significant new water resources. But the perplexing issue is, what will they be allowed to do with their water? Up to now, the Indians' right to water has been closely tied to irrigated farming by the "Winters" doctrine. The fact that the tribes even possess a reserved water right depends, at least on one interpretation, on the premise that they should become yeoman farmers. The "practically irrigable acreage" standard reflects the same bias toward agriculture. The 19th century idea that the U.S. government should "civilize" the tribes by promoting their transition from a hunting and gathering economy to a sedentary, agricultural one continues to influence Indian water rights policy on the threshold of the 21st century.

However, as we have stressed, farming is a vocation in decline. And irrigated commercial agriculture, which depends on massive, subsidized water projects and expensive technology, may not embody the Indians' best opportunity for long-term, stable employment on their reservations. Ideally, irrigated farms would raise high-value crops on land with a long growing season (such as California's Central Valley). By that standard, few Western reservations would be candidates for large-scale, profitable farming; indeed, most are located on land that white settlers did not want, precisely because it *was* marginal for agriculture. For example, on the Cheyenne River Sioux Reservation in South Dakota, 60 percent of Indian farmers either already have gone bankrupt or soon will. By one estimate, 40 percent of the 20,000 Native American farmers in the U.S. are in financial trouble.[56]

The "practically irrigable acreage" standard established in "Arizona v. California I" already has forced Native Americans to resort to elaborate, expensive research. To document the quantity of water to which they are entitled, tribes typically must hire hydrologists, agronomists, and engineers to carry out complex studies of soil conditions, suitability for agriculture, and so forth. They then present this material as evidence in court to demonstrate the amount of water they deserve to be allocated. But in the end, the studies often gather dust, since the tribes have no intention of using all their water for irrigated farming. In the paradoxical world of "Winters," one must pretend one will use water for irrigation in order to obtain it for other purposes.

In some cases, Indians actually have been held to the irrigation policy that is theoretically enshrined in "Winters." And if the "Cappaert / New Mexico" line of reasoning gains ground, the courts may eventually declare agriculture as the "primary purpose" of reservation water and thus exclude all other uses from reserved rights protection. The Pyramid Lake Paiutes' difficulties with the state of Nevada and the Interior Department have continued for years partly because they wanted water for fishing, not farming. Similarly, much of the discontent among the Tohono O'odham over their recent settlement stems from the fact that it commits them to irrigated farming on a tract of land that might have better uses.[57] Finally, the recent Wyoming state court ruling mentioned earlier denies the Shoshone and Arapaho on the Wind River Reservation the right to use water to maintain in-stream flows, since that is not considered a "beneficial use" under Wyoming law.

In our view, the time has come to rethink fundamentally the rationale of "Winters" and indeed of the whole reservation system. In the 19th century, when most reservations were created, government officials liked to describe them as educational institutions that would give Native Americans a chance to learn the arts of civilization and self-government. Implicit in this paternalistic, ethnocentric attitude lay the conviction that the reservation system eventually could be phased out: "the reservation was a way-station between the society prior to the advent of the European settlers and the society when reservations would no longer be needed."[58] The frequent calls for termination of the reservation system that have resounded in Western state capitals and the halls of Congress since that time simply reflect the persistence of this 19th century theory of the reservations' function. To many Anglos, especially those who would stand to benefit economically from the demise of the institution, the reservation system still seems an irksome, communitarian, collectivist exception to the prevailing rule of liberal individualism in American society. Why, they ask, shouldn't Indians own individual plots of land, handle their own private affairs, buy and sell property, water, or minerals as they see fit, and generally behave more like other citizens? Why not simply dismantle the reservation system and tribal government?

But there is another legal and moral tradition more open to treating Indian communities as distinct societies that will maintain their separate cultures, languages, and institutions for the foreseeable future. That tradition has been delineated by the noted legal scholar Charles Wilkinson. It begins with a trilogy of cases decided by Chief Justice John Marshall in the early years of the republic.[59] These cases—"Johnson v. McIntosh,"[60] "Cherokee Nation v. Georgia,"[61] and "Worcester v. Georgia,"[62]—affirmed the tribes' continuing (though limited) sovereignty and deduced it from their having been sovereign nations before the advent of European settlement. In Wilkinson's interpretation, the courts in recent years (partly under the influence of jurist Felix Cohen's work) gradually have revived the spirit of the Marshall decisions and tried to honor the implicit promise of the 19th century treaties and treaty substitutes to give Indians a "reservation homeland" accompanied by "measured separation" between them and the surrounding Anglo society.[63] In particular, the courts have been willing to recognize that Indian rights, such as water rights, land claims, and various attributes of sovereign power, do not lapse merely because they have fallen into desuetude.[64]

The Marshall-Cohen tradition of legal opinion (as Wilkinson calls it) has been fashioned piecemeal over many years. Its implicit "promise" of homelands for Indian nations has never been raised to the status of an explicit doctrine that would link tribal sovereignty to cultural survival and flourishing. Indeed, as we have noted, American courts have not always been receptive to the homelands doctrine in water rights cases. In our view, the persuasiveness of the homelands idea would be enhanced if it were more explicitly tied to a theory of "group rights." Such a theory would treat cultural groupings—not only Indian tribes, but all coherent, compact associations based on religion, language, or common descent—as permanent, irreducible features of the political landscape, and not, as is often the case now, as "interest groups."[65] In other countries, such as Switzerland, Belgium, Malaysia, Fiji, and Canada, ethnic and/or linguistic groups already have been recognized as distinctive, rights-bearing entities. Likewise, the United Nations and other international organizations have affirmed the duty of all nation-states to respect and promote indigenous and minority cultures and languages.[66] And in 1978, the U.S. Congress passed the Indian Religious Freedom Act, affirming the inherent worth of indigenous cultures and the role that traditional religious practices play in sustaining them.

The relationship between Indian water resources and the cultural integrity of the tribes has never been explicitly recognized, yet in some cases it seems ineluctable. Some tribes treat certain springs, streams, or waterfalls as sacred sites. As Susan Williams, one of the attorneys who argued the Shoshones' and Arapahos' case before the U.S. Supreme Court, has put it, "Water is the lifeblood of people and economies. Water entitlements establish or sustain a social order. And in Indian country, water often embodies important spiritual and other cultural values."[67] Other tribes have evolved cultures in which water and associated habitats sustain the traditional way of life (as we have already noticed in the case of the Sioux, Mandans, Arikara and Pyramid Lake Paiutes).[68] One Hualapai remarked, deploring the deleterious effects of Glen Canyon Dam on his tribe's portion of the Colorado River, "nature is our culture."[69] Thus, at least some indigenous peoples need their reserved water not only for the jobs it would create, but to shelter ways of life that would be threatened by massive commercial and industrial development.

American law and policy sensitive to the group rights of Native Americans would ensure that no water projects in the future inundated or otherwise damaged religiously and culturally significant places. Moreover, the government would ensure that indigenous people who wished to live in traditional ways would have enough water to maintain a nucleus of members on the reservation who could live, speak, and practice religion together, even if their agriculture or fishing did not pass the standard test of cost-effectiveness. For, without adequate water, life on Western reservations would become so difficult that many residents would drift away. Eventually, numbers there might fall below the level necessary to preserve ancient tongues, beliefs, and practices. Such a policy might require subsidizing water for Native Americans, but European-stock Americans have long received subsidies directly from the Department of Agriculture and indirectly from the BuRec via debt forgiveness and low repayment rates. If subsidies are good enough for Anglos, they ought to be good enough for Indians as well.

But irrigated agriculture cannot be the whole answer to the reservations' economic and social problems. And in fact most tribes that recently have won large supplies of water do not want to commit themselves unreservedly to irrigating their land; they want to be free to use the water as they choose to promote tribal prosperity on a number of fronts. In some ways, the most promising vista opening up to them would be to market their water to the highest bidder. There are, as we have noted, formidable legal and political obstacles to their doing so, but these may fall within the coming decades.[70] In theory, then, a tribe like the Utes in Colorado eventually could sell the water it would otherwise appropriate to electric utilities or to cities as far away as California. Native Americans on the Tohono O'odham and Fort Hall reservations will certainly be doing this on a limited scale in the near future. With the income they earn from water sales plus the tribal development funds provided in many of the settlements we have reviewed, some Western tribes should be able to reverse the exodus of their members from the reservations by creating good jobs for them at home.

Obviously, these are choices that Native Americans will have to make for themselves, and some sort of balance among irrigation, domestic and industrial uses, and marketing will have to be struck. It might be worthwhile to recall that once they restore artificially de-watered streams, many reservations will boast almost pristine environments. Except in a few cases (especially on the Navajo reservation), air and water pollution and toxic waste have not yet become serious problems. One suspects that ecological integrity, clean air, and clean water eventually could become so attractive that owners of certain light industries might want to relocate near the reservations simply to enjoy the quality of life that such an environment can offer.[71] Moreover, as representatives of the Wind River tribes have argued, there are economic opportunities in outdoor recreation. Clear, well-watered streams, such as the Wind River could remain if the state of Wyoming would allow the tribes to employ its water as they choose, might one day attract sport fishermen, kayakers, and other recreational users who would pump dollars into reservation economies. Once the iron bond between water rights and irrigated agriculture is broken, new possibilities for water use may arise that of yet have scarcely been considered.

NOTES

The authors express appreciation to staff members of the *High Country News* in Paonia, Colorado, for help in gathering information for this article. Steve Hinchman (no relation) of *HCN* and Professor Daniel McCool of the University of Utah kindly read an earlier draft and suggested many improvements. Susan Williams of the Albuquerque law firm Gover, Stetson, and Williams, P.C. responded to the authors' queries by sending along some helpful material.

1. *Times Independent*, Moab, Utah, March 26, 1992. (Report from the Montezuma Valley, Colorado *Journal*.)

2. For an account of the Pueblo Indians' ancient irrigation practices, see Charles T. Dumas, Marilyn O'Leary, and Albert E. Utton, *Pueblo Indian Water Rights*, (Tucson: University of Arizona Press, 1984), 7-8.

3. An acre-foot, the standard measure of water in the West, is enough water to cover one acre of ground one foot deep, or about 325,849 gallons.

4. See Marc Reisner, *Cadillac Desert*, (New York: Viking Books, 1986), 148-49.

5. The bureaucratic competition between the Army Corps of Engineers and the Bureau of Reclamation is skillfully described in Reisner, *Cadillac Desert*. See especially chapters 5-7.

6. Daniel McCool, *Command of the Waters*, (Berkeley: University of California Press, 1987), 33.

7. The California experience is discussed by Donald Worster, *Rivers of Empire*, (New York: Pantheon Books,

1985), 96-111, 191-256. See also Reisner, *Cadillac Desert*, 344-92.

8. Henry Caulfield, a past president of the Water Resources Council, cited these and other factors as reasons why the "Federal water development program is politically dying." Cited in McCool, *Command of the Waters*, 108.

9. Michael R. Moore, "Native American Water Rights: Efficiency and Fairness," *Natural Resources Journal*, 29 (Summer, 1989), 780, takes note of the cultural biases inherent in the beneficial use doctrine, which discounts fishing and growing low-value, subsistence crops as beneficial uses.

10. For discussions of "Winters" and its implications, see Monroe Price and Gary Weatherford, "Indian Water Rights in Theory and Practice: Navajo Experience in the Colorado River Basin," in Lawrence Rosen, ed., *American Indians and the Law*, (New Brunswick: Transaction Books/Duke University Press, 1976), 97-131; Marjane Ambler, *Breaking the Iron Bonds: Indian Control of Energy Development*, (Lawrence: University of Kansas Press, 1990), 213-20; William Veeder, "Winters Doctrine Rights: Keystone of National Programs for Western Land and Water Utilization," *Montana Law Review*, 26 (1956), 149-72; Walter Rusinek, "A Preview of Coming Attractions? 'Wyoming v. United States' and the Reserved Rights Doctrine," *Ecology Law Quarterly*, 17(2), (1990), 355-412; Susan M. Williams, "The 'Winters' Doctrine on Water Administration," *Proceedings of the Thirty-Sixth Annual Rocky Mountain Mineral Law Institute*, (New York: Matthew Bender and Company, 1991), Chapter 24, 1-48; Robert Dellwo, "Indian Water Rights: the Winters Doctrine Updated," *Gonzaga Law Review*, 216, (1971), 215-40; and Richard B. Collins, "The Future Course of the Winters Doctrine," *University of Colorado Law Review*, (1985), 481-94.

11. *Winters v. the United States*, 207 U.S. 564 (1908). For an analysis of some significant cases that followed "Winters" see Gerald R. Miller, "Indians, Water, and the Pelton Decision," *Utah Law Review*, 5, (1957), 495-510. Rusinek also analyzes the "Winters" case and its successors, with special emphasis on the putative purposes for which

Congress established Indian reservations, in "Reserved Rights Doctrine," 357-78.

12. See William H. Veeder, "Water Rights in the Coal Field of the Yellowstone River Basin," in Rosen, *American Indians and the Law*, 87.

13. For a helpful summary of these interpretations see Monroe E. Price, *Law and the American Indian: Readings, Notes and Cases*, (Indianapolis: Bobbs-Merrill, 1973), 316-24.

14. McCool, *Command of the Waters*, ably summarizes the irreconcilable differences between these two doctrines; see 2-4.

15. See John Locke, *Second Treatise of Government*, chapter 5. For analysis of Anglo/Lockean and Native American views of nature, see Annie Booth and Harvey Jacobs, "Ties That Bind: Native American Beliefs as a Foundation for Environmental Consciousness," *Environmental Ethics* 12(2), (1990), 27-43; Kathleen Squadrito, "Locke's View of Dominion," *Environmental Ethics*, 1(4), (1979), 255-62; O. Douglas Schwartz, "Indian Rights and Environmental Ethics: Changing Perspectives, and a Modest Proposal," *Environmental Ethics* 9(1), (1987), 291-302; and J. Baird Callicott, "Traditional American Indian and Western European Attitudes Toward Nature: An Overview," *Environmental Ethics*, 4(1), (1982), 293-318.

16. Dumars, et al., *Pueblo Indian Water Rights*, discuss possible interpretations of Pueblo water rights as (a) aboriginal, (b) "Winters"-derived, or (c) treaty-based. See 11-54.

17. This view of the federal courts as mostly well-disposed toward Indian water rights claims is defended by Lloyd Burton, *American Indian Water Rights and the Limits of Law*, (Lawrence: University of Kansas Press, 1991), 6-7, 33, and Richard Collins, "The Future Course of the Winters Doctrine," *University of Colorado Law Review*, 56, (Spring, 1985), 486. But see also Robert D. Dellwo, "Recent Developments in the Northwest Regarding Indian Water Rights," *Natural Resources Journal*, 20, (January, 1980), 101-20, who cites Supreme Court decisions from the 1970s that undermined tribal claims. Dellwo argues that the common denominator of these unfavorable decisions is an "assimilationist ideology," 103.

18. "Skeem v. U.S.," 273 F. 93, (1921). The court's position in "Skeem" was reaffirmed in "United States v. Ahtanum Irrigation District," 236 F. 2d 321, (1956).

19. "Arizona v. California," U.S., 373, (1963), 546.

20. Burton, *American Indian Water Rights*, 31.

21. For a discussion of "Arizona v. California II" in the context of legal conflicts over security of expectations and "finality" of property rights, see Charles Wilkinson, *American Indians, Time, and the Law*, (New Haven: Yale University Press, 1987), 43.

22. "Cappaert v. United States," U.S., 426, (1976), 128. On the other hand, "Cappaert" recognized the connection between the pumping of groundwater outside of a reserved-water area and the diminution of water supplies within. That finding has helped Arizona tribes whose well water supplies have been threatened by Anglo wells outside the reservation draining the underlying aquifers.

23. "United States v. New Mexico," U.S., 438, (1978), 696.

24. See Rusinek, "Reserved Rights Doctrine," 376.

25. "Colville Confederated Tribes v. Walton," 647 F. 2d 42, (9th Cir.), modified, 752 F. 2d. 397, cert. denied, U.S., 454 (1981), 1092.

26. "Colorado River Conservation District v. United States," U.S., 44, (1976), 800 and "United States v. Akin," 504 F. 2d 115, (10th Cir. 1974). For a review of the 1976 case and its aftermath see Burton, *American Indian Water Rights*, 36-40.

27. "Arizona v. San Carlos Apache Tribe," 103 S.Ct. 3201 (1983). An effective rebuttal of the Court's reasoning may be found in Mary Wallace, "The Supreme Court and Indian Water Rights," in Vine DeLoria, Jr., ed., *American Indian Policy in the Twentieth Century*, (Norman: University of Oklahoma Press, 1985), 197-200.

28. McCool, *Command of the Waters*, 118-19.

29. Statistics on Indian projects come from McCool, *Command of the Waters*, 159, and a Dec. 8, 1992 letter to the authors from Steve Hinchman, an expert on Western water issues.

30. Burton, *American Indian Water Rights*, 23.

31. McCool, *Command of the Waters*, 255.

32. See Martha Knack and Omer Stewart, *As Long as the River Shall Run: An Ethnohistory of Pyramid Lake Indian Reservation*, (Berkeley: University of California Press, 1984), 351-58.

33. Michael Moore estimated in "Native American Water Rights," 766, that Indian claims to water "involve 60 Western water basins and over 100 Indian communities" (as of 1989).

34. Ed Marston, "Colorado is the Appalachia of the West," *High Country News*, (August 19, 1985), 10.

35. See Tony Davis, "Arizona's Water Disaster," *High Country News*, (Aug. 10, 1992), 1, 10-13.

36. Sources for this section include Charles Du Mars and Helen Ingram, "Congressional Quantification of Indian Water Rights: A Definitive Solution or a Mirage?", *Natural Resources Journal*, 20, (1980); Lawrence Kelly, *The Navajo Indians and Federal Indian Policy, 1900-1935*, (Tucson: University of Arizona Press, 1968); Ambler, *Breaking the Iron Bonds*, 226-30; Michael Lawson, "The Navajo Indian Irrigation Project: Muddied Past, Clouded Future," *Indian Historian*, 9(1), (Winter, 1976), 19-29; Hanna Cortner, "The Navajo Environmental Protection Commission," *Indian Historian*, 9(4), (Fall, 1976), 32-37; Rosalie Martone, "The United States and the Betrayal of Indian Water Rights," *Indian Historian*, 7(3), (1974), 3-11; John Folk-Williams, *What Indian Water to the West: A Sourcebook*, (Santa Fe: Western Network, 1982), 13, 70-73; Price and Weatherford, "Indian Water Rights"; and Burton, *American Indian Water Rights*, 66-69.

37. Ambler, *Breaking the Iron Bonds*, 227.

38. Sources for this section include Ed Marston, "After Decades of Trying, Opponents Get the Central Utah Project into the Ring," *High Country News*, (Nov. 11, 1985), 6-7; Steve Hinchman, "The CUP Story: Why Utah Wants 'The Bureau' Out," *High Country News*, (July 15, 1991), 1, 6-15; Daniel McCool, "The Northern Utes' Long Water Ordeal," *High Country News*, (July 15, 1991), 8-9; Burton, *American Indian Water Rights*, 67-68, 78-79; and Folk-Williams, *What Indian Water Means*, 15, 88-91.

39. Sources for this section include Price, *Law and the American Indian*, 325-28; Burton, *American Indian Water*

Rights, 41-42, 65-66, 77-78; Knack and Stewart, *As Long as the River Shall Run*; The *Reno Gazette-Journal*, (Nov. 17, 1990); the *Lahontan Valley News*, (Nov. 17, 1990); and a letter to the authors from Steve Hinchman, Dec. 8, 1992.

40. "U.S. v. Orr Water Ditch Co. et al.," U.S. District Court for Nevada, Equity no. A-3 (1935).

41. "Pyramid Lake Paiute Tribe v. Rogers B. Morton, 2506-70 U.S. District Court for District of Columbia (1972); "U.S. and Pyramid Lake Paiute v. Truckee-Carson Irrigation District," U.S., 463, (1983), 110.

42. Sources for this section include Michael Lawson, *Dammed Indians: The Pick-Sloan Plan and the Missouri River Sioux, 1944-80*, (Norman: University of Oklahoma Press, 1982); Reisner, *Cadillac Desert*: Joseph Vincent Siry, "When the River Flows Upstream," *Indian Historian*, 11(2), (Spring, 1978), 6-14; Ambler, *Breaking the Iron Bonds*, 204-13; Peter Carrels and Lawrence Mosher, "Missouri: A River Basin at War," *High Country News*, (March 11, 1991), 1, 10-11; Marjane Ambler, "Standing Rock Sioux Moving to Enforce U.S. Water Regs," *High Country News*, (May 6, 1991), 5; Ed Marston, "In the Missouri River Basin: Let the Brawl Begin," *High Country News*, (Sept. 30, 1985), 1, 10-11; Glenn Emery, "Fighting to Preserve Culture Against a Flood of Incursions," *Insight*, (Sept. 1, 1986), 14-16.

43. Lawson, *Dammed Indians*, xiv. Something similar happened to the Yakima nation in Washington state in the 1940s when their key fishery, Celilo Falls, was inundated by the Dalles Dam on the Columbia River. See Glenn Emery, "Keeping the Past with the Future," *Insight*, (Sept. 1, 1986), 18.

44. See Lawson, *Dammed Indians*, 60.

45. Ibid., 184-85.

46. The government did pay the Sioux "rehabilitation" money, some of which went to develop new businesses and sources of income. But, except for livestock raising, few of these have panned out for the Indians.

47. Sources for this section include Burton, *American Indian Water Rights*, 69-73, 81-123, 138; Folk-Williams, *What Indian Water Means*, 37-43; McCool, *Command of the Waters*; Thomas R. McGuire, "Indian Water Rights Settlements: A Case Study in the Rhetoric of Implementation," *American*

Indian Culture and Research Journal, 15(2), (1991), 139-69; Price, *Law and the American Indian*, 477; Terrence J. Lamb, "Indian-Government Relations on Water Utilization on the Salt and Gila River Valleys of Southern Arizona, 1902-1914," *Indian Historian*, 10(3), (1977), 38-45; Sandy Tolan, "The Central Arizona Project is Designed to Water Homes," *High Country News*, (Feb. 20, 1984), 6-7; Sandy Tolan, "A Developer Seeks the Papago Tribe's CAP Water," *High Country News*, (Feb. 20, 1984), 10; and Tony Davis, "Arizona's Water Disaster," *High Country News*, (Aug. 10, 1992), 1, 10-13.

48. McGuire, "Indian Water Rights Settlements," 155.

49. Sources for this section include articles from Moab, Utah *Times Independent*; Ed Marston, "Reworking the Colorado River Basin," *High Country News*, (Nov. 10, 1986), 18-20; Russell Martin, "The Dolores Project is Man's Latest, and Most Grandiose, Attempt to Water Montezuma Valley," *High Country News*, (Mar. 5, 1984), 10-12; Ed Marston, "The Dolores Project Could Hurt its Most Ardent Suitors," *High Country News*, (Mar. 5, 1984), 13; Hotline, "Water Project Challenged," *High Country News*, (Mar. 9, 1992), 4; Folk-Williams, *What Indian Water Means*, 50-51; and Burton, *American Indian Water Rights*, 74-76, 83-85, 119, 127.

50. Comparative cost figures are derived from *High Country News*, Dec. 17, 1990, 10, and June 15, 1992, p. 10.

51. Sources for this section include Folk-Williams, *What Indian Water Means*, and Pat Ford, "Idaho Avoids the Courts," *High Country News*, (Aug. 27, 1990), 11, 15.

52. Sources for this section include Ambler, *Breaking the Iron Bonds*, 206, 209-10, 213, 217, 231; Katharine Collins, "Water: Fear of Supreme Court Leads Tribes to Accept an Adverse Decision," *High Country News*, (Oct. 19, 1992), 1; Katharine Collins and Debra Thunder, "Wyoming Tribes Lose Again in Court," *High Country News*, (July 13, 1990), 4; Ed Marston, "An Indian Water Victory Creates Turmoil in Wyoming," *High Country News*, (Nov. 25, 1985), 13; Geoffrey O'Gara, "Wyoming Tribes to Administer Wind River Water," *High Country News*, (May 6, 1991), 5; Geoffrey O'Gara, "Waterless in Wind River?" *High Country News*, (Aug. 7, 1990), 1, 10-11; Andrew Melynkovych, "Battle of the Big Wind River is Over!" *High Country News*, (Aug. 7, 1990), 10; Dave

Perry and Lawrence Mosher, "Indians Pursue Their Big Wind River Rights," *High Country News*, (Jan. 28, 1991), 11; Rusinek, "Reserved Rights Doctrine"; and Burton, *American Indian Water Rights*, 50-57.

53. Rusinek, "Reserved Rights Doctrine," 400.

54. Lisa Jones, "Animas-La Plata: Still Flawed," *High Country News*, (Dec. 17, 1990), 1.

55. For a pessimistic evaluation of negotiated settlements' achievements (and in particular their failure to assure finality and certainty) see Daniel McCool, "Intergovernmental Conflict and Indian Water Rights: An Assessment of Negotiated Settlements," *Publius* (forthcoming).

56. Both statistics are provided by Keith Jewett of the Cheyenne River Sioux. See *High Country News* special issue, "Tribes Struggle for Sovereignty and Power," (Nov. 25, 1985), 11.

57. For Tohono O'odham traditionalists, another issue has been the proper disposition of human remains found on lands under the San Xavier Development Project. Traditionalists fear that if these remains are disturbed, seven generations of Tohono O'odham will suffer "pain and disease"; see McGuire, "Indian Water Rights Settlements," 139.

58. Price, *Law and the American Indian*, 85. For a good statment of this 19th century justification for reservations, see "United States vs. Clapox," 35 F. 575 (D.C. Ore. 1888), reprinted in Price, 86-88.

59. See Wilkinson, *American Indians, Time, and the Law*, 24, 55-56.

60. U.S. (8 Wheat.), 21, (1823), 543.

61. U.S. (5 Pet.), 30, (1831), 1.

62. U.S. (6 Pet.), 31, (1832), 515.

63. Wilkinson, *American Indians, Time, and the Law*, 4, 31.

64. Ibid., 44.

65. On the question of group rights for Native Americans see Frances Svenson, "Liberal Democracy and Group Rights: The Legacy of Individualism and its Impact on American Indian Tribes," *Political Studies*, 27(3), (1979), 421-39, and two articles in Menno Boldt and J. Anthony Long, eds., *The Quest for Justice: Aboriginal Peoples and Aboriginal*

Rights, (Toronto: University of Toronto Press, 1985): William B. Henderson, "Canadian Legal and Judicial Philosophies on the Doctrine of Aboriginal Rights," 221-29, and James Youngblood Henderson, "The Doctrine of Aboriginal Rights in Western Legal Tradition," 185-220. For more general discussions of group rights consult the following works by Vernon VanDyke: "The Individual, the State, and Ethnic Communities in Political Theory," *World Politics*, 29(3), (1977), 343-69; "Justice as Fairness: For Groups," *American Political Science Review*, 69(2), (1975), 607-14; and "Collective Entities and Moral Rights: Problems in Liberal-Democratic Thought," *Journal of Politics*, 44(1), (1982), 21-44. For a defense of the liberal theory of rights vis-a-vis indigenous peoples, see Will Kymlicka, *Liberalism, Community and Culture*, (Oxford: Clarendon Press, 1991), especially chapters 7, 8, and 9.

66. A summary of international documents supporting cultural rights is provided by Sharon O'Brien, "Federal Indian Policies and the International Protection of Human Rights," in DeLoria, *American Indian Policy*. See also the works by Van Dyke cited in the previous footnote.

67. See Williams, "The "Winters" Doctrine on Water Administration," pp. 24-29. Williams' point may be illustrated by the example of the Snoqualmies and other Indian nations of the Pacific Northwest who consider Snoqualmie Falls sacred, and have fought against local power authorities who turn the waterfall on and off as electricity needs demand more or less diversion of water above it. See Brian Collins, "The Public Gets a Chance to Revamp Dams Built 50 Years Ago," *High Country News*, (Dec. 2, 1991), 1, 8-13. The Snoqualmie nation in particular, which has been in decline for decades, hopes it can initiate a cultural renaissance by restoring the falls, its main sacred site.

68. The Hopi and Pueblo tribes are especially sensitive to disruptions in their traditional uses of water, since "water is sacred [to them]. Their elaborate religion is all a prayer for rain to nourish their fields of corn, beans, squash and melons." George Hardeen, "The 'Moral Outrage' Over How Water is Used," *High Country News*, (Nov. 5, 1990), 7.

69. Quoted in Florence Williams, "Indian Tribe Pushes for a Natural River and Canyon," *High Country News*, (Aug. 26, 1991), 12.

70. For an analysis of cases that may lead the courts to expand "Winters" rights in the future to include non-agricultural uses, see Dellwo, "Recent Developments in the Northwest." The case for water leasing is presented in Bill Leaphart, "Sale and Lease of Indian Water Rights," *Montana Law Review*, 33, (1972), 266-76, and Williams, "The "Winters" Doctrine on Water Administration," 32-48. Collins, "Future Course of the Winters Doctrine," contends that "Congress should explicitly authorize Indians to lease water for periods long enough for lessees to amortize development interests" (p. 490). Some Indians object to the ecologically destructive "development" of their reservations for the sake of providing for profligate urban energy and water users; see, for example, Lawson, "Navajo Indian Irrigation Project," 27, and Ambler, *Breaking the Iron Bonds*, 230-32. In a typology laid out by Stephen Cornell, *The Return of the Native: American Indian Political Resurgence*, (New York: Oxford University Press, 1988), the goals of such Indians would be labelled "transformative-segregative" (chapter 9).

71. Recently, such a light manufacturing firm was located in Bluff, Utah; it employs significant numbers of Utes from a small reservation south of town. As reported in the Moab, Utah *Times Independent*, the owner was betting that the Utes' long tradition of craftsmanship would make them ideally suited for fine work with electronic components.

Native American Water Rights: Efficiency and Fairness

Michael R. Moore

ABSTRACT

This essay characterizes the setting for Native American water rights in economic, legal, and historical terms. A simple way of understanding the water claims, in part, is as a dispute over water between the Indian nations, as prospective water users, and established users of western water rights. The fewer opportunities to build new water-supply projects reduces the ability to sustain non-Indian use at historic levels and, simultaneously, to accommodate new Indian uses. This transforms Indian water rights into controversial resource disputes. The dilemma justifies considering a new approach to the issue.

Three premises guide the approach. Two of them argue that the federal government should recognize the legitimate property interests of both Indians and non-Indians. This essay supports the fairness of the first two premises. The government has the responsibility to pursue solutions to the conflict through some combination of developing new water supply, purchasing water rights, or substituting monetary compensation for water rights. The third premise gives to the government the authority to negotiate cost-efficient solutions to the disputes.

A generic approach to solving the water conflicts is recommended. The two parties to the dispute share equally the scarce water resource at issue. A government subsidy, then, sustains individual property rights by substituting money for the value of the water right. The two parties remain whole in their wealth status rather than in a physical, water-right status. Three other recommendations give additional substance to the procedure for quantifying Indian water rights, argue for subsidized water conveyance to the reservations, and suggest prospective sources of funds to earmark for the necessary government expenditures. A context of both the original goal of Indian water—to develop sustainable communities on the reservation lands—and the record of federal management of Indian and non-Indian water development supports the recommendations.

> The most intractable problem the Commission faced is the conflict between existing non-Indian users and newly initiated Indian withdrawals. While the Indians often have legal superiority to make use of water, a later initiated Indian use often would disrupt preexisting non-Indian uses representing large Federal, State, and private investments.
>
> *National Water Commission*[1]

There is urgency of a considerably grand scale to this need to channel the scattering forces and build predictable doctrine. . . . Indian water rights cases are typically as complex as major antitrust actions. Most of the great rivers of the arid West have major Indian holdings within their drainages and, while extensive litigation is inevitable, the scope of the cases can be narrowed by reasoned precedent.

Lack of a reasonably well defined matrix of doctrine also undercuts one of the most encouraging developments in Indian country—the increasing willingness of tribes and states to settle their differences extrajudicially. This growing atmosphere of cooperation is inevitably premised upon the existence of doctrinal benchmarks to guide parties at the bargaining table.

Charles F. Wilkinson[2]

INTRODUCTION

A great drama is unfolding in the American West: the assertion of Native American surface-water rights. The drama exists because the rights rested as fallow property since 1908; consequently, they conflict directly with traditional appropriative water rights. Further, they are members of the class of federal reserved water rights. Federal rights are altering the traditional state domain over surface water, which has been managed through the states' prior appropriation systems.

The transformation of Native American claims into water rights[3] will affect the economic efficiency of western water use, the economic and social status of both Indian and non-Indian communities, and the relationship between the western states and the federal government. This essay describes the setting for Native American claims, describes and supports three general premises that guide the reconciliation of the competing claims to surface water, evaluates the decisionmaking context for the existence and the scope of the Indian right, and makes four recommendations concerning the resolution of the issue.[4] The recommendations form a general, policy perspective for the scope of Indian water rights and for the management of conflicts over the allocation of water resources that they engender.

The adoption and implementation of the recommendations will set in motion a process that meets several objectives of sound public policy: fairness to the disputants, economic efficiency in water-resource use, and cost efficiency in the government's management of the dispute. Many commentators discuss the need to bring certainty and stability to the western waterscape so that water-resource planning and water markets can develop to allocate water resources efficiently. This essay provides a comprehensive perspective on a method to settle one major aspect of the current uncertainty in western water markets, the uncertainty surrounding Indian water claims.

THE SETTING

The U.S. Supreme Court, in the famous case of "Winters v. United States" in 1908,[5] found that when the Indian reservations were created, sufficient water was reserved implicitly for Indian tribes to sustain human communities on the arid and semi-arid reservation lands. The Court recognized at that time a new class of western surface water rights, the federal reserved water right (or "Winters" doctrine right). The Indian water right is the charter member of this class of water rights. For most of the century, "Winters" rights were treated as an illusion, and were ignored. In the case of "Arizona v. California" in 1963, the Supreme Court confirmed the reality of federal reserved rights by explicitly allocating to Indian reservations more than ten percent of the apportionment of the lower Colorado River.[6] The potential impact on western water allocation of "Winters" rights and, in particular, Indian water rights only now is being perceived.

Native American water claims are pervasive in the West: 60 of these cases already are in court, with the total volume of claims to water reaching 45 million acre-feet per year.[7] The claims involve 60 western water basins and over 100 Indian communities. Further, though frequently not mentioned, at least 100 (and probably more) non-Indian rural and urban communities are involved directly in the water-allocation decisions associated with Indian claims: they use water that reservations communities now claim.[8]

Native American water rights are of great symbolic value to the Indian nations.[9] A clear analogy exists, from their perspective, between ownership of their original homelands and ownership of water: they lost their homelands and feel threatened with the loss of their water rights.[10] Indian water, in this light, provides a rare opportunity for the reservation communities to develop, both culturally and economically. The symbolic value of water provides a new, common identity: it is a resource that the tribes learned to struggle for in the courtroom and that they are learning to manage in their best interest.[11] Further, water provides a renewable resource base upon which to foster the development of the reservations. This contrasts to a reliance on an exhaustible resource base, such as coal, oil, or uranium. Most tribes experienced only temporary increases in their standard of living from the extraction of their exhaustible resources.[12] In the era of Indian self determination with its renewed commitment to the reservations as Indian communities,[13] water rights represent a necessary resource endowment for achieving a measure of economic independence.

Two avenues are open to Indians once they file water claims: to participate in a general stream adjudication in state court[14] (which is subject to federal review), or to enter into settlement negotiations with the pertinent state governments, the federal government, and the affected established water users. The historic trend has been to rely on negotiation as the primary method to settle the water-resource disputes. This occurred for two reasons. First, successful negotiations attached Indian water onto federal water projects that were under construction, thereby effectively keeping the status of all the parties to the dispute constant, or whole, in the volume of water that they own.[15] Second, the litigation and adjudication processes are expensive and lengthy, with only uncertain results.[16]

In both legal proceedings and negotiated settlements, information on the quantity of the particular reservation's water right becomes important. The common quantification procedure establishes the volume of water required to irrigate the reservation lands.[17] The amount of land to be irrigated is described as the "practicably irrigable acreage" (PIA). The term "practicably" constrains the extensive margin of land use. The Supreme Court, in "Arizona v. California," adopted an economic-viability test, so that an approach applying benefit-cost analysis defines the PIA.[18]

A new chapter is beginning in the saga of Native American water rights. The ability to effect a negotiated settlement to the resource dispute solely in terms of water resources is diminishing as the opportunity for relatively inexpensive, new water supplies declines. The situation, naturally, parallels the common perspective on the status of western water: the era of structurally-oriented, water-resource development is ending; the era of water management is beginning. Rarely will all parties be kept whole in the physical volume of the water resource that they own. Indian water rights that are perfected in the future, consequently, will affect established appropriative water rights. They offer the prospect of a one-for-one transfer of the water right from established users to Indian tribes. Such a transfer may be sufficient impetus to force many established water users—primarily farmers—into bankruptcy.[19]

The new chapter in Indian water will likely be contentious.[20] Deloria, representing the Native American interests, warns that viewing water as either Indian water or non-Indian water will mire the western water system in legal procedures.[21] The U.S. Supreme Court cases in the 1980s indicate that the Court is addressing the more complex issue of balancing the variety of water-resource needs.[22] The cases give hope to established water users that Indian claims do not simply represent a transfer of water rights away from them. Yet the fact remains that the court system has no clear precedent for dividing water in the context of Indian water. American Indian law is a distinct body of law because of the unique status of Indian tribes in the United States.[23] Thus the equitable apportionment doctrine, which the Court uses to allocate water resources fairly between and among the states, does not strictly apply. Wilkinson emphasizes repeatedly the novel dilemma that persists in the general context of American Indians:

In most cases, a crucial issue—seldom mentioned in the opinions but implicitly a weighty presence to the parties and the judges—is how an old treaty, statute, or court decision should be applied in times bearing little resemblance to the era in which the words of law were originally written. . . . The Court, presented repeatedly with the option of honoring the old laws or of respecting the force of the changed circumstances, mostly has chosen to enforce the promises.[24]

A sensible, equitable approach to apportionment remains the major dilemma in the Indian water issue.

An opportunity exists for the congressional and executive branches of the federal government to clarify and specify the Indian water aspect of the "Winters" doctrine—in effect, to mold legal doctrine through statutory law rather than to wait for development of case law.[25] This essay describes a set of doctrinal guidelines in four recommendations to serve that purpose.[26] The recommendations concern the scope of the Indian water right and the division of water between Indians and established water users. Notably, they do not suggest a general legislative solution to the entire class of Indian water claims that contain specific water volumes and priorities, times and places. They focus, rather, on a general policy directive and a procedure to specify water-related property rights.[27] The recommendations intend to provide clear, basic principles for the negotiated settlement of the disputes on a case-by-case basis, with the federal government's participation at the negotiating table.

THE PREMISES

Three premises guide the content of the recommendations.

Premise One:
Indian communities on the reservations should be treated at least as well as the historical treatment of the agricultural communities in the West that

*were subsidized by the federal government
through development of irrigation water supplied
by the Bureau of Reclamation.*

The premise of "at minimum, equal treatment" derives from
four perspectives: the property-right foundation for Indian
water; the historic public policy of subsidizing the
establishment of irrigated agriculture and rural communities
in the West; the trust relationship between the federal
government and the Indian nations; and the federal
endorsement of the western states' authority to allocate and
administer their nonnavigable surface water.

Native American water rights were recognized in 1908
with the "Winters" decision.[28] They exist as a matter of
property law, co-existing with Indian rights to reservation
lands. Their origin is not a matter of *ex post* public policy. A
latent conflict between Indian water rights and traditional
appropriative rights has festered since that time.

Public policy has exacerbated the conflict. The Bureau
of Reclamation (BuRec), since its inception in 1902 as the
Reclamation Service, implemented the federal policy of
western development. The BuRec had two explicit goals: (1) to
stabilize the "colony" of the West by establishing communities
that relied on a renewable resource (surface water) rather
than on depletable resources (gold, silver, or other minerals),
and (2) to nurture the "small" men and women of the region
rather than to allow speculators and corporations to develop
the West's water resources.[29] The BuRec accomplished the
goals by subsidizing water storage and water delivery to the
farm-gate.[30]

The sole purpose of Indian water rights, in comparison,
is to enhance the ability of Indians to sustain viable
reservation communities through a tribal economy and
culture that, in the arid West, necessarily relies on water. The
purpose, importantly, is homologous to the institutional
purpose of the BuRec. Indian rights are homologous to
reclamation water rights, yet they remain to be developed.

The BuRec developed water resources that easily could
have been developed for the Indian reservations.[31] A portion
of the resources, in fact, was Indian property. The National
Water Commission vividly makes the point:

Following "Winters," more than 50 years elapsed before the Supreme Court again discussed significant aspects of Indian water rights. During most of this 50-year period, the United States was pursuing a policy of encouraging the settlement of the West and the creation of family-sized farms on its arid lands. In retrospect, it can be seen that this policy was pursued with little or no regard for Indian water rights and the "Winters" doctrine. With the encouragement, or at least the cooperation, of the Secretary of the Interior—the very office entrusted with the protection of all Indian rights—many large irrigation projects were constructed on streams that flowed through or bordered Indian Reservations, sometimes above and more often below the Reservations. With few exceptions the projects were planned and built by the Federal Government without any attempt to define, let alone protect, prior rights that Indian tribes might have had in the waters used for the project. Before "Arizona v. California," referred to hereinafter, actions involving Indian water rights generally concerned then existing uses by Indians and did not involve the full extent of rights under the "Winters" doctrine. In the history of the United States Government's treatment of Indian tribes, its failure to protect Indian water rights for use on the reservations it set aside for them is one of its sorrier chapters.[32]

The BuRec did not act independently. The U.S. Congress behaved with, and promoted, the attitude that distributive politics governed the construction of water projects. The feeble political power of the Indians is well known.

The federal government, collectively, also bears responsibility for the dearth of Indian water development because of its trust relationship with Indian tribes.[33] When no conflict of interest exists between the government and the competing established water users, the trust responsibility is like that of a private fiduciary relationship. Thus, the situation in which the BuRec as a matter of public policy developed water resources that conflicted with Indian water rights provides evidence of a breach of the trust responsibility.[34] That the Bureau of Indian Affairs (BIA), the primary representative of the federal government in the trust relationship, is a sister agency of the BuRec in the Department of the Interior only magnifies the breach. "Winters" rights, although originating in an independent legal doctrine with the status of federal superiority, failed to be asserted in favor of the "rule of capture" of the prior appropriation doctrine, to which reclamation rights subscribe.

The record of federal capital investment in irrigation illustrates the importance that the federal government placed on non-Indian water-resource development relative to Indian development (Table 1). New capital investment represents the effort to perfect water rights. The spending by the BIA relative to the BuRec was significant before 1940. After 1940, however, the relative effort of the BIA became paltry.

TABLE 1

Federal Investment in Irrigation (Thousands of Historical Dollars)

	Pre-1920	1920-1939	1940-1959	1960-1978
Bureau of Reclamation	129,510	120,736	1,206,483	2,156,419
Bureau of Indian Affairs	14,851	33,569	28,733*	36,743

*Bureau of Indian Affairs actually spent less than this amount in the period because the Census reports the figure as an aggregate along with other expenditures by minor irrigation organizations.

SOURCE: U.S. Department of Commerce, Bureau of the Census, Census of Agriculture: Census of Irrigation Organizations, Census Years 1950, 1959, 1969, 1978.

The final element of the federal role is the federal government's active endorsement of the western states' authority to allocate and administer their nonnavigable surface water. The endorsement began with the Desert Land Act of 1877,[35] endured many divisions of interstate water by compact and equitable-apportionment decree, endured the

BuRec's conformance with state water law when developing reclamation water,[36] and culminated with the recent federal willingness to adjudicate federal reserved rights in state proceedings for consistency with the McCarran Amendment.[37] It represents a tacit federal endorsement of the appropriative water rights that were developed solely with private capital. These rights, which represent the majority of western surface water development, also diminished the Indians' stature in water.

The conclusion is Premise One: the Indian communities should be treated at least as well as the historical treatment of the recipients of federal water subsidies. The conclusion derives from three facts: Indian water rights are property, the property was ignored, and the agent for the Indians did not adequately represent the interests of its client. It relies neither on a social-equity policy of affirmative action for past injustice nor on a social-welfare policy of a minimum income per capita. Rather, it relies on a public policy, now anachronistic in general, of developing the West with irrigated agriculture.

The provision that entertains the possibility of "better treatment" than their non-Indian neighbors recognizes the notion of the time value of money, that is, that a dollar payment 80 years ago, because it has had the opportunity to accrue interest, is more valuable than a dollar payment today. The subsidized development of Indian water could have occurred decades ago; Indians could have been receiving profit from water use for a long period. A comparable perspective holds that the Indian water rights, which are of high priority among western water rights, should receive an accumulated series of annual rental payments for their historic use.[38] Indians with legitimate water rights arguably deserve compensation equal to the present value of the foregone annual profit or rental, compounded from the date of the water's initial use to the present time. This premise's provision for "better treatment" is made in lieu of compensation of this nature.[39]

Premise Two:
The non-Indian, established water users whose appropriative and reclamation water rights

conflict with Indian water rights should not simply forfeit their water rights. Their financial status should continue at a level equal to their historical profit from water use. Maintaining the financial status, though, may require a combination of a water right, at a reduced volume, and monetary compensation.

Disputes over Indian water offer the prospect of a one-for-one transfer from the established water users to the reservation tribes. The transfer, notably, can be a direct taking of the resource without compensation.[40] This leads naturally to discussions of restraining the Indian right,[41] and to Indians' suspicion of non-Indians' law and motives.[42]

Two perspectives support Premise Two: the strong confirmation by the state and federal governments that appropriative and reclamation water rights represent secure property rights, and the policy supporting the development of western communities through irrigated agriculture. The federal government, as described earlier,[43] repeatedly placed the authority for water law with the individual state governments. Western communities, both rural and urban, made substantial capital investments in water-using infrastructure that depended on state law. They perceived that the investments were made in accord with law.

Two recent contributions edify these perspectives. Wilkinson recognizes that the non-Indian settlers of the West made good-faith investments in both land and water assets that properly belonged to Indian tribes.[44] He writes:

These [non-Indian] expectations cannot harden automatically into a right to be free of all tribal laws. The tribes had expectations, too, and they were merged into treaties and treaty substitutes that protected historic tribal prerogatives within reservation boundaries. Yet neither can the expectations of the non-Indian residents, themselves premised upon open invitations tracing to federal law, fairly be ignored. The recurrent, essential task for the judiciary in Indian law has been to construct a reconciliation of the laws to which the two sets of expectations trace.[45]

And elsewhere:

> If latter-day Indian claims seriously jeopardize good faith settlers, then Congress retains authority to reach legislative solutions based on the particularized needs and equities, as it did in resolving tribal claims to large areas in New Mexico, Alaska, and Maine.[46]

Huffaker and Gardner argue in a related context that reclamation water rights should not be retroactively restructured by unilateral action of the federal government as this would violate constitutional due process.[47] They conclude that the taking of appropriative and reclamation water rights generally fails a test of fairness. The task rests with either the Congress or the judiciary to reconcile the dispute.

The taking of the rights, moreover, counters the eighty-year public policy of nurturing sustainable western communities. A neutral policy of permitting the evolution of the communities, in response to economic incentives, from an agricultural base to an urban and industrial base seems sensible. An active policy of eroding the agricultural character of the West by transferring water away from its established users, in contrast, should be avoided. The possibility of forcing the users off the farm is real.[48] The importance of the cultural fabric of western agricultural communities should not be ignored in the process of recognizing the economic, cultural, and ethical imperatives of developing sustainable Indian communities.

Premise Three:
The federal government has the right and the responsibility to pursue a cost-effective resolution to the water disputes on a case-by-case basis. Premises One and Two constrain the government in the endeavor. The responsibility or cost efficiency stems from the government's representation of taxpaying citizens.

The third premise gives the federal government flexibility in the water-rights negotiations. The government uses the flexibility to achieve a cost-efficient settlement to each water conflict, that is, to minimize the federal expenditure required to satisfy the Indian and non-Indian interests. The U.S. Department of the Interior currently provides a similar type of mediation service with most Indian claims.[49] The set of premises, however, gives clarity to the stakes and responsibilities of the major interests.

Two factors guide the search for a cost-efficient settlement.[50] First, the water-supply situation in the pertinent area is a major variable: is the river basin fully appropriated, can existing water-storage projects be enlarged, can new water-storage projects be constructed, and/or is groundwater available to substitute for surface water? Second, the Indians and the non-Indians must be willing to accept a portfolio of water and money, rather than an endowment of only water, as a resolution to a water conflict. In effect, a nonstructural approach to the issue is feasible. The notion of substituting money for water, historically, was unacceptable. It now is common with the modern attitude of recognizing the commodity value of water. A complete substitution of money for water by the government, however, is impermissible because of the symbolic value of water in the West.

THINKING THROUGH THE ATTRIBUTES OF THE INDIAN WATER RIGHT: FICTIONS AND FALLACIES

Quantifying Indian water rights has developed into a reasonably well-defined procedure: benefit-cost analysis is applied to establish the reservation's practicably irrigable acreage and the associated irrigation water requirement. Indians' flexibility in using the water rights remains less clear. For example, must water be used for the "original purposes" of the reservation, and can water be transferred to non-Indians for use on or off the reservation?[51]

A thoughtful approach to structuring the issues requires the use of legal and economic fictions.[52] Fictions, as artifices, can be helpful in organizing information, guiding inquiry, and making "good" decisions. Indian water claims require fictions: water rights that were recognized in 1908, that date to the 1800s in priority, that frequently conflict with completely developed river systems, and that, now, must be made a reality, need a few conveniences. Some aspects that guide the inquiry into, and the decision's surrounding, Indian water rights must be accepted as the best approach to the issue although they may appear arbitrary when scrutinized. These are fictions. Fallacies, relatedly, fail close scrutiny. They are wrong, not merely arbitrary. The various fictions, along with some fallacies of benefit-cost analysis, follow.

Seniority of the Indian Water Right

The seniority trait of the Indian right has been treated consistently as coincident with the date of the individual treaty establishing each reservation. This treatment gives to Indian water rights a trait that corresponds to traditional appropriative water rights. This essay recommends that Indian water rights continue with a priority date set by the origin of the reservation. The recommendation relies on two reasons: to be generous in defining this trait of the water right as a means of compensating for the century of ignoring the Indian property (substantially Premise One) and to simplify the calculations required to quantify the right.

The Practicably-Irrigable-Acreage Standard

The practicably-irrigable-acreage (PIA) standard is a legal fiction for quantifying the Indian right. The standard simply states that the tribes should receive sufficient water to irrigate all of the irrigable reservation land. In contrast to the retrospective treatment of the Indian rights' priority, the PIA has been implemented using current economic variables (including irrigation technology).[53] The combination of these approaches leads to Indian rights of large volume and senior status.

The normative notion that Indians should develop agricultural communities on the reservations underlies the rationale for rooting the definition in agriculture. This notion was acceptable historically, as agricultural development was an original purpose of most reservation lands. The notion become outdated, however, in the modern context of a diversity of water uses and a general decline in agricultural water use. The fact that the quantification procedures use the

PIA standard, yet Indian water rights are not limited to agricultural uses, reflects the fictional nature of the standard.

The PIA standard benefits Indian tribes in some respects because of its land-based nature: most of the reservations are relatively extensive in land.[54] A population-based standard, for instance, likely would result in less Indian water. The provision for an expansive water right is by design. The U.S. Supreme Court, when adopting the PIA in 1963, chose the standard so that the "present and future needs" of the reservations would be achieved in a single adjudication.[55] The choice demonstrates remarkable foresight, as a land-based allocation links the endowment of water to the Indian nations' most binding long-run ecological constraint. A population-based standard, on the other hand, would be a difficult target for which to make a projection.

The discussion reveals the weakness of current attempts to limit the Indian water right to an amount that allows a reasonable standard of living to the extant generation of Indians. The reasoning of the PIA standard is to satisfy the current and future needs of the reservations. A replacement for the standard must provide for future needs. The PIA accomplishes that, in a logical fashion, at one moment for all time.

The simple truth is that Indian water rights represent a resource endowment—a wealth endowment—that is designed to make life possible on the reservations. Their symbolic value to Native Americans implies that the government cannot simply give Indians money, rather than water, to resolve the Indian water conflict. However, any quantification standard is a fiction.

Implementing the PIA Standard Through Benefit-Cost Analysis

The procedure of assessing practicably irrigable acreage has been implemented as an economic test, using a benefit-cost-analytic approach to measure the feasibility of irrigated agriculture. To reason that a benefit-cost test is required to ensure economically-efficient water use among sectors commits a fallacy. The reasoning violates the economic dictum that, once an initial endowment of a resource is made, a free choice by an individual necessarily results in economic efficiency.[56] The benefit-cost approach does guarantee an efficient allocation of water. However, it represents only one particular distribution among many feasible distributions of the resource that are efficient. Benefit-cost analysis in effect takes a narrow view of efficiency by focusing only on the final resource allocation (the resource-use product) rather than on the mechanisms that a society chooses to foster efficiency (the resource-allocation processes).[57] Economists emphasize voluntary exchanges in competitive markets as a resource-allocation mechanism that promotes efficiency. The initial endowment of the resource commonly is understood as an issue of fairness. The statement of water-allocation efficiency that is analogous to the general neoclassical dictum reads: regardless of the initial distribution of water rights among individuals, the ability to transfer the rights in competitive water markets guarantees an efficient final allocation of water. Once the Indian tribes establish their water rights, subsequent water-use decisions are efficient by definition provided that the rights are transferable.

The benefit-cost-analytical approach to water-allocation decisions frequently imposes a culturally-biased standard of water use on the Indians. For example, a particular tribe may prefer to leave water in the stream as part of a religious belief. Benefit assessment typically undervalues this activity. Another tribe may choose to grow low-value crops for its own subsistence rather than high-value crops for market. Benefit assessment assigns a value to the subsistence activity below the value of, say, raising vegetables in the winter for markets in the northern United States. Must the tribes develop golf courses and water fountains (or, for that matter, irrigated farms) as their route to economic improvement? Or can self-interested behavior and freedom of choice prevail?

The distinction, in essence, distinguishes between an economic-means test and an economic-efficiency test.[58] The accurate view of benefit-cost analysis, in this instance, is as an economic-means test. Benefit-cost poses the issue simply as: do the benefits of Indian water use exceed the costs of water development? The existence of transferable water rights and competitive markets, on the other hand, provides more compelling evidence of economic efficiency. The contemporary division of water resources among Indian tribes and non-Indian communities fundamentally represents an issue of fairness.

The view that benefit-cost analysis is unambiguous in its application demonstrates a second myth.[59] In the context of the PIA standard, for example, should it be implemented using the economic and technological variables that exist today, that existed in 1908 with the advent of the "Winters" doctrine, or that existed at the date of the reservation's origin? More subtly, should the institutional environment of federally-subsidized western water-resource development be included as a second class of variables in addition to the economic environment? The choices of output prices, irrigation-technology costs, water-conveyance costs, and BuRec water-subsidy rates affect the economic analysis that quantifies Indian rights using the PIA standard.

Finally, Burness, Cummings, Gorman, and Lansford demonstrate that the view of benefit-cost analysis as only a narrow efficiency criterion is a myth.[60] Benefit-cost analysis is a social-accounting approach; it differs markedly from private financial analysis. In this vein, they apply ethical principles to guide the choices of the economic and institutional environments for the benefit-cost analysis.[61] They make three recommendations: (1) use a low discount rate in the PIA evaluation; (2) subsidize the operating, maintenance, and repair costs of the hypothetical evaluation at the same rate as other BuRec water-development projects; and (3) pay for those subsidies by raising the electricity prices (that is, by reducing the electricity subsidies) paid by recipients of power generated by BuRec projects.

In conclusion, it is important to develop an educated view of benefit-cost analysis. Benefit-cost analysis is not the only means to efficiency, it has an important equity aspect, and it requires that many important choices be made during its application. Further, it simply is wrong to view the PIA standard as necessarily more than a quantification procedure. For example, if one is searching for a high rate-of-return for Indian water and is linking that return to quantification, merely pose the hypothetical: How much water could a Colorado River tribe sell to southern California at a profit? The benefit-cost analysis of this option surely results in quantifying a very large volume of Indian water rights. Implementing the PIA standard through benefit-cost analysis only represents a means of quantifying property rights, not of assuring either economic efficiency in water use or sustainable reservation communities.

The Native American Right: Analogous to an Appropriative or a Riparian Right?

Some commentators[62] argue that the Indian water right is appurtenant to the reservation lands, thereby effectively construing the right as a modified riparian water right. Two facts lead to their conclusion: the simultaneous creation of the rights along with the reservation lands and the absence of forfeiture of the rights through nonuse. Based on this, they argue that, like a riparian right, sales of Indian water separately from reservation land should not be permitted.[63]

The definition of the Indian water right as a riparian right is a fallacy rather than a useful legal fiction. The location of Indian reservations in the West implies strongly that, as Indian water claims are perfected, their integration into the prior appropriation system becomes an important goal. A ban on the transfer of Indian rights reduces the potential economic efficiency of western water use and, coincidentally, reduces the potential economic return to Indian tribes.[64] The fallacy of Indian rights as riparian rights has no redeeming virtue.

RECOMMENDATION ONE: QUANTIFICATION

The initial step toward resolving the issue of surface-water use involves establishing the volume of Native American rights. This recommendation adheres to the current procedure: using a benefit-cost approach to establish the reservation's irrigable acreage and the water required for its irrigation. Premise One, that Indians should be subsidized at a rate equal to or better than non-Indians, guides the features of the recommendation. The features are specific in places, although specific numbers should not be considered hard and fast rules. Within the structure of the recommendation, some numbers may be increased and others lowered provided that the recommendation retains its general intent.

(1) For the purpose of quantification, the Native American water right represents a right to water delivered to the reservation-gate at a cost subsidized by the federal government, that is, it is more than simply a right to water in the stream. This agrees with the historical policy of subsidizing water conveyance from the river to the farmgate. Use the weighted average of the unit cost of the water that the BuRec has under current contract as the unit cost of this delivered water.[65] In the economic analysis of agricultural feasibility, this would be the per unit cost of conveying water to the reservation-gate. As most of the water at issue comes from rivers flowing through the reservation, this may not be a major subsidy, but the Indians should not have to bargain away a portion of their water right to obtain this subsidy. The subsidy, effectively, is a distinct right. It treats equally Indians and their non-Indian neighbors.

(2) Use the unlined earthen canal as the on-reservation, water-conveyance technology for the analysis. Use either furrow or flooding irrigation technology, depending on the type of crop evaluated. Use modern water-pumping technology for lifting water to a higher elevation. Use current factor prices to calculate the cost of constructing the agricultural capital. This general provision has a generous impact on quantification.

(3) Treat capital costs in the analysis in a manner consistent with either the BuRec project-evaluation procedures before the cost-sharing era or the provisions of Section 2 of the Leavitt Act.[66]

(4) Use a two percent interest rate to evaluate the investment. This rate is below the market rate of the cost of capital as a premium to favor the financial feasibility of the project.

(5) Use product prices that include federal agricultural price subsidies. If farm-product

markets are deregulated in the future, then use current, stable prices in the analysis.

The recommendation for quantification, by necessity, forms an amalgam of old policy, old agricultural practices, and new prices and costs. By design, it translated hypothetical water rights into certain, adjudicated rights. It permits the passage of time to work in favor of Indian interests: the irrigation and conveyance technologies permit the pumping of water but do not demand the most recent water-conserving devices. This compensates for this century's dearth of Indian water-right perfection and water-resource development.

RECOMMENDATION TWO: SUSTAINABLE DEVELOPMENT ON THE RESERVATION

Keep perspective on the original purpose of the "Winters" doctrine, to develop sustainable communities. Two elements of the recommendation help to achieve this goal:

(1) Each tribe has a right to the subsidized delivery of its water to the reservation-gate. The right is distinct from the tribes' paper water right. It can be used at any time. In effect, the government fixes a rate of subsidy (analogous to the policy of the Bureau of Reclamation), and the tribe retains the option to use it, once, at the most beneficial time.

(2) Indians maintain a range of flexibility in using their quantified rights. They do not need to establish a conventional beneficial use of the water to perfect the right. They can choose to apply their water to non-agricultural uses. They can choose to sell or lease their water, on or off the reservation, subject to normal constraints of the prior appropriation doctrine, other state law, and interstate water law.[67]

Divorcing quantification and use of the Indian right becomes an important emphasis of the recommendation for sustainable development. The current method ties explicitly the development of a PIA analysis with both quantification and a project that uses the water. Pushing the Indians into agriculture rather than allowing a distinct Native American development path has had negative consequences. The case of the Navajo Indian Irrigation Project in northwestern New Mexico provides an example.[68] The components of the recommendation guarantee a subsidy, yet provide flexibility in its timing. Everyone benefits from this; in particular, the original goal of Indian water becomes attainable.

At the same time, to be balanced, a well-conceived plan tying together quantification and water-resource development should be acceptable. That is, separating quantification and development need only provide a conceptual distinction to alert Indian tribes to their property-right status. Tribes should reserve the right to pursue development along with quantification. The flexibility, in fact, allows for an inherently desirable quality of a negotiated settlement to the water-resource dispute: a mix of features to a comprehensive settlement may be the cost-effective approach to settlement; for example, combining water-storage and water-conveyance facilities, financial compensation, and a variety of water-supply sources may be the cheapest form of settlement.

RECOMMENDATION THREE: CONFLICT RESOLUTION

Enough time has elapsed since the modern recognition of Native American water rights in 1963 for the West to recover from an initial collective gasp at their prospect. It is incumbent, now, to resolve outstanding claims. The issue has clarified in some ways: the general format of the quantification procedure is established; the legal arena of jurisdiction—the state courts—is clear; the incentives to achieve a negotiated settlement are evident. Past experiences set a pattern for the future.

The successful negotiated settlements relied on creating new water supplies to resolve inherent conflicts between Native American rights and established appropriative rights. Both parties substantially remained whole in their water-resource endowments. Indian water claims were belatedly attached to water-development projects already under construction or awaiting construction. The recent negotiations relied on the same approach: to enlarge or create water-storage capacity.[69] The politics of the approach are self-evident, as it is the traditional way to obtain a federal subsidy by linking Indian water to the federal reclamation program.

Urging Indian nations to negotiate settlement of their water claims remains the prevailing approach. The future course of the settlements can take one of two directions. The Indians and the established users may coalesce effectively to persuade the federal government to subsidize the development of new, expensive water supplies as a means of settlement. Both Wilkinson and Collins argue that possibly a new niche has opened for the BuRec in developing water supplies to be shared between the Indians and the established users,[70] that is, to "wrap the project in an Indian blanket."[71]

Alternatively, the "iron triangle" of western water development—the coalition of Congress, the BurRec, and western water interests—may have dissolved. A nonstructural approach to resolving the generic Indian water conflict may dominate because of fewer opportunities to attach Indian claims to moderately cheap, new water-supply sources. Thorson writes of the new context:

> The "larger pot" era is coming to a close. There is more difficult competition for our existing water supply, and it is difficult to finance expensive new storage and delivery projects. The real test of negotiated settlements of Indian water disputes has yet to come. . . . There is room for creative new policies which identify and build upon mutual interest. But the overriding challenge will be for Indians and non-Indians to equitably and peacefully share limited water resources.[72]

A nonstructural approach, rather than the structural tradition, needs to be conceived of as a viable alternative.

The recommended approach to the general issue consists of searching for the cost-effective combination of water and money that, first, maintains the financial integrity of Indians and non-Indians and, second, provides a water endowment to both groups. The water-supply situation in a particular river basin represents the major variable in the search. The water in many western river basins is completely appropriated. A creative approach, when this is the case, is either to share the water supply on a pro-rata basis between the two parties or to construct a water-storage project that enhances the supply. A water-sharing arrangement requires compensatory financial payments to sustain material status. A water-storage project should be evaluated to account for both construction and environmental costs. The government chooses the cost-efficient alternative.

A generic approach to the case of scarce water supply follows.[73] The traits of the water resource at issue are those of one or more appropriative water rights. The traits include its relative priority in the water-rights queue (which establishes a probability of receiving water from the naturally varying water source), its volume, and its status as a direct-flow right or a storage right. A quantification proceeding establishes the Indian right to water in terms of priority and volume. The right, then, becomes like an established appropriative right. To clarify the stakes of the dispute, a one-to-one correspondence is identified between the Indian right and the established rights. That is, competing claims to the same water are identified.

One method of settling the property dispute—the nonstructural method—would be to share equally the water right between the Indian tribe and the appropriative-right owners with which it conflicts. This water-sharing agreement is analogous to a 50 percent pro-rata division of the water right. The annual economic benefit of water use in this case is denoted B_1; this magnitude simply is the aggregate revenue from the shared use of the existing water.

Monetary compensation paid to both parties keeps them whole. The benchmark for measuring wholeness is annual profit received by established water users from historical water use. The difference between historical profit and profit generated by using half of the original water right measures the monetary compensation due each party. Twice that amount, consequently, measures governmental expenditure. The amount of expenditure required to keep the parties whole becomes the measure of cost efficiency.

A federally financed water-storage project that keeps both parties whole by means of water endowment provides an alternative method of settling the dispute. The utility of a storage project comes from its reduction of the natural variability of supply. Indian users and established users share equally the water supply from the project. Denote as B_2 the economic benefit of a project; this represents the aggregate revenue of using the stored water supply. Monetary compensation may be needed to maintain the groups' endowments although at a lower rate than in the nonstructural approach. The project, further, has capital, operating, maintenance, and environmental costs; denote the costs, on an annualized basis, as C.

Adopting the maximum of either B_1 or $(B_2\text{-}C)$ establishes the settlement generating the highest aggregate net benefit.[74] This also corresponds to the perspective of cost effectiveness. It is cost-effective because it minimizes the money spent by the government to keep both groups whole in terms of monetary payments and storage project costs. Table 2 illustrates the two accounts of the alternatives.

TABLE 2

Account for Water-Sharing Agreement and Water-Storage Project

Alternative	Benefit	Cost	Net Benefit
Water-Sharing Agreement	B_1	0	B_1
Water-Storage Project	B_2	C	$B_2\text{-}C$

Cost-Efficient Alternative: Larger of B_1 or $(B_2\text{-}C)$

Many readers, and particularly those concerned with the Native American stake, recognize that a plan to share equally the existing water supply looks suspiciously like imposing the equitable apportionment doctrine on the settlement.[75] It is a *modified* equitable apportionment doctrine, with the modifications including: (1) an equal, pro-rata division of existing water rights at issue and (2) compensatory monetary payments to sustain the wealth from each parties' original water rights.

The equal-sharing of the water resource differs markedly from the recent evolution of the equitable apportionment doctrine to an economic-means test.[76] The compensation payments, in addition, provide novelty beyond the doctrine's traditional scope. Indian tribes probably would choose litigation if federal policy becomes a traditional equitable apportionment approach. Without the additional traits of the recommendation, an equal-sharing rule to resolve the water-resource disputes offers a poor bargain to them.

The case of groundwater availability is one other important water-supply situation. Surplus groundwater offers an opportunity to substitute groundwater for surface water in satisfying an Indian water claim; this may be a cost-effective approach. The federal government must guarantee the groundwater right's legitimacy, perhaps by its purchase. Further, the government and the Indians must be cognizant of the rising extraction cost of many groundwater reserves as depletion occurs, the government in a search for cost efficiency and the Indians in ensuring that they do not inherit a water supply whose cost increases through time because of groundwater mining. The basic notion of substituting between groundwater and surface water to minimize water supply costs, though, forms a tenet of enlightened state laws of conjunctive water use.[77] It warrants consideration in the Indian water context.

The courts currently do not have the ability to consider Native American claims and their associated water disputes in a framework similar to this recommendation. The stakes of the parties are evident in a courtroom setting. Established water users likely hope that the Supreme Court is lurching toward a pure equitable apportionment approach to the issue. They would prefer, in fact, an apportionment test based on the financial product of water use as it imposes a culturally biased standard. Indian nations likely fear an apportionment approach because it considers only a narrow set of issues; it is dissimilar to the modified version described above. As an alternative to the courts, a federal legislative proposal could define a clearer set of principles and goals to guide negotiations over Indian water rights.

RECOMMENDATION FOUR: SOURCES OF FUNDS

The prior recommendations require federal expenditures to meet a fundamental goal, fairness. A call for new government funding increasingly falls on deaf ears, however. The federal reclamation program provides one opportunity to earmark certain government revenues for use in resolving Indian water claims. Judiciously shaking the reclamation piggy banks in search of money has a certain logical appeal.

The federal government maintains the option of charging higher prices (and changing the mix of customers) for water and power services of BurRec projects when the current delivery contracts expire. Water-service and power-service contracts generally run for 40 years. Reimbursable aspects of projects are considered repaid when the contract elapses. At that time, the notoriously low administered prices of the BuRec can be raised to an equilibrium market price, for example, through the use of water-commodity auctions. The time profile of project construction suggests that revenues from free-market water could provide a sizeable source of funds after the year 2000.[78]

Provisions of the Reclamation Reform Act of 1982 may give a more immediate new source of revenue.[79] The Act furnishes incentive for irrigation districts to amend their current contracts, thereby agreeing to pay the full cost of water on leased land in excess of 960 acres, rather than being coerced to pay the full cost of water on leased land in excess of 160 acres.[80] The magnitude of the prospective funds will become clearer when final reports on implementation of the Act become available.

Federal and state policies to simplify reclamation-water transfers and to increase their potential market offer a third possibility. Voluntary market exchanges of water could be accompanied by a windfall profit tax, with its revenue earmarked for settling Indian water claims. Such a program could provide a source of revenue that bridges the gap to the major BuRec recontracting period after the year 2000.

The famous Reclamation Fund and the River Basin Funds represent final prospective sources of funds. The Reclamation Fund, in fact, is the general account for revenues from reimbursable reclamation services. It serves as the financial source for congressional appropriations to operate the BurRec, including project construction. In 1982, the unappropriated Reclamation Fund balance reached $785,432,000.[81] Additions since then exceeded $100,000,000 annually.[82] The River Basin Funds were designed to cross-subsidize the construction of irrigation projects with power projects.[83] The three major western river basins—Colorado River, Columbia River, and Missouri River—each have such a fund. An examination of the Funds may reveal some unappropriated money that could be earmarked for Indian water claims. For example, the power projects in the upper basin of the Colorado River—Flaming Gorge on the Green River and Curecanti on the Gunnison River—were designed to supplement funding of upper-basin projects. Many of the projects, though, will not be constructed in the foreseeable future. The importance of unresolved Indian water claims justifies a review of the Reclamation Fund and the River Basin Funds.

CONCLUSION

Water is central in the West. The conflict over Indian water claims is a central resource issue in the West. The depth and breadth of its impacts loom large.

Indian nations and established water users have an ethical and legal basis to persuade the federal government to become more involved in the issue. Federal participation according to this paper's recommendations has several positive economic consequences: sharing of Indian water with established water users avoids exacerbating the decline of rural economies; generous treatment of the Indian stakes promotes a sustainable economic development of reservation communities; the dispute-resolution process becomes clearer, thereby avoiding the money and time spent in litigation (which creates no new wealth); and reducing the pervasive uncertainty in western water promotes formation of more complex water markets (which create new wealth).

The custom in the West is to emphasize the need for comity in disputes over water resources. Comity, though, does not substitute for clear, well-defined procedural rules when reconciling a dispute. The prior appropriation doctrine, the equitable apportionment doctrine, and the opportunity for interstate compacts provide the procedural rules, traditionally, in western water matters. Indian water rights fall outside of the normal rules of western water. Inordinate amounts of comity do not begin to settle Indian water claims.

This essay integrates the law, economics, public policy, and history of western water development into a framework for evaluating Native American water rights. The framework, represented in three premises, specifies a context of fairness. The recommendations contained herein develop a comprehensive, cohesive approach for considering Indian claims. They outline a blueprint for a fair and cost-efficient resolution of the water disputes by defining specific rules for the reconciliation process. Simultaneously, traits of the recommendations provide incentive for economically efficient water-resource use.

Outstanding Indian water claims inject real uncertainty into the western waterscape. Extreme positions on the issue naturally exist, characterized by threats of leaving either non-Indians or Indians high and dry. The issue develops into a complex web of efficiency and fairness, of property rights and treaties, of good faith and questionable public policy. In this light, this essay offers a middle ground on Indian water, a central position for reasonable people who are concerned about western water matters.

NOTES

1. National Water Commission, *Water Policies for the Future*, (1973), 483.

2. C. Wilkinson, *American Indians, Time, and the Law*, (1987), 9.

3. "Rights" and "claims" are not used synonymously in this paper. The reservation tribes' rights to water are well established. Their water claims, as an assertion of the volume of the rights, may underestimate or overestimate the ultimate, legal water right. As a matter of bargaining, one expects that the claim exceeds the right. That is, either the volume of the claim may exceed the volume of the right or the claim itself may be inherently invalid. The distinction between rights and claims is made while recognizing its

negative connotation to Indians, represented by Deloria: "This initial step [of defining the traits of the right] is vitally important to the American legal system because the broadest scope of Indian rights can, in this context, be characterized as Indian 'claims' to water. As the legal system proceeds to narrow these claims, society can assure itself that it is merely 'defining rights,' not taking them away. Deloria, *A Native American View of Western Water Development,* 21 Water Resources Res. 1785, (1985).

4. The approach of stating premises and making recommendations parallels that of the National Water Commission in its chapter on Indian water rights. National Water Commission, *supra* note 1, 473. The fact that the commission devoted one of the 17 chapters of its final report to Indian water is important: the final report and the studies that contributed to it represent the most comprehensive and detailed study of water policy in this country. The federal government did not accept the commission's recommendations on Indian water. Consequently, the recommendations made in this paper are designed to achieve objectives similar to the commission's goals. This paper's recommendations have the advantage of 16 years of additional experience since publication of the commission's report. The commission's proposal remains important because so few recommendations from a general, objective perspective have been made on the topic. The commission's mandate was to draw conclusions and make recommendations "on the policies which it believes the Nation should adopt at this point in its history for the efficient, equitable, and environmentally responsible management of its water resources." Ibid. at iii.

5. U.S., 207, (1908), 564.

6. U.S., 373, (1963), 546, decree entered by "Arizona v. California," U.S., 376, (1964), 340, decree amended by "Arizona v. California," U.S. 383, (1966), 268, order amended by Arizona v. California, U.S., 466 (1984), 144. The decision allocated to five Indian reservations along the Colorado River more than 900,000 acre-feet per year. California received an annual allocation of 4.4 million acre-feet, Arizona 2.8 million acre-feet, and Nevada 300,000 acre-feet. Allocating water to Indians was necessary because of the blatant disregard for Indian water rights in the Colorado River Compact. According

to Norris Hundley, Jr., the noted historian of the Colorado River, "Their rights were considered 'negligible' and were dealt with perfunctorily in what [Herbert] Hoover called the 'wild Indian article': 'Nothing in this compact shall be construed as affecting the obligations of the United States of America to Indian tribes.'" Hundley, "The West Against Itself: The Colorado River—An Institutional History," in *New Courses for the Colorado River*, (1986), 18. Although "Arizona v. California" allocated a large volume of water to the tribes, approximately 20 outstanding Indian claims remain in the Colorado River basin.

The symposium that served as the basis for the aforementioned book began with an address by former Arizona Governor Bruce Babbitt and ended with a summary by Dr. Gilbert White. Babbitt identified Indian claims as one of two major issues of the Colorado River in the next century. White identified them as one of seven major unresolved issues of the river. See Babbitt, "Forward: The Future of the Colorado River," in *New Courses for the Colorado River*, (1986), xi; White, "A New Confluence in the Life of the River," id. at 220.

7. Riley, "The Water Wars," *Nat. L. J.*, 7, (Feb. 18, 1985), 1; See J. Folk-Williams, *What Indian Water Means to the West*, (1982). An exceptionally thorough description of the existing Native American water claims; C. Miklas and S. Shupe, eds. *Indian Water 1985: Collected Essays*, (1986). Discussion of many of the water policy and management issues associated with these claims.

8. For a detailed account of the location and nature of Indian water rights, see J. Folk-Williams, *supra* note 7.

9. See, e.g., A. Kneese and F. Brown, *Southwest Under Stress*, (1981); Weatherford, Wallace, and Harold, "Leasing Indian Water: Upcoming Choices in the Colorado River Basin," in *Water Marketing: Opportunities and Challenges of a New Era*, S. Shupe ed., (1986).

10. Deloria, *supra* note 3, 1785-86.

11. The American Indian Resources Institute, located in Berkeley, California, holds annual workshops on Indian water management. The 1986 course, for example, was entitled "1986 Summer Course on Tribal Water Management." It included the study of water law, policy,

economics, hydrology, administration, and management.

12. The economic status of reservation communities remains strikingly low by American standards. Unemployment among Indians on reservations was a steady rate of 35 percent throughout the early 1980s. U.S. Department of the Interior, Bureau of Indian Affairs, *Indian Service Population and Labor Force Estimates*, (1985), 2. Indians on reservations living below poverty levels in 1979 ranged from 5 percent to 100 percent, with a figure in the range of 30 percent to 50 percent typical. U.S. Department of Commerce, Bureau of the Census, *1980 Census of Population: General Social and Economic Characteristics, United States Summary*, (1980), 457.

13. Cornell traces the change in federal policy toward Native Americans from the period of segregation on the reservations, through the long period that had a goal of assimilating the Indians into the dominant American culture, to the episodic transition to self-government and economic independence. Cornell, "The New Indian Politics," *Wilson Quarterly*, (1986), 113; See also Weatherford, Wallace, and Harold, *supra* note 9, 27-29.

14. The Indian nations prefer their legal cases to be heard in federal court rather than in a state court's general adjudication. The McCarran Amendment of 1952, U.S.C., 43, (1982), 666, however, predisposes these cases to a state court adjudication, with the opportunity for federal review. See Amundson, "Recent Judicial Decisions Involving Indian Water Rights," in *Indian Water 1985*, *supra* note 7, 3; Williams, "Indian Natural Resource Development—The Impact on Poverty," in Part IV of *Rural Development, Poverty, and Natural Resources*, Workshop Paper Series, (1984), 29.

15. Thorson notes that, of the five major Indian water rights cases that have been settled, four of them were attached to existing water-supply projects: the Navajo Indian Irrigation Project in New Mexico, the Ak-Chin and Papago Indian settlements in Arizona, and the Ute Indian agreement in Utah. Thorson, "Resolving Conflicts Through Intergovernmental Agreements: The Pros and Cons of Negotiated Settlements," in *Indian Water 1985*, supra note 7, 32. Also, the recent settlement of the Ute Mountain Utes and the Southern Utes in Colorado is associated with the Animas-La

Plata Project, which will be constructed by the Bureau of Reclamation. Frazier, "Animas-La Plata is Just Inches Short of the Goal," *Rocky Mountain News*, (Sep. 20, 1986), 63.

16. For example, four stream adjudications cost the Navajo tribe over $10 million in legal fees, and the state government of Wyoming spent over $7 million in expert and legal fees opposing in court the water claims in the Big Horn River basin. Marston, "Indians Breathe Life into Old Treaties," *High Country News*, (Nov. 25, 1985), 1; Marston, "An Indian Water Victory Creates Turmoil in Wyoming," *High Country News*, (Nov. 25, 1985), 13.

17. Delimiting the Indian right through the amount of water required for irrigated agriculture is done for Indians with reservations whose original purpose was farming. Other tribes own a right that is based on alternative subsistence modes, the primary one being fishing. In the exceptional cases, alternative standards like a fishery-based standard provide appropriate substitutes for an agricultural standard. See J. Sax and R. Abrams, *Legal Control of Water Resources* (1986), 549.

18. Benefit-cost analysis was adopted by the Special Masters in both "Arizona v. California" in 1982, U.S., 466, (1984), 144 (amending order of U.S., 383, (1966), 268), and the adjudication of the Big Horn River System in Wyoming. The Special Masters' reports are, respectively, In the Supreme Court of the United States, (October Term, 1981), "Arizona v. California," Reported by Elbert P. Tuttle, Special Master, (Feb. 22, 1982), and Special Master, In Re: The general adjudication of all the rights to use water in the Big Horn River system and all other sources, State of Wyoming, 4993, Report of the Special Master (District Court of the Fifth Judicial District, State of Wyoming, December 15, 1982).

19. The notion that the current generation of irrigated-farm operators already receive an enormous subsidy for their water is, to a degree, a fallacy. Much of the value of subsidized water was capitalized into market prices of land to which the water is appurtenant. The first generation of owners of reclamation water rights and irrigation-district shares appropriated the subsidy when they sold their farms or ranches with associated water rights. For example, LeVeen and Goldman find that in the Westlands project, a relatively

youthful Bureau project, a majority of the irrigated land already had been sold. LeVeen and Goldman, "Reclamation Policy and the Water Subsidy: An Analysis of the Distributional Consequences of Emerging Policy Choices," *American Journal of Agricultural Economics*, 60, (1978), 929, 932. The degree to which the subsidies were appropriated throughout the federal reclamation projects needs research, as it also becomes important when considering markets in reclamation water rights and the fair appropriation of any ensuing windfall profits.

20. Thorson both discusses the stakes of the participants and searches for a common ground, yet is generally pessimistic about the future of negotiated settlements without a new approach. See Thorson, *supra* note 15, 28.

21. Deloria, supra note 3.

22. Claiborne, "Indian Water Rights in the Supreme Court: A Review and Preview" (paper presented at Conference on the Federal Impact on State Water Rights, Natural Resources Law Center, University of Colorado School of Law, 1984). Most recently, the U.S. Supreme Court has agreed to review the Wyoming Supreme Court's 1988 decision to allocate 480,000 acre-feet to Wyoming's Wind River Reservation. "Indian Water Resources," *Water Market Update* 8, (S. Shupe ed., May 1989). The Court agreed to review the practicably irrigable acreage standard.

23. C. Wilkinson, supra note 2, 53-63.

24. Ibid., 4-5. Wilkinson concludes: "After my long journey through this body of law, I have reached my own conclusion as to why the field has developed as it has, as to the deepest reasons why the Court has refused to allow American Indian tribes to be engulfed by the passage of time. . . . These old laws emanate a kind of morality profoundly rare in our jurisprudence. It is far more complicated than a sense of guilt or obligation, emotions frequently associated with Indian policy. Somehow, those old negotiations—typically conducted in but a few days on hot, dry plains between mid-level federal bureaucrats and seemingly ragtag Indian leaders—are tremendously evocative. Real promises were made on those plains, and the Senate of the United States approved them, making them

real laws. My sense is that most judges cannot shake that. Their training, experience, and, finally, their humanity—all of the things that blend into the rule of law—brought them up short when it came to signing opinions that would have obliterated those promises." Ibid., 121-22.

25. The Department of the Interior initiates and implements the vast majority of federal policy on Indian water rights. It favors the negotiated settlement of outstanding Indian water claims. In the area, the Department is more reactive to individual claims and disputes than proactive. See Claiborne, supra note 22, 9; U.S. Department of the Interior Departmental Working Group on Water Policy, "Summary of Activities," (October 29, 1986).

26. See infra, text accompanying notes 64-82.

27. The generality of the type of statutory law envisioned here is consistent with the second type (of three) of congressional action characterized by Wilkinson: "While many Indian statutes have dealt with individual tribes, a second kind of legislation is far more general. Congressional actions have often set broad Indian policy but have left implementation to subsequent legislation or administrative action." C. Wilkinson, supra note 2, 10.

28. See supra note 5.

29. The original Reclamation Act of 1902 defined a program of federal financing of western irrigation project construction with provisions stipulating an on-farm residency requirement for recipients of reclamation water and a 160-acre limitation on farm size. Stat. 32, (1902), 388, (current version in scattered sections of U.S.C., 43).

The twin goals of the Bureau of Reclamation followed Major John Wesley Powell's vision of the American West. Powell concluded that the federal government needed to construct major on-stream dams for water storage, and that irrigated farming should be done by family farmers in a cooperative mode. Powell envisioned a return to the Jeffersonian ideal of agrarian settlement in place of the tendency toward monopolization and speculation that he predicted for the unregulated development of the West. J. Powell, *A Report on the Lands of the Arid Region of the United States, with a More Detailed Account of the Lands of Utah* (2d ed., 1879). On the topic of Powell and western water, see W. Stegner, *Beyond the Hundredth Meridian*, (1953), and the recent accounts: D. Worster, *Rivers of Empire: Water, Aridity, and the Growth of the American West*, (1985); M. Reisner, *Cadillac Desert: The American West and Its Disappearing Water*, (1986).

30. Burness, Cummings, Gorman, and Lansford, "United States Reclamation Policy and Indian Water Rights," *Natural Resources Journal*, 20, (1980), 807.

31. Berkman and Viscusi present a series of case studies documenting the duplicity, as opposed to the benign neglect, of the Bureau of Reclamation in failing to recognize the Indian's water interests. They devote one of eight chapters to Indian water in their study of the Bureau. R. Berkman and W. Viscusi, *Damming the West*, (1973), 151. In addition, Reisner asserts, "[o]ne of the least-known consequences of water development in America is its impact on the Indians who hadn't already succumbed to the U.S. Calvary, smallpox, and social rot." Reisner, supra note 28, 194. He continues with a case study of the decision to locate a reservoir on the Fort Berthold Indian Reservation in North Dakota, which forced the displacement of the Indians, rather than to locate it on land occupied by non-Indians. Ibid., 194-98. "The Fort Berthold Indians have never recovered from the trauma they underwent. Their whole sense of cohesiveness was lost, and they adjusted badly to life on the arid plains and in the white towns." Ibid., at 198.

32. National Water Commission, supra note 1, 474-75.

33. Fine, "Off-reservation Enforcement of the Federal-Indian Trust Responsibility," *Pub. Land L. R. 117*, 7, (1986), 117. Fine notes that the entire federal government has a trust responsibility for Indians although the responsibility is primarily associated with the Bureau of Indian Affairs. Ibid. Also, the fact that the time period during which Indian water rights were unused coincides with the period of the federal policy of assimilating Indians into the majority culture is important: this is when the trust responsibility reached its peak because Indians could not rely on their traditional tribes and cultures for sustenance. Wilkinson emphasizes the importance of viewing Indian law and policy in the historical context of the tension between the disparate goals of assimilation and separatism. C. Wilkinson, supra note 2, 13.

34. The activities of the federal government in developing reclamation water rights and in implementing the federal Indian trust relationship are important to contrast. The original development of reclamation water by the Bureau of Reclamation is not the implementation of a fiduciary relationship with western settlers; rather, it is a public policy. The federal-Indian trust relationship is rooted in solemn promises and law. A conclusion, then, is that no conflict-of-interest existed in the original development of water for white settlers when the water was a "Winters" Doctrine right: the higher responsibility of the government was in representing the Indian interest in the manner of a private fiduciary; it had no fiduciary responsibility to develop reclamation water. The situation repeats itself frequently in the tension between reclamation water rights and Indian reserved water rights.

The U.S. Supreme Court ruled in its 1982 term, though, that the federal government's trust relationship with Indians had to be balanced with its responsibility for non-Indian water interests in a state water-right adjudication that was final in 1944. "Nevada v. United States," Supreme Court, 103, (1983), 2906. The Pyramid Lake Paiute Tribe asserted in the recent case that the federal government had a conflict-of-interest in representing both water interests, as the water that the Newlands Reclamation Project received in the adjudication should have been used, in the Tribe's opinion, to satisfy a reserved water right. The Court decided that no conflict existed: the government, in effect, had a fiduciary responsibility to both groups. See Amundson, supra note 14, 12.

The important point is the distinction between proximate and ultimate perspectives. The ultimate perspective is the earlier conclusion: the fiduciary responsibility of the government for Indian water interests was higher than the ex ante public-policy interest in reclamation water. In "Nevada v. United States" concerning the Pyramid Lake Paiute Tribe, the proximate perspective was litigated. The perspective was satisfactory in that context because the reclamation project already was operational. The context of this essay, though, correctly takes the ultimate perspective on the tension between the two genera of water rights, reclamation and reserved.

35. Ch. 107, *Stat.*, 19, (1877), 377. Codified as amended at U.S.C., 43, (1982), 321-39. The Desert Land Act recognized the western states' authority to administer water resources. See J. Sax and R. Abrams, supra note 17, 298-99.

36. As a matter of comity, reclamation water rights were established as traditional appropriative water rights. Comment, "Federal Appropriation and the Reclamation Act of 1902," *Neb. L. R.*, 57, (1978), 403, 405.

37. McCarran Amendment of 1952, U.S.C., 43, (1982), 666.

38. The U.S. Supreme Court recently resolved an interstate water dispute by requiring monetary compensation for a past violation of an interstate water compact. New Mexico was directed to pay Texas monetary damages for accumulating a 340,100 acre-foot deficit of Pecos River water over 34 years. "New Mexico, Texas Wrestle over River Flow Repayment," *U.S. Water News*, (December, 1987).

A numerical example edifies the concept of profits foregone by the absence of Indian water development. Assume that an acre-foot of water creates an annual marginal value of $5, which is reasonable in agricultural water applications, and that the real interest rate is 3 percent. Further, suppose that the Indian right to the water went unused for a 100-year period, e.g., from 1889 (the treaty date of a hypothetical reservation) through 1989. The current value in 1989 of using the acre-foot each year for 100 years to create an annual financial value of $5 is $3,180. (An annual value of $2.50 per acre-foot, for example, halves this amount.) The mathematical expression for the current value is:

$$\int_{t=0}^{100} 5 \cdot \exp[(.03)t]dt = \$3,180,$$

where exp is the exponential function, which is used in continuous-time compounding. The amount of $3,180 per acre-foot applies for the entire volume of a particular Indian water right. For perspective, the volumes of three established Indian rights range from 58,300 acre-feet per year for the Ak-Chin community and 76,000 acre-feet per year for the Papago Reservation in Arizona, to 370,000 acre-feet per year for the

Navajo Reservation in Northwest New Mexico and Northeast Arizona, to 900,000 acre-feet per year for the five tribes bordering the Colorado River in California and Arizona. J. Folk-Williams, supra note 7, 13, 14, and 20. Multiplying the Ak-Chin volume by the rate per acre-foot yields $185,394,000. This provides context for the topic of foregone profits from the absence of Indian water rights.

39. Wilkinson, notably, finds aspects of the Indian water right in which the passage of time works to the Indians' advantage: Thus "Arizona v. California I" [the 1963 decision] lets time work triply in the tribes' favor—in stark juxtaposition to the prior appropriation system, which locks in water rights at the time of their original use. Indian water rights are given an early date, no later than the date when the tribe puts the water to actual use. The rights can expand and include sufficient water for future needs and are not limited to those needs that prevailed at the time the reservation was established. The needs are defined by the quantity of land that up-to-date technology can make usable. To westerners, this is nothing short of heresy. C. Wilkinson, supra note 2, 71. This essay argues that the favorable intertemporal elements of the Indian right are necessary, in part, to compensate for the foregone intertemporal profit from early non-Indian use of Indian water.

40. That this transfer of property may be made without compensation is emphasized in Brookshire, Watts, and Merrill, "Current Issues in the Quantification of Federal Reserved Water Rights," *Water Resources Res.*, v. 21, (1985), 1777, and Weatherford, Wallace, and Harold, supra note 9, 26.

41. Collins recognizes the malleability of the "Winters" Doctrine. Collins, "The Future Course of the 'Winters' Doctrine," *University of Colorado Law Review*, v 56, (1985), 781.

42. Deloria, supra note 3, 1786.

43. See supra, text accompanying notes 34-36.

44. A close analogy exists between the cases of Indian reservation land and Indian water rights. As with the development of water rightfully attached to a reservation, the federal government encouraged the homesteading by non-Indians of reservation land. In general, the settlers were

unaware that their homesteads rested on Indian land. On the topic of conflicts over reservation land, see C. Wilkinson, supra note 2, 22-23.

45. Ibid., 23.

46. Ibid., 44-45.

47. Huffaker and Gardner argue this in the context of the Reclamation Reform Act of 1982. Huffaker and Gardner, "The 'Hammer' Clause of the Reclamation Reform Act of 1982," *Natural Resources Journal*, v. 26, (1986), 41.

48. See supra note 19.

49. See supra note 25.

50. The third major recommendation discusses the points in more detail. See infra, text accompanying notes 68-76.

51. Sax and Abrams present a textbook treatment of these and other current legal issues that are associated with Indian water rights. J. Sax and R. Abrams, supra note 17, 548-72.

52. One definition of "fiction" is as a legal term that means, "[s]omething accepted as fact without any real justification, but merely for the sake of convenience." *American Heritage Dictionary, 6th ed.,* (1976), 488. Adding the word to the vocabulary of economics makes explicit a common practice of economic reasoning: using devices that lack true empirical substance to aid in the development of both economic theory and economic pedagogy. For example, the notion of an equilibrium in an economic system permitted the advance of economic theory and facilitated the instruction of economics at the level of simple principles. An explicit recognition of economic fictions would improve the economist's ability to communicate within the profession and, more important, to engage in useful dialogue with other professions. For a compelling advocacy of the improvement of economic rhetoric, see McCloskey, "The Rhetoric of Economics," *Journal of Economic Literature,* v. 21, (1983), 481.

53. Brookshire, et al., argue, with good logic, that the Indian water right should be a set of water rights of varying seniority and volume to mimic the change in economic variables through time. Brookshire, Watts, and Merrill, supra note 39. However, they lack a general perspective on the issue

that this paper introduces with the explicit statement of premises and the use of the historical record of western water resource development.

54. Williams argues, though, that establishing the right based on a utilitarian value may diminish its volume. She refers to the Indians' cultural, religious, and aesthetic appreciation of water that transcends a value-in-use. Williams, supra note 14.

55. The PIA standard explicitly intends to satisfy present and future needs: "We . . . agree with the Master's conclusion as to the quantity of water to be reserved. He found that the water was intended to satisfy the future as well as the present needs of the Indian Reservations and ruled that enough water was reserved to irrigate all of the practicable irrigable acreage on the reservations. . . . We have concluded, as did the Master, that the only feasible and fair way by which reserved water for the reservations can be measured is irrigable acreage. "Arizona v. California," U.S., 373, (1963), 546-600.

56. The statement reflects the substance of the major theorem of modern welfare economics: a competitive market equilibrium is Pareto efficient, i.e., one individual's welfare cannot be improved without another's welfare being diminished. The theorem relies on the existence of competitive markets and an absence of externalities. See H. Varian, *Microeconomic Analysis*, (1978), 147.

57. Kneese and Brown adopt this limited view of efficiency in their section, "The Form of a Speculative Solution," proposing a solution to the allocational issue engendered by Native American rights. A. Kneese and F. Brown, supra note 9, 86. Other aspects of their solution are more enlightened, e.g., their recommendation of water use in any economic enterprise rather than only in agriculture. Brookshire, et al. also advocate the use of a narrow test of economic efficiency. They write, "Several solutions to this impasse are available. . . . For example, the opportunity cost of taking water from non-Indian users (if any) to irrigate Indian lands should also be considered. . . . Appropriate analyses, such as efficiency studies of water allocations, could be incorporated into these studies." Brookshire, Watts, and Merrill, supra note 39, 1783.

58. These perspectives on the limitations of benefit-cost analysis and on the distinction between an economic-efficiency test and an economic-means test are critically important in another major topic of water allocation, the division of water between and among the states. The same conclusion, that benefit-cost analysis and an economic-means test are only one route to allocative efficiency, applies to the equitable apportionment doctrine. Tarlock accurately states the point: Equitable apportionment actions require the Court to strike a balance, between the protection of existing uses and the initiation of new uses, that tends to maximize the value of the resource. . . . Existing uses may not be the most efficient use of the water, but it does not follow that an equitable apportionment is necessary to promote efficiency; the market is the best method of determining efficiency." Tarlock, "The Law of Equitable Apportionment Revisited, Updated, and Restated," *University of Colorado Law Review,* v. 56, (1985), 381, 411. Trelease is excellent on the related topic of how the equitable doctrine and the commerce clause should blend. Trelease, "State Water and State Lines: Commerce in Water Resources," *University of Colorado Law Review,* v. 56, (1985), 347.

59. Burness, Cummings, Gorman, and Lansford develop these ideas in an important line of research: *United States Reclamation Policy,* supra note 29; "The New Arizona v. California: Practicably Irrigable Acreage and Economic Feasibility," *Natural Resources Journal,* v. 22, (1982), 517; "Practicably Irrigable Acreage and Economic Feasibility: The Role of Time, Ethics, and Discounting," *Natural Resources Journal,* v. 23, (1983), 289.

60. Burness, Cummings, Gorman, and Lansford, "Practicably Irrigable Acreage and Economic Feasibility: The Role of Time," supra note 58.

61. The reader should delight in the irony of the process to broaden the benefit-cost criterion to include equity issues: the courts turn to economists by adopting an economic perspective to resolve the property-right interest; Burness, et al., economists, understanding the malleability of this perspective, infuse it with equity principles. Ibid.

62. See, e.g., Palma, "Considerations and Conclusions Concerning the Transferability of Indian Water Rights,"

Natural Resources Journal, v. 20, (1980), 91, 94.

63. Alienability of Indian water rights remains an issue that the federal government must consider because of article 12 of the Indian Non-Intercourse Act, ch. 161, Stat., v. 4, (1834), 729, 730-31 (codified at U.S.C., v. 25, (1982), 177). The act requires congressional approval of the sale of Indian lands as a means of protecting the Indians from non-Indians acting in bad faith. Its purview may extend to water rights.

64. Sax and Abrams make this point. J. Sax and R. Abrams, supra note 17, 556.

65. For example, Burness, et al. report that this unit cost is \$2.50 per acre-foot in 1977. Burness, Cummings, Gorman, and Lansford, supra note 29, 823.

66. See the three articles by Burness, Cummings, Gorman, and Lansford, supra notes 29 and 58, for a thorough review of BuRec procedures. The Leavitt Act of July 1, 1932, Stat., 47, (1932), 564, "defers repayment of construction costs only for projects irrigating Indian lands." DuMars and Ingram, "Congressional Quantification of Indian Water Rights: A Definite Solution or a Mirage?," *Natural Resources Journal*, v. 20, (1980), 17, 33.

67. The recommendation to integrate Indian water rights into traditional water law was controversial when settling the water claims of the Ute Mountain Ute and the Southern Ute tribes of southeastern Colorado. The major impediment to a negotiated settlement was the Ute tribes' attempt to have the right to transfer a portion of their water rights across state boundaries to the states of the lower basin of the Colorado River. Although, prima facie, this violates the Colorado River Compact, the tribes argued that they are not party to the Law of the River. For more information, see "Indian Tribes and Water Marketing," *Water Market Update,* 6 (S. Shupe and J. Folk-Williams, eds., January 1987).

68. DuMars and Ingram extensively document the Navajo situation. DuMars and Ingram, supra note 65.

69. See J. Folk-Williams, supra note 7, 22; Marston, "Indians Breathe Life into Old Treaties," supra note 16; Marston, "An Indian Water Victory Heats Turmoil in Wyoming," supra note 16.

70. Wilkinson, "Western Water Law in Transition," *University of Colorado Law Review*, v. 56, (1985), 317, 327;

Collins, supra note 40, 487.

71. Berkman and Viscusi write, "Nevertheless, it is often said on Capitol Hill that a Reclamation project has a better chance of passing if it is presented 'under an Indian blanket'—in other words, if the project includes some benefit for Indians. Unfortunately, it is usually true that Indians get only a blanket—a token," R. Berkman and W. Viscusi, supra note 30, 151.

72. Thorson, supra note 15, 45.

73. Moore presents additional details of this method of settlement. M. Moore, *An Economic Approach to Conflict Resolution: The Case of Native American Water Rights*, (1986) (unpublished manuscript).

74. In a simulation of the two alternatives, the equal-sharing alternative yielded an annual, aggregate expected profit of $1,233,820 ($B_1$ = $1,233,820) and the water-storage alternative yielded an annual, aggregate profit of $1,240,357 ($B_2$ = $1,240,357). The choice of the cost-efficient alternative, then, simplified to whether the total annual costs of the storage project were greater or less than $6,537. The analysis assumes that both the Indians and the non-Indians use their water in agricultural production. See ibid., 12.

75. The equitable apportionment doctrine provides one means of dividing among the riparian states the water of an interstate river. See Tarlock, supra note 57, 411. Indian interests do not trust an approach premised solely on the equitable apportionment doctrine as they perceive it as a means of diminishing their water right.

76. Ibid., 408-09. An economic-means test is different from an economic-efficiency test. As discussed previously, it is based on the product of resource use rather than the process of resource allocation. See supra, text accompanying notes 55-61.

77. Tarlock, "An Overview of the Law of Groundwater Management," *Water Resources Res.*, v. 21, (1985), 1751.

78. Huffaker and Gardner, supra note 46, 41.

79. U.S.C., 43, (1982), 390.

80. Huffaker and Gardner, supra note 46, 42.

81. Bureau of Reclamation, U.S. Department of the Interior, *1982 Summary Statistics: Volume II, Finances And Physical Features*, (1982), 89.

82. Bureau of Reclamation, U.S. Department of the Interior, *What Are Revenues?*, (1987) (unpublished manuscript).

83. Reisner describes the ironical twist in the economics of dam and project construction of cross-subsidizing irrigation with hydro-electricity: "With river-basin accounting, one could take all the revenues generated by projects in any river basin—dams, irrigation projects, navigation and recreation features—and toss them into a common 'fund.' The hydroelectric dams might contribute ninety-five cents of every dollar accruing to the fund, while the irrigation features might contribute only a nickel. . . . The beauty of river-basin 'accounting,' from the Bureau's point of view, was that it would be literally *forced* to build dams. The engineering mentality which, Robinson himself admits, came to dominate the Bureau's thinking in the 1930s and 1940s created an institutional distaste for irrigation projects. They were a necessary nuisance that provided the rationale for what Bureau men really loved to do: build majestic dams. In the past, however, the infeasibility of many projects put a damper on their ambitions, because if a project didn't make economic sense, they lost the rationale then needed to build a dam to store water. With river-basin accounting, the equation was stood on its head: a lot of bad projects—economically infeasible ones—created a rationale for building *more,* not fewer, dams. The dams—all with hydroelectric features, of course—would be required to compensate for the financial losses of the irrigation projects; the losses would miraculously vanish in the common pool of revenues." M. Reisner, supra note 28, 140-42.

Chapter XII

Tribal Enterprise

In order to combat tribal poverty and economic powerlessness, many Native American tribes are attempting to stimulate economic development in the reservations. Though only about ten percent of Native American tribes have access to a significant amount of investment capital, many of those which do enjoy such a benefit are embarking upon large scale and small scale enterprise ventures which promise to decrease unemployment and stimulate economic growth.

The creation of jobs on reservations is one of the top priorities of tribal economic planners. Currently, forty percent of Native Americans living on reservations are unemployed, and this figure soars to seventy five percent when we consider only the ten largest reservations. As a result, poverty, alcoholism, family violence, and disease plague Native American reservations.

Federal aid for Native Americans has been reduced drastically during the last twelve years. During the Reagan years alone, Indian aid was cut by one billion dollars per year. This has resulted in economic devastation for the already depressed economies of reservations. Over forty percent of all tribal income is derived from Federal and tribal jobs on reservations, so drastic reductions in aid equate to huge reductions in tribal income.

Beginning with the Nixon Administration, the Federal Government began to emphasize greater tribal autonomy and private economic development for reservations. This policy, accompanied by some tribes' realization of large court settlements and natural resource profits, has resulted in an increase in tribal enterprise during the last two decades. Many fortunate tribes possess large capital funds, or considerable resource bases, which promise to allow considerable investment opportunities.

There has been considerable disagreement among Native American leaders about the best way to invest such funds and develop such resources. Some leaders contend that large scale industrial concerns will best serve the interests of the community. Others contend that such ventures are not only economically ineffective, but also opposed to traditional Native American values. Rather, they argue, investment should be focused on small scale ventures, which promise the infusion of appropriate technologies on a scale which is both sustainable and renewable. It is better, they claim, to encourage investment in the product and distribution of basic services, on which Natives spend their money, than to focus on the production of military hardware or automobiles. In this way, the money spent by tribal members on basic goods and services can be kept in the tribal economy, thus sustaining and stimulating growth. Larger ventures, like tourism, gambling, and

341

industrial production, if they create growth at all, encourage artificial growth. Forty-three fortunate tribes which possess valuable natural resources on their lands have come together to form a cartel known as the Council of Energy Resource Tribes (CERT), which deals with the sale of Native American oil, mineral, timber, and fishing produce.

Native American leaders differ on the question of whether large scale or small scale investment will better serve to improve the self sufficiency of reservations and the living standards of tribal members. However, there is general agreement that the key to successful economic development through enterprise lies in consistent tribal leadership and a communal consensus on the road to development a particular tribe will choose to follow.

—RNW

Tribal Enterprise

Daniel Cohen

Last fall the Passamaquoddy Indians of Maine staged a financial coup that won Wall Street's admiration. Five years after engineering the first Indian-led leveraged buy out, to acquire New England's only cement plant, the tribe sold it at triple the purchase price. The $60 million profit in that deal left the 2,700-member tribe in control of one of Maine's largest investment funds and confirmed it as a major player in the state's economy.

Such an outcome flew in the face of what many Maine residents had predicted in 1980, when the Passamaquoddy and Penobscot tribes were together awarded $81.5 million in a landclaims settlement. The money was expected to pass quickly to non-Indians—and it might have done so, had the federal government's tradition of dividing spoils of this kind equally among tribal members been continued. Elsewhere such division has inspired spending sprees to the benefit of off-reservation merchants.

The Maine tribes, however, built into the settlement the right to buy 300,000 acres of timberland, and crafted a diversified investment strategy. "Their goal was to use the land-claims money to solve unemployment, create more wealth, and raise their status in the community," says Thomas N. Tureen, the chairman of Tribal Assets Management, which has provided financial advice to the tribes. The Passamaquoddy in 1982 bought one of the state's largest blueberry farms and two radio stations, and in 1983 the cement plant, which at the time was losing money almost as fast as it belched pollutants. Under the tribe's ownership it not only became profitable but also originated a patented pollution-control system that could help resolve the acid-rain crisis. When the tribe sold the plant, it kept ownership of the scrubber technology, which uses waste products to convert acidic emissions into salable by-products, and could become the tribe's next big money-maker. The Department of Energy and the Spanish buyers of the plant have since agreed to fund the construction of a $9.6 million prototype scrubber at the Maine plant.

As the first tribe to go shopping for investments, the Passamaquoddy became a potent symbol for other Indians. Partly in response, dozens of the nation's 500 federally recognized Indian tribes have in recent years sharpened their business skills and begun aggressively pursuing the kinds of deals—joint ventures with corporations, new factories to be built on reservations, and control of mining and drilling on their lands—that until a few years ago were widely viewed as instruments of outsiders' exploitation. The Mississippi Choctaws' five auto-parts factories and one greeting-card operation not only have raised tribal employment to more than 80 percent—the former unemployment rate—but also have made the tribe one of the state's fifteen largest employers, with 1,200 workers. Other tribes, such as the Salt-River Pima Maricopa, of Arizona, New Mexico's Jicarilla Apache, and the Devils Lake Sioux, of North Dakota, have likewise built well-managed tribal enterprises.

Large-scale reservation development, many tribal officials now believe, may represent the best chance in decades to improve Indians' living standards—and their status in the regions where they live. "The pressure for development coming from within tribal societies is far greater than anything coming from without," says A. David Lester, who was a health and human-services commissioner in the Carter and Reagan administrations and is the executive director of the Denver-based Council of Energy Resource Tribes, whose forty-three members are tribes with significant oil, mineral, timber, or fishery holdings. "The debate is pretty much over as to whether we should engage in economic development. The answer is affirmative."

But the chances that many other tribes will soon replicate the Passamaquoddy's success are slim. Formidable obstacles to economic development on Indian reservations remain, not only in the workings of the federal Bureau of Indian Affairs (BIA), which continues to exercise influence in nearly every area of tribal life, but also in terms of access to mainstream financial markets. And debate over the proper course of reservation development has in fact intensified, with some tribal factions arguing against the value of large-scale projects such as factories or mining on reservations, and some government and business groups challenging the government's role as trustee of Indian interests.

Zigzags in federal policy over the past hundred years have created many of the worst problems. The government has alternately sought to disband tribes and assimilate their members into the larger society (notably with the 1887 policy of allotment, which ostensibly tried to turn Indians into private farmers but shrank their land base by two thirds in fifty years) and to reinforce the tribal structures and land base (the New Deal's Indian Reorganization Act). The most recent turn in federal policy, taken under President Richard Nixon, has contributed to the burst of tribal capitalism. In 1970 Nixon repudiated the Eisenhower-era policy of "termination," which had led to the disbanding of 109 Indian tribes and the dispersal of their assets. Nixon endorsed tribal self-determination and supported the return of Blue Lake, a Taos Pueblo religious site, rather than forcing the Indians to accept cash for improperly taken lands. "The Nixon years were the best," says Suzan Shown Harjo, the executive director of the National Congress of American Indians. Her view is seconded by most Indian leaders today.

During the Nixon years Great Society programs run by the Office of Economic Opportunity and the Economic Development Administration, while being cut back elsewhere, were expanded in Indian country, funding legal services and tribally based development schemes; the EDA spent $495 million from 1965 to 1976. The EDA at first favored industrial parks and vacation resorts, few of which have been successful, though this strategy also led to the construction of water and sewer lines on many reservations that had had none. Those programs had another, perhaps unintended, effect: "OEO broke the stranglehold of the Department of Interior over Indian people and allowed new leadership to develop," LaDonna Harris, the president of Americans for Indian Opportunity, has said.

The energy crisis gave tribes an added boost in 1973 by increasing the value of resources under the reservations, including one third of the low-sulfur coal that can be strip-mined in the United States, and significant deposits of uranium, oil, and gas. Rapidly escalating mineral royalties and a series of land-claims settlements provided some tribes with large infusions of cash. Some Indian leaders also came to think about money in a new way. Instead of merely collecting fees from outside mining and drilling companies for the extraction of their reservations' resources, they began to look for potentially profitable production and marketing efforts of their own.

In the 1980s, however, oil prices plunged, and Indian mineral revenues with them. So did federal expenditures for Indian programs, which under the Reagan Administration were cut by $1 billion a year. Funding for job training and technical-assistance projects declined 56 percent from 1980 to 1984, for example, and per-capita funding for the Indian Health Service, the U.S. Public Health Service agency that provides medical care to one million Indians, shrank by about half. The cuts had an immediate negative effect on Indian employment, because 44 percent of Indians' personal income comes from federal and tribal jobs (in contrast, public-sector jobs provide 19 percent of salaries nationwide). Not surprisingly, overall Indian unemployment has in the past year climbed to 40 percent (by the BIA's reckoning, which is widely regarded as conservative), from a low of 38 percent in 1987. The figure averaged 75 percent on the ten largest reservations. "For practical purposes, there is no private-sector economy on many reservations," says Alan R. Parker, a Chippewa Cree who is the staff director of the Senate Indian Affairs Committee and a former president of the American Indian National Bank.

In December of 1985 the Cherokee chief Ross O. Swimmer, who had previously called for the abolition of the

Bureau of Indian Affairs, took over as its head and announced that it would be his goal to prod reluctant tribes into ending their dependence on federal aid and adopting business principles. "We hear the buzz word of economic development in Indian country, but some think that means a check, more federal expenditures," he told me last year. When Swimmer left office, last January, he conceded that he had made little headway in persuading tribes to be "self-sufficient instead of coming to Washington for more money."

He had succeeded, however, in raising fresh doubts about the efficacy of the $3 billion a year that the federal government spends on Indian programs. Some conservative observers argue that government aid to Indians amounts to "an experiment that failed" and that Indian "privileges" should be revoked. Unsuccessful initiatives and bureaucratic overhead do consume at least a third of the BIA's billion-dollar budget, but federal expenditures also include $1 billion annually for the Indian Health Service, plus rising sums for welfare grants to a population that is expanding at 2.8 percent a year—nearly twice as fast as the U.S. population overall. Federal aid has improved the Indians' health, although alcoholism, tuberculosis, diabetes, and fatal car accidents still claim Indian victims at rates two to four times higher than those for others. The infant-mortality rate among Indians is nine percent lower than that in the general population. At the same time, however, an alarming number of Indian children are born with fetal alcohol syndrome.

Although the BIA is no longer the unquestioned master on reservations, it remains a pervasive presence in tribal affairs, running schools for 200,000 Indian students, operating a special court system for Indian offenses, and employing more than a thousand tribal policemen, among other duties. It also must approve virtually every decision on the use of Indian resources—even the disposition of cash settlements that the Navajo and other tribes have won in lawsuits against the BIA itself. The BIA oversees the use of 53 million acres of Indian land, and its malfeasance has reached epic proportions—more than $1 billion a year is being lost in oil and gas royalties, according to estimates by the Interior Department and Congress. The bureau's $20 million a year in business-development funds scarcely begins to cover the losses caused by its faulty oversight.

The budget-cutting under Reagan prodded tribes to seek to develop the economy they have instead of waiting for federal aid. "The budget cuts made clear that there was a false economy sustaining reservation life," Alan Parker says. A series of Supreme Court rulings beginning in the 1950s has established that tribes are separate governments over which the states have no jurisdiction, and that Indians have extensive rights to the resources on their land. A 1982 law gave tribes the same powers of taxation and of issuing bonds that states have, extending their sovereignty.

As a result, the tribes' options have expanded. Bingo games and sales of tax-free cigarettes and gas have become money-makers on many reservations. Unfortunately, even when tribal governments endorse the concept of enterprise, they often focus on winning federal grants, not managing young businesses. "The tribe feels it's done its job by getting the money," says Chris Berry, a discouraged adviser to tribal entrepreneurs. Tribal businesses often founder because of classic start-up blunders—underpricing or having no marketing plan, for example, or overstaffing to increase employment, a constant temptation on job-poor reservations.

Indian culture and electoral priorities can make corrective measures highly unpopular. Creating jobs is a top priority of tribal enterprise, and favoring friends and relatives is often required, not frowned upon. In tribal elections, for which door-to-door campaigning remains essential, candidates may woo voters with promises of higher per-capita payouts from tribal enterprises, even when making such payouts is fiscally risky. Reinvestment of company earnings makes a poor platform, as tribal officials discover when entire councils are swept from office in elections, as has happened in some tribes. Suzan Harjo, of the National Congress of American Indians, explains, "If someone is going to give you a hundred and twenty-five dollars, that could feed a kid. Politics in Indian country is no different from politics anywhere else; it's just a more open process."

Politically successful chiefs have learned to manage that process while promoting development. Melvin J. Francis, the governor of the Pleasant Point Passamaquoddy, estimates that three out of four of his constituents support off-reservation investment. Nonetheless, he made sure that the cement-plant sale resulted in payments of $2,000 to each member of the tribe, along with the creation of a new-ventures fund.

The experience of the Penobscot contrasts with the Passamaquoddy's business successes. After an electoral rout of their sitting governor last fall, the Penobscot, who shared in the 1980 Maine land-claims settlement, severed their ties to Tribal Assets Management, which was formed after the settlement to help handle the tribes' investments. The new administration questioned the tribe's involvement with a profitable on-reservation audio-cassette factory, and looked at other higher-return (and higher-risk) investments. Envy of the Passamaquoddy may have figured in the change.

Resentment may cause problems within a tribe as well. When Joe J. McKay, a member of the Blackfeet tribe, took over the failing Blackfeet Indian Writing Company, a tribally owned pen and pencil manufacturer in Browning, Montana, in 1985, he quickly halved its payroll of 120 to keep the firm from bankruptcy, a highly unpopular action. Two years later the tribal council blocked McKay from using a $1.5 million line of credit to buy raw materials for a new calendar-printing operation—at peak production season.

"It all but ruined our credibility with suppliers whom we promised payment," McKay says. Partly as a result he has given up hopes of becoming a tribal leader and has returned to private law practice. "There should be development of individual businessmen, whether [in firms] totally held by tribal members or not," he says, admitting that he has come to agree with Ross Swimmer's view that tribal government often impedes the growth of industries it owns. McKay has two professional degrees, which he says brought him local resentment. Some at the pen and pencil factory say that hostility to McKay illustrates the famous Indian crab story—a bitter anecdote in which crabs at the bottom of a pail pull down one that is about to escape. For whatever reason, many talented Indians pursue their careers off-reservation—where nearly half of all Indians now live, owing in large part to federal relocation policies of the 1950s. That migration not only has deprived the tribes of badly needed skills but also causes a profound sense of dislocation among the people who have left.

Tribal enterprises are luring a growing number of professionally trained Indians. Indian lawyers, who number 600 now as against fewer than a dozen twenty-five years ago, have had an unmistakable impact on the jurisprudence of Indian affairs in the past decade. Interest among Indians in applying management training is only now emerging.

Growth in the talent pool of Indian professionals is, however, unlikely to generate the needed development by itself. The involvement of tribal government remains a nearly indispensable ingredient in any large-scale industry on reservations, because other sources of funds for investment are scant. Though Indian tribes may not sell or mortgage their land, their governments do have the authority to negotiate loans and issue development bonds. Thirty years ago Phillip Martin, who was then a member of the council of the Mississippi Choctaws, began a campaign for economic development; his tribe had few natural resources and no large cash settlement to invest. First he rewrote the tribe's constitution to stabilize its government and solidify its authority. "We went from two-year terms to four, and put the council on staggered terms," says Martin, who is now the chief of the 5,000-member tribe. The fortunes of the tribe have improved considerably over the years. The Choctaws have used government-insured loans and undertaken joint ventures with automobile manufacturers to build on tribal land five factories, where employees produce wire harnesses and audio systems for cars.

Martin himself has become a spokesman for bringing major industry to reservations. In east-central Mississippi, Martin believes, factor labor, while not perhaps the ideal, represents a realistic step in the reservation's development. "People don't have to go away to work; it develops infrastructure and promotes a better life," he says. Still more desirable job opportunities await Indians now completing their education, Martin argues: "A lot of jobs [on the reservation] require four years of college or better, and they now employ non-Indians."

That employment pattern likewise holds true at a number of defense plants on reservations, which manufacture parts for ground-to-air missiles and helicopters, camouflage netting, and other military hardware. Often constituted as joint ventures with majority tribal holdings in order to qualify for Defense Department set-asides, such plants are in fact generally directed by outside corporations. But these factories have been a source of steady employment in Indian country, and have provided management training for some tribal members.

As it happens, placing factories, particularly those of defense contractors, on Indian land has alienated a number of development activists who favor building individual or family businesses instead. The Seventh Generation Fund, an Indian-run "appropriate technology" foundation based in Forestville, California, promotes small-scale development that is "sustainable and renewable, in the control of the people, and culturally enhancing," according to Mike Myers, a Seneca who is a veteran of the 1969 Indian occupation of Alcatraz, and who is the fund's program director. Seventh Generation has backed an impressive array of smaller enterprises run, typically, by families or groups of friends. Its projects to date include a wild-rice marketing co-op among the Ojibwa in Minnesota, a women's shelter and quilt-making circle on the Pine Ridge Oglala Sioux reservation in South Dakota, and a center to build low-cost, energy-efficient housing at a Mohawk community in upstate New York. Creating only a handful of jobs at a time may bring change far more slowly than government officials would like, Myers concedes, but he argues that the change will at least be durable. "We need to rethink how rapidly development can happen," he says. "Corporate time lines don't fit."

In its critique of federally backed, large-scale tribal industries the Seventh Generation Fund echoes, from the left, conservatives' complaints that tribal councils have little expertise in managing a company for profit. "They get confused between being a business and being a government," Myers says. Projects like the ones Myers endorses often operate with little support from the tribal governments. A group of Navajo family farmers using Israeli drip irrigation, for example, found funding from Seventh Generation and the Department of Agriculture, not from the Navajo chairman, Peter MacDonald, who instead backed $30 million worth of high-tech development on the reservation. "MacDonald is absolutely committed to mega-development," claims an activist involved in the drip-irrigation project, which last year sold $230,000 worth of produce on and off the reservation.

Indians on reservations spend several hundred million dollars a year off-reservation for commodities ranging from groceries to auto parts, much of it in border towns where few if any businesses are Indian-owned. Many reservations remain barren of basic services. An extreme case is the Pine Ridge reservation, covering the nation's poorest county: only nine percent of the $82 million a year that comes into Pine Ridge is spent on the reservation.

The answer may lie not in importing industrial plants but in providing basic commercial services, from locksmithing to fencemending, that are now offered only informally or off-reservation. "The smallest amounts of money are hardest to find," says Rebecca Adamson, an Eastern Cherokee living in Virginia, who in 1979 founded First Nations Financial Project, to help tribes develop alternatives to federal funding. "We're dealing with people who have no credit history, no checking accounts, no credit cards." In 1986, after helping Pine Ridge put in place its first commercial code, to legalize debt collection, Adamson launched the Lakota Fund there and began to make unsecured loans of $1,000 or less to Oglala Sioux craftsmen and casual businesses at Pine Ridge. The $700,000 fund, raised from foundations, has made sixty of these small loans so far, and six larger ones. "There are fewer than forty-eight businesses on that reservation, but we found over a hundred activities that people do to get by, an economy that was ignored by federal funding," Adamson says.

Another benefit of tiny, indigenous businesses, in the view of many development specialists who favor them, is that they offer only small roles to non-Indians. That non-Indians often occupy prominent positions in tribal enterprises, as either advisers or executives, disturbs activists concerned with bolstering the skills and power of native people. "All that money has not been a cure-all," Mike Myers says, pointing to high rates of alcoholism and suicide among the Maine tribes. Although more than a score of tribes already own significant businesses requiring expert help that only non-Indians are now prepared to give, distrust of outsiders remains a thorny issue for many tribes.

Higher revenues from tribal enterprises or natural resources are the most likely source of significant new funds to invest in the future prosperity of Indian nations. Though federal funding for the BIA and the Indian Health Service has inched upward in recent years, any major increase in development outlays seems improbable. Not only must Indian programs compete with all other social programs for limited "discretionary" funds in the federal budget, but the welfare emergency on reservations has soaked up funds that might have been devoted to long-term development.

Both Congress and the Bush Administration continue to send conflicting signals on Indian policy. President Bush has promised to strengthen self-determination and to support tribal management of natural resources. But the head of the BIA, Eddie Brown, a Pascua Yaqui who formerly directed Arizona's Department of Economic Security (which is only a small fraction the size of the bureau) and who was nominated by Bush, has little policy background in the issues facing Indian people. Two bills now before Congress would encourage development, one by allowing entrepreneurs to reap tax and depreciation benefits for setting up on reservations, the other creating a $200 million Indian Development Bank, modeled on the World Bank. But the outlook for both remains clouded. As one of his last official acts, President Reagan pocket-vetoed the bill to launch the development bank, whose usefulness was questioned by the BIA and also some Indian activists.

In the meantime, pressure on Capitol Hill to restrict tribal autonomy has mounted. A Senate committee was convened last winter to investigate bureaucratic bungling by the BIA and fraud by energy companies that do business with Indians. Instead, it focused on corruption among tribal officials, notably the Navajo chairman Peter MacDonald, who was the leading symbol of free enterprise in Indian country. MacDonald, a flamboyant and high-living spokesman for tribal economic development (he has been called "the Marcos of Indian country"), has been accused of seeking a $50,000 kickback for arranging the sale of land to the Navajo tribe. The charges, which are already the subject of an Arizona grand-jury investigation and the cause of a constitutional crisis among the Navajo over the tribal council's attempt to impeach MacDonald, have led to renewed calls for greater federal oversight of the business dealings of Indian nations. Congress may try to pass legislation limiting tribal prerogatives, which could in turn strengthen the hand of the BIA and the major energy companies in Indian country— moves unlikely to enrich Indians.

Tribes with consistent leadership and consensus among members—the Choctaw, the Passamaquoddy—seem likely to consolidate their success. But only about one in ten tribes today has any means of producing a significant amount of revenue, and the proportion is unlikely to grow by much any time soon. The often vociferous debate over the tribes' business strategies signals the depth of interest among tribal leaders in taking control of their people's economic destiny. Proponents of big and small enterprises alike concede that it will be years before their projects have much impact on reservation economies. Another shift in government policy away from supporting tribal authority could destroy any difference they make.

Chapter XIII

Reservation Development in the United States: Peripherality in the Core

Vicki Page

Statistics indicate that American Indians form one of the most disadvantaged minority groups in the United States. Poor health, low-paying jobs, and low levels of education, along with high levels of unemployment, all contribute to the American Indian's seemingly endless state of poverty. Their cultural persistence, some argue, exacerbates the problem. Studies do indeed indicate that Indians generally maintain their cultural distinctiveness, even after their introduction and adjustment to an urban, industrial style of life. The fact that many reservations are pursuing industrial development as a strategy for attaining economic and cultural self-determination increases the ramifications of Indians' adjustment to the industrial way of life.

Federal policies and sociological analyses concerning American Indians in the past have failed to take into account long-term and world-wide system changes that not only impinge on the United States but which also have consequences for the United States government's relationship with American Indians and reservation development. Therefore, the major aim of this essay is to examine the intertwined "problems" of the persistence of Indian poverty and culture using the metropolis-satellite and world-system explanations. Focusing on the political and economic underpinnings of ethnic relations, these approaches allow not only the location of Indian-United States relations among more general, world-wide politico-economic processes but also a specification of these processes' impact upon the reservation economy and Indian ethnicity. A second aim is to illustrate

United States-world system relations as a possible basis for alternative United States-Indian policy considerations, and for addressing the cultural dilemma that Indians face in their efforts to industrialize.

METROPOLIS-SATELLITE

Historically, federal Indian policies have been based on the acculturation approach to Indian ethnicity and poverty, which posits that before white contact American Indians were backward and undeveloped, but that the Indian condition will constantly improve as they become more and more integrated into the mainstream social and economic milieu. This framework is similar to the larger modernization theory, which argues that "nation building involves a process of integration of formerly diverse social groups into one political economic order with a shared sense of identity," and that societies evolve more or less along uniform lines toward progress and modernity.[1] Both of these theories have failed, however, in that neither can account for the fact that diverse ethnicities within nation-states persist, along with underdevelopment across nation-states.

More recently, the political relations of the United States and American Indian reservations have been described as a metropolis-satellite situation in which the politico-economic relations are more imperative than the urban-rural dichotomy.[2] Economic surpluses are taken from rural areas and used for the benefit and growth of urban power centers. Thus, the backward condition of American Indian reservations is not due to the retention of traditional ways, "but result from the way in which United States' urban centers of finance, political influence, and power have grown at the expense of rural areas."[3] Results of this exploitation of Indian lands and resources by the United States metropolis include political oppression and neo-colonial subjugation, decimation of Indian populations, destruction of political and economic self-direction, and the burgeoning role of the Bureau of Indian Affairs and the Department of the Interior in conducting Indian affairs.[4] Increasingly, metropolis-based corporations are wielding considerable influence in the political arena, as well as in Indian affairs.

Jorgensen argues that the history of Indian/White federal relations has been a series of administrative attempts to civilize reservation Indians using an urban-development approach.[5] The resulting policies, instead, have plunged them into a state of perpetual economic and social poverty. First, as a result of the passage of the General Allotment Act (Dawes Act) of 1887, much Indian land was either tied up in heirship status or sold or leased to non-Indians. This situation left many Indians to depend upon family farming and ranching, which did not meet their subsistence requirements. Second, reflecting the notion that Indians themselves are to blame for their "backwardness," federal education policy used boarding schools to "white" educate and resocialize Indian children. This policy not only separated many Indian families but also, generally, failed to destroy "the so-called restrictive, backward influence of tribal life." Third, the termination and relocation policies of the 1950s were similarly designed to make American Indians "responsible citizens." In 1954, the House Concurrent Resolution 108 declared that the government was withdrawing federal responsibility and services from Indians as soon as possible (i.e., termination). This proved to be less than successful and in some cases disastrous, making destitute Indians who had already been poor.[6]

The Employment Assistance Program, better known as the relocation program, is intended for any Indian who is prepared to leave the reservation to seek employment in an urban area. It provides two basic services, the Direct Employment Program, and the Vocational Training Program. The former is designed to relocate individuals who have a marketable skill, while the latter is intended to provide vocational training in addition to job opportunities.[7] Although approximately half of the relocatees return to the reservations while many others end up in slums without steady employment, the relocation program has been considered successful "in terms of both return on the government's investment and the satisfaction of the Indian participants."[8]

WORLD-SYSTEM THEORY

In American sociology, world-system theory has developed out of opposition to the various versions of modernization theory as proposed by such authors as Rostow, Portes, and McClelland.[9] Modernization theory "tended to refuse the ideas that deep structural factors might prevent economic progress, and more importantly, that the very international context which was supposed to be spreading modernization might itself be such an obstacle."[10]

Recognizing these factors, world-system theory posits that "the existence of strong manufacturing powers with the ability to extend their markets and their political strength throughout the world re-directs the evolution of feeder societies."[11] Although both the metropolis-satellite and world-system theories draw on Frank's thesis of the "development of the underdevelopment," they explain uneven development on different levels.[12] On the one hand, the metropolis-satellite account of Indian and rural poverty is specific to the United States. While insightful, this explanation does not allow us to see what is unique, or not unique as the case may be, about the American Indians or the United States relative to political and economic relations with the rest of the world. World-system theory, on the other hand, explains uneven development on an international basis and allows an examination of modernization processes of which the United States-American Indian relationship is only one instance. Additionally, world-system theory addresses change in the structure of Indian societies; the metropolis-satellite thesis does not.

According to world-system theory, the growth of the global, capitalist division of labor and its processes divides the world into the core, periphery, and semi-periphery, as opposed to the metropolis-satellite theory, which emphasizes only two divisions (urban-rural) and the nation-state as the unit of analysis. The metropolis concept corresponds to the core, however, which can be described as strong, central, modern, diversified, industrial nations; in contrast, the satellite concept corresponds to the periphery, described as weak, marginal, monocultural, agricultural, or extractive nations.[13] The metropolis or core, as a center of economic and political power, extracts economic surplus from the rural-periphery areas, therefore growing at the latter's expense.

The two theories are also similar in that they attack the unilinear theories of development, but again at different levels of analysis. Specifically, the metropolis-satellite thesis is one of counter-acculturation, while world-system theory is one of counter-modernization. All nation-states, as well as regions within nation-states, have not developed evenly. Moreover, distinct local identities remain within supposedly uniformly modernized nations. Acculturation and modernization theories cannot account for these discrepancies. These theories have failed to explain why reservations remain underdeveloped, and why traditional Indian cultures still thrive. Both the metropolis-satellite and world-system explanations argue that uneven development is the result of modern nation-states expanding internationally or locally into undeveloped regions. Supposedly, as modern nation-states expand, they use resources extracted from undeveloped regions to fuel their continued development. This process not only blocks the development of these regions but also directs their change away from development. Frank's concept of underdevelopment is not only a lack of development, "but may also be a positive result of unfavorable economic relations—hence the phrase, 'development of underdevelopment.'"[14]

The changes wrought in what Hall terms non-state societies as a consequence of their interaction with more advanced societies is referred to as reactive change.[15] This change may be directed toward the impacting society, toward earlier forms of organization, or frozen at a specific level of development. The extent and permanence of change within non-state societies depend upon shifts in market articulation between the expanding national sector and the region being absorbed, and within the world economy. The more closely articulated a region is to the world groups, the more forceful are the pressures placed on local groups. If these pressures are strong and enduring, the change in the structure of local groups will be drastic and difficult to reverse; if not, as in the case of low levels of market articulation, the change will be not so profound nor so difficult to reverse.

As a specific illustration of reactive change among non-state forms in a modern or core nation, American Indian groups of autonomous bands have transformed (in some cases) into tribes as a result of the impact of absorption. As the needs of the United States and the rest of the world for more natural resources have increased through time, so has market articulation between reservations and the central sector. Because of the nation's increasing need for the natural resources found on many reservations, Indian tribes have taken on the same economic role in the primary industry sector, and to some extent are becoming amalgamated into a single labor force. This process of fusing ethnic and class solidarity has helped lead to the emergence of a new ethnic identity referred to as pan-Indianism.[16] According to Hall, new ethnic identities tend to take on distinctions that already exist in the cultural milieu.[17] In this light, then, pan-Indianism may be viewed as an ethno-political strategy similar to those of American blacks and Hispanics.

One reactive strategy of American Indians to corporate energy development on their reservations has been to form pan-tribal and tribal organizations that are very like modern corporate entities. Some of these include the Alaska Native Industries Cooperative Association, an economic and political organization composed of Indians, Eskimos, and Aleuts of western and interior Alaska; the National Indian Youth Council, the Council of Energy Resource Tribes, and the International Indian Treaty Council.

Furthermore, as members of a core society, American Indians occupy a special position in the class structure. In this regard, ethnicity or ethnic consciousness is defined in cultural terms, but has as its objective political and economic gain. According to Wallerstein, ethnic—as well as party— divisions are manifestations of class divisions.[18] A particular manifestation is influenced by a nation-state's position in the world stratification system and the relative efficiency of ethnic, party, or class organizations in promoting group interest.[19]

Ethnic divisions in the periphery are aligned with labor divisions. That is, when labor is plentiful, ethnic distinctions will coincide with indigenous distinctions; when labor is scarce, however, ethnic distinctions will resemble the division of labor. In contrast, core ethnicity tends to be a reactive phenomenon and responsive to the presence or absence of a cultural division of labor. And, in cases where ethnic groups are regionally located—many Indians are on reservations in the United States—the region will tend to have colonial-like relations with the central nation.[20] These colonial-like relations are analogous to those of the metropolis-satellite structure described earlier, and manifest peripherality in the core (e.g., industrial and governmental siphoning off and partitioning of reservation land and natural resources).

American Indians in this perspective, as an ethnic group which is located in peripheral-like regions of a core nation, therefore organize in order to enhance the possibility of their economic improvement. As internal colonies, however, American Indian reservations are economically and politically dependent upon the federal government and the Bureau of Indian Affairs, as well as on metropolis-based industry and corporations, for goods and services, and, in some cases, simple survival. This situation is exacerbated by the fact that reservations also supply the central United States with the raw materials (such as lumber, coal, oil, and natural gas) required for its further growth and development. Consequently, the persistence of Indian poverty can be explained in large part by the Indians' particular position within, and relations with the local and international division of labor in the capitalist world economy.

DEVELOPING THE UNDERDEVELOPED

In the past, knowledge of the value of Indian lands was limited, so corporate and government pressure on reservations to develop was slight. In the 1950s, however, the value of Indian resources became apparent. This discovery, coupled with the growing world energy crisis, increased demands on the energy supplies of the U.S., particularly those of American Indian reservations.[21] Thus, beginning about 1962, the Bureau of Indian Affairs expanded its "development" program of training and relocating to include actively promoting the industrialization of reservations. Cooperating with federal, state, and tribal organizations, civic organizations, and private businesses, the BIA contracts for development projects, usually dealing with reservations' natural resources. To hasten the process and add a competitive edge, the BIA offers inducements to firms to locate on reservations (as opposed to going outside of the United States). One such inducement is the promise of financial assistance to companies that will provide on-the-job training for Indians. This financial aid may take the form of direct subsidies, or payment for recruiting and screening services. Another is to offer to build the structural facilities for firms. Further incentive to companies to locate on reservations is the fact that employers would have few or no taxes to pay.[22]

Interested parties in the development of reservations include federal agencies (e.g., the Bureau of Indian Affairs, the Atomic Energy Commission, and the Department of Energy); state governments, which gain from taxes on extractive industries; and local, non-Indian communities, which see reservation development as a stimulus for their local economies. Pressure for development also comes from tribal governments as a strategy for strengthening reservation economies and creating jobs.[23] However, as reservation Indians become dependent upon the extraction of resources for the whole of their economic structure, continued development becomes a vested interest of the tribe, not just the tribal government. An example of "extraction dependence" is the fact that in 1975 approximately 70 percent of Navajo, Laguna Pueblo, and Arapahoe tribal revenues came from mining leases and extraction.

The relative accessibility of reservation resources and the possibility of large profits draws multinational corporations to become the major developers of reservations.[24] The Nixon administration's energy crisis and Project Independence brought many energy projects to Indian reservations, projects that resulted in development contracts with corporations including Anaconda Copper, Atlantic Richfield, Bethlehem Steel, Union Carbide, Texaco, Westinghouse, Peabody Coal, and Kennecott Copper.[25] By 1980, having been assisted further by BIA development policies and by their own economic and political clout, numerous multinational corporations such as Exxon, Kerr McGee, Amoco, Conoco, and Gulf Oil, had become involved in natural resource development on reservations.[26]

Several of the circumstances surrounding corporate development lend support to the metropolis-satellite and world-system explanations of Indian poverty (i.e., peripherality). One is that, generally, reservation industries are neither owned nor controlled by Indians. Second, these industries are primarily raw-material or agriculture related. And third, these non-Indian-controlled business operations generate relatively few employment opportunities and comparatively little income for reservation Indians.

In fact, despite resource development and increased federal appropriations for their affairs, American Indian poverty persists. Jorgensen attributes the failure of federal Indian policies partially to "mismanagement" by the BIA, arguing that the bureau encouraged the development of livestock operations at the same time quasi-cartels were taking over the industry, and that the bureau advised tribes to allow non-Indian corporations to exploit Indian resources.[27] Furthermore, many tribes have accused the BIA of failing to protect their interests with regard to controlling mineral leases (i.e., the BIA has consistently under-negotiated royalties or established low fixed royalties). This situation is exacerbated by the fact that many tribes have neither the capital nor the skills or adequate counsel to utilize their own resources.

THEORETICAL IMPLICATIONS AND DISCUSSION

Some of the natural resources currently being extracted from Indian lands are minerals such as copper, nickel, lead, chronite, zinc, vandium, titanium, and thorium, in addition to oil, coal, timber, and natural gas. Since 1980 the Northern Cheyenne have had an agreement with the Atlantic Richfield Company (ARCO) that allows the company to explore oil and gas reserves on the reservation for thirty-three years. The Northern Cheyenne get six million dollars, 25 percent of the production profits, and relatively no say in the exploration plans. Along with large profits, ARCO gets a twenty-year tax holiday and free access to the reservation's lands, roads, and water.[28] This contract is typical of other multinational corporations' development and exploration contracts with tribes such as the Chippewa, Potawatomi, Menominee,

Stockbridge-Munsee, Oneida, Winnebago, Navajo, and Hopi.[29]

Development of Indian reservations has brought increased revenue to one of the poorest minority groups in America. Notwithstanding, it has also resulted in litigation concerning delinquent royalty payments, the disturbance of Indian burial and religious sites, and inadequate health and safety practices, such as the high rate of lung cancer and fibrosis among Navajo uranium miners.[30] Other consequences of reservation development include community and kinship disruption, environmental destruction, and the loss of large quantities of natural resources, as well as the demise of traditional economies, such as fishing and herding.[31] One most recent example of community disruption concerns the Hopi-Navajo reservation re-partitioning and the consequent displacement of many of these peoples from their traditional homelands.

The apprehension of Indians concerning industrial development on their lands thus encompasses many concerns—environmental issues, the influx into and takeover of their economies by non-Indians, and a lack of tribal control over development, in addition to potentially devastating effects on their traditional cultures and ways of life. Similarly, Owens warns that if reservation control of development is not attained, "energy development will prove to be the latest and most devastating fiasco of federal Indian policy." She suggests actions that should be taken to gain economic control.[32] For instance, tribes must regulate business activities on their reservations by using appropriate laws and codes. In addition to this jurisdictional control, tribes must establish financial control through increased taxation, production-sharing and service contracts, and enforceable Indian-preference hiring clauses. Third, tribes must gain managerial control, the ability to conduct research and business operations, and to provide training programs for the full range of jobs available on the reservations. Finally, and alternatively, by building a commercial infrastructure to keep more dollars circulating on the reservation, tribes could create a diversified and self-sufficient economy.[33]

According to world-system analysis of Indian reservation development and poverty, the dynamics of the larger world economy impinge upon the United States economy, of which reservations are a part. Thus, by failing to take into account the wider systemic changes that confront Indians, Owens' strategies for self-direction, while well intended and liberally pro-Indian, are misdirected according to the world-system perspective. Wallerstein argues that the host-parasite relationship that exists between peripheral and core areas is a necessary condition for the maintenance and promotion of capitalism. Therefore, the chances for reservation-controlled development, even significant development itself, seem unlikely. Wallerstein argues that the only hope for change in regional economies within national metropolis sectors is change in the entire world economy.[34] More importantly, he posits that this change only will come via a world socialist revolution.[35] This solution is too broad and encompassing for the scope of this discussion. The point, however, is that since changes in the world economy account for changes in a region's articulation with the world economy, the dynamics of the so-called metropolis-satellite relations between the under-developed Indian reservations and the greatly developed urban United States have to be examined from both an international and a local perspective.

For instance, as the United States has become more closely articulated to the world capitalist economy, it has more forcefully impinged upon American Indian reservations. The general push by federal, state and local agencies to acculturate Indians through various programs of education and economic activity were and continue to be instances of this growing impingement, and are coincidental with the United States' increasing need for Indian resources, namely energy. This impingement is affected by the international political climate surrounding natural resources, particularly oil, and United States' relations with the primary suppliers. As a consequence of this impingement, reservations have not only become more industrially developed but also have become more clearly peripheral, while Indian cultures have become less distinct. This latter point speaks to the larger issue of an inherent contradiction in the development process, and the cultural dilemma that developing reservations, as well as Third World nations, face. That is, it seems impossible to maintain simultaneously both traditional Indian cultures and values and to develop economically. In order for Indians to remain culturally distinct, they must acquire the power and modern business skills necessary to control their building industries. In order to acquire this power and skill, however, they must acculturate (i.e., lose their cultural distinctiveness). Is there a solution to this dilemma, short of a "world socialist revolution"? Perhaps insight may be gained from within the world-system perspective itself.

Out of the world-system analysis of ethnic peripherality, the concept of reactive ethnicity has been expanded upon by Nagel and Olzak,[36] who argue that developmental processes promote the ethnic mobilization of increasing and organizing resource competition along ethnic boundaries.[36] In this analysis, ethnic development, whether economic or political, is seen as being relationally and situationally activated (e.g., Indian organizational development, which has occurred due to the impingement of the metropolis U.S. onto Indian reservations).

Specifically, Nagel and Olzak identify five developmental processes that are most likely to activate ethnic mobilization and development: urbanization; increased scales of organization; expansion of the secondary and tertiary sectors of the economy; expansion of the political sector; and establishment of supranational organizations.[37]

Urbanization promotes ethnic mobilization in that ethnic ties and networks aid in the urban transition of rural migrants: job competition in cities' "ethnically diverse labor markets" promotes organization along ethnic lines, which in turn enhances ethnic boundaries; differences among migrant ethnic groups become pronounced upon contact, and provide a convenient and salient basis for urban ethnic organization and mobilization.

Large-scale organizations arise from the competition that other large-scale organizations present at the national level. To be effective, ethnic groups must reorganize nationally or capture a large constituency. These national-level organizations produce national-level ethnic boundaries and provide a substructure for mobilization. In the case of American Indians, many tribes have joined together to combat resource colonialization by forming such organizations as the Council of Energy Resource Tribes (CERT) and the International Indian Treaty Council.

The expansion of secondary and tertiary economic sectors, and associated urbanization processes weaken segregated labor markets, resulting in ethnic competition; the increased material resources that economic development provides strengthen the political capabilities of peripheral ethnic populations in both peripheral states and regions within core states. Peripheral resource development (e.g., oil and coal in American Indian reservations and Native Alaskan territories) encourages ethno-regional solidarity as a response to the national sector's policies of extraction and exploitation.

Expansion of the political sector raises issues concerning national identity, creates an arena for competition for politically controlled resources—much of which is organized along ethnic lines (e.g., reservation boundaries)—and results in the formal recognition of ethnicity as a basis for resource competition. For example, certain ethnic groups become designated as deserving of special treatment, or become targeted for special legislation (e.g., U.S.-Indian treaties).

The rise of supranational organizations, such as the North Atlantic Treaty Organization (NATO), encourages interstate migration and provides economic and political incentive for ethno-regional movements, along with forums for self-determination claims and demands (e.g., attempts by tribes to claim perceived rights to ancestral territories, traditional lifestyles and religions, and payments for damages resulting from broken treaty agreements).

Perhaps, then, Nagel and Olzak's extension of the reactive perspective on ethnic persistence and mobilization in modern and modernizing states indicates that, short of a world socialist revolution, Indian peripherality can be overcome or at least combated by using creatively and politically the processes of peripheralization (i.e., urban, industrial, bureaucratic intrusion) either against themselves or to their own benefit.

Some of the most recent and most innovative strategies for reservation development oriented toward self-determination include (1) turning to small businesses for employment, rather than to large corporations; (2) persuading Indian businesspersons to build privately owned reservation enterprises instead of relying on government-funded, make-work jobs; (3) re-negotiating natural resource contracts for higher royalty payments; (4) instituting gambling, such as bingo and blackjack games or race tracks, as short-term money-making projects; and (5) using appropriate technologies and alternative energy sources in agriculture that do not require large initial capital investments, to grow organic foods.[38] Strategies such as these indicate that perhaps Indian ethnicity may not need to be forfeited for economic survival.

NOTES

1. Reinhard Bendix, "Tradition and Modernity Reconsidered," *Comparative Studies in Society and History* 9 (1967): 292-346.

2. Joseph Jorgensen, "Indians and the Metropolis" in *The American Indian in Urban Society*, ed. J. Waddell and M. Watson (Boston: Little, Brown and Company, 1971), 66-114; "Poverty and Work Among American Indians," in *American Minorities and Economic Opportunity*, ed. R. Kaplan (Itasca, Illinois: R. E. Peacock Publishers, Inc., 1977), 170-198.

3. Jorgensen, "Indians and the Metropolis," 85.

4. Ibid., 66-114.

5. Jorgensen, "Poverty and Work Among American Indians," 170-198.

6. League of Women Voters, "The Menominee: A Case Against Termination," in *The American Indian: Past and Present*, ed. R. Nichols (New York: John Wiley and Sons, 1971), 238-244.

7. Niles Hansen, *Rural Poverty and the Urban Crisis* (Bloomington: Indiana University Press, 1970), 86-114.

8. James Gundlach and Alden Roberts, "Native American Indian Migration and Relocation: Success or Failure," *Pacific Sociological Review* 21 (1978): 117-128; Hansen, *Rural Poverty and the Urban Crisis*, 166; Robert Weppner, "Socioeconomic Barriers to Assimilation of Navajo Migrant Workers," *Human Organization* 31 (1972): 303-314.

9. Walt W. Rostow, *The Stages of Economic Growth: A Non-Communist Manifesto* (London: Cambridge University Press, 1960); Alejandro Portes, "On the Sociology of National Development: Theories and Issues," *American Journal of Sociology* 82 (1976): 55-85; Donald McClelland, *The Achieving*

Society (New York: Free Press, 1967).

10. Daniel Chirot and Thomas Hall, "World Systems Theory," *Annual Review of Sociology* 8 (1982), 81-106.

11. Ibid., 83-85.

12. Andre Gunder Frank, "Latin America: Underdevelopment or Revolution," *Monthly Review* (1969): 21-94.

13. Thomas Hall, "Peripheries, Regions of Refuge, and non-State Societies: Toward a Theory of Reactive Social Change," *Social Science Quarterly* 64 (1983): 582-598; Immanuel Wallerstein, *The Modern World System: Capitalist Agriculture and the Origins of the European World-Economy in the Sixteenth Century* (New York: Academic Press, 1974).

14. Hall, "Peripheries, Regions of Refuge, and Non-State Societies," 583; Frank, "Latin America."

15. Hall, "Peripheries, Regions of Refuge, and Non-State Societies," 588-598.

16. Susan Olzak, "Contemporary Ethnic Mobilization," *Annual Review of Sociology* 9 (1983): 355-374.

17. Hall, "Peripheries, Regions of Refuge, and Non-State Societies," 592-598.

18. Immanuel Wallerstein, *The Capitalist World Economy* (London: Cambridge University Press, 1979), 165-230.

19. Ibid., 165-230; Michael Hechter, "Group Formation and the Cultural Division of Labor," *American Journal of Sociology* 84 (1978): 293-319.

20. Hecter, "Group Formation and the Cultural Division of Labor," 293-319.

21. Daniel Israel, "New Opportunities for Energy Development on Indian Reservations." *Mining Engineering* 32 (1980): 651-657; Allan Kneese and Lee Brown, *The Southwest Under Stress: National Resource Development in a Regional Setting* (Baltimore: Johns Hopkins University Press, 1981).

22. Hansen, *Rural Poverty and the Urban Crisis*.

23. Tom Barry, "New Mexico Pueblos Confront the Atomic Age," *American Indian Journal* 4 (1979): 10-13; John Butler and Richard LaCourse, "45 Indian Tribes in a Dozen States Form Heartland of Indian Oil Production," Washington D.C.: *CERT Report* 4 (1982): 1-7; Duane Champagne, "Sociocultural Responses to Coal Development: A Comparison of the Crow and Northern Cheyenne" (University of

Wisconsin; 1983): 2-20; Loretta Fowler, *Arapahoe Politics, 1851-1978: Symbols in Crisis of Authority* (Lincoln: University of Nebraska Press, 1982).

24. Israel, "New Opportunities for Energy Development on Indian Reservations," 651-657; James Boggs, "The Challenge of Reservation Resource Development: A Northern Cheyenne Instance," in *Native Americans and Energy Development II*, edited by J. Jorgensen (Boston: Anthropology Resource Center, 1984), 205-236; Stephen Cornell, "Crisis and Response in Indian-White Relations: 1960-1984," *Social Problems* 32 (1982): 44-60.

25. Rex Wyler, *Blood of the Land: The Government and Corporate War Against the American Indian Movement*, (New York: Vintage Books, 1982).

26. Boggs, "The Challenge of Reservation Resource Development," 205-236; Cornell, "Crisis and Response in Indian-White Relations: 1960-1984," 44-60; Richard Nafziger, "Transitional Energy Corporations and American Indian Development," in *American Indian Energy Resources and Development: Development Series* (2), edited by R. Ortiz (New Mexico: Native American Studies, University of New Mexico, 1980), 9-38; Lisa Young, "What Price Progress? Uranium Production on Indian Lands in the San Juan Basin," *American Indian Law* 9 (1981): 1-50.

27. Jorgensen, "Poverty and Work Among the American Indians," 170-198.

28. Boggs, "The Challenge of Reservation Resource Development," 205-236.

29. Weyler, *Blood of the Land: The Government and Corporate War Against the American Indian Movement*; Al Gedricks, "Resource Wars in Chippewa Country," in *Native Americans and Energy Development II*, ed. J. Jorgensen (Boston: Anthropology Resource Center, 1984), 175-194.

30. Weyler, *Blood on the Land: The Government and Corporate War Against the American Indian Movement*; Lynn Robbins, "Energy Development and the Navajo Nation: An Update," in *Native American and Energy Development II*, ed. J. Jorgensen (Boston: Anthropology Resource Center, 1984), 146-175.

31. Weyler, *Blood on the Land: The Government and Corporate War Against the American Indian Movement*;

Robbins "Energy Development and the Navajo Nation," 146-175.

32. Nancy Owens, "Can Tribes Control Energy Development," in *Native Americans and Energy Development*, ed. J. Jorgensen (Boston: Anthropology Resource Center, 1978), 62.

33. Ibid., 49-63.

34. Wallerstein, *The Capitalist World Economy*, 231-282.

35. Ibid.

36. Joane Nagel and Susan Olzak, "Ethnic Mobilization in New and Old States: An Extension of the Competition Model," *Social Problems* 30 (1982): 127-143.

37. Ibid.

38. Tom Arrandale, "American Indian Economic Development," *Editorial Research Reports* 1 (1984): 127-144; John Mohawk, "Small, Indian and Beautiful: Development Through Appropriate Technology," *Indian Studies* 1 (1984): 8-9.

Chapter XIV

The Changing Political and Economic Status of the American Indians: From Captive Nations to Internal Colonies

C. Matthew Snipp

ABSTRACT. *Resource development* on *American Indian lands* is bringing about a dramatic transformation of the political and economic status of *American Indians*. Recently, scholars observing this change have increasingly used *underdevelopment* theory to explain the nature of these changes. However, this discussion points out that as applied to *American Indians,* the perspective of underdevelopment theory is skewed in several important ways. Specifically, it fails to take into account the distinctive historical and political status of Indians in *American society.* A simple typology, *captive nations* and *internal colonies* is proposed for describing the *status* of *Indian tribes* before and after *development.*

I

Introduction

No other minority group in America can claim the sovereign legal and political status traditionally occupied by American Indians. This status stems from special agreements between American Indians and the Federal Government. The broader significance of these arrangements is seldom recognized by most social scientists. Even fewer are aware that the industrialized world's growing desire for inexpensive natural resources is moving Federal-Indian relations in significant new directions.

For sociologists interested in the global expansion of modern capitalism and its by-products, the changing status of American Indians graphically illustrates the processes related to political subjugation and economic exploitation. Against the background of two major themes in development literature, this paper sketches a simple typology for

371

describing the changing political status of Indian tribes, and the redefinition of their role in the national economy.

An exhaustive review of the development literature relevant to this typology is beyond the scope of this paper. Instead, a few key ideas are highlighted for the purpose of amplifying a concept advocated by historian D'Arcy McNickle and his colleagues.[1] They characterize the historic status of American Indians in law and public policy as "captive nations." This term describes the limited political autonomy of tribal governments, and reflects the relative isolation and detachment of Indians from the mainstream of American society and economic life.[2] As captive nations, tribes are subject to the higher political authority of the U.S. Government but in other respects, their lands are closed enclaves outside of American society.

Resource development on tribal land is reshaping the authority of tribal governments as they seek to control the flow of raw materials into the national economy. The relationship they have with American society is increasingly colonial and their insularity is steadily eroding. These changes signify a new political and economic status for American Indians as "internal colonies."

II

American Indians and Resource Development

The enigma of American Indians juxtaposes their low economic standing with their control of scarce and potentially valuable natural resources. In addition to large reserves of energy resources, American Indians also have substantial holdings in water, fishing, lumber, and pristine recreation areas.[3] For instance, in 1974 commercial forests occupied 5.5 million acres of Indian land and produced nearly $68 million worth of lumber.[4] Yet the median family income of Indian households was $13,724 in 1979 compared to $20,835 for White households in the same year.[5] Understanding how this situation came to exist, and what the eventual impact of development will mean for American Indians is complicated by their diversity. Vast differences exist between tribes in terms of their history, culture, views toward development, and sophistication in dealing with non-Indians. This diversity defies broad generalizations.

Tribal differences are especially critical because they provide the context and limiting conditions for statements about the changing status of Indians. In relation to natural resource development, three important distinctions include (1) the type of resource to which a tribe has access; (2) the scale of development, especially in capital intensity and, (3) the historical period in which development occurs. It would be a serious mistake to expect that all reservations are equally endowed with the same resources, or that the extent of development is consistent across reservations. Indeed, some tribes have consciously resisted development in favor of a more traditional lifestyle.

In recent years, federal bureaucrats, the popular press, academics, and some major U.S. corporations have taken an especially ardent interest in tribal affairs. This attention from disparate quarters of American society is primarily directed at a small group of tribes known for their reserves of energy resources. These tribes are frequently referred to as "energy resource" tribes and are represented by an organization known as the Council of Energy Resource Tribes (CERT) through a loose cartel agreement. They control vast amounts of energy-related resources such as coal, oil, gas, shale, and uranium. Some estimates suggest that 23 tribes control 33 percent of the nation's strippable low sulphur coal, 80 percent of U.S. uranium reserves, and between 3 and 10 percent of domestic reserves in gas and oil.[6] Only a small fraction of these reserves is being actively developed, and among these twenty-three tribes are some of the poorest segments of the Indian population, the Navajo and Cheyenne for example.[7]

Another important consideration is that Indian tribes do not share equally in resource development and exemplify a state of uneven development. In terms of development, some tribes have opted for actively exploiting their resources while others have acted with more restraint.[8] In absolute value, some tribes have resources which are larger or more valuable than others; a barrel of oil is worth more than a barrel of water. Likewise, some tribes have one type of resource while other tribes are rich in another type, and some have none at all. For example, the tribes in the plains and mountain states have energy related resources while most lumbering and fishing is limited to a few groups in the Pacific Northwest. For example, fourteen reservations collect 96 percent of all Indian timber revenues.[9]

Many studies of Indian resource development, especially those concerned with energy resource tribes,[10] operate within a narrow historical focus; often limited to a single tribe or a short time period. This is misleading because it creates the impression that the discovery of energy resources on Indian land is recent. The scale and scope of development is relatively new but energy development on Indian land has been on-going since the turn of the century. A small coal lease was negotiated with the Uinta of Utah in 1941 and earlier, in 1911, large reserves of petroleum were found on the Osage reservation of Oklahoma. As early as 1984, the Cherokees of Oklahoma unsuccessfully tried to develop petroleum leases on their land.[11]

III

American Indians and Models of Development

A complete review of development theory is far afield but two models are especially pertinent because they have been used to analyze the impact of social change on American Indians. The early literature on Indian development is dominated by cultural diffusion models emphasizing acculturation and assimilation.[12] Cultural diffusion models embrace themes found in the literature on modernization or "convergence" theory.[13] Recent analyses adopt "critical" or neo-Marxist perspectives that are heavily indebted to the development theories of Baran and Frank.[14] Modernization and critical perspectives both strive to (1) explain the impact of development on Indian tribes; (2) anticipate the likely changes among tribes seeking to become part of this process and, (3) predict the eventual status of tribes lacking resources or declining to develop them. As accurate guides for predicting the effects of development on American Indians, the achievements of the older development theories are dismal and the prospects for the newer theories are uncertain.

Convergence theory postulates a growing similarity between developing and developed nations as an inevitable outcome of economic advancement. As lesser developed societies expand and diversify their economies, they will increasingly resemble more highly industrialized nations in other facets of their social organization—the "melting pot" on a global scale. Cultural diffusion models embrace this idea by viewing economic development as an irresistible force of acculturation and assimilation. In this perspective, western cultural practices are an accoutrement of economic advancement and material well-being.

Cultural diffusion models further stipulate that prolonged contact between distinct cultural groups will eventually result in the adoption and diffusion of cultural practices. Over time, distinct groups become increasingly similar until they are no longer distinguishable as separate cultures.[15] For American Indians, a version of this model posits that cultural exchanges are asymmetric, and over time, they will be absorbed by the dominant White culture. Prolonged contact with White society ordains the disappearance of Indian culture,[16] as its loss facilitates higher levels of social development. The ethnocentrism of this view hardly needs mentioning. Berkhofer[17] notes that it discounts the possibility of cultural adaptation. Once exposed to White society, Indians are expected to adapt their own culture by discarding it.

For decades, this model dominated theoretical anthropology, and for decades, anthropologists awaited the eventual demise and disappearance of American Indians.[18] To their surprise, American Indians did not disappear. Studies repeatedly showed that they retained a strong attachment to traditional values and lifestyles, even in otherwise alien urban environments.[19] This instigated a theoretical crisis, causing one frustrated anthropologist to question "our earlier expectations concerning the rate of American Indian acculturation and why full acculturation to White American ways of life is not occurring in the contemporary American scene."[20]

The persistence of American Indian culture eroded the influence of cultural diffusion models as guides for understanding the impact of development. Besides their inability to explain cultural persistence, cultural diffusion models invited criticism by neglecting the role of social conflict, colonial relations of domination and subordination, and struggles for political power and other societal resources.[21] In their place, development models with an explicit interest in social conflict have become popular. These models posit the existence of two discrete social systems. Initially, these bodies are culturally, economically, and politically distinct. The development of social relations between these groups creates the opportunity for one group to dominate and exploit the other. Colonial relations, for example, are expressly established for domination and exploitation. In this situation, the powerful seek out the weak for their own enrichment.

The growing interest in colonial relationships does not signify a radical departure from the intellectual concerns expressed in cultural diffusion models. Differences between highly developed urban societies and the traditional, or "folk" social structures of native populations once dominated the interests of anthropologists.[22] A focus on colonialism pays less attention to the differences between more and less developed nations, in favor of a much stronger emphasis on the exploitation and inequality in their relationship. Baran's[23] analysis of neo-colonial relations has influenced several contemporary anthropologists.[24] He argues that the developed nations sustain their advantage in the world economy through an asymmetrical exchange of resources with less developed societies. Resources essential for economic production in western nations are extracted from less developed countries that in return, gain few benefits from their exports. In this manner, developed nations grow richer by depleting the resources of weaker countries.

To describe the structure of colonial relationships, Andre Gunder Frank coined the terms "satellite" and "metropolis."[25] According to Frank, less developed societies are economic satellites dominated by the influence of colonial powers, the "metropolis." As Jorgenson,[26] points out, it is important to notice that the "satellite-metropolis" typology does not readily imply a rural-urban distinction. Jorgenson explains that "the term 'metropolis-satellite' is used here rather than 'urban-rural' in a characterization of political economy because the latter implies a city, a locational unit filled with people. 'Metropolis' implies *the concentration of economic and political power and political influence.* 'Urban' and 'metropolis' are not, of course, completely independent. . . ."[27]

In his analysis of western capitalism and its impact on Latin America, Frank argues that Latin America is a satellite of capitalist interests in metropolitan North America and western Europe. In his words, this relationship has led to the "development of underdevelopment" in Latin America. The satellite-metropolis relationship not only fosters underdevelopment in the satellite; the growing impoverishment of the satellite also forces it to become increasingly *dependent* on the metropolis, especially for economic assistance. Dependency theory is also responsible for another idea: internal colonialism. Besides its global character, underdevelopment and dependency also occur between regions and locations within nations. When one area is exploited for the benefit of another, the exploited area is deemed an "internal colony."[28]

Internal colonies, also called periphery areas, are created when one area dominates another to the extent that it channels the flow of resources from the periphery to the dominant core area. Periphery economies are heavily concentrated in extractive or agricultural production that serves the development of the core area, especially by providing raw materials. Hechter[29] adds that ethnocentrism plays a role in the underdevelopment of periphery areas by offering a rationale for cultivating the disadvantaged status of periphery populations.

Since its introduction, the term internal colony has been applied to conditions in developing and developed nations. Applied to the U.S., it has been used to describe the plight of minority populations, especially Blacks.[30] In the last ten years, it also has become popular for describing the situation of native populations. Andre Gunder Frank[31] was one of the first scholars to apply this framework to indigenous societies in his analysis of the status of South American Indians. He argues that the regions they inhabit are internal colonies. These Indians are caught up in the larger forces affecting Latin American underdevelopment, except they suffer disproportionate hardships because they reside within the underdeveloped areas of underdeveloped societies.

Following Frank's example, the concepts of internal colonialism and underdevelopment have found popularity among students of North American Indians.[32] Most of these applications are used for describing the impact of resource development, especially energy resources, on Indian reservations. Analyzing conditions on reservations, these discussions closely follow the standard themes of underdevelopment theory. The underdevelopment perspective makes three points about the status of North American Indians. First, reservations are the exploited satellites and American society is the exploiting metropolis. Second, the relationship between the tribes and the Federal Government has nurtured underdevelopment and dependence in Indian communities. Third, resource development is an invitation for yet greater exploitation and underdevelopment.

This perspective emphasizes that the Bureau of Indian Affairs (BIA) has been instrumental in perpetuating the subordinate, colonized status of Indian reservations. The BIA is blamed for actively cultivating Indian dependencies and for being a willing accomplice to their economic exploitation.[33] Amid these accusations, Nafziger[34] suggests that the BIA is merely an instrument for carrying out policies that serve the interests of the dominant culture in general, and industrial capitalism in particular.

At first glance, models of underdevelopment are appealing explanations for the conditions on Indian reservations. The exploitation of American Indians and their dependence on federal authorities are well known and widely documented. The extraction of natural resources from Indian lands for the greater benefit of the U.S. economy fits especially well with underdevelopment models. However, a closer examination of this perspective reveals that it does not neatly fit the circumstances of American Indians.[35] An overarching problem is that the historical specificity of underdevelopment theory limits its generality from one setting to another. Underdevelopment theory was constructed around the events leading to the conquest and exploitation of Latin America. As useful as these insights may be, they bear no necessary relation to the circumstances of North American

Indians. In particular, the differences between North and South American Indians are sufficiently large that facile comparisons should be discouraged.

Frank[36] locates South American Indians in the periphery of Latin American national development because this population traditionally has been a cheap source of labor. As plantation and factory workers, Latin American Indians share with the peasants—the family and subsistence farmers—the exploitation which accompanies development. As Frank points out,[37] since the arrival of the Spanish, the Indian population of Latin America has provided a valuable source of labor either as slaves or as easily exploited peasants. Unlike their South American counterparts and especially compared to European immigrants, there is little to suggest that the labor of North American Indians, either as farmers or factory workers, made an important contribution to the development of American capitalism. After an analysis of historical data, Jacobson[38] concludes that "In the United States the corporations who benefited from colonization benefited for the most part from the exploitation of Indian lands rather than Indian labor." The mismatch between the original context of underdevelopment theory and the unique historical and political status of North American Indians can be improved by recognizing three special considerations.

IV

Some Amendments for Underdevelopment Theory

In its present form, the literature dealing with underdevelopment and colonialism has a number of shortcomings in its view of American Indians. In part, these liabilities arise because the special circumstances of North American Indians were never considered in the original discussion of this theoretical perspective. The mismatch between the original context of underdevelopment theory and the unique historical and political status of North American Indians can be improved by recognizing several special considerations.

First, American Indian tribes have a unique status as political sovereigns within the framework of the U.S. political system; no other ethnic minority group in the U.S. enjoys a similar status. Originally, tribal sovereignty was granted in recognition of American Indians as credible military threats. As this threat diminished over time, the authority of tribal governments became embedded in law through treaty negotiations and in federal case law. The authority granted by tribal sovereignty has waxed and waned since the early 19th century but it remains an accepted legal doctrine closely embraced by tribal governments and their supporters. This authority is subordinate to federal powers, but it grants tribal governments with control over reservation development and the power to enter negotiations with non-Indians on behalf of the tribe.[39]

Second, the political separation of American Indians has been reinforced by the geographic and social isolation of Indian tribes from American society. One result of this isolation is that, historically, there has been very little American Indian participation in the U.S. economy. In the 19th century, Indians were viewed as obstacles to progress and removed to isolated reservations away from the mainstreams of economic activity.[40] The cession of tribal lands made the expansion of American capitalism possible but only recently have many tribes and reservations had a role in the American economy, making their satellite status relatively new.

Third, developing Indian lands for the purpose of industrial production confronts Indian people with potentially profound changes in their traditional lifestyles. Before they were subjugated by European powers, American Indians practiced a lifestyle based on hunting and subsistence agriculture. Yielding to the political authority of the United States did not mean that this lifestyle was abandoned. Instead, it was relocated and adapted to the confines of reservations on Indian territory, as in Oklahoma; sometimes in the face of steep opposition from authorities. More recently, resource development poses a difficult dilemma for many tribes as they struggle to reconcile desires for traditional lifestyles with demands for the economic benefits offered by resource development. The interests of traditionalists, reinforced by traditional religious beliefs about the sanctity of nature, are served through the preservation of open land and especially pristine wilderness areas—often the same sites targeted for development. This conflict has been instrumental in slowing the rate of development on several reservations.[41]

Fourth, conquest and removal did not bring revolutionary changes in the economic base of many tribes; most American Indians continued hunting and agriculture for their livelihood. However, developments in the 19th century brought about major changes in their political status. Prior to economic development and their appearance in the periphery of the U.S. economy, American Indians practiced their traditional lifestyles in the face of an increasingly complex political environment affecting their right of self-government and notably, control over the use of their land. Unlike many colonial situations, military conquest and subsequent occupation of their land did not immediately lead to economic development. Instead, many tribes spent an earlier interregnum period during which they were quarantined from White society and made dependent on the agents of the Federal Government, especially the Bureau of Indian Affairs. During this period, there was a wholesale redefinition of the political status of American Indians which established the scope of control of federal authorities over Indian land, and especially how it eventually would be developed.

The earlier phase of development in Indian-White relations is important because it foreshadows the present satellite status of the tribes involved with resource development. For these tribes, the era preceding the development of their resources is critical because it describes the antecedent political conditions that facilitate existing economic relationships between Indian satellites and non-Indian metropolises. This also reveals a significant gap in underdevelopment theory in so far as it offers few insights about the structure of Indian-White relations preceding any satellite-metropolis configuration.

There is a conceptual element needed in the under-development vocabulary to express the pre-colonial status of American Indians. In this respect, a simple typology for describing the transition of Indian reservations from their isolated pre-development origins to their developing status as periphery regions fills an important gap in the conceptual framework of underdevelopment theory. Thoroughly exploring the implications of this typology is not possible in this brief discussion. However, the goal of this typology is to broadly outline how Indian-White relations are being altered by developing natural resources on tribal lands.[42]

Tribal land development, especially natural resource exploitation for consumption outside the reservation, signals a new era in tribal history and marks the end of an old one. This transition is significant because it represents a basic restructuring of the tribe's relationship with the U.S. economy. Framing this transition, the terms *"captive nations"* and *"internal colonies"* are a pair of simple, though heuristically useful categories for delineating two major stages of tribal development. The expression "captive nations"[43] defines the status of American Indian tribes prior to the development of tribal resources for nontribal consumption. For those tribes without resources or development, "captive nationhood" reflects their existing relationship with nonIndian society. For tribes in the midst of development, their situation can be plausibly compared with the conditions associated with internal colonialism. The term "internal colony," in its conventional usage, is a new status for many tribes as the resources they harbor become more valuable and sought after.

V

Discussion

Empirical data for documenting the transition from captive nation to internal colony is not readily available. By its nature, this process gradually occurs over long periods of time. For this reason, the rationale behind this typology is based on historical developments in the relationship between Indian tribes and the United States. These developments span a long period in American history beginning in colonial times and reaching into the present. In a subsequent article, I will review the major historical developments related to the emergence of internal colonies from captive nations. However, there are several key points to remember about this typology.

The first point is that the status of "captive nation" is defined mainly in political terms. Captive nationhood describes the limited amount of self-rule that Indian tribes exercised following their submission to the authority of the Federal Government. Prior to captive nationhood, many Indian tribes were fully independent of European powers. For example, tribes such as the Iroquois regularly maintained political alliances with the French and the English, and as recently as the Civil War, the Cherokee tribe established a formal alliance with the Confederacy. The redefinition of the political status of American Indians was accomplished through military and bureaucratic actions, yet the rights of political autonomy and self-government were not completely stripped. As a result, tribal authorities still enjoy a measure of political power that is highly circumscribed, not as independent nations but as captives. Some tribes such as the Creeks and Cherokees continue to refer to themselves as "nations."

As American Indians gave up their sovereign political powers to become captive nations, they did not experience a comparable revolution in their economic life. However, the status of captive nation paved the way for internal colonization by making formerly self-sustaining Indian tribes dependent upon federal authorities. As a matter of stated policy, for good and bad reasons, American Indians were made "wards" of the State with federal authorities, primarily the BIA, assuming extensive oversight responsibilities for the management of remaining Indian lands. Since becoming federal wards, Indians have continued to rely heavily on activities such as hunting, fishing and subsistence agriculture for their subsistence. However, as the resources on their land have become more valuable, many tribes are facing a revolution in their economic life unmatched since the redefinition of their political status in the 19th century.

The nature of this revolution is characterized by the changes which accompany the transition from captive nation to internal colony. The most profound change brought about by this transition is that American Indians are subject to entirely new forms of economic dominance, in addition to the older forms of political dominance exercised by the federal government. The types of economic relations associated with internal colonialism are a relatively new set of contingencies among people accustomed to relatively simple forms of economic activity. However, as resource development intensifies on Indian lands, internal colonization is almost certain to become more prevalent as the political dominance of earlier times gives way to newer and more complex forms of economic and political relations.

NOTES

1. D'Arcy McNickle, Mary E. Young, and Roger Buffalohead, "Captives Within a Free Society," in American Indian Policy Review Commission (AIPRC), *Final Report of the American Indian Policy Review Commission,* (Washington, D.C.: U.S. Government Printing Office, 1977), Chapter 1, 47-82.

2. McNickle, et al., are not the first scholars to use the expression "captive nation." Political scientists also use this term to describe the satellite status of Eastern Bloc nations in relation to the Soviet Union.

3. Americans for Indian Opportunity (AIO), *Indian Tribes as Developing Nations; A Question of Power: Indian Control of Indian Resource Development,* (Albuquerque, NM: Americans for Indian Opportunity, Inc., 1975), 1-9; Sar A. Levitan, and William B. Johnston, *Indian Giving: Federal Programs for Native Americans,* (Baltimore: Johns Hopkins Univ. Press, 1975), 124-150; Sam Stanley, ed., *American Indian Economic Development,* (The Hague: Mouton Publishers, 1978), Chapter 1, "Introduction," 2-14.

4. Levitan and Johnston, op. cit., 25.

5. U.S. Bureau of the Census, *Detailed Population Characteristics, United States Summary, Section A: United States,* (Washington, D.C.: U.S. Government Printing Office, 1984).

6. Joseph G. Jorgenson, Richard O. Clemmer, Ronald L. Little, Nancy J. Owens and Lynn A. Robbins, *Native Americans and Energy Development,* (Cambridge, MA: Anthropology Resource Center, 1978), 6.

7. Ibid., 5.

8. Stan Albrecht, "Energy Development: prospects and implications for Native Americans," paper presented at the annual meetings of the Society for the Study of Social Problems, 1977.

9. Levitan and Johnston, op. cit., 25.

10. Jorgenson et al., op. cit.; Roxanne Dunbar Ortiz, *Economic Development in American Indian Reservations,* (Sante Fe, NM: Native American Studies, University of Mexico, 1979); Lorraine Turner Ruffing, "Navajo Economic Development: a dual perspective," in Sam Stanley, ed., *American Indian Economic Development,* (The Hague: Mouton Publishers, 1978), 15-86.

11. H. Craig Miner, *The Corporation and the Indian: tribal sovereignty and industrial civilization in Indian territory, 1865-1907,* (Columbia, MO: Univ. of Missouri Press, 1976), 147-62.

12. J. Milton Yinger, and George Eaton Simpson, "The Integration of Americans of Indian Descent," *Annals of the American Academy of Political and Social Science,* 436, (1978), 137-51.

13. W. W. Rostow, *The Stages of Economic Growth,* (Cambridge: Cambridge Univ. Press, 1960); Bert F. Hoselitz, and Wilbert E. Moore, eds., *Industrialization and Society,* (Mouton: UNESCO, 1966); Neil J. Smelser and Seymour M. Lipset, "Social Structure, Mobility and Development," in Neil J. Smelser and Seymour M. Lipset, eds., *Social Structure and Mobility in Economic Development,* (Chicago: Aldine, 1966).

14. Paul Baran, *The Political Economy of Growth,* (New York: Monthly Review Press, 1957); Andre Gunder Frank, *Capitalism and Underdevelopment in Latin America: historical studies of Chile and Brazil,* (New York: Monthly Review Press, 1967).

15. Milton M. Gordon, *Assimilation in American Life: the role of race, religion, and natural origins,* (New York: Oxford Univ. Press, 1964).

16. Yinger and Simpson, op. cit., 142-43.

17. Robert F. Berkhofer, Jr., *The White Man's Indian: images of the American Indian from Columbus to the present,* (New York: Random House, 1979), 28-29.

18. Ralph Linton, *Acculturation in Seven American Indian Tribes,* (New York: Appleton-Century, 1940), Chapter 10, 501-20.

19. Prodipto Roy, "The Measurement of Assimilation: the Spokane Indians," *American Journal of Sociology* 67, (1962), 541-51; Joan Ablon, "Relocated American Indians in the San Francisco Bay Area: social interactions and Indian

identity," *Human Organization* 23, (1964), 296-304; Lynn C. White, and Bruce A. Chadwick, "Urban Residence, Assimilation, and Identity of the Spokane Indian," in Howard M. Bahr, Bruce A. Chadwick and Robert C. Day, eds., *Native Americans Today: sociological perspectives,* (New York: Harper and Row, 1972); Bruce A. Chadwick and Joseph H. Stauss, "The Assimilation of American Indians: the Seattle case," *Human Organization,* 34, (1975), 359-69.

20. Evon Z. Vogt, "The Acculturation of American Indians," *Annals of the American Academy of Political and Social Science,* 311, (1957), 137-46.

21. Joseph G. Jorgenson, "A Century of Political Economic Effects on American Indian Society, 1880-1980," *Journal of Ethnic Studies* 6, (1968), 1-82.

22. Redfield is credited with the distinction between "folk" and "urban" societies and for his work on analyzing the differences between these two types of cultures. Redfield's work was later disputed by Lewis which resulted in a major controversy in the anthropological literature. See Robert Redfield, "The Folk Society," *American Journal of Sociology,* 52, (1947), 293-298, and Oscar Lewis, "Tepoztlan Revisited," *Rural Sociology,* 18 (1953), 121-36.

23. Baran, op. cit.

24. Joseph G. Jorgenson, "Indians and the Metropolis," Chapter 2 in Jack O. Waddell and O. Michael Watson, eds. *The American Indian in Urban Society,* (Boston: Little, Brown and Company, 1971); Jorgenson, op. cit.; Nancy Oestreich Lurie, "Menominee Termination: from reservation to colony," *Human Organization,* 31 (1972), 257-70; Ruffing, op. cit.

25. Gunder Frank, op. cit.

26. Jorgenson, op. cit.

27. Ibid., 84.

28. Gunder Frank, op. cit.

29. Michael Hechter, *Internal Colonialism,* (Berkeley: Univ. of California Press, 1975).

30. Robert Blauner, "Internal Colonialism and Ghetto Revolt," *Social Problems,* 16 (1969), 393-408; William K. Tabb, *The Political Economy of the Black Ghetto,* (New York: W. W. Norton, 1970).

31. Gunder Frank, op. cit., 123-42. Although an early application, Andre Gunder Frank was not the first to use this

perspective. An even earlier discussion of colonialism and American Indians is Everett E. Hagen and Louis B. Schaw, *The Sioux on the Reservation: an American colonial problem,* (Cambridge, Mass.: Center for International Studies, 1960) and Everett E. Hagen, *On the Theory of Social Change,* (Homewood, Ill.: The Dorsey Press, 1962).

32. Lurie Oestreich, op. cit.; Nancy J. Owens, "Indian Reservations and Bordertowns: the metropolis-satellite model applied to the northwestern Navajos and Umatillas," Ph.D. Dissertation in anthropology, University of Oregon, (1976); Robert Bee, and Ronald Gingerich, "Colonialism, Causes, and Ethnic Identity: Native Americans and the National Political Economy," *Studies in Comparative International Development,* 12 (1977), 70-93; Mel Watkins, ed., *Dene Nation: the colony within,* (Toronto: Univ. of Toronto Press, 1977); Jorgenson, op. cit.; Turner Ruffing, op. cit.; Gary Anders, "The Internal Colonization of Cherokee Native Americans," *Development and Change,* 10, (1979), 41-55; Gary Anders, "Theories of Underdevelopment and the American Indian, *Journal of Economic Issues,* 40, (1980), 681-701; Gary Anders, "The Reduction of a Self-Sufficient People to Poverty and Welfare Dependence: an analysis of the causes of Cherokee Indian underdevelopment," *American Journal of Economics and Sociology,* 40, (1981), 225-37; Roxanne Dunbar Ortiz, *Economic Development in American Indian Reservations,* (Santa Fe, NM: Native American Studies, University of New Mexico, 1979); Roxanne Dunbar Ortiz, *American Indian Energy Resources and Development,* (Santa Fe, NM: Native American Studies, University of New Mexico, 1980); Richard Nafziger, "Transnational Corporations and American Indian Development," in Roxanne Dunbar Ortiz, ed., *American Indian Energy Resources and Development,* (Santa Fe, NM: Native American Studies, University of New Mexico, 1980), 9-38; Cardell K. Jacobson, "Internal Colonialism and Native Americans: Indian labor in the United States from 1871 to World War II," *Social Science Quarterly,* 65, (1984), 158-71.

33. Anders, "Internal" op. cit.; Anders, "Theories," op. cit.; Anders, "Reduction," op. cit.; Nafziger, "Transnational Corporations," op. cit., 9-38.

34. Nafziger, ibid.

35. These numbers are illustrative but they should be regarded with caution. Even in recent censuses, federal data are notoriously inaccurate for American Indians.

36. Gunder Frank, op. cit.

37. Ibid.

38. Jacobson, op. cit., 169.

39. It is true that petty exploitation was widely practiced by licensed traders and other agents of the Federal Government. Thomas Jefferson is generally credited with founding the trading outpost system which used a variety of deceits to keep Indians dependent on traders (DeRosier, 1970).

40. H. Craig Miner, *The Corporation and the Indian: tribal sovereignty and industrial civilization in Indian territory, 1865-1907,* (Columbia, MO: University of Missouri press, 1976).

41. Jim Richardson, and John A. Farrell, "The New Indian Wars," *Denver Post,* Special Reprint, November 20-27, 1983.

42. Another dimension of this issue concerns the wisdom of the trade-off between traditional lifestyles and economic development. According to Richardson and Farrell (1983, 19-25), many tribal leaders believe that economic development is possible without sacrificing too many elements of traditional culture. Whether this belief is justified remains to be seen.

43. This term is borrowed from McNickle et al., op. cit.

Chapter XV

Native American Gaming Operations

Due to extreme poverty, a lack of revenue-producing resources, and reductions in Federal aid, Native American tribes have recently become involved in the gaming industry in the hope of generating economic development and a higher degree of tribal self-sufficiency. Gaming, including high-stakes bingo, casino, and animal racing operations, has become a popular venture among Native American tribes since the first high stakes bingo parlor opened in Florida in 1979. In the last thirteen years, more than one hundred tribes in twenty-three states have hoped to improve their economic situations by taking advantage of their reservations' sovereign, tax-exempt status. In 1988, the United States Supreme Court ruled that a state is obliged to allow native tribes to engage in high stakes operation of any gaming venture legal in that state. In response to this ruling, the U.S. Congress passed the "Indian Gaming Regulation Act" in 1988, which established the National Indian Gaming Regulatory Commission (NIGC). The commission, headed by entertainer Bob Hope's son Tony Hope, is charged with the regulation of all legal gambling operations on Native American lands. Due to its slow start, low budget and laissez-faire philosophy, the NIGC has been largely ineffective. In spite of the commission's existence, many tribes have found that corruption, Mafia involvement, incompetence, and tribal warfare have prevented the generation of a sizable income for tribal education, medicine, and infrastructure.

A handful of tribes have enjoyed success in the gaming industry, and have seen their dreams of a better life for tribal members realized. Many other tribes, however, have seen their hopes dashed by greed, corruption, and warfare. In general, those tribes which have been successful have been those which have maintained direct control over their bingo parlors and casino resorts. Tribes which have allowed external concerns to operate on their lands in exchange for a percentage of the profit have generally found themselves victims of smooth, unscrupulous professionals.

Currently, the NIGC's only major role is to ensure that no convicted felon may serve as the manager of a Native American Gaming operation. The commission could prevent much of the corruption and tragedy of the industry by playing a more active role in the regulation of Native American gaming.

—RNW

389

The Future of Gambling in Indian Country

Gary Sokolow

Background and Scope

This article will analyze the legislative and legal issues that arise from gambling on Indian reservations. First, a general overview of Indian country gaming will be presented. Next, the federal government's attempt, through existing laws and proposed legislation, to deal with this situation will be discussed. A review of pending legislation will be emphasized. The existing case law will then be analyzed. Finally, an analysis of competing federal, tribal and state interests in gambling regulation will be discussed, followed by a look at future prospects.

The federal government has regulated gambling in Indian country only since 1924. Traditional Indian games were not the focus of these regulations. In that year, the Bureau of Indian Affairs (BIA) adopted tribal gaming ordinances for the purposes of its Code of Federal Regulation Courts.[1] Only recently has Indian gaming become a significant economic activity in Indian country.

In a June 17, 1986 survey, the Department of the Interior reported that 108 tribes had gaming facilities, 104 of them involving bingo.[2] Some tribes operate both bingo and card games, and others run only card games.[3] No tribes are currently known to operate pari-mutuel dog racing, horse racing, or jai-alai. Gross receipts of all tribes conducting such activities exceeds $100 million annually.[4]

The tribes, like other governmental entities, use these revenues largely for the economic, educational, and health benefit of their members. The expansion of gaming into Indian country and the recent proliferation of court decisions on the subject have aroused the interest of both the states and the Congress.

Federal Regulation of Gambling in Indian Country

Assimilative Crimes Act (ACA)

To date, Congress has not seen fit to directly regulate Indian gambling activities. However, the federal government is not without remedies to apply against the existence of such operations. These so-called "remedies" are in the form of criminal prosecutions, which seek to ban such activities, rather than merely regulate the time, place, and form of gambling. The first such possible "remedy" is the Assimilative Crimes Act (ACA), which allows federal officials to punish those crimes which are not included in the federal criminal code, by applying the applicable state law.[5] The ACA is an interstitial measure, reflecting the fact that the states, and not the federal government, are the usual arbiters of criminal conduct.[6] At least one commentator has suggested, however, that the ACA is not an independent basis of federal jurisdiction over these activities.[7] He suggested that the ACA is applicable to Indian reservations only through the General Crimes Act (GCA),[8] subjecting it to the exceptions of the GCA\CA, and as a result, since non-Indian matters are exempt from GCA coverage, the ACA would therefore not then apply to non-Indians.[9]

This interpretation is not unanimously accepted. Another writer takes the view that the ACA is a mere transformation of state law into federal law.[10] Under this view, federal regulation would simply turn on whether a state had outlawed such activity. Federal officials would then have to regulate gambling activity on a state-by-state basis, determining whether or not that state regulated or prohibited gambling. Such an analysis will be discussed later in the context of Public Law 280[11] and the civil/regulatory-criminal/prohibitory analysis. The ACA is not a very solid basis on which to regulate Indian gambling. The word "regulate" implies some form of permission, as opposed to the outright ban of the activity in question.

Gambling Devices Act

Another form of federal control of gambling, albeit a specialized one, is the Gambling Devices Act (GDA), which generally bans the use of certain gambling devices.[12] The GDA specifically prohibits the use of such devices as slot machines in Indian country.[13] However, the GDA prohibits only certain gambling paraphernalia, not the conduct of games per se. But if the federal government wants to stop the use of slot machines, for example, this act effectively cripples such gaming operations. That is what occurred in "United States v. Sousseur."[14] However, "Sousseur" relied on the ACA to allow the seizure of slot machines, since state law prohibited the use of such equipment. In "Sousseur," neither the United States nor the tribe had such a law or ordinance prohibiting the use of slot machines.[15]

Two federal cases which have construed the GDA held that while the United States may seize such gambling devices on Indian reservations, the GDA does not extend to the regulation of the conduct of gambling itself.[16] The GDA, like the ACA, is of limited application, especially in the bingo context, as many of the games do not utilize such equipment as the GDA defines.

Organized Crime Control Act of 1970

A far more potent weapon in the hands of federal regulators is the Organized Crime Control Act of 1970 (OCCA),[17] which is a general federal law of national application prohibiting large scale gambling. The OCCA makes it a federal crime to operate a gambling business "that is a violation of the law of a state . . . in which it is conducted."[18] As its name implies, the OCCA was passed largely to take aim at organized crime.[19] There is nothing in its legislative history which suggests that the authors of the act had Native American gambling activities in mind.[20] The wording of this statute raises two issues concerning its enforcement in Indian country.

The first question concerns infringement on the "ability of tribes to make their own laws and be governed by them"—the "Williams v. Lee"[21] infringement test. The Sixth

Circuit, in "United States v. Dakota," decided that the OCCA applies to Indian country in Michigan because the OCCA extends federal, not state jurisdiction into Indian country, thus precluding any infringement of state authority over Indian tribes.[22] That case found that the infringement test did not apply because the "Williams" test concerns state and not federal government infringement upon tribal sovereignty.[23] "Dakota" merely followed the prevailing analysis on this issue. The court also upheld the enforcement of the OCCA in Indian country, since the elements of the crime as set forth in the OCCA and the relevant state law were present.[24]

The second question involved is whether a general federal law such as the OCCA can be applied in Indian country, absent a clear indication by Congress to that effect. "United States v. Farris," a Ninth Circuit case, held that the OCCA does apply in Indian country.[25] The court simply reasoned that unless Congress says to the contrary, federal laws apply with equal force in Indian country.[26]

The implications raised in this second question in "Farris" are not nearly so clear as is the infringement issue. To take the "Farris" holding to its logical conclusion further modifies the well-established case law, which holds that tribes (at least those federally recognized) possess some measure of inherent sovereignty. Tribal sovereignty is again curtailed. To hold that all federal laws apply unless specifically exempted by Congress, greatly diminishes inherent tribal sovereignty. No nation expects to live by another sovereign's laws without that nation's consent. Nonetheless, the "Farris" view, echoing "United States v. Montana" and "United States v. Wheeler," is the prevailing view on that point.[27] Finally, "Farris" found that Congress never intended to allow Indians to freely engage in the very gambling activities that it forbade other citizens.[28]

The Public Law 280 status of a state is not a factor which affects the applicability of the OCCA in Indian country But we need not apply the prohibitory/regulatory dichotomy to the OCCA to determine whether or not gambling activity violates state law. "Dakota" and "Barona Group of Capitan Grande Band of Mission Indians v. Duffy" confirmed this, the latter case holding that the true test of the applicability of the OCCA is "whether [the] tribal activity is [a violation of state law] . . . depends on whether it is contrary to the public policy of the state."[29]

It should be realized that the OCCA, like the ACA and the GDA, does not give states themselves the right to enforce these laws, which would give rise to infringement problems. There is nothing in any of these acts which suggests that states may use them to enforce their own statutes, even though the ACA and the OCCA borrow state law in order to find violations of federal law. This "borrowing" of state law is consistent with constitutional and case law, which gives Congress "plenary" powers to regulate dealings with the Indian tribes.[30] To date, the United States Department of Justice has not vigorously enforced the OCCA, perhaps because recent federal policy supports tribal economic self-sufficiency.[31]

Proposed Congressional Regulation

Ninety-Eighth Congress

Only in the last few years has Congress moved to regulate gambling activity on Indian reservations. Congressional interest in this issue began in the Ninety-Eighth Congress with House Bill 4566, which sought to impose federal licensing requirements on Indian gambling enterprises, with a governmental commission within the Interior Department supervising the entire scheme.[32] The operation of this legislation was somewhat analogous to the Nevada Gaming Commission, which closely regulates the employment of workers, the licensing or gambling establishments, and the operating rules of the gaming industry. The Nevada commission also requires extensive disclosure of employee and operator financial interests.

House Bill 4566 was introduced in response to "Seminole Tribe of Florida v. Butterworth," which held that under certain circumstances, states cannot regulate bingo on an Indian reservation.[33] This bill died in committee and it was not heard from again in that Congress. Support for the bill was decidedly mixed among Indian communities. One group of tribes supported it as a clarification of existing law.[34] Other groups opposed it on grounds of infringement upon tribal sovereignty.[35]

Ninety-Ninth Congress

In 1985, with the Ninety-Ninth Congress, several bills on this subject were again introduced. The most noteworthy were Senate Bill 902, Senate Bill 2557, and House Bill 1920. Senate Bill 902 established certain federal standards for Indian gaming, with Secretarial approval required of tribal ordinances and management contracts.[36] A gambling commission was also established in that bill, but its powers and structure were not delineated. The standards for the tribal gaming ordinances and resolutions required that they be "at least as restrictive as [the] prevailing state law."[37] Thus, the tribe might as well adopt the state law on the subject, as it is left with no real choice of its own.

Much more comprehensive in scope than Senate Bill 902 was House Bill 1920, which set up a National Indian Gaming Commission, acting for the Secretary of the Interior, which again was required to approve of tribal ordinances and management contracts. This legislation also required that revenues generated from the gambling on the reservation only be used to support tribal governmental functions.[38] In this bill, for the first time three classes of gambling were established: Class I covered the traditional Indian forms of gaming and gave the tribes exclusive jurisdiction to regulate them; Class II included such games as bingo, which required commission approval of ordinances regulating same, thus giving the tribes and federal government concurrent jurisdiction over such gaming; and finally, Class III gaming included all other forms of gambling such as pari-mutual wagering on horse and dog racing, and jai-alai.[39] The jurisdictional aspects of Class III gambling are unclear from a reading of the bill.

Under House Bill 1920, the review of management contracts was the second area of major authority given the commission.[40] Evidently, there had been some overreaching by outside (non-tribal) management firms hired to run the gambling enterprises. Such overreaching occurred when the outsiders took a disproportionate share of the profits, when they did not account to the tribes for their income, and when they signed contracts for an unduly long period of years. On this last point, one case of a twenty-year contract term has been reported. House Bill 1920 curbs overreaching by setting a maximum contract term of five years, requiring strict accountability standards, and excluding felons from participating in these enterprises.[41] Under this bill, a member of the tribe's governing body is excluded from having any interest in the management contract.[42]

Finally, under House Bill 1920 a tribe need not be federally recognized to be subject to this bill. It is sufficient for the tribe merely to be eligible for services provided Native Americans by the Secretary of the Interior.[43] These two definitions are not necessarily the same. The latter one broadly includes those tribes ineligible for, or that may have not yet completed, the BIA's formal tribal acknowledgment process, but nonetheless under certain statutes qualify for certain services. Native Hawaiians are an example of one group who do not qualify for federal recognition as an Indian tribe, yet they are eligible for certain Native American programs administered by the Secretary of the Interior. Lands which fall subject to this bill include Indian reservations and, under certain circumstances, newly acquired tribal lands.

The Reagan Administration then had Senate Bill 2557 introduced as its answer to the emerging problems of Indian gambling.[44] This measure was a response to the perceived inadequacies of House Bill 1920. Assistant Attorney General John Bolton, in summarizing his objections to House Bill 1920, cited a lack of rigorous regulation in the form of strict licensing procedures and accounting and auditing procedures.[45]

There were several significant differences between Senate Bill 2557 and other bills which came both before and after it. Under this bill, tribally operated bingo would be forbidden in any state which does not also permit bingo, an apparent answer to court holdings which have construed Public Law 280 in a gaming context. The commission's operating expenses would be assessed against the tribally operated bingo operations. A major difference between this bill and others was its concentration on bingo, to the exclusion of other forms of gambling. Senate Bill 2557 regulated gambling in terms of bingo and little else. The regulatory scheme established by House Bill 1920, however, was more detailed than in any bills previously considered.

Like House Bill 1920, Senate Bill 2557 provided criminal sanctions in Title 18 of the United States Code for violations. Unauthorized gambling offenses would be handled in a manner similar to the ACA, inasmuch as these sanctions would apply prevailing state law and subject the offender to the same punishment as the state would mete out for like offenses.[46] A separate section on theft carried its own fines and imprisonment sanctions.[47] These sanctions effectively created concurrent state and federal jurisdiction over violations of state gambling laws in Indian country. Specific language in Senate Bill 2557 delegated to the states the jurisdiction to try such cases, unless the "circumstances justify" a federal prosecution.[48] Justifiable circumstances were not further clarified in the legislation. Lastly, the bill created a special class of crimes, using state law, which granted concurrent jurisdiction in both the federal and state governments.

One Hundredth Congress

These bills also died in Congress, failing to either come up for a vote in the appropriate House and Senate committee, or to get a do pass committee recommendation for a full House and Senate floor vote. More recently, the 100th Congress considered Senate Bill 555, introduced on Feb. 19, 1987 by Senators Daniel Inouye (D.-Hawaii) and Thomas Daschle (D.-S.D.). Both serve on the Select Committee on Indian Affairs, the former as committee chairman.

This bill was similar in form to the previous ones. Its authors justified it on the basis that the patchwork nature of Indian jurisdiction made application of criminal laws in Indian country somewhat unsettled. Further justification was the need to clarify the legal status of gambling in Indian country.[49] Inouye and Daschle also found the need to shield the tribes from the corrupting influences of organized crime (though only one such incident has been documented).

In the definitional section of the bill, "Indian lands" were defined as those within a reservation or held in trust by the United States for any person or tribe, or lands "held by any tribe or individual subject to restrictions by the United States against alienation and over which an Indian tribe exercises governmental power."[50] It is conceivable, then, that a gambling establishment could be put on land within the reservation which is owned by an individual tribe member, subject only to tribal jurisdiction. That individual would then be able to receive rent payments from that gaming operation on his land.

Under section 7 of this bill, a National Indian Gaming Commission would have wide-ranging powers to regulate the conduct of gambling. Only two of the five commission members must be members of a federally recognized Indian tribe. As a result, Indian gaming could be controlled by non-Indians. That possible result is clearly inconsistent with the often repeated federal policy of tribal self-determination. The Commission could conduct audits, inspect all books and gaming premises, and generally monitor Indian gaming activities.[51]

Like House Bill 1920, Senate Bill 555 established three classes of gaming, with the jurisdictional schemes remaining identical to the earlier bill. There were two requirements, however, for a tribe to engage in Class II gaming (bingo-type games). The first directed the tribe to enact an ordinance regulating such activity, and second, this gaming must not be of a type completely prohibited by a state.[52] For the purposes of the bill, if a state permits gambling in some form, however limited, then the second requirement for Class II gambling would be met. Apparently, that requirement was designed with the prohibitory/regulatory Public Law 280 analysis in mind. Such activity would be prohibited in Indian country if the state in which the reservation is located also prohibits it. The tribe may then regulate Class II gambling, subject to Commission supervision of certain details of the operation. A tribe must also meet the eligibility requirements for a state license. The conduct of Class III gambling would be made a violation of federal law, subject to some very narrow exceptions.[53]

Another restriction upon tribal sovereignty imposed by Senate Bill 555 was the requirement that all gambling revenues be dedicated only to tribal governmental operations or for the welfare of individual tribal members, tribal economic development, other charitable organizations, or to help local government agencies fund their operations. This last point is analogous to a federal grant of impact funds to state and local governments in order to compensate them for the loss of tribal trust lands from the property tax rolls. Tribes may make per capita payments to members, subject to some restrictions: 1) the tribe must have a Secretarial-approved plan for allocation, and 2) all such payments are expressly made subject to the federal individual income tax.[54]

Another significant portion of the bill provided for a transfer of tribal jurisdiction to the state, Public Law 280 notwithstanding, if the tribe elects to be freed from Commission regulation.[55] Any such transfer must be initiated by the tribe and then approved by the Secretary of the Interior, prior to it becoming effective.[56] The bill did not say whether the cessation of tribal jurisdiction is only in relation to civil and criminal incidents arising from the gambling enterprise.[57] Perhaps the ambiguities of this provision made it unlikely that the tribes would use it, fearing that such a consent will "open the floodgates" to the continued erosion of their sovereignty. Apparently, only Class III gambling transferred to state jurisdiction could be held exempt from state assessments for the costs of law enforcement, as long as the revenues derived therefrom are used solely for the general governmental purposes of the tribes.

Section 12 of the bill dealt with the issuance of management contracts, providing in part that contracts may not exceed a term of five years,[58] providing tribes a certain guaranteed minimum payment with a priority over the retirement of developmental and construction costs,[59] and strict financial disclosure (corporate and individual) accounting requirements.[60] The subsection dealing with the minimum guaranteed payment to the tribe was unnecessarily vague. It would allow the tribe to receive virtually nothing if the tribe became a victim of overreaching by an outside management company. A tribe, using its own consultants, could set up its own operation, with a minimum of outside help (at least one all-Indian consulting firm exists to do just that). A steadily increasing number of tribal members attending college would be equipped to make the tribes more self-sufficient, resulting in less dependence on outside help.

Section 14 dealt with civil penalties, allowing the commission chairman to fine and collect up to $25,000 for violations of this act.[61] The alleged violator could appeal such a levy to the full commission.[62] This provision would probably be challenged in court for a built-in conflict of interest, as such fines collected would be used to defray the operating expenses of the commission. The same people fine, collect and expend the funds.

Section 15 of Senate Bill 555 provided an aggrieved defendant the right to appeal a commission-imposed fine to the appropriate federal district court and thence the usual appeals route.[63] Decisions made by the full commission regarding licensure, fines, and other related matters would be considered final agency decisions for the purposes of the Administrative Procedures Act.[64] The Commission was vested with investigative and subpoena powers, but the Attorney General would have the discretion to either enforce or decline to enforce such subpoenas.[65]

Under section 18 of Senate Bill 555, the commission may tax, subject to certain limits, each tribal gaming operation to help defray its expenses.[66] If the tribe operates a thriving Class III gaming operation, it could reduce its tax burden by electing out of the commission's jurisdiction (and subsequent assessments) by requesting a transfer to state jurisdiction. A tribe might have a lower tax burden under state regulation. But the long run effect of such a move would bring with it some high costs, not the least of which would be a further erosion of tribal sovereignty. This would be an additional state encroachment in what has been an exercise of that tribal sovereignty.

Section 20 of the bill permitted, only under very narrow circumstances, the establishment of a gaming operation on newly-acquired (after the enactment date of this act) Indian trust lands. There appeared to be only one exception to the requirement that tribal gaming operations be conducted on new trust lands: the governor of the state involved must give his consent, after determining that such a move would not be "detrimental to the surrounding community."[67]

The effect of this section would likely foreclose a tribe obtaining land in a town or city, off the reservation, and then establishing a casino. A governor would probably accede to such a request only if 1) the area was economically depressed, 2) the tribe agreed to hire a significant number of non-Indian employees, 3) the gaming operation reimbursed the town or state for additional law enforcement expenses, and 4) it was politically safe or advantageous for the governor to do so. On this last point, there may be a great resentment against a tribe establishing what many non-Indians would perceive as an enterprise free of state taxation and regulation. Unfortunately for Native Americans, a vast amount of misinformation abounds regarding their political status as tribes. Citizens might not view such gubernatorial approval as a "righting of past wrongs," regardless of the nature of those wrongs.

At least tribes with an existing reservation could gain additional land with "gaming rights" through land acquired through the settlement of an outstanding land claim.[68] Terminated tribes restored to federal recognition could establish gaming houses on lands they re-acquire pursuant to such a re-recognition.[69] In the final analysis, an existing tribe such as the Oglala Sioux, for the purposes of gambling enterprises, would be subject to their present boundaries. The presumption built into Senate Bill 555 was that no newly acquired lands after the enactment of this bill could be used to establish any Class II or III gambling operations.

Section 23, the final major section of Senate Bill 555, addressed criminal sanctions for violations of this act. Unlike the previous bills that have been discussed, this section exempted Class I and II gaming already regulated by this act.[70] As did the other bills, this section likewise borrowed state law to see if a federal gambling offense has been committed.[71] The major difference between this and previous bills was that the United States has exclusive criminal jurisdiction for violations of this act, with transfer of such jurisdiction to the state subject to tribal consent.[72] To many tribes, this would surely be preferable to state jurisdiction, for historical reasons. Given the proliferation of Indian gaming enterprises, federal criminal sanctions would be sure to put additional burdens on the federal court and penal systems.

Under section 23, theft from gaming establishments by officers, employees, or any one else, was made punishable by fines up to $250,000 and prison terms of up to five years.[73] These criminal provisions would make for an ever-increasing federal presence on the reservations.

At the time of this writing, this bill was pending in the Senate Select Committee on Indian Affairs. House of Representatives Bill 964, which was introduced at the same time as Senate Bill 555, was substantially the same as its Senate counterpart.

Competing Tribal, Federal, and State / Local Interests

Tribal Interests

The concerns which were expressed on earlier bills are the same as those expressed for the currently pending legislation. Fundamentally, the entire argument comes down to the competing interests of all three sovereigns: tribal, federal, and state/local.

The most obvious interests of the tribes on this issue is that of economic development. For example, the Florida Seminole tribe grossed $20 million at all three of its bingo sites in 1982, with a net profit of $2.7 million dollars returned to its 1500 members that year.[74] This is welcome news to those tribes who do not possess an abundance of natural resources. The ability to attract tourists and non-Indian residents alike to the reservation represents a feasible way for a tribe to stabilize its economy.[75] One tribe sees these gambling bills as a way to "legitimize" the tribes' efforts to become truly self-sufficient.[76]

Aware of state concerns as to the stability of these enterprises, some of the tribes, such as the Fon Du Lac of Wisconsin, have enacted comprehensive bingo gambling ordinances which address many of the state and federal concerns of the bills.[77] It appears that the revenue raised from these ongoing enterprises is used to benefit the welfare of tribal members, through tribal expenditures on the health, welfare, and education of tribal members. Unfortunately, at the time of this writing, there is no survey available which indicates precisely how the gambling revenue earned by the various tribes is used. It is not doubted that gambling activities are potentially able to provide employment for members, and in turn, allow increased spending by both the tribe and its members, on and off the reservation. Indeed, tribes such as the small Cabazon Band of Mission Indians count such gambling revenues as its only source of income independent of state or federal government aid.

Tribal sovereignty is the final major Indian interest to be addressed here. The dilution of tribal powers as embodied by these bills is viewed by the tribes as the major problem with this legislation.[78] From the foregoing analysis of these bills, it is evident that just such a weakening of meaningful tribal self-determination may occur. Another layer of bureaucracy would be added within the federal government to "check up" on tribal activities. Federal or state standards, not tribal standards, would apply to the evaluation of prospective Indian gaming ordinances adopted pursuant to this legislation. These bills reach beyond mere Secretarial approval of tribal council ordinances to an ongoing audit and regulation of what are essentially those types of activities usually termed governmental police powers: those of regulating the conduct of business, social, or other enterprises on the reservation.

But at least one Indian group, a body of tribal chairmen solicited by the Interior Department for a study of this issue did not view this legislation as an incursion into tribal sovereignty.[79] Instead, they saw these bills as a way to protect tribal government rights.[80] Just how that would be accomplished was not explained.

Federal Interests

In fact, President Reagan embraced the Nixon Administration's goal of meaningful tribal self-determination.[81] It would appear that encouraging Indian gambling activities would accomplish just that. In a 1983 statement of federal Indian policy, Reagan encouraged tribes to reduce their dependence on the federal government by developing their economies, and in turn, their governments.[82]

Some people might view this statement as another attempt at termination of the federal-Indian trust relationship. Unfortunately, his statement offered little help in clarifying his views on gambling activities as a road to self-sufficiency. The President discussed self-sufficiency largely in terms of a tribe's natural resources, the lack of which seems to serve as the impetus for gambling activities on the reservations.[83] A rough pattern emerges here in that those tribes which already have abundant natural resources appear to have little interest in conducting gambling activities.

Unfortunately, there does not seem to be a unified federal response to this issue. While the BIA seems to favor Indian gambling as a means to self-sufficiency,[84] the federal courts and the Justice Department raise the specter of an infiltration of organized crime into Indian country.[85] This fear of organized crime is a recurring theme in the federal government's support of this legislation.[86] These same would-be federal regulators do not see the tribes as efficient self-regulators against this threat.[87] Yet to continually deny the tribe's ability to protect themselves undermines the very policy of meaningful self-determination. If the tribes are not seen as possessing abilities to be self-policing, then self-determination is virtually impossible. Mistakes made by the tribes in exercising their inherent sovereign powers serve as a pretext for the federal government to further limit their exercise of those dormant powers. Self-determination then becomes a mockery.

Congressman Norman Shumway (R.-Calif.), a prime sponsor of this legislation, makes much of this organized crime threat.[88] His district includes several rancherias which conduct gambling activities. He bases his conclusions of organized crime infiltration on reports by the California Attorney General's office.[89] His thoughts are but reflections of a lack of direction of federal policy makers in this area. On one hand, he supports the Indian effort to become self-reliant, but then he is concerned with possible crime problems.[90]

State Interests

There are two state interests affected by gambling in Indian country. The first is that of organized crime, as much a concern of states as it is the federal government. In "California v. Cabazon Band of Mission Indians,"[91] the state expressed concern that some non-Indian operators of one tribe's gambling operations were convicted in state court of murder and bribery.[92] This citation of organized crime infiltration into Indian country is the only one documented. Despite the expressed concerns of several state attorneys general of this crime threat, not one of them, except California's attorney general in "Cabazon," could allege any specific instances of organized crime infiltration into Indian reservations in their states. Indeed, the victory of the Cabazon Band in the recent U.S. Supreme Court decision on this subject indicates that the state, from an evidentiary point of view, has not demonstrated a compelling need for state intrusion into Indian country.

Essentially, the states have made their case for closer regulation of Indian gaming activities on the possibilities of what might happen.[93] They rely on the threat of organized crime infiltration, while not realizing that perhaps with federal cooperation, tribes may in time be able to effectively police these activities. Arguments also have been made that lower tribal standards may make policing more difficult.[94] One commentator, a member of the Nevada Gaming Commission, favors tight control over Indian gambling, arguing that even the legislation heretofore introduced greatly underestimates the complexity of the subject.[95] His argument for tight federal/state control is premised on his experience in Nevada, which had a history of criminal infiltration until tough regulatory laws were passed.[96] But the relatively new Indian experience in the area would enable tribes to account for previous non-Indian experiences when enacting their own gambling control ordinances. While corruption in Indian country is possible, as it is elsewhere, that possibility alone should not be seized as a pretext to burden all tribes with heavy federal or state regulation. All proposed legislation has failed to differentiate between those tribes with sophisticated law enforcement systems and those with none at all.

The second, but more subtle state interest in Indian gaming involves a threat to state sovereignty. Simply put, the states have argued that there is no justification for treating gaming activities differently by virtue of their location inside or outside of Indian country.[97] The argument has been made that a balancing test should be applied between the economic interests of the tribes and the interests of the state in protecting its citizens.[98] States naturally resent the lack of control of activities within their borders. But it is necessary that the states show some evidence of a compelling need for state regulation, a "test" implicitly reached by dicta in the "Cabazon" case.[99] In the final analysis, the status of gambling in Indian country, absent federal regulation, has rested on a judicial balancing test of tribal versus neighboring state interests. The days when the reservations were truly isolated from non-Indian communities are long past.

Case Law

Public Law 280 States

In response to the inevitable conflict among the three sovereigns, the courts have applied a variety of tests to attempt to solve the issue. The first test, the prohibitory/regulatory analysis, has its roots as an interpretational aid Public Law 280 states.[100] One purpose of this law was to attempt to bring some order to the chaos of determining the civil jurisdiction in Indian country. Criminal jurisdiction was, and is, a more settled area of Indian jurisdiction than is the civil side. The law was passed during the termination era of the 1950s, as a way to "mainstream" tribes into state jurisdictional analysis and to ease the federal government out of the "Indian business."

The legislative history of Public Law 280 indicates that Congress saw the need to extend state civil jurisdiction into Indian country, because the tribes were not fully developed according to Anglo-American concepts of law.[101] Many tribes are, of course, far more "developed" today than they were in 1953.

The first modern case to explore the applicability of Public Law 280 in a civil/regulatory-criminal/prohibitory context was "Bryan v. Itasca County."[102] That case involved the imposition of a state mobile home tax on an Indian in Indian country. A reading of Public Law 280 could lead to the conclusion that all jurisdiction which is not reserved to the tribes or federal governments such as subjects covered by treaty or matters of taxation, were delegated to the states.[103] Facially, Public Law 280 grants states "jurisdiction over offenses" and "civil causes of actions" arising in Indian country, and also mandates that state laws shall have the same force and effect in Indian country as they have elsewhere in the state.[104]

But "Bryan" rejected such a broad reading of the law. Looking at the law's legislative history, "Bryan" found that a major purpose of the act was to combat lawlessness on the reservations.[105] That court read Public Law 280 in pari materia with the 1950s-era termination acts and determined that if Congress had intended to give states general regulatory powers over Indian tribes, it would have expressly said so.[106] Since the termination acts themselves give states broad jurisdiction over tribal property, and allowed state taxation of income earned in Indian country, it must be presumed that Congress' failure to mention this in Public Law 280 excludes such powers. Such a reading is consistent with the canons of construction, generally construing ambiguous statutes in favor of Indian tribes.[107]

"Bryan" begins to develop the distinction between civil/regulatory and criminal/prohibitory laws for Public Law 280 states. The broad contours of this statute deal with conduct that is proscribed by law; i.e. criminal acts. The very essence of criminal law is to prohibit conduct which is deemed harmful to and by society. Of course such conduct may also be sanctioned by the imposition of civil penalties. Public Law 280 focuses on behavior which is generally prohibited, as opposed to that which is allowed, with restrictions.

Far less clear in the Public Law 280 case law are regulatory/civil acts which, by definition, may not be activities deemed so harmful that they must be banned altogether. For example, gambling or fireworks use are generally not thought to be so harmful that a total ban is required. Instead, such activities are regulated in order to minimize the harm to people. Such decisions rest on a state's public policy, as embodied in its legislative enactments. But in Public Law 280 states, mere labels are not determinative of whether that law can be used by a state to forbid gambling in Indian country.[108]

Such a determination of Public Law 280's applicability to Indian country gambling must be made on a case-by-case basis, analyzing the nature of the applicable state laws involved.

"Seminole Tribe of Florida v. Butterworth" was just such a case.[109] The case involved the Seminole Tribe's bingo operation in Indian country. The Hollywood, Florida bingo hall is right in the middle of a large metropolitan area, overwhelmingly populated by non-Indians. The state then has a great interest in regulating such an enterprise, both for revenue-taxation and law enforcement reasons. Nonetheless, instead of balancing competing interests, the Fifth Circuit chose to apply a narrow Public Law 280 analysis, Florida having recently assumed total Public Law 280 jurisdiction in Indian country.[110] The "Butterworth" court examined Florida gambling laws (particularly those pertaining to bingo) and found a regulatory and not a prohibitory intent in those laws.[111] Among the factors which militated in favor of the Tribe (a regulatory finding) were: 1) the state allows certain groups to gamble, and 2) the existence of an inference drawn from a reading of those laws that bingo is treated by Florida as a form of recreation, albeit closely regulated.[112] The "Butterworth" court found that a prohibitory interpretation of the Florida gaming laws could be implied—but using the canons of construction, it construed the ambiguities in favor of the Indians.[113] Once that court reached the opinion that Florida bingo gambling laws were civil/regulatory in nature, the racial identity of the parties, whether they be game operators or players, became irrelevant.[114] From the "Butterworth" case, it appears that when the law in question is found to be civil/regulatory in nature, the states are excluded from enforcing their bingo ordinances, even if the operators are non-Indian, as was the fact in this case.

Wisconsin, another Public Law 280 state, similarly lost its case in "Lac du Flambeau Band v. Williquette."[115] That state had a stronger case than did Florida. It historically had prohibited all forms of gambling, punishing violations with criminal sanctions including imprisonment.[116] Wisconsin's undoing was a recent state constitutional amendment, which exempted bingo and raffles from the gambling prohibition. In response to this change, the Lac du Flambeaus established a bingo hall on their lands in Indian country, and the state subsequently attempted to assert jurisdiction over such activity. The games conducted by the Lac du Flambeaus were precisely those permitted by the state and though the games were not state licensed, the court concluded that the Wisconsin bingo laws were civil/regulatory in nature, not the type of laws envisioned in the grant of Public Law 280 jurisdiction to the state.[117]

"Lac du Flambeau" followed "Oneida Tribe of Indians of Wisconsin v. State of Wisconsin," which earlier had reached the same result over state bingo laws.[118] "Oneida" also analyzed the state public policy and gambling laws, concluding that Public Law 280 jurisdiction must be denied Wisconsin in relation to gambling in Indian country.[119]

California, a third Public Law 280 state, similarly lost several cases which addressed this same issue. The first case involved was "Barona Group of Capitan Grande Band of Mission Indians v. Duffy," where under slightly different facts, the Indians prevailed. Unlike the previous cases mentioned, the Barona Indians lived on a very small reservation, with few enrolled members.[120] That court followed earlier decisions, ascertaining the intent and effect of the state gambling laws, whether or not such gambling was permitted elsewhere in the state, applying the canons, and finally accounting for the historical disfavor of state jurisdiction in Indian country, to find no state jurisdiction in this case.[121]

Recently, in "California v. Cabazon Band of Mission Indians," the United States Supreme Court upheld the criminal/prohibitory-civil/regulatory analysis as applied to Public Law 280 states.[122] The two bands of Indians (Morongo and Cabazon) in this case, like those in "Barona," were small, the Cabazon with twenty-five members and the Morongo with 730 members.[123] These bands conducted card and bingo games pursuant to tribal ordinance. The state sought to prohibit such games under both Public Law 280 and the OCCA.

In construing section 4 of Public Law 280,[124] which grants limited civil jurisdiction in Indian country to the state, the Court followed its earlier analysis in "Bryan" by looking at the legislative history of the law to determine that section

4 applied only to private civil litigation involving Indians.[125] "Bryan" involved a tax, unquestionably civil in nature. However, gambling can easily be considered both civil and criminal in nature, depending on a state's public policy towards such activity. With respect to Public Law 280, "Cabazon" held that whether the [gambling] conduct violates state public policy is the first test.[126] "Cabazon," as in numerous cases below, reviewed the state's widespread tolerance and encouragement of gambling—as manifested in the presence of a state lottery, pari-mutual horse racing, and numerous private bingo halls—and found that California's bingo laws are essentially civil/regulatory in nature.[127]

The state also attempted to argue that the presence of criminal sanctions in the bingo laws permit a criminal/prohibitory label to attach to such laws. The "Cabazon" court rejected such reasoning on the same grounds as did the "Butterworth" court.[128] The Supreme Court, adopting the "Butterworth" logic, reasoned that to permit such a result of labelling would permit a Public Law 280 state to merge tribal sovereignty into its own.[129] Such a scenario, given the history of state-Indian relations, would allow a state, under the rubric of Public Law 280, to reverse decades of federal Indian policy. All that the state need do to prevent the tribe from exercising its own jurisdiction in Indian country is to attach criminal sanctions to any laws it wishes to apply there. Inherent tribal sovereignty would then mean virtually nothing as a Public Law 280 state could then unilaterally extend its jurisdiction into Indian country.

Arguably, the 1968 Indian Civil Rights Act (ICRA)[130] could then operate to prevent such a result. The ICRA, which amended Public Law 280, required tribal consent to any further assumption of state jurisdiction in Indian country. No tribe that wants to establish gaming would likely assent to this.

Finally, once such laws are found to be regulatory in nature, the state is without jurisdiction in Indian country over any players or operators of gambling enterprises, whether or not they are Indian. The facts of "Cabazon" seem to indicate that all that is needed for immunity from regulation by a Public Law 280 state is a tribal ordinance controlling the gambling and state tolerance, however limited, of that activity. The site of the operation must meet the Indian country analysis of 18 U.S.C. § 1151 in order for the regulatory/prohibitory Public Law 280 analysis to be applied. If the site of the gaming is not in Indian country, then of course it would be subject to state jurisdiction like any other entity. While 18 U.S.C. § 1151 is a criminal jurisdictional statute, the Supreme Court in "DeCoteau v. District County Court"[131] and "McClanahan v. State Tax Commission of Arizona"[132] have held the section 1151 Indian country definition to apply also to questions of federal and tribal civil jurisdiction.[133] It appears then that the law is now relatively well settled, with respect to Indian country gambling issues in Public Law 280 states.

Non-Public Law 280 States with Special Jurisdictional Acts

It should be noted, however, that Public Law 280 applies only to a minority of states. What then is the rule in non-Public Law 280 states? Some of these states have special jurisdictional acts of Congress which authorize state criminal and/or civil jurisdiction in Indian country.

For example, in "Penobscot Nation v. Stilphen," the state relied upon the Maine Indian Claims Settlement Act of 1980 (MICSA),[134] to preclude the Penobscots, a federally recognized tribe from operating a high stakes beano parlor on its newly-established reservation.[135] That court rested its decision of state jurisdiction in Indian country on an interpretation of the state implementing act (authorized under MICSA), which allows tribes exclusive jurisdiction only over "internal tribal matters,"[136] Such "internal tribal matters" under title 30, section 6204 of the M.R.S.A., part of the state's Maine Implementing Act, did not mention gaming, traditional or otherwise, and the court did not find the conduct of beano to so qualify.[137] The "Stilphen" court relied on the fact that beano is not a traditional Indian game, nor "did it have any particular cultural significance to the [Penobscot] Nation."[138] The fact that the proceeds of the games were used to finance tribal activities did not qualify the games as internal tribal matters.[139] The Supreme Court dismissed an appeal of the Penobscot Nation on the grounds of a lack of a substantial federal question.[140]

Kansas, another non-Public Law 280 state, in "Iowa Tribe of Indians v. State of Kansas" also successfully assumed jurisdiction over the Iowa Tribe for the state law offense of selling pull-tabs cards (in connection with bingo games) on the reservation.[141] The state relied on the Kansas Act of 1940,[142] which gives the state jurisdiction over those crimes (so-called minor acts) not enumerated in the federal Major Crimes Act.[143] "Iowa Tribe" relied heavily on the legislative history of the Kansas Act to find that Congress meant to cede jurisdiction to the state for such "minor acts" and also that the tribes in Kansas do not possess and have not for many years possessed tribal courts.[144] In effect the "Iowa Tribe" court believed that the 1940 Act was passed to fill a void in tribal law enforcement in Kansas.[145] But that holding poses trouble for the oft-subscribed notion in federal Indian law of inherent tribal sovereignty. True sovereignty does not necessarily imply that the failure to exercise authority (i.e. the absence of tribal courts), causes tribes to lose that authority. No sovereign necessarily loses power by the failure to exercise its authority. Yet that is exactly what has happened here.

The state of Connecticut did not fare so well in "Mashantucket Pequot Tribe v. McGuigan."[146] Although Connecticut is not a Public Law 280 state, the "McGuigan" court nonetheless applied the regulatory/prohibitory analysis to determine that the state bingo laws only serve to regulate, not prohibit, bingo in that state.[147] The court employed that analysis because the Mashantucket Pequot Indian Claims Settlement Act[148] parallels Public Law 280's grant of "limited civil jurisdiction" to the states.[149] Thus, the act falls into that category of states covered by special Congressional enactments which cede to the state certain jurisdiction over Indian tribes in Indian country. The act was passed to settle land claims of the Indians there. The law established, inter alia, a new reservation in exchange for the extinguishment of long-standing land claims against the state and federal governments. So far, all cases examined involved either Public Law 280 states or those states with special jurisdictional acts of Congress.

States Without Public Law 280 or Special Jurisdictional Acts

The final group of states which remain subject to an analysis of state jurisdiction are all of the other non-Public Law 280 states—those without special jurisdictional statutes. The basis for an assumption of state jurisdiction, under these circumstances, is far less clear than it is in Public Law 280 states, now that the Supreme Court has spoken in the "Cabazon" case. The four basic theories advanced in these cases are an infringement on tribal sovereignty, the balancing of tribal/state/federal interests, the OCCA, and preemption. As is true of many issues in Indian law, there is no single standard or test which the federal or state courts apply.

In "State ex rel. May v. Seneca-Cayuga Tribe," a state court decision, the Seneca Tribe won only a partial victory.[150] The Oklahoma Supreme Court would permit state regulation of tribal bingo activities only to the extent that it affected non-member Indians or non-Indians.[151] By implication, then, member Indians involved in bingo are free of state regulation over such activities. That court allowed limited state jurisdiction under a balancing of the interests test, asserting that the state need for revenues and protection of Oklahomans from organized crime justifies limited state jurisdiction in Indian country.[152]

In "May," preemption and infringement are summarily dismissed, the latter on the ground that bingo is not a "traditional tribal activity."[153] The court, in attempting to balance the interests of all sovereigns, acknowledged the tribe's need for economic self-development, but not at the expense of the state.[154] From a full reading of the case, based on what was discussed (balancing), and what was not (infringement or preemption), it is clear that the court was seizing upon any possible pretext to permit some state jurisdiction over these activities. In "May," the state of Oklahoma did not appear to argue any compelling needs of the state such as tax revenue or a problem with organized crime. The lack of any meaningful discussion of these legitimate state interests, given the fact that the state relied on a balancing approach, is puzzling.

Another argument advanced by states is the applicability of the OCCA to Indian country. But federal court decisions have consistently held that while the OCCA makes gambling in federal enclaves a federal crime, if such activity is unlawful in the host state, the act cannot be used by state officials to assert state jurisdiction in Indian country.[155] In "United States v. Dakota," the United States, not the state of Michigan, brought a declaratory action against the Keweenaw Indian Bay Community for operating a gambling casino on its reservation.[156] That court declined to apply the Public Law 280 state.[157] Simply put, the court found that the casino violated state law, and therefore, the OCCA. Similarly, in "Farris," the Ninth Circuit upheld the convictions of both non-Indians and member Indians for a violation of the OCCA.[158] That court, notwithstanding the special tribal/federal trust relationship, or more specifically, the canons of construction, found that the OCCA, like other federal laws of general application throughout the United States, applies with equal force in Indian country.[159] In dicta, "Cabazon" permits only the federal government to apply the OCCA in Indian country.[160]

As to infringement analysis in non-Public Law 280 states, both "Farris" and "Cabazon" make it clear that the "Williams v. Lee" infringement test is inapplicable to a federal application of the OCCA in Indian country.[161] The "Williams" case concerned the attempted exercise of state jurisdiction on an Indian reservation. It noted the historical tension between state and tribal governments. But the OCCA is an exercise of federal, not state authority. States have virtually nothing to say about the enforcement of that act.

The next argument used by both tribes and states is that of preemption. Generally, preemption may be found to exist where a tribe or the federal government has a long or consistent history of self-regulation over the particular subject matter.[162]

In "Farris," the appellants argued that 15 U.S.C. § 1175 of the federal Gambling Devices Act served as a basis of federal preemption of an application of the OCCA. That court, however, rejected such an argument, primarily on the basis that section 1175 applies only to slot machines, while the OCCA applies to gambling in general.[163]

A much better argument for federal/tribal preemption of state gambling laws in non-Public Law 280 states was made by defendants-appellees in "Langley v. Ryder (Langley I)."[164] In that case, the defendants were arrested for gambling and other charges on the Alabama-Coushatta "reservation," near Shreveport, Louisiana. While the Coushatta lands were not an actual reservation, they were treated as Indian country for the purposes of this action. The "Langley I" court found for the preemption of state laws on several grounds.[165] The first base of preemption used was the Indian Commerce Clause,[166] which generally preempts state regulation of Indian affairs.[167] However, the court bowed to the realities of close contact between whites and Indians at the present time, tracing the softening of preemption through "Williams"[168] and "McClanahan,"[169] which permit state jurisdiction under certain conditions, even at the cost of some measure of tribal sovereignty.[170] Under the pressure of increasing close Indian-white contact, preemption nearly dissolves into a balancing test. "Langley I" found no particular overriding state interest, such as the "lost revenue" arguments made by Arizona in "McClanahan."[171] The latter case found the state asserting a great interest in lost revenue, if that state could not tax income earned by an Indian off the reservation. The crux of the state argument in "McClanahan" was that the state provides services to Indians both on and off the reservations.[172]

But in "Langley I," the state of Louisiana asserted no interests which might counter the preemption arguments of the defendants.[173] It was difficult to imagine why the state failed to argue the existence of state interests. Nonetheless, in "Langley v. Ryder (Langley II)," the state appealed the lower court finding of federal preemption of state law, and ultimately lost to the Coushatta Tribe.[174] The Fifth Circuit adopted the lower court's analysis of preemption.[175] Reflecting the state's failure to assert any compelling state interests in the conduct of bingo within Indian country, "Langley II" affirmed the district court in all respects.[176] The essence of "Langley II" was that there was no effective Congressional grant of jurisdiction to Louisiana within Indian country in order to defeat federal preemption, and thus vesting jurisdiction in Louisiana.[177]

In a state without Public Law 280 or a special jurisdictional act of Congress, the "Langley" cases offer a reasonably good basis for an Indian tribe to assert a tribal/federal preemption of state jurisdiction over tribal affairs. The Coushatta Tribe was a recently recognized tribe, on lands which were not in fact an established reservation in the usual sense. The land was donated to the Tribe and subsequently accepted for them by the United States Department of the Interior, in trust for the tribe as authorized by section 5 of the Indian Reorganization Act of 1934.[178] The current federal posture of permitting Indian gaming enterprises on reservations in the name of economic development suggests that the states will get little help in enforcing laws with respect to Indian-controlled gambling in Indian country.

However, the preemption test is not without limits. This test no longer rests on a "Williams v. Lee" analysis, but rather a balancing test, as the dicta in "Cabazon" suggests.[179] That case balanced the ample evidence of strong federal interests, manifested by President Reagan's emphasis of trial freedom from federal dependence, and a general federal promotion of bingo enterprises as against the state interests of containing organized crime.[180]

At first blush, it appears that these tribal interests might be diminished by the "Washington v. Confederated Tribes of the Colville Reservation" proscription against the mere "marketing of tax exemptions." But "Cabazon" distinguished "Colville" on the basis that the tribes there have significant interests not present in the latter case.[181] The material distinction in fact between these two cases on this point is that in "Colville," the tribes merely imported cigarettes for later resale, where in "Cabazon," the tribes committed significant financial resources and manpower towards the conduct of these gaming activities. In the earlier case, the tribes had already-existing smoke shops with no additional investment necessary in order to accommodate the cigarettes. The present case goes far beyond merely taking advantage of tax free status. In fact, the state's argument is focused not on taxation but the infiltration of organized crime. The case extends to the creation of a new industry on the California rancherias, that of recreation.

But this distinction exists only because the "Cabazon" case chose to deemphasize the marketing of tax exemption argument. Had the Supreme Court chose to follow "McClanahan" in this respect, the two cases are quite analogous. Both "McClanahan" and "Cabazon" in fact involve the marketing of an exemption from state regulation. The former case involved state taxation of the reservation sale of cigarettes, while the latter case involves state regulation of bingo establishments. In both cases, non-Indians would have no reason to patronize the Indian country businesses if they were subject to state regulation, either in the form of state taxes or the size of bingo jackpots. If the Court had found the marketing argument strong, "McClanahan" would have served as strong ammunition for the state of California.

The final analysis of the preemption/balancing test lies in the nature of the interests the state of California asserted in an attempt to demonstrate a compelling state interest, which would be enough to override tribal and federal interests. In "Cabazon," the state's assertion of a compelling state interest failed on evidentiary grounds.[182] The state felt that the threat of organized crime on the two reservations in this case was sufficient to escape preemption. The Court, in "Cabazon," found that argument unpersuasive for two reasons: 1) no actual proof was offered at trial that regulated off reservation games were free from organized crime and Indian country games weren't, and 2) the state didn't show that organized crime infiltration actually existed with respect to bingo and similar games, either on or off the reservation.[183] Such a lack of proof of the existence of organized crime or other law enforcement problems also existed in the "Cabazon" case at the Ninth Circuit level.[184] This same failure of proof existed both in the "Langley" cases and in recent congressional hearings on the subject.

Implicit in all of this is that with strong facts, where the state failed on a Public Law 280 analysis of their bingo statutes, they might have prevailed on a preemption or balancing test basis. As to preemption, Louisiana, like all other states, has a long history of gambling regulation. The "Langley" cases also suffered from this lack of proof. If Louisiana, a non-Public Law 280 state, had shown strong evidence of existing law enforcement problems, it could have made a credible case against federal preemption of state gambling laws. The "Cabazon" holding already implies that with solid evidence of past and/or present law enforcement problems, the state might have prevailed.[185] A showing of a compelling state interest might have also overcome the infringement test. In the context of Indian-white contact, the state almost automatically wins on a pure balancing of interests test, as most reservation populations are vastly outnumbered by the neighboring communities. In light of long standing rational and oft-demonstrated state and federal/tribal interests, a strong state showing could prevail, as it did in "McClanahan."

Conclusion

In predicting the future, the first step is to consider whether or not a given reservation (or land which meets Indian country definitions) is in a Public Law 280 state, a state which has specifically assumed some measure of criminal jurisdiction over the tribes. If so, absent congressional regulation of Indian gambling (as embodied in recent legislative proposals), the tribe's success will surely depend on whether or not the state permits the gaming activity which the tribe seeks to engage in. No cases have supported an exclusion of state jurisdiction in Indian country where the Public Law 280 state has totally prohibited that form of gambling. The "Cabazon" case infers that a total ban on such activities, even without proof of law enforcement problems, may be enough to permit state jurisdiction in Indian country.

Such a total ban would seriously weaken the preemption/balancing tests from the tribe's viewpoint. A non-gambling state would be able to point to a compelling need to maintain a gambling-free state. Permitting gambling, even in Indian country, would seriously weaken these state goals. A Public Law 280 analysis would, under "Seminole" and "Cabazon" rules, compel a decision in favor of a state. A total ban on such activities would take the state gambling law out of the civil/regulatory category and put it squarely into the criminal/prohibitory column—precisely the types of laws addressed by both the legislative history of Public Law 280 and "Bryan."

A total ban on gambling would also support any federal effort to halt gambling under the OCCA. This act could be applied to the reservation, but only by the federal government. However, existing federal policy makes any widespread federal prosecutions under the OCCA unlikely.

Like it or not, the concept of inherent tribal sovereignty, at least in the gambling context, has been considered softened since the heady days of "Williams v. Lee," where the infringement test placed a heavy burden on the states to overcome, which could be done only by showing some compelling state interest, such as a need to uphold law and order by applying state criminal law to reservations. This same burden also exists to some degree in the balancing test and the canons of construction.

"Cabazon" is merely a continuance of a gradually discernible trend of reducing tribal sovereignty in order to meet the exigencies of state interests. These exigencies manifest themselves as a result of ever increasing contact between whites and Indians. To move too fast against tribes (as was the case with the Termination Acts) would offend the sensibilities of all but the most ardent supporters of states (as opposed to Indian) rights.

The Public Law 280 analysis then becomes subsumed into the larger picture of competing state, federal, and tribal interests, in the name of infringement or balancing/ preemption tests. The Supreme Court's message in "Cabazon" appears to be that the Court stands ready, upon a good factual showing of compelling state interests, to blunt or jettison that Public Law 280 analysis in favor of a straight balancing-of-the-interests test. The Court surely indicated by inference, at least, that a strong factual showing of law enforcement problems by the state would have been enough to balance the interests in favor of state jurisdiction in Indian country.

The one sure fact of Indian law is that it is a fluid concept, subject to few permanent and enduring concepts. More than other areas of the law, Indian law is "fact driven." One only needs to look at both the courts and Congress to discern that fact. Tribal sovereignty, though never in fact unlimited after the Marshall Trilogy, is subject to gradual erosion as Indians and non-Indians live closer together, in ever-increasing numbers. As always, Indian rights, Public Law 280 or not, are either directly or indirectly dependent upon state law.

Addendum: An Update

Federal regulation of gambling in Indian Country has become a reality. On Oct. 17, 1988, President Reagan signed the Indian Gaming Regulatory Act (IGRA) into law.[186] The IGRA originated as Senate Bill 555, which was introduced in the first session of the 100th Congress, and subsequently amended. The major features of the IGRA were discussed previously in this article.

The one major difference between Senate Bill 555 and the IGRA concerns the issue of a transfer of criminal and civil jurisdiction from the tribe to the state, as it relates to gaming disputes. Under the original bill, a tribe wanting to conduct Class III gaming had to seek a transfer of civil and criminal jurisdiction from itself to the state. The tribe had to get Secretarial approval for this, and in fact, the Secretary was to be the vehicle for effecting the transfer. Under section 11(d) of the original Senate Bill 555,[187] in order for the tribe to conduct such gaming, the Secretary had to approve and, indeed, ask the state to assume jurisdiction over gambling related matters. The effect of this section would have put the tribe in the position of surrendering another piece of their sovereignty to the state as the price of conducting Class III gambling. The IGRA does not place the tribes in such a position.

To conduct Class III gambling, the IGRA still requires the tribes to adopt a gaming ordinance in conformity with the act, and the measure must then be approved by the Commission Chairman.[188] However, instead of the Secretary transferring jurisdiction from the tribe to the state, the tribe and state must now negotiate and agree to a compact which would govern both the actual conduct of the games and the allocation of related civil and criminal jurisdiction in Indian country. Such jurisdiction as assumed by the state, pursuant to the act, only allows the state to assess its law enforcement costs against the tribal Class III game.[189] Under the IGRA, the state is expressly forbidden to use the compact as precedent for imposing any revenue-raising taxes or assessment on any activities in Indian country, whether gambling-related or not, if there is not other legal basis for imposing such a tax or assessment.[190] In other words, a state is prevented from using the compact as a legal basis to collect taxes on other activities which take place in Indian country.

The burden to negotiate such a compact in good faith is initially shifted to the state. A tribe may seek an order from the appropriate federal district court to compel the recalcitrant state to negotiate in good faith for a compact.[191] The IGRA enumerates several factors for the court to consider in determining exactly what "good faith" means in this context. The IGRA also contains provisions for a mediation process to develop a compact in the event that both parties reach an impasse in their negotiations.[192]

In essence, the IGRA seeks to avoid the "all or nothing" result of transferring jurisdiction to the state at the expense of tribal sovereignty. This new approach mirrors the desire of Congress to strengthen the hand of the tribes in dealing with the jurisdiction issue.[193] Congress balanced the state concerns of crime prevention with the tribe's historic and continuing opposition to any imposition of state jurisdiction into tribal lands.[194] The IGRA now gives the tribes a significant voice as to the nature of state jurisdiction on gambling in Indian country.

Other differences are of a relatively minor nature, focusing mainly on exempting particular lands from provisions of the IGRA. At this point it is interesting to note that the revised version of Senate Bill 555[195] provided that a majority of the Commission members were to be members of federally-recognized tribes. The enacted version of Senate Bill 555, the IGRA, deleted that provision, leaving Indian members in a minority of two.[196] Nothing would prevent the President, of course, from appointing more than two Indian members to the Commission. One can only speculate as to the reasons why a provision calling for majority Indian membership on the Commission was deleted. Only time will tell how well the IGRA, discussed in Congress for over five years, actually works. At least the tribes and the states now have a framework in which to solve their differences over who should regulate gambling in Indian Country.

NOTES

1. S. Rep., 493, 99th Congress, 2nd Session, (1986), 2.

2. Ibid.

3. Ibid.

4. Ibid., 3.

5. "Assimilative Crimes Act," U.S.C. 18, (1969), 13.

6. "United States v. Marcyes," F.2d, 557, (9th Circuit Court, 1977), 1361, 1364.

7. Guzman, "Indian Gambling on Reservations," *Arizona Law Review*, 24, (1982), 209, 212.

8. "General Crimes Act," U.S.C., 18, (1988), 1153.

9. Guzman, supra note 7, 212.

10. Comment, "Indian Sovereignty Versus Oklahoma's Gambling Laws," *Tulsa Law Journal*, 20, (1985), 605, 622.

11. *Pub. L.* 280, Stat., 67, 588 (codified in U.S.C., 18, 1162(a), U.S.C., 28, (1984), 1360(a).

12. "Gambling Devices Act," U.S.C., 15, (1982), 1171-1178.

13. Ibid.

14. F. Supp., 87, (W.D.Wis. 1949), 225.

15. Ibid.

16. "United States v. Blackfeet Tribe," F. Supp., 369, (D. Mont., 1973), 562, 565; "United States v. Farris," F. 2nd, 624, (9th Cir. 1980), 890, 896.

17. U.S.C., 18, (1974), 1955.

18. Ibid.

19. H.R. Rep. No. 1549, 91st Congress, 2nd Session, (1970), 2.

20. Guzman, supra note 7, 212.

21. "Williams v. Lee," U.S., 358, (1959), 217.

22. "United States v. Dakota," F.2d, 796, (6th Cir. 1986), 186, 188.

23. "Dakota," F.2d, 796, (6th cir., 1986), 188.

24. Ibid.

25. "United States v. Farris," F.2d, 624, (9th Cir. 1980), 890.

26. Ibid., 893-94 (quoting "United States v. Wheeler, U.S., 435, (1978), 313, and "United States v. Montana," F.2d, 604, (9th Cir. 1979), 1162).

27. Ibid.

28. Ibid., 894.

29. "Barona Group of Capitan Grande Band of Mission Indians v. Duffy," F.2d, 694, (9th Cir. 1982), 1185, 1190, cert. denied, U.S., 461, (1983), 929; "Dakota," F.2d, 796, 188.

30. See, e.g, "Lonewolf v. Hitchcok," U.S., 187, (1903), 553; "Worcester v. Georgia," U.S., 31, (1832), (6 Pet.), 515.

31. *Weekly Comp. Pres. Doc.* 19, 98 (Jan. 24, 1983).

32. H.R. 4566, 98th Cong., 1st Sess. (1983).

33. "Seminole Tribe of Florida v. Butterworth," F.2d, 658, (5th Cir. 1981), 310.

34. "Indian Gambling Control Act: Hearings on H.R. 4566 Before the Committee on Interior and Insular Affairs, House of Representatives," 98th Cong., 2d Sess. (1984), 96-97, [hereinafter "House Hearings"].

35. Ibid., 101.

36. "S. 902," 99th Cong., 1st Session, (1985), 11.

37. Ibid., 5-6.

38. "H.R. 1920," 99th Congress, 2d Session, (1986), 11(b)(2)(i)-(iv).

39. Ibid., 19(5)(A)-(C).

40. Ibid., 12.

41. Ibid., 12.

42. Ibid., 12(e)(1)(A).

43. Ibid., 19(4).

44. Jones, "Gambling on Indian Reservations — Update February 17, 1987," Library of Congress: Congressional Research Service, (1987).

45. Ibid.

46. "S. 2557," 99th Cong., 2d Sess., (1986), 401.

47. Ibid.

48. Ibid.

49. "S. 555," 100th Cong., 1st Sess., (1987), 2.

50. Ibid., 4.

51. Ibid., 6-7.

52. Ibid., 4-5.

53. Ibid., 11(d).

54. Ibid., 11(b).

55. Ibid., 11(c), (d).

56. Ibid.

57. Ibid.

58. Ibid.

59. Ibid., 12(a)(2), (b).
60. Ibid.
61. Ibid., 14(a)(1), (b)(1).
62. Ibid.
63. Ibid., 14(b)(1), 15.
64. Ibid.
65. Ibid., 16-17.
66. Ibid., 17-19.
67. Ibid, 20.
68. Ibid.
69. Ibid.
70. Ibid., 23.
71. Ibid.
72. Ibid.
73. Ibid., 23-24.
74. De Domenecis, "Betting on Indian Rights," *California Lawyer*, (Sept. 1983), 29.
75. Ibid., 31.
76. "Gambling on Indian Reservations and Land: Hearings on 'S. 902' Before the Senate Select Committee on Indian Affairs," 99th Cong., 2d Sess., (1985), 83-85 [hereinafter "Senate Hearings"].
77. Ibid.
78. H. R. Rep. No. 488, 99th Cong., 2d Sess., (1986), 23.
79. "Senate Hearings," supra note 76, 84.
80. Ibid.
81. *Weekly Comp. Pres. Doc.*, 19, (Jan. 24, 1983), 98.
82. Ibid., 99.
83. Ibid., 100-101.
84. DeDeomenecis, supra note 74, 30.
85. "United States v. Farris," F.2d, 624, (9th Cir. 1980), 890, 895; see also "House Hearings," supra note 34, 67.
86. "House Hearings," supra note 34, 67.
87. S. Rep. No. 493, 99th Cong., 2d Sess., (1986), 28.
88. Letter from U.S. Rep. Norman Shumway to Gary Sokolow, (Mar. 2, 1987).
89. Ibid.
90. Ibid., 2.
91. U.S., 480, (1987), 202.
92. "Senate Hearings," supra note 76, 127.
93. Ibid.

94. Ibid., 158-60.
95. Ibid.
96. Ibid., 154.
97. H.R. Rep. No. 488, 99th Cong., 2d Sess., (1986), 31.
98. "Senate Hearings," supra note 76, 19.
99. "California v. Cabazon Band of Mission Indians," U.S., 480, (1987), 202, 221.
100. See supra note 11.
101. "1953 U.S. Code Cong. and Admin. News 2412."
102. F. Cohen, *Handbook of Federal Indian Law*, (1982 ed.), 362-63; "Bryan v. Itasca County," U.S., 426, (1976), 373.
103. F. Cohen, supra note 102, 363.
104. U.S.C., 18, 1162(a); U.S.C., 25, (1985), 1321(a), 1322(a); U.S.C., 28, 1360(a); F. Cohen, supra note 102, 363.
105. Bryan, U.S., 426, 378.
106. Ibid.
107. Ibid., 378-79.
108. Seminole Tribe of Florida v. Butterworth, F.2d, 658, (5th Cir. 1981), 310.
109. Ibid.
110. *Fla. Stat. Ann.*, (West 1975), 285.16.
111. "Butterworth," F.2d, 658, 316.
112. Ibid., 314.
113. Ibid.
114. Ibid.
115. "Lac du Flambeau Band v. Williquette," F. Supp., 629, (W.D. Wis. 1986), 689.
116. Ibid., 691.
117. Ibid., 692-93.
118. "Oneida Tribe of Indians of Wisconsin v. State of Wisconsin, F. Supp., 518, (W.D. Wis. 1986), 719.
119. Ibid.
120. "Barona Group of Capitan Grande Band of Mission Indians v. Duffy," 694, F.2d, 1185, 1187, (9th Cir. 1982), cert. denied 461 U.S. 929 (1983).
121. Ibid., 1190.
122. California v. Cabazon Band of Mission Indians, 480 U.S. 202, 209 (1987).
123. Ibid., 209 n.1.
124. U.S.C., 28, 1360(a).
125. "Cabazon," U.S., 480, 207-208.

126. Ibid., 209.
127. Ibid.
128. Ibid.
129. Ibid.
130. U.S.C., 25, 1301-1341.
131. "DeCoteau v. District County Court," U.S. 420, (1975), 425.
132. "McClanahan v. State Tax Commission of Arizona," U.S. 411, (1973), 164.
133. F. Cohen, supra note 102, 27.
134. "Pub. L. 96-420," Stat., 94, 1785 (codified U.S.C., 25, 1721-1735).
135. "Penobscot Nation v. Stilphen," A.2d, 461, (Me. 1983), 478.
136. Ibid.
137. Ibid., 490.
138. Ibid.
139. Ibid.
140. U.S., 464, (1983), 923
141. "Iowa Tribe of Indians v. State of Kansas," F.2d, 787, (10th Cir. 1986), 1434.
142. U.S.C., 25, (1940), 217(a).
143. "Act of June 25, 1948," Stat. 758, 62, 645, (codified at U.S.C. 18, 1153, 3242).
144. "Iowa," F.2d, 787, 1439.
145. "Iowa," 1439-40.
146. F. Supp., 626, (D.Conn. 1986), 245.
147. Ibid., 246.
148. "Pub. L. 98-134," Stat., 97, (1983), 851 (codified at U.S.C., 25, 1751-1760).
149. "McGuingan," F. Supp., 626, 248.
150. "State ex rel. May v. Seneca-Cayuga Tribe," P.2d, 711, (Okla. 1985), 77.
151. Ibid., 92.
152. Ibid., 91.
153. Ibid., 90.
154. Ibid., 90-91.
155. "California v. Cabazon Band of Mission Indians," U.S., 480, (1987), 202, 210-11; "United States v. Dakota," F.2d, 796, (6th Cir. 1986), 186, 186.
156. "Dakota," F.2d, 796, 186.

157. Ibid., 189.

158. "United States v. Farris," F.2d, 624, (9th Cir. 1980), 890, 890.

159. Ibid., 896.

160. "Cabazon," U.S., 480, 213.

161. Ibid.; "Farris," F.2d, 624, 896.

162. "Rice v. Rehner," U.S., 463, 713, rehearing denied, U.S., 464, (1983), 874.

163. "Farris," F.2d, 624, 896.

164. "Langley v. Ryder [I]," F. Supp., 602, (W.D.La. 1985), 335.

165. Ibid.

166. U.S. Const. art. I, 8, cl. 3.

167. "Langley, I," F. Supp., 602, 343.

168. "Williams v. Lee," U.S. 358, (1959), 217.

169. "McClanahan v. State Tax Comm'n of Arizona," U.S., 411, (1973), 164.

170. "Langley I," F. Supp., 602, 343.

171. Ibid.

172. "McClanahan," U.S. 411, 164.

173. "Langley I," F. Supp., 602, 335.

174. "Langley v. Ryder" [II], F.2d, 778, (5th Cir. 1985), 1096.

175. Ibid.

176. Ibid.

177. Ibid.

178. Ibid.

179. "California v. Cabazon Band of Mission Indians," U.S., 480, (1987), 202, 221.

180. Ibid., 211.

181. "Washington v. Confederated Tribes of the Colville Reservation," U.S. 447, (1980), 134; "Cabazon," U.S. 480, 215-16.

182. "Cabazon," U.S., 480, 219-21.

183. Ibid., 221.

184. "Cabazon Band of Mission Indians v. County of Riverside," F.2d, 783, (9th Cir. 1986), 900.

185. "Cabazon," U.S., 480, 202.

186. "Indian Gaming Regulatory Act Pub. L. 100-497," Stat., 102, 2467, *U.S. Code Cong. and Admin. News*, 3071, (1988) (to be codified at U.S.C., 25, 2701-2721; U.S.C., 18,

1166-1168).

187. S., 555, 100th Cong., 1st Sess., (1987), 11(d).

188. "Pub. L. 100-497," 11(d)(1).

189. Ibid., 11(d)(4).

190. Ibid.

191. Ibid., 11(d)(2)(B)(iii).

192. Ibid., 11(d)(7).

193. "S. Rep. No. 446," 100th Cong., 2d Sess., 13, reprinted in *U.S. Code Cong. and Admin. News*, (1988), 3083.

194. Ibid.

195. S., 444, 100th Cong., 2d Sess., (1988), 5(b)(3).

196. "Pub. L. 100-497," 5(b)(3).

Chapter XVI

Urban Native Americans

Today over half of Native Americans live in urban settings. There are large numbers of Native Americans living in Albuquerque, New Mexico, Buffalo, New York, Chicago, Illinois, Los Angeles-Long Beach, California, Minneapolis-St. Paul, Minnesota, New York City, Phoenix and Tucson, Arizona, San Francisco, California, and Tulsa, Oklahoma. The migration to the cities began during World War II and was accelerated by Bureau of Indian Affairs policies of termination and relocation during the 1950s and 60s. Another factor influencing Indian relocation to the city was extreme poverty and unemployment on Indian Reservations.

By moving off reservations the Native American jeopardizes his or her entitlements as an enrolled member of a federally recognized Indian tribe; health care, annuity money, subsidized housing, tax exemptions, etc. Only after Senator Edward Kennedy brought suit against the BIA in Federal District Court to require that urban Native Americans be covered by federal programs serving American Indians did federal programs begin to reach out to serve urban Native Americans. Even today the federal support system for urban Native Americans is incomplete and underfunded. As a group urban Native Americans remain as one of our foremost underprivileged minorities.

To replace the tribal institutions of the reservation, urban Native Americans have organized intertribal organizations to replace the support system provided by tribal institutions. Indian social clubs, community organizations, church run missions, bars, pow wows, forty-niners and ghettos are the urban substitutes for the tribal reservation system. These institutions provide services, support for new arrivals, social interaction and opportunities to participate in cultural ceremonies. Many of the leaders of the "Red Power" movement of the 1960s and 70s were urban Native Americans who had learned the organizational and mobilization techniques in the city.

A major challenge for urban Native Americans is preserving their Indian identity. The impersonal city does not provide the setting for the retention of traditional native values and cultural traditions. Native Americans are a small community in any urban setting and lack the political and economic leverage that other ethnic minorities possess. There is a continuous struggle to preserve the native languages, cultural traditions and historical identity in the face of urban institutions which encourage integration. Where numbers of Native Americans reside there is a strong interest in introducing Native language, history and culture in school curriculums.

As reservations were the repositories of native language and culture of the 19th and 20th centuries, the urban institutions of the present provide

429

the basis for preserving Indian identity and cultural distinctiveness in the 21st century for a majority of Native Americans. Increasingly Native Americans are moving off tribal reserves as the social and economic conditions deteriorate. There is no counterpart of the tribe or reservation system in the city but urban Native leaders have crafted institutions which seek to preserve Indian identity and resist the pull of the urban melting pot.

—RNW

Urban Indian Institutions in Phoenix: Transformation from Headquarters City to Community[1,2]

Edward D. Liebow

Phoenix, Arizona is a "Sunbelt" city whose explosive growth over the past thirty years provides us with an opportunity to refresh our thinking about such basic processes of urban social organization as ethnic institutionalization. Phoenix is also one of a few U.S. metropolitan areas where urban Indians have set about self-consciously creating a collective identity that is firmly tied to their metropolitan home. As in almost every city with more than a handful of Indian residents, the Phoenix area has urban Indian organizations, including dozens of urban Indian service organizations, advisory panels, recreational and social associations, as well as *ad hoc* groups that convene for special purposes. These groups draw urban Indian residents together and, generally, restrict access by non-Indians. Participation in organization-sponsored activities become points of reference in one's personal history (as in "I know 'so-and-so' from when we were on the Parents' Committee together"). Beyond engaging many urban Indians in an activity sphere that resists intrusion by outsiders, however, organizations are sometimes set in competition with one another, particularly social service contractors who depend on increasingly limited federal funds. To the extent that it exists, organizational factionalism undermines what little urban Indian influence there is in local governmental affairs. Further, factionalism dissipates organizational resources and individual energies that might otherwise be put to use in pursuit of more far-sighted political goals.

This paper examines urban Indian institutional development in metropolitan Phoenix, seen in the context of two competing models of ethnic institutionalization. One model holds that specific types of institutions follow one another in a stage-like sequence as the ethnic community matures, while the other holds that each type of institution develops in response to extra-local policy forces, and not some intrinsic cultural maturation process. Both models assume it is the ethnic community that creates institutions to serve its needs. I suggest that we focus instead on the process by which institutions create a community. Institutions have "careers"; new ethnic institutions are established when older institutions no longer accommodate the changing interests of those who are most actively engaged in supporting these institutions. To illustrate how a community can grow out of this succession of institutions, rather than the reverse, the careers of three different types of urban Indian institutions are reviewed: the Phoenix Indian Center's transition from a grassroots organization to a contractor agency; the State Commission on Indian Affairs in search of a governmental mission in the era of "new federalism"; and, finally, the urban Indian bars and their enduring qualities.

APPROACHES TO THE STUDY OF ETHNIC INSTITUTIONS

Urban Indian institutional development has been the subject of considerable discussion among anthropologists. Institutions are said to develop out of a need to reaffirm tribal identity,[3] or for fraternal and spiritual reasons.[4] According to the American Indian Policy Review Commission, "having lost the unity provided by the tribe, Indians have had to develop these (institutions) as places where their needs are represented."[5] Some scholars contend that urban Indian ethnic institutions develop in a sequence of stages characterized by a pattern of florescence and withering of different institutional types.[6] When this stage-like developmental sequence has been reconsidered in light of federal policy toward urban poor and ethnic minorities, different types of institutions are regarded as just as likely to co-exist and develop contemporaneously as they are to succeed one another.[7]

Both models assume that urban Indian institutions are service facilities, and that they are "ethnic based" because of their distinctive clientele. Further, they both assume that an ethnic "community" exists, and institutions form to serve community needs. The scholarly disagreement is over the forces that affect the formation of new institutions. One model invokes an underlying self-help dynamic that eventually plays itself out in one organizational incarnation, only to resurface in a freshly minted form as the ethnic community matures. Some intrinsic cultural process of adjustment to an unfamiliar social and economic setting is presumed to be at work here, in which case the development sequence should be relatively similar for many ethnic migrant groups.

The other model argues that this inclination to self-help is acted upon largely with the support of outsiders. In this view, ethnic institutional development is to be understood, at least partly, as a response to federal policy, in which case the development process that a particular ethnic group experiences should be distinctive, to the extent that policy towards this group is distinctive.

Price[8] observed that an urban pan-tribal ethnic culture has emerged among U.S. and Canadian Indians, complete with institutions formed on the basis of pan-tribal commonalities. In contrast to reservation institutions, whose control remains with outsiders (either directly or indirectly), these urban institutions have been established by, staffed by, and controlled by Indians. Price defines an institution as "an established social facility that provides some service, in the broadest sense of the term, to people." Ethnic institutions, in this view, are "simply those in which the ethnicity of the clients is significant." The staffing and design of ethnic institutions are almost always predominantly by people who are of the same ethnic group as the clients. To the extent that an institution shifts to a non-ethnic clientele, it ceases to function as an ethnic institution, and becomes an institution of the general population.[9]

According to Price, institutional development among urban Indians takes place in a stage-like developmental sequence. The first Indian ethnic institutions in the city are usually Indian bars, and perhaps some government and religious service agencies for Indians. These service agencies, where they appear, are said to be designed and staffed initially by non-Indians for lower-class Indians with little urban experience. Indian social cliques flourish in the urban bar culture and become the basis of the first urban Indian culture, but individuals are said to move away relatively quickly from this temporary setting. In time, urban-adapted Indians become middle-class and develop their own ethnic institutions, such as social centers, churches, pow-wow clubs, athletic leagues, political associations, and periodicals.[10]

The initial stage, in which the bar culture is said to dominate, is attributed to the historical efforts of non-Indians to actively restrict public, off-reservation settings in which Indians could drink. The bars are said to acquire a stigma because they are commonly located in "skid row" venues, and drinking is considered a "dysfunctional" adaptation to urban life. The second stage is characterized by the development of Indian centers and elaborated kinship-friendship networks. For some cities, where the urban Indian residents come primarily from reservations in the immediate region, Price sees a lag in the development of Indian centers. In these cities, one would expect to see more commuting back to the reservation on weekends, with less tribal diversity in the city, and people would tend to stick to people of their own tribal backgrounds, rather than engaging in activities of a pan-tribal nature:

> There is usually a decrease in the number of predominantly Indian bars during the second stage of ethnic institutionalization because (1) other institutions take over the social and educational functions for most migrants; (2) centers and networks take on the function of receiving newcomers; (3) people move away from the transient skid row area to more stable homes; and (4) people more often drink in their homes and at parties.[11]

The third stage of urban ethnic institutionalization comes when the ethnic institutions cover a broad range of common interest associations such as Indian athletic leagues, Indian Christian churches, pow-wow clubs, and political organizations. In the third stage, the Indians develop their own unique ethnic institutions, typically associated with promoting positive ethnic identity and expressions, rather than solving the "Indian problem" as perceived in such negative terms by the majority society. Institutions are then dominated by Indian staffs, who effectively put down much of the earlier social work style of paternalism. Based on what has happened to other urban ethnic groups, Price predicts that urban Indians should eventually develop a fourth stage of institutions with professional, academic, and entrepreneurial services.

In contrast to Price's stage-like developmental sequence, Fiske[12] suggests that the development of urban Indian ethnic institutions is determined by national policy. Borrowing from a model developed by Leeds,[13] Fiske examines institutions developed by the Los Angeles area Indian community, assuming that local institutions are constantly in competition and conflict with supralocal ones. The continual adjustment in the power relationship between non-local and local institutions affect the form, function, and rate of formation of local institutions. Voluntary organizations and other, less formal institutions that provide such services as information dispersal, financial, housing, and employment aid, child care, recreation and so forth exist like a "resilient layer" that cushions the local community of migrants when the state is "repressive." When repression is high, localities are said to turn to their own resources for sustenance.[14]

Fiske identifies a type of Indian organization whose existence Price did not predict: one that becomes incorporated into local decision-making bodies. Because they are integrated into local governmental units, these organizations are said to be different from institutions that were supported by federal and state funding, but existed differently from local policy-making entities. This institutional type also differs in that it is not a direct service provider, as almost all other urban Indian institutions have been from their earliest days. Instead, institutions of this type serve in an advisory or advocacy capacity, an investigative unit (into such "problem" areas as housing, health care, and employment), or funding units.

Fiske observes many different types of institutional adjustments to the urban environment—kin and friendship networks, bar cliques, common interest associations, incorporation into local government, and service organizations. She argues that these types of adjustments are as likely to exist and develop at the same time as they are likely to succeed each other. The development of institutions can better be understood as a response to the nature of federal policy toward poor and urban areas. In particular, the federal government is said to have "courted the poor" through programs sponsored by general revenue sharing policy and the Office of Economic Opportunity, through job training (e.g., Comprehensive Employment Training Act) and housing funds. The effect of these programs was dramatic, with the federally funded service program becoming "the focal point of urban Indian activity."[15]

Hansen[16] notes the extreme divisiveness that often characterizes urban Indian communities, as expressed in factionalism and a continually shifting and conflicting set of organizations. Using the Seattle area urban Indian community to illustrate her argument, Hansen attributes this characteristic factionalism not to the heterogeneous background of urban Indians, but rather to the conflict between local Indian political goals and the extra-local (i.e., federal) resources used to pursue these goals. To become eligible for federal funding, local organizations are often forced to restructure themselves, and may cut themselves off from effective participation in local politics as a result of this same restructuring.

INSTITUTIONAL DEVELOPMENT SEQUENCE IN PHOENIX

In Table 1, I have arranged in chronological sequence a comprehensive list of Phoenix metropolitan area urban Indian institutions, along with the categories that Price uses in his stage-development scheme.

The chronology reveals a more complex development sequence than either Price's "community maturation" or Fiske's "funding accommodation" models might suggest. Some of the organizations are "grassroots," self-contained / self-help responses to problem conditions facing the local Indian population. But many of the institutions in which urban Indians are actively engaged were founded by non-Indians, receive their support from outside the local Indian population, and must accommodate the interests of these non-Indian supporters, often in direct conflict with the interests of some portion of local urban Indian residents. They are included in the chronology, however, because they fit Price's definition of an ethnic institution, being service providers distinguished by their clientele.

Compared with Price's development scheme, in Phoenix the church-related organizations appeared earliest, and they were all established by non-Indian missionaries, until the First Indian Baptist Church was created in the mid-1960s. The reservation emigrants in the late 1940s and early 1950s created the first grassroots Indian organizations, and mobilized the state government to acknowledge a responsibility to support their efforts. A cadre of federal administrative workers, their civil service status offering an assuring measure of upward mobility, organized recreational activities and lent an ambiance to local taverns. In the early 1970s, federal education programs brought students to the metropolitan area community colleges and university in large numbers and campus student organizations emerged in a socializing context, but also against the backdrops of nationwide student activism in general, and Indian political activism in particular.

Also in the early 1970s, urban Indian residents directly felt the effects of general revenue sharing, and the federal policy of "maximum feasible participation" on the part of the community-based organizations through programs sponsored by the Office of Economic Opportunity, Housing and Urban Development, and Health, Education and Welfare. A welter of non-profit organizations sprang up to administer these programs, often staffed by former federal workers whose responsibilities had included administering the monies that were subsequently given over directly to the grassroots

TABLE 1
SEQUENCE OF URBAN INDIAN INSTITUTIONAL DEVELOPMENT IN PHOENIX

Stage 1 Bars & Non-Indian Orgs[a]	Stage 2 Service Org/Networks	Stage 3 Interest Assoc. & Church Orgs
Cook Christian Training School (early 1900s) Central Presbyterian Church (1930)		
	Phoenix Indian Center (1947) ASU National Indian Education Training Center (1948)	
		All Tribes Assembly of God (1952) American Indian Bible College (1952)
AZ Commission on Indian Affairs (1953) Ponderosa (early 60's) Esquire (early 60's)		
	Central Plains Club of Phoenix (1961) Basektball Bowling Softball Leagues (mid-60s) Native American Women's Association Indian Development District of AZ (1967)	
		First Indian Baptist Church (1967)
Can-Can (mid 60's) Lutheran Indian Ministry of AZ (1970)		

		Native American Students Clubs:
		  ASU (1971)
		  Mesa, Scottsdale & Phoenix
		  Colleges (1972)

	Inter-Tribal Council of AZ (1972) Metropolitan Phoenix Indian Coalition Urban Indian Advisory Committee (City of Phx)	
		Indian Adoption Project (1973) Affiliated Indian Centers of AZ (1974)[b] Indian Rehabilitation (1976) Urban Indian Law Project (1978) Kee N' Bah Day Care (1978) Indian Community Health (1978)[c] Guiding Star Lodge (1978)
	Arizona Indian Alliance on Alcoholism Assoc Native American Arts Coop (1982) ATLATL (Arts) (1984)	

NOTES:

[a] Arizona law prohibited the sale of alcoholic beverages to Indians (on or off the reservation) until 1954. It should not be surprising that there were no widely acknowledged public drinking places until this statute was revoked.

[b] According to a long-term employee of the Affiliation of Arizona Indian Centers, the directors of Indian centers in Tucson, Flagstaff, and Phoenix got

[continued]

[continued]
together in 1960 to form an organization that was conceived as an administrative and technical resource for all three. He also acknowledged, however, that the substantive beginning of Affiliation activities began with the 1974 passage of the federal Comprehensive Employment Training Act (CETA).

c The Phoenix Urban Indian Health Board was formed in 1978, and changed its name in 1983 to Indian Community Health.

groups. Because of the sometimes overlapping, sometimes conflicting purposes around which these organizations were formed, there then formed a series of meta-organizations to provide an arena for articulating an armistice. The short lifespans of these meta-organizations (e.g., Metropolitan Phoenix Indian Coalition, Urban Indian Advisory Committee) attest to both the depths of factionalism that had developed among the grassroots organizations, and the changes that the grassroots organizations themselves underwent in the late 1970s from community-based to contractor establishments.

Prominent for their persistence through much of the institutional metamorphoses over the past three decades are the Indian bars. Three of them are in town, and several more are located on the reservation borders at the outskirts of the urbanized area. The border area bars serve the reservation communities to which they are adjacent, with relatively few off-reservation residents travelling to these places to do their drinking. The in-town bars, however, serve both the reservation and off-reservation residents of the region. At these places, on any given evening, one might encounter a diverse mix of city dwellers, fun-seekers from the nearby reservations, and individuals who are in town on official business or just passing through on their way to a destination that may be yet a considerable distance away.

Indian bars are institutions in the same sense as the social service organizations, in that the bars also provide a service to a distinctive clientele. Although the service the bars provide is, admittedly, diffuse, at the very least they offer a congenial place to gather in the company of friends and familiar strangers, with access by non-Indians highly restricted. It is out of the activities that take place in these institutional contexts that a community forms, rather than having a community create institutions to serve its needs.

THREE CASES

The remainder of this discussion examines in some detail the process by which a community grows out of institutionalized activities. First, I trace the institutional career of the Phoenix Indian Center, which started as a grassroots organization but has turned to government contracts for the largest portions of its institutional support. Next, I describe the Arizona Commission on Indian Affairs, which was created by the state government in the early 1950s, and faces a serious threat to its existence because of statehouse politics. Finally, I offer an excursion to the area's Indian bars, which take their participants away from more visible public settings, and which endure while the flux in funding fashions hastens a changing of the agency guard.

THE PHOENIX INDIAN CENTER

The Phoenix Indian Center's (PIC) developmental career illustrates the manner in which, in order to persist, ethnic organizations restructure themselves in accommodation or conflict with forces within and outside the local population. The operation of outside constraints on local Indian organizations poses important problems for their continuation and political self-direction. The organization's response to outside forces affects its ability to actively engage urban Indian residents.

What started, in other words, as a grassroots—or self-contained / self-help—response to an unfamiliar and trying urban social environment, has been able to persist and mature largely due to the Indian Center's receipt of outside (i.e., government) support. As federal policy directives increasingly inform and support Center activities, however, the grassroots nature of its response to community problems and prospects has been fundamentally altered. At the same time, as its service orientation has become more formalized, it has become a forum for personal associations and local training and networking resource for other urban Indian organizations.

In 1947, the Center opened to provide a social gathering place and an information center for Indians visiting or recently moved to the city. The Center was first located in a downtown storefront with an alley entrance. It was placed there, in part, to placate merchants and city leaders who had grown concerned about the Indians who gathered in the downtown area. The building has since been torn down to make way for a city park, and the Center has moved several times before finding its most recent location in an office complex at the edge of the city's central business district.

At first, the Center's organizers met informally, and their storefront offered a place where out-of-town visitors and new arrivals could gather. By 1954, the group incorporated itself and looked to community members to support its modest activities. When it first incorporated, the Center had one paid staff member. The Center's need for assistance grew as its scope of activities increased, and the organization cast its net more broadly as it sought to keep in the business of serving the urban Indian community.

In its early days, the Center looked largely to private sources for support. Local business leaders were asked to provide jobs and job training. For new arrivals, temporary housing arrangements were channeled through church organizations and sympathetic residents. Help for other potentially problematic aspects of city living was later offered through Center-sponsored programs, but in the 1950s, problems with health care, individual legal and civil rights, drinking, and domestic relations were handled informally.

During the 1960s, the Center was in a strategic position as a grassroots organization to become the "social services delivery contractor" that administered some of the "Great Society" programs at the local level. The Center's role as "contractor" was expanded in the 1970s with the establishment of the Office of Economic Opportunity, Comprehensive Employment Training Administration (CETA), and the Administration for Native Americans.

By the mid-1980s, a retrenchment in social service programs had led to an increased demand for accountability regarding public expenditures for these services. This demand had taken the form of an explicit requirement that contractors turn their contracts into self-sustaining ventures, or demonstrate that it is in the public interest to continue these contract expenditures.

At the source of the Center's development has been a fundamental condition of urban Indian existence: once Indians arrive in the city, they enjoy only limited access to reservation services and amenities; yet, they remain members of a relatively isolated ethnic minority category as well. According to research among Indians living in the Los Angeles area,[17] most Indians prefer to rely on other Indians for help, rather than on non-Indians. Research also reveals that Indian people tend to mistrust or lack knowledge about the services of local government, and governments are often equally ignorant of Indians' rights to their services.[18] The Center's development has been an attempt to provide services to urban Indians similar to those enjoyed by their reservation and urban non-Indian counterparts.

Grassroots organizations that have gathered followers from a single, relatively narrowly defined local issue may expand as followers acknowledge a wider basis for concerted activity. An organization may also find itself floundering for a lack of support, and it may seek to preserve some organizational stability by recruiting what formerly had been considered outside sources of support. In either case, a point is reached in the career of most grassroots organizations when additional support for the organization's activities may be more easily obtained from sources outside its customary community base.

This certainly was the case for the Phoenix Indian Center in the late 1960s and early 1970s. Its local supporters could not sustain additional programs on their own. Chaudhuri[19] noted that, in 1970, 55% of all Indian households in metropolitan Phoenix were below the poverty income threshold. Money was available from a variety of federal programs designed to address the problems of impoverished urban minority populations. Federal policy at the time was to encourage "maximum feasible participation of the poor," and to encourage community organizations to deal directly with agencies such as the Office of Economic Opportunity and the

Department of Health, Education and Welfare. As Fiske points out:

> this particular policy or philosophy emerged in part from the advice of social scientists, who saw the apathy of the poor as a result of their powerlessness (e.g., the Moynihan Report). It resulted in community-centered groups that were organized around a target population that was defined as "disadvantaged." In effect, this policy bypassed local bureaucrats (i.e., on a city/county level).[20]

Why did the Center initially choose to pursue these sources of funding? Some long-time urban Indian residents suggest that the Center's leaders were predisposed to look to Washington for help, as their reservation experiences had shaped their perception of available funding. The Phoenix Indian Center is by no means the only Indian organization whose leaders have tended to turn first to Washington for support. By turning to Washington, furthermore, Indians could avoid local government officials, who were preoccupied with managing runaway metropolitan growth. Older Indian residents also had the clear memory of local government restrictions on Indian voting rights that had been struck down only by a 1948 Supreme Court decision, and municipal ordinances that persisted into the 1930s keeping Indians from certain sections of town unless they had some official business to conduct.[21]

Direct from Washington, then, came an infusion of support for grassroots groups like the Phoenix Indian Center. Because of its relatively long-standing presence, the Center offered a better track record than other, newer organizations could muster.

The support was not without its strings attached, however, and although government contracts have kept the Center going, decisions concerning the nature of help provided and those to whom help can be offered may no longer be within the province of the Center's staff, directors, or the population that it purports to serve.

How has control over Center programs shifted to funding agencies? Answers are to be found in the nature of the accountability that the public agency requires of its contractor, and the effect that this accountability requirement has on the contractor's regard for its clients' interests. A social services contract, typically, is negotiated by two parties whose agendas only partially overlap. The contractor and the funding agency both want needy clients to receive assistance, but the agency is responsible for seeing that public funds are stretched as far as they can among "deserving" or eligible clients. The contractor, for its part, often takes the position that it must keep its doors open and its staff paid if it is to provide any services to any clients. As a result, the contractor may calculate its projected costs first, and only then does it translate these calculations into the funding agency's terms.

Social service contracts usually specify the types of services that will be offered, and the discrete chunks—or "units"—into which each type is divided. Types of services are identified in terms of a "service unit taxonomy," and for each type of service to be offered, there is a numerical goal of "units" to be delivered. A typical Service Unit Contract with the City of Phoenix for the Senior Citizens Program is broken down in the manner illustrated in Table 2.

TABLE 2
SERVICE UNIT CONTRACT, CITY OF PHOENIX DEPARTMENT OF HUMAN RESOURCES DIVISION OF AGING, 1982-1983

Type of Service	Type of Unit	Goal (in Units)
Social & Recreational	15 minutes	36,000
Outreach	15 minutes	9,000
Information & Referral	1 contact	4,800
Transportation	1 one-way trip	432
Telephone Reassurance	15 minutes	5,500
TOTAL SERVICE UNITS		55,732
CITY OF PHOENIX BUDGET (1982-1983)		$12,948
COST PER UNIT OF SERVICE		$0.2323

Each unit of service is considered equivalent to the next, regardless of the incremental (or marginal) cost of providing services, economies of scale, or the relative importance of the service to the client. Written into the contract with the funding agency is the annual target (expressed in terms of units of service) that a contractor establishes on the basis of staff resources, program operating hours, and expected levels of client need or participation.[22]

If the contractor exceeds its overall target, then its subsequent budget requests will have to prove that these new targets are sufficiently ambitious. If the contractor fails to reach its overall target, then the funding agency will question the contractor's ability to realistically assess their organizational capabilities, and will decrease their subsequent contract awards accordingly. It is, therefore, to the contractor's advantage when securing funds for continuing programs to be able to demonstrate what the funding agency considers to be a sufficiently ambitious organization that has a realistic grasp of its service delivery capabilities. Both ambition and capability, in turn, are measured by calculating the contractor's actual cost per unit of service delivered, and by comparing per unit service costs with original estimates and with the performance of other contractors.

What are some of the consequences of using this "cost per unit of service" as the basis for evaluating contractor performance? For the funding agency, keeping tabs in this manner offers both program documentation and control over the expenditure of tax dollars. Simply put, the agency conditions its continuing support on the contractor's willingness to conform to agency expectations.

For the contractor, this form of accountability has direct effects on staff, program offerings, and the kinds of client needs that are met. Contract reporting requirements divert staff time from direct client service, with weekly, monthly, quarterly, and annual compilations commonly necessary for each funding source. Add to reporting requirements the grant-writing and bookkeeping specialists who secure funds and guide the organization through a maze of procurement regulations, and there is little wonder why the Indian Center's single largest category of employees is "Administrative."

Moreover, service unit taxonomies are established in a political arena that transcends ethnic and local boundaries, and the funding levels for various types of service offerings can fluctuate wildly from year to year. This often results in a staff full of generalists who must feel equally comfortable with whatever funding fashion has been recently instituted. The resulting on-the-job training costs are substantial when measured in terms of time and resources spent *not* with clients, but at workshops, conferences, and the like. As with many social service organizations, the Indian Center has a relatively high rate of staff turnover among the low-paying, stressful positions that deal directly with clients. The resources diverted to training because of funding fashion and staff turnover may not fall too short of the resources spent on direct client service. In this somewhat cynical view, one of the primary community development benefits that the Indian Center offers through its contractor services is the training that it provides to its staff.

Providing help for those in need remains the crucial concern. The mature organization, having dealt with uncertain resources and a transitory community base, is in a difficult position. The Center needs to keep its doors open to continue to offer programs, and its administrators feel that the funds that are most readily available to do so are from public agencies. But the Center has to cope with the conditions placed on the types and levels of services it can offer to the community with those funds, and it finds itself coping as much with service delivery contracts and the agencies from which these contracts originate as it finds itself providing help.

Has the Phoenix Indian Center's increased reliance on federal money isolated the Center from its local support base, or from other local Indian organizations? Active interest and participation in Phoenix Indian Center programs and events are far from universal. Many long-term urban residents regard the Indian Center as a social service agency. They do not feel they have the need for public assistance, and therefore have little occasion to become involved in the Center's activities. Says one young adult who has lived in the city all of her life:

> Our family has always gotten along just fine. My mother and father both worked. They both had

good jobs. We just didn't ever have the kinds of problems that they help you with over there. I know some of the people who work over there, from church, or growing up with them, so it isn't like we're snobs or anything. I don't know if it's true, but most (Indian) people you talk to will probably tell you that besides the (Native American Recognition Week) parade and pow wow, the Center's there if you've got food stamps or legal problems. Our family's never had either, that I know of.

It is significant, I think, that prominent urban Indian leaders feel strongly that the Center has *not* outlived its usefulness. They suggest, in general, that the Center's Board and administrators have found federal monies to be relatively easy to obtain in the past, and that this does not appear to be the case for at least the immediate future. They further suggest that the Center's leaders need to become more resourceful and willing to take greater risks than they have in the past in seeking program support. They point to other organizations in the metropolitan area that have more or less weaned themselves from federal funds, indicating that creative leadership could accomplish the same for the Indian Center, and in the process they will come to depend on one another to a greater extent than they have previously.

The Center's first risk-taking steps have not involved a shift away from federal funding sources. Within the federal government, however, the Center has turned to a few alternative sources in its efforts to offer programs that will attract a broader segment of the metropolitan area Indian population. Even with efforts to engage more people in an expanded array of Center-sponsored activities, it is difficult to overcome the "client service" approach with which Center staff members organize their excursions away from public assistance or counseling and into the realm of socializing and promoting urban Indian cultural awareness.

However, the Center's "client service" orientation has not required an elaborate institutional mechanism for handling public relations, both within and outside the metropolitan area Indian population. Without such a mechanism, the Center is not as well equipped as it might be to bring into its orbit people who have previously had little contact with the Center. For Center-sponsored activities that fall outside its conventional services, the Center can no longer rely on word-of-mouth contact. The metropolitan area Indian population is too dispersed, too diverse and apparently divided into two segments, one of which appears to be relatively cohesive, while the other is relatively transient and atomized.[23]

In addition, the population is too sophisticated a media audience to respond positively to ill-planned Center publicity. So long as it has been a social services agency, the Center has never had to be concerned about its public relations mechanism. It has received its public assistance, family and behavioral counselling, and employment seeking clients from referrals by the state and local welfare authorities. The Center has always been located in or near the part of town with the greatest concentration of Indians with social service needs, so its physical presence and accessibility have had a decidedly service orientation. If the Center wants to sponsor performing and visual arts presentations, or introduce Indian high schoolers to the humanities, it must compete for the attention and support of a following among the local Indian population. The Center needs to let Indians know that it is no longer just for social services, and it needs to present itself with a slickness that compares favorably with the sophisticated media techniques associated with non-Indian entertainment events and programs.

Up-to-date computerized mailing lists for direct mail advertising, periodical publications that are printed on time, active cultivation of contacts with the television, radio, and newspaper outlets in town—only very recently have these been instituted at the Phoenix Indian Center. They indicate that the Center is changing to accommodate funding sources outside the local area. These sources measure the value of their support in terms of the number of people benefiting from their money. By being responsive to outside funding sources, the Center hopes to demonstrate a potential for accomplishment that will increase its support in the local Indian population.

THE ARIZONA COMMISSION ON INDIAN AFFAIRS

As Fiske[24] noted, a distinctive type of urban Indian institution is incorporated into local governmental decision-making bodies rather than providing direct services. This type of institution serves instead in an advisory capacity, as an investigative unit (looking into such "problem areas" as housing, health care, and employment), or as a funding agency itself. The Arizona Commission on Indian Affairs is such an institution. It was established as a state agency at the request of tribal leaders in 1953, for the purpose of reviewing the conditions facing Arizona's Indian population. The Commission consists of 13 members, all appointed by the Governor: seven Indian members, two non-Indian members-at-large, and four who serve by virtue of their office. The *ex officio* members designated by the authorizing legislation are the Governor, Superintendent of Public Instruction, Attorney General, and Director of the Department of Health Services. The Commission has a staff of four, including an executive secretary, a field coordinator, an administrative assistant, and an office secretary. Its annual budget is extremely modest, less than $200,000 in fiscal year 1989.

State agencies in Arizona are required to undergo a performance audit every five years, and the auditor general's office recommended at the beginning of 1985 that the Commission not be continued after its funding was scheduled to expire in July 1986. The legislature ultimately decided not to eliminate the Commission, but the review process that led to this decision reveals a fascinating institutional history. In recent years, the Commission has been criticized for "not adequately addressing the major issues affecting Arizona's Indian population and State agencies serving Indian citizens."[25] The agency's function could be better handled, according to this recommendation, by "terminating the current Commission and restructuring it as an office of Indian affairs within the Governor's office."[26]

In strong language, the Commission's activities were characterized as inadequate. In its earlier years, it was expected to provide a forum in which discussions could take place that would clarify jurisdictional ambiguities, and clarify state responsibilities to its Indian citizens. More recently, the

Commission has been expected to articulate mutual interests between state and tribal governments. These interests reside in such areas as economic development, taxation, education and health care, water management (especially the federally- and locally-sponsored Central Arizona Project), and transportation planning. The auditor general's report states, however, that:

> Although there is a need for state involvement to provide coordination between the State and tribes to address important issues, the Arizona Commission of Indian Affairs does not fulfill this need. The Commission does engage in worthwhile activities; however, the majority of the staff's activities are small scale and do not address important State-tribal issues. Intergovernmental concerns are not addressed because the Commission and its staff lack direction and leadership.[27]

The "small scale" activities in which the Commission has been engaged include the sponsorship and organization of ten "Indian Town Halls" bringing state and tribal officials together to discuss specific issues. Topics have included water rights, tribal sovereignty, contracting for state-provided public services, and control of natural resources. The Commission also developed a proposal to obtain federal funding for an economic development center for Indian entrepreneurs. It publishes an updated directory listing key tribal officials in the state each year.

The bulk of Commission staff activity seems to be taken up with honoring requests for information, or appearances at speaking engagements by the executive secretary and field coordinator. A survey of state agencies and tribal officials indicated that the Commission was not used to assist in "resolving significant problems." Moreover, the Commission was accused of meeting infrequently and failing to provide sufficient direction to its staff to permit the agency to fulfill its legislatively-specified goals.

Representatives from the Commission responded to charges of inadequacy by blaming the legislature. The executive secretary claimed that the Commission was not designed as a "super agency" to deal with the state's Indian population. He said that the legislative mandate is to "consider and study conditions among Indians residing in the state," and that the Commission is doing this job as well as it can be expected, given the budget limitations imposed on it by the legislature. In response to the auditor general's finding that the Commission had failed to involve itself as closely as it could with coordinating state-tribal exchanges of information, the executive secretary said that he has no inclination to "interfere" with tribal governments, and that such interference on the part of the state agency would be inappropriate at best, an infringement on the essential sovereignty of the tribes.

In the Fall, 1985, hearings were conducted by The Arizona Legislative Committee on Intergovernmental Relations concerning the auditor general's performance review of the Commission. At these hearings, the Commission's representatives, as well as tribal officials from around the state, were given a chance to respond to the recommendation that the agency be abolished, with its functions being taken over by a branch of the governor's office. Several tribal chairmen addressed the committee, each suggesting that placing the Commission's functions within the Governor's Office would be "too political," and would subject Indians to even more outside control than they already experience with the BIA looking over their shoulders. The initial legislation authorizing the Commission was blamed for the perceived inadequacies reported by the Auditor General, and could be remedied by drafting revisions that would restructure the Commission and offer a clearer statement of the Commission's purposes. Even the legislative committee members acknowledged that "the Commission was created as a symbol, and it has always been funded as a symbol, thereby rendering it ineffective."

The relationship between the state's Commission on Indian Affairs and the tribes' Intertribal Council of Arizona (ITCA)—the extent to which the two organizations duplicate and complement one another's activities—figured prominently in the legislature's decision concerning the Commission's ultimate fate. If there is already an organization that is fulfilling the responsibilities for which the Commission was created, the legislators reasoned, and if it is doing so without state funding, then the State could save some money by eliminating the agency.[28]

ITCA lobbies for legislation and policy at all levels of government—federal, state, and local—on behalf of all its member tribes, which include all reservations in Arizona but the Navajo. When state issues are at stake, in the areas of roads, water, education, taxes, and tourism, for example, the Commission is the state agency through which the ITCA makes its voice heard.

The chairman of the O'Odham Tahono (Papago) tribe, a prominent Arizona Indian leader who was once the director of the State's Indian Education programs, a Commission board member, and a member of the board of directors of ITCA, testified at one of the legislative hearings concerning the Commission. After clarifying the nature of the relationship between ITCA and the Commission, he was asked for his frank assessment of the Commission's value. He said that while he was a Commissioner, he found himself frustrated by the low attendance at Commission meetings—the Governor had not gotten around to filling vacant appointments. He assured the legislative committee that there is sufficient expertise within the Indian community to overcome past limitations that the Commission has been justly described as having.

This reassurance of adequate organizational capacities has a familiar ring to it. The theme of a 1984 National Indian Education Association congress held in Phoenix, "organizational capacity building" became a rallying cry in the world of Indian service institutions. It is probably best understood as a response to the critical assessment leveled against earlier federal policies that were guided by the dictum: "maximum feasible participation." In the wake of inner-city violence and the failure of local governments to listen seriously to urban ethnic minority groups, the federal government sought to fund ethnic community organizations directly. The premise was that community-based organizations were more likely than local government agencies to succeed in addressing community development problems, because people were more likely to listen to organizations than to government representatives. If the minority group members felt they had some control over the ways in which problems were defined and solutions were considered, as they might if the local governments (often perceived as the source of the problems) were bypassed, then they would more actively participate in community-based organizational activities. Housing projects, health care and day care facilities, schools, and consumer organizations were reorganized at what was termed the "grassroots" level, although the money was coming directly from federal agencies.

More often than not, however, the local organizations had formed in order to take advantage of the funds being made available directly to contractors. Hence the spurt of organizing activity that resulted in the clump of Phoenix urban Indian service organizations in the mid-1970s (see table 1). Perhaps it was the need for community organizing that led Congress to make funding available, but it was the availability of funds that provided the immediate stimulus for creating the organizations—they simply had not existed before federal funds were available. With relatively short prior histories, many of these organizations had not had opportunities to establish their credibility and visibility among community members. Even if they had a more or less substantial community support base, they had little experience in administering service contracts. As a result, the whole program of distributing money directly to community organizations through block grants and revenue sharing mechanisms met with the harsh and often warranted criticism that these organizations simply did not have the capacity to assume the responsibilities offered by the promise of maximum feasible participation.

Although it is a state agency, and not a community organization, the state's Commission on Indian Affairs is treated by the legislature and the auditor general's office as though it were a service agency. The Commission is faulted for not having adequately "served" either the state's Indian population, or the state's administrative departments in their dealings with Indians in the state. The Commission's board of policy makers is appointed directly by the governor, and its staff members are subject to the same civil service requirements as non-Indian state employees in positions of comparable responsibility. Yet the competence of its organizational capacities is evaluated as though the Commission were a service contractor to the state, and its performance as a contractor is evaluated in terms of the cost per units of service delivered. Even as an institutional type that has been incorporated into the government decision-making apparatus, the Commission is expected to offer assurances that the Indian community can provide administrators with sufficient ability to justify the Commission's continued existence.

THE INDIAN BARS

One type of Indian institution whose continued existence does not seem to be in question is the Indian bar. Of course, there are many other contexts for gathering sociably besides bars. Indeed, avoiding the bars and drinking altogether is a prime motivation for a number of informally instituted recreational pursuits. Nevertheless, Indian bars are an enduring social institution among Phoenix urban Indians. Price suggests that socializing at bars becomes very important to urban Indians because in this context they are known and respected, and through bar cliques they can enjoy city life.[29] Waddell[30] argues that by drinking publicly, and by taking part in the bar scene in particular, an individual can make it clear to himself and to other Indians that he too is Indian. In a city like Phoenix, where Indians constitute a small minority, bars are highly sociable gathering places where Indians become a localized majority. Bars, however, are by no means the only public places in which urban Indian drinking occurs. Drinking also takes place in a few public parks, behind specific public buildings and in alleys, in parking lots outside of dance halls and athletic arenas where Indian events are taking place, and in the yards of Indian residences.[31] There is more to the bar scene than drinking, however. Drinks in a bar cost more than they would in another setting, and penalties for driving while intoxicated in Arizona are among the stiffest in the country, making the risk of bar-hopping or driving home after a night on the town relatively costly.

Price[32] observes that urban Indian bars are often located in the same parts of town in which homeless "street people" congregate, and that, as a result of these skid row locations, the Indians who retain a strong point of reference to the bars are often ill-equipped to adjust successfully to city life. People who are a part of the urban Indian bar culture, in Price's view, usually either leave town for the reservation after a relatively short stay, or they find longer-term employment and housing in the city, reducing or eliminating their involvement in the bars.

In Phoenix, the Indian bars are not "skid row" bars. Phoenix's version of "skid row," a jumble of adult movie theaters, single room occupancy (SRO) hotels, public parks with benches and shade trees, missions, and taverns, is located along eight to ten blocks of several streets stretching between the Greyhound bus terminal on the east and state capitol complex on the west. Known for many years as "The Deuce," this area is rapidly being redeveloped. Older buildings are being torn down to make way for new office and commercial complexes. In September 1985, the City of Phoenix succeeded in having the area designated as a "slum" in accordance with U.S. Housing and Urban Development guidelines in order to qualify for federal aid in building an ambitious governmental mall. As central business district workers arrive each morning, they see dozens of men stirring to shake off the early dampness. As the workers evacuate the area each evening, they might pass the homeless men queuing up in the front of the local CBS affiliate's television studios on their way to get their mission soup kitchen supper.

The bars in the Deuce are unseemly places, even to the vast majority of the area's street people. Long-term patrons of such places as Lil's, the Silver Dollar, and Harry's feel they are often at risk of being rolled or robbed, as there are always newcomers who grow fortified by their fill of drink and the knowledge that one must have some cash to remain off the street. Unlike the original Skid Road in Seattle,[33] or the districts in Canadian cities to which Price is referring, the concentration of Indians among the SRO hotel and homeless populations in Phoenix has probably never been greater than 10%.[34] Thus, it is understandable that the bars of the Deuce and the Indian bars in Phoenix are not the same places.

Price's comments about the "dysfunctional" nature of the bar culture and the bar clique for urban Indians may be more appropriate in cities where the Indian bars are found in the skid row section of town.

Just as they are not the "dysfunctional," altogether disreputable places that they may be in other cities, as social institutions, the Indian bars in Phoenix do not closely resemble service agencies or part of the metropolitan political apparatus. There are three of them in town,[35] and each has maintained a distinctive clientele among urban residents, those who come into town for the evening from nearby reservations, and those who are merely passing through town. One is located within a couple of blocks of the Phoenix Indian Medical Center and IHS District administrative offices. It caters to an older crowd, many of whom are employed in career jobs with the federal government. The other two bars, on the other hand, cater to a younger crowd, and more of their patrons are likely to be out-of-towners than at the one near the medical center. The three bar owners are non-Indians, and they each own establishments by the same names in Gallup, New Mexico.

None of the three are particularly fancy places. The one near the medical center, the Ponderosa, is the smallest, with a single room containing an undersized pool table and three Naugahyde booths in addition to its bar. On a crowded Friday or Saturday night, there might be as many as thirty people in the place. The Esquire has two rooms, one with five booths and two pool tables, the other with the bar, three booths, and a tiny bandstand and dance floor that together take up half the main room. Filled to capacity on a night where dancing to live music is featured, the Esquire might hold 100 people, two or three of whom might be non-Indian companions. The Can Can was the largest, and probably the rowdiest of the bars. Not coincidentally, it has moved locations more than the other two. In its earliest incarnation, it was located within easy walking distance of the central city neighborhoods in which even today there remains the greatest concentration of poor Indian households. The "Can" moved in 1978 slightly further from the neighborhoods to a building that had formerly been a good-sized restaurant on the northern edge of the city's central business district. It had two rooms, one of which had a large dance floor and several tables in addition to the bar, the other with two pool tables, and several booths and tables for drinking patrons. Live music was featured Thursday, Friday, and Saturday evenings, and the crowds would get so large that they would spill over into the parking lot and across a major commercial artery to the parking lot of an office complex and adjacent fast food hamburger restaurant.

Not all urban Indians go to the bars, holding in low regard the prevalence of drunken comportment and associated "time out" during which the clock of social responsibility is temporarily halted.[36] All three are congenial places, however, where patrons no longer feel conspicuous in a crowd of non-Indians. Drinks are generously exchanged, and friendly gambling occurs over a vast array of pool and dice games. Beyond a certain level of proficiency at the pool table, this gambling assumes a redistributive function, as the difference between winning and losing is more a matter of turn taking, and not dependent on one's virtuosity with a cue stick.

There is an inescapable impression that the urban Indian bars are decidedly not "citified." In fact, it may be their non-city trappings that constitute one of the main sources of the bars' appeal for those who go frequently. An increasing number of Indians have some post-secondary or vocational educational experience, and many work in office settings as tribal and federal government employees or for social service agencies. At the bars, however, the mode of dress includes boots, hats, Levis, fancy belt buckles, and western shirts. The juke boxes carry country and western tunes, and the dance bands most often feature similar music, offering a comforting familiarity to those who seek it. Not surprisingly, Phoenix Indians do not find such bars uniformly appealing. Those who avoid such places include individuals who regard themselves as urban and cosmopolitan, those who do not wish to be reminded of a part of their past, in addition to those for whom drinking is not a part of socializing.

Will the bars persist as social institutions as the urban Indian population in Phoenix becomes increasingly city-born and raised? Although the current temperance movement may limit bar patronage, individuals who are otherwise conspicuous for their minority status have few other opportunities to fade into a crowd of friends and familiar strangers as part of a highly localized majority. It seems more likely that the ambiance of the bars will change to reflect more urbanized tastes in music and dress, but their essential character will remain as congenial places appealing to the many individuals for whom alcohol is an ingredient in socializing behavior.

SUMMARY AND CONCLUSION

The explosive growth of Sunbelt cities offers an opportunity to refresh our thinking on such fundamental urban processes as political mobilization through ethnic institutions. Phoenix, Arizona is essentially a new city, having increased in population nearly twenty-fold since the end of World War II. Written on a sprawling blank slate in the central Arizona desert, at least for off-reservation metropolitan area Indian residents, is the legacy as formally instituted federal administrative activities and the opportunities created for channeling of common interests and actions into ethnic institutions, permitting the transfer of information, resisting intrusion of outsiders, and promoting the material improvement of urban Indian life.

The case of the Phoenix Indian Center is instructive because it illustrates the career of the institution, flexible and resilient as it changed from its initial service orientation reliant on private support, through its days as a service delivery contractor with the associated advantages and limitations, to the emerging cultural organization faced with the challenge of appealing to a sophisticated market. The State Indian Commission case reviewed here is also instructive, especially noting a critical juncture in the Commission's history when its very purpose and necessity were called into question. It illustrates the intra-group competition for resources, including talented staff, while recognizing the need to exist not just in the world of the Indian service population but in the broader context of state politics. In the terms used by students of urban ethnicity, one can't simply define one's purpose and make it stick—other ascription is equally important. The bars' enduring character is rooted in their appeal to many for whom alcohol is an ingredient in socializing along with athletics and other recreational pursuits, creating a more diffuse, informally instituted set of activities growing out of work.

From a policy perspective, it is the local political arena in which urban Indians will find themselves more centrally engaged in the years to come. Increasingly left exposed by shifting federal policy, the material interests of urban Indians will perhaps best be served by a political mobilization strategy that focuses inward on distinctively *Indian* concerns. In the longer term, once the urban Indian community has better established itself as a local political force to be reckoned with, its collective interests may be better served by joining with the ethnic minority groups that greatly outnumber it at present. For now, however, ties between urban Indians and their Hispanic and Black counterparts appear so attenuated that to strengthen these ties would divert organizing efforts from the more immediate community development tasks at hand.

If that is exclusionary in its outlook, it is only modestly so. The community's institutional network represents an important material resource that can be strengthened through self-conscious effort. The tangible benefits that can be achieved in this manner are exceeded only by the feelings of comfort that are generated by the knowledge that a familiar realm persists amidst the change and uncertainty heralded by the future.

NOTES

1. This work was supported by the National Science Foundation (grant #BNS8317262) and the Wenner Gren Foundation for Anthropological Research (Grant-in-aid #4350). Research assistance was provided by Alyce Sadongei. Additional assistance was provided by Tammy Sixkiller, Phyllis Bigpond, and Sandra Wilks at the Phoenix Indian Center. James Eder, Donald Bahr, Brian Foster, Robert Trennert, and John Aguilar provided most helpful commentary regarding this research.

2. The term "urban Indian" carries with it connotations that some metropolitan area Indian residents find

objectionable. The term can be used with at least two possible senses. It may simply designate an urban area resident, or it may convey a sense that an individual considers the urban area to be his/her "home," rather than some reservation community or ancestral lands. People who take the term in this second sense often feel that to be referred to as an "urban Indian" is to be considered somehow "less Indian." I use the term here with the first of these two meanings, referring simply to those metropolitan area residents who consider themselves to be Indians.

3. James Hirabayashi, William Willard and Louis Kemnitzer, "Pan-Indians in the Urban Setting." In T. Weaver and D. White (Eds.), *The Anthropology of Urban Environments.*" Society for Applied Anthropology Monograph No. 11. (Boulder, CO: The Society for Applied Anthropology, 1972), 78-87.

4. Hazel W. Hertzberg, *The Search for an American Indian Identity: Modern Pan-Indian Movements.* (Syracuse: Syracuse University Press, 1971).

5. American Indian Policy Review Commission, *Final Report on Urban and Non-Reservation Indians.* Task Force 8, (Washington, DC: U.S. Government Printing Office, 1976), 41.

6. John A. Price, "U.S. and Canadian Urban Ethnic Institutions," *Urban Anthropology* 4, (1975), 35-52; Wayne Bramstedt, "Corporate Adaptations of Urban Migrants: American Indian Voluntary Associations in the Los Angeles Metropolitan Area." Ph.D. dissertation Anthropology Department, University of California, Los Angeles, 1977.

7. Shirley J. Fiske, "Urban Indian Institutions: A Reappraisal from Los Angeles." *Urban Anthropology* 8 (2), (1979), 149-171.

8. Price, "U.S. and Canadian Urban Ethnic Institutions," (1975), 35-52.

9. Ibid., 38.

10. Ibid., 36.

11. Ibid., 42.

12. Fiske, "Urban Indian Institutions," (1979), 149-171.

13. Anthony Leeds, "Locality Power in Relation to Supralocal Power Institutions." In Aidan Southhall (ed.), *Urban Anthropology*, (Oxford: Oxford University Press, 1973), 15-41.

14. Ibid., 150.

15. Ibid., 66.

16. Karen Tranberg Hansen, "Ethnic Group Policy and the Politics of Sex: The Seattle Indian Case," *Urban Anthropology* 8 (1), (1979), 29-47.

17. Joan Weibel, "Native Americans in Los Angeles: A Cross Cultural Comparison of Assistance Patterns in the Urban Environment," Ph.D. diss. (Los Angeles: University of California Anthropology Department, 1977).

18. Sister Mary Rose Christy, "American Urban Indians—A Political Enigma. A Case Study: The Relationship Between Phoenix Urban Indians and Phoenix City Government." M.A. Thesis, (Tempe, AZ: Arizona State University Political Science Department, 1979).

19. Joyotpaul Chaudhuri, *Urban Indians of Arizona: Phoenix, Tucson, Flagstaff*, (Institute of Government Research, Arizona Government Series, No. 11, University of Arizona Press, 1974).

20. Fiske, "Urban Indian Institutions," (1979), 164.

21. Michael J. Kotlanger, "Phoenix, Arizona: 1920-1940." Ph.D. diss. (Arizona State University Press, Department of History, 1983).

22. For example, the Senior Citizens Program activities take place 6 hours a day, 3 days a week, 52 weeks a year, or 936 hours annually. Thus, the maximum number of recreational/social service units an individual client could receive in the course of a year is 3,744. To meet its service unit contract for this category of services, the Program has to average about 10 regular participants throughout the year.

23. Edward B. Liebow, "Category or Community? Measuring Urban Indian Social Cohesion with Network Sampling." *Journal of Ethnic Studies* 16 (4), (1989), 67-100.

24. Fiske, "Urban Indian Institutions," (1979).

25. Auditor General, State of Arizona, *A Performance Audit of the Commission of Indian Affairs*, (Phoenix: Office of the Auditor General, State of Arizona, Jan. 22, 1985).

26. Ibid., 19.

27. Ibid., 12.

28. A digression on state fiscal policy is in order here. In the late 1970s and early 1980s, a taxpayers' movement swept through the U.S., protesting excessive increases in state and

local taxes. Reducing the tax burden can be accomplished in either of two ways: one can limit the amount of revenue collected, or one can limit government spending. In 1978, Californians adopted Proposition 13, which cut government revenues by limiting state property tax rates. Two years later, Arizonans approved a measure that had a similar effect, but accomplished in a different manner. Where California's landmark legislation placed limits on tax revenues, Arizonans opted for a measure that restricted spending. State budget increases were tied to increases in aggregate personal income among state residents. Thus, the Arizona state budget cannot grow any faster than the personal income in the state. As a result, the Arizona Legislature is constantly looking for ways to cut from its budget any costs that could be born directly by the Arizonans who receive the benefits of government services. In this manner, legislators are considering whether the state's tribes would be willing to help fund Commission activities by paying a membership fee, as they do to support the ITCA. This, in effect, would represent an unprecedented requirement that tribal governments fund a state agency. It is not likely to meet with widespread approval among the state's Indian politicians.

29. Price, "U.S. and Canadian Urban Ethnic Institutions," (1975), 35-52.

30. Jack O. Waddell, "Drinking As A Means of Articulating Social Values: Papagos In An Urban Setting." In J. O. Waddell and M. W. Everett (eds.), *Drinking Behavior Among Southwestern Indians: An Anthropological Perspective* (1980), 37-82.

31. Ibid., 45.

32. Price, "U.S. and Canadian Urban Ethnic Institutions," (1975), 35-52.

33. James Spradley, *You Owe Yourself A Drunk: An Ethnography of Urban Nomads*, (Little Brown, 1970).

34. Phoenix South Community Mental Health Center, *The Homeless of Phoenix: A Profile.* Prepared by Carl Brown, Ron Paredes, and Louisa Stark, (Phoenix: Phoenix South Community Mental Health Center, The Salvation Army, St. Vincent De Paul Society, September, 1982); Phoenix South Community Mental Health Center, The Homeless of Phoenix: Who Are They? and What Should be Done? Prepared for the

Consortium for the Homeless, (Phoenix: Phoenix South Community Mental Health Center, St. Vincent De Paul Society, and the Salvation Army, June 1983).

35. The Can Can was forced to vacate the building it had occupied between 1979 and 1985, when the building was sold and torn down to make way for an office and hotel complex. It relocated to a former storefront on north 7th Avenue, but was not able to re-open right away, because of the need for interior remodeling in the bar's new venue. As of July 1989, it had still not re-opened.

36. C. MacAndrew and Robert B. Edgerton, *Drunken Comportment: A Social Explanation*, (Aldine, 1969).

Chapter XVII

Native American Women

Before the arrival of the Europeans, the women of Native American cultures were valued members of society. Because they were considered extensions of the Spirit Mother, women were extremely important in the spiritual aspect of Native culture. Many of the Spirits the Indians called upon for guidance were female. In their role of mother and head of the family, women were appreciated for their contribution to the continuation of cultural knowledge and for the survival of the tribe itself. Although there were gender specific duties, women who wished to perform the masculine tasks were often allowed to become warriors, chiefs, etc. In many tribes, women formed a part of tribal government and were heads of household. As women became older, their status in the tribe increased and they were looked to for advice and wisdom. It is important to note that the status of women did vary from tribe to tribe in traditional cultures.

Women's status changed dramatically when western culture was brought to North America. Traditional Indian religion and society was replaced by Christianity and the European lifestyle. Women lost their spiritual role in the patriarchal new belief system and their other duties lost the prestige they once were given. A combination of changes—men working off the reservation, the breakdown of the extended family, girls leaving school prematurely to help out at home and inadequate, and often destructive, B.I.A. schooling led to women's increased dependence on the men and their lack of marketable job skills outside the home. Women's roles were further devalued by non-Natives who misinterpreted the traditional Indian lifestyle and perpetuated the myth that Native women were submissive and secondary within their own culture.

Education has not been encouraged among Native Americans. Only thirty-one percent of all Indian adults received their high school diplomas. When Native women decide to go on to college, they are discouraged by their family and the other members of their tribe. They are faced with the knowledge that they are going against their cultural standards and are decreasing their chances of marrying a Native man, since they will rarely marry a more educated woman.

Education is just one area where women must try to live by the standards of two very different cultures. To succeed, a woman learns to cope with the mental strain produced by the conflict. However, Native Americans see mental illness as the result of weakness, so they do not often seek psychological counseling. Those who do often complain of the cultural conflicts arising between western psychological ideals and Native American culture. Those who do not seek professional help find their own ways of

463

coping. Unfortunately, coping often involves drugs and alcohol, which only magnifies the problem.

Recently, there has been a trend toward retraditionalizing the roles of Native American women. Traditional roles of guardian and teacher are integrated into the modern roles that today's Native women have established for themselves. In tribes where retraditionalization is being practiced,women are becoming leaders once again. Because they take on these positions as capable, traditional people, they are not only able to perform their duties well, they also do so with the idea that the preservation of the tribe is as important as their own personal achievement. Through their success, Native American women are returning to the respected position they once held within the tribe.

—RNW

Changing and Diverse Roles of Women in American Indian Cultures

Teresa D. LaFromboise, Anneliese M. Heyle, and Emily J. Ozer

This article explores traditional and contemporary sex roles of Indian women. It emphasizes the renewing power of the feminine—a creative, healing balance that arises as traditional and contemporary strengths are brought together. The survival of the extended family throughout two hundred years of government policy attests to Indian women's resilience despite continuous role readjustment, value conflict, and economic pressure. Tribal diversity and predominantly egalitarian structural similarities are affirmed in this work through reviews of ethnographic studies addressing the roles of Indian women prior to European contact. The conventional and alternative roles of Indian women in traditional times are examined with an eye toward the spiritual source of Indian women's strength. Studies outlining the emotional and spiritual costs of contemporary Indian women living bicultural lifestyles, especially those pursuing advanced educational training, highlight the continued use of traditional Indian coping mechanisms. Finally, the current movement toward retraditionalization of roles of Indian women as caretakers and transmitters of cultural knowledge is posited as an effective means of overcoming problems and achieving Indian self-determination.

A fundamental methodological issue in the study of sex roles of Indian women concerns the recognition of original diversity and eventual change in the social structures of American Indian societies.[1] Because traditional American Indian social systems and life patterns have been tremendously disrupted by White colonization and expansion, it is critical to consider gender roles over time and in several contexts: A study of American Indian women's activities and spheres of power must include an examination of their specific tribes' traditional structures, the varying direct and indirect effects of White culture on the tribe, the mediating factors affecting the magnitude and direction of White influence, and the personal and professional responses and adaptations of Indian women to cultural pressures and changes.[2]

There is a dearth of empirical research focused on American Indian women and written from an Indian cultural perspective. The extremely limited empirical research presented on contemporary Indian women provides more information regarding health and economic indicators than on sex roles and the status of women. In fact, there has been scant research on contemporary Indian women outside of a clinical or pathological perspective. While it is true that many current Indian practices and social structures now mirror Anglo culture as a result of forced acculturation, Christianization, and economic change (to name just a few significant forces), Indian women are a dynamic and diverse cultural group whose strength, contemporary lifestyles, and social structures merit increased empirical study and documentation.[3]

There is an increasing body of evidence to support the claim that the non-Indian, male-centered biases of traditional social science research has provided both inaccurate and incomplete depictions of American Indian social systems and behavior. Predominantly male, non-Indian ethnographers of American Indian cultures have selectively chosen to study and have had more access to male activities and male informants. This has led to indirect and distorted descriptions of Indian women's activities and beliefs.[4] The tendency to ignore fundamental female roles, blur tribal variations, and misunderstand the centrality of the Spirit World in Indian life suggests that the veracity of this body of work is questionable.[5]

Ethnographic analysis has also been heavily influenced by stereotypical images, myths, and fantasies which limit Indian women to dichotomous princess/squaw roles.[6] Koehler[7] provides an excellent bibliography of the existing literature regarding Native American women. He points out that the inappropriate perspectives of previous custom studies which focused on isolated aspects of Indian women's lives without understanding their complexity and cultural contexts are finally being supplemented by Indian women's own reflections and research.

Theories and data generated by "outsider" observers regarding American Indian women not only reflect non-Indian expectations and stereotypes regarding Indian women[8] but for the most part also represent the sex roles, status of women, and behavior only while the group conducted its external affairs or interacted with outsiders.[9] In some tribes, dealing with outsiders was a sex-differentiated activity fulfilled by men; non-Indians often overestimated male power within the tribe because they had little experience with women's spheres of power and activity.[10]

Furthermore, considering the widespread, long-term history of violence and oppression waged against Indian people by non-Indians, it would be hard to imagine why Indian women would trust outsiders with the knowledge of their intimate rituals, thoughts, or feelings. Many observer-researchers attempting to "study" American Indian women succeeded more in studying their useful defense mechanisms and coping strategies—such as passive resistance and secrecy—rather than their internal personalities or behavior patterns.[11] Male-centered assumptions—both Indian and non-Indian—have led to interpretations of Indian rituals and traditions now contested by American Indian women.

ROLES OF WOMEN IN TRADITIONAL INDIAN LIFE

A woman's identity in traditional Indian life was firmly rooted in her spirituality, extended family, and tribe.[12] Women saw themselves as collective beings[13] fulfilling harmonious roles in the biological, spiritual, and social worlds: Biologically, they valued being mothers and raising healthy families; spiritually, they were considered extensions of the Spirit Mother and keys to the continuation of their people;[14] and socially, they served as transmitters of cultural knowledge and caretakers of their children and relatives.[15] Great value was ascribed to these traditional female roles.

Many western North American tribes—such as the Klamath—were based on egalitarian systems of reciprocity in which separate, complementary, and equally essential tasks were assigned to each sex.[16] Contemporary Indian social scientists and writers argue that these social systems were misinterpreted by non-Indian observers socialized to equate difference with inequality and hierarchy.[17] Tribal diversity must be stressed: The current claim is not that women in all tribes shared equal status and power with men, but that the high frequency of egalitarian relationships has been greatly underrepresented.

Allen[18] and Beiswinger and Jeanotte[19] emphasize the fundamentality of the Spirit World and tribal members' intensely personal relationships with particular spirits in the social structure and gender roles in traditional Indian life. In this traditional world view, everything in the universe, including a woman's (and man's) power and identity was derived from direct connections to the Spirit World.[20] Many tribes looked to women spirits or mythological forebears of the people like Thought Woman of the Keres, Clay Lady of the Santa Clara Pueblo, Changing Woman of the Navajo, or White Buffalo Calf Woman of the Sioux for an understanding of life and guidance concerning how to behave.[21] Although tribes may have had conventional ideals of behavior for each gender group, nonconformity was identified and sanctioned through dreams or ceremonial connections with particular spirits.

Role and gender variations and sex-differentiated spheres of social and governing power differed according to the social structure and traditions of each tribal group.[22] Although in most tribes there were distinct areas of female and male production, this diversion was not entirely rigid and women's roles and tasks were often extremely variable. In some tribes, women enjoyed significant flexibility and latitude in their gender role and lifestyle preferences.[23] In these societies, free expression of sexuality and nonconformist gender roles were permitted, with nontraditional males and females, gays, and lesbians accepted to varying degrees within the group.[24]

Recent research demonstrates the existence of institutionalized alternative female roles alongside roles that have been interpreted as traditional. Women in Plains tribes, such as Canadian Blackfeet, have typically been pictured as chaste, submissive, and hard-working wives. There is evidence within this tribe for such institutionalized roles as: the independent and aggressive "manly-hearted women," the sexually promiscuous "crazy women," and chief or "sit-by" wife, and the important religious role of the Sun Dance woman. Other examples of alternative female roles in Plains tribes include daring Cheyenne women horse-riders and Lakota girls who were named "child beloved" and were honored by participation in the Buffalo Ceremony and Virgin Fire. There is also evidence from the Apache, Crow, Cheyenne, Blackfeet, and Pawnee tribes that the "warrior woman" role was widespread across the continent.[25]

As the "manly-hearted" and "warrior woman" names suggest, some of the Indian females' alternative roles specifically allowed them to express masculine traits or participate in male-associated occupations without dressing as men or assuming their social roles.[26] Other roles, however, such as the "berdache," which was socially sanctioned at various levels in at least 33 tribes, involved a woman's thorough shift to the male social and occupational role sometimes accompanied by homosexual marriage or sexual relationships (although the berdache's assumed lesbianism is a subject of debate).[27] The "berdache" role is also termed a "cross-gender" role.[28]

Gender identification in pre-colonial Indian tribes, unlike that in Anglo culture, seemed to center on an individual's participation in gender-specific ceremonies and tasks rather than on her sexual anatomy or choice of sexual partners.[29] Transition to a male gender role could be prompted and validated by a girl's interest in traditionally male tasks or a refusal to perform female tasks; Kaska families that had all daughters yet desired a son would encourage the child with the most inclination to become "like a man" to participate in puberty initiation ceremonies and customs for boys instead of girls. Involvement in these activities publicly validated the role change. In the Cocopa tribe, cross-gender females followed the male custom of nose-piercing rather than getting their chins tattooed as did other women.

Although the socializing process differed from tribe to tribe, community recognition and validation of the women's new cross-gender role was acquired through acceptable channels. In the southwest, for example, dream experience was very important in ritual life as an avenue to gain special powers and social sanction of the use of those powers. In such tribes, such as the Mohave, all cross-gender individuals reported dreaming about their role change.

Cross-gender women could not marry men because they could not perform traditional female-specific tasks; in order to gain the household and kinship benefits of marriage, they married women and fulfilled the household, community, and ritual obligations of a male. Cross-gender individuals were often unusually good providers and were valued for their economic contributions to the family and tribe; households with a cross-gender partner were often more wealthy than the norm, probably because they focused on work rather than on children.[30]

There is considerable anthropological debate regarding the defining characteristics, sexual behavior, degree of social acceptance, and prevalence of the cross-gender or "berdache" status; clarifications are often difficult due to confusion and disgust on the part of early non-Indian observers and social scientists. Callender and Kochems[31] provide an excellent review of the contradictory "berdache" literature and highlight the methodological biases and limitations of the assessment of this alternative role. They indicate that outsider cultural biases against transvestitism, cross-gender roles, and cross-sexual behavior made for research that condemned rather than examined the existence of berdaches. Observer bias contributed to Indian reticence regarding berdache acceptance and prevalence, and perhaps led to within-tribe cultural sanctions against the berdache status.[32]

There is substantial support for the view that women were respected and rewarded for successful cross-gender role activity;[33] manly-hearted women and female berdaches earned high reputations[34] and were differentiated from other women by their wealth, status, boldness and efficiency. But although males in the berdache role could earn great respect for success and efficiency in traditionally feminine spheres of work, womanliness was certainly not the typical Indian male ideal.

The status of Indian woman, however, increased with their age (in contrast with Anglo culture's youth emphasis): A post-menopause woman, as the Winnebagos put it, was "just like a man."[35] Older women's age and wisdom were revered and their opinions regarding tribal history, herbal medicines, and sacred matters were valued.[36] Thus, in some tribes it was possible for women to achieve status levels equal to men, but they earned equal status by accumulating years or success in cross-gender tasks.

Some Indian social systems, however, including the Cherokee, Montagnais-Naskapi, Navajo, Iroquois, Mandan, Hopi, Zuni, Northern Paiute and Eastern Pueblo tribes, provide clear evidence that women played critical economic, political, and spiritual roles in tribal life without the advantages of age or cross-gender task success.[37] In these tribes, matrilineal patterns of inheritance were observed and in those with agricultural economies, the land, crops, houses, and tools were owned by the women while the men cultivated the gardens and were responsible for much of the labor. Even in non-agricultural economies women's close relationship to food and the supply of food conferred great power upon her.[38]

Women sometimes exercised formal governing authority on the basis of their spiritual power, as was the case in the pre-colonization Cherokee gynocracy, or "petticoat government," whose Women's Council had a significant influence on tribal decisions. The "Beloved Woman of the Nation," or head of the Women's Council of the Cherokee, was believed to speak the words of the Great Spirit.[39]

Before the tribe's conversion to Catholicism, the Montagnais-Naskapi social system was striking in its women-centeredness and flexibility. Women exercised a great deal of control over family decisions (such as planning when to move) and other household affairs; in fact, missionaries reported, with dismay, that men followed their wives' advice and would not act against their wishes.[40] Women also enjoyed a tremendous amount of freedom regarding issues of sexuality, marriage, and divorce. In general, the Montagnais-Naskapi and Huron cultures were non-authoritarian and peaceful;

children were not punished and women were encouraged to be independent and decisive.[41]

Although males might have monopolized public roles and positions of authority, important family and tribal decisions were also determined in the private sphere; therefore, the reality of power was often very different from its public manifestation.[42] Realizing the importance of private power is critical to understanding Indian cultural systems because—in general—Indian women exercised almost complete control over the home, the children, and belongings inside the home.

IMPACT OF ACCULTURATION ON GENDER ROLES, POWER, AND STATUS

The effects of acculturation on American Indian gender roles of course depend on the original role and status of women before colonization and the nature of the acculturation strategies inflicted upon a woman's particular tribe. The overwhelming result of acculturation has been a breakdown of the complementary nature of male-female relations and a general increase in Indian male dominance and control over Indian women.[43] With the collapse of traditional religion and culture, women lost not only some very fundamental spiritual roles but also lost the significance and ritual power of the sex-specific activities and roles that they were allowed to maintain, such as puberty, menstruation, child-bearing, and domestic responsibilities.[44]

Colonizers considered tribal gender role flexibility, matrilocal and extended family patterns, complementarity in gender power relations, and sexual freedom on the part of women subversive to the intended European-style political, social, and religious order. Sometimes, as in the case of the Montagnais-Naskapi and the Iroquois, Indian men collaborated with the colonizers and helped to subjugate Indian women by the establishment of male-dominated religious and social organizations within the tribe.[45]

Anderson[46] analyzes the relationship between the advent of commodity exchange and production systems and the subordination of women through an examination of the interaction between 17th-century French missionaries and the Montagnais-Naskapi and Huron tribes along the St. Lawrence River. The power of the missionaries to support the tribes' matriarchal and egalitarian social systems in which women were in no way subservient to men fundamentally lay in the colonizer's ability to capitalize on environmental conditions and then completely control the tribe's livelihood and society.

More recently, changes in the traditional economic system of the largest American Indian tribe, the Navajo, have also been identified as contributing to the decrease in women's status and power within the family and the transformation of the extended family pattern into independent households. Navajo women and men originally occupied complementary roles with a system of female inheritance; Navajo women made the family's financial decisions and had at least as much influence as their husbands in all spheres of life.[47]

With men's increased participation in off-reservation employment, there was a shift toward independent families. some families moved to the outskirts of the reservation or to border towns. Women became more dependent on their husbands—characterized by Hamamsy[48] as often erratic and irresponsible providers—for cash income. Men, however, began to claim that their wage labor earnings belonged to them and not to the family group. Complementary roles disintegrated. Women's troubles were compounded by the erosion of the extended family network because they no longer had extensive family help in raising their children. Sometimes Navajo girls were taken out of school to help at home, contributing to their limited education and outside job skills.[49] Recently, higher rates of hypertension were reported among elderly Navajo women than Navajo men due to acculturation, especially among the women who were most educated and isolated.[50]

A major agent of acculturation started in the late 19th century in the practice of removing young Indian children from their homes to attend BIA boarding schools. Numerous studies in the past two decades attest to the psychological trauma and adjustment problems caused by experiences within these boarding schools.[51] Recent research indicates that the stress associated with Indian women's forced attendance in schools away from home during adolescence has apparently been manifested in lowered self-esteem and inhibitions associated with maternal capabilities.[52]

Many of the boarding schools were extremely regimented and Indian girls' education was eventually degraded into domestic labor for the school and for community homes and businesses. Indian girls were given less classroom instruction than Indian boys[53] and were beaten if they resisted the work. Many tried to run away.[54] When female students returned to their reservations, they found that their domestic and cooking skills were not appropriate to the technology or culture of the reservation and they were often mocked or shunned for their "White ways." Some left the reservation to return to the cities, to become maids, prostitutes, and dance hall girls.[55]

The establishment of both the boarding schools and the BIA field matron program represented only two efforts on the part of the U.S. government to teach Indian women how to behave (and work) like White women and thereby rescue them from the perceived drudgery and backwardness of their traditional lives.[56] Even attempts to elevate Indian women to the status of White women through Indian New Deal policies seriously ignored the traditional, political roles Indian women played at that time.[57] It was thought that if Indian women were shown the superiority of White lifestyles, they would then return to the reservation to "civilize" their own people.

Despite traumatic and confusing experiences such as the BIA boarding schools and other modes of forced acculturation, there is evidence that Indian women have been somewhat better able to adapt to acculturation than have Indian men.[58] Perhaps Indian women were seen as less threatening than Indian men. Their tradition of accepted role flexibility may have facilitated a readiness to take on work roles within the dominant society that Indian men would be unwilling or offended to pursue.

Women in some tribes, such as the Oglala Sioux, and Northern Paiute have been more effective than their male counterparts as landowners, political leaders, and liaisons with Whites, thereby increasing their relative power and status.[59] In the case of the Northern Paiute and Oglala Sioux, women received advanced training (primarily in the area of education and social welfare) under federal policies and were then able to better fulfill professional and governmental roles.[60] However, despite isolated accounts of positive advances resulting from acculturation (only relative to Indian men, of course, who have also suffered tremendous reductions in power and status), acculturation has been severely destructive to the status, power, and role flexibility that Indian women in many tribes once enjoyed. Acculturation brought about rigid, Christianized societies intolerant to religious freedom, traditional lifestyles, nonconformist gender and sex roles, and sexual freedom.[61]

BICULTURAL LIFESTYLES

Living in two different cultural worlds, the Indian and the Anglo, can be "a feast of appreciation for human ingenuity, or it can be the bitterest trap."[62] Regardless of an Indian woman's profession, lifestyle, or geographical base, she retains a sense of homeland and duty to her people.[63] Adapting to the majority culture—by moving to cities, attending college or university, or seeking professional jobs and training—can provide greater economic and political opportunities for Indian women and the communities they represent but can also be a major source of conflict and stress[64] and can increase individuals' vulnerability to the development of psychological problems.[65]

Although the high frequency of severe social and economic problems can make reservation life extremely bleak, an Indian woman within her own cultural context at least have the social support of her extended family network and community of people who share her values and practices. Off the reservation, Indian women may become geographically and culturally isolated from their families and may find it extremely difficult to adjust—cognitively and socially—to "White" or majority culture.

In general, the majority culture espouses a work ethic centered around individual achievement, competitiveness, and the accumulation of property and titles; cultural traditions and family ties are often considered of secondary importance compared with personal social and professional mobility. Majority values and societal pressures clearly conflict with primary Indian communal concerns which emphasize observance of tradition, responsibility for extended family and friends, cooperation, and group identification.

Educational Issues

Studies of adolescent Indian females in academic and athletic competition reveal that they (like many women from other cultures) do not focus on their individual success when competing against males but rather will inhibit their own performance level, especially when the men are not performing well.[66] Indian girls' behavior is consistent with their cultural training which stresses cooperation and group cohesion but is clearly counter-productive in Anglo contexts in which individuals are regarded through success in competition.

American Indian college students are clearly anomalies in communities characterized by illiteracy and tremendously high drop-out rates.[67] Nearly one-third of all Indian adults are classified as illiterate and only 31% of all Indians have a high school education.[68] American Indian women must work hard to break down powerful social and psychological barriers just to get into college.[69] Recent empirical research concerning American Indian college women provides evidence that they experience tremendous difficulties in adapting to the competitive culture of higher education institutions[70] and face a multitude of bicultural, conflicting pressures and expectations. Family and community members often discourage Indian women from pursuing post-secondary education and a survey of 61 Indian female undergraduates indicates that almost 90% of the students felt that they were going against their culture by attending college.[71] Furthermore, attending college limits Indian women's chances for marrying within their culture because Indian men without college degrees will seldom marry a university graduate.

In light of the multitude of immediate and concrete pressures working against Indian college women's motivation and ability to lead a productive academic lifestyle, it is not surprising that their college completion rates—which unfortunately must be inferred from statistics for both Indian women and men—are extremely low: 18% for Indian undergraduates, 1% for masters' degree candidates, and .2% for doctoral degree candidates.[72]

Mental Health Issues

American Indian communities are distinguished by many ties among tribal members and strong group cohesion, particularly in time of crisis. Indian people have concerns about psychological concepts such as "mental health," "personality," and "self" because of the absence of naturalistic or holistic tenets in the design and implementation of therapeutic techniques. Traditional healing systems involved a collective process which helped the psychologically troubled individual and also reaffirmed the norms of the group.[73]

Conceptions of mental health are clearly culture-bound. In the Lakota (Sioux) language, mental health is defined as *ta-un*, or "being in a state of well-being."[74] In most Indian cultures, a person is considered to be in a state of well-being when peaceful and exuding strength through self-control and adherence to Indian cultural values. Many American Indians believe that mental illness is a justifiable outcome of human weakness or the result of avoiding the discipline necessary for the maintenance of cultural norms and community respect.[75]

It is significant that conventional "Western" psychology and traditional Indian culture differ in the definition and treatment of psychological troubles.[76] The quantitative research reported in this discussion provides information shaped by the disease-oriented, clinical categories and paradigms of conventional psychology. While extensive empirical studies are critical—especially in determining intervention needs and in assessing the effectiveness of existing mental health programs—their cultural assumptions must be recognized.

There are few data concerning the frequency rates of psychiatric disease and treatment for American Indian women. Only three community-wide American Indian epidemiological studies of psychopathology exist, and the results of these research efforts are not analyzed by sex.[77] Neuroses, alcoholism, psychoses, and drug abuse and dependence are the most frequent problems and account for

40% of all visits to Indian Health Service mental health programs.[78] An unpublished summary of a random sample of caseloads in three urban health clinics reveals that 30% of the patients were seeking medical help for problems psychological in nature.[79]

A recent annual report by the Social and Mental Health Services of the IHS presented percentages for those Indian women who do utilize services according to the following leading problem categories/diagnoses: alcohol misuse in the family (82%), adult-child relationships (78%), grief reactions (77%), depression (76%), child management/abuse (72%), and marital conflict (72%).[80] Many women seeking IHS services have experienced incest, rape, and sexual assault and the incidence of females seeking IHS treatment for violent behavior is 38%.[81] In one recent survey, at least 80% of Indian women clients at a regional psychiatric center serving a five-state area had experienced sexual assault. In 1979, the Navajo Times reported that rape was the most prevalent crime on the Navajo reservation, and there was a trend of organized gang rape on reservations in which a group of males take premeditated revenge on a selected woman.[82]

Despite findings which indicate that the prevalence of depression within select Indian communities may be four to six times higher than previous estimates[83] and that female high school students in tribal-operated boarding schools are more prone to depression and phobic reactions (e.g., performance anxiety) than their male counterparts, IHS records report extremely low rates of psychiatric treatment for women. "Mental disorders" account for 7% of male and 3% of female hospital stays.[84]

Considering the preponderance within both reservation and off-reservation communities of intense life stressors, it appears that American Indian women are significantly underutilizing mental health services. Several surveys suggest that a primary cause of this phenomenon is that American Indians needing help are less aware of the kinds of psychological services available to them than are most Americans.[85]

Even those aware of available services underutilize them because of perceptions that the existing services are unresponsive to their needs.[86] Many American Indians who manage to obtain psychological services do not continue treatment.[87] Dukepoo[88] identified fear, mistrust, and insensitivity as major barriers to mental health service utilization in the Southwest. In addition, Indians often perceive young IHS personnel and doctors as incompetent and inexperienced; in a culture which equates age with wisdom, Anglo doctors and health professionals—who are often young because of college load reductions received for working on Indian reservations—are seen as second-rate.[89]

Cultural distance—expressed as differences in values and expectations between counselors and clients—has been identified as a cause of inappropriate and ineffective therapy with American Indian service populations. American Indians who engage in individual therapy often express concern about how conventional Western psychology superimposes biases onto American Indian problems and shapes the behavior of the client in a direction that conflicts with Indian cultural life-style orientations and preferences. The incompatibility between conventional counseling approaches and indigenous perspectives has been discussed by Jilek-Aall,[90] LaFromboise, Trimble, and Mohatt,[91] and Trimble and LaFromboise.[92] Many American Indians recognize the need for professional assistance, only when informal community-based networks are unavailable.

Besides cultural obstacles in the counselor-client relationship, Indian underutilization of psychological services can also be attributed to neglect by representatives of the U.S. Government and the psychology profession itself in promoting adequate mental health services or health maintenance activities.[93] There is a critical need for more preventive services and rehabilitative interventions for substance abuse and other problems.

With utilization of mental health services low, American Indians often rely on their own coping skills or "self-medication" to manage stress and emotional disturbance. The use of alcohol and drugs as responses to stress is frequent among American Indian women and men and the overall rates of alcohol and drug abuse are high.[94] It has also been known that drugs and alcohol are contributing factors in the frequency of accidental deaths, homicide, suicide, sexual violence, child abuse and neglect, and fetal alcoholism syndrome.[95] As previously stated the rate of death due to alcoholism among American Indian men and women, although declining, is still alarmingly high.

A Congressional hearing on Indian juvenile alcoholism and drug abuse reported that 52% of urban Indian adolescents and 80% of reservation Indian adolescents engaged in moderate to heavy alcohol or drug use as compared to 23% of their urban, non-Indian counterparts.[96] A recent study of high school students in tribal-operated boarding schools indicated differential patterns of drug use between males and females: Female students showed much higher levels of drug use than did their male counterparts and also used drugs at all times of the day compared with more time-restricted male drug use.[97]

Recent research, however, supports the view that alcohol use in some Indian tribes with high rates of alcohol-related deaths is less widespread than in the general U.S. Population. Only 13 to 55 percent of the women in the Navajo and Plains tribes drink alcohol,[98] compared to 60% of non-Indian women.[99] A minority of women in these tribes have serious alcohol abuse problems, despite the alarming statistics on adolescent alcohol experimentation and the pervasive "drunken Indian" stereotype.

To restore or maintain a state of psychological well-being, Indian women and their families are exerting impressive reservoirs of strength and coping mechanisms in the face of harsh environmental realities.[100] Indian women's complex repertoire of coping differs according to age, tribe, and environmental setting. While older women from the Cherokee and Appalachian tribes most often responded to stressful events with inaction or information-seeking techniques,[101] a recent survey of Indian female college students under stress indicates that they rely while coping most heavily on social support.[102] Social support from family and community members—especially for the aged—is a primary value in many American Indian cultures. By pooling resources, energy, ideas, and compassion, social networks insulate people from severe crises and life stress and often help them generate the means of coping with life problems.[103]

In the LaFromboise[104] study referred to earlier, Indian college women employed the following strategies to overcome the stress associated with bicultural conflicts: seeking social support (35%); cognitive methods such as self-talk, problem-solving, and recalling personal and cultural beliefs associated with spirituality (22%); and behavioral actions such as working harder or exercising to relieve tension (18%). Seventeen percent of the college women in the LaFromboise[105] study sought help from formal support systems such as counseling, Alcoholics Anonymous, or financial aid offices, while 5% reacted to stress by employing strategies such as eating, smoking, and using drugs or alcohol.

As indicated earlier, an Indian woman's conception of mental health is often rooted in her sense of order and balance within a holistic framework of family, community, tradition, and universe. Acculturation and bicultural demands often place Indian women in a position of having to fulfill multiple and perhaps conflicting social roles; due to professional or academic pressures, they might also be unable to participate in culturally-valued activities or discharge tribal responsibilities.

Traditional psychological well-being is impossible if integration and balance of these roles is not achieved; furthermore, a woman experiencing bicultural stress may be isolated from the community and tribal context which can provide the social support and cultural framework to help her resolve any conflicts. The problem of community isolation has been remedied in part by the development of "reconstituted" Indian networks; the parameters of the extended family have widened considerably in recent years and reconstituted, intertribal extended families are becoming increasingly common.[106] These families provide Indian women with child care as well as the emotional support and strength to help withstand the stress of multiple commitments to tribe, self, and profession.[107] Informal networks and communities of Indian professional women have also been formed, with colleagues nationwide providing valuable contacts and support in environments often not well understood by families and other members of women's original Indian community. Through reconstituted family networks, Indian women can participate in valued cultural roles they might be unable to fulfill by themselves (e.g., a woman without time or desire for a family may be able to play the caretaking "aunt" role to another woman's child).

RETRADITIONALIZED ROLES OF CONTEMPORARY INDIAN WOMEN

Retraditionalization—or the extension of traditional care-taking and cultural transmission roles to include activities vital to the continuity of Indian communities within a predominantly non-Indian society—represents a major current attempt on the part of Indian women to integrate traditional and contemporary demands in a positive, culturally-consistent manner.[108] The structure of the cultural system remains intact, but the specific jobs are modernized in accordance with social change.

Many Indian women are increasingly visible in professional roles such as social workers, psychologists, writers, artists, political leaders with the intent of serving their communities and tribes. Some noteworthy examples of Indian women leaders include: La Donna Harris (Comanche), president and director of American Indians for Opportunity; Wilma Mankiller, Chief of the Cherokee Nation; Jo Ann Sarracino (Laguna), developer of the Native American Mineral Engineering and Science Program; and Nancy Wallace (Comanche/Creek), manager of the Industrial Engineering Department at Digital, the third largest computer company in the world. These "retraditionalized" American Indian women have achieved success by exhibiting independence, leadership, confidence, competitiveness, and emotional control. Without ignoring their cultural heritage, losing acceptance among their people, or forfeiting the ability to behave appropriately within Indian cultures, Indian women leaders have increased respect and status for Indian people and gained professional recognition for themselves.

Women's political power in a substantial number of tribes is significant and on the rise. Their interest and position in the policy-making arena has stemmed from traditional concerns for the community and has often found a foundation in existing or vestigial female networks and power bases within the tribe. In a study of 10 tribal councils of Nevada reservations, Lynch[109] reports that women constituted the vast majority of local committee and service clubs and that only one tribal council did not have women members.

On the Northern Paiute reservation, matrilocal marriage patterns still in effect—28 out of 32 households contained married men born and raised off of the reservation—facilitated women's ability to take active political roles within the tribe. Women's kinship connections and long-term concerns for community issues, along with the historical importance of women's contributions to the families' existence and their experience in coordinating people in social activities and common goals contributed to their effectiveness as leaders.[110]

Oglala Sioux women—who are steadily occupying more positions as tribal council members, judges, and decision-makers—also credit women's traditional family skills and experiences as important factors in their leadership ability; one Oglala Sioux woman judge explained that as a mother, she was accustomed to making unpopular decisions and making people "stick" to them.[111] Although Oglala women of all ages have become politically active and many have led or participated in protests for treaty rights, few would consider themselves political activists but rather see themselves as people fulfilling vital tribal needs.[112]

Thus, for many Indian women, positions of authority and prominence are natural evolutions of their caretaking role and they see their actions as personal rather than organizational. Their goal is to be productive yet humble leaders by virtue, not position.[113] It is important to recognize that retraditionalization efforts on the part of Indian women are often inconsistent with some goals of the current majority-culture women's movement. Non-Indian feminists emphasize middle-class themes of independence and androgyny whereas Indian women often see their work in the context of their families, their nations, and Sacred Mother Earth.[114] Preservation and restoration of their race and culture is at least as important to Indian women as are their individual goals for professional achievement and success, although many Indian women clearly have made important professional commitments and value the role of work in their lives.

By maintaining their past traditions rather than shedding them, major social and political changes on the part of Indian women may take many years; however, these changes will be firmly based on a solid sense of identity and will involve lowered levels of psychological and interpersonal conflict. Indian women are in the process of redefining identities long-obscured by the stereotypes and misconceptions of others. Despite potential loss of their traditional spiritual base and traditional social and economic roles due to acculturation and the advent of male-centered cultural norms, Indian women have maintained their responsibilities to family and tribe and have continued to work to develop themselves and their communities. With a respect for the past and clear agendas for the future, Indian women remain as a strong force in their own land.

NOTES

1. P. G. Allen, *The Sacred Hoop*, (Boston: Beacon Press, 1986); B. Medicine, "American Indian Women: Spirituality and Status," *Bread and Roses*, 2(1), (1980), 15-18.

2. Ibid.

3. G. Hudson, "Participatory Research by Indian Women in northern Ontario Remote Communities," *Convergence: An International Journal of Adult Education*, 13(1-2), (1980), 24-33.

4. E. Leacock, "Women, Power and Authority," in L. Dube, E. Leacock and S. Ardener (Eds.), *Visibility and Power: Essays on Women in Society and Development*, (Delhi: Oxford University Press, 1986), 107-135.

5. P. G. Allen, "Lesbians in American Indian Cultures," *Conditions* 7, (1981), 67-87; R. Green, "The Pocahontas Perplex: The Image of Indian Women in American Culture," *Massachusetts Review* 14, (1976), 698-714; Medicine, "American Indian Women," (1980), 15-18.

6. Green, "The Pocahontas Perplex," (1976), 698-714; Medicine, "American Indian Women," (1980), 15-18; M. Powers, *Oglala Women: Myth, Ritual and Reality*, (Chicago: University of Chicago Press, 1986); J. N. Terrell and D. M. Terrell, *Indian Women of the Western Morning: Their Life in Early America*, (New York: Dial Press, 1974); D. Welch,

"American Indian Women: Reaching Beyond the Myth." In C. Calloway (Ed.), *New Directions in American Indian History*, (Norman: University of Oklahoma Press, 1987), 31-48.

7. L. Koehler, "Native Women of the Americas: A Bibliography," *Frontiers* 6(3), (1982), 73-101.

8. R. Christensen, "Indian Women: A Historical and Personal Perspective," *Pupil and Personal Services Journal* 4, (1975), 13-22; R. Green, *Native American Women: A Contextual Bibliography*, (Bloomington, IN: Indiana University Press, 1983); N. O. Lurie, "Indian Women: A Legacy of Freedom," in R. L. Lacopi and B. L. Fontanta (Eds.), *Look to the Mountaintop*, (San Jose, CA: Gousha Publications, 1972), 29-36; C. Metoyer, "The Native American Woman," in E. Snyder (Ed.), *The Study of Women: Enlarging Perspectives on Social Reality*, (New York: Harper and Row, 1979), 329-335.

9. V. Brady, S. Crome, and L. Reese, "Resist! Survival Tactics of Indian Women," *California History* 63, (1984), 140-151.

10. N. Parezo, "Navajo Sandpaintings: The Importance of Sex Roles in Craft Production," *American Indian Quarterly* 6, (1982), 25-48.

11. Brady, Crome, and Reese, "Resist!," (1984), 140-151.

12. Allen, *The Sacred Hoop*, (1986); R. Green, "Native American Women," *Signs: Journal of Women in Culture and Society* 6(2), (1980), 248-267; M. A. Jaimes, "Towards a New Image of American Indian Women," *Journal of American Indian Education*, 22(1), (1982), 18-32; T. LaFromboise, *Circles of Women: Professionalism Training for American Indian Women*, (Newton, MA: Women's Educational Equity Act Press, 1989); Welch, "American Indian Women," (1987), 31-48; S. H. Witt, "Native Women Today: Sexism and the Indian Woman," *Civil Rights Digest*, 6(3), (1974), 29-35.

13. S. Benally, "Guest Editorial," *Winds of Change* 3(3), (1988), 6.

14. Allen, *The Sacred Hoop*, (1986); K. Jencks, "Changing Women: The Navajo Therapist Goddess," *Psychological Perspectives* 17(2), (1986), 202-221.

15. C. Niethammer, *Daughters of the Earth*, (New York: Macmillan, 1977).

16. E. Blackwood, "Sexuality and Gender in Certain

Native American Tribes: The Case of the Cross-Gender Females," *Signs: Journal of Women in Culture and Society*, 10, (1984), 27-42.

17. P. Albers and B. Medicine, *The Hidden Half: Studies of Plains Indian Women*, (New York: University Press of America); Green, "The Pocahontas Perplex," (1976), 698-714.

18. Allen, "Lesbians in American Indian Cultures," (1981), 67-87.

19. J. N. Beiswinger and H. Jeanotte, *Medicine Women*, (Grand Forks, ND: University of North Dakota Press, 1985).

20. For a detailed account of the intertribal life and power of a Mohawk medicine woman, see H. H. Tanner, "Coocoochee: Mohawk Medicine Women," *American Indian Culture and Research Journal* 3(3), (1979), 23-41.

21. Jencks, "Changing Women," (1986), 202-221; N. C. Zac, "The Earth Mother Figure of Native North America," *Reviston* 10(3), (1988), 26-36; N. C. Zack, "Sacred and Legendary Women of Native North America," in S. Nicholson (Ed.), *The Goddess Re-Awakening: The Feminine Principle Today*, (Wheaton, IL: Theosophical Publishing House, 1989), 232-245.

22. B. Medicine, *The Native American Woman: A Perspective*, (Austin, TX: National Educational Laboratory Publishers, Inc., 1978); Medicine, "American Indian Women," (1980), 15-18.

23. K. Anderson, "Commodity Exchange and Subordination: Montagnais-Naskapi and Huron Women, 1600-1650," *Signs: Journal of Women in Culture and Society*, 11(1), (1985), 48-62; Blackwood, "Sexuality and Gender in Certain Native American Tribes," (1984), 27-42; L. Hamamsy, "The Role of Women in a Changing Navajo Society," *American Anthropologist* 59, (1957), 101-111; Medicine, "American Indian Women," (1980), 15-18; Metoyer, "The Native American Woman," (1979), 329-335; Parezo, "Navajo Sandpaintings," (1982), 25-48; Welch, "American Indian Women," (1987), 31-48.

24. Allen, "Lesbians in Native American Indian Cultures," (1981), 67-87; Allen, *The Sacred Hoop*, (1986); Blackwood, "Sexuality and Gender in Native American Tribes," (1984), 27-42; S. E. Jacobs, "Berdache: A Brief Review of the Literature," *Colorado Anthropology* 1, (1977), 25-40.

25. K. M. Buchanan, *Apache Women Warriors*, (El Paso, TX: Texas Western Press, 1986); M. Liberty, "Hell Came with Horses: Plains Indian Women in the Equestrian Era," *Montana* 32, (1982), 10-19; B. Medicine, "Indian Women: Tribal Identity as Status Quo." In M. Lowe and R. Hubbard (Eds.), *Woman's Nature: Rationalizations of Inequality*, (New York: Pergamon Press, 1983), 63-73.

26. O. Lewis, "Manly-hearted Women Among the Northern Piegan," *American Anthropologist* 43, (1941), 173-187.

27. Allen, "Lesbians in American Indian Cultures," (1981), 67-87; Blackwood, "Sexuality and Gender in Certain Native American Tribes," (1984), 27-42; C. Callender and L. Kochems, "The North American Berdache," *Current Anthropology* 24(4), 443-470; P. McCormack (Ed.), "Cross-sex Relations and Native Peoples" [special issue], *Western Canadian Journal of Anthropology* 6(3), (1976).

28. Blackwood, "Sexuality and Gender in Certain Native American Tribes," (1984), 27-42.

29. Callender and Kochems, "The North American Berdache," (1983), 443-470.

30. Ibid.

31. Ibid.

32. Ibid.; A. B. Gatshet, "The Karankawa Indians, The Coast People of Texas," *Papers of the Peabody Museum of Archaeology and Ethnology* 1(2), (1891); McCoy, I., "His Presence was so Disgusting." In J. Katz (Ed.), *Gray American History*, (New York: Crowell, 1976), 300; J. R. Swanton, "Indian Tribes of the Lower Mississippi Valley and Adjacent Coast of the Gulf of Mexico," *Bureau of American Ethnology Bulletin* 43, (1911).

33. Lewis, "Manly-hearted Women Among the Northern Piegan," (1941), 173-187.

34. Niethammer, *Daughters of the Earth*, (1977).

35. Witt, "Native Women Today," (1974), 32.

36. Metoyer, "The Native American Woman," (1979); Lurie, "Indian Women," (1972).

37. Allen, *The Sacred Hoop*, (1986); Anderson, "Commodity Exchange and Subordination," (1985), 48-62; C. S. Kidwell, "The Power of Women in Three American Indian Societies," *Journal of Ethnic Studies* 6, (1979), 113-121; R.

Lynch, "Women in Northern Paiute Politics," *Signs: Journal of Women in Culture and Society* 11(21), (1986), 352-366; Witt, "Native Women Today," (1974).

38. E. Seton and J. Seton, *The Gospel of the Redman: An Indian Bible*, (Santa Fe, NM: Seton Village, 1953).

39. Allen, *The Sacred Hoop*, (1986).

40. Anderson, "Commodity Exchange and Subordination," (1985), 48-62.

41. Allen, *The Sacred Hoop*, (1986); Anderson, "Commodity Exchange and Subordination," (1985), 48-62.

42. E. Friedl, "The Position of Women: Appearance and Reality," *Anthropological Quarterly* 40, (1967), 97-108.

43. Brady, Crome, and Reese, "Resist!," (1984), 140-151; Welch, "American Indian Women," (1987), 31-48.

44. Allen, *The Sacred Hoop*, (1986).

45. Anderson, "Commodity Exchange and Subordination," (1985), 48-62; K. Livingston, "Contemporary Iroquois Women and Work: A Study of Consciousness of Unequality," Ph.D. diss., (Ithaca: Cornell University, 1974), *Dissertation Abstracts International* 35, 3194A.

46. Anderson, "Commodity Exchange and Subordination," (1985), 48-62.

47. Hamamsy, "The Role of Women in a Changing Navajo Society," (1957), 101-111.

48. Ibid.

49. Ibid.

50. S. Kunitz and J. Levy, "The Prevalence of Hypertension Among Elderly Navajos: A Test of the Acculturation Hypothesis," *Culture, Medicine, and Psychiatry* 10, (1990), 97-121.

51. C. Attneave and A. Dill, "Indian Boarding Schools and Indian Women: Blessing or Curse?" In National Institute of Education (Ed.) *Conference on the Educational and Occupational Needs of American Indian Women*, (Washington, D.C.: U.S. Department of Education, 1980); M. Beiser, "A Hazard to Mental Health: Indian Boarding Schools," *American Journal of Psychiatry* 131, (1974), 305-306; E. Dlugokinski and L. Kramer, "A System of Neglect: Indian Boarding Schools," *American Journal of Psychiatry*, 131, (1974), 25-31; J. Kleinfeld and J. Bloom, "Boarding Schools: Effect on the Mental Health of Eskimo Adolescents,"

American Journal of Psychiatry 134(4), (1977), 411-417.

52. A. Metcalf, "From Schoolgirl to Mother: The Effects of Education on Navajo Women," *Social Problems* 23, (1976), 535-544.

53. M. Szasz, "'Poor Richard' Meets the Native American: Schooling for Young Indian Women in Eighteenth-Century Connecticut," *Pacific Historical Review* 49(2), (1980), 215-235.

54. R. Trennert, "Educating Young Girls at Non-Reservation Boarding Schools," *Western Historical Quarterly* 13, (1982), 271-290.

55. Ibid.

56. H. Bannan, *True Womanhood on the Reservation: Field Matrons in the United States Indian Service*, (Tucson, AZ: Southwest Institute for Research on Women, University of Arizona, 1974); Trennert, "Educating Young Girls at Non-Reservation Boarding Schools," (1982), 271-290.

57. A. Bernstein, "A Mixed Record: The Political Enfranchisement of American Indian Women during the Indian New Deal." In W. Williams (Ed.), *Indian Leadership*, (Manhattan, KS: Sunflower University Press, 1984), 13-20.

58. C. L. Attneave, "American Indian and Alaska Native Families: Emigrants in their own Homeland." In McGoldrick, J. K. Pearce and J. Giordano (Eds.), *Ethnicity and Family Therapy*, (New York: Guilford Press, 1982), 55-83; L. Spindler and G. Spindler, "Male and Female Adaptations in Culture Change." *American Anthropologist* 60, (1958), 217-233.

59. Lynch, "Women in Northern Paiute Politics," (1986), 352-366; M. Mead, *The Changing Culture of an Indian Tribe*, (New York: Columbia University Press, 1982); Powers, *Oglala Women*, (1986).

60. Lynch, "Women in Northern Paiute Politics," (1986), 352-366; Powers, *Oglala Women*, (1986).

61. Allen, *The Sacred Hoop*, (1986).

62. S. H. Witt, "Past Perspectives and Present Problems." In Ohoyo Resource Center Staff (Ed.), *Words of Today's American Indian Women: Ohoyo Makachi*, (Wichita Falls, TX: OHOYO, Inc., 1981), 11.

63. Witt, "Native Women Today," (1974), 29-35.

64. E. R. Barter and J. T. Barter, "Urban Indians and Mental Health Problems," *Psychiatric Annals* 4, (1974), 37-43;

T. LaFromboise, *Cultural and Cognitive Considerations in the Coping of American Indian Women in Higher Education,* Unpublished manuscript, (Stanford: Stanford University School of Education, 1988).

65. L. S. Kemnitzer, "Adjustment and Value Conflict in Urbanizing Dakota Indians Measured by Q-Sort Techniques," *American Anthropologist,* 75, (1973), 687-707; Spindler and Spindler, "Male and Female Adaptations in Culture Change," *American Anthropologist* 60, (1958), 217-233.

66. C. Weisfield, G. Weisfield and J. Callaghan, "Female Inhibition in Mixed-Sex Competition Among Young Adolescents," *Ethology and Socialbiology* 3, (1982), 29-42; C. Weisfield, G. Weisfield, R. Warren and D. Freeman, "The Spelling Bee: A Naturalistic Study of Female Inhibition in Mixed-Sex Competition," *Adolescence* 18(71), (1983), 695-708.

67. T. Coladarci, "High School Dropout Among Native Americans," *Journal of American Indian Education* 23, (1983), 15-22; D. Jacobson, *Alaskan Native High School Dropouts,* Report Prepared for Project ANNA, (Anchorage, AK: Alaska Federation of Natives, 1973), (ERIC Document Reproduction Service No. ED 088651); D. Sanders, "Cultural Conflicts: An Important Factor in a Southern Baffin Island Eskimo Settlement," *Canadian Psychiatric Association Journal* 19, (1974), 363-367.

68. U.S. Bureau of the Census, *1980 Census of the Population: Characteristics of the Population.* U.S. Summary, PC80-1-B1, (Washington, D.C.: U.S. Department of Commerce, 1983).

69. T. LaFromboise, "Professionalization of American Indian Women in Postsecondary Education," *Journal of College Student Personnel* 25, (1984), 470-472.

70. J. L. Edgewater, "Stress and the Navajo University Student," *Journal of American Indian Education* 20, (1981); LaFromboise, *Cultural and Cognitive Considerations in the Coping of American Indian Women in Higher Education,* (1988).

71. C. A. Kidwell, "The Status of American Indian Women in Higher Education." In National Institute of Education, *Conference on the Educational and Occupational Needs of American Indian Women,* (Washington, D.C.: U.S. Department of Education, 1976), 83-123.

72. National Research Council, *Summary Report 1988 Doctoral Recipient from United States Universities*, (Washington, D.C.: National Academy Press, 1986); R. Ryan, "The Federal Role in American Indian Education," *Harvard Educational Review* 52, (1982), 423-430.

73. B. Kaplan and D. Johnson, "The Social Meaning of Navajo Psychopathology and Psychotherapy." In A. Kiev (Ed.), *Magic, Faith, and Healing*, (New York: Free Press, 1964); B. Perrone, H. Stockel and V. Krueger, *Medicine Women, Curanderas, and Women Doctors*, (Norman, OK: University of Oklahoma Press, 1989).

74. B. Medicine, "New Roads to Coping—Siouan Sobriety." In S. Manson (Ed.), *New Directions in Prevention Among American Indian and Alaska Native Communities*, (Portland, OR: National Center for American Indian and Alaska Native Mental Health Research, 1982), 189-212.

75. T. LaFromboise, "American Indian Mental Health Policy," *American Psychologist* 43, (1988), 388-397.

76. J. E. Trimble, S. M. Manson, G. Dinges, and B. Medicine, "American Indian Concepts of Mental Health: Reflections and Directions." In P. Pedersen, N. Sartonus, and A. Marsella (Eds.), *Mental Health Services: The Cross-Cultural Context*, (Beverly Hills, CA: Sage, 1984).

77. C. Roy, A. Chaudhuri, and D. Irvine, "The Prevalence of Mental Disorders Among Saskatchewan Indians," *Journal of Cross-Cultural Psychology* 1, (1970), 383-392; B. M. Sampath, "Prevalence of Mental Disorders in a Southern Baffin Island Eskimo Settlement," *Canadian Psychiatric Association Journal* 19, (1974), 363-367; J. H. Shore, J. D. Kinzie, D. Thompson and E. M. Pattison, "Psychiatric Epidemology of an Indian Village," *Psychiatry* 36, (1973), 70-81.

78. E. R. Rhoades, M. Marshall, C. L. Attneave, M. Echohawk, J. Bjork and M. Beiser, "Mental Health Problems of American Indians seen in Outpatient Facilities of the Indian Health Service," *Public Health Reports* 96, (1980), 329-335.

79. American Indian Health Care Association, *Six Studies Concerning the Assessment of Mental Health Needs in the Minneapolis-St. Paul Area: A Summary*, Unpublished manuscript, (Minneapolis, MN: American Indian Health Care

Association, 1978).

80. Indian Health Service, *A Progress Report on Indian Alcoholism Activities*, (Rockville, MD: U.S. Department of Health and Human Services, Public Health Service, 1988).

81. Ibid.; P. Old Dog Cross, "Sexual Abuse: A New Threat to the Native American Woman: An Overview." *Listening Post: A Periodical of the Mental Health Programs of the Indian Health Services* 6(2), (1982), 18.

82. Ibid.

83. S. Manson, J. Shore and J. Bloom, "The Depressive Experience in American Indian Communities: A Challenge for Psychiatric Theory and Diagnosis." In A. Kleinman and B. Good (Eds.), *Culture and Depression* (Berkeley, CA: University of California Press, 1985).

84. U.S. Department of Health and Human Services, *Indian Health Service Chart Series Book*, (Washington, D.C.: U.S. Government Printing Office, 1988).

85. N. Dinges, J. Trimble, S. Manson, and F. Pasquale, "The Social Ecology of Counseling and Psychotherapy with American Indian and Alaska Natives." In A. Marsella and P. Pedersen (Eds.), *Cross Cultural Counseling and Psychotherapy*, (New York: Pergamon Press, 1981); J. G. Red Horse, R. L. Lewis, M. Feit, and J. Decker, "Family Behavior of Urban American Indians," *Social Casework* 59, (1978); J. E. Trimble, S. M. Manson, N. G. Dinges, and B. Medicine, "American Indian Concepts of Mental Health: Reflections and Directions." In P. Pedersen, N. Sartorius and A. Marsella (Eds.), *Mental Health Services: The Cross Cultural Context*, (Beverly Hills, CA: Sage, 1984).

86. E. R. Barter and J. T. Barter, "Urban Indians and Mental Health Problems." *Psychiatric Annals* 4, (1974), 37-43; B. Medicine, "Native American Women Look at Mental Health," *Plainswoman* 6, (1982), 7.

87. S. Sue, "Community Mental Health Services to Minority Groups: Some Optimism, Some Pessimism." *American Psychologist* 32, (1977), 616-624.

88. P. C. Dukepoo, *The Elder American Indian*, (San Diego, CA: Campanile, 1980).

89. Powers, *Oglala Women*, (1986).

90. L. Jilek-Aal, "The Western Psychiatrist and his Non-Western Clientele." *Canadian Perspectives* 17(2), (1986), 202-

221.

91. T. LaFromboise, J. Trimble, and G. Mohatt, "Counseling Intervention and American Indian Tradition: An Integrative Approach." *The Counseling Psychologist* 18, (1990).

92. J. E. Trimble and T. LaFromboise, "American Indians and the Counseling Process: Culture, Adaptation and Style." In P. Pedersen (Ed.), *Handbook of Cross Cultural Mental Health Services*, (Beverly Hills, CA: Sage, 1985), 127-134.

93. D. Liberman and R. Knegge, "Health Care Provider—Consumer Communication in the Miccosukee Indian Community." *White Cloud Journal* 1(3), (1979), 5-13.

94. D. B. Heath, "Alcohol Use Among North American Indians: A Cross-Cultural Survey of Patterns and Problems." In R. G. Smart and F. B. Glaser (Eds.), *Research Advances in Alcohol and Drug Problems*, (New York: Plenum Press, 1983), 343-396; P. May, "Substance Abuse and American Indians: Prevalence and Susceptibility." *International Journal of Addictions*, 17(7), (1982), 1185-1209; E. R. Oetting, B. A. Edwards, G. S. Goldstein and V. G. Mason, "Drug Use Among Adolescents of Five Southwestern Native American Tribes." *International Journal of the Addictions* 15, (1980), 539-445; R. K. Thomas, "The History of North American Indian Alcohol Use as a Community Based Phenomenon." *Journal of Studies on Alcohol* 9, (1981), 29-39.

95. P. A. May, K. J. Hymbaugh, J. M. Aase, and J. M. Samet, "Epidemology of Fetal Alcohol Syndrome Among American Indians of the Southwest." *Social Biology* 30(4), (1983), 374-387; Powers, *Oglala Women*, (1986); R. White and D. Cornely, "Navajo Child Abuse and Neglect Study: A Comparison Group Examination of Abuse and Neglect of Navajo Children." *Child Abuse and Neglect* 5, (1981), 9-17.

96. U.S. Senate Select Committee on Indian Affairs, *Indian Juvenile Alcoholism and Eligibility for BIA Schools*, Senate Hearing 99-286, (Washington, D.C.: U.S. Government Printing Office, 1985).

97. U.S. Department of Health and Human Services, *Indian Health Service Chart Series Book*, (1988).

98. J. E. Levy and S. J. Kunitz, *Indian Drinking: Navajo Practices and Anglo American Theories*, (New York:

Wiley, 1974); L. C. Longclaws, C. Barnes, L. Grieve and R. Dumoff, "Alcohol and Drug Use Among the Brokenbend Djibwa." *Journal of Studies on Alcohol* 41, (1980), 21-36; J. O. Whittaker, "Alcohol and the Standing Rock Sioux Tribe: A Twenty Year Follow Up Study." *Journal of Studies on Alcohol* 43, (1982), 191-200.

99. National Institute on Alcohol Abuse and Alcoholism, *Alcohol and Health* (4th ed.), (Washington, D.C.: U.S. Government Printing Office, 1981).

100. M. Chovan and W. Chovan, "Stressful Events and Coping Responses Among Older Adults in Two Sociocultural Groups." *Journal of Psychology* 119(3), (1984), 253-260; LaFromboise, "Cultural and Cognitive Considerations in the Coping of American Indian Women in Higher Education," (1988); H. Light and R. Martin, "American Indian Families." *Journal of American Indian Education* 26(1), (1986), 1-5; Special Populations Subpanel on Mental Health of American Indians and Alaska Natives, *A Good Day to Live For One Million Indians*, (Washington, D.C.: U.S. Government Printing Press, 1978).

101. Chovan and Chovan, "Stressful Events and Coping Responses Among Older Adults in Two Sociocultural Subgroups," (1984), 253-260.

102. LaFromboise, "Cultural and Cognitive Considerations in the Coping of American Indian Women in Higher Education," (1988).

103. C. L. Attneave and R. V. Speck, "Social Network Intervention in Time and Space." In A. Jacobs and W. Spradlin (Eds.), *The Group as Agent of Change*, (New York: Behavioral Publications, 1974); Chovan and Chovan, "Stressful Events and Coping Responses Among Older Adults in Two Sociocultural Subgroups," (1984), 253-260.

104. LaFromboise, "Cultural and Cognitive Considerations in the Coping of American Indian Women in Higher Education," (1988).

105. Ibid.

106. J. G. Redhorse, "Family Structure and Value Orientation in American Indians," *Social Casework* 6(8), (1980), 25-48.

107. R. A. Ryan, "Strengths of the American Indian Family: State of the Art." In R. Hoffman (Ed.), *The American*

Indian Family: Strengths and Stresses, (Isleta, NM: American Indian Social Research and Development Associates, 1980).

108. R. Green, *Native American women: A contextual bibliography*. (Bloomington, IN: Indiana University Press, 1983).

109. Lynch, "Women in Northern Paiute Politics," (1986), 352-366.

110. Ibid.

111. Powers, *Oglala Women*, (1986).

112. Ibid.

113. L. Campbell, "The Spirit Need Not Die. A People in Peril" [special issue], *Anchorage Daily News*, (1988).

114. Green, *Native American Women*, (1983); B. Medicine, "Warrior Women—Sex Role Alternatives for Plains Indian Women." In P. Albers and B. Medicine (Eds.), *The Hidden Half: Studies of Plains Indian Women*, (Lanham, MD: University Press of America, Inc., 1983), 267-280.

Chapter XVIII

Canadian-United States Indian Policies

For Native Peoples in Canada the negotiations over the federal constitution are critical to their emergence as a legally recognized distinct political culture. Their goal is to have the Canadian Government insert in the new constitutional document a recognition of their aboriginal rights and right to self-determination. In the United States the goals of tribal sovereignty and self-determination are no less important but have had a longer period of historical development and actual practice. Though neither Canada nor the United States can lay claim to enlightened and humane treatment of its indigenous peoples, the rights of tribal sovereignty and internal self-government have deeper historical roots in United States law and practice.

Even though there are many similarities in the ways in which Native Peoples in both countries have been treated by their governments, there are also important differences which distinguish the development of Indian policy in both countries. The legal status of Indian peoples and tribes in the United States has a stronger legal basis as a result of the extensive treaty process, federal court rulings and Congressional enactments. American Indians have not been encumbered by an "Indian Act" in the manner in which that legislation has constrained native self-determination in Canada for over a century. Until recently, there have been substantially more constraints placed on the political authority of the 500 Indian Bands (tribes) in Canada. Also, by law, it is estimated that over a million Native People (metis) in Canada have no legal status as Indians and therefore do not qualify for federal protection and services under the Indian Act. Much of Canada's north and British Columbia are claimed by Native Peoples, including the Inuit, and is the subject of a series of involved land claims negotiations. Conversely there is no existing aboriginal title in the United States and what land claims exist are as a result of the failure to adhere to federal law in the early years of the republic.

The extensive negotiations over the Canadian Constitution has enabled Native Peoples in Canada to bring forth their claims to legal status, aboriginal title and political self-determination. Also beginning with the "Sparrow" decision by the Supreme Court of Canada, the legal rights of Natives regarding land claims, status and self-government have been enhanced. The Assembly of First Nations, the status Indian national organization representing the 500 recognized bands, has also played a prominent role in the constitutional process.

The main barriers to Tribal Sovereignty and self-determination in the United States are legal and economic. Recent federal court decisions have made serious incursions into the civil and criminal jurisdiction of Indian

495

Tribes. The economic status of Native Americans is precarious. Federal cutbacks and economic depression among reservation communities stifle tribal government and the goals of the 1975 Indian Self-Determination and Education Act. Moreover states have begun to encroach on areas which have been identified historically as exclusive tribal domain.

The evolution of Indian Policy in Canada awaits the conclusion of the constitutional process. Whatever the outcome, Native Peoples will have an enhanced political and legal status and a defined role in Canadian Confederation. The outlook in the United States is more mixed. Over half of Native Americans live off reservation and their needs need to be formally addressed by the federal government. The courts and state action have cut into historical prerogatives of tribal sovereignty and immediate legislative action is necessary to address this incursion. Moreover the economic status of all Native Americans in the United States has deteriorated badly due to reduction in federal funding and the prolonged economic slump in the United States.

Note: Since the publication of Professor Johnson's article, the Inuit of the eastern Northwest Territories, Canada, signed a land claim agreement with the Canadian Government in June 1993. Under the agreement the Inuit (the Turgavik Federation of Nunavut) receive direct ownership of 353,610 square acres and a cash payment of 1.4 billion dollars over fourteen years. They will be the largest private land owners in Canada and will have legal control over their territory and self-government in 1999.

—RNW

FRAGILE GAINS: TWO CENTURIES OF CANADIAN AND UNITED STATES POLICY TOWARD INDIANS

Ralph W. Johnson

Abstract: The United States and Canada share a common history in their policies toward and legal treatment of the Native Americans that historically have occupied both countries. The Royal Proclamation of 1763 established a policy of recognizing Aboriginal title and treating with Indians that was binding on the colonies that preceded both countries, and influenced both governments in later dealings with tribes. Assimilationist themes are evident as well in the national policy toward Indians in both countries. Nevertheless, historically and in the present, national policies and laws of the two governments can be contrasted. This Article sets forth a detailed comparison of the historical events surrounding white settlement and displacement of Indians from their Aboriginal lands. It further describes trends in the creation and development of Indian law, in the United States Congress and the Canadian Parliament, and in the courts of both countries. United States Supreme Court Justice John Marshall first recognized tribal sovereignty in developing a federal common law that has been extremely influential in the Indian jurisprudence of both countries. Presently in the United States, however, the Supreme Court is hostile toward tribal sovereignty and will not review federal legislative actions toward tribes, while Congress is an increasing champion of tribal self-government and economic self-development. Conversely, the Canadian Parliament continues in its assimiliationist legislative attitudes, refusing to recognize inherent powers of sovereignty in tribal government. Nevertheless, aboriginal rights of the Indigenous peoples of Canada were codified in the 1982 Constitution, and the Canadian Supreme Court has recently taken unto itself the power to scrutinize legislative action in light of those rights.

INTRODUCTION

Native Americans[1] of Canada and the United States have struggled for more than 200 years, largely beneath the surface of mainstream history, to retain their cultural identity, to keep or recapture Aboriginal lands, and increasingly to protect their rights to self-determination and self-government.

This is a comparative study of United States and Canadian policies and laws towards Native Americans. Both Canada and the United States share the same "mother country." Both are federations, with populations that share similar racial problems and social systems; both share the common law system; and, both share similar moral, ethical, and political values. Differences in the two nations' Indian policies are partly based on demographics. More often, however, they reflect conscious choices about dealing with the "Indian problem." This Article analyzes these choices and their impacts on the lives of Native Americans and non-Native Americans. The Article evaluates both successful and unsuccessful policies of the two countries. It is my hope that these comparisons will afford improved understanding and awareness of this complex subject and will contribute constructively towards the continuing debate about the enlightened and successful national policies that should be adopted towards Indians.

I. THE HISTORICAL SETTING

A. Aboriginal Claims

Historically, the conqueror governments of Canada and the United States have exhibited persistent, negative attitudes towards Indians and their aboriginal claims. For example, in 1855, Congress enacted a law allowing contract suits to be brought against the United States in the newly created Court of Claims.[2] When it became apparent that Indian tribes might file suit under this Act for treaty violations, Congress, in 1863, amended the Act specifically to deny Indians access to the new court.[3] Thereafter, an Indian tribe had to obtain a special Act of Congress to bring suit for treaty violations. It was not until after the 1946 Indian Claims Act that the United States paid most claims, and then only partially.[4] In 1955, the United States Supreme Court held that the taking of aboriginal title by the United States did not give rise to an Indian claim for fifth amendment[5] compensation.[6] In fact, until the 1930s, even the taking of title "recognized" by treaty, agreement, or statute, by the federal government was not clearly compensable.[7]

Canada likewise refused to give credence to First Nation Aboriginal claims. From 1927 through the early 1930s, it was a crime to assist a First Nation in Canada to file suit against the government based on Aboriginal title.[8] In 1969, a government white paper recommended that all Aboriginal claims be ignored and forgotten.[9] It was not until the 1973 case of "Calder v. Attorney-General,"[10] the Constitution Act of 1982,[11] and the 1990 decision in "Sparrow v. The Queen,"[12] that the Canadian government began recognizing Aboriginal rights.

B. National Policies v. Implementation

Early national laws and policies were sometimes directly damaging to Native American tribes. More often, however, it was the implementation of laws,[13] or the lack thereof, that needlessly damaged or destroyed Indigenous peoples' culture, religion, health, and self-esteem.[14] Time and again, the lofty statements and high policies of the two national governments were ignored or consciously thwarted: first, by avaricious prospectors and settlers who embraced Manifest Destiny as an excuse to take Indian land and resources, legally or otherwise; and second, by local politicians and land developers. The dominant society's belief in its own moral, cultural, and religious superiority was based on western conceptions of civilization, on attitudes of racial superiority, and on an often religious, ethnocentric view of life that denied validity to Native American cultures, religions, and lifestyles. The historical literature about Indian/White relations is replete with examples of this attitude.[15] A typical problem for United States tribes was that when they would move to their assigned reservation they would find it already occupied by white settlers. The response of the national government was not to call out the troops and expel the white trespassers, but to coerce and cajole the Indians into ceding more land or moving to some other, usually less desirable, area.[16] At other times, tribes who had been assigned and were already living on a reservation would discover settlers infiltrating, taking gold, water, and timber, and settling on reservation lands.[17] Seldom did the United States require settlers to move. It was the Indians who had to move, adjust, and absorb the loss.

The history of treaty implementation[18] is, unfortunately, not within the scope of this Article. But that history should be kept in mind as background against which to measure the choice and the impact of laws and policies.

C. Knowledge of Indian History

One of the sad truths about policies towards Indians is the fact that the public, as well as most political leaders, historians, and lawyers, have had very little knowledge of or interest in Indian history. For most of this century, school children have learned how the West was "won" by pioneers, cowboys, gold seekers, and railroad builders. Indians play a minor role, being "bad" and impeding white "progress," or, in some cases, being "good" and cooperating with whites.[19] Rarely taught are historical events such as the Yakima War, fought for four long years, from 1855 to 1859, in which the vigilante Oregon "Volunteers," independent of the United

States Army, committed atrocities against Indian men, women, and children.[20] Eventually, of course, the industrialized, "civilized" society won. The war was a military, political, and economic disaster for the Indians.

This was a monumentally important event in the lives of the Yakima, Nez Perce, Walla, Cayuse, and Umatilla tribes. Similar cataclysmic events occurred with other Indian tribes throughout both nations, yet the dominant society treats these events as curiosities rather than significant historical events. This lack of understanding continues to contribute to legislative myopia in policymaking and unfair interpretations of statutes and treaties by courts and administrators.

The study of Native American history teaches that the overriding, but rarely articulated, policy of Canada and the United States towards Aboriginals was to get them out of the way so their land could be settled and developed by whites.[21] The second most pervasive policy, governmental action taken "for the good of the Indians," effectively abolished Indian religion, culture, and lifestyle. These policies were sometimes motivated by altruism, to the extent that they were designed to do as little harm as possible to the Indians while achieving the overriding goal of eliminating Aboriginal occupancy, religion, and culture. In spite of high-toned rhetoric about tribes and First Nations freely signing treaties, the land acquisition policy was only occasionally accomplished by fair, arms-length transactions. Most of the time the government acquired lands by a combination of coercion, fraud, threat of force, or actual military force. While the earliest acquisitions by the British Crown along the eastern seaboard were made by purchase,[22] later ones were produced by coercion. It is absurd to argue that Aboriginal tribes knowingly and voluntarily gave up their claims to these lands. If the westward-bound settlers in either Canada or the United States had asked the indigenous occupants whether they would prefer (1) to be removed from ancient homelands, hunting, fishing, and food gathering grounds, forced often to live on distant, strange, hostile lands,[23] be squeezed onto tiny reservations with other often incompatible tribes, made totally dependent on the white man for the most meager of rations,[24] even survival, and have their cultures, customs, and religions ridiculed, prohibited, and debased, or (2) remain on their ancestral lands, continue their traditional lifestyles, be treated with dignity and respect, and choose their own time, place, and method for adopting or rejecting industrialization and technological advances, does anyone doubt the answer?

Manifest Destiny, the Oregon Trail, and Westward Ho were not rallying cries for square-dealing with Aboriginal tribes. These concepts gave mythical and moral support to westward-bound settlers in both Canada and the United States, the Indigenous peoples be damned. These powerful ideas were based on the profoundly held faith that the West, in both countries, was there to be won by white men. The Aboriginals were savage heathens, obstacles to progress, to be battled if necessary and overcome, like wild animals, the weather, and the desert. It was inconceivable to whites that these natives had any "right" to stop the westward march of Christian civilization, carried by prospectors, farmers, and settlers.

In the late 1880s, the western United States had been largely "settled," boundaries had been set between Canada, the United States, and Mexico, and the Aboriginal peoples subdued and required to live on reservations. Most of the reservations to be created were in place by then. By 1887, the plight of the Native population was so bad it bothered the conscience of the white society and government. Something had to be done. That something proved to be the Dawes Act of 1887,[25] yet another disaster for Indigenous people.

Congress intended, through the Dawes Act, to break up reservations and make landowners of the Indians. At the same time, a new government policy was initiated declaring as surplus reservation land that was not parcelled out as allotments to individual Indians and arbitrarily opening that land to white settlement. Although Congress eventually stopped the allotment and surplus land practices, by 1934 these programs had transferred two-thirds of reservation lands from Indian to white ownership. Land ownership has remained in this pattern to the present self-determination era.

In Canada, Parliament never enacted a Dawes type of legislation. Frequently, however, land-hungry settlers pushed aside First Nations, which lost their Aboriginal lands without benefit of negotiations, cession, or reservation. Both countries have consistently promoted ethnocentric assimilation policies, overlooking or ignoring Native American traditions, lifestyles, religions, and cultures. Quite remarkably, instead of being assimilated and disappearing, Indigenous people have demonstrated surprising resilience and today are moving to reaffirm their history, religion, and cultural identity.

One contributing factor in this self-determination movement has been the accessibility of better legal talent for Indian tribes. For example, the University of New Mexico Indian Center student program has encouraged several hundred Indian lawyers to enter the law, and most of them now represent Indians and Indian tribes. The civil rights movement and especially the introduction of young lawyers to the field of Indian law through the Office of Economic Opportunity Program enhanced the competence of tribal representation. The creation of the Native American Rights Fund in 1968 markedly improved the competence of lawyering for Indian tribes. This enhanced legal representation has facilitated negotiation of Indian claims.

Historically, states, provinces, and local governments[26] ignored Indian claims of treaty, statutory, or other rights until tribes commenced litigation and secured court decisions affirming their legally enforceable rights. Typically, successful tribal lawsuits have convinced state or local governments to negotiate rather than litigate. This scenario plays out again and again. Officials of the State of Maine ignored the claim of the Passamaquoddy and Penobscot Indians to most of the state until court decisions put both respect and fear into the hearts of these officials.[27] Non-Indian water users ignored Indian water rights claims until litigation was under way, or concluded with an Indian victory.[28] Washington also refused to recognize Indian treaty fishing rights until the federal courts ruled that the tribes were entitled to catch fifty percent of the harvestable fish under treaties of the 1850s.[29] The State of Washington refused to negotiate settlement of the Puyallup Tribe's ownership claims to tidelands and a river bed in the City of Tacoma until various suits were filed, and some brought to conclusion.[30]

In Canada, the national and provincial governments paid little attention to First Nation Aboriginal land claims until the 1973 case of "Calder v. Attorney-General"[31] raised a realistic possibility that Aboriginal rights might receive favorable consideration by the courts. National policy toward Aboriginal claims changed from open hostility in the 1930s, to recommending they be ignored in the late 1960s, to recommending recognition and settlement of these claims after "Calder."

Other historical factors condition contemporary negotiations with Indian tribes. In Canada, the British North America Act of 1867 and the Constitution Act of 1930 bestowed on the provinces ownership of the natural resources within their borders, including rivers.[23] The provinces thus hold title to public lands not yet conveyed to private owners. The Canadian national government owns relatively little land in comparison to the United States federal government, which owns approximately one-third of the United States, including half of the land in the eleven western states, and ninety-five percent of Alaska.[33] Provincial ownership of land enhances the power of the provinces in negotiations with First Nations on Aboriginal claims concerning land, water, hunting and fishing, environmental rights, and governmental powers.

This Article examines several sharply defined differences in Indian law and policy between Canada and the United States. United States courts have held that Congress has "plenary" power over Indians,[34] and that, under "Lone Wolf v. Hitchock,"[35] judicial review is not available to test acts of Congress against the federal trust responsibility to Indians. Canadian courts historically applied the same rules,[36] until the Canadian Supreme Court held in "Sparrow v. The Queen"[37] that the 1982 Constitution Act requires judicial review to assure that legislation truly advances the interests of First Nations. The court detailed the methodology for this review, which resembles remarkably the "strict scrutiny" examination given to racially based legislation in the United States.[38] Canadian law is thus very different from current United Sates law with regard to Indians. Canadian courts review legislation to assure consistency with the government's trust responsibility, whereas United States courts refuse to undertake such review.

In the United States, Indian tribes assert broad sovereign governing powers over their reservations, including criminal jurisdiction over tribal members and civil jurisdiction over non-member Indians and non-Indians as well as tribal members. In Canada, the First Nations exercise minimal self-governing powers, lacking sovereignty even over their own members. The governing powers they do exercise are controlled by exceedingly detailed federal laws, primarily the Indian Act.

The following pages are divided into five sections that help explain the relationship of Native Americans to the national and state/provincial governments, and the growing tribal insistence on self-government. Each heading starts with a discussion of United States law and policy, followed by a discussion on Canadian law and policy. Comparisons are generally made in the sections on Canadian law.

II. HISTORICAL POLICY TOWARDS INDIANS

A. The United States: A Historical Perspective

> In the past this [federal/tribal] relationship has oscillated between two equally harsh and unacceptable extremes.[39]

Historically, United States national policy towards Indians[40] has swung widely, urging assimilation into the dominant culture, or favoring self-determination and tribal identity. In 1763, before the United States became a separate nation, Great Britain issued a Royal Proclamation designed to separate the Aboriginal and non-Aboriginal populations, and set aside an enormous land reserve for Aboriginals in what is now western Canada and the western United States.[41] The Proclamation provided that no part of the reserved land could be acquired by purchase or otherwise unless by consent of the Crown. The United States continued this policy of exclusive federal jurisdiction by enacting the Trade and Intercourse Acts.[42] The continuing policy of separating the Indians and non-Indians ultimately resulted in the removal of many eastern tribes to the western United States.

From the nation's birth until about 1815, military defense dictated national Indian policy. Treaties with the great Iroquois Confederacy and other confederations and tribes gained allies for the new nation or neutralized military threats. Some tribes retained enough power to threaten the new nation's existence.[43] Indian support or opposition could affect battles, sometimes even wars. After approximately 1815, this was no longer true.

Between 1815 and about 1845, the national government policy favored removal, designed to clear Indians off the land and to reduce conflict with non-Indians.[44] As early as 1803, President Thomas Jefferson favored the idea of removal. He urged William Henry Harrison, governor of the Indiana Territory, to convince the Indians to move voluntarily and, if they resisted removal and took up the "hatchet" while trying to remain in their homeland, to seize their land and drive them across the Mississippi.[45] President Monroe sent a message to Congress in 1825, emphasizing the importance of removal, saying that it should only be done "to promote the interest and happiness of those tribes" and on terms "satisfactory" to them.[46] Andrew Jackson, who was President when the Cherokee removal occurred,[47] advised the tribes to voluntarily move to the west or else submit to state laws because the Constitution did not provide for Indian tribal governments.[48] Secretary of War Eaton wrote to Cherokee leaders,

[b]eyond the Mississippi your prospects will be different. There you will find no conflicting interests. The United States power and sovereignty, uncontrolled by the high authority of state jurisdiction, and resting on its own energies, will be able to say to you, in the language of your own nation, the soil shall be yours while the trees grow, or the streams run.[49]

The removal policy was discarded during the 1840s and 1850s, not because it fell into disfavor, but because Indian country was overrun by gold and land-hungry prospectors and settlers.[50] Violence between Indians and whites often resulted. Whites wanted the land, but the Indians had to be removed first. National policy changed to one of creating reservations in the west and cajoling, coercing, or forcing tribes, including western tribes as well as previously "removed" eastern tribes, to squeeze onto these reservations.

1. Treaties as Land Transactions

Between 1815 and 1871, when treaties were banned by Congress, treaties looked increasingly like land exchange transactions. The Indians ceded to the United States aboriginal title to their hunting grounds in return for title to specific reservation areas. After 1871, reservations continued to be created, but by statute, agreement approved by Congress, or executive order, rather than by treaty.[51]

2. Treaties Construed in Favor of Indians

[The lower court decided that] the Indians acquired no rights but what any inhabitants of the territory or state would have. Indeed, acquired no rights but such as they would have without the treaty. This is certainly an impotent outcome to negotiations and a convention which seemed to promise more, and give the word of the Nation for more. And we have said we will construe a treaty with the Indians as "that unlettered people" understood it. . . .[52]

Treaties and other documents creating reservations frequently contained general, unspecific, and ambiguous terms. Rules of construction gradually evolved to aid in interpreting these documents, based on the fact that the treaties and agreements were negotiated in English, a strange language to the Indians, and used white man's legal concepts, also unfamiliar to the Indians. These rules provided that treaties and agreements were to be construed as the Indians understood them.[53] Executive orders and statutes were to be construed in favor of the Indians.[54] The courts even read new provisions into treaties if the intent of the parties could be so construed.[55] For example, where a desert reservation was created with the intent that Indians become capitalist farmers, the Supreme Court held that the treaty reserved sufficient water from streams flowing along or across the reservation to carry out the purposes of the reservation.[56] In most cases, the United States intended that the Indians become irrigation farmers. The courts have held the tribes are entitled to sufficient water to irrigate all the irrigable land on the reservation,[57] or to propagate fish if that was the Indian goal.[58]

The reservation era in the United States lasted from roughly 1850 to almost 1900. An occasional reservation was created thereafter, and may still be created, but only by statute.[59]

3. The 1887 Allotment Act: Assimilation Accelerated

> It is a part of the Indian's religion not to divide his land.
>
> . . . .
>
> . . . [W]hen thirty or forty years shall have passed and these Indians shall have parted with their title, they will curse the hand that was raised professedly in their defense to secure this kind of legislation. . . .
>
> . . . .
>
> This is a bill that, in my judgment, ought to be entitled "A bill to despoil the Indians of their lands and to make them vagabonds on the face of the earth."[60]
>
> Indian tribes [even today] face tremendous Congressional pressure to sell their land, divide the assets, and disperse.[61]

Prior to the 1860s, assimilation was a secondary national policy, designed to absorb Indians into the larger society. When removal became impossible, empty lands no longer remaining, the assimilation policy became dominant. "Eastern philanthropists wanted to civilize the Indian; western settlers wanted Indian land."[62] The assimilation policy gained strength through the 1860s and 1870s, culminating in the Dawes Act, or General Allotment Act of 1887.[63]

Senator Henry L. Dawes of Massachusetts favored the total Americanization of the Indian, to be accomplished by breaking up reservations.[64] The Act authorized the Secretary of the Interior to allot tracts of reservation land to individual Indians, eighty acres to a single person and 160 per couple, to encourage them to become farmers instead of hunters and fishers. Congress reasoned that ownership of a plot of land would automatically turn the Indians away from their communal lifestyle to become farmers. The historian Francis Paul Prucha has written that the Dawes Act was part of the "drive to individualize the Indian that became the obsession of the late-nineteenth-century Christian reformers."[65] "Lacking all appreciation of the Indian cultures, they were intent on forcing upon the natives the qualities that they themselves embodied. It was an ethnocentrism of frightening intensity, and it set a pattern that was not easily eradicated."[66]

Indians were able to become United States citizens when they received their allotments.[67] If he/she were deemed "competent" the allottee could apply for a fee patent after a period of years. Between 1910 and 1920, however, the Secretary of the Interior issued thousands of "forced fees" to Indians who were not competent to manage their land and who neither requested nor knew of the patent issuance.[68]

The Dawes Act was yet another disaster for the Indians.[69] Often in dire need of subsistence food and housing, especially during the period from 1910 to 1920, the Indians lost their land after patent, by selling or mortgaging to obtain cash.[70] At the same time, a new federal policy emerged that declared reservation lands "surplus" when not needed for allotments. The government invited white settlers to homestead these "surplus" lands. They often settled the best reservation lands. As a result of the allotment, surplus land policies, and subsequent refinements of the allotment policies, Indian land ownership dropped from 138 million acres in 1887 to forty-eight million acres by 1934. Moreover, Indians lost not only eighty percent or more of their land value held in 1887, but more than eighty-five percent of the land value of all the allotted lands as well.[71] Congress belatedly stopped the allotment process with the 1934 Indian Reorganization Act.[72]

The allotment process created checkerboard land ownership on many reservations, with fee simple, allotment tracts, and tribally owned lands intermixed. Non-Indians now range from a small minority[73] to an overwhelming majority of the reservation population.[74] The Supreme Court has held these checkerboard reservations remain Indian Country and that tribes still govern them.[75] The presence of so many non-Indians, however, has affected the Court's assessment of the nature and extent of tribal governmental powers, especially where these powers impact non-Indians who cannot vote in tribal elections. Large non-Indian holdings have also enabled states to claim jurisdiction over lands and activities on the reservation.[76]

4. The 1934 Indian Reorganization Act and Self-Determination

> Some Indians proud of their race and devoted to their culture and their mode of life have no desire to be as the white man is. They wish to remain Indians, to preserve what they have inherited from their fathers . . . .[77]

The Meriam Report of 1928 revealed the deplorable health, education, and economic conditions of reservation Indians as well as the adverse impact of the loss of most of their lands under the Dawes Act and the surplus land policy. John Collier, a strong advocate for Indian rights, was appointed by President Franklin D. Roosevelt as Commissioner of Indian Affairs in 1933. Collier used the Meriam Report to lobby for passage of the Indian Reorganization Act of 1934[78] which stopped the allotment process. It was not retroactive, however, and allotted land retains that same status today. The 1934 Act encouraged economic development, enhanced self-determination and cultural identity, and provided the tribes recognizable legal status. It enabled tribes to create governments with federally-approved constitutions, that would be recognized by non-Indian bankers, and state and local officials.[79] Tribes began to create federally-chartered corporations to engage in business activities.[80] A new era appeared to shine on the horizon. This is the first time Indians were given any choice about whether to be affected by a national law. The Great Depression, however, curtailed the budget appropriations necessary to assist tribes to achieve the Act's goals. World War II indefinitely delayed budget allocations to the tribes.

5. The Termination Policy: Public Law 280

THESE PEOPLE SHALL BE FREE.[81]

By the end of World War II in 1945, national policy began again to tilt toward the opposite pole. "Termination," enthusiastically embraced by the 1953-1960 Eisenhower administration, became the new national Indian policy. This policy curtailed the sovereignty and governing powers of many Indian tribes, disbanded reservations, gave states jurisdiction over Indians and their lands, and terminated all special federal relationships with some Indians. Congress expressed its intent in House Concurrent Resolution 108,[82] adopted in 1953 by unanimous vote for both houses.[83]

Within a year after adopting H.C.R. 108, Congress began passing individual acts dismantling reservations. Some 109 tribes were eventually terminated,[84] including two large tribes, the Menominee in Wisconsin and the Klamath in southern Oregon.[85] In 1953, Congress enacted Public Law 83-280 (P.L. 280) empowering states to assert jurisdiction over reservations, with or without tribal consent.[86] Many states asserted such jurisdiction,[87] further eroding the prospects for Indian self-government and autonomy.

6. Self-Determination Adopted as National Policy

Indians, Congress, and executive officials increasingly criticized termination during the late 1950s and early 1960s.[88] By 1970, the pendulum had swung through the arc again. Termination was roundly discredited, to be replaced by a policy of self-determination and economic self-sufficiency, more like Collier's original proposals in the 1934 Indian

Reorganization Act. In 1970, President Richard Nixon put the termination policy to rest:

> Because termination is morally and legally unacceptable, because it produces bad practical results, and because the mere threat of termination tends to discourage greater self-sufficiency among Indian groups, I am asking the Congress to . . . expressly renounce, repudiate and repeal the termination policy as expressed in House Concurrent Resolution 108. . . .[89]

President Nixon also proclaimed the new policy of self-determination, which has been embraced by all administrations since 1970.[90]

Support for termination still exists, however, and advocates of this policy continue to seek new ways to express this philosophy. Barsh has argued persuasively that the Department of Interior follows a policy of "administrative termination" of Indian tribes.[91] The Secretary has evolved a pattern of withdrawing federal services from a tribe and then requiring that the tribe challenge this action by filing a petition for "acknowledgment."[92] In this way, tribes' continuing eligibility for federal services depends on their ability to satisfy spot checks.[93] To meet this onerous burden, the tribe must go through the same lengthy and expensive evidence-gathering process required for tribes seeking initial federal recognition.[94]

7. Whittling Sovereignty Away: The Supreme Court's Recent Trend

a. Tribal Court Criminal Jurisdiction

The judiciary is simultaneously whittling away at both tribal legislation and judicial jurisdiction. Cases in the early 1800s held that, because of their dependent status, the tribes had lost their capacity to engage in international relations,[95] and their ability to convey title to real property without the consent of the United States.[96] In 1883, the Supreme Court held that a crime committed on a reservation by a non-Indian against a non-Indian fell under state court rather than tribal or federal court jurisdiction.[97] Further, Congress has decided that crimes committed by non-Indians against Indians should be tried in the federal courts, although state law controls the trial.[98] Jurisdiction stood thus until 1978, when the Supreme Court decided "Oliphant v. Suquamish Indian Tribe,"[99] ruling that tribal courts did not have criminal jurisdiction over non-Indians who violate tribal codes on the reservations. In 1990, the Supreme Court took an even more serious bite out of tribal court jurisdiction by holding that tribal courts do not have criminal jurisdiction over non-member Indians, that is, Indians who are members of other tribes.[100] Congress legislatively reversed this decision in November 1990 for a period of one year.[101]

Criminal jurisdiction in Indian Country is a confusing maze, raising the question whether a competent law and order system is possible on reservations. Matters are further complicated where states also exercise jurisdiction under Public Law 280.[102] The Yakima Tribe raised this question in the Supreme Court in 1979. The Tribe argued that its members were denied equal protection under the federal Constitution because of the complexity in criminal law enforcement brought about by P.L. 280 in Washington. The Supreme Court rejected the Yakima argument, and in a holding remarkably insensitive to Indian aspirations and to the federal policy of self-determination, volunteered in dicta that if the tribe did not like the complicated partial jurisdiction imposed by the state it could simply request full state jurisdiction.[103]

b. Tribal Court Civil Jurisdiction: Preemption Analysis

In civil matters, a similar judicial trend is apparent. Until 1973, "sovereignty," as defined in "Worcester v. Georgia,"[104] shielded the tribes against state law intrusions on the reservation. In "Williams v. Lee,"[105] the Court held that state law did not apply on reservations where it "infringed on the right of the Indians to govern themselves."[106] "Williams" thus suggests a balancing approach to determine jurisdiction. In "McClanahan v. State Tax Commission,"[107] however, the Court introduced preemption analysis as a new method for determining whether state law applies on Indian reservations. "McClanahan" relegated sovereignty to a "background" status. Preemption analysis, in most cases, constitutes a balancing process. The issue is congressional intent but, because congressional intent frequently is not spelled out, decisions turn not on whether events took place in Indian Country, but instead on the degree of "Indianness" of the events. If Indian interests are strong and the state or local government interests are weak or modest, the Court is likely to find preemption. If the reverse is true, then federal preemption will be rejected in favor of state jurisdiction. The decisions of the present Supreme Court reflect a trend against finding federal preemption.[108] The Supreme Court instead appears headed towards a goal of permitting Indians to govern only Indians and Indian-owned lands. Indian governments will lack jurisdiction over non-Indians or non-member Indians except in rare circumstances.

B. Canada

In contrast to the radical swings in Indian policy in the United States,[109] "the most singular feature of Canadian legislation concerning Indians is that the governmental policy established therein, that of 'civilizing the Indians,' has shown almost no variation since the early 19th century when the government assumed responsibility for the society and welfare of the Indian population."[110]

The national government explicitly announced an assimilation policy in the Civilization of Indian Tribes Act of 1857.[111] This Act authorized the "enfranchisement" of Indians who were "sufficiently advanced," that is, who could assume the duties and responsibilities of "citizens" and could support themselves, at which time they attained the right to vote but lost their right to register as Indians.[112] The enfranchisement law was repealed in 1985. "There is now no way for a person who is an Indian within the meaning of the Indian Act to cease being one."[113]

Both Canada and the United States negotiated treaties with Aboriginal tribes. In eastern Canada, the French were the first to deal with the First Nations.[114] Unlike the British, the French made no pretense of recognizing Aboriginal title to land. As a result, they signed no land cession treaties in Quebec and the Maritime Provinces.[115] In 1763, following the British takeover of French lands, Great Britain issued a Royal Proclamation announcing its first Aboriginal policy, designed to minimize contact between Aboriginals and non-Aboriginals.[116] The Proclamation created a huge reserve in the west, encompassing an area from southern Ontario to the Gulf of Mexico, and from the Appalachian highlands to the Mississippi River. It also provided that no one but the Crown could purchase land from the Aboriginal tribes, and prohibited squatting or trespassing on Aboriginal lands.[117] The Proclamation was, however, limited geographically. The Maritime Provinces ignored it altogether and the Proclamation's coverage of the far West was uncertain.

Beginning in 1783, British policy toward First Nations changed from protecting Indigenous people from white encroachment to purchasing their lands for settlement and military purposes. This new direction corresponded with a change in the way the British perceived the First Nations. Their importance as warriors, either as allies or enemies, decreased as the white population grew. They became less a military presence and more a hindrance to white expansion. National policy changed accordingly, as it did in the United States a few years later.[118]

"Until Confederation the imperial government put no restraints upon the power of the [Canadian] colonies to control [First Nations'] reserves and lands. The [Indigenous people] had to look to the local governments for protection of their lands and interest."[119]

1. Assimilation Policy Formally Adopted

> [W]hile the purpose of the Indian Act is to protect the rights and interests of the Indians . . . it is not right that the requirements of the expansion of white settlement should be ignored, that is, that the right of the Indian should be allowed to become a wrong to the white man.[120]

The Civilization of Indian Tribes Act of 1857 explicitly articulated the policy of assimilation,[121] although it had been national policy since the 1830s in a more obscure form.[122] Under this policy, the government first collected the Aboriginals onto reservations. Reserves were meant to be temporary, useful merely to educate and Christianize the Aboriginals and establish agriculture as their primary economic base. This process, advocates argued, could accelerate assimilation by giving the Aboriginals fee simple title to their property and engendering pride of ownership.[123] By the 1840s, however, opponents defeated this policy by arguing that it would cause the Aboriginals to lose their land and their reserves.[124] Interestingly, this debate took place in Canada during the 1830s, while the United States was still preoccupied with removal. Later, during the 1880s, when Congress considered the Allotment Act, it rejected the argument that allotment would cause the Indians to lose their land. Not until the 1920s and 1930s, after the Indians had lost two-thirds of their land, did the United States admit that this prediction was accurate.

Since the late 1800s, the Indian Act in Canada has been the primary vehicle for dealing with First Nations in Canada. Bartlett traces the form of the modern Indian Act[125] to an 1867 Act[126] and an 1869 amending statute entitled "Act for the Gradual Enfranchisement of Indians and the Better Management of Indian Affairs."[127] This amendment gave the Superintendent General broad powers over reserve lands and reserve income, giving only token encouragement to Indian self-government. The government has insisted on dominating governance and land rights[128] of First Nations, severely limiting First Nations' rights and abilities to self-government.[129]

The consolidation of Aboriginal laws first appears in the Indian Act of 1876,[130] but that Act contained little new material. In contrast, the Dawes (Allotment) Act passed by the United States Congress just eleven years later differed markedly from prior policy in establishing a powerful national program of breaking up reservations through allotments to individual Indians.

Comparison of Canadian and United States Indian policies during the 1800s reveals that the differences stem both from demographic factors and from conscious choices in policy. Settlement came earlier in the western United States than in western Canada, and this population pressure caused problems that directed policy choices. In the United States, pioneer migration into the Mississippi and Ohio valleys and the South triggered the removal policy. Manifest destiny and the migration of prospectors and settlers into the West prompted creation of the reservation policy. Assimilation in the United States was an early and ongoing policy, but it was secondary until 1887, when the Dawes Act was passed.

2. Treaty Interpretation in Canada

The Canadian government, created in 1867, continued Britain's practice of signing treaties with the First Nations. The same year that Congress barred further treaties with Indian tribes in the United States, 1871, marks the beginning of Canada's most active treaty-making period. The Robinson Treaties, covering the northwestern part of upper Canada, were signed in 1850.[131] Between 1850 and 1853, Vancouver Island bands signed fourteen treaties covering about one-fortieth of the Island. Between 1871 and 1921, all of the "numbered" treaties were signed, covering vast tracts of interior Canada, the largest area touched by treaties. The signing of Treaty 11 in 1921 essentially concluded the treaty making era in Canada.[132] Approximately half the aboriginally occupied lands of Canada, including most of British Columbia, the Yukon, the Northwest Territories, and parts of Quebec, were never the subject of treaties, and the treaties in the Maritimes established peace and friendship between the parties, rather than land surrenders.[133]

Rules of construction for treaty interpretation in Canada are very much like the rules applied by courts in the United States. Treaties with Indigenous peoples are often ambiguous, and sometimes leave out terms clearly intended, such as the right to use waters on or adjacent to the reserve. The courts apply rules of construction to interpret these ambiguities and omissions. Ordinarily the "plain meaning" of the words in an agreement will control.[134] The Supreme Court of Canada, however, recently held that "plain meaning" interpretation is inappropriate for Indian treaties and statutes. In "Nowegijick v. The Queen,"[135] a unanimous Court declared that "treaties and statutes relating to Indians should be liberally construed and doubtful expressions resolved in favor of the Indians. . . ."[136] Affirming this principle in "R. v. Simon," the Court approved not only the principle of resolving doubtful expressions in favor of the Indians, but also held that these agreements should be interpreted as the Indians understood them.[137] These rules of construction are consistent with those applied by United States courts.[138]

The recent decision of the Canadian Supreme Court in "Attorney General of Quebec v. Regent Sioui,"[139] adds significantly to Canadian treaty law. Defendant Sioui and other Huron Indians were convicted of cutting down trees, camping, and making fires in places contrary to regulations of the Jacques-Cartier Park.[140] Defendants admitted the acts charged but claimed they were practicing ancestral religious rites which were the subject of a treaty between the Hurons and the British.[141] The document in question is only one paragraph long,[142] and fails to describe the territory covered. The Court held the document was a treaty, that it had not expired from lack of use, and that it had not been extinguished by laws creating and regulating the Jacques-Cartier Park. The Court spoke against extinguishment in strong terms:

> It must be remembered that a treaty is a solemn agreement between the Crown and the Indians, an agreement the nature of which is sacred. . . . The very definition of a treaty thus makes it impossible to avoid the conclusion that a treaty cannot be extinguished without the consent of the Indians concerned. Since the Hurons had the capacity to enter into a treaty with the British, therefore, they must be the only ones who could give the necessary consent to its extinguishment. . . .[143]

The Court followed "Simon" in construing this minimal and incomplete treaty in favor of the Indians.

The province also argued that a different treaty, the Treaty of Paris, signed by England and France on February 10, 1763, abrogated the treaty between the Hurons and the English. The Court rejected this argument, however, holding that "England and France could not validly agree to extinguish a treaty between the Hurons and the English. . . ."[144] This is, of course, a very different position from that taken by the United States cases, which hold that although treaties are the supreme law of the land, a treaty with an Indian tribe may be abrogated either by later statute, or later treaty.[145]

In "Sioui," the Attorney General of Quebec argued that the territorial scope of the treaty did not extend to cover the park.[146] The Hurons argued that the treaty gave them personal rights, which included the right to practice religion in the park, as part of the territory they occupied in 1760.[147] The Attorney General of Canada argued that treaty rights equalled territorial rights. The Court rejected both extremes and held that the treaty covered an area large enough to meet the Hurons' need to exercise their religious practices and customs, including sites within the park, "so long as the carrying on of the customs and rights is not incompatible with the particular use made by The Crown of this territory."[148] It was "up to the Crown" to prove that it could not accommodate its occupancy of the territory to reasonable exercise of the Hurons' rights.[149]

For the exercise of rites and customs to be incompatible with the occupancy of the park by the Crown, it must not only be contrary to the purpose underlying that occupancy, it must prevent the realization of that purpose.

> First, we are dealing with Crown lands, lands which are held for the benefit of the community. Exclusive use is not an essential aspect of public ownership. Second, I do not think that the activities described seriously compromise the Crown's objectives in occupying the park. . . . [The unique qualities of this area are not threatened.] These activities . . . present no obstacle to cross-country reaction.[150]

The Court concluded that the Attorney General had failed to establish that the park purposes were incompatible with the exercise of Huron rites and customs.[151]

In light of the rulings and language in "Sioui" and "Horseman" there is serious doubt whether Parliament has power to modify or extinguish a First Nation's treaty without the consent of that Nation, except where the federal action is taken for the benefit of the Indigenous people or with their consent. "Sioui" teaches that the courts will carefully scrutinize legislation concerning treaties to ensure that it is indeed for the benefit of the Native Americans, or at least not detrimental without justification.[152] This is consistent with current Canadian government policy of negotiating with tribes for settlement of Aboriginal claims.

In the United States, by comparison, the courts have not deviated from "Lone Wolf v. Hitchcock," which held that Congress has plenary power to abrogate Indian treaties if it chooses to do so for any reason whatsoever.[153] Further, the courts will not review legislation to assure that it advances the government's trust responsibility, or benefits the Indians.

3. Subjugation Under the Indian Act

The Great Depression of the 1930s "appears to have been the high water mark of government regulation and interference in the daily lives" of the Canadian Indians.[154] Parliament made numerous detailed amendments to the Indian Act before and during the Depression years. Only a few have been made since. None of the amendments changed the basic policy of "civilizing" the Indigenous peoples and denying the First Nations meaningful self-government.[155]

In the United States, the 1950s were dominated by the termination policy. In Canada, 1951 was significant for passage of a new Indian Act,[156] which, for all its changes, looked more like the 1868 Indian Act than anything new.[157] It increased the imposition of provincial laws and standards on First Nations. The new Act did remove some of the cultural control and lessened excess government control of local affairs on the reserves, but it did not alter the policy of encouraging assimilation through award of citizenship. Nor did the Act bestow any broader powers of self-government on First Nations. The concept of termination, as conceived in the United States, did not reach Canada until 1969, and then was short-lived, appearing only as a "proposed" policy without any follow-up legislative implementation.[158]

In the United States, self-determination became the dominant national policy by the late 1960s. The Indian Civil Rights Act, enacted in 1968, permitted tribal retrocession from state jurisdiction under P.L. 280 and enhancement of tribal courts. In 1970, President Nixon made his landmark speech flatly rejecting termination and endorsing a strong and comprehensive policy of self-determination for Indian tribes.

4. Termination in Canada: A Short-Lived "Era"

In the late 1960s, while the United States was moving rapidly towards self-determination, Canada was going in the opposite direction. In 1969, the Canadian government issued a policy statement called a "White Paper" on Indian Policy.[159] This Paper set forth a formula for termination and reads remarkably like H.C.R. 108[160] adopted by the United States Congress in 1953 to launch the termination era. Bartlett describes the White Paper:

> [The Paper] . . . declared that total assimilation must occur within a short period of time—the Indian Affairs Branch should be abolished in five years. All legislation specially pertaining to Indians was to be repealed, thereby denying special rights of Indians. Instead, all services were to be provided by the provinces; the statement rejected treaties and land-claims as insignificant in the debate on the future of the Indians. The Federal Government's goal of total assimilation would be accomplished according to the Statement, by short-term economic aid. The 1969 Policy did not contain any major positive suggestions regarding the well-being of the Indians. Its essence was the severing of all ties between the Indians and the Federal Government.[161]

The 1969 White Paper generated immediate opposition. In 1970, the Indian Chiefs of Alberta presented their "Red Paper"[162] to the Trudeau cabinet, opposing the entire concept of termination and arguing for greater recognition of treaty rights, Aboriginal claims, and rights to self-government. Passage of the Alaska Native Claims Settlement Act in 1971 influenced Canadian policy, as did the "Calder" case, decided in 1973. On August 8, 1973, shortly after "Calder" was decided, "the federal government issued a Statement on Aboriginal Claims, in which it declared its willingness to negotiate" these claims with First Nations peoples.[163] The 1969 White Paper proposal was dead. In 1977, the Mackenzie Valley Pipeline inquiry, headed by Thomas Berger, recommended recognition and settlement of native claims.[164] In 1981, the federal government further developed its policy in publication titled *In All Fairness: A Native Claims Policy, Comprehensive Claims.*[165]

5. Canada Begins To Recognize Aboriginal Rights

In the 1970s, Canadian policy began to reverse itself. The 1973 "Calder"[166] decision posed the very real possibility that the courts might recognize Indian claims to aboriginal titles and rights. In 1982, Canada adopted a new Constitution Act. Section 35(1) of the Act recognized and affirmed First Nation Aboriginal rights. In 1990, the "Sparrow" Court interpreted this language to mean that Aboriginal fishing rights are not extinguished merely because they are regulated in detail, and that the government has a heavy fiduciary duty, reviewable in the courts, when dealing with Aboriginal rights. "Sparrow" represents a remarkable turnaround for Canada.

6. Academics and Lawyers Take Up the Indian Cause

The "Sparrow" decision is unusual in the Court's heavy reliance on academic writings to support its analysis. The Court notes that:

[Until 1966] there was a virtual absence of discussion of any kind of Indian rights to land even in academic literature. By the late 1960s, Aboriginal claims were not even recognized by the federal government as having any legal status. . . . It took a number of judicial decisions and notably the "Calder" case in this court (1973) to prompt a reassessment of the position being taken by government.[167]

The Court then cites and quotes from numerous academic articles, all written after 1980, when academics realized that these problems should be studied.[168] In the United States, a similar pattern of scholarship emerges, although the Canadian scholarship has influenced the Canadian Supreme Court more profoundly. Cohen published his landmark treatise, *Handbook of American Indian Law*, in 1942. It was revised ineptly in 1957, but remained virtually the only example of legal scholarship with regard to Indian law until the 1970s. The field was then "discovered" by academics and, since 1975, dozens of fine articles and books have appeared.[169]

Paralleling the discovery of this field by academics has been the discovery and participation in the field by competent Indian and non-Indian lawyers. Competent legal representation has had a significant impact on the achievement of Indian goals. Until the 1960s competent legal counsel were seldom available to Indian tribes.[170] They were relegated to relying on government counsel who had unfettered discretion as to whether to represent a tribe in a given case. The government lawyers are located in the Solicitor's office and the Department of Justice and have (with a few recent exceptions) established a very checkered history of advocacy on behalf of Indian tribes.

The civil rights movement of the 1950s and 1960s produced a cadre of young, capable lawyers dedicated to minority causes, some of whom became expert in the unique field of Indian law. Lawyers in the Office for Economic Opportunity (War on Poverty Legal Service Program) became knowledgeable in Indian law. By 1969, some forty Legal Services lawyers were working on reservations throughout the nation.[171] More importantly, the University of New Mexico law student program[172] encouraged several hundred Indians themselves to attend law schools throughout the country. Most of these lawyers have returned to work on behalf of their communities. Law schools began teaching federal Indian law only in the late 1960s and early 1970s.[173] It is now a widely taught subject in western law schools. Law school casebooks[174] and law review articles began to appear during the same period. In 1982, the revised edition of the 1942 "Felix S. Cohen's Handbook of Federal Indian Law" was published after being completely rewritten over a seven year period.[175]

In 1966, Congress enacted a law permitting Indian tribes to file suit in their own names if the United States declined to sue for them.[176] Many such suits were filed. In the 1970s and 1980s, the United States dedicated more resources to litigation on the Indians' behalf. The Native American Rights Fund (NARF) in Boulder, Colorado, created in 1968, provides exceptional legal talent to tribes around the nation.[177] The totality of these changes means that Indian tribes, for the first time, have access to competent legal assistance, an accessibility that is essential for survival in modern United States. Treaty, statutory and other rights held by the tribes, long dormant, are now increasingly recognized and enforced by the courts.

III. ABORIGINAL RIGHTS

A. *The United States*

> Conquest gives a title which the courts of the conqueror cannot deny. . . . The conqueror prescribes its limits. . . . [T]he Indian inhabitants are to be considered merely as occupants . . . incapable of transferring the absolute title to others.[178]

In the United States the issues surrounding aboriginal title have nearly all been resolved, through treaty cessions and through the 1946 Indian Claims Commission Act. In Canada, these issues are now at center stage and are the major preoccupation of the Indian community.

Aboriginal rights and titles are recognized in both Canada and the United States. In "Johnson v. M'Intosh," Justice Marshall affirmed the existence of such title:

> They were admitted to be the rightful occupants of the soil, with a legal as well as just claim to retain possession of it, and to use it according to their own discretion; but their rights to complete sovereignty, as independent nations, were necessarily diminished, and their power to dispose of the soil at their own will, to whomsoever they pleased, was denied by the original fundamental principle that discovery gave exclusive title to those who made it.[179]

The Supreme Court has stated that the Indians' right of occupancy is "as sacred as the fee-simple of the whites."[180] The Indians' possessory right is a "federal" right,[181] so that a tribe is entitled to recover rent from a persistent trespasser on Indian title land.[182]

Indian aboriginal claims are founded on immemorial custom. Such claims are proven by establishing exclusive use and occupancy of the land[183] from time immemorial,[184] which the court defines as prior to the assertion of sovereignty by the United States.[185] The Ninth Circuit has held that proof of aboriginal hunting and fishing rights can create possessory rights in native Villages of Alaska.[186]

Aboriginal title is good against all but the United States, which has the exclusive power to extinguish such title.[187] While Indians are generally not entitled to compensation when aboriginal title is extinguished by the United States,[188] Congress usually awards compensation as a matter of policy. Once Indian title has been recognized by treaty, agreement, or statute, compensation is required when the title is taken by the United States.[189] This is not true of executive order reservations.[190]

Very few aboriginal title claims remain unsettled in the United States.[191] The federal government largely abolished Indian title during the reservation era, 1850-1857, forcing Indian tribes to give up their ancestral hunting grounds in return for "recognized" title to reservations. Throughout the first half of this century, Indian tribes bitterly complained that they were forced, coerced, or induced by fraud to leave their ancestral lands and move onto reservations, and maintained that the United States should return the land or at least pay for the taking. Before 1946, such claims could not be filed in court unless Congress passed special legislation waiving sovereign immunity and authorizing suit on each claim.[192] Over 140 such special bills had been passed. Deciding this process was too cumbersome,[193] Congress, in 1946, enacted the Indian Claims Commission Act[194] establishing a special forum to settle Indian claims without special legislation for each lawsuit. The Commission made monetary awards to several hundred tribes between 1946 and 1978,[195] thereby resolving most aboriginal claims. A few claims remained against states[196] or subdivisions of states,[197] based on violation of the Trade and Intercourse Acts[198] for entering into treaties or agreements with Indian tribes in the late 1700s.

B. Canada

The Canadian law of Aboriginal rights remained fairly constant throughout the Canadian history until the 1973 decision in "Calder,"[199] the Constitution Act of 1982,[200] and the 1990 Supreme Court decision in "Sparrow v. The Queen."[201]

1. Canadian Hostility Toward Aboriginal Rights

Prior to the 1982 Constitution Act, the federal government had both unilateral and exclusive power to deal with, or terminate, Aboriginal title and rights.[202] The 1867 Constitution Act provides that the federal government has exclusive jurisdiction over "Indians and lands reserved for Indians."[203] The federal government retains exclusive power to deal with Aboriginal rights, as against the provinces, but that power is now constrained by the 1982 Constitution Act.

The Canadian government has recently declined to extinguish title without consent. By negotiating settlements of Aboriginal claims, it has engaged in a process with all the earmarks of earlier treaty negotiations.[204] Several settlement agreements have been concluded in recent years.[205]

Because treaties covered only about half the nation, First Nations still assert claims of Aboriginal title to large areas of Canada. Until recently, the Canadian government looked unkindly on attempts to assert or litigate these Aboriginal claims. In 1927, for example, the Indian Act was amended making it a "federal crime to take Indian claims to court, to raise money to pursue Indian claims or in fact to organize to pursue Indian claims."[206] Although this provision was repealed in the 1930s, the federal government believed as late as 1969 that Aboriginal claims were so ill-defined that "it is not realistic to think of them as specific claims capable of remedy."[207] By 1973, the Canadian government's perspective had altered. The government recognized Aboriginal title when it indicated a commitment to negotiate outstanding claims, including those based on Aboriginal title.[208]

2. Recent Canadian Recognition of Aboriginal Rights

In 1973 the Supreme Court started down the path toward recognizing Aboriginal rights when it decided "Calder v. Attorney-General."[209] The Nishga people of northwestern British Columbia sought a declaration that they had Aboriginal title to their land and that this title had not been terminated. The Nishgas based their claim on the fact that their ancestors had occupied and used the land from time immemorial. Justice Hall, speaking for three members of the Supreme Court of Canada, agreed that the Nishgas had existing Aboriginal title derived from original occupancy and use.[210] Justice Judson, speaking for three other members of the Court, held that whatever title the Nishgas may have had had since been terminated.[211] Justice Pigeon, the seventh judge, wanted to dismiss the Nishgas' application because the Tribe had failed to comply with a British Columbia statute requiring the Lieutenant Governor's consent to litigation involving the Crown's title to land.[212] Because of the 3-3 stalemate between the other judges on the substantive issues, Pigeon's procedural argument is the sole reason "Calder" is binding legal authority. The real significance of "Calder," however, lies in its ruling that Aboriginal title is not necessarily limited to the confines of the Royal Proclamation of 1763, but may be based on the concept of prior occupation of lands.[213]

Until 1982, it was generally assumed that the Canadian government could unilaterally abrogate Aboriginal rights and title. Section 91(24) of the 1867 Constitution Act stood as authority for this position. This section granted the federal government jurisdiction over "Indians, and Lands reserved for the Indians."[214] This view has changed with the adoption of the 1982 Constitution Act, which provides in section 35(1) that "[t]he existing Aboriginal and treaty rights of the Aboriginal peoples of Canada are hereby recognized and affirmed."[215]

The 1982 Constitution Act appears to "constitutionalize" Aboriginal and treaty rights prospectively. Extinguishments that occurred prior to 1982 are still effective, but future attempts by Parliament to extinguish or alter such rights would be void. In 1985, Hogg wrote that section 35:

> operates as a limitation on the legislative power of both the federal Parliament and the provincial Legislatures: neither level of government is competent to impair aboriginal or treaty rights. The entrenchment of aboriginal or treaty rights means . . . that future extinguishments of such rights could be implemented only by the process of constitutional amendment.[216]

The one exception would occur when a First Nation voluntarily agreed to the extinguishment.

3. *Sparrow v.* The Queen *Requires Judicial Review of Laws*

Although the 1982 Constitution Act does not define Aboriginal rights, or how they should be treated by the courts, "Sparrow v. The Queen"[217] provides both a methodology and substantive answers to the meaning of section 35(1). The defendant was charged under the Fisheries Act[218] for fishing with a driftnet longer than permitted by his band's food fishing license. He admitted the facts but claimed an Aboriginal right to fish under section 35(1) of the 1982 Constitution Act.[219] The court remanded the case for trial on the constitutional issue, and provided criteria for reviewing legislation to assure that it advances rather than hinders First Nation interests.[220]

The "Sparrow" Court said the Government has a fiduciary duty to Aboriginal peoples.[221] The role of the Government is "trust like," rather than adversarial.[222] Contemporary recognition and affirmation of Aboriginal rights must be defined in light of this historic relationship.

Important differences exist between the aboriginal title and rights of First Nations in Canada and the United States. Many more outstanding claims of Aboriginal title exist in Canada than in the United States. Canada never created an equivalent to the United States Indian Claims Commission. Aboriginal title and its proprietary incidents are important, contemporary issues in Canada and are the basis for numerous claims now being pursued through legal and political avenues.

Justice Hall described Aboriginal title as "a right to occupy the lands and to enjoy the fruits of the soil, the forest, and of the rivers and streams."[223] In "Sparrow," the Court, in interpreting the 1982 Constitution Act, found that the scope of the defendant's Aboriginal fishing right should not be limited to mere subsistence, but could incorporate evolving and contemporary[224] uses as well.

IV. FEDERAL POWERS REGARDING NATIVE AMERICANS AND NATIVE CANADIANS

A. *The United States*

1. *The Plenary Power of Congress over Indians and the Indian Commerce Clause*

The United States Supreme Court has said that the federal government has plenary power over Indians and Indian tribes.[225] Early cases attributed this power to the treaty clause of the Constitution, the property clause, and the war power. In "United States v. Kagama,"[226] the Supreme Court attributed the power to enact the Major Crimes Act[227] to the trust relationship. The Court rejected the Indian commerce clause as a basis[228] because the clause only authorized Congress to legislate about commerce, and crimes are not commerce. More recent judicial opinions[229] have rejected the trust relationship as a source of congressional power and have attributed such power to the commerce clause.

The Supreme Court has not always identified a specific constitutional clause as the source of the federal government's power over Indian tribes. In "Johnson v. M'Intosh,"[230] the Court held that Indian tribes have no power to convey title to lands to anyone other than the federal government because "discovery" denied them that power. An act of Congress is required to authorize a tribe to convey real property. This includes water rights, which are considered real property.[231]

2. All Indian Treaties Have Been at Least Partially Abrogated

Congress has asserted its authority over Indian tribes by disestablishing some tribes,[232] by authorizing states to impose state jurisdiction over tribes either with or without tribal consent,[233] by authorizing highways and reservoirs to be built on Indian lands,[234] and by enacting other legislation altering tribal sovereignty.[235]

The Supreme Court has approved Congress's unilateral authority to abrogate Indian treaties[236] and agreements, just as treaties with other nations can be abrogated.[237] If Indian property rights are damaged or destroyed by such abrogations the Indians are entitled to compensation under the fifth amendment.[238] If, however, the federal government takes land or resources held under aboriginal title, which it clearly has power to do, the Indians have no constitutional right to compensation,[239] although in recent years Congress has usually made a political judgment to award compensation.[240]

Congress can enact special criminal laws applicable only to Indians who commit crimes in Indian country.[241] Enactment of these laws, applying only to Indians and Indian tribes, does not violate the Equal Protection Clause of the United States Constitution,[242] because the Court has said that they are based upon a political classification (tribes), rather than a racial classification.

3. The Trust Relationship in the United States

The United States has a special relationship toward Indian tribes, known as the "trust relationship." This includes general moral and political obligations to deal fairly with Indians,[243] as well as legally enforceable obligations.[244] The courts are often unclear which dimension of the trust relationship is at issue and the line between these two concepts is often blurred.

Chief Justice Marshall's opinion in "Cherokee Nation v. Georgia"[245] is the source of the trust relationship. Marshall characterized the tribes as "domestic dependent nations"[246] with a right of occupancy of the land until the federal government chooses to extinguish their title. He said "[m]eanwhile they are in a state of pupilage. Their relation to the United States resembles that of a ward to his guardian."[247]

The trust obligation of the federal government constrains congressional authority much less than it constrains executive authority. As applied to Congress, the trust obligation imposes only a moral or political obligation. No court has ever struck down congressional legislation concerning Indians on the basis of the trust relationship.[248] On the other hand, the trust relationship imposes justiciable duties on the executive. The Court has held that where a treaty required the United States to pay funds to tribal members, it was liable when it instead paid the money to the tribal government which was known to be misappropriating it. The government was "more than a mere contracting party," it was to "be judged by the most exacting fiduciary standards."[249] In the 1980s, the Supreme Court defined the trust relationship further, holding that when the government assumes comprehensive control over some aspect of Indian resources, such as timber harvesting, a trust obligation arises:

> [A] fiduciary relationship necessarily arises when the Government assumes such elaborate control over forests and property belonging to Indians. All of the necessary elements of a common-law trust are present; a trustee (the United States), a

beneficiary (the Indian allottees), and a trust corpus (Indian timber, lands, and funds).[250]

The Court then held the government liable for damages for the breach of its fiduciary duties.[251]

"Mitchell" and other trust cases indicate that the Court will find an enforceable trust responsibility as to the executive but only when a statute or course of government conduct supports that relationship, that is, no general trust relationship will be found arising out of the common law. The trust relationship tends to reinforce the rules of construction that doubtful statutes shall be construed in favor of the Indians, and that treaties and agreements will be construed as the Indians understood them.[252]

B. Canada

"The federal Parliament has taken the broad view that it may legislate for Indians on matters which otherwise lie outside its legislative competence, and on which it could not legislate for non-Indians."[253] This view is based on interpretation of section 91(24) of the 1867 Constitution Act.[254]

Can Parliament, by legislation, abrogate treaties with Indians? Pentney writes that "[i]n practice . . . virtually all of the important terminations of treaty obligations have been involuntary, in the form of legislative enactments."[255] The termination of treaty rights has usually arisen in connection with hunting and fishing rights. The leading case in "Regina v. Sikyea,"[256] which upheld the Migratory Birds Convention between Great Britain, on behalf of Canada, and the United States and Mexico, despite the fact that it substantially restricted treaty hunting rights. This case established that federal law could supersede treaty rights, and has been followed in later cases.[257]

The Canadian Bill of Rights guarantees equality before the law and specifically prohibits discrimination by reason of race. Yet section 91(24) of the 1867 Constitution Act establishes a basis for special laws for Indians and reserves. In fact, as Hogg says:

such laws are the sole reason for s. 91(24). Indeed, legislation enacted in relation to "Indians" . . . must normally be confined to Indians, that is to say, it must employ a racial classification in order to be constitutional. Legislation in relation to "lands reserved for the Indians" . . . need not necessarily employ a racial classification.[258]

In the United States, congressional legislation dealing with Indians does not violate the equal protection clause because, the Court says, it refers to a political classification—Indian tribes—and not to Indians as a racial group.[259] Such legislation is also sustained by the Indian commerce clause of the Constitution.[260]

1. The Indian Act Stifles Tribal Governments

Under the Indian Act in Canada, traditional Indian governments were replaced by band councils that function as agents of the federal government, exercising a limited range of delegated powers under close federal supervision.

The basic Canadian law dealing with Aborginals is the Indian Act, originally passed in 1876.[261] It determines who is a status[262] Indian in Canada by enumerating which bands are recognized or chartered,[263] and provides for a registration system for individuals of those bands. The Act specifically excludes Metis[264] and Indians who are enfranchised, that is, fully assimilated into Canadian majority society.[265] Status Indians and Inuit are generally accorded the same rights in terms of Aboriginal title and treaty agreements.[266]

The 1982 Constitution Act recognizes and affirms existing Aboriginal and treaty rights, which were preserved in the Royal Proclamation of 1763.[267] No new legislation is necessary to create or delegate those rights. A special committee to the House of Commons recommended in 1983 that legislation be enacted to occupy all areas of competence necessary to permit First Nations to govern themselves and to ensure that provincial laws would not apply on Indian lands except by agreement of the Band government.[268] No such legislation has yet been enacted and there is little chance that such enactment will soon occur.

2. *The Trust Relationship in Canada*

In Canada, the law concerning trust obligations and Indians is considerably less developed than in the United States. It has largely blossomed since the 1982 Constitution Act, and partly because of that Act. Nonetheless Canadian and United States laws are similar.

Some form of fiduciary relationship has been recognized in Canada from early times. Woodward notes that the fiduciary relationship was first enunciated in the Royal Proclamation of 1763,[269] but the case that primarily developed the relationship was "Guerin v. The Queen."[270]

The trust relationships of the United States and Canadian governments towards Indians are generally parallel. Canadian courts have tended to adopt rules similar to those supplied by courts in the United States, largely because the issues have frequently arisen and been decided earlier in the United States. Bartlett says:

> The history of the Aboriginal peoples and of their relationship to governments in the United States closely parallels circumstances in Canada. Not surprisingly, Canadian courts have paid considerable regard to United States jurisprudence. The Supreme Court of Canada has accentuated this practice in recent years. When "Guerin" was appealed to the Supreme Court of Canada, all parties relied on United States jurisprudence.[271]

The trust obligation in Canadian law was given more power in "Guerin v. The Queen,"[272] where the Court held that the federal government must deal in good faith, and keep its word, when managing tribal property held in trust. "The Musqueam Band surrendered reserve lands to the Crown for lease to a golf club. The terms of the lease actually obtained by the Crown were much less favorable than those approved by the Band at the surrender meeting."[273] The Court found that when the Crown took the land in order to lease it, a fiduciary relationship was created in its place: "[t]he *sui generis* nature of Indian title and the historic powers and responsibility assumed by the crown constituted the source of such a fiduciary obligation."[274] The property had appreciated since the breach of trust. The court affirmed damages of ten million dollars, quoting an Australian opinion on common law principles concerning damages in breach of trust: "a defaulting trustee must make good the loss by restoring to the estate the assets of which he deprived it notwithstanding that market values may have increased in the meantime."[275]

In 1990, however, in "Sparrow v. The .Queen,"[276] the Canadian Supreme Court tied the trust relationship together with the honor of the Crown. The "Sparrow" Court opined that the "honour of the Crown" is at stake when interpreting documents involving First Nations. In addition, "the special trust relationship and the responsibility of the government vis-a-vis Aboriginal people must be the first consideration in determining whether the legislation or action in question can be justified."[277]

The Court said that legislation affecting the exercise of Aboriginal rights is valid only if it meets the test for "justifying" an interference with a right "recognized and affirmed" under section 35(1). The Court then set forth criteria to determine if legislation is "justified," one of which is the extent of legislative or regulatory impact on an Aboriginal right.

> [F]ederal power must be reconciled with federal duty and the best way to achieve that reconciliation is to demand the justification of any government regulation that infringes upon or denies aboriginal rights. Such scrutiny is in keeping with . . . the concept of holding the Crown to a high standard of honourable dealing.[278]

This level of judicial review provides "a measure of control over government conduct and a strong check on legislative power."[279]

The Court stated that section 35(1) requires judicial review of legislation. The broad legislative power over Indians provided in the 1867 Constitution Act is now modified by the judicial review power imposed by section 35(1). The government bears the burden of justifying legislation[280] that has a negative effect on any Aboriginal right protected under section 35(1).[281] The first question a court should ask is whether the legislation interferes with an Aboriginal right. If so, it represents a prima facie infringement of section 35(1). To decide whether a prima facie case is established, the court must determine whether the limitation is unreasonable.[282] Second, the court must determine whether the regulation imposes undue hardship. Third, the court must determine whether the regulation denies holders of their preferred means of exercising that right.[283]

At this point, analysis moves to the issue of justification.[284] Is there a valid legislative objective? If the objective is conserving and managing a natural resource, it will probably be valid.[285] Also valid would be objectives purporting to prevent the exercise of section 35(1) rights that would cause harm to the general populace, or to Aboriginal peoples themselves.[286]

If a valid legislation objective is found, the analysis proceeds to the second part of the justification issue, considering whether the "honour of the Crown" has been upheld.[287] Food fishing including fish for ceremonial and social occasions, is to be given priority over the interests of other user groups.[288] Additional questions must be addressed, such as whether there has been the least infringement possible, whether fair compensation is available if an expropriation is involved, and whether the Aboriginal group has been consulted with respect to the conservation measures.[289]

3. Does the "Sparrow" Concept Fit the United States?

The American public has difficulty believing . . . [that] injustice continues to be inflicted upon Indian people because Americans assume that the sympathy or tolerance they feel toward Indians is somehow "felt" or transferred to the government policy that deals with Indians. This is not the case.[290]

Two comparisons come to mind when considering "Sparrow" and United States Indian law. The first involves the Pacific Northwest Indian fishing rights dispute in which the courts were asked to interpret treaties that reserved to the tribes the right to fish off-reservation at their usual and accustomed fishing sites "in common with the citizens of the territory."[291] In 1968, the United States Supreme Court held that under this treaty language, the state may regulate Indians "in the interest of conservation, provided the regulation meets appropriate standards and does not discriminate against the Indians."[292] Later, in 1974, a federal court found that state regulations failed to meet the conservation standard or were discriminatory, and enjoined their implementation.[293] Conservation, the court said:

> is limited to those measures which are reasonable and necessary to the perpetuation of a particular run or species of fish. In this context . . . "reasonable" means that a specifically identified conservation measure is appropriate to its purposes; and "necessary" means that such purpose in addition to being reasonable must be essential to conservation.[294]

The state has the burden of proving the regulation is reasonable and necessary. To do so, the state must show that the conservation purpose cannot first be satisfied by restricting non-Indian fishing. The court said: "[i]f alternative means and methods of . . . conservation regulation are available, the state cannot lawfully restrict the exercise of off reservation treaty right fishing, even if the only alternatives are restriction of fishing by non-treaty fishermen, either commercially or otherwise, to the full extent necessary for conservation of fish."[295]

Two observations are pertinent. First, the United States rules evolved out of a treaty interpretation case, whereas the "Sparrow" rule evolved from an Aboriginal rights case. Secondly, the United States Supreme Court has ruled that Indians may fish commercially, because they bartered fish from prehistoric times.[296] The "Sparrow" Court declined to decide this issue because it was not raised in the lower courts.[297]

A second analogy may be drawn between Canadian and United States law. The "Sparrow" rule reminds one of the equal protection analysis of the United States Supreme Court.[298] The fifth and fourteenth amendments to the federal Constitution require the federal and state governments respectively to provide equal protection to all individuals. The concept governs governmental actions which classify individuals for different benefits or burdens under the law. It requires that persons similarly situated should be treated alike.[299] It guarantees that legislative classifications will not be based on impermissible criteria or arbitrarily used to burden a group of individuals.[300] A statutory classification that is based on economics will be tested by the milder "rational basis" standard: the question is whether it is conceivable that the classification bears a rational relationship to an end of government that is not prohibited by the Constitution. Nearly all legislation tested by this standard is sustained.

On the other hand a statutory classification that affects a fundamental right such as voting,[301] or the right to travel,[302] or a classification that is based on race or national origin, receives "strict scrutiny"[303] by the courts. Under this test a court strikes down the legislation unless it is "necessary" to achieve a "compelling" governmental interest. Almost all legislation tested by this standard fails.[304]

Nowak, Rotunda and Young have concisely described the Supreme Court's strict scrutiny test:

> The strict scrutiny test means that the justices will not defer to the decision of the other branches of government but will instead independently determine the degree of relationship which the classification bears to a constitutionally compelling end. The Court will not accept every permissible government purpose as sufficient to support a classification under this test, but will instead require the government to

show that it is pursuing a "compelling" or "overriding" end—one whose value is so great that it justifies the limitation of fundamental constitutional values.

Even if the government can demonstrate such an end, the Court will not uphold the classification unless the justices have independently reached the conclusion that the classification is necessary to promote that compelling interest. Although absolute necessity might not be required, the justices will require the government to show a close relationship between the classification and promotion of a compelling or overriding interest. If the justices are of the opinion that the classification need not be employed to achieve such an end, the law will be held to violate the equal protection guarantee.[305]

Returning to the field of Indian law, the Supreme Court held in "Lone Wolf v. Hitchcock,"[306] that Congress is the sole arbiter of its own good faith and of the question whether legislation advances or damages Indian interests. No judicial review applying strict scrutiny or any other standard constrains Congress.[307] In Canada the "Sparrow" decision holds differently. If the good faith or trust responsibility of Parliament is in question, the court will give the law careful "scrutiny."[308]

Although "Sparrow" dealt with an Aboriginal fishing right, the language used by the Court to describe the fiduciary duty of the government seems to reach more broadly, as where the Court says "the Government has the responsibility to act in a fiduciary capacity with respect to aboriginal peoples. The relationship between the government and aboriginals is trust-like, rather than adversarial, and contemporary recognition and affirmation of aboriginal rights must be defined in light of this historic relationship."[309] This broad language suggests that the trust relationship protects not only Aboriginal title and fishing rights, but also, perhaps, the right to self-government.

The "Sparrow" doctrine of judicial review of Indian legislation is predicated partly on the 1982 Constitution Act. Given the general terms of that Act, however, the "Sparrow" interpretation is significantly attributable to the Canadian Supreme Court's embracement of a general trust obligation. The United States Supreme Court took a different turn in "Lone Wolf v. Hitchcock," ruling that while congressional legislation about Indians should demonstrate "perfect good faith," no judicial review of that issue was justified.[310] "United States v. Sioux Nation of Indians"[311] reflects a judicial tempering of this view and a possible inclination to re-examine the "Lone Wolf" rule. In that re-examination United States courts could benefit from a study of the Canadian jurisprudence, specifically "Sparrow v. The Queen."

V. STATE AND PROVINCIAL POWER OVER INDIANS

A. *United States*

In the United States, states historically had no judicial or legislative power over Indian country,[312] because the tribes were semi-sovereign under federal protection. Only the federal government had authority to negotiate with the tribes. The Court blurred this "bright line" doctrine slightly in 1882 when it decided that an offense committed by a non-Indian against a non-Indian on a reservation fell under the jurisdiction of state courts and state criminal codes.[313] Congress further eroded tribal immunity from state law in 1953 when it enacted P.L. 280, empowering forty-five states to make a limited extension of state jurisdiction onto Indian reservations with or without Indian consent.[314] Many states enacted laws asserting jurisdiction over reservations, sometimes with Indian consent and sometimes without.[315] The courts have limited P.L. 280,[316] construing it to apply only to state laws of general application such as state criminal laws.[317] States cannot impose state taxes, or state or local regulatory laws, such as zoning, on reservations.[318] P.L. 280 explicitly denied states jurisdiction over Indian hunting, fishing, and water rights.[319] The United States Supreme Court has further eroded Indian immunity from state law by changing its analytical approach to the issue of state jurisdiction in Indian country. In 1973, the Court decided that immunity from state law no longer depends on "sovereignty," but now depends on "preemption" analysis.[320] Preemption analysis asks whether the federal government has so fully occupied the field of law that there is no room left for state action. When sovereignty was the key issue, the reservation boundary was quite impervious to state law, except when Congress explicitly breached it by clear legislation such as P.L. 280, or termination legislation. Under preemption analysis, however, the court considers each case on its own facts[321] in deciding whether the federal government has so fully occupied the field that no room is left for state action. In general, the courts easily find preemption where the controversy is among Indians, or between an Indian and a tribe.[322] Preemption is difficult to find if the controversy is among non-Indians.[323] Uncertainty occurs when the controversy is between a non-Indian and an Indian.[324] In the meantime, "sovereignty" has been relegated to "backdrop" status.[325]

Where an Indian and a non-Indian are involved, state laws will apply on the reservation even though Congress has never so legislated if the tribal interest is modest and the state interest great.[326] State and local law have been held to apply to zoning of non-Indian land on a checkerboarded part of a reservation where approximately 50% of the land is owned by non-Indians.[327] Conversely, a few members of the Court said state zoning laws do not apply on a "closed" portion of the reservation where more than 90% of the land was tribally owned.[328] State law applied to non-Indians fishing on non-Indian lands on a reservation where the tribe was not seriously affected by the fishing and failed to show historic, aboriginal reliance on fish as a source of food.[329] State jurisdiction failed when a state imposed taxes on the non-Indian builder of a school on a reservation because federal policy and money encouraged the educational program for Indian children.[330] In yet another case, the state was barred from imposing a "transactions privilege tax" on a non-Indian machinery seller who made a one-time-only tractor sale on the reservation to a member of the tribe.[331] The Court said the non-Indian seller was a "trader" and was comprehensively regulated by the federal Indian Trader

Statutes.[332] A state also failed in its attempt to impose taxes on a non-Indian motor carrier that hauled logs on the reservation from an Indian logging operation.[333] The logs were hauled over BIA or tribal roads, and the logging operation was strongly encouraged and partly financed by the federal government, thus preempting state jurisdiction. On the other hand, the state is not preempted from controlling water distribution to non-Indian landowners on the reservation where the water is surplus to the Indians' needs, and the source river starts above the reservation and flows on below it.[334]

Federal law controls the question of Indians' rights to water under the "Winters" doctrine. Under the 1952 McCarran Amendment,[335] however, state courts have jurisdiction to adjudicate Indian water rights and determine the amount of water to which the Indians are entitled.[336] State courts must still apply federal law in these proceedings, and the Indians, or the United States on their behalf, can petition the United States Supreme Court for review if they feel the state court misconstrued or misapplied federal law. Several such state court adjudications have now been completed in the western United States.[337] Others are still pending in the courts.[338]

B. Canada

Canada has no foundation court decision similar to the "Worcester v. Georgia"[339] holding that state law does not apply on an Indian reservation. In Canada, detailed federal laws control much of Aboriginal life. In addition, federal power over Aboriginals has been transferred to the provinces through a number of legislative enactments. Perhaps the most important delegation of federal legislative power over First Nations is found in a 1951 amendment to the Indian Act.[340] Section 88 permits extension of provincial laws of general applicability over Indians, subject to the terms of treaties and federal laws.[341] This statute has spawned voluminous litigation, particularly with regard to off-reserve hunting and fishing rights. The extent to which section 88 permits application of provincial laws to Indian lands and resources is unsettled.[342] Provincial laws generally apply to

Indians on as well as off reserves.[343] This is true of wildlife,[344] environmental, and other laws. This rule, however, is subject to several exceptions. Provincial laws do not apply to First Nations where Aboriginal rights are protected by section 35(1) of the 1982 Constitution Act, are expressed in a treaty, or appear in a federal statute such as the Indian Act.[345] Further, provincial laws may not single out Indians for special adverse treatment or affect their "Indianness."[346] Sanders describes "Indianness" as covering the "political, social and economic life of the community."[347] Woodward says it covers "laws which affect the essential characteristics of a people as Indian people," and notes that these "essential characteristics have not yet been elaborated on by the Courts."[348] In "Derrickson v. Derrickson," the Court ruled that provincial laws may not interfere with First Nation possessory rights to reserve land, which are exclusively a federal matter.[349] In "Surrey v. Peace Arch Enterprises,"[350] the Court found that provincial zoning laws cannot apply on reserve lands. Thus, a municipality could not zone reserve lands even within municipal boundaries. In the United States, the prevailing doctrine is that state laws do not apply in Indian country unless Congress says so,[351] or when the issue is not central to Indian life.[352] In Canada, the opposite theory prevails. Provincial law applies to Indian reserves except when the provincial law is contrary to section 35(1) of the 1982 Constitution Act, contrary to a treaty, or contrary to federal law.[353] Significantly, the Allotment Act of 1887 in the United States, which created checkerboard ownership on many reservations, has no parallel in Canada. In the United States, this checkerboarding is one reason that state law has been allowed to intrude onto reservations. In Canada, of course, provincial law applies to reserves regardless of land ownership.

VI. INDIAN SELF-GOVERNMENT

The act establishing the [Cherokee] Standing Committee . . . provided for Warriors in National Council Assembled. The committee was to consist of thirteen members each serving two year terms. . . . The resolution further provided that "affairs of the Nation shall be committed to the care of the standing committee . . . but acts of this body shall not be binding in our common property on the Nation without unanimous consent of the members and Chiefs of the Council.[354]

A. *The United States*

In the United States, tribes have all the powers of self-government except as those powers have been changed by clear action of Congress, or lost by necessary implication arising from their dependent status.[355] Over the years, these sovereign powers have gradually but consistently diminished. Early decisions held that tribes, because of their dependent status, lost their power to enter into treaties or agreements with other nations.[356] Also, due to the guardian-ward relationship, tribes lost their capacity to convey title to their real property, including water rights, except with the consent of the United States.[357] In 1881, the Supreme Court held that a crime committed by one non-Indian against another non-Indian was to be tried in state court, under state law.[358] Tribal courts had no jurisdiction. In 1886, the Court held that Congress had power to enact the Major Crimes Act,[359] applicable to Indians in Indian Country, without necessarily obtaining the consent of the Indians.[360]

Government policy seriously eroded traditional Indian governance in the late 1800s by breaking up reservations under the 1887 Dawes Act[361] and by administrative policies designed to individualize Indians and discourage their communal lifestyle.[362] Congress intended gradually to terminate the reservations and thus saw no need to plan the best form of tribal governments. The tribes would simply disappear.[363] The IRA sanctioned tribal governments, but operated to promote governments with limited powers and non-Indian forms and procedures. In 1953, Congress enacted P.L. 280 authorizing forty-five states to impose their jurisdiction over Indian reservations either with or without Indian consent.[364] In 1968, the Indian Civil Rights Act

(ICRA)[365] changed the law to require Indian consent to state jurisdiction. The ICRA, however, also applied a variation of the Bill of Rights to Indian tribal courts and governments, and limited tribal court criminal jurisdiction to fines of $500 and imprisonment of six months.[366]

Modern court decisions have contributed to the erosion of tribal government. In 1978, the Supreme Court held that tribal courts did not have criminal jurisdiction over non-Indians committing crimes against the tribal code.[367] In 1990, the Supreme Court held that tribal courts lack jurisdiction over non-member Indians.[368] In 1973, the Supreme Court adopted preemption as the formula for analyzing whether state laws applied on the reservation.[369] In practice, this meant that state laws apply in many situations where they would earlier have been excluded, such as where a county zones property owned by a non-Indian on a checkerboarded part of the reservation.[370] Thus, the sovereignty and self-governing powers of Indian tribes have gradually been eroded in these multiple and diverse ways. Tribal governmental powers nonetheless are still substantial.

> [I]n addition to the power to punish tribal offenders, the Indian tribes retain their inherent power to determine tribal membership, to regulate domestic relations among members, and to prescribe rules of inheritance for members . . . . But exercise of tribal power beyond what is necessary to protect tribal self-government or to control internal relations is inconsistent with the dependent status of the tribes, and so cannot survive without express Congressional delegation.
>
> Indian tribes retain inherent sovereign power to exercise some forms of civil jurisdiction over non-Indians on their reservations, even on non-Indian fee lands. A tribe may regulate, through taxation, licensing, or other means, the activities of nonmembers who enter consensual relationships with the tribe or its members, through commercial dealing, contracts, leases, or other

arrangements. . . . A tribe may also retain inherent power to exercise civil authority over the conduct of non-Indians on fee lands within its reservation when that conduct threatens or has direct effect on the political integrity, the economic security, or the health or welfare of the tribe.[371]

Several cases have been decided by the federal courts since "Montana" and illustrate how the lower federal courts apply the "Montana" test.[372] The Supreme Court itself addressed the question of tribal zoning power over non-Indian land on the reservation in "Brendale,"[373] holding in a highly fractured opinion that the tribe had exclusive zoning power over the "closed" part of the Yakima reservation, predominantly Indian land and population, while the tribe and county shared zoning power over the "open" part of the reservation, predominantly non-Indian occupied and owned. The county zoned non-Indian-owned lands, while the tribe zoned trust and tribally-owned lands within the "open" area.

One of the most comprehensive legislative intrusions in Indian governance occurred in the Indian Reorganization Act of 1934 (IRA).[374] This Act encouraged renewal of tribal governments, but in a different form. The Act authorized tribes to draw up constitutions for approval of the Secretary of the Interior. When a constitution was approved it gave the tribe status of an IRA tribe with certain legislative powers and protections. These constitutions created governments with a tribal chairperson, and tribal councils elected by the tribal membership.

In spite of the fact that the tribes had federally approved constitutions, they operated on the basis of inherent sovereignty.[375] Federal policy encouraged tribal courts to grow and become more proficient. Acceptance of the IRA form of government was voluntary. Each tribe voluntarily decided whether to accept this form of government.[376] Over two-thirds of the nation's tribes became IRA tribes.[377] Over the years, however, nearly all tribes (except for the theocratic Pueblos of New Mexico) adopted constitutions and the chairperson/council form of government similar to the IRA tribes.[378]

1. *Federal delegation of Environmental Control to Indian Tribes*

> What happens to the Earth happens to the children of the Earth. Man has not woven the web of life. He is but one thread. Whatever he does to the web, he does to himself.[379]

In the United States, Congress and the courts have affirmed tribal governmental power by delegating authority to implement federal environmental laws to the tribes, and by enabling tribes to receive federal grants toward this goal in the same way as states. In Canada, no similar legislative delegations have occurred.[380]

Seven major federal environmental statutes authorize delegation of authority to Indian tribes: the Clean Water Act (CWA),[381] the Clean Air Act (CAA),[382] the Safe Drinking Water Act (SDWA),[383] the Comprehensive Environmental Response, Compensation and Liability Act (CERCLA),[384] the Federal Insecticide, Fungicide, and Rodenticide Act (FIFRA),[385] the Surface Mining Control and Reclamation Act of 1977 (SMCRA),[386] and the Resource Conservation and Recovery Act (RCRA).[387] Only a few tribes have received these delegations, primarily because of the lack of federal funds to hire the essential experts.

The CWA is illustrative of these delegations. Enacted in 1972, it gave the federal government, rather than the state governments, primary authority to prevent, reduce, or eliminate pollution in the nation's waters. A national waste discharge permit system was established that could be delegated to the states for implementation.[388] The Environmental Protection Agency (EPA) has authority to approve and delegate, or disapprove and decline to delegate, state programs.[389] If a state chooses not to have a program, the EPA will itself implement pollution control in that state. Amendments to the CWA in 1987[390] provide that the EPA shall treat tribes similarly to the states for most purposes including implementation of the permit program and the non-point source control program. Tribes are also defined as "municipalities" in the CWA,[391] making them eligible for federal grants for construction of sewage treatment facilities.

Each of the other environmental statutes listed above has similar delegation clauses, except for RCRA.[392]

RCRA is the only federal environmental statute that does not authorize Indian tribes to be treated as states for implementation of the Act, which regulates disposal of solid and hazardous wastes to protect underground water sources. RCRA is intended to track hazardous wastes from their origin to their final disposition. As with the CWA, tribes are defined as "municipalities," and thus are eligible for financial assistance for facilities planning, legal assistance, economic and other studies.[393]

In a recent case, the state of Washington attempted to exercise RCRA jurisdiction over reservations.[394] The EPA, however, approved the state program only as to non-Indian lands on reservations. The Court held that Indian tribes possess inherent sovereignty, which the EPA recognizes, and Indian reservations are not subject to state regulation under the Act. The EPA may approve tribal jurisdiction, or if a tribe declines implementation, then the EPA may regulate in the tribe's place.[395]

These delegations of environmental authority to Indian tribes illustrate how Indian tribal governments are entrenched in the statutory and case law of the nation. Their existence denies the "disappearing Indian" myth, and illustrates how Indian governments and institutions have become a permanent part of the governmental structure of the nation.

2. The Power to Exclude

Indian tribes generally have the power to exclude persons from the reservation.[396] This power sometimes is provided for in treaties, but it exists as an inherent sovereign power whether or not found in a treaty, statute, or other government source.[397] Tribes clearly have the power to exclude non-members from trust lands.[398] Whether the tribe can exclude a non-member from fee patent land depends on the circumstances. Certainly the tribe could not exclude a person from his or her own land on the reservation, or from road access to that land. Whether a tribe could exclude a non-member from all non-Indian owned land on the reservation has not been answered by the courts.

3. Tribal Legislatures and Tribal Courts

All but a few Indian tribes have legislative bodies,[399] much like a typical city council. These legislatures enact laws which are then enforced by the executive branch of government,[400] and by tribal police. Tribal legislative bodies exist whether or not the tribe has a constitution approved by the Secretary of the Interior under the 1934 Indian Reorganization Act.[401]

In the past twenty years, tribal councils have become increasingly active in passing legislation. In earlier times the principal law adopted by most tribes was a criminal code dealing with misdemeanors.[402] This has changed. In recent years tribal councils have enacted laws concerning inheritance, domestic relations, traffic control, adoption, taxation, and a multitude of other topics.[403] These enactments demonstrate the intention of tribal governments to exercise their powers of self-government and to control their own destinies.

Approximately 130 tribal courts operate on reservations in the United States.[404] Most tribal courts are courts of general jurisdiction that derive their authority from the inherent sovereignty of the tribe, as reflected in the tribal constitution and ordinance. Under their inherent sovereign powers tribal courts start with unlimited criminal and civil jurisdiction. Limitations, however, have been placed on tribal court jurisdiction by Congress, the Supreme Court, and in some instances by tribal laws. Federal law limits tribal court criminal jurisdiction to punishments of no more than one year in jail and $5000.[405] "Oliphant v. Suquamish Indian Tribe"[406] restricts tribal court jurisdiction to Indians, and "Duro v. Reina"[407] limits that jurisdiction to members of the tribe where the court sits. In other words, tribal courts have no criminal jurisdiction over either non-Indians or non-member Indians. On the civil side, tribal courts' general jurisdiction is not limited by federal law in extent or type of case. Where P.L. 280 applies,[408] some tribes exercise concurrent civil jurisdiction with state courts.

Tribal courts were not historically part of Indian dispute resolution. In 1883, the BIA began creating a system of Courts of Indian Offenses, similar to the Indian courts now operating under the Code of Federal Regulations.[409] Few tribal courts existed at the time. Enactment of the IRA in 1934 encouraged rapid growth of tribal courts based on inherent sovereignty. The trend dwindled during the termination era, but developed rapidly again after the Indian Civil Rights Act of 1968.[410] Most tribal courts are not significantly different from state courts, although they occasionally apply customary tribal law. The Bill of Rights of the federal Constitution does not constrain tribal governments,[411] but they are bound by the legislated Indian Civil Rights Act, which is very similar to the federal Bill of Rights.[412] Tribal courts have civil jurisdiction similar to state courts over matters occurring on the reservation. To the extent that the tribe has legislative jurisdiction over environmental matters on the reservation, the tribal court has civil enforcement powers against non-Indians, and both civil and criminal enforcement power as to tribal members. The tribal court also has jurisdiction over suits for nuisance, negligence, or riparian rights, depending on the applicable statutory and common law as determined by each tribe.

B. Canada

As Canada evolved from colonial status to independence, the Indigenous people were largely ignored, except where the government negotiated agreements to obtain more land for settlement.[413] The Aboriginals played no part in negotiating the Confederation or in drafting the British North America Act of 1867, which assigned legislative authority with respect to "Indians and Lands reserved for the Indians" to the federal government.[414] The government assumed increasing legislative control over Indian communities, leading to the 1876 Indian Act, which, with minor modifications, remains in effect today.[415] The result over the years has been the wholesale erosion of First Nation governmental powers.[416]

Initially, the federal government recognized traditional native governments for the purpose of signing treaties and surrendering land. In spite of the fact that a Legislative Assembly study of 1858 recommended that traditional First Nation internal government be allowed,[417] the government nonetheless soon imposed controls on tribal governments. Subsequent detailed legislation deprived the tribes of most of their self-governing powers.[418]

In 1869, Parliament passed the Act for the Gradual Enfranchisement of Indians and the Better Management of Indian Affairs.[419] The provisions of this Act have been only slightly altered since that time. Section 10 of the Act provided for elections for office to be held for a three year term. The officers were subject to removal by the governor "for dishonesty, intemperance or immorality."[420] Especially in small communities, this "elective method" appears to have been less democratic than existing Indian customs and tradition. The three year term and the limited powers of removal vested in the Governor denied the immediate control of the Chiefs formerly possessed by the community.[421]

Parliament intended to introduce the Indigenous people to the dominant society's forms of government, and inculcate a spirit of individuality in place of the communal life and hereditary leadership of the traditional past.[422] The Indian-elected governments were given only trivial powers, and generally were subjected to stifling supervision by government. An 1880 amendment gave the Governor in Council broad discretion over the bands, to make decisions "[w]henever the Governor in Council deems it advisable."[423] The Indian agent was empowered to call and reside over all band council meetings. The Department's blindness to First Nation objections to this intrusion into tribal powers of self-government is unfortunate. The same ethnocentrism that has plagued Indian policy in the United States has plagued Canadian Aboriginal policy.

The band council elective system was fully developed by 1884.[424] The First Nations consistently resisted it. In 1951, the Indian Act was again amended by legislation that returned the form of the Act to its 1868 concepts. The policy of self-determination apparently was never seriously considered in Canada.[425]

Many experts assert the First Nations still have sovereign governmental powers, even though seldom used and yet unrecognized by the federal government.[426] Some suggest that it is not the sovereign governmental powers of Indigenous people that are ill-defined, but the recognition of these powers in Canadian law.[427] The federal government has so occupied the internal affairs of First Nations, however, that precious little room is left for self-government. Federal regulation defines bands, amalgamates bands, permits the government to abrogate band custom councils, determines how the councils of certain bands are elected, determines who shall be a member of the band, determines how a band council may make decisions, determines how a band may spend its money, and defines the legislative power of a band council.[428]

Although many bands claim rights to self-government and to their own tribal courts[429] as an Aboriginal right never divested,[430] the Indian Act historically and today does not recognize such claims.[431] The powers of band councils to make by-laws have been virtually unchanged since 1886 and are confined to matters with which a rural municipality might normally be concerned. They are, however, expressly subject to regulations that the Governor in Council might make consistently with the Indian Act and the power of disallowance of the Minister of Indian Affairs. The power to make money by-laws—the taxation of interests in reserve land and of band members—is confined to those bands declared to have "reached an advanced stage of development."[432] In the Province of Saskatchewan there are sixty-seven bands with a population of approximately 45,000—none of the bands has been declared to have "reached an advanced stage of development."[433]

Two kinds of band councils operate in Canada: those selected by customary means (about 35%) and those elected under terms of section 74 of the Indian Act (about 65%).[434] Band councils selected by custom exercise customary powers but can be stripped of these powers by Parliament. Disagreement exists as to the powers of the section 74 councils.[435] Some courts take the view that their powers derive strictly from the Indian Act. Others contend they have broader powers, but no court has taken the position of "Worcester v. Georgia"[436] that Indian tribes have all powers of government unless specifically removed by federal statute or by their dependent status.

In 1983, the Report of the Special Committee of the House of Commons on Self-Government recommended that the rights of Indian peoples to self-government be explicitly stated and entrenched in the Canadian Constitution.[437] Indian governments would then form a distinct order of government. The Committee recommended that, while waiting the constitutional entrenchment, Parliament should fully occupy the field, ousting Provincial jurisdiction, and then vacate those areas of jurisdiction to recognize First Nation governments. Different agreements would be entered into with each First Nation concerning the extent of that tribe's jurisdiction, including land and water management, revenue raising, and economic and commercial development.[438] A bill was introduced in parliament based on the Committee recommendations,[439] but fell far short of implementing the Report's recommendations and was never passed.[440] Bartlett observes that "[t]he Bill did not provide for self-government or even self-management. It merely provides for the possibility of negotiating with the minister an agreement which could confer powers of self-management over Indian lands."[441]

"In spite of [intrusive provincial policies], the concept of a homeland has been gaining strength. . . . The idea of a homeland for Aboriginal peoples seems now to be an accepted part of provincial and federal government policy for Indians, Inuit and Metis."[442]

1. Federal Delegation of Environmental Control to First Nations

No delegation of Canadian national environmental laws to First Nations has occurred in Canada. One obvious reason is the paucity of governmental authority held by these Nations. Without some type of on-going governmental operation it is unlikely that the national government would delegate governing authority to Indian tribes.

2. *Tribal Courts*

Tribal courts, drawing authority from inherent sovereignty, do not operate in Canada, although that may change if the movement toward self-determination, self-government and independence continues to grow. Alternatively, First Nations may attempt to establish courts on the basis of existing Indian Act authority. Woodward believes that "as government by band by-law becomes more and more common, it may be expected that bands will attempt to establish their own courts and tribunals to enforce and interpret those laws."[443] He concludes, however, that the Indian Act provides a "thin" basis upon which to build a judicial system to enforce band by-laws.[444]

VII. CONCLUSION

Although similarities exist between Canadian and United States policies concerning Native tribes and bands, the differences are substantial. Neither country deserves accolades for dealing fairly with the Aboriginal tribes within their borders.

The official national policy of both countries has always been to negotiate voluntary treaties and agreements with Indigenous tribes. The Royal Proclamation of 1763 first stated this policy. The 1763 Proclamation also pronounced that only the national government could sign treaties with First Nations, a position later adopted by both Canada and the United States.

In spite of these official declarations, the real policy of both governments was to move the Aboriginals off the land and make it available for prospecting, logging, farming, and settlement by non-Indians. The policies of treaty negotiation, removal, assimilation, and reservations were all designed to accomplish this overriding goal. In practice, treaties and other cessions were seldom concluded with willing Indian tribes. The tribes usually knew that they must either cede their lands and put their welfare and survival at the mercy of the dominant government, or be pushed aside without even a small reservation to call home.

The swings in United States policy have been more extreme than in Canada: from removal in the first half of the nineteenth century, to a reservation policy for the second half of that century, to assimilation under the 1887 Allotment Act, to self-determination in 1934, to termination in the 1960s and back to self-determination in the 1970s and 1980s. Canada has maintained a consistent policy of individualization and assimilation from 1763 to recent time.

Both nations recognize Aboriginal land rights, and in both only the national government has legal authority to abrogate such rights. In the United States virtually no aboriginal rights remain, having been eradicated largely by Indian cessions in the reservation era of the 1800s. Claims still alive went to the 1946 Indian Claims Commission where tribes received partial monetary compensation for their lost land.[445] Except for a few remaining claims, aboriginal land rights are no longer an issue in the United States. The situation is quite different in Canada. Although some cessions occurred in treaties and agreements establishing reserves in Canada, these documents were used more sparingly than in the United States, resulting not so much from any conscious policy as from the fact that central and western Canada were settled later than the western United States and had fewer population pressures. Canada has only recently attacked this problem and under national policies promulgated in the 1970s and the Constitution Act of 1982, is now attempting to negotiate settlement of Aboriginal claims.[446] Other Canadian First Nation claims are in the courts for resolution. Nothing comparable to the United States Indian Claims Commission is anticipated in Canada. The Canadian policy of negotiation poses a long and arduous journey, but has the distinct advantage of showing respect for tribal claims.

The United States Congress and the Canadian Parliament both have extremely broad powers to legislate about Indian affairs, under the United States Constitution and the several Constitution Acts of Canada. Until recently these governments could abrogate treaties, disestablish reservations in whole or part, take Indian property in condemnation proceedings, determine who is an Indian, and determine the nature of tribal government. Canadian law has changed with "Sparrow v. The Queen."[447]

In 1903, the United States Supreme Court ruled in "Lone Wolf v. Hitchcock"[448] and Congress should act "with perfect good faith" towards Indians, but held that Congress, not the Court, was the arbiter of its own good faith.[449] In contrast, the Canadian Supreme Court ruled in "Sparrow" that the courts will give careful scrutiny to legislation adversely impacting Native Americans.[450]

This ruling is reminiscent of two separate doctrines in the United States. With regard to off-reservation treaty fishing rights in the Pacific Northwest, the courts have held that states can regulate these rights, but only when necessary for conservation, and only when regulation of non-Indian fishermen cannot accomplish the same purpose.[451] The states, in other words, must regulate the non-Indians first, before regulating the treaty tribes.

The second parallel with "Sparrow" concerns the constitutional rights of "equal protection" set forth in the fifth and fourteenth amendments to the federal Constitution. Under the cases interpreting these constitutional rights, a legislative classification based on a fundamental right (e.g., voting, travel), or upon race, ethnic origin, or religion, will be given "strict scrutiny" by the courts. The courts reject any presumption of validity. The legislation will be upheld only if it is necessary to achieve a "compelling governmental interest." An examination of the cases reveals that very few statutes that trigger strict scrutiny pass this test. The "Sparrow" approach implements the fiduciary relationship, and ought to be considered carefully by courts in the United States. The question is whether the legislation about Indians is consistent with the government's fiduciary responsibility, whether it advances Indian interests or does them harm. Such a test is needed because of the often cavalier and sometimes disastrous ways that Native American tribes and their governments are treated by congressional and state legislation. Such a test would be particularly relevant where Congress enacts legislation adversely impacting tribal self-government. Such legislation can totally destroy the all important rights to self-government, can even destroy the tribe as a political entity, without the payment of compensation—because no "property" is taken.

"Sparrow" also implies that compensation will be required if the government takes any Indian aboriginal right. In the United States, no compensation is required when the federal government takes aboriginal lands or rights.[452]

In the United States, the 1832 decision of "Worcester v. Georgia" ruled that state laws do not apply on Indian reservations.[453] But that brightline doctrine has been chipped away to the point that today state laws often apply on reservations, for example, where a crime or civil wrong is committed by one non-Indian against another non-Indian, where states have asserted jurisdiction under P.L. 280, and where county zoning applies to predominantly non-Indian owned areas of reservations. Nonetheless, Indian tribes in the United States still retain many characteristics of sovereign government. Tribes enact their own civil and criminal laws, establish and empower their own tribal courts, exercise criminal jurisdiction over their members, determine criteria for tribal membership, control inheritance rights, and retain civil jurisdiction over non-Indians where a vital tribal interest such as health or safety is involved—and they do all of these things with about the same degree of success as state and local governments. In Canada, a combination of federal and provincial law smothers tribal governments. Virtually no self-governing powers exist.

The Canadian attitude toward Indian self-government is anomalous in that the government acknowledged the legitimacy of tribal government for the purpose of signing treaties and ceding land, but has since refused to acknowledge that Indians are capable of self-government. If anything, the Canadian government's policy towards Indian self-government has been more denigrating and stifling than policies of the United States. In the past thirty years self-determination and economic self-sufficiency have become the official national United States policy towards tribes. Nearly all Indian tribes in the United States have self-created governments, constitutions, tribal courts, tribal police, and other accoutrements of government. In a sense these governments have become "constitutionalized," and are now accepted as a permanent part of the legal landscape of the United States. In Canada, the movement toward self-determination and self-government is at a very different stage. Almost no self-government exists, even though many Indian tribes and academic scholars believe that self-governing powers based on inherent sovereignty could be exercised by the tribes. The recent Report of the Special Committee of the House of Commons, "Indian Self-Government in Canada," makes a strong case for creating, or recognizing, the independence, self-governing powers, and right to self-determination of Canadian Indian tribes. But Indian self-government is not a widely accepted concept in Canada, as it is in the United States. The prevailing law in Canada for reservations emanates from a federal or provincial source rather than from tribal legislative bodies as in the United States.

In the United States, termination was the official Indian policy in the 1950s. More than 100 tribes were terminated under this policy, and P.L. 280 was enacted authorizing states to impose jurisdiction over Indian reservations either with or without tribal consent. In Canada, the idea of a termination policy did not officially appear until a 1969 government White Paper. This document was met with such strong opposition that the policy was dropped and never effectuated. The impact of termination in the United States was especially great in its destruction of tribal governments.[454] Canadian termination policy would have had its greatest impact in destroying Aboriginal claims, because no tribal governments exist. In both countries, special health and welfare programs would have terminated.

In both Canada and the United States, the role of academics has been significant in forming contemporary government policy and law. Academic legal literature dealing with Indians was virtually nonexistent in both countries until the 1970s. In the 1980s, however, the trickle of the late 1970s became a flood. This literature has informed the courts of important theories, historical and anthropological data, analytical approaches, and policy considerations. It is noteworthy that the great bulk of academic legal literature on both sides of the border tends to take a pro-Indian point of view.

Canada deals with Indian tribes through the comprehensive Indian Act, a single statute that defines and controls nearly all Indian relations between Indians and the government. In the United States, there is no single statute comparable to the Indian Act. Statutes dealing with Indians and Indian tribes are scattered, and frequently uncoordinated.

In the United States, tribal courts are now woven into the legal fabric of the nation. They provide law and order and dispute resolution for the reservations. Their successful operation, especially since the Indian Civil Rights Act of 1968, is viewed with justifiable pride by the Indian community. With their unlimited civil jurisdiction, and significant criminal jurisdiction, they serve a critically important function on the reservations. The competence of the judges and other court personnel continues to improve. An increasing number of these courts are staffed with lawyers. Full faith and credit is usually given to their judgments by state courts.[455] In Canada, no tribal courts exist. In the past few years Canadian natives have shown great interest in the tribal court system in the United States. Some Canadian Indians believe there is sufficient residual sovereignty in Canadian tribes to support a tribal court system, but it is clear that the Indian act would have to be overhauled before an effective tribal court system could be created in Canada.

The policy of self-determination, combined with economic self-sufficiency, is the most enlightened policy choice ever adopted by the United States toward American Indians. This policy permits Indians to determine what is best for themselves, rather than thrusting federally designed programs at the tribes. Self-determination furthers two key goals. It fosters a genuinely pluralistic society; and it provides Indians with legal and political space to define themselves in their own way. Congress has effected this policy through a variety of legislative enactments, while the Executive branch has embraced the policy for the past twenty years.

Until recently, United States Supreme Court decisions supported and reinforced self-determination. Unfortunately, the contemporary Court has begun to undercut this policy, through decisions denying Indian tribal courts jurisdiction over non-member Indians, allowing state taxes to apply on reservations, refusing to find federal preemption in key situations, and denying Indians the protection needed for exercising their religious beliefs. It will be unfortunate, indeed, if the Supreme Court undercuts this policy, which took so long and so many tragic mistakes to evolve. Historically, the federal courts in the United States were the guardians of Indian rights, a role that now appears to be changing.

At the same time, the Canadian Supreme Court is headed in the opposite direction, toward greater judicial protection of First Nations and Aboriginal rights. The "Sparrow" decision enhances the trust responsibilities of the courts in Canada, giving them substantive review powers over legislation affecting aboriginal land claims and self-government. These powers assure consistency between governmental action, the trust relationship, and the honor of the Crown.

In the United States, tribal governments, tribal courts, and tribal businesses have established themselves as legally valid, politically justified, and economically sound endeavors. State and local governments increasingly respect them, engage in joint programs with them, and cooperate in areas of mutual interest. Congress may now be the preferred forum in which to press toward institutionalizing these gains, and assuring that Indian tribal self-determination and self-government are permanently woven into the fabric of society.

NOTES

1. In the United States the term "Indian" is normally used to describe aboriginal Americans. The term "tribe" (alternatively "nation") is used to describe both ethnological groups of Native Americans as well as the contemporary legal-political groups (often comprised of several ethnological tribes) that occupy and govern modern-day reservations. F. Cohen, *Handbook of Federal Indian Law 3*, (1982), 19. An exception is Alaska where aboriginals are usually referred to as "Alaska Natives," and the legal-political groups of Natives are usually identified as "Villages," although at times the terms "tribes" and "bands" are still used. D. Case, *Alaska Natives and American Laws*, (1984), 10.

In Canada the term "Indian" is sometimes used to describe all Aboriginals, but not the Metis. The preferred terms now are "First Nation," Indigenous People, or

Aboriginal. In the literature the term "band" is often used in Canada rather than "tribe." J. Woodward, *Native Law*, (1990), 2-14. The above definitions are the most widely used in the literature and legislation, however the definition of these terms often depends on the legislative intent of Congress or Parliament. The precise meaning must be determined by context, and requires a particularized analysis.

Douglas Sanders has said that if there is a legal definition of the word "Metis," it must mean the people who took "half-breed" grants under the Manitoba Act of 1870 or the Dominion Lands Act, or the descendants of those people. Sanders, "Aboriginal Peoples and the Constitution," *Atlanta Law Review* 19, (1981), 410, 419-420. Other definitions can be found in J. Woodward, *Native Law*, (1990), 54-55.

2. Act of Feb. 24, 1855, ch. 122, § 1, 10 Stat. 612 (currently codified as amended at 28 U.S.C. § 171 (1988)).

3. The 1863 statute was allegedly enacted to punish Indians for the hostilities of some tribes against the United States. See H.R. Rep. No. 1466, 79th Congress, 1st Session, 2 (1945).

4. The Indian Claims Commission awarded judgments for the value of the land when it was taken by the United States in the 1800s, and refused to award interest on those sums for the years up to the date of the Commission award. The normal rule is that interest is awarded for fifth amendment takings. *United States Indian Claims Commission, Final Report*, (1978), 11.

5. U.S. Constitution, amendment V.

6. "Tee-Hit-Ton v. United States," U.S. 348, (1955), 272.

7. See "United States v. Cook," U.S. 86, (Wall 19), (1873), 591; see also "Pine River Logging and Improvement Co. v. United States," U.S. 186, (1902), 279; Op. Att'y Gen. 19, (1890), 710; Op. Att'y Gen. 19, (1888), 194.

8. See note 206 and accompanying text.

9. *Statement of the Government of Canada on Indian Policy* (1969).

10. "Calder v. Attorney-General," S.C.R. (1973), 313, aff'g D.L.R. 3d 13, 64; W.W.R. 74, (1970), 481.

11. "Constitution Act, 1982," *Can. Rev. Stat.* app. II, No. 44 (1985).

12. "R. v. Sparrow," S.C.R. 1, (1990), 1075.

13. See, e.g., United States v. John, U.S. 437, (1978), 634, 641-632: "The account of the federal attempts to satisfy the obligations of the United States both to those [Choctaws] who remained [in Mississippi] and to those who removed, is one best left to historians. It is enough to say here that the failure of these attempts, characterized by incompetence, if not corruption, proved an embarrassment and an intractable problem for the Federal Government for at least a century.

14. Some historians have chronicled the numerous disasters that occurred to Indians in the implementation of national Indian policies. See A. Debo, *A History of the Indians of the United States*, (1970); B. Dipple, *The Vanishing American*, (1982); W. Hagan, *American Indians*, (rev. ed. 1979); F. Prucha, *The Great Father*, (abr. ed. 1986).

15. See generally A. Debo, *A History of the Indians of the United States*, (1970); Felix Cohen, *Handbook of Federal Indian Law*, (1942); F. Prucha, *The Great Father*, (1986); see also R. Berkhofer, Jr., *The White Man's Indian*, (1978); D. Brown, *Bury My Heart at Wounded Knee*, (1970); V. Deloria, Jr., *Custer Died for Your Sins*, (1969); B. Dipple, *The Vanishing American*, (1982).

16. The history of the Puyallup Indian Tribe in Washington state, which recently negotiated a multi-million dollar land claims settlement, provides a good example of this problem. See Draft White Paper—Puyallup Indians Negotiations Project (on file with the *Washington Law Review*); see also "Puyallup Tribe of Indians v. Port of Tacoma," F. Supp. 525, (W.D. Wash. 1981), 65, 71-74, aff'd, F.2d 717, (9th Cir. 1983), 1251, cert. denied, U.S. 465, (1984), 1049.

17. See, e.g., F. Prucha, *The Great Father*, (1986), 211-16; Report of Henry Knox on White Outrages (Secretary of War to the Continental Congress) (July 18, 1788), reprinted in *Documents of United States Indian Policy*, (F. Prucha 2d ed. 1990), 11; see also "United States v. Sioux Nation of Indians," U.S. 448, (1980), 371, 377-379, (describing events surrounding the dismantling of the great Sioux reserve).

18. The United States Congress banned further treaty signing with Indian tribes in 1871. Some 389 treaties were negotiated between the United States and various Indian tribes. Treaty making, however, has not been as dominant as

often thought. "Of the 52 million acres of trust land now held by the tribes and individual Indians, only about 20 million were originally recognized by treaty." C. Wilkinson, *American Indians, Time, and the Law*, (1987), 8. Of the balance, 23 million acres were set aside by executive orders between 1855 and 1919, and the rest were established by agreements, which were approved by Congress, or by federal statute. Treaties and agreements covered nearly 95% of the United States public domain. *U.S. Indian Claims Commission, Final Report*, (1978), 1. After that date reservations were created by statute, congressionally approved agreement, or executive order. In Canada, treaties were still being signed after World War II, and treaties cover nearly half of the nation. P. Cumming and M. Mickenberg, *Native Rights in Canada* 13, (2d ed. 1972), 53.

19. P. Limerick, *The Legacy of Conquest*, (1987), 219-221. Older "westerns" are repeatedly replayed on television, with their stereotyped savage Indians on display.

20. W. Brown, *The Indian Side of the Story*, (1961).

21. See S. Cornell, *The Return of the Native-American Indian Political Resurgence*, (1988).

22. "Worcester v. Georgia," U.S. 31 (6 Pet.), (1832), 515, 545.

23. After the early 1800s, when the British-Canadian and United States governments attained dominance over the less-developed native groups, many tribes in the United States were removed from their homelands and forced to live in distant places, thus opening their traditional lands to settlement by pioneers. Multiple tribes were often consolidated on a single confederated reservation, including tribes with diverse cultures and sometimes backgrounds of outright hostility towards each other. Traditional cultures, religions, and self-governance systems foundered. The Indians became the poorest and smallest minority in both Canada and the United States, conditions which prevail today. A. Debo, *A History of the Indians of the United States*, (1970), 117; F. Prucha, *The Great Father*, (1986), 64, 78.

24. Historian Hagan concludes: "That starvation and near-starvation conditions were present on some of the sixty-odd reservations every year for the quarter century after the Civil War is manifest." Hagan, "The Reservation Policy: Too

Little and Too Late," in *Indian-White Relations: A Persistent Paradox*, (1976), 161.

25. Act of Feb. 8, 1887, ch. 119, 24 Stat. 388 (codified as amended at U.S.C. 25 (1988), 331).

26. In "United States v. Kagama," U.S. 118, (1886), 375, the Court remarked: "Because of the local ill feeling, the people of the States where they [Native Americans] are found are often their deadliest enemies." Ibid., 384.

27. In "Joint Tribal Council of Passamaquoddy Tribe v. Morton," F.2d 528, (1st Cir. 1975), 370, the court held that the United States had a trust obligation to the Passamaquoddy tribe. This led the United States to file suit against the State of Maine under the Trade and Intercourse Act of 1789. Even the filing of suit did not initially get the attention of Governor James Longley who "refused to consider the Indian land claim a serious matter." P. Brodeur, "Annals of Law: Restitution," *New Yorker*, (Oct. 11, 1982), 102. Ultimately a Justice Department opinion frightened state officials sufficiently that they engaged in serious negotiations and settled the Indian's claims. Ibid., 104-105.

28. This issue is highly divisive. Negotiation is especially difficult because the waters of many streams are already fully allocated. Recognizing the Indian claim, even though legally prior in time, will likely reduce the water available to lower priority non-Indians. Even an Indian victory in court, however, does not necessarily produce "wet" water for the Indians. The cost of construction and the impact on water and land areas off the reservation normally require that Congress enact a law to implement the Indians' rights. Congress is loathe to do this if it will deprive non-Indian irrigators of essential water. See McCool, "Indian Water Rights: Negotiation; Agreement; Legislative Settlement," in *Indian Water Rights and Water Resources Management*, (1989), 127.

29. See "Washington v. Washington State Commercial Passenger Fishing Vessel Association," U.S. 443, (1979), 658. Sports and commercial fishermen in the Pacific Northwest criticized the Indians for years, in the 1950s and 1960s, about demonstrations and "fish-ins" in support of their treaty rights. The Indians should use the court system like civilized people, the critics said. The Indian tribes finally did go to

court—a federal court, not an Indian court—and won the right to harvest 50% of the fish under their treaties, instead of 3% which is the amount the state had limited them to in the past. "United States v. Washington," F. Supp. 384, (W.D. Wash. 1974), 312, aff'd, F.2d, 520, (9th Cir. 1975), 676, cert. denied, U.S. 423, (1976), 1086.

After the Indian victory some non-Indians said the Indians were being greedy. But let us assume that a non-Indian corporation was advised by its lawyers that if it filed suit against the state on a property right issue it might win a judgment of hundreds of millions of dollars. Would we expect the corporation to voluntarily forego filing such a suit? Hardly!

30. See "Puyallup Indian Tribe v. Port of Tacoma," F.2d, 717, (9th Cir. 1983), 1251, cert. denied, U.S. 465, (1984), 1049.

31. S.C.R. (1973), 313.

32. "British North America Act, 1867," Canadian Rev. Stat. app. II, No. 5, ch. 3, (1985), 92(10),(16); "Constitution Act, 1930," Canadian Rev. Stat. app. II, No. 26, ch. 26 (1985).

33. See U.S. Public Land Law Review Commission, *One Third of the Nation's Land, A Report to the President and to the Congress,* (1970), 22-23.

34. "United States v. Sandoval," U.S. 28, (1913), 231; "United States v. Kagama," U.S. 375, (1886), 118.

35. U.S. 553, (1903), 187.

36. Aboriginal title "is subject to regulations imposed by validly enacted federal laws." "Kruger v. R.," [1978], S.C.R. 1, (1977), 104, 116 (citation omitted). Although the government now holds a fiduciary relationship regarding Indians, that relationship is relatively recent. "R. v. Sparrow," S.C.R. 1, (1990), 1075, 1108 (citing "Guerin v. R.," [1984] S.C.R. 2, 335; "R. v. Taylor & Williams," 34 O.R.2d 360 (1981)). Woodward concludes that "[i]n the United States Indian Tribes are considered to be . . . subject to the full power of Congress to interfere with internal self-government by express legislation (citation omitted). Although never clearly expressed as such by any court, the situation in Canada is probably similar." J. Woodward, supra note 1, at 90-91; see also "R. v. Sparrow," S.C.R., 1, (1990), 1103.

37. S.C.R. 1 (1990), 1075, 1108-1109.

38. Few statutes survive strict scrutiny. "Loving v.

Virginia," U.S. 388, (1967) 1, 11; "Bolling v. Sharpe," U.S. 347, (1954), 497, 499.

39. H.R. Doc. No. 363, 91st Congress, 2d Sess., (1970), 2. (President Nixon's message to Congress transmitting recommendations for Indian policy).

40. The Department of the Interior has "recognized" 306 Indian tribes in the lower 48 states and 197 Native Villages in Alaska. Fed. Reg. 53, (1988), 52, 829. Dozens of other Native groups are seeking recognition. See infra notes 91-94. Still other reservations and their governments have been disestablished.

41. Royal Proclamation of 1763, Canadian Rev. Stat. app. II, No. 1, (1985). See R. Surtees, *Canadian Indian Policy*, (1982), 22.

42. Act of July 22, 1790, chapter 33, 1 Stat. 137. This first act and the next three, enacted in 1793, 1796, and 1799 were temporary. A permanent Act was enacted in 1802 and has been reenacted several times since. It is now found in U.S.C. 18, (1988) 1152, 1160, 1165; U.S.C. 25, (1988), 177, 179-80, 193-194, 201, 229-230, 251, 263, 264. See generally F. Prucha, *American Indian Policy in the Formative Years*, (1962).

43. F. Prucha, *The Great Father*, (1986), 17.

44. For a detailed history of these eras see F. Cohen, *Handbook of Federal Indian Law* 3, (1982), 78 (describing "removal").

45. See Letter from President Jefferson to William Henry Harrison, governor of Indiana Territory, (February 27, 1803), reprinted in Prucha (Ed.), *Documents of United States Indian Policy*, (1990), 22-23. Jefferson urged Harrison to convince the Indians to move west of the Mississippi, saying: "[W]e presume that our strength and their weakness is now so visible that they must see we have only to shut our hand to crush them. . . . Should any tribe be foolhardy enough to take up the hatchet at any time, the seizing the whole country of that tribe, and driving them across the Mississippi, as the only condition of peace, would be an example to others. . . ." Ibid, 23.

46. *Documents of United States Indian Policy*, (1990), 39.

47. In 1830, Congress passed the Indian Removal Act,

ch. 148, Stat. 4 (1830), 411, under which numerous tribes were re-settled in the West.

The Five Civilized Tribes, Choctaw, Chickasaw, Cherokee, Creek, and Seminole were removed from their ancestral homes in what is now Georgia and Florida to Oklahoma. Some 4,000 died on the winter journey to the west, out of 13,000 who started the trek. F. Cohen, *Handbook of Federal Indian Law 3*, (1982), 92. Numerous other tribes were also removed, including the Delawares, Kickapoos, Quapaws, Shawnees, Kaskaskias, Peorias, Piankashaws, Weas, Winnebagoes, Chippewas, and Ottawas. F. Prucha, *The Great Father*, (1986), 78-83, 88-90.

48. Prucha, *Documents of United States Indian Policy*, (1990), 47-48.

49. Letter written by Secretary of War John H. Eaton to a Cherokee delegation to the Government (April 18, 1829), 46.

50. Control of Indian affairs was transferred from the Army to the newly created Department of the Interior in 1849. This had only modest effect on the administration of policy, however, because the Indian Office in the Department of the Army had become a civilian bureau in 1834. F. Cohen, *Handbook of Federal Indian Law 3*, (1982), 119-20.

51. Ibid., 127-28.

52. "United States v. Winans," U.S. 198, (1905), 371, 380. Some state courts have obstinately refused to follow the Supreme Court on treaty interpretation issues. "A treaty can only exist between independent, sovereign powers. Several generations ago the United States government entered into a so-called treaty of peace with the nation of the Ute Indians. . . .

. . . [T]he descendants of the inhabitants of that nation are now citizens of the United States. . . . [The] treaties are no longer of any force or effect. . . ." "Brough v. Appawora," P.2d 553, (1976), 934, 935, vacated, U.S. 431, (1977), 901.

The premise of Indian sovereignty we reject. The treaty is not to be interpreted in that light. At no time did our ancestors in getting title to this continent ever regard the aborigines as other than mere occupants, and incompetent occupants, of the soil.

These arrangements [for treaties and reservations] were but the announcement of our benevolence which, notwithstanding our frequent frailties, has been continuously displayed. Neither Rome nor sagacious Britain ever dealt more liberally with their subject races than we with these savage tribes, whom it was generally tempting and always easy to destroy and whom we have so often permitted to squander vast areas of fertile land before our eyes. "State v. Towessnute," Wash. 89, (1916), 478, 481-82, 154 P. 805, 807.

53. See, e.g., Winans, U.S. 198, (1886), 380-81 (citing "Choctaw Nation v. United States," U.S. 119, (1886), 1). Later, in "Washington v. Washington State Commercial Passenger Fishing Vessel Association," U.S. 443, (1979), 658, the Court construed the Indians' treaty right to fish at their usual and accustomed stations off the reservation "in common with the citizens of the territory" to mean that today the treaty tribes are entitled to half the harvestable fish in most Washington waters. Morisset, "The Legal Standards for Allocating the Fisheries Resource," *Idaho Law Review* 22, (1985-1986), 609, 612-613; see also F. Cohen, *Handbook on Federal Indian Law 3*, (1982), 221-224.

54. F. Cohen, *Handbook on Federal Indian Law 3*, (1982), 224.

55. Implied water rights exist whether the reservation was created by treaty, agreement, executive order, or statute. "Arizona v. California," U.S. 373, (1963), 546, 598.

56. "Winters v. United States," U.S. 207, (1908), 564, 576.

57. "Arizona v. California," U.S. 373, (1963), 601.

58. "United States v. Adair," F.2d 723, (9th Cir. 1983), 1394, 1409, cert. denied, U.S. 467, (1984), 1252; "Colville Confederated Tribes v. Walton," F.2d, 647, (9th Cir.), 42, 48, cert. denied, U.S. 454, (1981), 1092.

59. The practice of creating Indian reservations by executive order was discontinued in 1919. See Act of June 30, 1919, ch. 4, 27, 41 Stat. 3, 34.

60. Congressional Record 11, (1881), 780-81, 783, 934-35, (statement of Sen. Henry M. Teller during the Senate debate on Land in Severalty (the Dawes Act)), reprinted in Prucha (Ed.), *Americanizing the American Indians*, (1978), 134, 137.

61. V. Deloria, Jr., *We Talk You Listen—New Tribes New Turf*, (1990), 115.

62. F. Cohen, *Handbook on Federal Indian Law 3*, (1982), 132.

63. General Allotment (Dawes) Act of 1887, ch. 199, Stat. 24 (1988), 119 (codified as amended at U.S.C. 25, (1988), 331-34, 339, 341-342, 348-349, 354, 381).

64. Prucha (Ed.), *Americanizing the American Indians*, (1978), 6-7. Dawes had the backing of the prestigious Lake Mohonk Conference that met annually during the 1880s and later. The participants at these conferences were a tightly unified group who shared a common outlook and who were religiously oriented, in the evangelical Protestant tradition. Ibid., 8. Prucha describes their goals: "All three of these main lines of Indian policy reform converged in one ultimate goal: the total Americanization of the Indians. All were aimed at destroying Indianness, in whatever form it persisted. The aim was to do away with tribalism, with communal ownership of land, with the concentration of the Indians on reservations, with the segregation of the Indians from association with good white citizens, with Indian cultural patterns, with native languages, with Indian religious rites and practices—in short, with anything that deviated from the norms of civilization practiced and proclaimed by the white reformers themselves. Failing to perceive a single element of good in the Indian way of life as it existed, they insisted on a thorough transformation. The civilization which they represented must be forced upon the Indians if they were unwilling to accept it voluntarily." Ibid., 7-8.

The Conference was made up of clergymen, congressmen, academics, and public leaders. Ibid., 5-6. It had a strong religious orientation. Although a voluntary group, its views carried great weight in setting national Indian policy. Ibid. at 9. Lyman Abbott, a noted Congregational clergyman, spoke at the conference saying that "it may be taken for granted that we [the conference participants] are Christian men and women; that we believe in justice, good-will, and charity, and the brotherhood of the human race." Ibid., 32. He stated that the treaties and reservations should be canceled, and the reservation system was "hopelessly wrong." Ibid., 35. "We have no right to do a wrong because we have covenanted to [do so]." Ibid., 33. Abbott suggested that the treaties were expedient at the time they were negotiate, but should then be ignored. He concluded that the reservation system was evil: "I hold to immediate repentance as a national duty. Cease to do evil, cease instantly, abruptly, immediately. I hold that the reservation barriers should be cast down and the land given to the Indians in severalty." Ibid., 35.

William Strong, former United States Supreme Court Justice, disagreed about breaking the treaties. Ibid., 40. Merrill E. Gates, president of Rutgers College, argued that Americans were the Christian "children of the light." Ibid., 288. He concluded that Indian society was disdained and contemptible; that tribes were political anomalies, unchristian and anticivilizing; and that the reservations should be broken up. Ibid., 45-56.

Richard H. Pratt, a retired army officer who founded the famous Carlisle School in Pennsylvania for Indian children, said: "In a sense, I agree with the sentiment [that a good Indian is a dead Indian], but only in this: that all the Indian there is in the race should be dead. Kill the Indian in him, and save the man." Ibid., 260-261. Pratt was critical of missionaries for encouraging Indians to remain separate and apart from white civilization, Ibid., 266, saying that "Carlisle has always planted treason to the tribe [in its students] and loyalty to the nation at large." Ibid., 269.

65. F. Prucha, *The Great Father*, (1986), 224.

66. Ibid., 199. See also H. Jackson, *Century of Dishonor*, (1981), where she argued that deeding tribal lands to individual Indians would simply result in loss of those lands to the white community. This result may, indeed, have been one reason the law was passed, although most of Congress apparently believed that allotment was best for the Indians too. "The main purpose of this bill is not to help the Indian, or solve the Indian problem, or provide a method for getting out of our Indian troubles, so much as it is to provide a method for getting at the valuable Indian lands and opening them up to white settlement." H.R. Rep. No. 1576, 46th Cong., 2d Sess. (1880), 7-10, reprinted in Prucha (Ed.), *Americanizing the American Indians,* (1978), 128.

67. F. Prucha, *The Great Father,* (1986), 226. In 1924, federal law bestowed citizenship on all Indians born in the continental United States, if they did not already have this status (about two-thirds were already citizens under earlier

statutes) (Act of June 2, 1924, ch. 233, Stat. 43, (1988), 253) (codified as amended at 8 U.S.C. (1988), 1401(b)).

68. LaFave, "South Dakota's Forced Fee Indian Land Claims: Will Landowners Be Liable for Government's Wrongdoing?," S.D.L. Rev. 30, (1984), 59.

69. F. Prucha, *The Great Father*, (1986), 304.

70. See generally F. Cohen, *Handbook of Federal Indian Law*, (1982), 136-137; F. Prucha, *The Great Father*, (1986), 304-305.

71. Hearings on H.R. 7902 Before the House Comm. on Indian Affairs, 73d Cong., 2d Sess. (1934), 16-18, (memorandum of John Collier).

72. F. Cohen, *Handbook of Federal Indian Law*, (1982), 148.

73. For example, in 1974, the Navajo Reservation, most of which was not allotted, had a Navajo population of approximately 150,000 and a non-Indian population of approximately 5,000. *U.S. Department of Commerce, Federal and State Indian Reservations and Indian Trust Areas*, (1974), 63.

74. In 1978, the Port Madison Reservation was occupied by about 50 Indians and 3000 non-Indians. "Oliphant v. Suquamish Indian Tribe," U.S. 435 (1978) 191, 193 n. 1.

75. "Seymour v. Superintendent of Wash. State Penitentiary," U.S. 368, (1962), 351.

76. See, e.g., "Brendale v. Confederated Tribes and Bands of Yakima Indian Nation," U.S. 492, (1989), 408, where the U.S. Supreme Court allowed the county to zone non-Indian owned land on a checkerboarded but predominantly non-Indian owned part of the Yakima Reservation, at the same time noting that the tribe had exclusive jurisdiction to zone the allotment and tribally owned lands. The population on this portion of the reservation was about evenly split. The court rejected a claim of concurrent jurisdiction, holding that the tribe lacked any power to zone non-Indian owned lands in these circumstances. In "Duro v. Reina," S. Ct. 110, (1990), 2053, the Court denied tribal courts jurisdiction over non-member Indians emphasizing the voluntary character of tribal membership and the fact that only members could participate in "tribal government, the authority of which rests on consent." Ibid., 2064. But see Department of Defense

Appropriations Act, 8077, Pub. L. No. 101-511, Stat. 104, (1990), 1892, in which Congress restored tribal criminal jurisdiction over non-member Indians for one year.

Non-members cannot vote in tribal elections, hold tribal office, or serve on tribal juries. The Court has noted that the Bill of Rights of the Constitution does not apply in tribal courts, and while the Indian Civil Rights Act of 1968, U.S.C. 25, (1988), 1301-1303, does apply, it does not give rise to a federal cause of action against the tribe for violations of its provisions. The only remedy for someone denied their civil rights is either in tribal court, or by habeas corpus in federal court. "Santa Clara Pueblo v. Martinez," U.S. 436, (1978), 49, 50.

77. Institute for Gov. Research (Brookings Institute), *The Problem of Indian Administration* (Meriam Report) (1928), reprinted in Prucha (Ed.), *Documents of United States Indian Policy*, (1990), 219.

78. U.S.C. 25, (1988), 461-479.

79. Cohen, *Handbook of Federal Indian Law*, (1982), 147.

80. Ibid.

81. Senator A. Watkins, *Annals* 311, (1957), 47-50, 55, reprinted in Prucha (Ed.), *Documents In United States Indian Policy*, (1990), 239, (arguing in favor of termination of special federal relationships with Indian tribes).

82. H.R. Con. Res., Stat. 108, 67, (1953), B132.

83. H.C.R. 108 states: "Whereas it is the policy of Congress, as rapidly as possible, to make the Indians . . . subject to the same laws and entitled to the same privileges and responsibilities as are applicable to other citizens, . . . to end their status as wards of the United States, and to grant them all of the rights and prerogatives pertaining to American citizenship; and

Whereas the Indians within the territorial limits of the United States should assume their full responsibilities as American citizens: Now, therefore, be it Resolved by the House of Representatives (the Senate concurring), That it is declared to be the sense of Congress that, at the earliest possible time, all of the Indian tribes and the individual members thereof located within the states of California, Florida, New York, and Texas, and all of the following named

Indian tribes and individual members thereof, should be freed from Federal supervision and control and from all disabilities and limitations specially applicable to Indians: The Flathead Tribe of Montana, the Klamath Tribe of Oregon, the Menominee Tribe of Wisconsin. . . . It is further declared to be the sense of Congress that, upon the release of such tribes and individual members . . . from such disabilities and limitations, all offices of the Bureau of Indian Affairs . . . whose primary purpose was to serve any Indian tribe or individual Indian freed from Federal supervision should be abolished. It is further declared to be the sense of Congress that the Secretary of the Interior should examine all existing legislation dealing with such Indians, and treaties between the . . . United States and each such tribe, and report to Congress at the earliest practicable date, but not later than January 1, 1954, his recommendations for such legislation as, in his judgment, may be necessary to accomplish the purposes of this resolution." Ibid.

84. See Wilkinson and Biggs, "The Evolution of the Termination Policy," *American Indian Law Review* 5, (1977), 139, 151.

85. Ibid. Both tribes have since been restored to their former status by Congress. Menominee Restoration Act of 1973, 25 U.S.C. 25, (1988), 903-903f; Klamath Indian Tribe Restoration Act, U.S.C. 25, (1988), 566.

86. U.S.C. 18, (1988), 1162; U.S.C. 28, (1988), 1360.

87. See generally, Goldberg, "Public Law 280: The Limits of State Jurisdiction Over Reservation Indians," *U.C.L.A. Law Review* 22, (1975), 535, 546-547.

88. See, e.g., S. Rep. No. 604, 93d Congress, 1st Session, (1973) 4.

89. H.R. Doc. No. 363, 91st Congress, 2nd Session 3, (1970), (President Nixon's message to Congress transmitting recommendations for Indian policy).

90. Ibid., 4.

91. Barsh, "The Rocky Road to 'Recognition,'" *Ann. W. Indian L. Symp.* 4, (1990), 407, 416.

92. Ibid., 414-416. See C.F.R. 25, (1990), 83, (federal acknowledgment process).

93. Barsh, "The Rocky Road to Recognition," (1990), 416.

94. Comment, "The Imprimatur of Recognition:

American Indian Tribes and the Federal Acknowledgment Process, *Wash. L. Review* 66, (1991), 209, 217-19.

95. "Worcester v. Georgia," U.S. 31 (6 Pet.) (1832), 515, 59; "Cherokee Nation v. Georgia," U.S. 30 (5 Pet.), (1831), 1, 17.

96. "Johnson v. M'Intosh," U.S. 21, (8 Wheat.), (1823), 543.

97. "United States v. McBratney," U.S. 104, (1882), 621.

98. Assimilative Crimes Act, U.S.C. 18, (1988), 13; Indian Country Crimes Act, U.S.C. 18, (1988), 1152. Criminal jurisdiction on Indian reservations is very complicated. See Clinton, "Criminal Jurisdiction Over Indian Lands: A Journey Through a Jurisdictional Maze," *Arizona Law Review* 18, (1976), 503.

99. U.S. 435, (1978), 191.

100. "Duro v. Reina," S. Ct. 110, (1990), 2053.

101. Department of Defense Appropriations Act, 8077, Pub. L. No. 101-511, Stat. 104, (1990), 1892.

102. U.S.C. 18, (1988), 1162(a); U.S.C. 28, (1988), 1360(a). For example, in Washington state, P.L. 280 applies to Indians on fee patent land on the reservation, to non-Indians anywhere in Indian country, and to Indians on trust land for certain subjects such as divorce, mental health, and driving on public highways. *Washington Review Code*, (1989), 37.12.010. Thus jurisdiction depends both on the geography of land ownership and on subject matter.

103. "Washington v. Confederated Bands and Tribes of the Yakima Indian Nation," U.S. 439, (1979), 463, 499.

104. U.S. 31 (6 Pet.), (1832), 515, 556-57.

105. U.S. 358, (1959), 218.

106. Ibid., 223.

107. U.S. 411, (1973), 164, 172.

108. "Montana v. United States," U.S. 450, (1981), 544; see also "Brendale v. Confederated Tribes and Bands of Yakima Indian Nation," U.S. 492, (1989), 408. Somewhat earlier cases appeared to favor preemption. "White Mountain Apache Tribe v. Bracker," U.S. 448, (1980), 136. But note that Rehnquist dissented in those cases and the mix of court members has changed.

109. Some scholars argue that United States policy was quite consistent, at least until the 1970s. See R. Berkhofer,

supra note 15; B. Dipple, supra note 14.

110. Bartlett, "The Indian Act of Canada," *Buffalo L. Rev.* 25, (1978), 581, 582 [hereinafter Bartlett, "The Indian Act of Canada"]; see also R. Bartlett, *Indian Reserves and Aboriginal Lands in Canada: A Homeland* (1990), 25 [hereinafter R. Bartlett, *A Homeland*].

The exact numbers of Aboriginal people, in bands and on reserves in Canada, is unknown. Recent data placed the registered Indian population at just over 300,000, among 573 bands residing on 2,242 reserves. The 1981 census recorded 75,110 non-status Indians and 98,260 Metis. These figures are much disputed. See Morse, "Aboriginal Peoples and the Law," in *Aboriginal Peoples and the Law: Indian, Metis and Inuit Rights in Canada*, (B. Morse ed. 1985), 5.

The precise number of treaties and agreements concluded between native groups and the government is also unknown. The federal Department of Indian and Northern Affairs lists 67 treaties and 26 land grants concluded between 1680 and 1929. G. Brown and R. Maguire, *Indian Treaties in Historical Perspective* xvi-xxiv, (1979). Uncertainty exists, however, because of the informal nature of early agreements, particularly in the Maritime provinces, and the ambiguous nature of French treaty activity following discovery of Quebec territories. Ibid., 10, 20.

111. Ch. 26, Can. Stat. 1857, 1984.

112. This was the era of active reservation creation in the United States, when tribes were forced to stop their roaming and live on reservations. At the same time, in the United States, there was an opposite undercurrent towards allotment and assimilation. Some of the pre-Dawes Act allotments were accomplished by treaty and some by statute. Sometimes, similar to the Canadian enfranchisement policy, "[a]llottees surrendered their interests in the tribal estate and became citizens subject to state and federal jurisdiction." F. Cohen, *Handbook of Federal Indian Law*, (1982), 130.

113. J. Woodward, *Native Law*, (1990), 30.

114. G. Brown and R. Maguire, *Indian Treaties in Historical Perspective*, xvi-xxiv, (1979), 10.

115. S. Weaver, *Making Canadian Indian Policy—The Hidden Agenda 1968-1970*, (1981), 32.

116. "Royal Proclamation of 1763," *Can. Rev. Stat.* app.

II, No. 1, (1985).

117. Ibid. This prohibition against squatters and trespassers in Indian Country was ignored by the miners and prospectors who refused to leave. P. Cumming and N. Mickenberg, *Native Rights in Canada*, (1971), 70, 71. The United States also often failed to uphold its own agreements with Indian tribes. See notes 232-242 and accompanying text.

118. G. Brown and R. Maguire, *Indian Treaties in Historical Perspective* xvi-xxiv, (1979), 24-25.

119. R. Bartlett, *Indian Reserves and Aboriginal Lands in Canada*, (1990), 21.

120. Ibid., 28 (quoting the Canada Minister of the Interior, House of Commons Deb., 3d Sess., 11th Parl., 1 & 2 Geo. 5, (1910-1911), 7826.

121. Bartlett, *The Indian Act of Canada, supra* note 110, at 583 (citing 1857 Can. Stat., ch. 26).

122. Ibid., 583 n.8.

123. R. Bartlett, *Indian Reserves and Aboriginal Lands in Canada*, (1990), 20-21.

124. Ibid.

125. Can. Rev. Stat. ch. I-5, (1985).

126. Department of the Secretary of State Act, ch. 42, Can. Stat. 1868, 91.

127. Ch. 6, Can. Stat. 1869, 22; see Bartlett, "The Indian Act of Canada," (1978), 583.

128. The omnipotence of the federal government in relation to Indian bands is unequivocally expressed in section 18(1) of the Indian Act, *Can. Rev. Stat.* ch. 1-5, (1985): "Subject to this Act, reserves are held by Her Majesty for the use and benefit of the respective bands for which they were set apart, and subject to this Act and to the terms of any treaty or surrender, the Governor in Council may determine whether any purpose [sic] for which land in a reserve are used or are to be used is for the use and benefit of the band." See Bartlett, "The Indian Act of Canada," (1978), 603.

In the United States, similar power over reservation lands is held by the federal government. This results in part from the Trade and Intercourse Acts adopted by Congress from 1790 on, Act of July 22, 1790, ch. 33, Stat 4, 1, 137, and partly from the guardian/ward relationship developed by the Supreme Court in "Johnson v. M'Intosh," U.S. 21 (8 Wheat.),

(1823), 543. See F. Cohen, *Handbook of Federal Indian Law*, (1982), 510, 511 n.6. It is often said that Congress has "plenary" power over Indians and Indian lands. The principal remedy for a tribe whose land is "taken" by the federal government is a right to compensation.

129. The Indian Advancement Act, ch. 28, Can. Stat. 1884, 116, reflects this inconsistency. It provided for wider powers for the Band Councils, including the raising of money, but then appointed the government's Indian Agent Chairman of the Council.

130. Ch. 18, Can. Stat. 1876, 43. It is interesting to note that it was also in 1876 that the battle of Little Bighorn took place, where Custer and his troops were defeated by the Sioux.

131. G. Brown and R. Maguire, *Indian Treaties in Historical Perspective*, (1979), xxv.

132. See Morse, *Aboriginal Peoples and the Law*, (1985), xxxix-xiv (Chronology of Key Events).

133. S. Weaver, *Making Canadian Indian Policy*, 36.

134. "R. v. Johnston," D.L.R.2d 56, (1966), 749, 752.

135. S.C.R. 1, (1983) 29. The Court quoted from the landmark United States case of "Jones v. Meehan," U.S. 175, (1899), 1, 11 where "it was held that Indian treaties 'must . . . be construed, not according to the technical meaning of [their] words . . . but in the sense in which they would naturally be understood by the Indians.'" Ibid., 36.

136. Ibid. This principle was recently stated in "Horseman v. The Queen," S.C.R. 1, [1990], 901. Horseman, an Indian, went moose hunting to feed his family, pursuant to a treaty right. He shot and killed a moose, skinned it, and hurried home to obtain assistance from other Band members to haul it out of the bush. When they arrived a grizzly bear was eating the moose, claiming "valid possessory title." Ibid., 924. Faced with a conflicting claim, the bear charged Horseman, who displayed cool courage and skill under attack by shooting and killing the charging bear. He skinned the bear and took the hide. Horseman did not have a license to hunt grizzly bears or sell their hides. A year later, in spring of 1984, Horseman found himself out of work and in need of money to support his family. Under this financial pressure he decided to sell the grizzly hide. Before doing so he applied for

and was issued a grizzly bear hunting license entitling him to hunt and kill one bear and sell the hide to a licensed dealer. He made use of the license to sell the hide of his adversary of the year before to a licensed dealer for $200. He was then charged with a crime.

The majority of the Supreme Court upheld Horseman's conviction, stating that his treaty hunting rights had been limited by the Albert Natural Resources Transfer Agreement of 1930, under which he could hunt only for food. Ibid., 932-36. Horseman received the minimum fine. Ibid., 926.

137. S.C.R. 2, (1985), 387, 402; see also "R. v. White & Bob," W.W.R. 52, (B.C. 1965), 193, 232-33, aff'd, S.C.R. (1965), vi; "R. v. Taylor and Williams," O.R.2d 34, (1981), 360, 367.

138. "Winters v. United States," U.S. 207, (1908), 564, 576-77. On treaty interpretation generally, see Wilkinson and Volkman, "Judicial Review of Indian Treaty Abrogation: 'As Long As Water Flows, Or Grass Grows Upon The Earth'—How Long A Time Is That?," *California Law Review* 63, (1975), 601.

139. S.C.R. 1, (1990), 1025.

140. Ibid., 1030.

141. Ibid., 1031.

142. The treaty states: "These are to certify that the Chief of the Huron tribe of Indians, having come to me in the name of His Nation, to submit to His Brittanick Majesty, and make Peace, has been received under my Protection, with his whole Tribe; and henceforth no English Officer or party is to molest, or interrupt them in returning to their Settlement at Lorette; and they are received upon the same terms with the Canadians, being allowed the free Exercise of their Religion, their Customs, and Liberty of trading with the English; — recommending it to the Officers commanding the Posts, to treat them kindly." Ibid.

143. Ibid., 1063 (citation omitted).

144. Ibid.

145. F. Cohen, *Handbook of Federal Indian Law*, (1982), 63.

146. S.C.R. 1, (1990), 1066.

147. Ibid., 1066-1067.

148. Ibid., 1070.

149. Ibid., 1072.

150. Ibid., 1073.

151. Ibid.

152. "The very definition of a treaty thus makes it impossible to avoid the conclusion that a treaty cannot be extinguished without the consent of the Indians concerned." Ibid., 1063.

153. U.S. 187, (1903), 553.

154. Bartlett, "The Indian Act of Canada," (1978), 585.

155. R. Bartlett, *Indian Reserves and Aboriginal Lands in Canada*, (1990), 177-78.

156. Ch. 29, Can. Stat. 1951, 131.

157. Bartlett, "The Indian Act of Canada," (1978), 586.

158. *Statement of the Government of Canada on Indian Policy*, (1969).

159. Ibid.

160. H.R. Con. Res. 108, Stat. 67, (1953), B132; see notes 82-83.

161. Bartlett, "The Indian Acts of Canada," (1978), 588.

162. Ibid., 588-89.

163. R. Bartlett, *Indian Reserves and Aboriginal Lands in Canada*, (1990), 49.

164. Ibid.

165. Canada, Dep't of Indian and Northern Affairs (1981); see R. Bartlett, *Indian Reserves and Aboriginal Lands in Canada*, (1990), 51.

166. "Calder v. Attorney-General," S.C.R. (1973), 313, aff'g, D.L.R. 3d 13, 64, W.W.R. 74, (1970), 481.

167. "R. v. Sparrow," S.C.R. 1 (1990), 1075, 1103-1104.

168. B. Schwartz, *First Principles, Second Thoughts,* (1986), 353-364; Little Bear, "A Concept of Native Title," Can. Legal Aid Bull. 2-3, (1982), 99; Lyon, *An Essay on Constitutional Interpretation*, Osgoode Hall L.J. 26, (1988), 95; McNeil, *The Constitutional Rights of the Aboriginal Peoples of Canada*, Sup. Ct. Law Review 4, (1982), 255; Pentney, "The Rights of the Aboriginal Peoples of Canada in the Constitution Act, 1982, Part II, Section 35: The Substantive Guarantee," U. Brit. Colum. L. Rev. 22, (1988), 207; Sanders, "Pre-Existing Rights: The Aboriginal Peoples of Canada," in *The Canadian Charter of Rights and Freedoms*, 2d ed. (1989); Slattery, "Understanding Aboriginal Rights," Can. B. Rev. 66, (1987), 727; Slattery, "The Hidden

Constitution: Aboriginal Rights in Canada," *American J. Comp. Law.* 32, (1984), 361. This is not to suggest that academics always, or even usually, turn out to be any more enlightened than anyone else. In this instance, however, they have served an important purpose in revealing the legal, social, and economic mistreatment of Canadian and United States Indians.

169. F. Cohen, *Handbook of Federal Indian Law*, (1982); M. Price and R. Clinton, *Law and the American Indian* 2nd ed., (1983); R. Strickland, *Fire and the Spirits—Cherokee Law From Clan to Court*, (1975); Wilkinson, *American Indians, Time, and the Law*, (1987); Chambers, "Judicial Enforcement of the Federal Trust Responsibility to Indians," *Stanford Law Review* 27, (1975), 1213; Clinton, "Criminal Jurisdiction Over Indian Lands," (1976); Collins, "Indian Allotment Water Rights," *Land and Water Law Review* 20, (1985), 421; Getches, "Water Rights on Indian Allotments," *S.D.L. Review* 26, (1981), 405; Johnson, "The States Versus Indian Off-Reservation Fishing: A United States Supreme Court Error," *Washington Law Review* 47, (1972), 207; Johnson and Crystal, "Indians and Equal Protection," *Washington Law Review*, 54, (1979), 587; Strickland, "The Absurd Ballet of American Indian Policy or American Indian Struggling with Ape on Tropical Landscape: An Afterword," *Maine Law Review*, 31 (1979), 213.

170. Attorneys for the Solicitor's office were sometimes dedicated and competent, and sometimes not. Frequently, they were, and are, up against highly competent, and highly paid private counsel when negotiating natural resources agreements on reservations. Government attorneys are hampered by conflicts of interest, as where they advise both the Bureau of Indian Affairs and the Bureau of Reclamation on water allocation disputes.

The other group of lawyers who became expert in aspects of Indian law represented tribes in claims before the United States Indian Claims Commission. These attorneys became specialists on the historic claims of tribes, what lands the tribes originally occupied, and when and how the United States "took" those lands. Only a few claims attorneys became involved in current Indian litigation. *U.S. Indian Claims Commission, Final Report*, (1978), 21.

171. Price, "Lawyers on the Reservation: Some Implications for the Legal Profession," *Law and Social Order*, (1969), 161.

172. Twenty-five to thirty-five Indian pre-law students have attended the summer program at the University of New Mexico Indian Law Center each year since 1968. After a six week summer introduction to law they attend law schools throughout the nation.

173. Professor Fred Hart, University of New Mexico, and Professor Monroe Price, UCLA Law School, began to teach this subject in 1971. The author started teaching Indian law in 1969.

174. Monroe Price of UCLA Law School, authored the first such casebook, *Law and the American Indian*, (1973). This book has been revised and the third edition is now co-authored by Robert Clinton and Nell Newton. D. Getches and C. Wilkinson have published a casebook, *Federal Indian Law*, 2d ed., (1986).

175. The original treatise was published in 1942 and was authored by Felix S. Cohen. It became the dominant authority in the field. The 1982 edition was written by a group of academic scholars. The board of authors and editors includes Rennard Strickland, editor-in-chief, Charles F. Wilkinson, managing editor, Reid Peyton Chambers, Richard B. Collins, Carole E. Goldberg-Ambrose, Robert N. Clinton, David H. Getches, Ralph W. Johnson, and Monroe E. Price.

176. U.S.C. 28, (1988), 1362.

177. Started by David H. Getches as a spin-off of California Indian Legal Services, it continues its tradition to excellence under the leadership of John Echohawk. Narf employs about 20 lawyers. It generally is involved in about 70 cases at any one time, throughout the nation.

178. "Johnson v. M'Intosh," U.S. 21 (8 Wheat.), (1923), 543, 588-591.

179. Ibid., 574.

180. "Mitchel v. United States," U.S. 34 (9 Pet.), (1835), 711, 746.

181. "Oneida Indian Nation v. County of Oneida," U.S. 414, (1974), 661, 670.

182. "County of Oneida v. Oneida Indian Nation," U.S. 470, (1985), 226, 236.

183. "United States v. Alcea Band of Tillamooks," U.S. 329, (1946), 40, 46.

184. "Confederated Tribes of Warm Springs Reservation v. United States," Ct. Cl. 177, (1966), 184.

185. "Village of Gambell v. Clark," F.2d 746, (9th Cir. 1984), 572, 774.

186. "Alaska v. Udall," F.2d 420 (9th Cir. 1969), 938.

187. "Oneida Indian Nation v. County of Oneida," U.S. 21 (8 Wheat), (1823), 543; "Worcester v. Georgia," 31 U.S. (6 Pet.) 515 (1832); "Johnson v. M'Intosh," 21 U.S. (8 Wheat.) 543 (1823).

188. "Tee-Hit-Ton Indians v. United States," U.S. 348, (1955), 313.

189. "United States v. Shoshone Tribe of Indians," U.S. 304, (1938), 111.

190. See "Hynes v. Grimes Packing Co.," U.S. 337, (1949), 86; "Sioux Tribe of Indians v. United States," U.S. 315, (1942), 317. In spite of those cases, the "modern practice" of Congress has been to provide compensation to tribes for the taking of property on executive order reservations. F. Cohen, *Handbook of Federal Indian Law*, (1982), 496.

191. One such claim was recently put forth by several Alaska Native Villages to aboriginal hunting and fishing rights on the outer continental shelf. The Alaska Native Claims Settlement Act of 1971 (ANCSA) abolished all aboriginal hunting, fishing, and land rights of Natives "in Alaska." U.S.C. 43, (1983), 1601-1628. The Ninth Circuit held, in "Village of Gambell v. Hodel," F.2d 869, (9th Cir. 1989), 1273, 1279, that the outer continental shelf is not "in Alaska." Thus aboriginal rights on the outer shelf were not abolished by ANCSA.

192. See F. Cohen, *Handbook of Federal Indian Law*, (1982), 160.

193. U.S. Indian Claims Commission, Final Report 2-3 (1978).

194. Indian Claims Commission Act of 1946, Pub. L. No. 79-726, Stat. 60, 1049. The Commission terminated in 1978 (omitted at U.S.C. 25, (1988), 70v).

195. These damage awards were challenged by various Indian tribes. The tribes objected to the fact that (1) they could only obtain money damages under the Act, they could

not reclaim the land, (2) they received the value of their land at the date it was taken, usually sometime in the 1800s, (3) they received no interest on this valuation after the date of the taking, (4) the United States ardently contested each claim, sometimes attempting to offset the cost to the government of "removing" the tribe from its eastern homeland to Indian territory in the West, and (5) the Commission would only entertain claims by tribes, not individual Indians. See generally, *U.S. Indian Claims Commission, Final Report*, (1978), 1-21.

196.   See "Joint Tribal Council of Passamaquoddy Tribe v. Morton," F.2d 528, (1st Cir. 1975), 370, (tribal claim against the state of Maine).

197.   See "County of Oneida v. Oneida Indian Nation," U.S. 470, (1985), 226.

198.   Several of the Acts were passed by Congress in the late 1700s and early 1800s. See, e.g., Trade and Intercourse Act of 1793, Stat. 1, 329. They provided that no agreement with an Indian tribe could be valid unless approved by Congress.

199.   S.C.R. 1973, (1970), 313, aff'g, W.W.R. 74, (1970), 481.

200.   Can. Rev. Stat. app. II, No. 44 (1985).

201.   S.C.R. 1, (1990), 1075.

202.   J. Woodward, *Native Law*, (1990), 138-39; see, e.g., "R. v. Sparrow," S.C.R. 1, (1990), 1075, 1097-99; see also, "R. v. Derrickson," S.C.R. 2, (1976), D.L.R. 3d 71 (1976), 159, aff'g D.L.R. 3d 60, (1975); Bartlett, "The Indian Act of Canada," (1978), 581.

203.   Can. Rev. Stat. app. II, No. 5, (1985), 91(24).

204.   It seems clear that the constitution authorizes cession of Aboriginally held lands as part of a voluntary settlement and no further constitutional amendment is necessary to accomplish this. P. Hogg, *Constitutional Law of Canada* 2nd ed, (1985), 565-566.

205.   See, e.g., *Canada, Editeur Officiel Du Quebec, the James Bay and Northern Quebec Agreement* (1976), and *Canada, Dep't of Indian and Northern Affairs, The Western Arctic Claim—The Inuvialuit Final Agreement* (1984). The Inuvialiut Agreement came into force after the 1982 Constitution Act and has been constitutionalized, as was the

James Bay Agreement.

206. Many Fingers, "Commentaries: Aboriginal Peoples and the Constitution," *Alta. L. Rev.* 19, (1981), 428, 429. The potlach tradition of the Six Nations of Iroquois was outlawed by the Canadian government and jail sentences handed down to all violators; attendance at potlatch functions was prohibited by law as late as 1951. *Can. Rev. Stat.,* ch. 43, (1886), 114, (repealed 1951). See Canada House of Commons, Special Committee on Indian Self-Government, Indian Self-Government in Canada, (1983), 13 [hereinafter Indian Self-Government].

207. *Statement of the Government of Canada on Indian Policy,* (1969).

208. Morse, "The Resolution of Land Claims," in *Aboriginal Peoples and the Law,* (1985), 617.

209. S.C.R., (1973), 313.

210. Ibid., 375, 422 (Hall, J., dissenting).

211. Ibid., 333, 344.

212. Ibid., 426-427 (Pigeon, J., concurring).

213. See "Guerin v. R.," S.C.R. 2, (1984), 335, 376-377.

214. British North America Act, 1867, *Can. Rev. Stat.* app. II, No. 5, 1867, (1985); see, e.g., J. Woodward, *Native Law,* (1990), 88, 94, 95.

215. Constitution Act, 1982, *Can. Rev. Stat.* app. II, No. 44, (1985), 35(1).

216. P. Hogg, *Constitutional Law of Canada,* (1985), 566.

217. S.C.R. 1, (1990), 1075.

218. *Can. Rev. Stat.,* ch. F-14, (1970), 34, 61.

219. The issue of commercial fishing as an Aboriginal right was not raised in the lower courts, and thus was not discussed by the Supreme Court.

220. It is interesting to note that the "Sparrow" court cited and relied on "Johnson v. M'Intosh," U.S. 21 (8 Wheat.), (1823), 543, where the Supreme Court recognized Indian aboriginal title while at the same time recognizing broad federal power over that title. S.C.R. 1, (1990), 1103. "Johnson," and the two Cherokee opinions by Justice John Marshall, are frequently cited by Canadian courts and scholars. These issues arose in the United States earlier than in Canada because of the earlier settlement and conflict

between Indians and non-Indians. This may also explain in part why United States courts seldom cite Canadian cases in the Indian law field.

221. S.C.R. 1, (1990), 1108.

222. Ibid.

223. "Calder v. Attorney-General," S.C.R., (1973), 313, 352 (Hall, J., dissenting).

224. S.C.R. 1, (1990), 1093, 1099-1101.

225. "Delaware Tribal Business Commission v. Weeks," U.S. 430, (1977), 73; "Shoshone Tribe v. United States," U.S. 299 (1937), 476. See the definitive study by Newton, "Federal Power Over Indians: Its Sources, Scope, and Limitations," *U. Pa. L. Rev.*, 132 (1984), 195, 199.

226. U.S. 118, (1886), 375.

227. The Major Crimes Act, U.S.C. 18, (1988), 1153, makes it a crime for Indians to commit certain crimes on reservations, e.g., murder, manslaughter, rape, arson. In Kagama, U.S. 118, 384-85, the Court upheld the constitutionality of the Act against the challenge that it was beyond Congress' power.

228. U.S. Const. art. I, 8, cl. 18. That clause states: "[t]he Congress shall have Power To . . . regulate Commerce with foreign nations, and among the several States, and with the Indian Tribes."

229. See, e.g., "McClanahan v. State Tax Comm'n," U.S. 411, (1973), 164, 172 n.7 (the source of federal authority over Indian matters has been the subject of some confusion, but it is now generally recognized that the power derives from federal responsibility for regulating commerce with Indian tribes and for treaty making).

230. U.S. 21 (8 Wheat.), (1823), 543.

231. See P. Sly, *Reserved Water Rights Settlement Manual*, (1988); G. Weatherford, M. Wallace, and L. Storey, *Leasing Indian Water—Choices in the Colorado River Basin*, (1988).

232. See "Rosebud Sioux Tribe v. Kneip," U.S. 430, (1977), 584; "DeCoteau v. District County Court," U.S. 420, (1975), 425.

233. This 1953 law, H.R. 1063, 83d Cong., 1st Sess., is commonly known as P.L. 280 (codified as amended at U.S.C. 18, (1988), 1162(a) and U.S.C. 28, (1988), 1360(a)).

234. "Seneca Nation of Indians v. Brucker," F.2d 262, (D.C. Cir. 1958), 27, cert. denied, U.S. 360, (1959), 909.

235. See Newton, "Federal Power Over Indians: Its Sources, Scope, and Limitations," (1984).

236. "Lone Wolf v. Hitchcock," U.S. 187, (1903), 553.

237. Few treaties with foreign nations have been abrogated by Congress, whereas every Indian treaty has been abrogated to some extent.

238. See "United States v. Creek Nation," U.S. 295, (1935), 103, 111.

239. "Tee-Hit-Ton Indians v. United States," U.S. 348, (1955), 272.

240. The most important example of this policy is found in the Alaska Native Claims Settlement Act of 1971, U.S.C. 43, 1601-1621, where the federal government extinguished all aboriginal claims to land and to hunting and fishing rights in Alaska and in return awarded the Natives nearly a billion dollars, confirming title in newly-created Native Corporations to approximately 44 million acres of land.

241. Major Crimes Act, U.S.C. 18, (1988), 1153; see "United States v. Antelope," U.S. 430, (1977), 641.

242. "Morton v. Mancari," U.S. 417, (1974), 535, 554; "United States v. Antelope," U.S. 430, (1977), 641; see Johnson and Crystal, "Indians and Equal Protection," (1979).

243. Chambers, "Judicial Enforcement of the Federal Trust Responsibility to Indians," (1975).

244. "United States v. Mitchell (Mitchell II)," U.S. 463, (1983), 206.

245. U.S. 30, (5 Pet.), (1831), 1.

246. Ibid., 17.

247. Ibid.

248. See "Lone Wolf v. Hitchcock," U.S. 187, (1903), 553; Comment, "Sparrow and the Lone Wolf: Native American Rights, Congress, and the Trust Obligation in the United States and Canada," *Washington Law Review* 66, (1991).

249. "Seminole Nation v. United States," U.S. 316, (1942), 286, 296-297.

250. "United States v. Mitchell," U.S. 463, (1983), 206, 225.

251. Ibid., 228.

252. "United States v. Winans," U.S. 198, (1905), 371,

380.

253. P. Hogg, *Constitutional Law of Canada*, ed ed., (1985), 565-566. Hogg writes that the most conspicuous examples of this super legislative authority are the provisions of the Indian Act that govern succession to the property of deceased Indians. There are also provisions for administration of the property of the mentally ill and infants. Ibid.

254. *Can. Rev. Stat.* app. II, No. 44, (1985).

255. Pentney, "The Rights of the Aboriginal Peoples of Canada in the Constitution Act, 1982, Part II, Section 35," (1988), 46.

256. "R. v. Sikyea," W.W.R. 46, (N.W. 1964), 65, 74-75, aff'd, S.C.R. (1984), 642.

257. See Pentney, "The Rights of the Aboriginal People of Canada and the Constitution Act, 1982—Part I: The Interpretive Prism of Section 25," *U. of British Columbia Law Review*, 22, (1988), 21, 48.

258. P. Hogg, *Constitutional Law of Canada*, end ed., (1985), 565-566.

259. "Morton v. Mancari," U.S. 417, (1974), 535; "United States v. Antelope," U.S. 430, (1977), 641.

260. U.S. Constitution, art. I, 8.

261. See *Can. Rev. Stat.*, ch. 43, (1886). Although amended several times, this Act remained nearly the same until significant revisions occurred in 1951. The 1951 edition has been amended, but is substantially the same at present. *Can. Rev. Stat.*, ch. 32, (1985).

262. "Status" Indian in the Canadian literature means an Indian who is registered or who is entitled to be registered under section 2(1) of the Indian Act. Sometimes they are referred to as "treaty" Indians where their land is covered by a treaty. J. Woodward, *Native Law*, (1990), 7.

263. See J. Woodward, *Native Law*, (1990), 12.

264. Metis are commonly thought to be persons of mixed white and Indian blood. See, e.g., Metis Betterment Act, *Alta, Rev. Stat.*, ch. 233, (1970) amended by ch. 26, 1982 Alta. Stat. 251. Woodward suggests the definition should include facts or circumstances, such as "whether a person's ancestors received 'scrip,' or a grant of land under the Manitoba Act, 1870 . . . [or] under any of the Dominion Lands

Acts, or were entitled to such a grant." J. Woodward, *Native Law*, (1990), 54-55.

265. Some enfranchised Indians may get their status back under 1985 revisions to the Indian Act. *Can. Rev. Stat.*, ch. I-5, (1985), 61(1)(e); see also J. Woodward, *Native Law*, (1990), 22-23.

266. The Metis, despite initial agreements reserving a land base to them, were later excluded from treaty activity as a group, their claims being settled through individual payments of land or scrip. G. Brown and R. Maguire, *Indian Treaties in Historical Perspective*, (1979), 28, 31-35.

267. Canada House of Commons, *Special Committee on Indian Self-Government, Indian Self-Government in Canada*, (1983), 44.

268. Ibid., 59.

269. J. Woodward, *Native Law*, (1990), 63.

270. S.C.R. 2, (1984), 335.

271. Bartlett, *Indian Reserves and Aboriginal Lands in Canada*, (1990).

272. S.C.R. 2, (1984), 335.

273. "R. v. Sparrow," S.C.R. 1, (1990), 1075, 1108 (discussing Guerin, S.C.R. 2, (1984), 345-48.

274. Ibid. (discussing Guerin, S.C.R. 2, (1984), 348-350, 376, 382).

275. Guerin, S.C.R. 2, (1984), 361 (quoting Re Dawson; "Union Fidelity Trustee Co. v. Perpetual Trustee Co.," N.S.W.W.N. 84, (1966), 399, 404-406).

276. S.C.R. 1, (1990), 1075.

277. Ibid., 1079.

278. Ibid., 1109.

279. Ibid., 1110.

280. See the comparison of the "Sparrow" criteria with United States equal protection analysis, notes 298-305 and accompanying text.

281. "Sparrow," S.C.R. 1, (1990), 1110.

282. Ibid., 1112.

283. For example, in "Sparrow" the test involved asking whether either the purpose or the effect of the restriction on net length unnecessarily infringed the interests protected by the fishing right. Were the Musqueam forced to spend undue time and money per fish with a shorter net?

284. Sparrow, S.C.R. 1, (1990), 1113.

285. Ibid., 1113-1114.

286. The court rejected the test, whether the legislation or regulation is in the "public interest" as too vague. Ibid., 1113.

287. Ibid., 1114.

288. Ibid., 1101, 1116.

289. Ibid., 1119.

290. L. Silko (Laguna Pueblo author), Foreword to *Now that the Buffalo's Gone*, (A. Josephy, Jr. ed.), (1982).

291. Treaty of Point Elliott, Jan. 22, 1855, Stat. 12, 927; Treaty of Point No Point, Jan. 26, 1855, Stat. 12, 933; Treaty of Medicine Creek, Dec. 26, 1854, Stat. 10, 1132.

292. "Puyallup Tribe v. Department of Game," U.S. 391, (1968), 392, 398.

293. "United States v. Washington," F. Supp. 384, (1974), 312 aff'd, F.2d 520, (9th Cir.), 676, cert. denied, U.S. 423, (1975), 1086.

294. Ibid., 342.

295. Ibid.

296. Ibid., 332-33.

297. "R. v. Sparrow," S.C.R. 1, (1990), 1075, 1101.

298. When a status infringes on a fundamental right, such as the right to vote or travel, or if the statute is based on a suspect classification such as race or national origin, the courts apply "strict scrutiny" to the legislation. Under this often fatal test the classification must be "necessary" to achieve a "compelling governmental interest" for the law to stand. See "San Antonio Independent School District v. Rodriguez," U.S. 411, (1973), 1; "Shapiro v. Thompson," U.S. 394, (1969), 618; "Harper v. Virginia State Bd. of Elections," U.S. 383, (1966), 663.

299. Tussman and tenBroek, "The Equal Protection of the Laws," 37 *Calif. L. Rev.*, 37, (1949), 341, 344.

300. J. Nowak, R. Rotunda and J. Young, *Constitutional Law*, 3d ed., (1986), 523.

301. Harper, U.S. 383, (1966), 663.

302. Shapiro, U.S. 394, (1969), 618.

303. Strict scrutiny has been called "strict in theory and fatal in fact." Gunther, "The Supreme Court 1971 Term, Foreword: In Search of Evolving Doctrine on a Changing

Court: A Model for Newer Equal Protection," *Harvard Law Review*, 86, (1972), 1.

304. Gunther, "The Supreme Court 1971 Term, Forward," *Harvard L. Rev. 89*, (1972), 1.

305. J. Nowak, R. Rotunda and J. Young, *Constitutional Law*, (1986), 530.

306. U.S. 187, (1903), 553, 567-568.

307. "United States v. Sioux Nation of Indians," U.S. 448, (1980), 371. This case called for judicial review of treaty dealings with the Sioux tribe. The case is unique in that Congress passed a special statute asking the courts to make such a review. Act. of March 13, 1978, Pub. L. No. 95-243, Stat. 92, (1978), 153. Lone Wolf, 187, (1903), 553 still stands as the law absent such special legislative authority. See also Comment, "Sparrow and the Lone Wolf," (1991).

308. This exact term is used twice in Sparrow. "The extent of legislative or regulatory impact on an existing aboriginal right may be scrutinized so as to ensure recognition and affirmation" of the Aboriginal right. "R. v. Sparrow," S.C.R. 1, (1990), 1075, 1110. "'[R]ecognition and affirmation' incorporate the fiduciary relationship referred to earlier and so import some restraint on the exercise of sovereign power. . . . [F]ederal power must be reconciled with federal duty and the best way to achieve that reconciliation is to demand the justification of any government regulation that infringes upon or denies aboriginal rights. Such scrutiny is in keeping with . . . a high standard of honourable dealing with respect to the aboriginal peoples of Canada. . ." Ibid., 1109.

309. Ibid., 1108.

310. U.S. 187, (1903), 553, 566.

311. U.S. 448, (1980), 371.

312. "Worcester v. Georgia," U.S. 31, (6 Pet.), (1832), 515.

313. "United States v. McBratney," U.S. 104, (1881), 621.

314. Act of Aug. 15, 1953, ch. 505, Stat. 87, (1988), 588-590 (codified as amended in U.S.C. 18, (1988), 1151, 1162, and U.S.C. 28, (1988), 1331, 1360).

315. E.g., Wash. Rev. Code, (1989), 37.12.010 (amended 1963).

316. E.g., "Bryan v. Itasca County," U.S. 426, (1976),

373.

317. E.g., "Santa Rosa Band of Indians v. Kings County," F.2d 532, (9th Cir. 1975), 655, cert. denied, U.S. 429, (1977), 1038.

318. Ibid.

319. U.S.C. 18, (1988), 1162(b); U.S.C. 28, (1988), 1360(b).

320. "McClanahan v. State Tax Comm'n," U.S. 411, (1973), 164, 172.

321. See "Ramah Navajo School Bd. v. Bureau of Revenue," U.S. 458, (1982), 832; "White Mountain Apache Tribe v. Bracker," U.S. 448, (1980), 136; "Central Mach. Co. v. Arizona State Tax Comm'n," U.S. 448, (1980), 160.

322. "White Mountain Apache Tribe v. Bracker," U.S. 448, (1980), 150-51.

323. In no case has a court found preemption where two non-Indians are involved.

324. "White Mountain Apache Tribe v. Bracker," U.S. 448, (1980), 144; "Washington v. Confederated Tribes of the Colville Reservation," U.S. 447, (1980), 134, 155-56.

325. "McClanahan v. State Tax Comm'n," U.S. 411, (1973), 164, 172.

326. See "Brendale v. Confederated Tribes and Bands of Yakima Indian Nation," S. Ct. 109, (1989), 2994.

327. Ibid., 3009.

328. Ibid., 3015.

329. "Montana v. United States," U.S. 450, (1981), 544.

330. "Ramah Navajo School Bd. v Bureau of Revenue," U.S. 458, (1982), 832.

331. "Central Mach. Co. v. Arizona State Tax Comm'n," U.S. 448, (1980), 160.

332. See U.S.C. 25, (1988), 261-264.

333. "White Mountain Apache Tribe v. Bracker," U.S. 448, (1980), 136.

334. "United States v. Anderson," F.2d 736, (9th Cir. 1984), 1358. Where the source river was entirely contained on the reservation, the court held that state law did not apply to the non-Indian landowner in his use of surplus water. "Colville Confederated Tribes v. Walton," F.2d 647, (9th Cir. 1981), 42, cert. denied, U.S. 454, (1981), 1092.

335. Act of July 10, 1952, ch. 208(a)-(c), Stat. 66, (1988),

560 (codified at U.S.C. 43, (1988), 666).

336. "Colorado River Water Conservation Dist. v. United States," U.S. 424, (1976), 800; see also "United States v. District Court," U.S. 401, (1971), 520.

The term "adjudication" means to bring into one lawsuit everyone who claims a water right within a given river basin or sub-basin so that all water rights are determined at one time. It does not allow suits against the United States for determination of Indian water rights by a single, or even several plaintiffs. Every claimant must be included.

337. Two such agreements are representative: the Big Horn River System, Wyoming, see In re Big Horn, P.2d 750, (1988), 681, and the Fort Peck, Montana Compact, see Mont. Code Ann., (1990), 85-20-201.

338. P. Sly, *Reserved Water Rights Settlement Manual*, (1988); G. Weatherford, M. Wallace and L. Storey, *Leasing Indian Water*, (1988).

339. U.S. 31, (6 Pet.), (1832), 515.

340. The Indian Act, ch. 29, Can. Stat. 1951, 131, 161.

341. *Can. Rev. Stat.* ch. I-5, (1985), 88. This power is presumably now subject also to the constitutional entrenchment of Aboriginal and treaty rights under the Constitution Act, 1982, *Can. Rev. Stat.* app. II, No. 44, (1985), 35(1).

342. "Derrickson v. Derrickson," S.C.R. 1, (1986), 285, 297-299. Questions of title and rights of possession concerning reserve lands are exclusively within Parliament's federal authority. Ibid., 293, 296. "It is far from settled that s. 88 contemplates referential incorporation [of provincial laws] with respect to lands reserved for Indians." Ibid., 297.

343. "The basic principle is that provincial laws apply [to Indians and Indian lands] unless excluded by one of these rules." J. Woodward, *Native Law*, (1990), 120. For "these rules," see notes 345-346 and accompanying text.

344. "Dick v. R.," S.C.R. 2, (1985), 309.

345. Sanders delineates two basic principles that have emerged from the cases: (1) provincial laws apply to Indians if they do not discriminate against Indians and are not in conflict with federal laws; and (2) provincial laws apply to Indian reserve lands if they do not directly affect the use of those lands, do not discriminate against Indians, and do not

conflict with federal law. Sanders, "The Application of Provincial Laws," in *Aboriginal Peoples and the Law*, (1985).

346. Sanders, "Hunting Rights—Provincial Laws—Application on Indian Reserves," Sask. L. Rev. 38, (1974), 234, 242.

347. Ibid., (citing "Dick v. R.," S.C.R. 2, [1985], 309, 323).

348. J. Woodward, *Native Law*, (1990), 121.

349. S.C.R. 1, (1986), 285, 296.

350. W.W.R. 74, (1970), 380, 383.

351. See, e.g., U.S.C. 18, (1988), 1162(a); U.S.C. 28, (1988), 1360(a) (authorizing states to impose state jurisdiction on reservations).

352. For example, where a non-Indian commits a crime against a non-Indian, or where zoning applies mostly to non-Indians and non-Indian-owned lands.

353. Under P.L. 280, the tribes may have retained concurrent jurisdiction with the state, so the tribes did not *lose* any jurisdiction. State jurisdiction was merely added and made concurrent with tribal jurisdiction. This issue is now being tested in "Confederated Tribes of the Colville Reservation v. Superior Court," No. 89-35829 (9th Cir. filed Nov. 30, 1989).

354. R. Strickland, *Fire and the Spirits—Cherokee Law from Clan to Court*, (1975), 62.

355. "The areas in which such implicit divestiture of sovereignty has been held to have occurred are those involving *the relations between an Indian tribe and non-members of the tribe. . . .*" "Montana v. United States," U.S. 450, (1981), 544, 564 (emphasis in original) (citing "United States v. Wheeler," U.S. 435, (1978), 313, 326).

356. "Cherokee nation v. Georgia," U.S. 30 (5 Pet.), (1831), 1.

357. "Johnson v. M'Intosh," U.S. 21 (8 Wheat.), (1823), 543.

358. "United States v. McBratney," U.S. 104, (1881), 621.

359. U.S.C. 18, (1988), 1153.

360. "United States v. Kagama," U.S. 118, (1886), 375. The courts still have not decided whether the Major Crimes Act eliminated tribal court jurisdiction over the same crimes.

Tribal and federal jurisdiction are probably concurrent.

361. General Allotment Act of 1887, ch. 119, Stat. 24, 388.

362. F. Cohen, *Handbook of Federal Indian Law*, (1982), 129-30.

363. Ibid., 139.

364. Many states imposed jurisdiction on tribes, sometimes with, and sometimes without their consent. See Goldberg, "Public Law 280: The Limits of State Jurisdiction Over Reservation Indians," U.C.L.A. L. Rev. 22, (1975), 535, 546-547.

365. Title II, 201-203, Pub. L. No. 90-284, Stat. 82, (1988), 77 (codified at U.S.C. 25, (1988), 1301-1303, 1321-1322).

366. Ibid., 202. The penalties were increased in 1986 to $5,000 and one year of confinement. U.S.C. 25, 1302(7).

367. "Oliphant v. Suquamish Indian Tribe," U.S. 435, (1978), 191.

368. "Duro v. Reina," S. Ct. 110, (1990), 2053. But see Department of Defense Appropriations Act, 8077, Pub. L. No. 101-511, Stat. 104, (1990), 1892 (legislatively reversing the Duro holding for one year).

369. "McClanahan v. State Tax Commission," U.S. 411, (1973), 164.

370. "Brendale v. Confederated Tribes and Bands of Yakima Indian Nation," U.S. 492, (1989), 408.

371. "Montana v. United States," U.S. 450, (1981), 544, 564, 565-566.

372. In "Segundo v. City of Rancho Mirage," F.2d 813, (9th Cir. 1987), 1387, the court held that a municipal rent control ordinance could not be applied to a mobile home park operated by non-Indians on an Indian-owned allotment land on the Agua Caliente Reservation in California. Both tribal trust land and allotment land fall under the exclusive regulatory authority of the tribe. In "Knight v. Shoshone and Arapaho Indian Tribes," F.2d 670, (19th Cir. 1982), 900, the court ruled that the tribe could zone non-Indian land on the reservation and prevent it from being subdivided by private developers. This met the "police power" aspect of the "Montana" test in that the development would have a direct effect on the health and welfare of the tribe. The county had

no zoning ordinance for the area in question. The fact that the code applied to and affected non-Indians who could not participate in tribal government was immaterial.

The Ninth Circuit Court of Appeals, in "Cardin v. De La Cruz," F.2d 671 (9th Cir. 1982), 363, cert. denied, 459 U.S. (1982), 967, held that the Quinault Indians' tribal health and safety regulations applied to non-Indian owners of a grocery store within the reservation. The facts satisfied both the concensual commercial relationship aspect of the "Montana" test, and represented conduct that directly threatened tribal health and welfare, which met the second aspect of the "Montana" test.

The federal district court in "Lummi Indian Tribe v. Hallauer," Ind. L. Rep. (Am. Indian Law Training Program) 9, (W.D. Wash. 1982), 3025, approved a tribe's requirement that non-Indians hook up to the tribal sewer system. The health and welfare of the reservation residents was clearly involved there.

In "Confederated Salish and Kootenai Tribes v. Namen," F.2d 665, (9th Cir. 1982), 951, cert. denied, U.S. 459, (1982), 977, the Ninth Circuit held that the Flathead Tribe could regulate the riparian rights of non-Indian landowners on the reservation. The non-Indians owned land fronting on a lake, the bed of which was part of the reservation. The exercise of these riparian rights directly affected the health and welfare of the tribes. In a recent district court case in California, "Pinoleville Indian Community v. Mendocino County," F. Supp. 685, (N.D. Cal. 1988), 1042, the court upheld an injunction against an asphalt and cement plant on non-Indian owned land within the boundaries of the rancheria (a reservation-like holding in California). The court found that the plant would affect the health and welfare of the tribe.

In "Colville Confederated Tribes v. Walton," F.2d 647, (9th Cir. 1981), 42, cert. denied, U.S. 454, (1981), 1092, the court held that the tribe could regulate surplus water use on non-Indian-owned land on the reservation where the source stream started and died within the boundaries of the reservation. In a subsequent case, "United States v. Anderson," F.2d 736, (9th Cir. 1984), 1358, the court ruled that the tribe could not regulate non-Indian water use on fee land where the source river started above the reservation and flowed on beyond it downstream. The court recognized the tribe's interest in regulation but concluded the state's interest was greater than in "Walton" because only a small portion of the source river was located on the reservation.

373. "Brendale v. Confederated Tribes and Bands of Yakima Indian Nation," U.S. 492, (1989), 408.

374. U.S.C. 25, (1988), 461-492.

375. F. Cohen, *Handbook of Federal Indian Law*, (1982), 149, 232, 239.

376. U.S.C. 25, (1988), 478.

377. F. Cohen, *Handbook of Federal Indian Law*, (1982), 150 n.48.

378. F. Prucha, *The Great Father*, (1986), 390.

379. Attributed to Chief Seattle (Duwamish Indian Tribe, 1855). See *How Can One Sell the Air? A Manifesto of an Indian Chief*, (1984).

380. Only a few tribes in the United States have taken advantage of this opportunity to manage their water quality environment. Most show a relative disinterest, or lack of capacity to manage water quality effectively.

381. U.S.C. 33, (1988), 1251-1387.

382. U.S.C. 42, (1988), 7401-7642.

383. U.S.C. 42, (1988), 300f-300j.

384. U.S.C. 42, (1988), 9601-9675. The statute was amended by the Superfund Amendments and Reauthorization Act of 1986 (SARA), Pub. L. No. 99-499, Stat. 100, 1613 (codified in scattered sections of Titles 10, 26, 29, and U.S.C. 42), and Pub. L. No. 99-563, Stat. 100, 3177 (codified at U.S.C. 42, 9671-9675).

385. U.S.C. 7, (1988), 136-136y.

386. U.S.C. 30, (1988), 1201-1328.

387. U.S.C. 42, (1988), 6901-6992.

388. U.S.C. 33, (1988), 1342(a)-(b).

389. Ibid., 1342(b).

390. Title V, 506, Pub. L. No. 100-104, Stat. 101, 77 (codified at U.S.C. 33, 1377(h)).

391. U.S.C. 33, (1988), 1362(4).

392. The CAA provides that the redesignation or change of air quality standards on an Indian reservation can be done by the tribal, not the state government. If either a state or a tribe permits a new emission source that

contributes to air pollution greater than that permitted by the receiving government's area, either may request the EPA to arbitrate the dispute. If it cannot be arbitrated, then the EPA has authority to decide the issue. U.S.C. 42, (1988), 7474.

The SDWA protects drinking water supplies, including sources and distribution systems, from contamination. Amendments in 1986 authorized the EPA administrator to treat Indian tribes the same as states and delegate implementation power to them for most purposes. Alternatively, if a tribe does not seek or obtain EPA approval, this federal agency is empowered to implement the program itself. U.S.C. 42, (1988), 300(h)-1(3).

CERCLA (the "Superfund" Act) is designed to facilitate cleanup of hazardous waste sites and oil spills. In 1986, SARA authorized tribes, as well as states and the United States to recover for losses to natural resources from, hazardous waste disposal or oil spills. Tribes also are authorized to enter into cooperative agreements with states to join in an effort to clean up hazardous waste sites. U.S.C. 42, 9604(d)(1).

FIFRA regulates pesticide handling and use. In its original enactment in 1978 Congress empowered the EPA Administrator to delegate almost complete operating authority to Indian tribes as well as states. U.S.C. 7, (1988), 136u.

The SMCRA recognizes that surface coal mining creates serious environmental problems and that regulation is necessary to require operators to reclaim the land after mining is completed. From its initial enactment this law has mandated that tribes be treated as states for most purposes under the Act. U.S.C. 30, 1235(k).

Tribes will be granted primacy under the CWA, CERCLA, and the SDWA only if they meet certain conditions concerning governmental powers and the capacity to implement these federal statutes. They also need federal funding, which has been totally inadequate to date.

393. U.S.C. 42, (1988), 6903(13).

394. "Washington Dep't of Ecology v. EPA," F.2d 752, (9th cir. 1985), 1465.

395. Ibid., 1472.

396. "Oliphant v. Suquamish Indian Tribe," U.S. 435, (1978), 191; "Worcester v. Georgia," U.S. 31, (6 Pet.), (1832),

515, 561.

397. F. Cohen, *Handbook of Federal Indian Law*, (1982), 252.

398. "Montana v. United States," U.S. 450, (1981), 544, 557; "Merrion v. Jicarilla Apache Indian Tribe," U.S. 455, (1982), 130, 136-37.

399. F. Cohen, *Handbook of Federal Indian Law*, (1982), 247.

400. In some tribes implementation is not by a separate executive branch. Instead, staff works under direct control of the council. See R. Johnson (ed.), *Indian Tribal Codes*, (1988).

401. F. Cohen, *Handbook of Federal Indian Law*, (1982), 247.

402. Ibid., at 250.

403. Johnson, *Indian Tribal Codes*, (1988).

404. About 17 BIA courts, or Courts of Indian Offenses, also operate in the United States. These courts are regulated by C.F.R. 25, pt. 11, (1990). They draw their authority as well as their pay from the BIA and are considered arms of the federal government; judges are hired and fired by the BIA. Tribal courts draw their authority from "sovereignty" and are independent of the federal government. F. Cohen, *Handbook of Federal Indian Law*, (1982), 250.

Since 1970, the National American Indian Court Judges Association has conducted extensive training programs for tribal judges, many of whom are now lawyers.

405. U.S.C. 25, (1988), 1302(7).

406. U.S. 435, (1978), 191.

407. S. Ct. 110, (1990), 2053, 2064-2065. But see Department of Defense Appropriations Act, 8077, Pub. L. No. 101-511, Stat. 104, (1990), 1892, (legislatively reversing the "Duro" holding for one year).

408. Act of Aug. 15, 1953, ch. 505, Stat. 67, (1988), 588 (codified as amended at U.S.C. 18, (1988), 1162, U.S.C. 25, (1988), 1321-1326 and U.S.C. 28, (1988), 1360); see notes 102-103 and accompanying text.

409. C.F.R. 25, pt. 11, (1990); see F. Cohen, *Handbook of Federal Indian Law*, (1982), 736-37.

410. U.S.C. 25, 1302.

411. F. Cohen, *Handbook of Federal Indian Law*, (1982), 664-666; see "United States v. Wheeler," U.S. 435,

(1978), 313; "Talton v. Mayes," U.S. 163, (1886), 376.

412. F. Cohen, *Handbook of Federal Indian Law*, (1982), 666-670; see "Santa Clara Pueblo v. Martinez," U.S. 436, (1978), 49.

413. *Canada House of Commons, Special Committee on Indian Self Government, Indian Self-Government in Canada*, (1983), 39.

414. *Can. Rev. Stat.* app. II, No. 5, (1985), 91(24). Neither did Indians play a part such as this in the United States.

415. *Can. Rev. Stat.* (1985), ch. I-5.

416. See generally, *Canada House of Commons, Special Committee on Indian Self Government, Indian Self-Government in Canada*, (1983).

417. Bartlett, "The Indian Act of Canada," (1978), 593.

418. Ibid., 594-603.

419. Ch. 6, Can. Stat., (1869), 22; see J. Woodward, *Native Law*, (1990), 93 n.59.

420. Ch. 6, 10, Can. Stat., (1869), 22, 24.

421. Bartlett, "The Indian Act of Canada," (1978), 594.

422. Ibid., 582-583.

423. Ch. 28, 72, *Can. Stat.*, (1880), 202, 223.

424. Bartlett, "The Indian Act of Canada," (1978), 596.

425. *Canada House of Commons, Special Committee on Indian Self Government, Indian Self-Government in Canada*, (1983), 42.

426. Ibid., 43.

427. J. Woodward, *Native Law*, (1990), 82-83; *Canada House of Commons, Special Committee on Indian Self Government, Indian Self-Government in Canada*, (1988), 43-45.

428. *Can. Rev. Stat.*, ch. I-5, (1985), 2(1), 2(3)(6), 9(1), 10(1)(a), 17(1)(a), 61(1), 74, 74(1), 81, 83, 85.1; J. Woodward *Native Law*, (1990), 90-91.

429. Hemmington, "Jurisdiction of Future Tribal Courts in Canada: Learning from the American Experience," Can. Native L. Rep. 2, (1988), 1.

430. *Canada House of Commons, Special Committee on Indian Self Government, Indian Self-Government in Canada*, (1983), 43.

431. Bartlett, "The Indian Act of Canada," (1978), 593.

432. *Can. Rev. Stat.*, ch. I-6, (1970), 83(1).

433. Bartlett, "The Indian Act of Canada," (1978), 600.

434. J. Woodward, *Native Law*, (1990), 164.

435. Ibid.

436. U.S. 31 (6 Pet.), (1832), 515, 556-57.

437. *Canada House of Commons, Special Committee on Indian Self Government, Indian Self-Government in Canada,* (1983), 41, 44, 141.

438. Ibid., 59, 64, 76.

439. C-52 (1984) ("Indian Self-Government Act") (on file with the *Washington Law Review*).

440. R. Bartlett, *Indian Reserves and Aboriginal Lands in Canada*, (1990), 160-61.

441. Ibid., 162.

442. Ibid., 178.

443. J. Woodward, *Native Law*, (1990), 378.

444. Ibid.

445. It was only partial because values were determined as of the date of the taking, and no interest was allowed on the years since the taking. *U.S. Indian Claims Comm'n, Final Report*, (1978), 11.

446. See note 205 and accompanying text.

447. S.C.R. 1, (1990), 1075.

448. U.S. 187, (1903), 553, 566.

449. Ibid., 567-568.

450. "Sparrow," S.C.R. 1, (1990), 1109-1110.

451. "United States v. Washington," F. Supp. 384, (1974), 312, 333, 342, aff'd, F.2d 520, (9th Cir. 1975), 676, cert. denied, U.S. 423, (1976), 1086.

452. "Tee-Hit-Ton Indians v. United States," U.S. 348, (1955), 272.

453. U.S. 31, (6 Pet.), (1832), 515.

454. But, at the same time, it was undoubtedly a major factor in the development of pan-tribal political activism and support for tribal self-determination. See S. Cornell, *The Return of the Native American Indian Political Resurgence*, (1988).

455. See, e.g., "Fredericks v. Eide-Kirschmann Ford," N.W. 2d 462, (1990), 164.

GLOSSARY OF TERMS

Acculturation/Assimilation. A policy pursued by the federal government beginning in the second half of the 19th century. Major instruments of this policy were Indian boarding schools, the 1887 General Allotment Act, missionary activity on tribal reservations and Bureau of Indian Affairs administration of tribal affairs and reservation life.

AIPRC (1977) (American Indian Policy Review Commission). Congress directed a comprehensive study of Indian affairs and the Commission produced a ten-volume report and a series of recommendations. Unfortunately, the report and recommendations were largely ignored.

BIA (1849) (Bureau of Indian Affairs). The federal agency primarily responsible for the formulation and supervision of Indian policy.

Boarding Schools Circa (1880). Boarding schools were the centerpiece of federal educational policy for Indians. They removed Indian children from reservation life and instructed them in the "civilized virtues" of white society. By 1886, there were over seven thousand Indian children in boarding schools, three times the number attending day schools. The boarding schools were central to carrying out a policy of forced assimilation and acculturation.

Board of Indian Commissioners. Established on June 3, 1869, this board was made up of Protestant men who were appointed by the President. Their job consisted of monitoring the distribution of funds allocated by Congress for use by Native Americans and by those working to help the Natives, supplying policy and reform advice to the Secretary of the Interior and the Commissioner of Indian Affairs, and supervising all Protestant appointments to agency positions.

Carlisle Indian Industrial School. Established in 1879 by Richard H. Pratt, the school was the first off-reservation boarding school for Native Americans. The school had two main goals: to Americanize the Native children and to prove to the public that it was possible to educate Indians. The Carlisle School became a model for future Native boarding schools.

Cherokee Nation v. The State of Georgia (1831). After the Indian Removal Act of 1830 took effect, three of the five major southern tribes had left their tribal land. The Cherokee nation did not leave and decided to fight to keep their land in the Supreme Court. The court, under Chief Justice John Marshall, ruled for the Cherokees, affirming their right to the land, stating that Native Americans were not subject to state laws. However, the court ruled that the Cherokees were not sovereign nations, but a state dependent on the United States government. Despite an apparent Cherokee victory, President Andrew Jackson refused to enforce the ruling and the Cherokees eventually lost their land.

CERT (Council of Energy Resource Tribes). A grouping of 43 Indian tribes which has water, energy, and mineral deposits on its tribal lands. The group coordinates its resource leasing and royalty policy to maximize tribal earnings on tribal holdings.

Civil Rights Act of 1968. This act contained an "Indian Bill of Rights" which provides protection for Native Americans from tribal authority, similar to the protection provided to the individual by the original Bill of Rights. Prior to this act, these rights could not be guaranteed. Opponents believed this was an imposition of a white legal system and felt that the development of a native legal system would be more appropriate.

Dawes Act on Severality (1887) (General Allotment Act). Billed as Indian reform legislation, this act was perhaps the strongest attack on Indian land base and tribal integrity. Between 1887 when the law was passed and 1934 when its provisions were rescinded, Indians and Indian tribes lost two-thirds of their 180 million acres of land.

Federally Recognized Tribe. An Indian tribe which is authorized to receive federal protection and services from the United States Government. There are over 300 federally recognized Indian tribes.

Ghost Dance (1889). A nativist revitalization movement led by a Paiute Indian prophet named Wovoka. Wovoka claimed that in a visit to the spirit world he saw the Great Spirit and dead Indian ancestors all alive and happy in a beautiful land with abundant game. His message was to work hard, live in harmony with the white people and, eventually, they would be reunited with the dead in a world without sadness, old age or death. He brought back a dance which would bring about this transformation if the dance was properly performed. The Ghost dance spread like wild fire among the several tribes on the Great Plains.

IHS (Indian Health Service). A division of the U.S. Public Health Service responsible for Indian Health.

Indian Civilization Act (1819). This act appropriated $10,000 annually toward Indian education in reading, writing, arithmetic and agricultural techniques.

Indian Claims Commission. Created by the Indian Claims Act of 1946, this commission heard tribal suits against the United States for past mistreatment and wrongdoings by the United States government.

Indian Country. A term with legal, geographical and cultural meaning. Indian Country is "federal trust land" on which most tribal Indian people live. Geographically, Indian Country is the area west of the Mississippi, the twenty-six states which have been historically home to the majority of Native Americans and their historical homelands. In Indian law, Indian Country comprises all those lands and easements which come under the federal trust responsibility and are inhabited by Indian people.

Indian Trade and Intercourse Act (1790). A law which asserted federal jurisdiction over non-Indians in Indian territory, regulated trade with Indian tribes and placed limits and restrictions on Indian land transactions.

Indian Removal Act (1830). This act granted the government of the United States the power to relocate the Southern Indians to land west of the Mississippi and to appropriate Indian lands by creating a new set of treaties. Despite strong opposition from many northern legislators, the act was signed into law by President Andrew Jackson on May 30.

IRA (1934) (Indian Reorganization Act). Established elected form of tribal government, partially restored Indian land base and provided for tribal incorporation.

Meriam Report (1928). A report prepared for the Secretary of Interior by the Brookings Institution to investigate Indian Health, economic conditions, education and tribal management. It was a major indictment of Indian policy and led to reforms under BIA Commissioner John Collier.

NARF (Native American Rights Fund). Established in 1970 with the aid from a Ford Foundation grant, NARF is the principal national Indian interest law firm.

NCAI (National Congress of American Indians) (1944). A successor intertribal organization to the Society of the American Indians. The organization promotes Indian awareness, cultural heritage, treaty rights, tribal sovereignty and Indian welfare in general.

NIYC (National Indian Youth Council) (1961). Founded by young, educated Indians at a conference of Indian college students in Chicago, Illinois. Their confrontational style heralded a new strategy in resolving Indian-non Indian differences. Many of the leaders of the Washington "Fish-ins" and the A.I.M. "Red Power Movement" emerged from the NIYC experience.

NTCA (National Tribal Chairmen's Association). The principal advocacy group for tribal Indians. Founded in the

1960's with Community Action monies, the NTCA has vigorously supported federal programs to support tribal programs on the reservations.

PL 83-280 (1953). A companion piece of legislation to HCR-108. This law transferred criminal and civil jurisdiction on Indian reservations and provided that any other state could assume such jurisdiction, if it wished, without Indian consent.

PL 93-638 (1975). Indian Self-Determination and Education Assistance Act provided for Indian tribes to take over management and supervision of education, economic development and social and health services on their reservations. Its success has been hampered by lack of funding and BIA boot dragging.

Relocation (1951). A vocational training and job placement program initiated by the BIA to encourage Indians to leave the reservation. By 1975, 160,000 Indians had participated in the program.

Sequoia. A Cherokee Indian who developed an 85 symbol written language in 1821.

Termination (1953). Under the provisions of House Concurrent Resolution 108, a specific number of Indian tribes were to be removed from federal supervision "at the earliest possible time." Subsequently, 200 Indian tribes and rancheros were terminated.

Treaty Relationship. The principal relationship between the United States government and Native Americans until 1871. The relationship involved several types of treaties: those of peace and friendship, cession, removal, allotment and acknowledgement of United States sovereignty. Initially, U.S. negotiators respected the Indian treaty rituals of the peace pipe and wampum belt, but later forced the Indians to follow white customs. The negotiations would often be carried out with a portion of the tribe, ignoring those who would not comply.

Trail of Tears (1838). The removal of eighteen thousand Cherokee Indians from their tribal land to land west of the Mississippi. Four thousand people died during the long and difficult journey.

United States Indian Peace Commission. Approved by Congress on July 20, 1867, the commission was ordered by President Johnson to pacify relations with the Native Americans by removing the causes of the discord and to put in effect a policy of concentration. This policy called for the relocation of western Indians onto three larger reservations.

Wounded Knee (1890). On September 29, over two hundred Sioux Indians, including women and children who had surrendered to the U.S. Seventh Cavalry, were killed by soldiers en route to the Pine Ridge Indian Agency.

NOTES ON CONTRIBUTORS

Mark Allen, Boston College Environmental Affairs Law Review.

Gary Carson Anders is a Professor of Economics at Arizona State University West. His research on the economic development of American Indians and Alaska Natives has been published in a number of academic journals and books. Of Native American descent, Dr. Anders combines his interest in Native economic issues with Asia nad non-western approaches to economic organization.

Curtis Berkey is a staff attorney with the Indian Law Resource Center in Washington, DC.

Gregory R. Campbell is an associate professor of anthropology, University of Montana, Missoula. His research interests include Native American health and demography, ethnicity, and political economy.

Ward Churchill (Creek/Cherokee Metis) is director of the Educational Development Program at the University of Colorado at Boulder and co-director, with Glenn Morris, of the Colorado chapter of the American Indian Movement.

Daniel Cohen is a journalist and resides in Hoboken, NJ.

Anneliese M. Heyle, Stanford University.

Lewis P. Hinchman is associate professor of political science at Clarkson University, Potsdam, NY. He is the author of *Hegel's Critique of the Enlightenment* and the co-editor of *Hannah Arendt: Critical Essays*. He has written articles on many topics, including human rights, autonomy, individuality, and deep ecology.

Sandra P. Hinchman is professor and former chair of the government department at St. Lawrence University, Canton,

606

NY. The co-editor of *Hannah Arendt: Critical Essays*, she has also written on Joan Didion and on deep ecology.

Ralph W. Johnson is a professor of law at the University of Washington in Seattle.

Teresa D. LaFromboise, Department of Counseling Psychology, School of Education, University of Wisconsin—Madison.

Dan Lamont is a Seattle-based photojournalist specializing in land-use issues. His work often appears in *Time*, *Newsweek*, and *Smithsonian*.

Edward D. Liebow is a research scientist on the staff of the Battelle Human Affairs Research Center at 4000 NE 41st St., Seattle, WA 98105.

Thomas R. McGuire holds an appointment with the Bureau of Applied Research in Anthropology, University of Arizona, Tucson, Arizona 85721.

Michael R. Moore is a resource economist with the Resources and Technology Division, Economic Research Service, U.S. Department of Agriculture.

Emily J. Ozer, Harvard and Radcliffe Colleges.

Vicki Page is an adjunct professor of sociology at the University of Texas at Dallas.

Paul Schneider writes frequently for *Esquire*, *Mirabella*, and other magazines. This is his first article for *Audubon*.

C. Matthew Snipp, Ph.D., is professor of rural sociology and sociology, and director, American Indian Studies, University of Wisconsin—Madison.

Gary Sokolow, J.D., 1988, University of South Dakota. He received the first place award for the 1987-88 *American Indian Law Review* writing competition.

BIBLIOGRAPHY

Native American Resurgence and Renewal

Native American Reference Sources

Abler, Thomas S. et al. *A Canadian Indian Bibliography, 1960-1970.* Ann Arbor: Books on Demand.

Corley, Nora Teresa. *Resources for Native Peoples Studies.* Ottawa: Resources Survey Division, Collections Development Branch, National Library of Canada, 1984.

Dunn, Lynn P. *American Indians: A Study Guide and Sourcebook.* San Francisco: R and E Research Associates, 1975.

Frazier, Gregory W. *American Indian Index: A Directory of Indian Country, U.S.A.* Denver: Arrowstar Publishers, 1985.

Haas, Marilyn L. *Indians of North America: Methods and Sources for Library Research.* Hamden, CT: Library Professional Publications, 1983.

Hill, Edward E. *Guide to Records in the National Archives.* Washington, D.C.: National Archives and Records, 1984.

Hirschfelder, Arlene B. *Guide to Research on North American Indians.* Chicago: American Library Association, 1983.

Hodge, William H. *A Bibliography of Contemporary North American Indians: Selected and Partially Annotated with Study Guides.* New York: Interland Publishers, 1976.

Hoxie, Fred, and Harvey Markowitz. *Native Americans: North America—An Annotated Bibliography.* Pasadena: Salem

Press, 1991.

Kelso, Dianne R., and Carolyn L. Attneave. *Bibliography of North American Indian Mental Health*. Greenwood, NY: Greenwood Press, 1981.

Klein, Barry T. ed. *Reference Encyclopedia of the American Indian*. New York: Todd Publications, 1986.

Lass-Woodfin, Mary J. *Books on American Indians and Eskimos*. Chicago: American Library Association, 1977.

Prucha, Francis Paul. *Atlas of American Indian Affairs*. Lincoln: University of Nebraska Press, 1990.

Russell, Thornton. *Sociology of American Indians: A Critical Bibliography*. Bloomington: Indiana University Press, 1980.

Sharma, H.D. *Indian Reference Sources: An Annotated Guide to Indian Reference Material, Social Sciences and Pure and Applied Sciences, v.2*. Fayetteville, AR: University Books, Ltd., 1989.

Smith, Dwight L. *Indians of the United States and Canada: A Bibliography*. Santa Barbara: ABC-Clio, 1974-1983.

Native American Journals/Periodicals

American Anthropologist, first published 1899.

American Ethnologist, first published 1974.

American Indian Culture and Research Journal, first published 1974.

American Indian Law Review, first published 1973.

American Indian Quarterly, first published 1974.

Canadian Ethnic Studies, first published 1969.

Canadian Review of Sociology and Anthropology, first published 1964.

Current Anthropology, first published 1960.

Ethnic and Racial Studies, first published 1973.

Ethnohistory, first published 1954.

Ethnology, first published 1962.

Journal of American Indian Education, first published 1962.

Journal of Anthropological Research, first published in 1964. (Formerly *Southwestern Journal of Anthropology*, first published 1945.)

Journal of Ethnic Studies, first published in 1973. Final publication 1992.

National Geographic, first published 1959. (Formerly *National Geographic Magazine*, first published 1888.)

Smithsonian Contributions in Anthropology. (Formerly *Bureau of American Ethnology Bulletin*, first published in 1887.)

Urban Anthropology and Studies of Cultural Systems and World Economic Development, first published in 1985. (Formerly *Urban Anthropology*, first published in 1972.)

Wassaja, the Indian Historian, first published in 1982. (Formerly *The Indian Historian*, first published in 1964. Final publication 1979.)

Western Historical Quarterly, first published 1970.

History

ARTICLES

"1491: America Before Columbus." *National Geographic* 180 (October 1991):1-99.

Johnson, R.W. "Fragile Gains: Two Centuries of Canadian and United States Policy Toward Indians." *Washington Law Review* 66 (July 1991):643-718.

Landers, Robert K. "Is America Allowing Its Past to be Stolen?" *Editorial Research Reports*, January 18, 1991, pp. 34-47.

Morris, C. Patrick. "Termination by Accountants: The Reagan Indian Policy." *Policy Studies Journal* 16 (Summer 1988):731-50.

Murphey, Dwight D. "The Historic Depossesion of the American Indian: Did it Violate American Ideals?" *The Journal of Social, Political and Economic Studies* 16 (Fall 1991):346-68.

Prucha, Francis Paul. "American Indian Policy in the Twentieth Century." *The Western Historical Quarterly* 15 (January 1984):5-18.

BOOKS

Brown, Dee. *Bury My Heart at Wounded Knee: An Indian History of the American West*. New York: Dell, 1971.

Cahn, E. *Our Brother's Keeper: The Indian in White America*. New York: World Publishing Co., 1969.

Calloway, Colin G. *New Directions in American Indian History*. Norman: University of Oklahoma Press, 1988.

Cronon, William. *Changes in the Land: Indians, Colonists, and the Ecology of New England.* New York: Hill and Wang, 1983.

Debo, Angie. *A History of the Indians in the United States.* Norman: University of Oklahoma Press, 1970.

Deloria, Vine Jr. *American Indian Policy in the Twentieth Century.* Norman: University of Oklahoma Press, 1985.

_____. *Custer Died for Your Sins: An Indian Manifesto.* New York: University of Oklahoma Press, 1969.

_____. *Of Utmost Good Faith: The Case of the American Indian Against the Federal Government.* San Francisco: Straight Arrow Books, 1971.

Deloria, Vine Jr. and Lytle, Clifford M. *American Indians, American Justice.* Austin: University of Texas Press, 1983.

Driver, Harold E. *Indians of North America.* Chicago: University of Chicago Press, 1970.

Fixico, Donald L. *Termination and Relocation: Federal Indian Policy, 1945-1960.* Albuquerque: University of New Mexico Press, 1986.

Foreman, Grant. *Indian Removal.* Norman: University of Oklahoma Press, 1932.

Gibson, Arrell Morgan. *The American Indian: Prehistory to the Present.* Lexington, MA: D.C. Heath, 1980.

Hagan, William T. *American Indians.* Chicago: University of Chicago Press, 1979.

Hoxie, Frederick E. *A Final Promise: The Campaign to Assimilate the Indians.* Lincoln: University of Nebraska Press, 1984.

Jackson, Helen. *A Century of Dishonor: The Early Crusade for Indian Reform*. New York: Harper and Row, 1955.

Josephy, Alvin M. Jr. *The Indian Heritage of America*. New York: Knopf, 1968.

_____. *Now That the Buffalo's Gone: A Study of Today's American Indians*. New York: Alfred A. Knopf, 1982.

McNickle, D'Arcy. *Native American Tribalism: Indian Survivals and Renewals*. New York, 1973.

Martin, Calvin. *The American Indian and the Problem of History*. New York: Oxford University Press, 1987.

Nichols, Roger. *The American Indian: Past and Present*. New York: International Publishers, 1981.

Olson, James S. and Wilson, Raymond. *Native Americans in the Twentieth Century*. Provo, Utah: Brigham Young University Press, 1984.

Oswalt, Wendell H. *This Land Was Theirs: A Study of the North American Indian*. New York: Wiley, 1966.

Prucha, Francis Paul. *The Great Father: The United States Government and the American Indians*. Lincoln: University of Nebraska Press, 1984.

Spicer, Edward H. *A Short History of the Indians of the United States*. New York: Van Nostrand Reinhold, 1969.

Stuart, Paul. *Nations Within a Nation: Historical Statistics of American Indians*. New York: Greenwood Press, 1987.

Talbot, Steve. *Roots of Oppression: The American Indian Question*. New York: International Publishers, 1981.

Trennert, Robert A. *Alternative to Extinction: Federal Indian Policy and the Beginnings of the Reservation System, 1846-1851*. Philadelphia: Temple University Press, 1975.

Washburn, Wilcomb E. *The Indian in America*. New York: Harper and Row, 1975.

Wise, Jennings C. *The Red Man in the New World Drama*. New York: Macmillan, 1971.

Wissler, Clark. *Indians of the United States: Four Centuries of their History and Culture*. New York: Doubleday, Doran and Co., 1940.

Canadian Indians

ARTICLES

Allison, Derek J. "Fourth World Education in Canada and the Faltering Promise of Native Teacher Education Programs." *Journal of Canadian Studies* 18 (Fall 1983):102-18.

Boldt, Menno, and Anthony J. Long. "Tribal Traditions and European-Western Political Ideologies: The Dilemma of Canada's Native Indians." *Canada's Journal of Political Science* 17 (September 1984):537-53.

Came, Barry. "In Search of Pride" (contrasting Indians of Canada and the United States). *Maclean's* 102 (July 3, 1989):40-41.

Cassidy, Frank. "Aboriginal Governments in Canada: An Emerging Field of Study." *Canadian Journal of Political Science* 23 (March 1990):73-99.

Donohue, M.A. "Aboriginal Land Rights in Canada: A Historical Perspective on the Fiduciary Relationship." *American Indian Law Review* 15 (1991):369-389.

Farlinger, Brian. "Aboriginal Entrepreneurs and the Banks" (providing loans and non-credit services). *Canadian Banker* 98 (March/April 1991):50-54.

Griffiths, Curt Taylor, Linda F. Weater, and Colin J. Yerbury. "Canadian Natives: Victims of Socio-structural Deprivation?" *Human Organization* 46 (Fall 1987):277-82.

Haig-Brown, Celia. "Border Work." *Canadian Literature* 124/125 (Spring/Summer 1990):229-41.

Hedican, Edward J. "On the Ethno-politics of Canadian Native Leadership and Identity." *Ethnic Groups* 9 (1991):1-15.

Jackson, M. "Looking Up Natives in Canada." *University of British Columbia Law Review* 23 (1989):215-300.

Jamieson, Ron L. "A Canadian Challenge: Providing Opportunities for Native Business." *The Canadian Business Review* 17 (Winter 1990):33-35.

Johnson, R.W. "Fragile Gains: Two Centuries of Canadian and United States Policy Toward Indians." *Washington Law Review* 66 (July 1991):643-718.

Long, J. Anthony. "Political Revitalization in Canadian Native Indian Societies." *Canadian Journal of Political Science* 23 (December 1990):751-73.

Macklem, P. "First Nations Self-Government and the Borders of the Canadian Legal Imagination." *McGill Law Journal* 36 (April 1991):382-456.

Morgan, E.M. "Self Government and the Constitution: A Comparative Look at Native Canadians and the American Indians." *American Indian Law Review* 12 (1984):39-56.

Paquette, Jerald. "Policy, Power and Purpose: Lessons from Two Indian Education Scenarios." *Journal of Canadian Studies* 24 (Summer 1989):78-94.

Ryan, Joan. "Aboriginal Peoples in Canada." *The American Indian Quarterly* 11 (Fall 1987):315-23.

Sanders, Douglas. "The Supreme Court of Canada and the 'Legal and Political Struggle' Over Indigenous Rights." *Canadian Ethnic Studies* 22 no.3 (1990):122-132.

Sorenson, Jean. "Truck Loggers Look at Indian Land Claims." *Forest Industries* 118 (April 1991):44.

Weaver, Sally M. "A New Paradigm in Canadian Indian Policy for the 1990's." *Canadian Ethnic Studies* 22 no.3 (1990):8-18.

Young, T. Kue. "Indian Health Services in Canada: A Sociohistoric Perspective." *Social Science and Medicine* 18 no.3 (1984):257-64.

BOOKS

Asch, Michael. *Home and Native Land: Aboriginal Rights and the Canadian Constitution*. Agincourt, Ontario: Methuen Publications, 1984.

Boldt, Menno and Long, J. Anthony. *Pathways to Self Determination: Canadian Indians and the Canadian State*. Toronto: University of Toronto Press, 1984.

Cardinal, Harold. *The Rebirth of Canada's Indians*. Edmonton, Alberta: Hurtig, 1977.

_____. *The Unjust Society: The Tragedy of Canada's Indians*. Edmonton, Alberta: Hurtig, 1969.

Frideres, James. *Native Peoples in Canada: Contemporary Conflicts*. Scarborough, Ontario: Prentice-Hall, 1988.

Jeness, Diamond. *The Indians of Canada*. Toronto: University of Toronto Press, 1977.

Culture — General

ARTICLES

Clifton, James A. "Cultural Fictions." *Society* 27 (May/June 1990):19-28.

La Fromboise, Teresa D., Anneliese M. Heyle, and Emily J. Ozer. "Changing and Diverse Roles of Women in American Indian Cultures." *Sex Roles* 22 (April 1990):455-76.

Miller, Bruce G. "Women and Politics: Comparative Evidence from the Northwest Coast." *Ethnology* 31 (October 1992):367-83.

Nichols, Roger L. "Native American Survival in an Integrationist Society." *Journal of Ethnic History* 10 (Fall 1990/Winter 1991):87-93.

Ragsdale, J.W. Jr. "Indian Reservations and the Preservation of Tribal Culture: Beyond Wardship to Stewardship." *UMKC Law Review* 59 (Spring 1991):503-54.

Ridington, Robin. "Omaha Survival: A Vanishing Indian Tribe that Would Not Vanish." *The American Indian Quarterly* 11 (Winter 1987):37-51.

Shively, JoEllen. "Cowboys and Indians: Perceptions of Western Films Among American Indians and Anglos." *American Sociological Review* 57 (December 1992):725-34.

Snipp, C. Matthew. "Sociological Perspectives on American Indians." *Annual Review of Sociology* 18 (1992):351-71.

BOOKS

Blossom, Katherine E. *Culture, Change and Leadership in a Indian Community: The Colorado River Indian*

Reservation. Cherokee Publishers, 1979.

Fey, Harold E. and McNickle, D'Arcy. *Indians and Other Americans: Two Ways of Life Meet*. New York: Harper and Brothers, 1959.

Fritz, Henry J. *The Movement for Indian Assimilation*. Philadelphia: University of Philadelphia Press, 1963.

Hoxie, Frederck E. *A Final Promise: The Campaign to Assimilate the Indians, 1880-1920*. Lincoln: University of Nebraska Press, 1984.

Joe, Jennie R. ed. *American Indian Policy and Cultural Values: Conflict and Evaluation*. Los Angeles: University of California American Indian Studies Center, 1987.

Snipp, C. Matthew. *American Indians: The First of This Land*. New York: Russell Sage Foundation, 1989.

Spicer, Edward H. ed. *Perspectives in American Indian Culture Change*. Chicago: University of Chicago Press, 1961.

Unger, Steven ed. *The Destruction of American Indian Families*. New York: Association on American Indian Affairs, 1977.

Culture — Religion

ARTICLES

Booth, Annie L., and Harvey M. Jacobs. "Ties that Bind: Native American Beliefs as a Foundation for Environmental Consciousness." *Environmental Ethics* 12 (Spring 1990):27-43.

"Constitutional Law-Liberty or Luxury? The Free Exercise of Religion in the Aftermath of Employment Division,

Department of Human Resources v. Smith." *Wake Forest Law Review* 26 (1991):1297-1347.

Johnson, Trebbe. "The Four Sacred Mountains of the Navajos." *Parabola* 13 (Winter 1988):40-47.

"Just Say No to Judicial Review: The Impact of Oregon v. Smith on the Free Exercise Clause." *Iowa Law Review* 76 (May 1991):805-33.

Michaelson, Robert S. "We Also Have a Religion": The Free Exercise of Religion Among Native Americans." *The American Indian Quarterly* 7 (Summer 1983):111-42.

Ortiz, Bev. "Mount Diablo as Myth and Reality: An Indian History Convoluted." *The American Indian Quarterly* 13 (Fall 1989):457-70.

Talbot, Steve. "Desecration and American Indian Religious Freedom." *The Journal of Ethnic Studies* 12 (Winter 1985):1-18.

Warrior, Robert Allen. "Indian Country's Real Struggles." *Christianity and Crisis* 51 (October 7, 1991):302-04.

BOOKS

Hultkrantz, Ake. *Belief and Worship in Native North America*. Syracuse: Syracuse University Press, 1981.

GOVERNMENT DOCUMENTS

United States. *Joint Resolution, American Indian Religious Freedom*. Washington, D.C.: U.S. Government Printing Office, 1978.

U.S. Senate Select Committee on Indian Affairs. *Native Americans Right to Believe and Exercise their Traditional Native Religions Free of Federal Government*

Interference: Report. Washington, D.C.: U.S. Government Printing Office, 1978.

Economic Development

ARTICLES

Ambler, Marjane. "Settling Accounts." *Across the Board* 28 (June 1991):43-49.

Anderson, Terry L., and Dean Lueck. "Land Tenure and Agricultural Productivity on Indian Reservations." *The Journal of Law and Economics* 35 (October 1992):427-54.

Arrandale, Tom. "American Indian Economic Development." *Editorial Research Reports* 1 (1984):127-44.

Blanchard, David. "High Steel! The Kahnawake Mohawk and the High Steel Construction Trade." *Journal of Ethnic Studies* 11 (Summer 1983):41-60.

Carey, Richard Adams. "Approaching the Millennium." *The Massachusetts Review* 28 (Summer 1987):343-49.

Cohen, Daniel. "Tribal Enterprise." *The Atlantic* 264 (October 1989):32-34+.

Cornell, Stephen, and Joseph P. Kalt. "Pathways from Poverty: Economic Development and Institution-Building on American Indian Reservations." *American Indian Culture and Research Journal* 14 no.1 (1990):89-125.

Farlinger, Brian. "Aboriginal Entrepreneurs and the Banks (providing loans and non-credit services)." *Canadian Banker* 98 (March/April 1991):50-54.

Haycox, Stephen. "Economic Development and Indian Land Rights in Modern Alaska: The 1947 Tongass Timber Act." *The Western Historical Quarterly*, February 1990, 21-46.

Jacobsen, Cardell K. "Internal Colonialism and Native Americans: Indian Labor in the United States from 1871 to World War II." *Social Science Quarterly* 65 (1984):158-71.

Jamieson, Ron L. "A Canadian Challenge: Providing Opportunities for Native Business." *The Canadian Business Review* 17 (Winter 1990):33-35.

Katzer, Bruce. "The Caughnawaga Mohawks: The Other Side of Ironwork." *Journal of Ethnic Studies* 15 (Winter 1988):39-55.

La Duke, Winona, and Ward Churchill. "Native America: The Political Economy of Radioactive Colonialism." *Journal of Ethnic Studies* 13 (Fall 1985):107-132.

Meyer, Melissa L. "We can not get a living like we used to: Dispossession and the White Earth Anishinaabeg, 1889-1920," *The American Historical Review* 96 (April 1991):368-94.

O'Hare, William. "The Best States for Indians in Business." *American Demographics*, December 1991, 33.

Ourada, Patricia K. "Indians in the Work Force." *Journal of the West* 25 (April 1986):52-58.

Page, Vicki. "Reservation Development in the United States: Peripherality in the Core." *American Indian Culture and Research Journal* 9 (1985):21-35.

"Reviving Native Economies: Native Americans Working to Reverse Columbus' Legacy." *Dollars and Sense*, October 1991, 18-20.

Sandefur, Gary D., and Arthur Sakamoto. "American Indian Household Structure and Income." *Demography* 25 no.1 (February 1988):71-80.

Sandefur, Gary D., and Wilbur J. Scott. "Minority Group Status and the Wages of Indian and Black Males." *Social Science Research* 12 (March 1983):46-68.

Snipp, C. Matthew, and Alan L. Sorkin. "American Indian Housing: An Overview of Conditions and Public Policy." In *Race, Ethnicity, and Housing in the United States*. Edited by Jamshid A Momeni. Westport, CT: Greenwood Press, 1986.

Snipp, C. Matthew. "The Changing Political and Economic Status of the American Indians: From Captive Nations to Internal Colonies." *The American Journal of Economics and Sociology* 45 (April 1986):145-57.

BOOKS

Adams, Evelyn C. *American Indian Education: Government Schools and Economic Progress*. Morningside Heights, N.Y.: King's Crown Press, 1976.

Browe, F. Lee and Ingram, Helen M. *Water and Poverty in the Southwest*. Tucson: University of Arizona Press, 1987.

Carlson, Leonard Albert. *The Dawes Act and the Decline of Indian Farming*. Ph.D. Dissertation, Stanford University, 1977.

Champagne, Duane. *Politics, Markets and Social Structure: The Political and Economic Responses of Four Native American Societies to Western Impacts*." Ph.D. Dissertation, Harvard University Press, 1982.

Geisler, Charles C. et al. *Indian S.I.A.: The Social Impact Assessment of Rapid Resource Development on Native Peoples*. Monograph no. 3, Ann Arbor: Natural Resources Sociology Lab, University of Michigan, 1982.

Hansen, Niles. *Rural Poverty and the Urban Crisis*. Bloomington: Indiana University Press, 1970.

Lukaczer, Moses. *The Federal Buy Indian Program: Promise vs. Performance*. Reseda, CA.: Mojave Books, 1976.

Ortiz, Roxanne D. ed. *Economic Development in American Indian Reservations*. Albuquerque: University of New Mexico Native American Studies, 1979.

Reno, Phillip. *Navajo Resources and Economic Development*. Albuquerque: University of New Mexico Press, 1981.

Stanley, Sam ed. *American Indian Economic Development*. Chicago: Aldine, 1978.

Weiss, Lawrence D. *The Development of Capitalism in the Navajo Nation: The Political-Economic History*. Minneapolis: MEP Publications, 1984.

GOVERNMENT DOCUMENTS

U.S. Congress Committee on Interior and Insular Affairs. *Indian Economic Development Act: Hearings Before the Committee on Interior and Insular Affairs, House of Representatives, May 15 and October 2, 1986*. Washington D.C.: U.S. Government Printing Office, 1987.

U.S. Congress Joint Economic Committee and U.S. Congress Joint Economic Committee Subcommittee on Economy in Government. *American Indians: Facts and Future: Toward Economic Development for Native American Communities*. New York: Arno Press, 1970.

U.S. Congress Select Committee on Indian Affairs. *An American Indian Finance Development Finance Institution: a Compendium of Papers Submitted to the Senate Select Committee on Indian Affairs*. Washington, D.C.: U.S. Government Printing Office, 1987.

U.S. Congress Select Committee on Indian Affairs. *Buy Indian Act Amendments of 1989: Report*. Washington, D.C.: U.S. Government Printing Office, 1989.

Education

ARTICLES

Allison, Derek J. "Fourth World Education in Canada and the Faltering Promise of Native Teacher Education Programs." *Journal of Canadian Studies* 18 (Fall 1983):102-18.

Barquist, Rose, and Mary Lewis. "Growing up in the Alaska Bush with Head Start." *Children Today* 19 (May/June 1990):6-11.

Beaulieu, David. "The State of the Art: Indian Education in Minnesota." *Change: The Magazine of Higher Learning* 23, 2 (March/April 1991):31-35.

Brod, R.L., and J.M. McQuiston. "American Indian Adult Education and Literacy: The First National Survey." *Journal of American Indian Education* 1 (1983):1-16.

Carnegie Foundation for the Advancement of Teaching. "Native Americans and Higher Education: New Mood of Optimism." *Change* 22 (January/February 1990):27-30.

Coladarci, T. "High School Dropout among Native Americans." *Journal of American Indian Education* 23 (1983):15-22.

Ellis, Howard. "From the Battle in the Classroom to the Battle for the Classroom." *The American Indian Quarterly* 11 (Summer 1987):255-64.

Gipp, Gerald E. and Fox, Sandra J. "Education: The Real Hope for American Indians." *National Forum* 71 (Spring 1991):2-4.

Gipp, Gerald E. and Fox, Sandra J. "Promoting Cultural Relevance in American Indian Education." *The Education Digest* 57 (November 1991):58-61.

Haig-Brown, Celia. "Border Work." *Canadian Literature* 124/125 (Spring/Summer 1990):229-41.

Hill, Norbert. "AISES: A College Intervention Program That Works." *Change: The Magazine of Higher Learning* 23, 2 (March/April 1991), 24-30.

Kidwell, Clara Sue. "The Vanishing Native Reappears in the College Curriculum." *Change* 23, 2 (March/April 1991):19-23.

Mankiller, Wilma. "Education and Native Americans: Entering the Twenty-First Century on Our Own Terms." *National Forum* 71 (Spring 1991):5-6.

McCarty, T.L. "The Rough Rock Demonstration School: A Case History with Implications for Educational Evaluation." *Human Organization* 46 (Summer 1987):103-12.

_____. "School as Community: The Rough Rock Demonstration." *Harvard Educational Review* 59, 4 (November 1989):484-503.

McQuiston, John M., and Rodney L. Brod. "Structural and Cultural Conflict in American Indian Education." *The Education Digest* 50 (April 1985):28-31.

"Native Americans." *National Forum* 71 (Spring 1991):2-35.

"Native Americans and Higher Education: New Mood of Optimism." *Change* 22 (January/February 1990):27-30.

O'Brien, Eileen M. "Indians in Higher Education." *Research Briefs* 3, 3 (Washington, D.C.: American Council on Education, 1992).

_____. "The Demise of Native American Education." Three-part series. *Black Issues in Higher Education* (March 15, March 29, and April 12, 1990).

Paquette, Jerald. "Policy, Power and Purpose: Lessons from Two Indian Education Scenarios." *Journal of Canadian Studies* 24 (Summer 1989):78-94.

Ryan, F. "The Federal Role in American Indian Education." *Harvard Educational Review* 52 (November 1982):423-30.

Sanders, D. "Cultural Conflicts: An Important Factor in the Academic Failures of American Indian Students." *Journal of Multicultural Counselling and Development* 15 (1987):81-90.

Tierney, William G. "Native Voices in Academe: Strategies for Empowerment." *Change* 23, 2 (March/April 1991), 36-39.

Tierney, William G., and Clara Sue Kidwell, eds. "American Indians in Higher Education." (Special section with editorial comments by Tierney and Kidwell), *Change* 23 (March/April 1991):4-5, 11-26, 31-46.

"Tribal College Enrollment and Funding Statistics." American Indian Higher Education Consortium. Unpublished tabulations. (1992).

Wells, Robert N. Jr. "Indian Education from the Tribal Perspective: A Survey of American Indian Tribal Leaders." Unpublished paper. (January 1991).

_____. "The Native American Experience in Higher Education: Turning Around the Cycle of Failure." Presentation at Minorities in Higher Education conference sponsored by Hofstra University, March 10, 1989.

_____. "Tribal Cooperation in Educational Opportunities for Native Americans: Twenty Years of St. Regis

Mohawk-St. Lawrence University Association." Western Social Science Association Meeting. Denver, Colorado, April 30, 1988.

Wright, Bobby, and William G. Tierney. "American Indians in Higher Education." *Change* 23 (March/April 1991):11-18.

BOOKS

Adams, Evelyn C. *American Indian Education: Government Schools and Economic Development.* Morningside Heights, N.Y.: King's Crown Press, 1976.

Association of American Indians. *To Sing Our Own Songs: Cognition and Culture in Indian Education.* New York: Association of American Indians, 1985.

Astin, A.W. *Minorities in Higher Education.* San Francisco: Bass, 1982.

Carmack, William et al. *Native American Research Information Service.* Los Angeles: University of California American Indian Studies Center, 1983.

Fuchs, Estelle and Havighurst, Robert Jr. *To Live on this Earth: American Indian Education.* Garden City, N.Y.: Doubleday, 1972.

Gilliland, Hap. *Teaching the Native American.* Dubuque, Iowa: Kendall/Hunt Pub. Co., 1988.

Guyette, Susan and Heth, Charlotte. *Issues for the Future of American Indian Studies.* Los Angeles: University of California American Indian Studies Center, 1985.

Hyer, Sally. *One House, One Voice, One Heart: Native American Education at the Santa Fe Indian School.* Santa Fe: Museum of New Mexico Press, 1990.

Johnson, Basil. *Indian School Days*. Toronto: Key Porter Books, 1988.

La Fromboise, T. *Circles of Women: Professionalizaton Training For American Indian Women*. Newton, MA: Women's Educational Equity Press, 1989.

Nichols, Claude A. *Moral Education among the North American Indians*. New York: Teachers College, Columbia University, 1930.

Philps, Susan U. *The Invisible Culture: Communication in Classroom and Community on the Warm Springs Indian Reservation*. New York: Longman: 1983.

Reyhner, Jon. *Teaching the Indian Child: A Bilingual/Multicultural Approach*. Billings: Eastern Montana College, 1988.

Roessel, Robert A. *A Navajo Education, 1948-1978: Its Progress and its Problems*. Chinle, AZ: Rough Rock Press, 1979.

Selinger, Alphonse D. *The American Indian High School Dropout. The Magnitude of the Problem*. Portland: Northwest Regional Educational Laboratory, 1968.

Senese, Guy B. *Self Determination and the Social Education of Native Americans*. New York: Praeger, 1991.

Szasz, Margaret Connell. *Education and the American Indian: The Road to Self-Determination Since 1928*. Albuquerque: University of New Mexico Press, 1977.

Trennert, Robert A. *The Phoenix Indian School: Forced Assimilation in Arizona*. Norman: University of Oklahoma Press, 1988.

Unrau, William E. and Miner, H. Craig. *Tribal Dispossession and the Ottawa Indian University Fraud*. Norman: University of Oklahoma Press, 1985.

U.C.L.A. American Indian Studies Center. *Multicultural Education and the American Indian*. Los Angeles: University of California American Indian Studies Center, 1979.

Wax, Murray et al. *Formal Education in an American Indian Community: Peer Society and the Failure of Minority Education*. Prospect Heights: Waveland Press, 1989.

GOVERNMENT DOCUMENTS

Fries, Judith E. *The American Indian in Higher Education, 1975-76 to 1984-85*. Washington, D.C.: Center for Education Statistics, Office of Educational Research and Improvement, U.S. Department of Education, 1987.

Greenbaum, Paul. *Nonverbal Communications Between American Indian Children and their Teacher*. Lawrence, Kansas: Native American Research Associates, 1983.

Indian Education Training. *Alternatives in Indian Education: A Final Report*. Albuquerque: Indian Education Training, Inc., 1981.

Indian Nations at Risk Task Force, U.S. Department of Education. *Indian Nations at Risk: An Educational Strategy for Action*. Washington, D.C.: U.S. Government Printing Office, 1991.

Kidwell, Clara Sue. *Motivating American Indians into Graduate Studies*. Las Cruces, N.M.: ERIC Clearinghouse on Rural Education and Small Schools, 1986.

Tonemah, Stuart. *Trends in American Indian Education: A Synthesis and Bibliography of Selected ERIC Resources*. Las Cruces, N.M.: ERIC Clearinghouse on Rural Education and Small Schools, New Mexico State University; Tempe, AZ.: Center for Indian Education, Arizona State University, 1984.

U.S. Bureau of Education Staff. *Bilingual Education for American Indians*. New York: Arno Press, 1978.

U.S. Bureau of Indian Affairs Staff. *Statistics of Indian Tribes, Agencies and Schools*. Washington, D.C.: U.S. Government Printing Office, 1903.

U.S. General Accounting Office. *The Bureau of Indian Affairs Should Do More to Educate Indian Students*. Washington, D.C.: The Office, 1977.

U.S. Senate Select Committee on Indian Affairs. *Indian Juvenile Alcoholism and Eligibility for B.I.A. Schools*. Washington, D.C.: U.S. Government Printing Office, 1985.

U.S. Senate Select Committee on Indian Affairs. *Culturally Early Education Programs: Hearing Before the Senate Select Committee on Indian Affairs, November 24, 1987*. Washington, D.C.: U.S. Government Printing Office, 1988.

U.S. Senate Special Subcommittee on Indian Education. *Indian Education: A National Tragedy—A National Challenge. 1969 Report of the Committee on Labor and Public Welfare*, (91st Congress, 1st Session). Washington, D.C.: U.S. Government Printing Office, 1969.

Gambling

ARTICLES

Angle, Marth. "High Stakes Bingo to Continue: Congress Clears Legislation to Regulate Indian Gambling." *Congressional Quarterly Weekly Report* 46 (October 1988):2730.

Berg, Senator Charles A. "Gambling and Cities." *Minnesota Cities* 76 (November 1991):6-11.

DeDomenecis. "Betting on Indian Rights." *California Lawyer* 29 (September 1983):29-31.

Guzman. "Indian Gambling on Reservations." *Arizona Law Review* 24 (1982):209-12.

Sokolow, Gary. "The Future of Gambling in Indian Country." *American Indian Law Review* 15 no.1 (1990):151-83.

BOOKS

Eadington, William ed. *Indian Gaming and the Law*. Reno: University of Nevada Press, 1990.

GOVERNMENT DOCUMENTS

United States. *An Act to Regulate Gaming on Indian Lands*. Washington, D.C.: U.S. Government Printing Office, 1988.

United States Congress. *Indian Gaming Regulatory Act: An Act to Regulate Gaming on Indian Land*. Washington, D.C.: U.S. Government Printing Office, 1988.

United States Congress Committee on Interior and Insular Affairs. *Indian Gaming Regulatory Act: Hearing Before the Committee on Interior and Insular Affairs, June 25, 1987*. Washington, D.C.: U.S. Government Printing Office, 1989.

United States Congress Senate Select Committee on Indian Affairs. *Establish Federal Standards and Regulations for the Conduct of Gaming Activities Within Indian Country: Hearing Before the Senate Select Committee on Indian Affairs, June 17, 1986*. Washington, D.C.: U.S. Government Printing Office, 1986.

United States Congress Senate Select Committee on Indian Affairs. *Gambling on Indian Reservations and Lands: Hearing Before the Senate Select Committee on Indian Affairs, June 26, 1985*. Washington, D.C.: U.S. Government Printing Office, 1985.

Health — General

ARTICLES

Barsh, Russel Lawrence. "Are Anthropologists Hazardous to Indians' Health?" *The Journal of Ethnic Studies* 15 (Winter 1988):1-38.

Boyum, W. "Health Care: An Overview of the Indian Health Service." *American Indian Law Review* 14 (1989):241-67.

Campbell, Gregory R. "The Changing Dimension of Native American Health: A Critical Understanding of Contemporary Native American Health Issues." *American Indian Culture and Research Journal* 13 nos. 3&4 (1989):1-20.

Haroldson, Sixten S.R. "Health and Health Services Among the Navajo Indians." *Journal of Community Health* 13 (Fall 1988):129-42.

"Health Care for Indigent American Indians." *Arizona State Law Journal* 20 (1988):1105-148.

Mazzola, Lars Charles. "The Medicine Wheel: Center and Periphery." *Journal of Popular Culture* 22 (Fall 1988):63-73.

Samet, M.J. et al. "Uranium Mining and Lung Cancer Among Navajo Men." *New England Journal of Medicine* 310 (1984):1481-484.

Young, T. Kue. "Indian Health Services in Canada: A Sociohistorical Perspective." *Social Science and Medicine*

18 no.3 (1984):257-64.

BOOKS

Locust, Carol. *American Indian Beliefs Concerning Health and Unwellness.* Tucson: Native American Research and Training Center, College of Medicine, University of Arizona.

Torrey, E. Fuller et al. *Community Health and Mental Health Care for North American Indians.* New York: MSS Information Corp., 1975.

GOVERNMENT DOCUMENTS

U.S. Congress Committee on Energy and Commerce. Subcommittee on Health and the Environment. *Indian Health Care: An Overview of the Federal Government's Role: a staff report.* Washington, D.C.: U.S. Government Printing Office, 1984.

U.S. Congress Committee on Interior and Insular Affairs. *Indian Health Care Improvement Act: A Report of the Committee on Interior and Insular Affairs, U.S. House of Representatives,* Washington, D.C.: U.S. Government Printing Office, 1976.

U.S. Department of Health and Human Services. *Indian Health Service Chart Series Book, April 1988.* Washington, D.C.: U.S. Government Printing Office, 1988.

U.S. Indian Health Services. *Indian Health Service: A Comprehensive Health Care Program for American Indians and Alaska Natives.* Rockville, MD.: U.S. Department of Health and Human Service, Public Health Service, Health Resources and Services Administration, Indian Health Service, 1985.

U.S. Office of Technology Assessment. *Indian Health Care.* Washington, D.C.: U.S. Government Printing Office, 1986.

U.S. Office of Technology Assessment. *Indian Health Care: A Summary.* Washington, D.C.: U.S. Government Printing Office, 1986.

U.S. Office of Technology Assessment. *Survey of Urban Indian Health Programs.* Washington, D.C.: U.S. Government Printing Office, 1985.

U.S. Senate Select Committee on Indian Affairs. *The Urban Indian Health Equity Act: A Report.* Washington, D.C.: U.S. Government Printing Office, 1990.

Health — Alcoholism

ARTICLES

Edwards, E. Daniel, and Margie E. Edwards. "Alcoholism Prevention/Treatment and Native American Youth: A Community Approach." *Journal of Drug Issues* 18 (Winter 1988):103-14.

Fisher, A.D. "Alcoholism and Race: The Misapplication of Both Concepts to North American Indians." *The Canadian Review of Sociology and Anthropology* 24 (February 1987):81-98.

Grobsmith, Elizabeth S. "The Relationship Between Substance Abuse and Crime Among Native American Inmates in the Nebraska Department of Corrections." *Human Organization* 48 (Winter 1989):285-98.

Lamarine, Roland J. "Alcohol Abuse Among Native Americans." *Journal of Community Health* 13 no. 3 (Fall 1988):143-55.

May, Philip A. "Alcohol and Drug Misuse Prevention Programs for American Indians: Needs and

Opportunities." *Journal of Studies on Alcohol* 47 (May 1986):187-95.

_____. "Substance Abuse and American Indians: Prevalence and Susceptibility." *International Journal of the Addictions* 17 (1981):1185-209.

Oetting, E.R., Fred Beauvais, and Ruth Edwards. "Alcohol and Indian Youth: Social and Psychological Correlates and Prevention." *Journal of Drug Issues* 18 (Winter 1988):87-101.

Watts, Thomas D., and Ronald G. Lewis. "Alcoholism and Native American Youth: An Overview." *Journal of Drug Issues* 18 (Winter 1988):69-86.

Weibel-Orlando, J. "Substance Abuse Among American Indian Youth: A Continuing Crisis." *Journal of Drug Issues* 14 (1984):313-33.

BOOKS

Brown, Donald N.; Everett, Michael W.; and Waddell, Jack. *Drinking Behavior Among Southwestern Indians: An Anthropological Perspective.* Tucson: University of Arizona Press, 1978.

Eitzen, D. Stanley. *Social Problems.* Boston: Allyn and Bacon, 1983.

Frederick, Calvin J. *Suicide, Homicide and Alcoholism Among American Indians: Guidelines for Help.* Rockville, MD: National Institute of Mental Health, 1973.

Hamer, John H. *Alcohol and Native Peoples of the North.* Lanham, MD: University Press of America, 1980.

Leland, Joy H. *Firewater Myths: North American Indian Drinking and Alcohol Addiction.* New Brunswick, N.J.: Rutgers Center of Alcohol Studies, 1976.

National Institute of Alcohol Abuse and Alcoholism. *Alcohol and American Indians.* Rockville, MD: National Clearinghouse for Alcohol Information, 1980.

GOVERNMENT DOCUMENTS

U.S. Congress. *Indian Alcohol and Substance Abuse Prevention and Treatment Act of 1986.* Washington, D.C.: U.S. Government Printing Office, 1986.

U.S. Congress Select Committee on Indian Affairs. *Indian Juvenile Alcohol and Drug Abuse Prevention: Hearing Before the Senate Select Committee on Indian Affairs.* Washington, D.C.: U.S. Government Printing Office, 1985.

U.S. Congress Select Committee on Indian Affairs. *Indian Juvenile Alcoholism and Eligibility for B.I.A. Schools.* Washington, D.C.: U.S. Government Printing Office, 1985.

U.S. Indian Health Service. *A Progress Report on Indian Alcoholism Activities.* Rockville, MD.: U.S. Department of Health and Human Services, Public Health Service, 1988.

U.S. Indian Health Service. *Alcoholism: A High Priority Health Problem.* Washington, D.C.: U.S. Government Printing Office, 1977.

Vandarwagen, Craig; Mason, Russell D. and Owan, Tom Choken. *IHS Alcoholism/Substances Abuse Prevention Initiative: Background, Plenary Session, and Action Plan.* Rockville, MD.: U.S. Department of Health and Human Services, Public Health Service, Health Resources and Services Administration, Indian Health Service, Office of Health Programs, Alcoholism/Substance Abuse Program Branch, 1985.

Health — Mental Health

ARTICLES

Bagley, Christopher. "Poverty and Suicide Among Native Canadians: A Replication." *Psychological Reports* 69 (August 1991):149-50.

Berlin, I.N. "Prevention of Adolescent Suicide Among Some Native American Tribes." *Adolescent Psychiatry* 12 (1985):77-92.

_____. "Psychopathology and its Antecedents Among American Indian Adolescents." *Advances in Clinical Child Psychology* 9 (1986):125-52.

Kelso, Dianne R., and Carolyn L. Attneave, eds. *Bibliography of North American Indian Mental Health.* Greenwood: Greenwood Press, 1981.

La Fromboise, Teresa. "American Indian Mental Health Policy." *American Psychologist* 45 no. 51 (1988):388-97.

Levy, Jerrold E. "Navajo Suicide." *Human Organization* 24 (1965):308-18.

Levy, Jerrold E. and Stephen J. Kunitz. "Suicide Prevention Program for Hopi Youth." *Social Science and Medicine* 25 (1987):931-40.

May, Phillip A. "Suicide and Self-Destruction Among American Indian Youths." *American Indian and Alaska Native American Mental Health Research: Journal of the National Center* 1 no. 1 (June 1987):52-69.

Mc Shane, Damian. "Mental Health and North American Indian/Native Communities: Cultural Transactions, Education, and Regulation." *American Journal of Community* 15:95-116.

Medicine, B.   "Native American Women Look at Mental Health." *Plainswoman* 6 no. 7 (1982).

Meketon, Melvin Jerry.   "Indian Mental Health: An Orientation." *American Journal of Orthopsychiatry* 53 (January 1983):110-15.

Old Dog Cross, P.   "Sexual Abuse: A New Threat to the Native Woman: An Overview." *Listening Post: A Periodical of the Mental Health Programs of the Indian Health Service* 6 no. 2 (1982):18.

BOOKS

Bachman, Ronet. *Death and Violence on the Reservation: Homicide, Suicide and Family Violence in American Indian Populations.* Dover, MA: Auburn House, Forthcoming.

McIntosh, John L. *Suicide Among U.S. Racial-Ethnic Minorities 1985-1988: A Comprehensive Bibliography.* Monticello: Vance Bibliographies, 1988.

Pedersen, P. ed. *Handbook of Cross-Cultural Mental Health Services.* Beverly Hills, CA: Sage, 1985.

Torrey, E. Fuller et al.   *Community Health and Mental Health Care Delivery for North American Indians.* New York: MSS Information Corp., 1974.

GOVERNMENT DOCUMENTS

Attneave, Carolyn L. *Mental Health Programs of the Indian Health Service.* Rockville, MD : Department of Health, Education, and Welfare, Public Health Service, Health Service Administration, Indian Health Service, 1975.

Harras, A. *Issues in Adolescent Indian Health: Suicide.* Washington, D.C.: U.S. Department of Health and

Human Services, 1987.

U.S. Office of Technology Assessment. *Indian Adolescent Mental Health*. Washington, D.C.: Congress of the United States, Office of Technology Assessment, 1990.

Health — Violence

ARTICLES

Bachman, Ronet. "An Analysis of American Indian Homicide: A Test of Social Disorganization and Economic Deprivation at the Reservation County Level." *Journal of Research in Crime and Delinquency* 28 no. 4 (November 1991):456-71.

_____. "The Social Causes of American Indian Homicide as Revealed by the Life Experiences of Thirty Offenders." *The American Indian Quarterly* 15 (Fall 1991):469-92.

Fischler, R.S. "Child Abuse and Neglect in American Indian Communities." *Child Abuse and Neglect* 9 (1985):95-106.

Old Dog Cross, P. "Sexual Abuse: A New Threat to the Native Woman: An Overview." *Listening Post: A Periodical of the Mental Health Programs of the Indian Health Service*. 6 no. 2 (1982):18.

Peak, Ken and Jack Spencer. "Crime in Indian Country: Another 'Trail of Tears.'" *Journal of Criminal Justice* 15 no. 6 (1987):485-94.

Reed, Little Rock. "The American Indian in the White Man's Prisons: A Story of Genocide." *Humanity and Society* 13 no. 4 (November 1989):403-20.

BOOKS

Bachman, Ronet. *Death and Violence on the Reservation:*

Homicide, Suicide and Family Violence in American Indian Populations. Dover, MA: Auburn House, Forthcoming.

Pagelow, M.D. *Family Violence.* New York: Praeger, 1984.

Identity

ARTICLES

Cornell, Stephen. "The Transformation of Tribe: Organization and Self-Concept in Native American Ethnicities." *Ethnic and Racial Studies* 11 (January 1988):27-47.

Harmon, Alexandra. "When is an Indian not an Indian? The 'Friends of the Indian' and the Problems of Indian Identity." *Journal of Ethnic Studies* 18 (Summer 1990):95-123.

Jarvenpa, Robert. "The Political Economy and Political Ethnicity of American Indian Adaptations and Identities." *Ethnic and Racial Studies* 8 (January 1985):29-48.

Landsman, Gail H. "The 'other' as Political Symbol: Images of Indians in the Woman Sufferage Movement." *Ethnohistory* 39 (Summer 1992):247-84.

"Native Americans: In Search of an Identity." *Scholastic Update* 121 (May 26,1989):2-12.

Porter, Frank W. "In Search of Recognition: Federal Indian Policy and the Landless Tribes of Western Washington." *The American Indian Quarterly* 15 (Spring 1990):113-32.

Snipp, C. Mathew. "Who are American Indians? Some Observations About the Perils of Data for Race and Ethnicity." *Population Research and Policy Review* 5 no. 3 (1986):337-52.

Warrior, Robert Allen. "Indian Youth: Emerging into Identity." *Christianity and Crisis* 50 (March 19, 1990):82-86.

BOOKS

Ashabranner, Brent. *To Live in Two Worlds: American Indian Youth Today.* New York: Putnam Publishing Group, date not set.

Clifton, James A. *Being and Becoming Indian.* Belmont, CA.: Dorsey, 1988.

Fritz, Henry L. *The Movement for Indian Assimilation.* Philadelphia: University of Pennsylvania Press, 1963.

Hertzberg, Hazel W. *Search for an American Indian Identity: Modern Pan-Indian Movements.* Syracuse: Syracuse University Press, 1971.

Hoxie, Frederick E. *A Final Promise: The Campaign to Assimilate the Indians, 1880-1920.* Lincoln: University of Nebraska Press, 1984.

Trafzer, Clifford E. *American Indian Identity: Today's Changing Perspective.* New Castle, CA: Sierra Oaks Publishers, 1989.

Trennert, Robert A. *The Phoenix Indian School: Forced Assimilation in Arizona.* Norman: University of Oklahoma Press, 1988.

GOVERNMENT DOCUMENTS

Warm Springs Reservation Committee. *Being Indian Is...* Washington, D.C.: National Institute of Education, U.S. Government Printing Office, 1981.

Land Tenure/Claims

ARTICLES

Carey, Richard Adams. "Approaching the Millennium." *The Massachusetts Review* 28 (Summer 1987):343-49.

Churchill, Ward. "American Indian Lands: The Native Ethic Amid Resource Development." *Environment* 28 (July/August 1986):72-77.

Drew, Lisa. "Here is Your Land, Now Make Money." *National Wildlife* 30 (December 1991, January 1992):38-45.

Erdrich, Louise, and Michael Dorris. "Who Owns the Land?" *The New York Times Magazine*, September 4, 1988:32-35.

Gordon-McCutchan, R.C. "The Battle for Blue Lake: A Struggle for Indian Religious Rights." *Journal of Church and State* 33 (Autumn 1991):785-97.

Hall, G. Emlen. "Land Litigation and the Idea of New Mexico Progress." *Journal of the West* 27 (July 1988):48-58.

Haycox, Stephen. "Economic Development and Indian Land Rights in Modern Alaska: The 1947 Tongass Timber Act." *The Western Historical Quarterly*, February 1990:21-46.

Slagle, Al Logan. "Unfinished Justice: Completing the Restoration and Acknowledgement of California Indian Tribes." *The American Indian Quarterly* 13:325-45.

Sorenson, Jean. "Truck Loggers Look at Indian Land Claims." *Forest Industries* 118 (April 1991):44.

Whyte, Kenn. "Aboriginal Rights: The Native American's Struggle for Survival." *Human Organization* 41 (Summer 1982):178-84.

BOOKS

Berry, Mary C. *The Alaska Pipeline, the Politics of Oil and Native Land Claims.* Bloomington: Indiana University Press, 1975.

Cronon, William. *Changes in the Land: Indians, Colonists, and the Ecology of New England.* New York: Hill and Wang, 1983.

Deloria, Vine Jr. *We Talk, You Listen: New Tribes, New Turf.* New York: Macmillan, 1970.

Gordon-McCutchan, R.C. *The Taos Indians and the Battle for Blue Lake.* Santa Fe: Red Crane Books, 1991.

Kinney, J.P. *A Continent Lost-A Civilization Won: Indian Land Tenure in America.* New York: Arno Press, 1975.

McDonnel, Janet A. *The Dispossession of the American Indian.* Bloomington: Indiana University Press, 1991.

Matthiessen, Peter. *Indian Country.* New York: Viking Press, 1984.

Parker, Linda S. *Native American Estate: The Struggle over Indian and Hawaiian Lands.* Honolulu: University of Hawaii Press, 1989.

Slattery, Brian. *Ancestral Lands, Alien Laws: Judicial Perspective on Aboriginal Title.* Saskatoon, Saskatchewan: Native Law Centre, University of Saskatchewan, 1983.

Sutton, Imre. *Indian Land Tenure: Bibliographical Essays and a Guide to the Literature.* New York: Clearwater, 1975.

_____. *Irredeemable America, The Indian's Estate and Land Claims.* Albuquerque: University of New Mexico Press, 1985.

Vecsey, Christopher and Starna, William A. *Iroquois Land Claims.* Syracuse: Syracuse University Press, 1988.

Resources — General

ARTICLES

Allen, Mark. "Native American Control of Tribal Natural Resource Development in the Context of the Federal Trust and Tribal Self-Determination." *Boston College Environmental Affairs Law Review* 16 (Summer 1989):857-95.

Magnuson, Jon W. "Little Big Victory." *Christianity and Crisis* 49 (March 20, 1989):85-87.

Snipp, C. Matthew. "American Indians and Natural Resource Development: Indigenous People's Land, Now Sought After, has Produced New Indian-White Problems." *The American Journal of Economics and Sociology* 45 (October 1986):457-74.

BOOKS

Americans for Indian Opportunity. *Indian Tribes as Developing Nations: A Question of Power: Indian Control of Indian Resource Development.* The Hague: Mouton Publishers, 1978.

Burton, Lloyd. *American Indian Water Rights and the Limit of the Law.* Lawrence: University of Kansas Press, 1991.

Geisler, Charles C. et al. *Indian S.I.A.: The Social Impact Assessment of Rapid Resource Development on Native Peoples.* Ann Arbor: Natural Resources Sociology Research Lab, University of Michigan, 1982.

Matheny, Ray T. and Berge, Dale L. eds. *Symposium on Dynamics of Cultural Resource Management.*

Albuquerque: Department of Agriculture, Forest Service, Southwestern Region, 1976.

Reno, Phillip. *Navajo Resources and Economic Development.* Albuquerque: University of New Mexico Press, 1981.

Resources — Energy

BOOKS

Iverson, Peter. *The Plains Indians of the Twentieth Century.* Norman: University of Oklahoma Press, 1985.

Jorgenson, Joseph G. *Native Americans and Energy Development II.* Boston: Anthropology Resource Center and Seventh Generation Fund, 1984.

Jorgenson, Joseph G.; Clemmer, Richard O.; Little, Ronald L.; Owens, Nancy J. and Robbins, Lynn A. *Native Americans and Energy Development.* Cambridge: Anthropology Resource Center, 1978.

Wilson, Terry P. *The Underground Reservation: Osage Oil.* Lincoln: University of Nebraska Press, 1985.

Resources — Fishing/Hunting

ARTICLES

Boxberger, Daniel L. "The Lummi Indians and the Canadian/American Pacific Salmon Treaty." *The American Indian Quarterly* 12 (Fall 1988):299-311.

Gmelch, George. "Two Rivers, Two Cultures." *Natural History* 97 (May 1988):52-63.

Meyers, G.D. "Different Sides of the Same Coin: A Comparative View of Indian Hunting and Fishing Rights in the United States and Canada." *U.C.L.A. Journal of Environmental Law and Policy* 25 (1991):67-121.

Ott, Brian Richard. "Indian Fishing Rights in the Pacific Northwest: The Need for Federal Intervention." *Boston College Environmental Affairs Law Review* 14:313-43.

Parman, Donald. "Inconstant Advocacy: The Erosion of Indian Fishing Rights in the Pacific Northwest, 1933-1956." *Pacific Historical Review.* 53 (May 1984):163-89.

Parmentier, David. "Mississippi of the North." *The Humanist* 49 (September/October 1989):17-1+.

Reynolds. "Indian Hunting and Fishing Rights: The Role of Tribal Sovereignty and Preemption." *North Carolina Law Review* 62 (1984):743.

"Where do the Buffalo Roam? Determining the Scope of American Indian Off-reservation Hunting Rights in the Pacific Northwest." *Washington Law Review* 67 (January 1992):175-94.

Wilkinson, Charles F. "To Feel the Summer in the Spring: the Treaty Fishing Rights of the Wisconsin Chippewa." *Wisconsin Law Review* no. 3 (1991):375-414.

BOOKS

Cohen, Fay G. et al. *Treaties on Trial: The Continuing Controversy over Northwest Indian Fishing Rights.* Seattle: University of Washington Press, 1986.

GOVERNMENT DOCUMENTS

U.S. House Committee on Merchant Marine and Fisheries. Subcommittee on Fisheries and Wildlife Conservation and the Environment. *Indian Fishing Rights—Fishery Management: Hearings Before the Subcommittee on*

Fisheries and Wildlife Conservation. Washington, D.C.: U.S. Government Printing Office, 1980.

U.S. Senate Select Committee on Indian Affairs. *Clarifying Indian Treaties and Executive Orders with Respect Fishing Rights: A Report.* Washington, D.C.: U.S. Government Printing Office, 1987.

Resources — Minerals

ARTICLES

La Duke, Winona. "The History of Uranium Mining." *Black Hills/Paha Sapa Report.* 1 no.1 (1979).

GOVERNMENT DOCUMENTS

United States. *Indian Mineral Development Act of 1982.* Washington, D.C.: U.S. Government Printing Office, 1983.

U.S. Senate Select Committee on Indian Affairs. *Indian Mineral Development: Hearings Before the Select Committee on Indian Affairs, U.S. Senate, February 12, 1982.* Washington, D.C.: U.S. Government Printing Office, 1982.

U.S. Senate Select Committee on Indian Affairs. *Regulation of Coal Mining on Indian Reservation Lands: Hearing Before the Select Committee on Indian Affairs, U.S. Senate, February 10, 1992.* Washington, D.C.: U.S. Government Printing Office, 1984.

U.S. House Committee on Interior and Insular Affairs. Subcommittee on Energy and the Environment. *Regulation of Surface Mining on Indian Lands: Oversight Hearing Before the Subcommittee on Energy and the Environment, March 19, 1984.* Washington, D.C.: U.S. Government Printing Office, 1984.

Resources — Water

ARTICLES

Burton, L. "The American Indian Water Rights Dilemma: Historical Perspective and Dispute Settling Policy Recommendations." *U.C.L.A. Journal of Environmental Law and Policy* 7 (1987):1-66.

Dumars and Ingram. "Congressional Quantification of Indian Water Rights: A Definite Solution or a Mirage?" *Natural Resources Journal* 20 (1980).

Membrino, J.R. "Indian Reserved Water Rights, Federalism and the Trust Responsibility." *Land and Water Law Review* 27 (1992):1-31.

Moore, Michael R. "Native American Water Rights: Efficiency and Fairness." *Natural Resources Journal* 29 (Summer 1989):763-91.

Shupe. "Water in Indian Country: From Paper Rights to a Managed Resource." *University of Colorado Law Review* 57 (1986):561.

Wilkinson, Charles F. "To Feel the Summer in the Spring: The Treaty Fishing Rights of the Wisconsin Chippewa." *Wisconsin Law Review* 3 (1991):375-414.

BOOKS

Browe, F. Lee and Ingram, Helen M. *Water and Poverty in the Southwest*. Tucson: University of Arizona Press, 1987.

Burton, Lloyd. *American Indian Water Rights and the Limits of the Law*. University of Kansas, 1991.

McCool, Daniel. *Command of the Waters: Iron Triangles, Federal Water Development and Indian Water*. Berkeley: University of California Press, 1987.

Treaties

ARTICLES

Boxberger, Daniel L. "The Lummi Indians and the Canadian/American Pacific Salmon Treaty." *The American Indian Quarterly* 12 (Fall 1988):299-311.

"Congressional Abrogation of Indian Treaties: Reevaluation and Reform." *Yale Law Journal* 98 (February 1989):793-812.

Morse, Mary. "New Battle over Indian Rights." *Utne Reader*, May/June 1990:39-40.

Nicolai, Dan. "Parmenter, David. "Mississippi of the North." *The Humanist* 49 (September/October 1989):17-19+.

BOOKS

Akwasasne Notes. *Trail of Broken Treaties: "B.I.A.: I'm Not Your Indian Anymore."* Mohawk Nation, Rooseveltón, N.Y.: Akwasasne Notes, 1974.

Deloria, Vine Jr. *Behind the Trail of Broken Treaties: An Indian Declaration of Independence.* Austin: University of Texas Press, 1985.

Du Puy, Henry F. *A Bibliography of the English Colonial Treaties with the American Indians.* Irvine: Reprint Services, 1988.

Jennings, Francis and Fenton, William. *The History and Culture of Iroquois Diplomacy: An Interdisciplinary Guide to the Treaties of Six Nations and their League.* Syracuse: Syracuse University Press, 1985.

Juricek, John T. *Early American Indian Documents, Treaties and Laws.* Washington, D.C.: University Publications of America, 1987.

Morris, Alexander. *The Treaties of Canada with Indians of Manitoba and Northwest Territories.* Toronto: Willing and Williamson, 1880.

Vaughan, Alden. *Early American Indian Documents: Treaties and Laws, 1607-1789.* Washington, D.C.: University Publications of America, 1979.

GOVERNMENT DOCUMENTS

Kappler, Charles J. *Indian Affairs: Laws and Treaties.* Washington, D.C.: U.S. Government Printing Office, 1904-1941.

Tribal Sovereignty

ARTICLES

"The Aftermath of Duro v. Reina: A Congressional Attempt to Reaffirm Tribal Sovereignty through Criminal Jurisdiction over Non-member Indians." *Cooley Law Review* 8 (1991):573-607.

Ambler, Marjane. "Settling Accounts." *Across the Board* 28 (June 1991):43-49.

Annette, Jaimes M. "Federal Indian Identification Policy: Usurpation of Indigenous Sovereignty." *Policy Studies Journal* 16 (1988):788-98.

Bee, Robert L. "The Predicament of the Native American Leader: A Second Look." *Human Organization* 49 (Spring 1990):56-63.

Berkey, Curtis. "Indian Nations Under Legal Assault: New Restrictions on Native Sovereignty: Are they Constitutional? Are the Moral?" *Human Rights* 16 (Winter 1989/1990):18-23+.

Brandfon, Fredric. "Tradition and Judicial Review in the American Indian Tribal Court System." *U.C.L.A. Law Review* 38:991-1018.

Core, M. Allen. "Tribal Sovereignty: Federal Court Review of Tribal Court Decisions—Judicial Intrusion into Tribal Sovereignty." *American Indian Law Review* 13 (1985):175-92.

"The Decline of Tribal Sovereignty: The Journey from Dicta to Dogma in Duro v. Reina, 110 S. Ct. 2053." *Washington Law Review* 66 (April 1991):567-86.

Emerson, L. "Self Determination through Culture and Thought Processes." Paper presented at The Indigenous Peoples' World Conference, Vancouver, University of British Columbia, Canada.

Iverson, Peter. "Building Toward Self Determination: Plains and Southwestern Indians in the 1940's and 1950's." *The Western Historical Quarterly* 17 (April 1985):167-73.

Morgan, E.M. "Self Government and the Constitution: A Comparative Look at Native Canadians and the American Indians." *American Indian Law Review* 12 (1984):39-56.

"Native Americans." *National Forum* 71 (Spring 1991):2-35.

Newton, N.J. "Federal Power over Indians: Its Sources, Scope and Limitations." *University of Pennsylvania Law Review* 132 (January 1984):195-288.

O'Brien, Sharon. "Tribes and Indians: With Whom Does the United States Maintain a Relationship?" *Notre Dame Law Review* 66 (1991):1461-94.

Peak, Ken. "Criminal Justice, Law and Policy in Indian Country: A Historical Perspective." *Journal of Criminal Justice* 17 no.5 (1989):393-407.

Pommersheim and Pechota. "Tribal Immunity, Tribal Courts and the Federal System: Emerging Contours and Fronteirs." *South Dakota Law Review* 31 no. 553 (1986).

Porter, R.B. "The Jurisdictional Relationship Between the Iroquois and New York State: An Analysis of 25 U.S.C. 232, 233." *Harvard Journal on Legislation* 27 (Summer 1990):497-577.

"A Proposed Solution to the Problem of State Jurisdiction to Tax on Indian Reservations." *Gonzaga Law Review* 26 (1990/1991):627-59.

Quinn, William W. Jr. "Federal Acknowledgement of American Indian Tribes: The Historical Development of a Legal Concept." *American Journal of Legal History* 34 no. 4 (1990):331-64.

Resnik, Judith. "Dependent Sovereigns: Indian Tribes, States and the Federal Court." *University of Chicago Law Review* 56 (1989):671-759.

Reynolds. "Indian Hunting and Fishing Rights: The Role of Tribal Sovereignty and Preemption." *North Carolina Law Review* 62 (1984):743.

"Self-determination for Native Americans: Land Rights and the Utility of Domestic and International Law." *Columbia Human Rights Law Review* 22 (Spring 1991):361-400.

"Self-determination: Indians and the United Nations—The Anomalous Status of America's 'Domestic Dependent Nations.'" *American Indian Law Review* 8 (Summer 1980):97-116.

"Tribal Businesses and the Uncertain Reach of Tribal Sovereign Immunity: A Statutory Solution." *Washington Law Review* 67 (January 1992):113-32.

Trosper, Ronald L. "Multicriterion Decision-Making in a Tribal Context." *Policy Studies Journal* 16 (Summer 1988):826-42.

Vachon, Robert. "Political Self-Determination and Traditional Native Indian Political Culture." *Interculture Journal* 12 (1979).

Volkman, John. "Tribal Sovereignty and Federal Indian Policy." *Christianity and Crisis* 49 (September 11, 1989):265-68.

Williams, Walter L. "Twentieth Century Indian Leaders: Brokers and Providers." *Journal of the West* 23 (July 1984):1-6.

Worthen, K.J. "Sword or Shield: The Past and Future Impact of Western Legal Thought on American Indian Sovereignty." *Harvard Law Review* 104 (April 1991):1372-92.

BOOKS

American Indian Resource Institute. *Indian Tribes as Sovereign Governments*. Oakland, CA: American Indian Lawyer Training Program Inc., 1987.

Barsh, Russel Lawrence and Henderson, James Youngblood. *The Road: Indian Tribes and Political Liberty*. Berkeley: University of California Press, 1981.

Cornell, Stephen. *The Return of the Native: American Indian Political Resurgence*. New York: Oxford University Press, 1988.

Deloria, Vine Jr. and Lytle, Clifford M. *American Indians, American Justice*. Austin: University of Texas Press, 1983.

_____. *The Nations Within: The Past and Future of*

American Indian Sovereignty. New York: Pantheon Books, 1984.

Goldberg, Carole E. *Public Law 280: State Jurisdiction over Reservation Lands.* Los Angeles: University of California American Indian Culture and Research Center, 1975.

Little Bear, Leroy et al. *Pathways to Self Determination: Canadian Indians and the Canadian State.* Toronto: University of Toronto Press, 1984.

Lopach, James J. et al. *Tribal Government Today: Politics on Montana's Indian Reservations.* Boulder, CO: Westview, 1990.

McBeath, Gerald and Morehouse, Thomas A. *The Dynamics of Alaska Native Self Government.* Lanham, MA: University Press of America, 1980.

Miner, Craig H. *The Corporation and the Indian: Tribal Sovereignty and Industrial Civilization in Indian Territory, 1865-1970.* Norman: University of Oklahoma Press, 1989.

O'Brien, Sharon. *American Indian Tribal Governments.* Norman: University of Oklahoma Press, 1989.

Philp, Kenneth R. *Indian Self-Rule: First-Hand Accounts of Indian-White Relations From Roosevelt to Reagan.* Salt Lake City: Howe Brothers, 1986.

Tickner, J. Ann. *Self Reliance vs. Power Politics: American and Indian Experiences in Building Nation-States.* New York: Columbia University Press, 1987.

Urban Indians

ARTICLES

Burt, Larry W. "Roots of the Native American Urban

Experience: Relocation Policy in the 1950's." *The American Indian Quarterly* 10 (Spring 1986):85-99.

Fine. "Off-Reservation Enforcement of the Federal Indian Trust Responsibility." *Public Land Law Review* 7 (1986):117-33.

Fiske, Shirley J. "Urban Indian Institutions: A Reappraisal from Los Angeles." *Urban Anthropology* 8 no.2 (1979):149-71.

Liebow, Edward D. "Category or Community? Measuring Urban Indian Social Cohesion with Network Sampling." *Journal of Ethnic Studies* 16 no.4 (Winter 1989):67-100.

_____. "Urban Indian Institutions in Phoenix: Transformation from Headquarters City to Community." *Journal of Ethnic Studies* 18 (Winter 1991):1-27.

Mucha, Janusz. "American Indian Success in the Urban Setting." *Urban Anthropology* 13 (Winter 1984):329-54.

_____. "From Prairie to the City: Transformation of Chicago's American Indian Community." *Urban Anthropology* 12 (Fall/Winter 1983):337-71.

Philip, Kenneth. "Strive toward Freedom: The Relocation of Indians to Cities: 1952-1960." *The Western Historical Quarterly* 16 (April 1985):175-90.

Sandefur, G.D. "American Indian Migration and Economic Opportunities." *International Migration Review* 20 (1986):55-68.

Shoemaker, Nancy. "Urban Indians and Ethnic Choices: American Indian Organizations in Minneapolis, 1920-1950." *The Western Historical Quarterly* 19 (November 1988):431-47.

Tax, Sol. "The Impact of Urbanization on American Indians." *The Annals of the American Academy of Political and*

Social Sciences 436 (1978):121-35.

BOOKS

Anderson, David L. et al. *The Dynamics of Government Programs for Urban Indians in the Prairie Provinces.* Montreal: Institute for Research on Public Policy, 1984.

Dosman, Edgar J. *Indians: The Urban Dilemma.* Toronto: McClelland and Steward, 1972.

Guillemin, Jeanne. *Urban Renegades: The Cultural Strategy of American Indians.* New York: Columbia University Press, 1975.

Hansen, Niles. *Rural Poverty and the Urban Crisis.* Bloomington: Indiana University Press, 1970.

Katznelson, Ira. *City Trenches: Urban Politics and the Patterning of Class in the United States.* New York: Pantheon, 1981.

Neils, Elaine M. *Reservation to City: Indian Migration and Federal Relocation.* Chicago: University of Chicago Department of Geography, 1971.

Thornton, Russell; Sandefur, Gary D.; and Grasmick, Harold G. *The Urbanization of American Indians.* Bloomington: Indiana University Press, 1982.

Waddell, Jack O. and Watson, O. Michael. *The American Indian in Urban Society.* Boston: Little and Brown, 1971.

GOVERNMENT DOCUMENTS

National Council on Indian Opportunity. *Public Forum Before The Committee on Urban Indians in Los Angeles, CA, December 16-17, 1968.* Washington, D.C.: U.S. National Council on Indian Opportunity, 1969.

_____. *Public Forum Before The Committee on Urban Indians in Minneapolis-St. Paul, MN, March 18-19, 1969.* Washington, D.C.: U.S. National Council on Indian Opportunity, 1969.

_____. *Public Forum Before The Committee on Urban Indians in Phoenix, AZ, April 17-18, 1969.* Washington, D.C.: U.S. National Council on Indian Opportunity, 1969.

_____. *Public Forum Before The Committee on Urban Indians in San Francisco, CA, April 11-12, 1969.* Washington, D.C.: U.S. National Council on Indian Opportunity, 1969.

U.S. American Indian Policy Review Commission, Task Force Eight. *Report on Urban and Rural Non-reservation Indians: Final Report to the American Indian Policy Review Commission.* Washington, D.C.: U.S. Government Printing Office, 1976.

U.S. Senate Select Committee on Indian Affairs. *The Urban Indian Health Equity Act: Report.* Washington, D.C.: U.S. Government Printing Office, 1990.

INDEX

ABOUT THE AUTHOR

ROBERT N. WELLS, JR. (A.B., M.A., Ph.D., Michigan) is the Munsil Professor of Government and Coordinator of Native American Programs at St. Lawrence University, Canton, New York. For 25 years, he has been actively involved in teaching courses on Native American education, law and tribal government on the St. Lawrence campus and its extension program on the St. Regis (Akwesasne) Mohawk Reservation. Dr. Wells regularly publishes articles on Native American affairs and recently completed two national studies of Native American education at the pre-collegiate and college levels. In addition to his scholarly interest in Native Americans, Dr. Wells teaches and publishes articles in the field of international relations. He recently edited a book of readings and bibliography, *Peace by Pieces — United Nations Agencies and Their Roles* (Scarecrow, 1991).